Temple and Contemplation

ISLAMIC TEXTS AND CONTEXTS

Also available in this series:
Cyclical Time and Ismaili Gnosis
by Henry Corbin

Temple and Contemplation

Henry Corbin

Translated by Philip Sherrard
with the assistance of Liadain Sherrard

KPI
London and New York
in association with
ISLAMIC PUBLICATIONS
London

First published in French as Temple et Contemplation *by Flammarion et Cie, Paris 1980. This English edition first published in 1986 by KPI Limited*
11 New Fetter Lane, London EC4P 4EE
Distributed by
Routledge & Kegan Paul, Associated Book Publishers (UK) Ltd
11 New Fetter Lane, London EC4P 4EE
Methuen Inc., Routledge & Kegan Paul
29 West 35th Street, New York, NY 10001, USA

Set in Baskerville
by Hope Services, Abingdon
and printed
by
Unwin Brothers Ltd
Old Woking, Surrey

ISBN 0-7103-0129-4 (cloth)
ISBN 0-7103-0130-8 (paperback)

The Institute of Ismaili Studies, London

The Institute of Ismaili Studies was established in December 1977 with the object of promoting scholarship and learning in Islam, and a better understanding of its relationship with other faiths, beliefs and practices.

Its programmes are designed to encourage a balanced study of Islam, and the strength and diversity of the Islamic heritage within the fundamental unity of faith. They also deal with issues of modernity that arise as Muslims seek to relate their heritage to the contemporary situation.

In carrying out its programmes, the Institute collaborates with different universities. It has been affiliated to McGill University since April 1980, and also works closely with the University of London Institute of Education. With the co-operation of McGill University, the Institute runs a Department of Graduate Studies and Research (London and Paris), by whom the series "Islamic Texts and Contexts" is edited jointly with the Publications Department.

The views expressed in this series are those of the respective authors.

"Réalisme et Symbolisme des Couleurs en Cosmologie Shī'ite" was delivered at the Eranos conference of 1972, whose general theme was "Le Monde des Couleurs", and was published in *Eranos-Jahrbuch* XLI (1972);

"La Science de la Balance et les Correspondances entre les Mondes en Gnose Islamique" was delivered at the Eranos conference of 1973, whose general theme was "Le Monde des Correspondances", and was published in *Eranos-Jahrbuch* XLII (1973);

"Temple Sabéen et Ismaélisme" was delivered under the title "Sabian Ritual and Ismaili Exegesis of the Ritual", at the Eranos conference of 1950, whose general theme was *Mensch und Ritus*. The paper was published in Eranos-Jahrbuch XIX (1950);

"La Configuration du Temple de la Ka'ba comme Secret de la Vie Spirituelle" was delivered at the Eranos conference of 1965, whose general theme was "Form als Aufgabe des Geistes" and was published in *Eranos-Jahrbuch* XXXIV (1965);

"L'Imago Templi face aux Normes Profanes" was delivered at the Eranos conference of 1974, whose general theme was "Avenir et Devenir des Normes", and was published in *Eranos-Jahrbuch* XLIII (1974).

Published as a collection, "Temple et Contemplation", by Flammarion, Paris 1980.

Contents

Books by Henry Corbin available in English translation

Avicenna and the Visionary Recital (Bollingen Series. LXVI), translated by W. R. Trask, New York, 1960; reprinted Spring Books. Dallas, 1980 (paperback edition).

Creative Imagination in the Ṣūfism of Ibn 'Arabī (Bollingen Series, XCI), translated by Ralph Manheim, Princeton University Press, 1969, Routledge & Kegan Paul, 1970.

Spiritual Body and Celestial Earth: From Mazdean Iran to Shī'ite Iran (Bollingen Series, XCI:2), translated by N. Pearson, Princeton University Press, 1977.

The Man of Light in Iranian Sufism, translated by N. Pearson, Shambhala Publications Inc., Boulder and London, 1978.

Cyclical Time and Ismaili Gnosis (Islamic Texts and Contexts), translated by R. Manheim and J. Morris, Kegan Paul International and Islamic Publications, London, 1983.

Editorial Note

This volume brings together five lectures which were originally delivered at different sessions of the famous *Eranos* Conferences in Ascona, Switzerland. Henry Corbin himself had outlined the plan for this book, whose title suggests that these diverse studies converge on a common spiritual centre.

The last three studies explicitly ask us to reflect on the role of the heavenly Temple, or the archetype of the Temple, in the spiritual traditions of the Religions of the Book. No other work of Henry Corbin brings out more clearly the hermeneutic correspondences among spiritual visions belonging to those religions—religions which differ in their outward aspect, but whose inner dimension (the *bāṭin*) reveals many comparable forms and structures.

Thus it is that the "astral" religion of the Sabians, far from being a simple natural worship of the Heavens and their Spheres, is on the contrary one which sees in this universe the threshold beyond which there begins the world of the Angels; and the "celestial temple of the mediating Angels" must lead one beyond toward the invisible and unknowable God. The temple of the Imamate, for the *Ikhwān al-Ṣafā'* and other Ismaili authors, likewise has this mediating function. Each Angel of the esoteric Heavens, each Prophet in the Cycles of metahistory, is like a buttress or wall of that Temple, with the Imam of the Resurrection crowning and completing that structure. But this "spiritual form" of the Temple is not simply the esoteric aspect of the Cosmos, any more than the Imam is a simple reality external to the heart of his true follower. The Temple becomes the inner form of the person, and "the ritual celebrated by man in the temple of his being is his own metamorphosis, the bringing to birth within himself of that Form of himself which conforms to the angelic archetype" (p. 169).

This was how Henry Corbin came to interpret the remarkable theosophy of the Temple created by the Shiite philosopher Qāḍī Saʿīd Qummī. There the Temple of the Kaaba is "brought back" to its invisible archetypes. It leads one back to a hierarchy of worlds and heterogeneous times, passing from the most dense to more and more subtle ones. For the "House of God" has an inner correspondence with the Throne of divine Unity, which is the pure noetic, intelligible Temple.

Now if this Shiite hermeneutics is thereby able to ascend beyond the Temple visible to our physical eyes, which is only the crypt of the true Temple present in the Imaginal world, so it also makes possible a comparative hermeneutics of Images of the Temple. It is this same hermeneutics, moving in an ascent from the sensible form to the world of the revealed Divinity, which permits and justifies the correlations and correspondences among the different manifestations of a single and unique *Imago Templi*. In this last study, whose very scope demands our appreciation, Henry Corbin brings out the intimate inner homology between Jewish mysticism (centered around the notion of the *shekhinah*), and Hellenistic Judaism, as well as the spirituality of Qumrān and the Christian theology of the Temple.

The two essays that open this collection might wrongly appear "out of place" in the perspective that has just been mentioned. Henry Corbin gave them their place precisely to point out that Shiite hermeneutics necessarily leads to a theosophy of the Temple—just as the Temple itself has no meaning, if we do not have a method and ontology that can lead us there.

The "science of the Balance" is in fact a general theory of *ta'wīl*, of spiritual exegesis, which interprets numbers and dimensions, and which makes possible the construction of remarkable "diagrams" in which intelligible proportions become visible and imaginal forms descend into the visible world. For the function of this hermeneutics is not to set up mere abstract concepts in opposition to the sensible, material reality, but rather to make a visionary reality manifest to the eyes of the soul, as a *visible reality* giving a subtle body to the theophanic reality. Like the Temple which comes to be present in the soul, so also Haydar Amulī's diagrams express the structures of the divine Names, of Prophetology and of Imamology by safeguarding them from abstraction. They arrange those structures according to a pure space in which they are no longer subject to the limitations of discourse, but are instead grasped all together as a single symbolic pleroma, the simultaneous manifestation of the Unknowable at the centre of the diagram.

Without such a *ta'wīl* the spiritual theology of the Temple would be impossible. With it, the visible domain is no longer limited to the physical universe, and the intelligible world is not reduced to a few names and abstract ideas. Thanks to it, the world of the Soul and that of the Intelligences come to possess their own Earth, their own Heaven, time and space.

Finally, just as the Imaginal world, being the pure space of symbols, lies beyond the sensible space of material bodies, so likewise colours lead beyond to their subtle being, to a supra-sensible light. "Light is the Angel of colour", as the spiritual Temple is the angelic form of the material Temple. Hence the Imaginal world is not simply made up of living numerical or geometric dimensions expressing the structures of the divine worlds; for those worlds are not without tone and colour. Since they raise the visible world up to their own level, thereby making themselves accessible to the eyes of the soul, so they too are adorned with spiritual colours.

Now one can understand why Henry Corbin wished to link "Temple" and "Contemplation": the theory of visionary perception allows for the emergence of the Temple, but the processes of visionary knowing are themselves based on the eternal presence of the *Imago Templi*. Their union in man's spiritual organism is active contemplation: "When man is thus, man is truly the Temple" (p. 387).

Christian Jambet
Translated by James W. Morris

All is mere ashes and dust —
all, except the Temple within us.
It is ours, and with us for ever.
VLADIMIR MAXIMOV

I

The Realism and Symbolism of Colours in Shiite Cosmology

According to the "Book of the Red Hyacinth" by Shaykh Muḥammad Karīm-Khān Kirmānī (d. 1870)

PROLOGUE

Various aspects of the phenomenon of colour have been discussed in both Islamic philosophy and theosophy. Several years ago, I myself was able to make a study of it, taking as my guide one of the greatest masters of Iranian spirituality: the fourteenth-century 'Alāuddawlah Simnānī. I was thereby led to the heart of a physiology of the subtle body, whose every centre is both defined as a "prophet of your being", and characterized by a colour, an *aura*, visionary perception of which reveals to the mystic the degree of his advancement upon the spiritual Way.*[1]

There is, moreover, a long Hermetic tradition in Islam, whose testimony makes one ask what perception of colour and colour phenomena it was that enabled alchemists to interpret them in the way they did. Thus, with regard to both subtle physiology and alchemy, one is faced with a question which is essentially one of phenomenology: in what does the *phenomenon* of colour consist for our authors? How is one to understand correctly what they say about it, when their interpretation seeks to "preserve its appearance", that is, to explain it in accordance with what they perceive?

* *Translator's note*: Where an English translation of a work by Corbin exists, the reference is to this translation. Not all his works, however, have been translated.

1 Cf. my book, *The Man of Light in Iranian Sufism*, trans. Nancy Pearson (Shambhala Publications, Boulder & London 1978). For more detailed information regarding the psycho-cosmic constitution of the organs or subtle centres (the *laṭīfah*), see my *En Islam iranien: aspects spirituels et philosophiques*, III, book IV (Paris, Gallimard, 1971–1972; new edition, 1978), pp. 330 ff.

The best way to answer this question was to have recourse to a treatise, if one could be found, in which our authors would themselves provide an answer. I was able to find such a treatise—of recent date, certainly, but this, far from detracting from its value, actually increased its scope. The work stems from a school of Iranian Shiism, the Shaykhi school, derived from Shaykh Aḥmad Aḥsā'ī (d. 1826), notable for its intention to preserve in its integrity the theosophical tradition of the Imams of Shiism. This treatise is the work of Shaykh Muḥammad Karīm-Khān Kirmānī (d. 1870), who was second in succession to Shaykh Aḥmad Aḥsā'ī and whose work, like that of other shaykhs of the same school, is evidence of a tremendous fertility, comprising as it does about three hundred titles.[2] Muḥ. Karīm-Khān Kirmānī was a kind of universal genius whose interest extended to all branches of learning, like the masters of our own Renaissance; and he was thereby led to write on scientific questions which he consistently envisaged from a theosophical point of view. His theory of colours has already given us occasion to speak of him as a sort of Iranian Goethe, in the same way that the theory of our mystics concerning visions of coloured light led me to evoke the "physiological colours" of Goethe's *Farbenlehre*.[3]

The treatise which I propose to analyse and briefly comment upon was written in Arabic in 1851, and was provoked by the question of a tiresome person whose indiscretion our shaykh does not hesitate to condemn. It was written very rapidly, in two days, and comprises about sixty pages. I have used a photocopy of the autograph manuscript. It is, to be sure, an occasional piece, but because of the author's extensive and intimate grasp of the subject, it is also remarkably concentrated. It is one of many unedited works, and is entitled *Risālat al-yāqūtat al-ḥamrā'*, the "Book of the red hyacinth" (the allusion being to the precious stone of that name). We shall have more than one occasion to make it clear that the title was not chosen at random.[4] It is divided into two books of more or less equal length. The first book, comprising eight chapters, deals with the concept and the reality of colour. Book II, which contains nine chapters, is concerned more particularly with the colour red, with its "descent from

2 On the life and work of Muḥammad Karīm-Khān Kirmānī, see *En Islam iranien . . .*, op. cit., IV, book VI (The Shaykhi School).
3 Cf. *The Man of Light . . .*, op. cit., pp. 139 ff.
4 On this treatise, see my report in *Annuaire* of the Section des Sciences religieuses de l'École pratique des Hautes-Études, 1972–1973.

the world of archetypes", and with a hermeneutics of this colour linked directly with the esoteric hermeneutics of the Koran. This last is particularly original, rich in presuppositions and consequences.

In order to appreciate our author's point of view—which he realizes is probably unique—we should take stock of the research that has been done into the theory of colour in Islamic philosophy. Let me say at once that this research is still very limited.[5] Our assessment would lead us to consider the various theories proposed by Aristotle on the subject, as well as what was known about it by Islamic philosophers, notably by Fārābī, Avicenna, Ibn al-Haytham, and so on. It would appear that the greatest advance was made by the philosopher Avempace (= Ibn Bājjah, twelfth century A.D.), who was perhaps the "best leader" of the Andalusian philosophical school. Because his optical doctrine contradicted generally accepted ideas, it was examined at length by Averroes, who found it *valde difficilis*, very difficult to understand in the terms put forward by Avempace, for these went so far as to propose that colour exists here and now *in potentia* in darkness.[6] But however interesting these studies may be—as are those of Alhazen (Ibn al-Haytham), whose treatise, translated into Latin, had considerable influence in the West, as well as that of his commentator Kamāluddīn Fārsī (d. 1320 A.D.)—there is still a basic divergence, possibly an abyss, between the statements of these philosopher-opticians and those of a theosophist like Muḥ. Karīm-Khān Kirmānī. The latter was himself perfectly aware of this, and never misses an opportunity of showing how beside the point were the philosophers' speculations in this field.

Before going further, we should specify three points fundamental to our shaykh's colour theory:

5 The best and most recent study of this question is Helmut Gätje's 'Zur Farbenlehre in der muslimischen Philosophie', in *Der Islam*, 43/3 Berlin 1967), pp. 280–301. The starting-point of this study is actually a reference in Goethe's *Farbenlehre* to the theory of colour in Avempace and Averroes.

6 Avempace's theory regarding the relationship between light and colour marks a break with the thesis, commonly held, that the effect of light on a transparent medium can be produced only in so far as the latter is transparent in actuality. For Avempace, light is already a sort of colour (*aliquis color*); any effect produced by the colour on the transparent medium is equivalent precisely to the actualization of this transparency as such. If light is necessary for the perception of colours, it is because colours already exist *in potentia* in the darkness, and because light actualises them in the sense that the colours then suscitate the transparent medium. Cf. H. Gätje, op. cit., pp. 293 ff. On Avempace (Ibn Bājjah), cf. my *Histoire de la philosophie islamique*, I, pp. 317 ff. A work by Avempace has recently been discovered which contains a chapter important for his theory of colours: *Kitāb al-Nafs* (The Book of the Soul), ed. M. S. H. al-Ma'sūmī (*Majallat al-Majma'al-'Arabī*, 33–35) (Damascus, 1958–1960); M. S. Ḥasan al-Ma'sūmī, *Ibn Bājjah's 'Ilm al-Nafs*, English trans. (Karachi 1961).

1. It is important to make a clear distinction between the existence (*wujūd*) and the manifestation (*ẓuhūr*) of colour. It was failure to make this distinction that nullified the labours of the philosophers. Colour may *exist*, yet not be *manifested*. One must therefore determine the relationship between light and colour.

2. This relationship cannot be established on the level merely of the physical conditions of our world. Although our author's attitude may appear to be one of rigorous, even extreme, Platonism, it is in fact nourished by the whole substance of Shiite theosophy. A verse of the Koran (15:21) is both its *leitmotiv* and its explanation: "There are no things whose treasures (*khazā'in*) do not exist alongside Us. We make them descend only in determined proportions." For our author and his colleagues, the Koranic concept of "treasures" here signifies nothing less than *archetypes*. All the phenomena of our terrestrial world, including the phenomenon of colour, are to be explained by a "descent of archetypes" from superior worlds.

3. As a corollary to this, the notion of "composite" (*murakkab*) applies to all levels of the universe, including those universes that are supra-sensible. Consequently, the phenomenon of colour extends equally to the totality of these universes, so that a hermeneutic of colour would employ not an abstract symbolism, but a symbolics founded on an integral spiritual realism.

1. *On a concept of colour encompassing the totality of universes.* In the course of the first two chapters of Book I of his treatise, our shaykh undertakes a critical examination of the views of the philosophers concerning the phenomenon of colour; we will note only his conclusions. According to him, that which makes up the essence and the reality of colour has eluded the most famous of the philosophers: these wise men have gone astray in their researches. Avicenna notably, in his *Shifā'*. got no further than the idea—and this with much hesitation—that colour possesses a certain existence *in potentia*; but after a lengthy development of this idea, he confesses wearily that what constitutes the essence of colour is beyond his grasp. In a general sense our shaykh rejects the usual postulate of the philosophers: that in all cases where colour exists, it must be visible.

To this physics, which confuses the existence of colour with its manifestation, our shaykh opposes another physics based on the idea of "subtle matter", the *laṭīfah*, whose implicit link with Simnānī's subtle physiology is easily discernible.[7] There is a subtle component, a *laṭīfah*, which disposes the nature of beings and objects into three categories. 1. That in which the subtle component predominates. The object is then a source of light that is not only manifest and visible of itself, but in addition manifests and renders visible other objects by virtue of its intrinsic nature. 2. That in which the *laṭīfah*, the subtle component, is equal with the other components. In this case, the object, although manifest and visible of itself, even in darkness, is powerless to manifest other objects and make them visible. By way of example he cites red light (one could no doubt think of cases of what we call phosphorescence). 3. That, finally, in which the *laṭīfah*, the subtle component, is less predominant than the other components. In this instance, the object is not even visible of itself; it needs to be manifested by another object in which the *laṭīfah*, the subtle element, does predominate.

According to our author, this last eventuality does not mean that bodies do not possess colour in themselves; it means that their colours, in order to manifest themselves—that is to say, in order to be not only illuminated but illuminating—have need of a light that will bring them to fulfilment. Yet fulfilment concerns the *manifestation* of the colours, not their actual existence; for colour is an integral part of the body's very nature. In other words, it is wrong to think, like certain philosophers, that a body as such is deprived of colour, because the fact of its being what it is presupposes a "descent of archetypes"; and part of this descent is the descent of the colour which is proper to the body in question. Its colour in this world is not merely the result of the conditions which prevail in this world, but corresponds to what it is here and now in other worlds that, ontologically speaking, precede this one; it simply happens not to be manifest in this world. So much is this the case that, in agreement with the Koranic verse (6:1), "He has established Darkness *and* Light", it must be said that Darkness is not purely and simply the absence of manifestation, for it entails a manifestation of its own—which is, precisely, its manifestation as Darkness. If colours are invisible to us in the Darkness, it is due to their

7 Cf. the references in note 1 above. The modalities of each of these *laṭīfahs* confer their particular modes of the colours which in their turn communicate the modalities to the imaginative perception. Each *laṭīfah* is an independent act of coloured light, which actualizes the *imaginal* transparent medium. For the theosopher, the realm of sensible perception, with which the philosopher-opticians are exclusively concerned, is only one realm among others, the level of which is determined precisely with reference to the gradations of *laṭīfahs* which themselves determine the scale of the levels of being.

weakness or the paucity of their subtle element, their *laṭīfah*; it is not due to a basic non-existence of colour (one could, on the other hand, recall the "black light" of certain subterranean caves).

In the end, therefore, one may justifiably speak of a "manifestation *in potentia*", but not of an "existence *in potentia*"; for colour, even if invisible, is present here and now. We can see, then, what distinguishes our theosophical shaykh both from philosophers such as Fārābī (for whom "colours do not exist in themselves", but are due to the action of the light-source on surfaces) and from all the philosopher-opticians who went so far as to admit that colour possesses a certain potentiality of existence.[8] "All these great men", he says, "remained in a state of perplexity. They had no knowledge of the meaning and concept of colour. When they did write about it, it was in a conjectural fashion and without arriving at any definite conclusion."

By contrast, here is a first premiss postulated by our shaykh, the importance of which is evident throughout the rest of the treatise: "The truth is", he says, "that every composite possesses a colour in itself, whether that composite is one of the bodies manifest in *time* in this world (*ajsām ẓāhirah zamānīyah*), or the subtle bodies of the *imaginal* world of the *barzakh* (the intermediary world, *ajsām mithālīyah barzakhīyah*), or the bodies of the sempiternal world of the Soul (the *Malakūt*, *ajsām dahrīyah nafsānīyah*), or is one of the composites of the *Jabarūt* (*murakkabāt jabarūtīyah*). The gradations of colour differ according to the differences of the composites: if the composite belongs to the subtle world (*laṭīf*), the colour is likewise subtle; if it belongs to the world of density and opacity (*kathīf*), the colour is likewise opaque."

It is important to stress the originality and audacity of this premise, for they typify the position of the theosophist when compared with that of the philosopher:

a. The banal dualism between spirit and flesh disappears. Along with

8 In contrast to Fārābi, Ibn al-Haytham (Alhazen) adopts an intermediate position: colour "is born between the eye and the light", and he concedes that it may possess real existence. In this connection his commentator, Kamāluddīn Fārsī (d. 720/1320), defines the relationship between light and colour, and makes colour conditional upon light, although conceding that colour possesses existence *in potentia*. Cf. H. Gätje, op. cit., p. 300. For Muḥ. Karīm-Khān Kirmānī, however, the relationship between *wujūd* and *ẓuhūr* is not one between potential existence and actual existence. These are the hesitations of the philosopher-opticians to which he alludes in order to go beyond them.

the idea of a composite, the idea of the body is progressively sublimated until it comes to denote a body belonging to superior universes: there are the subtle bodies of the intermediary *mundus imaginalis*, perceived not by the senses but by the active Imagination; there are the subtle bodies of the world of Souls of the *Malakūt*; there are even bodies belonging to the world of the Intelligences of the *Jabarūt*. This world-structure conforms perfectly to that found in Mullā Ṣadrā Shīrāzī, in whose writings the idea of the body is ultimately sublimated to that of a "divine body" (*jism ilāhī*). The structure conforms equally to the physics and the metaphysics of the Resurrection to be found in Shaykh Aḥmad Aḥsā'ī, from whom our author is spiritually descended, and in whose writings the differentiation between the two *jasad* and the two *jism* ultimately links up with the theory of the *okhēma* (Gk. ὄχημα), the *currus subtilis* of the soul, of the Neoplatonist Proclus.[9]

b. This spiritualization of the idea of the body derives from a concept of *tajarrud* (a state separate from matter, Greek χωρισμός), which represents a break with the spirituality which the Islamic philosophers had inherited from the Greek philosophers. Yet it is thanks to this break that such a sublimation is possible. The concept of *tajarrud* has always created difficulties for the strict theologians of Islam, for whom it can only actually refer to the creative Principle, not to any of the beings deriving from it. We are thus presented with the paradox of a theosophist like Shaykh Aḥmad Aḥsā'ī taking the side, against the theologian Majlisī, of those philosophers who do not attribute the *tajarrud* to any created thing.[10] Even the cherubic Intelligences of the *Jabarūt* are composed of a matter and a form, of an existence and a quiddity or essence: Light is their being, their "matter", and Mercy (*Raḥmah*) is their dimension of shadow, their quiddity. All beings, on whatever level, are composed of this Light and this Mercy.

c. Thus, more than a theory is needed. We need a phenomenology of colours which will "unveil" (*kashf*) to us, at every level both sensible and

9 On the whole of this doctrine, see my book, *Spiritual Body and Celestial Earth: from Mazdean Iran to Shi'ite Iran*, trans. Nancy Pearson (Bollingen Series XCI:2, Princeton University Press, 1977), pp. 90–96. (*Translator's note*: this is a translation of the 1960 Buchet-Chastel edition, not the 1979 revised edition to which Corbin refers and of which no translation exists. However, this does not affect the references to it either here or below.)

10 See *En Islam iranien . . .*, op. cit., IV, general index, s.v. *tajarrod.*

supra-sensible, the mode of reality of colours; which will account for both their existence and their manifestation. Our shaykh could not find such a phenomenology either in Aristotle or in the philosophers whom Aristotle inspired. On account of this, the line he takes is an extension of traditional Shiite theosophy.

d. We can now divine the significance of what we observed a moment ago. The phenomenon of colour is not limited to our sensible world. Indeed, in this world it simply betokens the archetypes that are here active. It is certainly in order to speak of the symbolism of colour; nevertheless, this must be understood not purely in terms of a language of signs, but in the sense that colours "symbolize with each other", in the same way as their state in this world symbolizes with their state in other, supra-sensible universes. Symbolism will here possess the quality of a visionary realism.

In support of this realism, our shaykh adduces a group of Koranic verses (chapter II) of which the most important is the verse, quoted above, referring to "treasures" or "archetypes". All these verses are called upon to witness that colours are in fact objectively real: they are neither imaginary nor a purely subjective impression resulting from an admixture of the element of Air with the light-rays. Were the latter the case, the colours would belong not to the bodies but to the light-rays. In a way, the Koranic verses are called upon to witness against Newton.[11] Finally, our shaykh refers to a long conversation between the sixth Imam, the Imam Ja'far al-Ṣādiq (d. 765 A.D.) and his disciple and *famulus* Mufaḍḍal al-Ju'fi (chapter III). This conversation is really the equivalent of a treatise *De sensu et sensato*, that is to say a treatise on the faculty of sensible perception and its object. For each faculty there is a corresponding object, and *vice versa*. Between the two—between the sense and the sensible object—there are mediators, as, for example, the light which makes colour manifest. Our shaykh invites us to meditate on each of the terms used by the Imam Ja'far, who speaks of light as that which *manifests* colour, not that which produces it and makes it *exist*. It is not the object that needs complementing, but our visual faculty. Light performs this task, but light is neither a

11 Essentially, these verses are 30:22: "The diversity of your languages and your colours"; 35:27: "In the mountains there are white paths and red paths"; 16:13: "That which He has multiplied for you on earth in different colours"; 18:31: "They [the inhabitants of Paradise] are clothed in green garments" (cf. 76:21); 3:106: "On the day of the Resurrection there will be white faces and black faces", etc.

realization nor a fulfilment of the existence of colour; it is the cause of the *manifestation* of colour, not of its *existence.*

All that has just been said refers to the lights of this world; but there are many traditions (*ḥadīth* and *akhbār*) concerning the existence of colours in the supra-sensible worlds: *ḥadīth* about the coloured lights of the cosmic Throne (of which we will say more below), an account of the Prophet's vision of his God, all the Koranic verses on the joys of Paradise—which, contrary to the claims of a prudish apologetic, are not of the material sensible order, but of the *imaginal* order—and so on. In short, colours exist in all the worlds; and in the face of this thesis the sum of the labours of the philosophers, as of the scholastic theologians of the *Kalām* (the *Mutakallimūn*), is seen to be sadly negative. The fact is that they did not know how to bridge the gap between the Illumination of the revealed Book and their own opinions (ash'arites, mu'tazilites, *falāsifah*). Already Mullā Ṣadrā Shīrāzī was maintaining that, of all the schools of Islamic thought, only the Shiites had succeeded in bridging this gap. For by following the teaching of their Imams which unveiled the esoteric and the exoteric, the hidden interior and the visible exterior, they had learned to understand, to "save the phenomena". The phenomenon in this case is that of colour; and to preserve it in all its integrity, philosophy is not enough. What is needed is a divine wisdom, a *theosophia.*

2. *On the true relationship between light and colour.* Light and colour are different things, light being the cause not of the existence but of the manifestation of colour,. and colour being manifested on all levels of the universes, sensible as well as supra-sensible. How, then, should one understand the true relationship between them? The answer to this question is given in a second proposition put forward by our author, and he leads us towards it by deploying his theory of archetypes and of their mode of action.

He begins by stating (chapter IV) that certain bodies whose composition is qualitatively different can display the same colour; the colour may become more or less intense, but it remains *this* particular colour. Thus, colour is not something produced in the way the philosophers say it is. According to them, if the qualitative modality (*kayfīyah*) of one body were contrary to that of another, its colour would likewise have to be contrary to that of the other. This, however, is not the case. Let each of us, he says, have recourse to his own innate intelligence (*fiṭrah*), and reject the ready-made opinions which he hears being formulated around him. He will at once discover that the object of his vision or contemplation requires two things: first, a light which is the product of a light-source, and second, a colour which belongs essentially to the qualitative modality of the object in question. Anyone who doubts the differentiation between these two things and declares that where there is no light, colour itself does not exist, is like a man who says that if no-one looks at the sky, the sky does not exist, or that if no-one looks at the shadow of a person in the sun, the shadow quite simply does not exist. Similarly, one would be correct in saying that brightness is something which happens to a colour and makes it bright; one might even pay more attention to the brightness than to the colour, or *vice versa*. But the fact remains that even if brightness manifests colour, it does not cause it to exist (*inna'l-barīq yuẓhiru'l-lawn wa-lā yūjiduh*).

This being said, our shaykh formulates five premisses which every investigator should take to heart (chapter V).

1. There is a difference between the mode of being of the archetype which produces the signature (the *mu'aththir*, vestigium; cf. the notion of *signatura* in Paracelsus), and the signature that it imprints (*athar*, *mu'aththar*). The world above is exempt from the limitations that condition the world below (*ḥudūd al-dānī*). The archetype remains "henadic" (*aḥadī*) in the sense that this technical term possesses in Proclus. It is the Unific, the Unificient, of all that is unique; it is not itself a unity constituted among other unities, that is to say, a signature among the signatures which its archetypal activity constitutes into so many unities. It is the first and last explanation because it is not itself explicable by any other thing; and it is more epiphanic than all its epiphanies. Such is the meaning of the invocation attributed to the third Imam, the Imam Ḥusayn ibn 'Alī: "Could there be another than You in possession of an epiphany which you did not possess, so that this Other would be that-which-manifests-you when you were hidden; or could you have need of a pointer to indicate You, so that the signatures provided the means of approaching You?" No indeed; the light that *enables one to see* is the sufficient cause of the light which *is seen*, precisely because it makes the latter visible, not the other way round. It is the colour's archetype which is its principle, not *vice versa*. The archetype manifests itself in the signature, and the concept of this latter is the manifested archetype. This, again, is suggested by the mystical invocation:

"No light is visible in things except Your light; no sound is perceptible in things except Your sound."

2. Our author refers to a parallelism as familiar in Islamic theosophy as in our Western theosophical traditions (notably that of Paracelsus and his disciples): the parallelism between the *Liber mundi* and the *Liber revelatus*, between the great Book of the world and the Book of sacred revelation. Indeed, the fundamental phenomenon is the same for all prophetic religions, and hence for all prophetic philosophies: it is the "phenomenon of the Book of sacred revelation". As the two books are simply two versions of the same book, it is possible to apply to both of them the same hermeneutics (*ta'wīl*): in the end we shall see, with some astonishment, the colour red undergo an esoteric hermeneutic whose phases reproduce exactly the phases of the esoteric hermeneutics of the Koran. Nevertheless, even here our shaykh asks us to consider a difference between the epiphany of being, or ontological epiphany (*ẓuhūr kawnī*), and scriptural epiphany (*ẓuhūr shar'ī*)—between, that is to say, the phenomenon of being and that of the sacred Book. This difference derives from the fact that primary Manifestation, which is the manifestation of being, does not possess an opposite, for non-being is pure negativity; non-being is not merely the opposite of being, otherwise both being and non-being would have to be included within a genus common to both of them. Thus, the manifestation of being is so all-inclusive that, as we observed a short while back, it embraces both Light and Darkness simultaneously: the phenomenon of being manifests both apparition and occultation, visibility and invisibility. It is the total signature, the signature *without absence*. As for the phenomenon of the sacred Book, which is as it were a signature begotten on a signature (the phenomenon of the Book begotten on that of being), it consists of the manifestation of what is exoteric, but at the same time it is the occultation of what is esoteric, an esoteric which, as such, remains hidden. We are no longer dealing with an all-inclusive manifestation *without absence*, as in the case of the primary manifestation of being; we are dealing with a manifestation which includes an *absence*, because beneath the revealed appearance (the exoteric) lies the sense which remains concealed (the esoteric), and because you start off by *being absent* from this esoteric, just as it remains absent from you. In other words, the phenomenon of being reveals to us both apparition and occultation: it renders them *present* to us. The phenomenon of the Book reveals occultation to us

as an *absence*, a veiling. How, then, is one to go beyond this *absence*, to cross the threshold of the esoteric?

3. The investigator should now have his attention drawn to a third point: the conditions of Manifestation *a parte subjecti*. For there may exist between you and other things a screen which is none other than yourself, your own body; or there may be an obstacle emanating from the thing itself. In the first of these cases, your cognizant soul is immured within the secrecy of your body, which constitutes a screen between your soul and sounds, scents and colours. The soul's gates must be opened to these things. Yet is it simply a question of the faculties of sense? For to which things, ultimately, should the soul's gates be opened?

4. They should be opened to precisely those things which you cannot perceive until the obstacle that prevents you from doing so is removed (conditions of Manifestation *a parte objecti*). At this point, our shaykh refers once again to his theory of the *laṭīfah* or subtle components, whose disposal of things into three categories we have already glanced at. Now it is the subtle component, the *laṭīfah*, which is the actual signature, the signature of the henadic archetype. If this subtle component predominates in an object, or at any rate is equal to the other components of that object, then there occurs that manifestation or epiphany (*ẓuhūr*) which is actually the *expansion*, the unfolding (*inbisāṭ*) of the Image-archetype (*al-mithāl al-a'lā*), the superior *Imago* projected into the self-ness (*huwīyah*) or individuality which is its receptacle. We shall see later how this *Imago* is the personal lord (*rabb*) of a being, and in what way it is decisive for the phenomenon of colour. Thus, all obstacles must be simultaneously removed from both object and subject in order for "absence to withdraw". This is why it is not just any sound that can be heard, or any colour that can be seen, and so on. Our physics would express this in terms of waves and vibrations; our shaykh, with his purely qualitative physics, speaks of the *laṭīfah*, the subtle element in a being or a thing. The degree to which the *laṭīfah* is present does not depend on the physical conditions; rather, it is the *laṭīfah* which determines the state of these conditions, and is itself the work, the *signatura* or *vestigium* of the archetype.

5. This introduces the fifth premiss that the investigator must take to heart. Either the *laṭīfah* is too weak and the object remains occulted, *absent*, so long as this *laṭīfah* is not strengthened; or else the *laṭīfah*, the subtle

aspect of a thing, is sufficiently strong in itself, and occultation ceases without anything else being required.

The application of these five fundamental premisses has still to be demonstrated, and this is done by showing us the archetype in action—that is to say, the activity of the world above as it imprints its signatures on the world below. What is colour? It is a qualitative modality which comprises, among other things (*min sha'ni-hā*), the capacity of being made manifest to sight. The application of the five principles noted above enables us to affirm that an object is manifest only in so far as the superior agent produces its own signature in that object (*al-'ālī al-mu'aththir*). Only the activity of the archetype repulses the *absence* accompanying the manifestation of which we spoke above in relation to the phenomenon of the Book, and which applies equally in the case of the phenomenon of colour. For the veil to be lifted, the *absence* to withdraw, and for what had been occulted to be de-occulted, the *laṭīfah* needs to be intensified, elevated, kindled; and this is brought about by the same superior agent that imprints the signature. Such intensification of the *laṭīfah* consists so entirely in the withdrawal of the absence that our author explains it in terms of the remoteness of the archetype being succeeded by its greater proximity. In every case, and in whatever situation they occur, it is the archetypal principle that nourishes and substantiates its signatures, that is to say, the multiple lights—whether these are manifested to the fleshly eyes of terrestrial beings or to the *imaginal* eyes of the intermediary world of the *barzakh*, to the pure gaze of the Souls of the *Malakūt* or to the Intelligences of the *Jabarūt*. All is due to the superabundancy of the Manifestation of the archetype or superior agent, which produces its signatures in the mirrors constituted by the receptivities of beings and objects in their various states.

This is true for the phenomenon of colour in so far as colour is in the position of being manifested to sight. When closest to its Principle, it is at its most manifest, and is given the name of light and brilliance (*ḍaw'*). When, on the other hand, it is furthest away from its Principle, it certainly exists, but in a non-manifest state: it is occulted, as the esoteric sense of the Book is occulted in the phenomenon of the sacred Book. It is this that permits us to define the *true relationship between light and colour*, which our shaykh does in advancing a second proposition that he formulates in two ways, both of them equally representative of the spirit of Shiite theosophy.

1. Light is the subtle aspect of colour (*laṭīf al-lawn*) or colour in its subtle state. It is, *eo ipso*, the strong aspect of colour (*qawīy al-lawn*) or colour in its strong state, whereas colour is light in an opaque (*kathīf*) state, thicker and more dense. Needless to say, both light and colour proceed from the same genus, otherwise there could be no interaction between them: light would not be able to receive the "tincture" of colour (*ṣibgh*, *tinctura* in the alchemical sense) any more than it is able to assume the "tincture" of scent; and correspondingly colour would not be capable of reinforcement by light. In point of fact, light contains the hidden secret of colour; but unless two things are in the same "field", one cannot act on the other. A mediating element is needed between sight and the object of vision; and it is the idea of this mediating element that brings the author to the second way of formulating his proposition. He announces it with a warning: "Firmly grasp what I tell you, for it is extremely subtle. Study it thoroughly in order to perceive its truth. Divine exception apart, no other philosopher or wise man will have opened your eyes to what I say here."

2. "Light", says our shaykh, "is the spirituality [the spiritual element or *angel*] of colour (*rūḥānīyat al-lawn*), that is to say, colour in the spiritual state or spiritualized (*lawn mutarawwaḥ*), while colour is the corporeity (the corporeal element or *jasadānīyah*) of light, that is to say, light in a materialized state (*ḍaw' mutajassad*). " We must remember here that the notion of "body" is not limited to the notion of the physical body of this world. The shaykh continues: "Both light and colour are two things from the point of view of the individual and the species, but a single thing from the point of view of genus (*jins*). Analogous to their relationship is *that of spirit and body*, for spirit and body are two things according to one point of view, but one and the same according to another." (Our alchemists, of whom the shaykh was one, speak of the spirit as "light in fusion", and of the body as "light solidified".) Nothing could be clearer: spirit and body, light and colour, are distinct yet inseparable one from the other, the one being manifested by the other. Light is mediated by colour, and *vice versa*; and it is thus mediated that they enter our field of vision. Later on we will see this relationship expressed as the relationship between *rabb* and *marbūb*: lord and vassal imply and mediate each other.

That is why Muḥ. Kārim-Khān Kirmānī rejects any hypothesis put forward by the philosophers conducive to the idea of a pure light that is without colour. "All light is manifested colour, whether it be the brilliance of celestial luminaries or that of fire. Where would you look for the idea of a light to illumine crystal, without that light being itself a colour?" Whether one speaks of the whiteness of moonlight or the yellow of sunlight, lamplight and firelight, a certain colour is always involved; and it is this that causes the hue in a sapphire-coloured garment to vary according to whether one looks at it by daylight or lamplight (it turns from blue to green, like the enamelled cupolas of the mosques of Isfahan). Hence there can no more be light without a colour than there can be spirit manifested without a body either physical, or subtle and spiritual. Light, without any doubt, is closer to the Principle. And here the author uses the term *ḥikāyah*, a term loaded with meaning and connoting both a *story* and an *imitation*—which is the case with the parable, the cryptography of all mystical narrations. Light is the supreme *ḥikāyah* of the Principle, whereas colour is further removed from it. Here again, proximity to and distance from the archetype are invoked in order to explain the gradation of colours. Without light, colour is certainly there, but it is inert and inanimate, like a body without its spirit. The author puts forward a comparison: the Sky (the subtle mass of the Sphere animated by the *Anima caelestis*) is a body, as the Earth is a body. Nevertheless, the Sky, because of the proximity of the Principle, is alive, mobile and conscious, while the Earth, because of its remoteness from the Principle, is inanimate, immobile and unconscious. In the same way, the closer a colour is to the Principle, the more it is manifest unaided, like the *blue* of Saturn, the *white* of Jupiter, the *red* of Mars, the *yellow* of the Sun, and so on. When it is remote from the Principle it needs to be assisted by an excess of light falling on it, just as the Earth, in order to live, needs the celestial vital spirit (*rūḥ ḥayawānīyah falakīyah*).

3. *How every composite, whether it belongs to the sensible or to the supra-sensible world, has a colour.* Now that he has given us an explanation of colours in terms of the activity (proximity or distance) of their respective archetypes, and has defined the relationship between light and colour as a relationship between spirit and body, our author can proceed to his original purpose: the elaboration of a phenomenology and thence of a hermeneutics of colour which accounts for and "preserves the phenomenon" of colour at all levels of the entire hierarchy of worlds.

We have seen the importance of the concept of the signature (*athar*, vestigium). We must now analyse this concept; and this analysis will lead us to a third proposition: a signature acquires reality only when it occurs in terms of one of the four possible modalities. The author arrives at this proposition by means of a physics of the Elements which appears to be peculiar to himself.

It should be noted that the principle which allows our shaykh to deduce the four elementary qualities—that is to say, the quadruple modality under which a signature may occur (chapter VI)—should be dependent on a metaphysical consideration: the movement whereby a signature severs itself from the action of that which gives it existence. Now, the very idea of movement implies the idea of the production of heat and dryness. One can thus consider the signature in relation to the movement which gives it existence, in which case the qualitative modality is that of *hot* and *dry*. Or one can consider it in itself, in its dimension of passivity with regard to the active agent, in which case the qualitative modality is that of *cold* and *dry*. Because heat and dryness are contiguous to the superior dimension which is the active agent, they move of their own accord in an *upwards* direction, whereas cold and dryness move of their own accord downwards.

Our shaykh clearly means to distinguish himself from the classical physicists who have discussed the Elements and the elemental qualities. He refuses to see the first two elemental qualities as united in the idea of a *dryness* that is common to both of them. The dryness of the element of Fire, which dryness is by nature fiery, is totally different from the dryness of the element of Earth, which dryness is by nature earthly. Fiery nature, which is hot and dry, is characterized by an extreme suppleness and an unrestricted tendency to assume all forms; earthly nature, which is cold and dry, is characterized by a hostility towards new forms, by a resistance to metamorphoses ("Fire is seventy thousand times more supple than Earth, seven hundred times quicker than Water to assume a form"). Classical physics concerning the Elements considered the humid modality as the most apt to acquire and conserve form. If, therefore, Fire is now said to possess this aptitude *par excellence*, we must invert classical physics and declare Fire to be *humidity* (*fa'l-nār raṭbah*), which is precisely the paradox that the alchemists opposed to the logic of peripatetic physics. Moreover, a Koranic verse (21:30) says: "We made all living things by means of Water", and certain *ḥadīth* state that "Water is the first thing that God created". Now, as we have just seen, Fire is the first thing (hot and dry) that emerges at the initial stage, when the signature separates from the archetype. Consequently, if one considers it from the point of view of its flexibility and subtlety, its promptness to assume form (the metamorphoses of its flames), and the fact that it is the principle and the life of all living things, one might say that *Fire is Water*. If one considers it with reference to the fact that it is the first to emanate from the movement which imparts existence, it is Fire. (Fire is humidity, Fire is Water: these are paradoxes familiar to the alchemists.)

Thus, we have two opposite terms: hot and dry here correspond to the masculine, cold and dry to the feminine. But by means of what mediating dialectic may we proceed from one to the other, uniting the two so as to produce a *quaternity*? At this point, like a true alchemist, our author resorts to the hermeneutic of a Koranic verse which transfers to the physics of the Elements a disposition made by the Prophet with regard to conjugal matters. The verse in question is 4:35, and it prescribes that in the case of a possible disagreement between husband and wife, two arbiters should be chosen, one from the family of the husband and one from that of the wife. This is precisely what happens in the physics of the Elements. The arbiter chosen from the husband's side (Fire, hot and dry) will be what is hot and humid (Air); the arbiter chosen from the side of the wife (Earth, cold and dry) will be what is cold and humid (Water). The reconciliatory quality of what is hot and humid and what is cold and humid is here quite obvious.[12] When husband and wife are reconciled, there is stability and perfect equilibrium. Earth, which is feminine, prevents Fire, which is masculine, from ascending, because Earth is suspended from Fire. Fire, which is masculine, prevents Earth, the feminine, from descending, because Fire is suspended from Earth. The result is the perfect nuptial union of Fire and Earth.

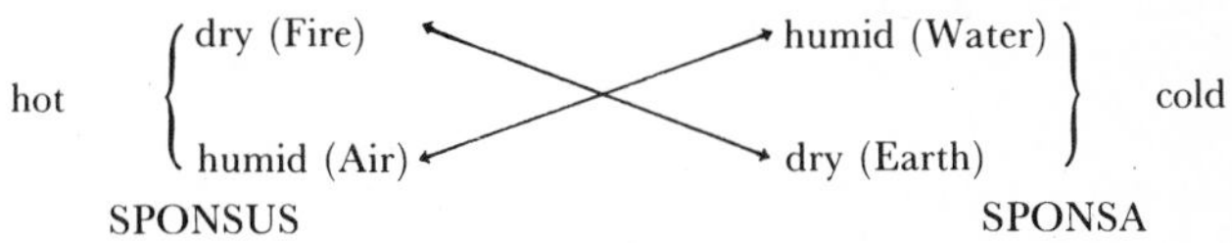

It is interesting to note here how far our shaykh takes this nuptial imagery. What happens in the case of Fire (the husband) and Earth (the

12 The diagram below is intended to illustrate this more clearly.

wife) is the same as what happens in the case of the love between Zayd and Zaynab. In both cases we have a pair. For the pair to be perfect, the two partners who constitute it must become *four*. Zayd is not in fact one of the partners in a couple until his isolated state is shattered, and until the shadow of Zaynab has fallen upon him and he is in the shadow of Zaynab. The same is true of Zaynab, until the shadow of Zayd falls on her. What makes two partners not simply two isolated terms but two partners of a couple is precisely the aspect that is added to each of them, the event which doubles each of them, as was the case with both Zayd and Zaynab. It is in this way that the two terms, in forming a pair, become four, since the being of each as it is for the other is added to the being of each as it is in and for itself. Here Muḥ. Karīm-Khān Kirmānī offers us a kind of intuition which anticipates the idea of quaternity as it is expounded by C. G. Jung. Fire is Zayd; in order for him to form a pair with the Earth-Zaynab, the element Air must mediate. Earth is Zaynab; to form a pair with the Fire-Zayd, the element Water must mediate. In each case, the mediator doubles the partner by adding to him or her an existence which is his or her existence *for the other*. As Water corresponds to the *spousality* of Zaynab, so Air corresponds to the *spousality* of Zayd. One could thus say that the element Air is in some way the *Animus* of Zaynab or the element Earth, while Water is the *Anima* of Zayd or the element Fire.

Without pushing these instructive analogies any further, we can conclude that our shaykh has now completed the analysis which will allow him to put forward his third proposition: that a signature, whatever it may be, only acquires reality thanks to the four qualitative modalities known in current physics as Fire, Air, Water and Earth, in order of their increasing distance from the Principle. One might say that these four elemental modalities with their respective colours are the *ḥikāyah*, the imitation, the history, the parable, of the archetypal world. But on the level of Earth, the remoteness is so great that the superior world only manifests itself to Earth by veiling itself in it.

It is this that enables our shaykh to say: "The degrees of light are three in number, whereas the degree of darkness is unique. Hence, the sources of light are three, while the sources of colour are four." It must be noted that the source of colour is by no means reduced to the action of Darkness conquering light. Because the sources of colour are four, they include also those of light. The four sources correspond to the modalities described above; and it is the intervention of the terrestrial element that alone is responsible for the visibility of colour in this world, since, without the element Earth, the colours of the other three elements remain invisible to us. That is why the shaykh vigorously denies the opinion of the philosophers for whom the scale of colours is situated in the interval contained between white and black. This is not the case at all. The shaykh enumerates the stages of greyness and dullness whereby one proceeds from white to black: they have nothing to do with the phenomenon of colour. Colours, therefore, must have other sources. The theme will be taken up again in connection with the four pillars of coloured light which support the cosmic Throne of Mercy. For the moment, the author confines himself to naming them: the primordial sources of colours in our world are *white*, *yellow*, *red* and *black*.

We have made considerable progress. We now know that the phenomenon of colour is due to the activity of the world above, to the activity of the archetypes. We have seen how the range of colours is determined by the four modalities which are designated as the four Elements. A further step will establish this more specifically by showing us how, contrary to what was held by ordinary physics to be the case, all transparent bodies—for example, the Elements in their simple state—possess light and colour; but that this colour, while *existing*, is invisible to our fleshly eyes as long as these bodies do not become dense. As for the colour that is manifested at the level of the sensible world, it corresponds to the colour already possessed by these bodies at the supra-sensible level.

The totality of modes of perception actually revolves around three axes (chapter VII). a) There is perception by penetration and impression. Unfortunately, the forms of the world above are not such that they can imprint themselves on the organs of the lower world—that is, the apparatus of the sensible faculties. b) There is perception by embodiment (*iḥāṭah*); such is the perception that can be had of the imprinted signature by that which imprints it, but not vice versa. c) There can be perception by unitive union (*ittiḥād*); such is the perception that a being has of itself. But the world above is not "itself" the world below; thus, perception of the world above by the world below is not possible except by means of a manifestation (*ẓuhūr*) of the former, that is to say, by means of a theophany or hierophany. In this way, we are led to conceive of a perception of colour deriving from a perception which is theophanic or hierophanic.

Nothing, however, is perceptible to our vision unless it has acquired the *tinctura* of Earth.

The celestial Spheres, for example, are transparent, and that is why they are invisible. If the stars set in the Spheres are visible to us, it is because they are a sort of condensation of sidereal matter, in the same way that water becomes visible to us when it turns foamy. Equally, the transparency of Fire, Air and Water in their elemental state makes them invisible to us, and the same applies even to Earth in the case of glass and crystal. Our shaykh is thus able to formulate a fourth proposition: "So long as these transparent and diaphanous (*shāffah, shafīf*) bodies remain in their subtle (*laṭīf*) state, their colours and lights are not perceptible to our senses, for they too are in a subtle state. But this does not in the least mean that they do not possess colour and light. How could this be the case, when it is precisely light and colour which are the manifestation of the world above in the world below, and when the closer a thing is to the Principle, the more intense is its manifestation and its light, and the more vigorous its colour? This is why light and colour in transparent bodies are more intense and vigorous [than in opaque bodies]. Nevertheless, the force and intensity of their colour are not perceptible to our sight. But lack of visibility is not due to the fact that light and colour do not exist; it is due rather to the proximity of the Principle." We had been told from the start that we must distinguish between the existence of colour and its manifestation; we now learn that the invisibility of colour may be due not to its absence or to its obscuration but, on the contrary, to its extreme intensity. The same is true of all reality which is subtle and transparent; and, as we have already noted, it is here that the theosopher's perception differs from everything that the philosopher-optician could envisage.

To follow this up is to go beyond the banal proposition current among the philosophers: that it is light which makes colour manifest itself. Henceforth we must recognize two things: firstly, that it is colour which makes light manifest itself, for it is by means of colour that light becomes visible, in the same way as the spirit is made manifest by the body; and secondly, that the relation between light and colour is the same as that between spirit and body. In a formula reminiscent of Suhravardī's *Ishrāq*, the shaykh specifies: "Light is the Orient made visible (*al-mashriq al-mar'īy*), it is the manifestation of the Principle (the theophany) *tinctured* by something which possesses density and which is therefore the cause of its visibility."

The shaykh has already outlined the gradations of this visibility: that of red light, of yellow light, and of white light. "In short," he concludes, "so long as the transparent body stays transparent, it may possess a light and a colour, but both are invisible to us. It is the earthly *tinctura* that accords it a form of manifestation (*maẓhar*) accessible to us." The shaykh cites by way of example the case of gold and silver in their molten state, glass, crystal, and so on.

A further step has to be taken (chapter VIII) in order to consolidate what has been indicated from the start. If even a transparent body has a light and a colour, then all composites, all bodies, whether of the sensible or of the supra-sensible world, must also possess a light and a colour. Here the theosopher enters a field of exploration in which the philosophers, the *falāsifah*, were unable to find their way.

What is more, our shaykh's manner of proceeding here assumes a remarkable character, for his phenomenology of colour links up with the highest mystical speculations of an Ibn 'Arabī. He is no longer concerned with the signature as presenting the quadruple, qualitative modality previously analysed. He is concerned with it as a structure composed of two "dimensions" or aspects (*jihāt*):one dimension "from the side of its Lord" (its *rabb*), and one dimension "from its own side", or in other words a divine and lordly dimension or condition (*rubūbīyah*), and a human dimension or condition, as the vessel of its divine lord (*marbūbīyah*). It is this relationship which, as we have just seen, puts light and colour in a position that permits each to be mediated and manifested by the other. Thus what is in question is the pair or the bi-unity of *rabb* and *marbūb*; and the idea of bi-unity is of fundamental importance in the mystical doctrine of Ibn 'Arabī. The lord who is the *rabb* is not the hidden unknowable deity, the *Absconditum*, not the terrifying, transcendent and all-powerful God. He is the God created in faith and revealed in the love of each being; between this lord and the being to whom he reveals himself as such, a solidarity is established which renders them interdependent in the manner of lord and vassal, companions in destiny who cannot do without each other. From now on, the relationship between this personal God and his faithful vassal is a chivalric one.

Ibn 'Arabī expressed this bond admirably and often, saying for example: "If he has given us life and existence through his being, I, too, give him life through knowing him in my heart." This same reciprocity of roles is expressed, no less admirably, by one of our own Western mystics, Angelus Silesius, when he says: "God does not live without me; I know that God cannot for one moment live without me. If I become nothing, he too must give up his life."[13] It is an extraordinary intuition, one that tells us that God's every death is necessarily preceded by the death of man; but it is equally extraordinary that the phenomenology of colour should here take us to the heart of the solidarity which makes the divine lord and his earthly knight, the *rabb* and the *marbūb*, responsible for each other, precisely because light and colour are in a similar relationship to one another.

Our shaykh explains this as follows. The signature's lordly dimension—elsewhere called the imperishable Face or inner Imam of a being (the theme will reappear at the end of this study)—is precisely the Image-archetype, the *Imago* which, as we were told earlier, is the signature projected into the concrete individuality that is its receptacle. This *Imago* is the dimension of the signature which is "towards its lord", its "lordly dimension"—that is to say, the manifestation of this lord by means of the *Imago* to the concrete individual, and by the individual to others. Its "dimension towards itself"—human and vassal—is that of its occultation, for it is only manifested through its lord (as in the invocation quoted above: "Could another than You possess a manifestation which was not Yours?").

What does this mutual solidarity have to do, ultimately, with the phenomenon of colour? Briefly, in the absence of light, colour would not be manifested but would remain in an inert state, like a corpse. But the process works both ways; for, as we have seen, without colour light would not be manifest to us precisely because of the excessive intensity of its manifestation. In the same way the *marbūb*, the vassal or knight, is maintained in being by his *rabb* or feudal lord; yet the latter would be unknown and invisible without his vassal, because his lordly condition would not be manifested, as the spirit would not be manifested without the body, or light without colour. The consequences of this are far-reaching: the world of colours, according to this analysis, is part and parcel of an entire service of mystical chivalry, of which the *rabb-marbūb* relationship is the type *par excellence*. We will see an example of this shortly.

Our shaykh explains himself here by means of a diagram that is to be

13 Cf. my book, *Creative Imagination in the Sufism of Ibn 'Arabī*, trans. Ralph Manheim (Bollingen Series XCI, Princeton University Press, 1969), p. 129.

found in another of his books—significantly enough, one analogous to it figures among the diagrams in a work by Robert Fludd, the great seventeenth-century English doctor and alchemist, who was also a Rosicrucian.[14] The relationship between *rabb* and *marbūb*, between lord and knight, light and colour, can be illustrated by two interpenetrating spheres or more clearly still, in the world of surfaces, by two interpenetrating triangles.

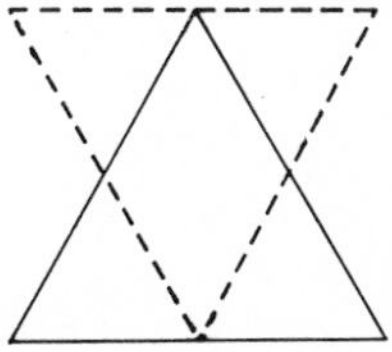

The base of the triangle which represents the lordly dimension (indicated here by the dotted line) is above, close to the Principle, while the tip of its cone touches the base of the triangle which represents the human dimension, the lord's vassal. Conversely, the base of the triangle which represents the human dimension (indicated by the continuous line in the diagram) is at the extreme lower limit, while the tip of its cone touches, above, the base of the divine dimension of lordship.

Our shaykh explains, in his turn, what is already to be found in Ibn 'Arabī: the Manifestation (*qiyām al-ẓuhūr*) of the divine or lordly dimension subsists by virtue of the dimension of the soul, or human dimension, for the *rabb* would not be manifested without the *marbūb*, nor light without colour. Equally, the reality (*qiyām al-taḥaqquq*) of the human dimension owes its subsistence to the divine dimension. Without the human dimension, the divine dimension would not be manifested, but without the divine lordly dimension the human dimension would be deprived of reality, as colour without light would remain in the inert state of a body deprived of life. Such is the whole secret of the *Imago* at the heart of man, the sole reality that man may meaningfully invoke as "My God", and towards whom (for that very reason) he is capable of supreme devotion.

14 On this diagram, which appears in another of our shaykh's works, see my *Spiritual Body and Celestial Earth* . . . , op. cit., pp. 228–229 (the "triangle of light and the triangle of darkness"). See also Serge Hutin, *Robert Fludd (1574–1637) alchimiste et philosophe rosicrucien* (Paris, "Omnium Litteraire", 1972), pl. X, p. 126.

This is why the phenomenon of colour leads us back to the famous *ḥadīth* which dominates the horizon of Islamic theosophy, and which is deliberately recalled here by our shaykh: "I was a hidden Treasure. I desired to be known; that is why I created creatures"—that is, creatural limits, so that I might manifest myself to and by these very limits. This is to say that God only manifests himself to created beings by means of these created beings themselves. The parallel is not a difficult one to follow. Light, because of its intensity, would remain invisible if it did not receive the *tinctura* of colours. The divine Treasure would likewise remain concealed—not by darkness, but by its excessive light. This light must take on the *tincture* of created beings, must limit its intensity, if it is to become visible. This is the "theophany within limits" (*al-tajallī fī'l-ḥudūd*), the secret of the *Imago* and hence of the Gnostic profession of faith: *Eum talem vidi qualem capere potui* (I saw him according to my capacity to perceive him).

In order to obtain a complete phenomenology of colour, it only remains to consider its modalities through all the levels of the hidden Treasure's ladder of theophanies. The limits of this ladder belong to the "human dimension", their sources being six in number: time, space, *situs*, rank, quantity and quality. They also go by the name of "the six days of Creation", that is to say, the six limits constitutive of created beings. Among these limits are those which derive from the four qualitative modalities that we analysed earlier. For the creatural dimension of the signature, the qualitative modality which derives from Fire is colour; from Air, sound; from Water, touch; and from Earth, taste. That which is palpable to touch derives from the combination of qualitative modalities which possess something in common.

It follows that light and colour are a qualitative modality which exists in every composite, by virtue of the fiery nature (the element of Fire) that each composite contains. Just as no composite is deprived of this fiery nature (the element of Fire), so no composite is without a certain light. The totality of the lights existing in things derives from this Fire. When the world above projects its *Imago* into the world below, its manifestation in each Nature acquires a *tincture* that corresponds to the nature that is below. Through each Nature, each Element, it manifests itself to one of the faculties of perception, the faculty created by this same Nature (manifestations by colour, sound, scent and so on). This is how the "hidden lord", who is allied to his knight, his *marbūb*, is manifested to the organ of created vision: he is manifested through the fiery nature of things, through the elemental Fire that each thing contains. This is so because the light that is the manifestation of this lord through the fiery nature, through the elemental Fire concealed within the signature, is only perceptible to the organ of vision created by that same Fire. "Like alone knows like" is a principle effective both for the theory of coloured photisms in Najmuddīn Kubrā and for Goethe's *Farbenlehre*.[15]

If it is true, therefore, that the eye cannot perceive transparent things or lights in a subtle state until they have undergone a certain condensation, then every signature and composite possesses colour and light, regardless of whether it belongs to the material bodies of this world or to the *imaginal* realities of the *barzakh*, to the spiritual forms of the Soul's *Malakūt* or to those of the *Jabarūt* of the cherubic Intelligences. This is why the shaykh, in anticipating the deductions stemming from his consideration of the theme of the cosmic Throne, specifies the scale of colour distributed over seven levels of the universe as follows: 1. The colour of the world of Intelligence is *white*. 2. The colour of the world of Spirit is *yellow*. 3. The colour of the world of Soul is *green*. 4. The colour of the world of Nature is *red*. 5. That of the world of Matter is *ashen*. 6. That of the world of the Image is *dark green*. 7. That of the material body is *black*.

He warns his readers that they will find no mention of all this either in the *Mutakallimūn* or in his writings of the professional philosophers. "You will perceive," he says, "their inability to grasp the question decisively . . . Such is our way. As for their way, I call God to witness that they know only the appearance and the outer aspect of the life of this world; they are unaware of the other world (cf. Koran 30:7)." This other world will be revealed to us in the second part of the "Book of the red hyacinth" by means of an astonishing esoteric hermeneutic of the colour red, preceded by an analysis of the way in which colours are generated in the sensible and supra-sensible worlds.

4. *How colours are generated in the sensible and supra-sensible worlds*. From the point we have reached we can catch a glimpse of the goal envisaged by our shaykh: a goal at which the hermeneutics of the Koran converges in an astonishing way with the hermeneutics of colour in general, and in par-

15 Cf. my book, *Man of Light* . . . , op. cit., index, s.v. Goethe, Najmoddīn Kobrā.

.ticular with that of the colour red which is the theme of the "Book of the red hyacinth". Before attaining this goal, however, there is a stage of some difficulty to be gone through. It will include an analysis of the way in which colours are generated, while its recapitulation should make it possible for us to profit from what we have learned up to now. Very briefly, this stage consists of three phases: A. We need a doctrine dealing with the primordial sources of colour; this will be the subject of the discourse on the cosmic Throne of the Merciful One, supported by four pillars of coloured light. B. On the basis of this doctrine, we have to deduce the manner in which colours are generated and distributed in terms of the four fundamental qualitative modalities which we considered earlier. C. When we have reached this point, we will be in a position to confirm the intial proposition, that every composite in both the sensible and the supra-sensible world possesses its own particular colour. To this end, the author returns briefly to the theme of the signature's double dimension of *rabb* and *marbūb*, lord and knight, light and its colour. This is what makes it possible for us to understand how at each of the seven or eight levels of the universe, there is an *anamnesis* of the colours that we contemplate in this world; and the theory of *anamneses* or correspondences makes possible in its turn a transcendental hermeneutic of the colour red which plumbs what is most esoteric in its esoteric reality. This constitutes our shaykh's goal, and the consummation of his book.

A. We cannot understand either the significance and source of the colour red, or the qualitative modality of its appearance, its exoteric dimension (*ẓāhir*), without having first acquired an understanding of the sources of the other colours (II, chapter I). As we saw, it is absolutely out of the question for these sources to be limited to black and white; or, rather, between black and white, as between the two extreme terms of Fire and Earth, two fundamental colours must interpose themselves and assume the role of mediators. The general proposition is that in the subtle world of transparent colours, where earthly darkness does not intrude, the sources of colour are four in number: *white*, *yellow*, *red* and *green*. But in our physical, terrestrial world, the four sources are white, yellow, red and *black*; because in this world black replaces the green of the subtle worlds.

Generally speaking, the predication of these four sources constitutes one of the great themes of Shiite theosophy, the theme of the Throne of Mercy or of the Merciful One (*'Arsh al-Raḥmah*, *'Arsh al-Raḥmān*), which rests on four cosmic supports. When the Koranic verse (15:21) states that "There are no things whose treasures (archetypes) do not exist alongside Us" or "with Us" (*'indanā*), "with Us" is interpreted as signifying the theophany that is accomplished in the creation of the universes.[16] The theme is stated in a *ḥadīth* which is recorded in the great *corpus* of Kulaynī and is attributed to the first Imam: "God created the throne out of four lights: a red light whereby the colour red *becomes red*; a green light whereby the colour green *becomes green;* a yellow light whereby the colour yellow *becomes yellow*; a white light whence *whiteness* is derived." Briefly, this *white* light characterizes the upper right-hand pillar of the Throne; it is the world of the cherubic Intelligences, the summit of the *Jabarūt* typified by the archangel Seraphiel.

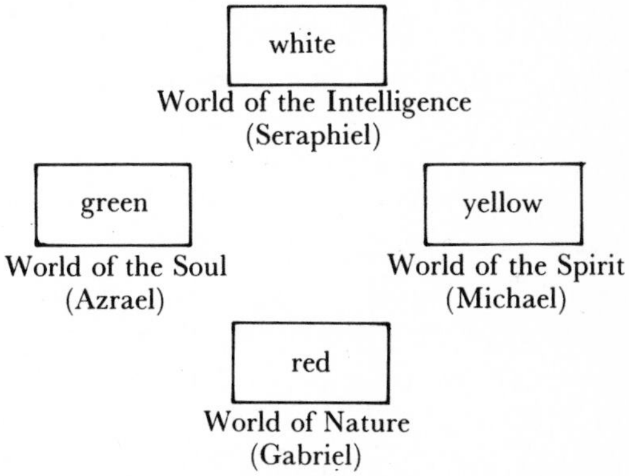

The four pillars of the cosmic Throne of Mercy

The *yellow* light characterizes the lower right-hand pillar of the Throne; it is the world of the Spirit (*Rūḥ*) typified by the archangel Michael. The

16 On the theme of the Throne, see Mullā Ṣadrā Shīrāzī, *Le Livre des pénétrations métaphysiques (Kitāb al-mashā'ir)*, Arabic and Persian texts with French translation by H. Corbin (Bibliothèque iranienne, vol. 10; Paris, Adrien-Maisonneuve, 1964), p. 167. The *ḥadīth* of the Throne recorded by the Imams and quoted below does not mention the colour blue as being one of the fundamental colours. In this connection, the ancient Arabs distinguished only three fields of colour: blue-green (*akhḍar*), red-brown (*aḥmar*), and yellow-brown (*asfar*). The other terms relating to colour refer only to degrees of greater or lesser clarity in these fundamental colours. On this point, see Wolfdietrich Fischer, *Farb-und Formbezeichnungen in der Sprache der alt-arabischen Dichtung* (Wiesbaden 1965) (review by Ewald Wagner in *Der Islam*, 43/3, 1967, pp. 316 ff.). On the other hand, we know that Aristotle in his *Meteora* groups the colours of the rainbow into three classes: purple, green, red-brown. Cf. H. Gätje, op. cit., p. 290. An entire study is called for, comparing the Greek, Arabic and Persian vocabularies that relate to colour.

green light characterizes the upper left-hand pillar of the Throne; it is the summit of the *Malakūt* or world of the Soul, typified by the archangel Azrael. The *red* light characterizes the lower left-hand pillar of the Throne; this is the world of Nature and is typified by the archangel Gabriel because he is the demiurge of our world. He is the Holy Spirit of the Koran; the philosophers identified him with the Tenth Hierarchic Intelligence or active Intelligence, that for humankind is both the angel of knowledge and the angel of revelation.

This theme has been developed in many ways, a synthesis of which would be a considerable task and one that has not yet been attempted.[17] In the course of previous researches, I was able to ascertain (in the writings, for example, of the seventeenth-century theosophist Qāḍī Sa'īd Qummī) that the theme of the Throne was actually *eo ipso* that of the heavenly Temple, archetype of all temples, and that it is in fact possible to substitute the word *Temple* for *Throne*. In addition, wherever we come across this theme in Islamic theosophy, we are dealing with the same theme as it appears in some form or other in the Jewish Cabbalah, as well as with the theme of the Temple in the tradition of Christian esotericism—I am thinking in particular of the theme of the interiorization of the Temple in the work of the great eighteenth-century mystic Willermoz.[18] In the present case, too, the hermeneutics of colour leads to just such an interiorization.

For the contemplative exploration of the cosmic Throne of Mercy reveals that the four lights typified by the archangelic tetrad are the sources around which the totality of lights revolves, including the lights of the supra-sensible world. They are the absolute and universal lights, from which all partial lights are derived. Each manifestation of these partial lights is a *ḥikāyah* (imitation, story, recital, parable) of the supreme Lights, which are themselves not the result of any intermixture but are primordial "acts of light". I will merely refer in passing to the question that suggests itself to our author, namely, whether white is a colour like the others or,

17 Cf. below, the study "The Configuration of the Temple of the Ka'bah as a Secret of Spiritual Life, according to the work of Qāḍī Sa'īd Qummī (1103/1691)". See also Mullā Ṣadrā, op. cit., pp. 166–167, 218 ff.

18 I owe my knowledge of this to the very fine unedited document presented by Antoine Faivre in the appendix to his edition of René le Forestier, *La Franc-maçonnerie templière et occultiste aux XVIIIe et XIXe siècles* (Paris, Aubier-Montaigne, 1970), pp. 1023–1049.

properly speaking, not a colour at all. In fact, this question is first suggested in a variant reading of the *ḥadīth* of the Throne quoted above,[19] as well as by the fourth Imam, 'Alī Zaynal-'Abidīn, when he says that white light is the "Light of Lights", while red, yellow and green light are themselves the light of which white is the light. That is why white light can acquire any *tincture*, although no colour can be *tinted* by it. It is therefore the most simple of colours, the most faithful *ḥikāyah* of the supreme world that lies beyond the universes accessible to our contemplation.

B. Now that we know these sources, the archetypes of colour as they exist in the cosmic Throne of Mercy, we have to describe their mode of generation according to the four elemental qualitative modalities analysed earlier. It is clear (II, chapter II) that each of these modalities possesses its own exigency and aptitude. When the light of the Principle manifests itself through one of these modalities, it does so through the colour which is specific to the modality in question. Here we have the conditions necessary for a hermeneutic of colour: each of the four modalities can be a form of manifestation; a particular manifestation is produced according to the colour that is specific to a particular modality. All colour, therefore, is a *phainomenon* that "symbolizes with" the light of its Principle, and the meaning should be interpreted in accordance with this manifestation.

We have seen the four elemental modalities emerge on the level of the world of Nature, itself typified as the lower left-hand pillar of the cosmic Throne of Mercy, whose light is red. It is self-evident, then, that the first modality—Fire—which issues from this Nature will have red as its specific colour. The four constitutive modalities of the world of Nature are thus seen as manifesting, each at one level of this Nature, the four colours of the Throne.

a) *Heat and dryness* in a substance postulate the substance's stability in

19 The text of the *ḥadīth*, as it is recorded by the first Imam, mentions (as distinct from the other colours): "A white light from which whiteness proceeds." Thus, he does not speak of it as a *tinctura*, as though things were *tinted* by it. This text supports those who hold that *white* is not a colour but the *pole* of all colours, and exempt from the definitions that apply to them; all of them have recourse to it, while it has recourse only to itself. By contrast, the same *ḥadīth* as recorded by one of the other Imams says: "A white light whereby whiteness *becomes white*." This variant reading supports those who hold that white is a colour in the same class as other colours, that is, that the white object is similarly *tinted* by whiteness. Furthermore, white is a colour in that it is postulated by the elemental Natures or qualities, since it is the colour specific to the element of Water.

the shadow of its Principle and its orientation towards that Principle, in other words coherence and cohesion, subtlety and ascending motion (*ṣu'ūd*). Its configuration or *Gestalt* is the upright stance: the Arabic letter *alif* (I) in its vertical solitude, or the Pen, or the tall flame, or the cypress tree thrusting straight at the sky-line. All this is the result of the tendencies of a substance's constitutive parts to move towards *one* centre, *one* area of being. When all these properties are united in one substance which is the first to emanate from its *henadic* principle (here the lower left-hand pillar of the Throne), they require this substance to be *red* in colour, because that is what the colour red *is*, at least when we are dealing with the subtle component parts (the *laṭīfah*). If, however, the colour red acquires an extreme intensity in the parts which are dense, these will turn a verdigris green (*zangār*) in colour. (What we call the oxidization of copper or silver, for example, is interpreted here in terms of a rigorously qualitative physics, which posits at the origin of a colour only the state of density or subtlety of its parts, its proximity to or distance from the Principle.)

That, in short, is why the colour of Fire is *red*. Since it is the most subtle of the elements, its colour is equally subtle and is hidden from our eyes of flesh, created out of opaque Earth. This Earth must itself take on the *tincture* of Fire before Fire can be seen by us as red and in a state of density, as we observe it to be in the case of a lump of coal, a candle, or a piece of red-hot iron. And while this may be the only Fire we can see, it is also the Fire that Zoroastrian cosmology denounces as that of Ahriman, because it is a fire that ravages, whereas the subtle Fire of Ormazd neither ravages nor destroys. The significance of this differentiation will become clear to us at the conclusion of our enquiry. Let us observe in passing that it should not surprise us if in Persian miniatures, as in the ritual paintings of the Byzantine Empire down to our Middle Ages, natural tints are not reproduced as the artist may have seen them with his eyes of flesh; what counts above all is the colour's symbolic, hermeneutic, sacramental value.

b) When *heat and humidity* are in a substance, they result in swelling, expansion, the opposite to the effects of dryness. Nevertheless, here too heat demands ascending motion, which is why the figuration or *Gestalt* that typifies such a substance in the world of volumes is the conical form of a pine-cone or, in the world of surfaces, the triangle pointing upwards (△). The internal cohesion that such a substance owes to its heat would postulate, as in the preceding case, the colour red; but its expansiveness postulates the colour white. The result is an intermediary, mediating colour (a *barzakh*-like in-between colour, like the arbiter between man and wife of which mention was made above). Thus, the colour of the element Air is *yellow*, but in order to be visible to our eyes of flesh, it must take on an earthly *tincture* (the author gives the example of the yellow colour of bile, thus relating the theory of colours to traditional medicine).

c) When *cold and humidity* come together in the same substance, the humidity demands expansion, as in the case of Air, while the cold demands movement downwards (*tasafful*), the absence of all spontaneous upward impulsion. Such a substance revolves upon itself; its *Gestalt* is the spherical form (O), the most corpulent of all forms. Because of their lack of compactness and cohesion, its constituent parts tend towads dispersion and thus towards transparency; and when the Principle manifests itself through it, it does so through the substance's swelling and expansiveness. The colour deriving from these two properties is *white*, and thus the colour of the element Water is white. Once again, to be visible to us it must congeal or agglomerate as foam (or, in another medical reference, as phlegm, *balgham* = φλέγμα).

d) Finally, when *cold and dryness* are the determining factors of a substance, the dryness postulates the compactness and cohesion of the parts, while the cold demands movement downwards, as in the case of Water. The resulting colour is *black*, the colour of the terrestrial Earth (on the other hand, the colour of the celestial Earth of Hūrqalyā is green); and black forms a screen before the lights of the Principle. That is why the Earth is tenebrous, inert and lifeless. Its *Gestalt* is a toothed form (*shakl mutaḍarras*) with angles and dents (ʌʌʌ), composing a screen.

We now have a succession of morphological types (I O △ ʌʌʌ) attributed to the four modalities which are characterized by their respective colours. For the moment, we do not possess any terms of comparison; as our shaykh says at this point: "Take all this in with care, for you will not find it in any book, neither will anyone speak to you of it."

C. Now we know the sources of the basic colours in the archetypal Throne or Temple, and we have seen them emerge in each of the four constitutive elemental modalities. To achieve a transcendental hermeneutic, we have to see whether we can find a correspondence to these four constitutive modalities at all levels of the universe. To this end, let us bear in mind the initial proposition, to the effect that all composites, whether of the sensible or the supra-sensible world, possess a colour. This proposition implies a differentiation between the existence of colour and its manifestation. Opposing it was the proposition of the philosophers, which either confused existence with manifestation or at most granted a potential existence to colour—that is to say, existence in a state of invisibility, of non-actualization in the darkness. Conversely, when our theosophers speak of colours actually existing in a non-manifest state, they are envisaging something quite other than the philosopher-opticians, for the simple reason that the latter took into account only the level of our physical world, and that for them colour was a manifestation which had reference only to our physical world. The invisible colours of which the theosophers speak are certainly actualized, but they are invisible because of their extreme subtlety and luminescence. That is to say, their invisibility is due not to the darkness but to a light which is too intense for our terrestrial eyes of flesh. Yet our contemplative Imagination, through the exercise of an inner vision, is able to imagine in each of the superior universes an *anamnesis* of the sensible colours of our world.

These subtle composites are colours possessing the "oriental" *tinctura*, in the metaphysical sense of the word (*alwān musharraqah*, II, chapter III).[20] Such colours are the *ḥikāyah* (imitation, parable) of their Principle; they are not something that needs to be illuminated in order to be actualized, but are themselves acts of the Light which acquires their *tincture* in the subtle state, so subtle and pure that this Light is not perceptible to our eyes and remains occulted. This is why the light of the Throne of Mercy cannot be perceived, even though it is seventy times brighter than the light of the firmament (*Kursī*). In the same way, the light of the firmament cannot be perceived, even though—or rather because—it is seventy times brighter than the light of the sun. Here the shaykh valorizes the postulates of traditional Shiite cosmology (the *ḥadīth* of *Kāfi* by Kulaynī), in which the recurrence of the number seven and its augmentations make it clear that the numerical signs possess an arithmosophic value, not the statistical value of a quantitative science. According to a *ḥadīth* by the sixth Imam, "the sun is one 70th of the light of the firmament. The light of the firmament (*Kursī*) is one 70th of the light of the Throne (*'Arsh*). The light of the Throne is one 70th of the light of the Veil (*nūr al-Ḥijāb*). The light of

20 The word *musharraq* can also mean "tinted red"; the allusion is particularly apposite in our text.

the Veil is one 70th of the light of the Curtain (*nūr al-Sitr*)"—Veil and Curtain, beyond the Throne, are possibly a reminiscence in this cosmology of the esoteric meaning of the structure of the Temple of Solomon—"And yet all these lights are invisible."

What needs to be emphasized is the fact that it is not the darkness but extreme light that is the cause of this invisibility. We perceive these subtle realities, not when they finally emerge from obscurity and darkness but, on the contrary, when by condensation and thickening the light encloses itself in the darkness. The colours that our eyes perceive in bodies or in the most magnificent of landscapes are not present in their purity, in the state in which they are in the simple Elements that are invisible to us. They are mixed with darkness and the black colour of the Earth, because only thus are colours perceptible in the terrestrial world and to our earthly eyes. The light here is an "oriental", illuminating *colour*, while colour is *light* in a state of density, and both, as we know, are in the same relation to each other as spirit and body.

We have reached a crossroads; for this composition of light and colour that is the structure of every signature is raised and repeated at every level of the sensible and supra-sensible worlds. This is the way we have to follow. From the start, our author once again reminds us of the signature's double dimension, typified in the vocabulary of Ibn 'Arabī as a lordly and suzerain dimension (*rabb*), and a human dimension that is in the service of this divine dimension to the same degree as the latter is dependent on it (II, chapter IV). The sixth Imam, Ja'far al-Ṣādiq, has commented magnificently on this: "The human condition (that of vassal, servant, the *marbūbī-yah*) is a gem whose hidden base is the lordly and divine condition (*rubūbīyah*). What remains occulted in the divine condition is accessible in the human condition. And what is lacking or absent in the human condition can be found in the divine condition." (We may recall the diagram, specified above, of two interpenetrating triangles.) Thus we are at a crossroads, because at this point the phenomenology of colours intersects with the highest mystical experience. All we are able to perceive of colours in our world, and with our eyes of flesh, is their condition as *marbūb*, as servant in the service of the light. But at the same time it is possible for our contemplative vision to imagine them in their divine dimension (*rabb*), their lordly condition. "What you have learned to know in the world of sensible phenomena and the human condition, learn now to know in the supra-sensible world (*absent* from our senses) and in the divine condition (*fī'l-ghayb wa'l-rubūbīyah*)." Learn, that is, to know the gem hidden in the phenomenon of colour which is accessible to our senses.

Where on the scale of being is our present world situated? Many *ḥadīth* have been composed by the Imams on this subject: "God created millions of universes and millions of Adams, and you are in the last of these universes, and you yourselves are the adamic humanity of this last universe." All that we find and see in our world "descends" from the universes that precede it. In place of the current term of correspondence and symbolism between these universes, our shaykh employs a term of remarkable realism, the term *dhikr*, which signifies a calling to mind (anamnesis) or naming of something. In the current vocabulary of Sufism, the term *dhikr* designates the practice of invoking a divine Name until the endless repetition seals up the soul's energies and produces a state of ecstatic intoxication.

Here, the word has a sense that is more sober and strict. The shaykh means that in every universe there is an *anamnesis* (*dhikr*) of what we perceive in this world (the word anamnesis here signifying something similar to "evocation" as it is used in connection with music and painting). In every universe, each thing, being or state that we perceive in our universe possesses an *anamnesis* which corresponds to the state of that universe. There cannot be a *hiatus*: it is not possible for a signature to be situated at such an extreme distance from its Principle that the intermediary degrees lack an *anamnesis* of it, that is to say, something that calls it to mind and corresponds to it. Colours, therefore, possess an *anamnesis* in the superior universes over which the Treasures or archetypes have ascendency. Obviously, however, one cannot know the modality of these anamneses without a profound knowledge of what they *call to mind*—that is, the four possible modalities of every signature. The point is that in these superior universes, every signature possesses these modalities, but in each universe the modalities exist in accordance with the requirements imposed by the particular nature of that universe.

This is the root of the law which requires that we distinguish between *existence* and *manifestation*, a law so rigorous that the Shaykhi School, of which Muḥ. Karīm-Khān Kirmānī was a leading figure, had to remind the Shiites that it was the basic law of their esotericism, prescribed by the holy Imams themselves. In affirming the existence of an esoteric hierarchy, they affirmed the existence of certain perfect Shiites, the *Kāmilān-i shī'ah.*[21] This scandalized the exoteric Mullas, in whose eyes those who proclaimed the necessary existence of such beings could only be claiming for themselves the status of "perfect Shiites". But this was not the case: the Shaykhis, although they were not always understood, responded tirelessly to this accusation by saying that their affirmation had reference to a category of spiritual persons in this world but that under no circumstances did it ever permit the naming of such persons. A spiritual qualification is a secret between God and his worshipper; it never is and never can be an exoteric prerogative, worldly, social or profane. The existence of these "perfect Shiites" is absolutely necessary if the world is to continue to be, for they are its mystical pillars. Yet though their existence is a necessity, not only is their manifestation not necessary, but it is precisely their occultation that is necessary and inevitable under the present conditions of our world. If they were to manifest what they are, they would *eo ipso* cease to exist as such. One might say that they are under the same strict laws as the knights of the Grail. The esoteric conception of these perfect Shiites, who are unknown to the majority of men, is in a certain respect reminiscent of that of the "unknown, secret, just men (Saddiqīm)" of the Jewish tradition;[22] while in another respect it recalls those "unknown Superiors" of a particular esoteric Occidental tradition, provided that the word "Superiors" is understood in the metaphysical and spiritual sense.

It should be emphasized that the necessity for the occultation of these "perfect Shiites" from the eyes of the world is equally applicable to the divine dimension as "a gem occulted in the human condition", in the words of the Imam Ja'far. It also applies to the occultation of the "divine dimension" or the "lordly" aspect of colour, as our shaykh invites us to contemplate it in the universes that precede that of the earthly Adam. It is this lordly aspect or "divine dimension" of colour which is necessarily and inevitably occulted from the common perception of our world. Our shaykh pursues a characteristic line, on which, unfortunately, we cannot elaborate here. He presents us with a hierarchy consisting not just of seven but of

21 On this theme, which links up with what is called the "fourth pillar" (*rukn-i chahārum*), see *En Islam iranien . . .*, op. cit., IV, book VI (The Shaykhi School).

22 Cf. Gershom Scholem, 'Three Types of Jewish Piety', *Eranos-Jahrbuch* XXXVIII, 1969, pp. 346 ff.

eight levels of universe, because mention is now made of the world of the hidden deity at the summit, a world that transcends all the theophanic universes concentrated in the Temple of Mercy. To signify the distance separating one universe from the next, the shaykh reiterates that every superior world is of a light seventy times more intense than that of the world immediately inferior to it. We have already seen that this figure, with its arithmosophic value, is meant essentially to tell us that the distance is beyond our quantitative measures.

1. The highest of these universes is "the world of the intimate depths and light of God" (*'ālam al-fu'ād wa-nūr Allāh*). The lights of which we have been speaking up till now exist there as lights that are true and real: they are the light of the Lord of lords, and even the pure cherubic Intelligences are unable to perceive them. There, colours are united in a transcendent, unific (henadic) union, without admitting plurality of any sort. It is to these that the inspired (*qudsī) ḥadīth* alludes when it speaks of seventy Veils of light. "If these Veils were to be lifted, the splendours of his Face would set on fire all that met his gaze."[23]

2. Next come the "four pillars of the Throne". This is the universe of the cherubic Intelligences (*'ālam al-'uqūl*); and here the lights are united in a union which as yet admits only a plurality and multiplicity that are wholly inner, ideal (*ma'nawī*), not exterior (white light).

3. This is the universe of Spirits, of subtle Forms (*barzakhīyah*) intermediate between the Intelligences and the Souls. Colours are differentiated according to a difference equally intermediate between ideal plurality and exterior plurality (yellow light).

4. This is the world of *Malakūt*, the world of Souls separated from the matter of this world (*al-nufūs al-mujarradah al-malakūtīyah*). Here colours are differentiated according to their exterior form (*tamāyuz sūrī*) (green light).

5. This is the world of Nature, in which colours are differentiated by nature and genus (*tamāyuz tabi'ī wa-jinsī*), by a diversification accessible to the senses (red light).

6. Below is the world of Cloud (*'ālam al-habā'*). Colours are differentiated by a material difference (*tamāyuz māddī*) (ashen colour).

23 Here, the shaykh brings together two quotations—that of the Prophet: "Know God through God himself", as God may not be known save through God; and that of the (anonymous) poet: "She saw the Moon in the sky, and she remembered me—Each of us two comtemplates a single Moon—But I contemplate it through her eyes, and she contemplates it through my eyes."

7. This is the *mundus imaginalis* (*'ālam al-mithāl*), where colours are differentiated by individual differences, like images seen in mirrors—these last being the lower level of the *mundus imaginalis*, still linked to material bodies (dark green; cf. the green light of the *Malakūt*).

8. Finally there is the world of material bodies, where colours are differentiated in a way we are able to observe (black).

"Such," concludes our shaykh, "are the Treasures (archetypes) of colours, from which they descend and towards which they ascend. Their subtlety or density is in proportion to the subtlety or density of each of these universes." He is aware that he has dealt very summarily with the question of the *anamnesis* of colour in each universe, but "if we wished," he says, "to comment on these problems in a more profound fashion, with prolegomena of prolegomena, the Moon would disappear before we had completed our elucidation, for as the Koranic verse (18:110) says: 'If the sea were ink for the words of my God, the sea would be exhausted before my God's words were exhausted, even if we had another sea like the first to provide us with ink.'"

5. *The hermeneutics of the Koran and the hermeneutics of colour.* The analysis of these anamneses has of necessity been an incomplete one; nevertheless the idea we have been given of them is enough to justify our shaykh in his sense of having attained the goal envisaged from the start. From this vantage-point he will be able to undertake a hermeneutic of the phenomenon of colour, and particularly of the colour red, which parallels step by step the esoteric hermeneutics of the Koran. It is a grandiose undertaking, the consummation of an entire theosophy which pivots on the phenomenon of the sacred Book; and it suggests many fruitful comparisons with other esoteric commentaries on the Koran as well as those on the Bible. Here I will simply recall the *ḥadīth* of the Prophet proclaiming the seven esoteric depths of the Koran, in connection with the undertaking of the great fourteenth-century Iranian mystic 'Alāuddawlah Simnānī. By means of a radical interiorization of prophetology, Simnānī relates all Koranic references to the prophets to the seven centres of subtle physiology. These centres, which typify the "prophets of your being", are each characterized by a colour, an *aura*, that belongs to it alone. In the case of our shaykh, the undertaking is comparable in scope but follows a different schema from that of Simnānī. As we observed earlier, it illustrates in a remarkable way

what is common to the phenomenon of the Book both as *Liber mundi*, the "Book of being" to which colours pertain, and as the *Liber revelatus*, the holy Book; for the same hermeneutic leads to an understanding of both of these.

The vocabulary to be used needs careful defining. The word *ta'wīl* is the key-word of this hermeneutic procedure. Our shaykh defines the *ta'wīl* (II, chapter V) as "consisting in referring the literal appearance back to one of the archetypes [or in 'exchanging' the literal value for one of the treasures or archetypes],[24] with the understanding that this archetype determines what the object is, whether it belongs to the sensible or to the supra-sensible world." This definition accords perfectly with that given by Ismaili theosophy: "The *ta'wīl* consists in leading back, in returning a thing to its principle or archetype" (in Persian: *chīzī-rā bi-aṣl-i khvud rasānīdan*). Thus, the idea of the *ta'wīl* implies the action of rising up again, the idea of an ascensional, *anagogical* way. As an esoteric hermeneutic, the *ta'wīl* is essentially an "anagogical hermeneutic".

The starting point of this hermeneutic is the *ẓāhir*, the exoteric dimension. At every hermeneutic level there is both an esoteric dimension (*bāṭin*) to discover and a *ta'wīl* to accomplish. Thus there is a *ta'wīl* of the esoteric as well as of the exoteric dimension, and this *ta'wīl* in its turn contains an esoteric dimension. In order to clarify the route we still have to traverse, we will recapitulate its stages in the following schema:

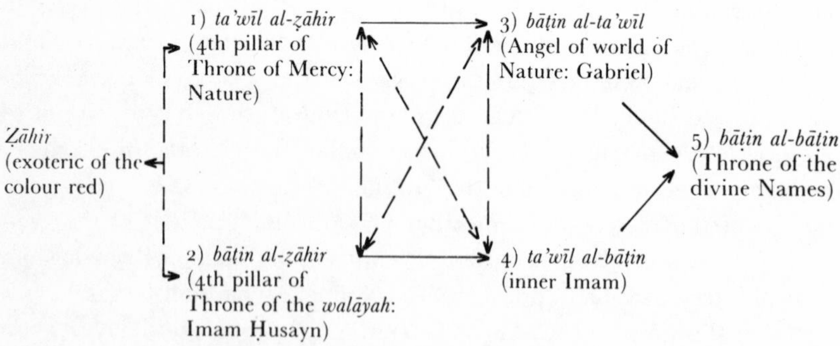

24 According to the double meaning connoted by the root *ṣrf*: send back, expedite; exchange; change the direction of something (whence, in grammar, the *ṣarf* signifies declension and conjugation); *taṣarruf* means "to dispose freely of something"; *ṣarrāf* means "he who changes". The spiritual hermeneutist is in some sense an "exchanger" of value and a "changer" of direction.

The shaykhs of the Shaykhi School discussed certain chapters of the Koran according to this complete schema, and one can well imagine that it would require an entire library to make a commentary on the Koran in this fashion from one end to the other. In order to make it clear from the start what the process of the *ta'wīl* comprises, the shaykh takes as an example a verse from the Koran, an example which has the virtue of showing us how the colour red belongs to the phenomenon of the sacred Book, and how as a result the same hermeneutic can be applied to it.

The Koranic verse (13:17) is as follows: "He makes water descend from the sky, so there are torrents that flow according to their measure." By means of the *ta'wīl*, the sky is elevated to the level of the divine creative Will (the *mashī'ah*) which is itself subject and object, organ and source of Creation, the active dimension (*jihat al-fā'il*) of that which is set in motion (the *mutaḥarrak*). The *water* descending from the sky is *being*—not absolute being, but the determined and delimited being (*muqayyad*) that descends from this Will. It is the Water whereby every thing in the act of being has been made to live (we have already seen how, in alchemical terms, this Water is the equivalent of the primordial Fire); by this Water, corpses, which are vessels of being in a state of expectation, are aroused to life. The torrents are precisely these vessels of being; they are torrents whose beds are empty and dry until the "Water of being" flows into them. This, according to the shaykh, is how the *ta'wīl* is employed, as the anagogical hermeneutic of all verses of the Koran and all traditional recitals.[25] But he emphasizes that the initiative with regard to its use cannot be left to the first comer: only he has the capacity and the right to assume responsibility for the *ta'wīl* who has first acquired a perfect understanding of the "data" which the literal revelation (*tanzīl*) provides for the *ta'wīl*, and who is fully apprised of the modalities according to which the universes intercorrespond, as well as of the meaning of the *anamneses* to be found in all of them. For this universality of universes forms the *Liber mundi*, the Book of being, the immense register-book (*Kitāb tadwīnī*) which God wrote with the *Pen* of the creative Act, the Pen which signifies the first Intelligence, the first-created Logos.[26]

25 Cf. for example 7:143: when God manifests himself on the mountain (Sinai), he reduces it to dust; for the *ta'wīl*, the mountain is the body itself of Moses, and Moses falls down in a swoon; similarly, the four Elements are the four humours of the human body, etc.

26 Cf. the *ḥadīth*: "The first thing that God created was the Pen. Then he told it:

Other Koranic verses attest that what is posited is a *book*, as for example the following: "You will remain in the *Book of God* until the day of Resurrection" (30:56); and again: "What, then, did the past generations desire?" asks Pharoah of Moses, who replies, "The knowledge of that is close to my God in a certain Book" (20:51–52). This Book is the glorious Word that God will utter and that is wholly a Book,[27] comprising genera (homologous to the large sections of the Koran), species (homologous to the chapters), categories (the verses or "signs", *āyāt*), and individuals (homologous to the words made up of letters).[28]

Such being the case, the colour red is in one sense a letter (*ḥarf*) of this Book; in another sense it is a word, a verb (*kalimah*); in yet another sense it is an entire verse (a "sign", *āyah*). In this way it corresponds to all the components of the phenomenon of the Book ("And among His *āyāt* . . . is the diversity of your languages and your colours" (30:22)).[29] That is why, concludes the shaykh, recapitulating everything that correlates the two aspects of the phenomenon of the Book, "the colour red contains a *ta'wīl* as the Book contains a *ta'wīl*." The science of Nature and the science of the Book are two aspects of the same science of the Spirit.

1. The *ta'wīl of the exoteric dimension of the colour red (ta'wīl al-ẓāhir)*, that is to say, the immediate term to which the *ta'wīl* leads the colour back, is Nature in the act of being, or being as Nature: the lower left-hand pillar of the cosmic Throne of Mercy. A *ḥadīth* attributed to the first Imām has already informed us that this pillar is characterized by red light, "whereby the colour red becomes red". All red colour in our world derives from the essential red light of this pillar; thus, the pillar is the Treasure or arche-

---

'Write!'—'What shall I write?' asked the Pen.—'That which is and that which will be until the Day of the Resurrection.' And the Pen wrote. Then God put a seal over the mouth of the Pen and, having written, it did not declare the hidden meaning."

27 On the transition from the Word as uttered—from its state as Logos—to the Word as it is when set down in scripture, in its state as the Book, cf. Mullā Ṣadrā Shīrāzī, op. cit., pp. 193–194 of the French text; cf. also the index s.v. *Kalām Allāh*, Livre.

28 "The Most High God designates its categories by the word *āyāt* (verses, Signs). He says: 'We will show them our Signs [that is to say, the categories of the Book written by the Pen] both on the horizons and within themselves' (41:53). And he designates its individuals by the word *kalimah* (word, Logos), as he does in the case of Jesus: 'By one of his Words, whose name shall be Christ' (3:45), and with reference to his name as a sign (*āyāt*): 'We have made of Maryam's son and of his mother a Sign' (23:50). And he calls the whole by the name of *Book*, as you have just heard."

29 This is the verse already quoted (see above, note 11), as a Koranic testimony in favour of the thesis that colours are actually in things themselves, not merely in our perception.

type whence the colour red "descends" into this world, and it is the explanation of the colour. To complete the picture, our author reminds us that this fourth pillar of the Throne—Nature—comprises the four elemental modalities characterized respectively by the four basic pillars: Fire (red), which is the very nature of being; Air (yellow), which is its exemplary Image (*mithāl*); Water (white), which is its matter; Earth (black), which is its body. It is to be observed that the descending order of the Elements (beginning with Fire, that accords with the supra-sensible world) is reversed in our temporal and phenomenal world (in which we ascend from Earth up to the element Fire).

A certain legend alludes to this *ta'wīl* of the colour red when it recounts how the Creator produced a "red hyacinth" (the words that form the title of our shaykh's work) and that he contemplated it with admiration. Under his gaze, the red hyacinth melted and turned into Water (once again, the alchemical idea of the reciprocity of Water and Fire). Out of the foam on this Water, God created the Earth; out of its vapour (the subtle part) he created the Heaven. The shaykh explains that the red hyacinth typifies Nature: it turns into Water which is Nature's matter; the Heaven, which is the *mundus imaginalis* (*'ālam al-mithāl*), is created out of its subtle vapour; while from its Earth is created the telluric mass, which is the world of bodies. In this way, the symbol of the red hyacinth embraces the totality of the four fundamental modalities.[30]

2. The *esoteric dimension of the colour red (bāṭin al-ẓāhir*, the esoteric of its exoteric, II, chapter VI), takes us from the cosmic Throne or Temple of Mercy to another Throne or Temple, which is in perfect symbolic accord with the former. The second Throne is in fact the hierocosmic Throne of Shiite esotericism, and is named the *Throne of the "walāyah"* (*'Arsh al-walāyah*). We know that the word *walāyah* is one of the key words in Shiite theosophy, for it is at the heart of the Imamology that goes hand in hand with prophetology. The *walāyah* (Persian *dūstī*) is the gift of love, the divine love or favour that renders eternally sacred the "Friends of

30 The author has added later, in the margin of the text, a number of possible *ta'wīlāt*: "We can also *lead back* the colour red to violence, anger, murder, or to the bile that is in the human body, or to fierce beasts, or to fire, or to the planet Mars, to the sun, to political power, to the Turks, to the sword, to copper, or to the elixir of gold and other, similar things." Doubtless on re-reading what he had written, the author added this inventory haphazardly; the rules of the *ta'wīl* that are thereby demonstrated are not clear, whereas he is extremely precise when speaking of the correspondences between the Thrones.

God", that is to say, using the term in its proper sense, the Twelve Imams, and through their mediation all those whose attachment (*walāyah*) to the Imams makes them likewise "Friends of God".

The *walāyah* transforms the religion of the Law into the religion of love. As a gift imparted to the Imams, it is defined as the "esoteric dimension of prophecy", and is thus prophecy's indispensible support. The vocation of *nabī* or prophet presupposes a previous state as *walī* or friend. Thus, just as the four pillars typified by the archangelic tetrad are the supports of the cosmic Throne of Mercy in its function as creator of the universes, the tetrad made up out of four of the twelve Imams is the support of the Throne of the *walāyah*. On this Throne is established that Mercy which is called here prophecy or prophetic grace (*Raḥmān al-nubuwwah*).[31]

The correspondences between the structures of the two Thrones are perfect, and they demonstrate the breadth of the cosmic function of the *walāyah* as the word is used in Imamology. I cannot, unfortunately, give more than a brief description of them here: anything more would require a full commentary on Imamology. The pillar of *white* light is here the mystical figure of the twelfth Imam, the Imam of our times, the "Imam hidden from the senses but present to the hearts of those who believe in him". He is never named without the interpolation, "May God hasten our joy of him!" This joy is his future advent as the Imam of the Resurrection, Renewer of the world, he who will restore the world to the state of purity that it possessed originally, at its creation (restoration, *apokatastasis*). This no doubt accounts for his role as the keeper of the white light. He bears the forename of the Prophet; he is the secret of the *walāyah*, which as we have just seen is itself the secret or esoteric dimension of prophecy, of the prophetic vocation and message. The twelfth Imam is the crown and fulfilment of the pleroma of the Twelve Imams, and is consequently placed at the apex as the "upper right-hand pillar" of the Throne of the *walāyah*. Finally, he is the pole of the *futuwwah*, the mystical order of chivalry made up of all those who aspire to be numbered among the "companions of the twelfth Imam".

The lower right-hand pillar of yellow light typifies the first Imam, Imam 'Alī ibn Abī-Ṭālib, the Prophet's *alter ego*. The upper left-hand

31 On the whole of this theme, see my study 'Juvénilité et chevalerie', *L'Homme et Son Ange* (Paris, Fayard, 1984). See also *En Islam iranien . . .*, op. cit., IV, general index s.v. *fotowwat*, *walāyat*.

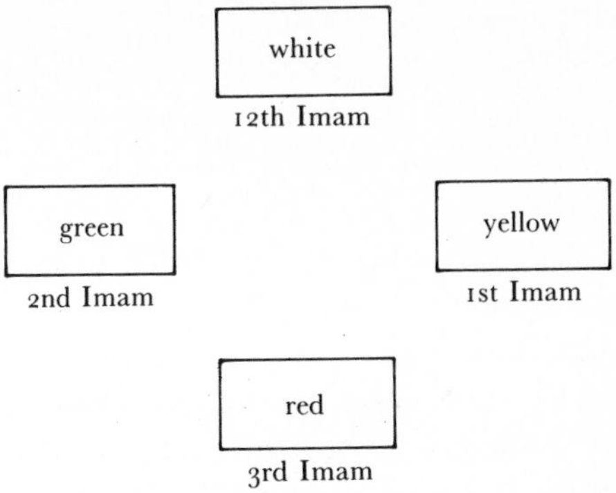

The four pillars of the Throne of the *walāyah*

pillar of *green* light typifies the second Imam, Ḥasan ibn 'Alī. Finally, the lower left-hand pillar of *red* light typifies the third Imam, Ḥusayn ibn 'Alī, whom the tragedy of Karbalā made into the "prince of martyrs" (*sayyid al-shuhadā'*). Thus, then, the Throne or Temple of the *walāyah* of the Imams is the esoteric dimension (the *bāṭin*) of the cosmic Throne of creative Mercy. The fourth pillar, made crimson by the red light of the martyred Imam Ḥusayn, is the esoteric dimension of the fourth pillar, that of Nature, which is characterized by red Light in the cosmic Throne.

One should meditate at length on this correspondence, this mysterious *anamnesis*. I shall do no more than mention the beautiful legend recounted by our shaykh, which tells how one feast day, when the two child-Imams Ḥasan and Ḥusayn asked their grandfather the Prophet to give them a new garment as a present, two robes came down out of the sky. The robes were white, but the two boys declared that they would not be satisfied until they were dyed the colour they wanted. Ḥasan asked for his garment to be green as the emerald, while Ḥusayn wanted a colour like that of the red hyacinth. This was brought about through the ministration of the angel Gabriel, the angel of Revelation. But while the Prophet rejoiced, the angel shed tears; and when the Prophet asked him the reason, he could not but announce the fate that awaited the two young Imams in this world. Ḥasan would perish through poison, Ḥusayn would be assassinated. Another tradition expresses, with delicate symbolism, the link between the Imam Ḥusayn, fourth pillar of red light of the Throne of the *walāyah*, and the archangel Gabriel, fourth pillar of red light of the Throne of Mercy. The tradition tells us that "the Prophet clothed Ḥusayn in a garment woven of the archangel's hair". Other traditions express the same secret (*sirr*) link by saying that the castle of al-Ḥasan in paradise is of emerald green, while the castle of al-Ḥusayn is of red hyacinth. It becomes more and more clear how the title of his book was imposed on our author.

3. Next comes *the esoteric dimension of the ta'wīl of the colour red (bāṭin al-ta'wīl*, II, chapter VII): for the conclusion reached by the first phase of the process, the *ta'wīl* of the exoteric dimension, contains in its turn its own esoteric meaning. The *ta'wīl* of the exoteric dimension of the colour red led us back to the fourth or lower left-hand pillar of the cosmic Throne of Mercy, that is to say, to the hypostasis of Nature (red light). On the other hand, what is called the esoteric dimension of Nature or the esoteric dimension of a heaven is the angel of that nature or that heaven. In the archangelic tetrad that supports the cosmic Throne, it is the archangel Gabriel who is the angel of our world of Nature. Such a hermeneutic accords perfectly with the role ascribed to the archangel Gabriel by the philosophers and theosophers of Islam. As we saw, he is the Tenth hierarchic Intelligence, and he is the demiurge of our world. (Here again, tradition offers us a delicate symbol: "The red rose is an effusion of the archangel Gabriel"). By the same token, it is he who, on the mystical Sinai, is the goal of the pilgrim in Suhravardī's romances of initiation. In this way, a strict correspondence between the tetrad of theophanic universes, the archangelic tetrad, and the tetrad of the *walāyah* is established; and we can see how in each tetrad there is an *anamnesis* of the colour red.

Our shaykh indicates other possible interpretations. This esoteric dimension of the *ta'wīl* of Nature, typified in the colour red, could also be the Imam of the Resurrection (*Qā'im al-Qiyāmah*); or his companions battling at his side; or the *walāyah* itself inasmuch as it is an elixir poured out over the bodies which are human hearts; or it can be the gnosis (*ma'rifah*) and the sciences of love (*'ulūm al-maḥabbah*). Does not the Imam Ja'far speak of love as a "Fire that unexpectedly invades the depths of the heart and consumes all that is not the beloved object"? There is certainly no need to reject any of these symbolisms; but the one initially offered has the advantage of applying in all respects from one hermeneutic level to another.[32]

32 It is worth emphasizing that our shaykh is remarkably aware of the danger inherent in the *ta'wīl* when it is used by the ignorant: "I cannot provide a more extended

4. A further step permits us to accomplish the *ta'wīl of the esoteric dimension of the colour red (ta'wīl al-bāṭin*, II, chapter VIII). In the third phase of the process, our shaykh has unveiled to us the esoteric dimension of the *ta'wīl* of the exoteric dimension, that is to say, of the *ta'wīl* which formed the first phase of our hermeneutical operation. This *ta'wīl* led us back, in the first phase, to the world of Nature; and, as we saw in the third phase, the esoteric dimension of this Nature is the angel Gabriel. Now he offers us the *ta'wīl* of the *esoteric* dimension, that is to say, of the dimension discovered during the second phase in the person of the Imam Ḥusayn (cf. the schema above). This fourth phase is decisive for Shiite spirituality, for it brings about a radical interiorization of Imamology. In the second phase, the esoteric dimension (*bāṭin*) of the colour red was shown to us in the person of the Imam Ḥusayn, the "prince of martyrs" (lower left-hand pillar of the Throne of the *walāyah*). The third phase showed us the esoteric dimension of the *ta'wīl* of the colour red, that is to say, the esoteric dimension of Nature; and this dimension is the angel of this Nature, the angel Gabriel. Now, corresponding symmetrically to this third phase which disclosed the "esoteric dimension of the *ta'wīl*", the fourth phase consists in accomplishing the "*ta'wīl* of the esoteric dimension" of the colour red, the dimension that the second phase disclosed to us in the person of the Imam Ḥusayn. To whom, then, does the present *ta'wīl* lead us? To the *Imam within*, the secret personal guide of each of us, to the *rabb* or lord, of whom each faithful vassal is the knight.[33]

---

commentary now, or, rather, such commentary is not permitted. For there is always a tendency in the hearts of men to deviate from the truth. Once they have understood the matter of the *ta'wīl* and the *bāṭin* in all their aspects, they start doing the *ta'wīl* of all religious laws in conformity with the object of their desires; they lead themselves and others astray." On the other hand, there are the doctors of the Law, the *fuqahā'*, who deny the *ta'wīl* and the esoteric dimension. Both these categories of person should be reminded of the tradition attributed to the Imam Ja'far al-Ṣādiq: "There are people who believe in the exoteric while denying the esoteric. This does not profit them in the slightest, for there is no exoteric faith save through an esoteric, and *vice versa*, no esoteric faith save through an exoteric." This simultaneous dual affirmation of the *ẓāhir* and the *bāṭin* expresses the whole spirit of Shiite gnosis. One can never say to symbols: "Vanish, you have been explained!" Does the colour red vanish once we have explained its genesis and symbolism?

33 It should be observed, in the diagram given above at the start of the present section of this essay, what correspondences are indicated by the direction of the arrows. There is a *ta'wīl* of the *ẓāhir* and a *ta'wīl* of the *bāṭin*; there is a *bāṭin* of the *ẓāhir* and a *bāṭin* of the *ta'wīl*, and so on. The relationship between the *bāṭin* of the *ta'wīl* and the *ta'wīl* of the *bāṭin* indicates the relationship between the Angel Gabriel and the inner

According to our shaykh, there is an Imam Ḥusayn within each man: his intellect, whose divine splendour is a light that derives from the Imam. But this inner Imam is surrounded by enemies, and these are all the powers of the carnal soul that issue from the shadow of the Imam's enemies. Within every man there unfolds a tragedy of Karbalā. "In the *Karbalā of his heart*, it may happen that the powers of the carnal soul kill the intellect and the angelic companions who assist it, and uproot all traces of them from man's heart. Then indeed there is accomplished in each one of us, word for word (*ḥarfan bi-ḥarfin*), the *ta'wīl* of the tragedy of Karbalā." Such is the *ta'wīl* of the esoteric dimension of the colour red, the *ta'wīl al-bāṭin.*

By proceeding in this way Shaykh Muḥ. Karīm-Khān Kirmānī places himself at the forefront of the great spiritual tradition of Shiism. The idea of the "Imam within" is to be found in the greatest spiritual masters: Najmuddīn Kubrā, Mullā Ṣadrā Shīrāzī, and so on.[34] I cannot do better than translate the shaykh's own words at this point: "God has in fact two sorts of witness[35] before men: the outer Imam (or witness) (*Ḥujjah ẓāhirah*), in the person of each of the Twelve Imams, and the inner Imam (or witness) (*Ḥujjah bāṭinah*). The Imam within is each individual intellect, such an intellect being the irradiation (*shu'ā'*) of the outer Imam; for the Shiites, the initiates of the Imams, have been created out of the rays of their light, and light is proportional to the source of light." Thus, the process of interiorization is accomplished spontaneously, since this light that is in man, or at any rate in the man who is an initiate of the Imams, is actually a ray of their own light; and so the light, both exterior and interior, is one and the same. The shaykh continues: "While the esoteric dimension of the colour red is the Imam Ḥusayn [see above, phase 2],

Iman. It is the same relationship as that established in the *Ishrāqīyūn* of Suhravardī between the Angel Gabriel as the Angel of humanity, and Perfect Nature as the guide and angel of each human individual. The interiorization of Imamology leading to the idea of the Imam within (the "Gabriel of your being") is of capital importance for the understanding of Shiite spirituality. See my *The Man of Light . . .*, op. cit., and *En Islam iranien . . .*, op. cit., index s.v. Imam, *shaykh al-ghayb*, Nature Parfaite.

34 Ibid., index s.v. guide intérieur.

35 This teaching is also to be found in the works of Mullā Ṣadrā. The term *Ḥujjah* (proof, guarantee, witness) applies, above all, to the Imam. In the technical vocabulary of the Ismailism of Alamūt, which is also marked by a tendency towards interiorization, the term signifies the dignitary who is the companion closest to the Imam, and who forms a bi-unity with him.

because he died a martyr's death at Karbalā, the *ta'wīl* of this esoteric dimension [that is, the term to which the *ta'wīl* of the Imam leads us back] is man's intellect, because all intellects derive from the irradiation and the light of this esoteric dimension [that is to say, from the Imam], intellects that can be murdered by the carnal soul and its assistants", whether these latter are typified by the men of Mu'āwiyah or by Ahriman's auxiliaries. This is the entire mystery of the Imamate within man. It is a theme that could be developed at length, but the shaykh, in his prudence, chooses to say no more.[36]

5. Finally, there is the *esoteric dimension of the esoteric* (*bāṭin al-bāṭin*, II, chapter IX), a subject on which our authors are usually fairly reticent. Muḥ. Karīm-Khān Kirmānī even gives us the motive for this reticence here when he refers to the Pharoah and his troops who immolate the sons of the believers but spare their wives. These sons are the initiates of esotericism, while the wives who are spared are the initiates of exotericism. The reference is transparent: it alludes to all those, East and West, who represent the priesthood of the Grand Inquisitor. And the shaykh says: "Neither is it permitted to reveal plainly the esoteric dimension of the esoteric." Nevertheless, some marginal references to it are permitted. To understand them it is enough simply to pursue the hermeneutical line we have taken up till now.

We should keep this line clearly in mind. On the one hand, the *ta'wīl* of the exoteric dimension of the colour red leads us back to the lower left-hand pillar of the cosmic Throne, to the world of Nature whose esoteric dimension is the archangel Gabriel (the esoteric dimension, that is to say, of the *ta'wīl*). On the other hand, the esoteric dimension of the colour red was revealed to be the lower left-hand pillar of the Throne of the *walāyah*, typified in the person of the third Imam, the Imam Ḥusayn, martyr of Karbalā. Next, the *ta'wīl* of this dimension disclosed the "Imam within" to each believer. Finally, what of the esoteric dimension of this esoteric dimension, that is to say not merely of the interiorization of the Imam through the *ta'wīl*, but of the essence of his essence in all its secret theosophical meaning? It now appears that the esoteric dimension of this

36 Here, the shaykh recalls that these *ta'wīlāt* are *arcana*. He does not wish to say more, for he has no confidence in the questioner who made him bring up the question of the colour red, and who belongs to that class of people whose constant questioning is only intended to embarrass the wise. The shaykh has answered here simply out of respect for the person who is acting as intermediary.

esoteric dimension can only be the Imam—seen not as he is in the dramatic action of his fugitive appearance on earth, but in his metaphysical essence, in the pleroma, that is, of the "eternal Muhammadan Reality", the *Ḥaqīqah muḥammadīyah*, the primordial theophany of the *Absconditum*, the pleroma of the "Fourteen Immaculate Ones" in their persons of light. By reason of its primordial theophanic function, this "eternal Muhammadan Reality" is assigned an essential cosmogonic function. And it is precisely about this that it is inadvisable to speak before the Pharoah and his troops, that is to say before the exotericist Mullās.

Nevertheless, this is the direction in which our shaykh appears to be steering us. He writes: "When the colour red is exalted to the world of the Imperative [by which he means the world not of the intermediate creation, *'ālam al-khalq*, but that which is the immediate response to the KN, the creative *Esto*, *'ālam al-Amr*, the world of the Imperative], this colour thereupon falls to the lot of the Perfect Word (*al-Kalimah al-tāmmah*) before which the Great Abyss draws back; for this Word possesses several degrees: the dot, the initial *alif*, the letters, the words [in short, all the components of the "Book of being", as we saw earlier]. And when the colour red is exalted to the divine Name, it is assigned exclusively to the level of the perfect Epiphany (*al-Ẓuhūr al-tāmm*), since these levels are four in number."[37] These four levels make up the Throne of the divine Names (*'Arsh al-Asmā'*), which corresponds symbolically to the cosmic Throne of the archangelic tetrad and to the Throne of the *walāyah*, both described above.

In speaking of the Throne on which Mercy is established, the Mercy in question signifies creative Mercy (the *Raḥmah* that is so close to the *Sophia* of other gnoses) which is at once subject and object (active and passive), the instrumental and the ablative of the act of Mercy which constitutes the liberation of being, the "absolution of being", setting being free to be.[38] Four of the divine Names are here the pillars of the Throne. First there is *al-Qābiḍ*, literally "he who seizes"; this is Mercy seizing "hold" of itself in a way that, through creative autophony, is transmuted into an act of being.

37 These are, says the shaykh without entering upon explanations, 1) the esoteric; 2) the esoteric according to its occultation; 3) the exoteric; 4) the exoteric according to its manifestation.

38 For the context of what is here referred to only briefly, see the teaching of Shaykh Aḥmad Aḥsā'ī, with which all Shaykhi thinkers are imbued. Cf. the *Fawā'id* (The Book of Teachings), (Tabriz 1274), pp. 37 ff. See my conference reports in: *Annuaire* of the Section des Sciences Religieuses de l'École pratique des Hautes-Études, 1966–1967, pp. 109 & 113; 1967–1968, pp. 142–145.

The other three Names are: "He who inaugurates" (*al-bādi'*), "He who brings death" (*al-mumīt*), "He who resuscitates" (*al-bā'ith*) (cf. Koran 30:40). According to the shaykh, it is the name *al-Qābiḍ* that sustains the colour red, which in its turn manifests itself in partial Names such as the Avenger, the Conqueror, the Dominator, the Protector, and so on. These names, however, are perhaps allusions to the twelfth Imam, the Imam of the Resurrection, who dominates the "heaven of the *walāyah*".

Our shaykh does not explain how the colours are divided between the other three Names, but concludes that forms of knowledge are endless and limitless. That which is first projected into intellects still imperfect is knowledge of the exoteric; then, progressively, an increasing knowledge of the esoteric is projected into them. "You must understand the concise words with which I have attempted to convey what I have conveyed. Then the exoteric will convert itself into the esoteric, and *vice versa*. For, if the esoteric dimension of the esoteric is concealed within the esoteric, it is because of its Manifestation within Manifestation itself. It is occulted because of the intensity of its Manifestation, and veiled because of the sublimity of its Light." This recapitulates everything that we have been taught by the "Book of the red hyacinth" about invisible lights and colours, the reasons for their occultation, and the true relationship between light and colour. The theory and hermeneutics of colour lead us to the heights of metaphysical theosophy. On the final point, the esoteric dimension of the esoteric, our shaykh has exercised discretion, and it behoves us to follow his example.[39]

39 The shaykh underlines the motives for his discretion by alluding to some verses by an anonymous poet: "If our age were not united in rejecting the truth, I would speak of it here. Nevertheless, I can be forgiven; I am jealous for you of everyone other than myself, even of myself—I am jealous of you, of the time and space that you occupy—Even were I to have you before my eyes—Up to the Day of the Resurrection, it would not suffice me." The "Seal of the book", which is its conclusion, returns to the question that was asked initially by a troublesome man in conversation with the person who reported it to Muḥammad Karīm-Khān Kirmānī. The troublesome man hoped to put the shaykh in a difficult position by provoking him to speak of the modality of the tint of the red carpet (which actually came from Kirmān!) upon which the questioners were seated. The analysis that we have given here makes evident the level to which the shaykh raised the question in order to answer it. In his conclusion, he analyses briefly the impulses that arise from the depths of the human being. The desires which are "tinted" only by the colour red are related to each other with the aid supplied to them by Mars and the Sun, as astrology explains in detail. Finally, the shaykh says: "As for the manner of tinting a carpet red with shellac, that is something over which dyers argue, even though in

EPILOGUE

The task which now suggests itself is one of comparative research. We should study the consequences of this colour theory for the theory and practice of alchemy, of which our shaykh was an initiate. We would need to discover what his doctrine of light and colour in the supra-sensible world has in common with the doctrines of other theosophical schools, notably with that of Swedenborg in the West. We would doubtless have to learn to look with new eyes at Persian miniatures, and also perhaps at the fiery windows of our own cathedrals. But we must postpone this task. Instead, I will conclude without going beyond the Iranian world, and will attempt to perceive in that world the deep resonance of all that shaykh Muḥ. Karīm-Khān Kirmānī has proposed for our meditation.

In this connection I shall recall some recent incidents, some conversations I happened to have at Persepolis in October 1971, during the celebrations of the twenty-fifth centenary of the founding of the Persian Empire, and during the international congress of Iranology which was being held at Shiraz at the same time and in honour of the same occasion. The previous month, at the beginning of September, what is now called the annual festival of Shiraz had taken place, though it is actually held among the grandiose ruins of Persepolis. A work by Xenakis had been performed, which, in the hill setting of the mountain that surrounds the ruins, made allusions to the myth of Prometheus. I was struck to observe, among some Iranian friends, not incomprehension of the Promethean allusions but, on the contrary, a comprehension so perfect that it resulted in a feeling which can only be called indignation. Now, this is one of the myths whereby Western consciousness has affirmed its pride: Fire, and hence permanent possession of the light, stolen from the gods, from celestial beings, by means of man's Promethean audacity.

In powerful contrast, the fundamental conceptions of Iranian cosmology, be they those of ancient Zoroastrian Persia with the Light of Ormazd, or those of Shiite Persia with its Muhammadan Light of the *walāyah*, are quite the opposite of the myth of Prometheus. For the believer who

---

our country none of them know about it. I willingly give the recipe as a gift to anyone who is interested." After that come detailed instructions on how to proceed. The autograph is signed by the author and dated Thursday 27 Dhū'l-Ḥijjah of the year 1267 A.H. (September 1851).

experiences the Iranian concept of Light at the heart of his being, the myth of Prometheus cannot but seem a violent perversion of the reality of things, for Fire and Light are the sacred gift given to men by the Powers of Light. Moreover, the Celestials and the Terrestrials are partners, allied together in defending this Light against the infernal Powers. Ormazd needs the help of the Fravartis (the celestial entities of the beings of light) in defending the fragile world of Light against Ahriman; and this conflict will continue until the end of our *Aiōn*. The Zoroastrian believer is a knight fighting alongside the lord of Light, who is not the "Almighty". For him there can be no question of betraying his lord, or of deserting the struggle.

We have had occasion to analyse the continuance of this sentiment from Zoroastrian Persia into Shiite Persia, passing from the heroic epic of the heroes of the Avesta to the chivalry of the mystical epics of Islamic Persia. The same ethic links the Zoroastrian "companions of *Saoshyans*" with the Shiite "companions of the twelfth Imam". How is it conceivable that man should have used force and stolen fire and light from Celestial Beings, when he is their comrade-in-arms in the defence of these very things? How can the idea of the heavenly gift be perverted into that of Promethean theft? When he commits such a perversion, is not man simply taking the place and part of Ahriman? This, perhaps, is the first episode of the "philosophical disfiguration of man" which Gilbert Durand has analysed so profoundly.[40]

Yet this is not all. The celebration of the twenty-fifth centenary included, one evening among the ruins of Persepolis, a "Sound and Light" spectacle. It was one of moving grandeur and beauty, but inevitably it evoked the burning of Persepolis, traditionally imputed to Alexander. On this occasion, I heard similar manifestations of vehement indignation. The motives for these were clearly expressed. There are two Fires: that of Ormazd and that of Ahriman. The Fire of Ormazd is a flame of pure light, resplendent and illuminating, which neither ravages nor destroys. It is the burning Bush, which illuminates without being consumed. The fire of Ahriman is fire as we experience it in our world of "admixture", in the state resulting from Ahriman's invasion that violates the world of Light and brings corruption and death into it. It is an opaque fire which ravages and

40 Gilbert Durand, 'Défiguration philosophique et figure traditionelle de l'homme en Occident', *Eranos-Jahrbuch* XXXVIII, 1969, pp. 46–93.

destroys, and is darkened by thick smoke. How, then, could the burning of Persepolis be evoked as though it were an act of natural fire, when it was actually burned by Ahrimanian fire? How could such a catastrophe have been brought about by the Angel of Fire (the *Rabb al-naw'*)? In this connection, a speaker recited to me an entire page of Suhravardī, *shaykh al-Ishrāq*, which I myself felt deeply, and not without cause. The uneasiness of the Iranian spectators was thus due to the fact that the "Sound and Light" spectacle has surreptitiously staged a demonic spectacle, had staged in ignorance the demonic act which corrupted Creation and the Elements.

What is striking about these protests is how closely they tally with what our shaykh has set forth for us in his "Book of the red hyacinth", leading us to distinguish between the lights and colours of the subtle, transparent beings in the supra-sensible world, and the lights and colours of our world which only become visible to us through a process of obscuration. Between his theosophy of light and colour, and the theory of colour professed by the philosopher-opticians, the distance is the same as that between the Zoroastrian believer who is outraged by the myth of Prometheus or the burning of Persepolis, and the Western spectator who is indifferent because he is unaware of the true facts about the drama he is watching.

I have just referred once again to the idea of the pact which binds an entire mystical order of chivalry to the service of the celestial world of Light which it is its duty to defend. This is something that we have previously tried to clarify by tracing the course of the *futuwwah* back to Zoroastrian Persia. I am struck by the fact that our shaykh's entire theory of colours leads us in the end to the very source of this chivalric idea. We were told that it is Fire, the fiery nature, that manifests the hidden Treasure, and hence that heavenly *Imago* of the Lord of Light which is projected into each of us and is for each of us the lord to whose service we pledge ourselves as soon as we recognize him. This is the whole secret of the relationship between *rabb* and *marbūb*. We have seen how this relationship is one of a reciprocal solidarity: the lord needs his knight in order to be manifested, while the knight needs the lord in order, quite simply, to be. It is the introduction of this mystical structure into the shaykh's theory of colour that is possibly the most significant thing it has to teach us. *Rabb* and *marbūb*, lord and knight, are related in the same way as light and colour: it is true to say that the *marbūb* literally "wears the colours" of his lord; and this is perhaps the intuition that lies at the source of heraldry—heraldic science, the science of emblems—as a science of the sacred.

Finally, the theory of colour has led us to the confluence of mystical experience and prophetic experience, two forms of spiritual experience which have sometimes been placed in opposition to each other, but which are in fact interlinked, at least in the theosophies represented in the three branches of the tradition that stems from Abraham. The theme of colour is elevated to the point at which light and colour possess a prophetic meaning that derives from a prophetic philosophy. We were given a brief but striking indication of this in the elucidation of the esoteric dimension of the colour red which refers us to the Throne of the *walāyah*, which is the esoteric dimension and the support of prophecy.

This is why the implications of the hermeneutics of colours as developed by Muḥ. Karīm-Khān Kirmānī may not be fully appreciated unless we bring it into line with Simnānī's hermeneutic. We have already seen how this great mystic interpreted the verses of the Koran in terms of seven subtle centres which he calls the seven "prophets of your being", each of which is discernible to mystical perception as a colour or *aura* specific to itself. Now, the tradition of the *futuwwah* envisages the mission of each prophet, beginning with Abraham, as knightly service (*fatā*). This tells us how we should understand the vocation of each "prophet of your being", until we attain the mystical degree which, according to the teaching of Simnānī, is the Seal of the prophets of our being. Then the relationship between *rabb* and *marbūb* reveals itself to be truly such that if the knight falters or dies spiritually, it is his lord himself, his *rabb*, who perishes. Who, ultimately, is this Lord, the "divine dimension", simultaneously himself and another? He is the superior Self, the Self who objectifies the "I" by saying, for instance, "I know myself". It is the Self whom one addresses as Thou. Bearing in mind the *Intelligentia agens* of the philosophers, one could call this Self the *Imago agens*, the Image that is active, effective, motorial: the Image-archetype because it is the *Imago Dei* projected into each being, our shaykh reminds us, as its "divine dimension", and by the same token inspiring, in the man who recognizes it, the total devotion of a knight.

This Image or personal divine lord is he who imparts his mission to the prophet of my being that is assigned to me: myself sent to myself by Myself. Shiite prophetology distinguishes a multitude of *nabīs* or prophets:

the *nabī* sent with a Book, the *nabī* sent to a village, to a community or to a family. There is also the *nabī* sent to himself. And it is this, perhaps, that the prophetic wisdom of the theory of colours re-affirms, in so far as this theory permits us to see the relationship between light and colour as that between *rabb* and *marbūb*. This, too, is what a great mystic of the Arabic language discloses to us, in a couplet with which we will conclude this study:

"I was a prophet sent to myself from Myself,
And it is myself who, by my own Signs, was guided towards Myself."[41]

Thus sang the mystic, Ibn al-Fāriḍ . . .

Paris, July 26, 1972.

41 *Ilayya rasūlan kuntu minnī mursalan—wa-dhātī bi-āyātī ʿalayya istadallat.*

2

The Science of the Balance and the Correspondences Between Worlds in Islamic Gnosis

according to the work of Ḥaydar Āmulī, 8th/14th century

1. The Science of the Balance

In Islamic gnosis, the metaphysical and mystical basis of the science of correspondences is called the "science of the Balance" (*'ilm al-Mīzān*). This science, with which the name of Jābir ibn Ḥayyān is particularly associated, was practised *par excellence* by the alchemists. This being the case, it is important to free as far as possible the actual concept of alchemy from the ambiguities surrounding it; for only thus can we understand how the alchemical process, and the hermeneutical processes that are the subject of this study, both pertain to the "science of the Balance".

To be sure, we know from Jābir that "the idea of the Balance comprises a number of aspects, and varies according to the objects to which it is applied. There are balances for measuring the Intellect, the Soul of the World, Nature, Form, the Celestial Spheres, the stars, the four natural qualities, the animal world, the vegetable world, the mineral world, and lastly there is the Balance of letters, which is the most perfect of all."[1] There will be occasion to study here several examples of this last type of Balance. But there is something still more important: if "the Balance is the principle that measures the intensity of the Soul's desire during its descent through Matter", or if, in other words, the Balance "is the principle which measures the quantities of the Natures that the Soul has appropriated for the purpose of forming their bodies",[2] then it seems to us both exaggerated and improper to take the word "measure" in the sense in which it is used by the science of today, and to regard the science of the Balance as

1 Cf. Paul Kraus, *Jābir ibn Ḥayyān*, II: 'Jābir et la science grecque' (Cairo, 1942), pp.187–188.
2 Ibid., p. 161.

"having as its purpose the reduction of all the data of human knowledge to a system of quantity and measure, thereby conferring on them the character of an exact science."[3] Such an attitude stems from the desire to discover, at all costs, precursors of the exact sciences. There are other ways of valorizing and justifying these so-called precursors.

The numbers used or formulated by the science of the Balance do not conduce to the constitution of an exact science as we understand the term today. They possess a value and significance that are themselves qualitative, totally different from the function of number in our statistics. To reduce these to one identical concept is, in short, to confuse the task of the chemist with that of the alchemist. Formerly, both the chemist and the alchemist could work wholly or in part on the same material; but the hermeneutical level of their respective operations was completely different. "To measure the desire of the Soul of the World" is essentially to release transmutative psycho-spiritual energies; as Jaldakī (fourteenth century A.D.) says, it is to transfer gold from its natural mine to the mine of the philosophers, or in other words *extrahere cognitionem*—to free the thought, the spiritual energy, which is immanent in the metal.[4] This is something quite other than the "chemical" analysis carried out nowadays. The science of the Balance does not make alchemy a chapter in the pre-history of our modern chemistry; it does not lead to the formulation of "mathematical laws" any more than it leads, in the examples we are about to study, to conclusions precursive of our philosophies of history.

Yet this, precisely, is where its interest lies, in the very real degree to which the now forgotten science of correspondences offers us a recourse against so-called "modern" ideologies, which are altogether devoid of the

3 Ibid., p. 187. Cf. the reservations that I have already expressed in my study 'Le Livre du Glorieux de Jābir ibn Ḥayyān', *Eranos-Jahrbuch* XVIII (Zurich, 1950), pp. 83–84; to be published with the article "De l'alchimie comme art hiératique: Le Livre des sept statues d'Apollonius de Tyane, conservé en arabe par l'alchimiste Jaldakī", Editions de l'Herne, with an introduction by Pierre Lory.

4 I am thinking here of the commentary by the alchemist Jaldakī (a native of *Jaldak* in the Khurasan, not of *Jildak*) on the "Book of the seven statues" (K. al-aṣnām), attributed to Apollonius of Tyana. The statute of the "Sun's son", who delivers the first of the seven sermons that compose the work, is made out of philosophical, not natural, gold. On this statue, see my report in *Annuaire* of the Section des Sciences religieuses de l'École pratique des Hautes-Études, 1973–1974; see also my article 'De l'alchimie comme art hiératique: Le Livre des sept statues d'Apollonius de Tyane, conservé en arabe par l'alchimiste Jaldakī, to be published by Editions de l'Herne (*supra*, n. 3). On the Soul's alchemy and energetics, cf. my 'Livre du Glorieux', loc. cit.

dimension represented by such a science. Thus, although real balances were of course used in antiquity (such as the one mentioned by Zosimus, or Archimedes' hydrostatic balance), these are not what we mean when we speak about the basis of the science of correspondences. We mean a Balance the very concept of which expresses essentially the harmony and equilibrium of things: a concept exalted, as Jābir ibn Ḥayyān very well understood,[5] to the level of a metaphysical principle—so much so, in fact, that the principle of the Balance is superior to all our categories of knowledge, in the sense that it is the cause of all determinations and the object of none.

By the same token, one can grasp its importance in the vocabulary of religion and in all speculative theosophy. The idea of the *equilibrium* of things and that of divine equity (*ʿadl*) go together, affirming themselves in the symbol of the Balance as an eschatological symbol (cf. Koran 21:49 and *passim*). In Islamic gnosis, the Balance signifies the equilibrium between Light and Darkness. In Ismaili gnosis, for example in the writings of Ḥamīduddīn Kirmānī (died c. 408/1017), the Balance of things religious (*mīzān al-dīyānah*) makes it possible to specify the correspondence between the earthly esoteric hierarchy and the celestial angelic hierarchy and, more generally, the correspondences between the spiritual and corporeal worlds.[6] The visible aspect of a being presupposes its equilibration by an invisible and celestial counterpart; the apparent and exoteric (*ẓāhir*) is equilibrated by the occulted and esoteric (*bāṭin*). Modern agnostic dissent, by ignoring this law of integral being, simply mutilates the integrality of each being. Against those who think that a being's invisible and celestial counterpart is merely the object of a hypothesis or an act of faith, the science of the Balance affirms the principle which creates and ensures this counterpart's ontological necessity. Viewed in this way, the analogical form of knowledge that typifies the science of correspondences is always an *anaphora* (the act of raising up), an *anagoge* (the act of lifting up or elevating); the *analogical* method follows the *anagogical* path, the path which leads upwards. In other words, it follows the gradations of the hierarchy of beings which is itself determined by the spiritual or esoteric function assigned to each level.

5 Cf. P. Kraus, op. cit., p. 311.
6 Ibid., p. 313 ff. Cf. my *Trilogie ismaélienne*, Bibliothèque Iranienne, vol. 9 (Tehran/Paris 1961), index, s.v. Balance, hiérarchie.

This, broadly speaking, is what we will try to elicit from a work of Twelver Shiite theosophy which is currently being edited in Tehran. The author, a great thinker and spiritual master of fourteenth-century Iranian Shiism, was Ḥaydar Āmulī (born 720/1320, died after 787/1385). Spiritually, Ḥaydar Āmulī was a disciple of the great Andalusian visionary theosopher, Ibn 'Arabī (died 638/1240), in whose voluminous work he was able to rediscover the positive elements present in Imamite Shiism, although he maintained a spirit of great critical freedom with regard to Ibn 'Arabī's own Imamology. As a result, Ḥaydar Āmulī's writings are of great significance in the relationship between Shiism and Sufism. This considerable work, written partly in Persian and partly in Arabic, had for long remained unpublished; it was only a few years ago that we were able to make a start on its reconstruction and publication.[7] In this study, we will analyse several chapters of one of his works written in Arabic. It is entitled "The Text of Texts", and is an immense commentary on the *Fuṣūṣ al-ḥikam* (The Gems of the Wisdom of the Prophets), a book in which Ibn 'Arabī had condensed the doctrines spread over the tens of thousands of pages in his other writings.[8]

The prolegomena to this "Text of Texts" are characterized by, among other things, a large number of diagrams (twenty-eight, to be precise), ingeniously constructed by the author. The purpose of these diagrams is to make the structure of the spiritual worlds perceptible on the level of the *imaginal*, which is intermediary between sensible perception and intellective intuition. They thus possess the virtue of being experimental verification *sui generis* of metaphysical exploration. The function they fulfil in the work of Ḥaydar Āmulī is the same as that fulfilled by the "Book of Figures" in the work of Joachim of Fiore. Several of them constitute an illustration relevant to the "science of the Balance". Their circular form invites us,

7 On Ḥaydar Āmulī, see my *En Islam iranien: aspects spirituels et philosophiques*, III (Paris, Gallimard, 1971–1972; new edition, 1978), pp. 149–213. See also Ḥaydar Āmulī, *La Philosophie shī'ite: 1. Somme des doctrines ésotériques (Jāmī' al-asrār); 2. Traité de la connaissance de l'être*; published, with a double introduction, by H. Corbin and O. Yahya, Bibliothèque Iranienne, vol. 16 (Tehran/Paris, Adrien-Maisonneuve, 1969).

8 See Ḥaydar Āmulī, *Le Texte des Textes* (*Naṣṣ al-Nuṣūṣ*, abbreviated henceforth to N. al-N.), *prolégomènes au commentaire des "Fuṣūṣ al-ḥikam" d'Ibn 'Arabī*, published with a double introduction by H. Corbin and O. Yahya, Bibliothèque Iranienne, vol. 22 (Tehran/Paris, Adrien-Maisonneuve, 1974). In spite of its size, this compact work contains only the prolegomena to the commentary. An edition of the entire commentary would run to three or four volumes of equal length.

particularly where sacred history is concerned, to an apprehension of things by means of an Image. This Image is altogether different from that of the indefinite, rectilinear progression of time presupposed by evolutionist theory, and by explanations of things in terms of historical causality.

This Image is of circles, cycles, or "cupolas", as they are called in certain Nuṣayrī texts,[9] which not only show us temporal succession finally stabilized in the order of spatial simultaneity, but are also unique in their capacity to make possible and illustrate an application of the science of the Balance to sacred history. They can do this because the figures and personages distributed respectively within the circles do not constitute the historical causes of their succession to one another, but are the homologues of each other and assume a permanent function according to their respective places and ranks. Only this mode of perception effectively makes possible something like a science of correspondences.

Still speaking in general terms, we could say that Ḥaydar Āmulī's subject-matter weighs three great books "in the balance".[10] By virtue of a Koranic verse (41:53) he calls one of these books the "Book of Horizons" or of the macrocosm (*Kitāb āfāqī*); then there is the "Book of Souls", the book of the microcosm or the world of man (*Kitāb anfusī*). These two books correspond to what Paracelsus, in his *Astronomia Magna* or *Philosophia Sagax*, calls the "exterior Heaven" and the "interior Heaven"; and we could also refer to Swedenborg. Finally, there is the third book, which is the revealed book, the Koran. When the science of the Balance is applied to the homologous figures that correspond with each other in the three books, it formulates not "mathematical laws" as we understand them today, but arithmological relationships, which alone are able to "measure" the place and function of these homologous figures.

We shall examine, in succession, the "Balance of the Seven and the Twelve" (the correspondences between the astronomy of the visible Heaven and that of the spiritual Heaven, between the esoteric hierarchy and its cosmic correspondences); the "Balance of the Nineteen", which "measures" the epic of divine Mercy descending and ascending from world to world; and the "Balance of the Twenty-Eight", which is an aspect of the balance of sacred history. Finally, the mysterious personages known as the

9 On this Nuṣayrī concept of the "cupolas" of sacred history, see my article 'Une liturgie shī'ite du Graal', in *Mélanges H.-C. Puech* (Paris, 1974).

10 Cf. *N. al-N* (see above, note 8), §§ 669, 736.

"horsemen of the Invisible" may enlighten us more fully as to the nature of the world of correspondences.

II. The Balance of the Seven and the Twelve

The different applications of the science of the Balance induce us to study *six* of the great diagrams constructed by Ḥaydar Āmulī. Each of these presupposes an entire preliminary study with the diagram presented at the end of it, because it is only then that its purpose and structure become comprehensible. The first two bring into operation the Balance of the Seven and the Twelve, illustrating, as we have just seen, the theme of the esoteric hierarchies and their cosmic correspondences. Such a theme requires that we bear in mind the inspired *ḥadīth* in which God declares in person: "My Friends are beneath my tabernacles (or beneath my cupolas). No one knows them, other than myself." In addition, then, to acknowledging the existence of these mysterious personages whom eighteenth-century occidental esotericism designated as the "unknown Superiors", such a *ḥadīth* tells us that their function and qualification are purely spiritual. It follows, too, that one speaks only of categories of persons, without being permitted to apply the *ḥadīth* to any particular individual currently known among men in this world. Hence we should not expect the schemas outlining the hierarchy of these "Friends of God" to be as precise and uniform as an administrative blue-print. Besides, there are many points on which all the Shiite and Sufi writers on this subject differ considerably.[11] An entire book would be needed to expound these variants and to coördinate them.

In addition to his personal inspiration, Ḥaydar Āmulī is guided on this point mainly by two great masters, Ibn 'Arabī and Sa'duddīn Ḥamūyah (died 1252 A.D.). The first question to be posed is one of vocabulary, that is, of the meaning of the terms used to indicate the degrees of the esoteric hierarchy. As all its members are called the "Friends of God" (in Persian, *Awliyā-yi Khudā*, *Dūstān-i Ḥaqq*, a term found among the *Gottesfreunde* of the Rhenish mystical school, as I have remarked elsewhere), what in the first place is the exact significance of the term *walī*, pl. *awliyā'*?

It has most commonly, and totally inadequately, been translated by the

11 For a brief survey of these variants, see my *En Islam iranien . . .* op. cit., I, pp. 120–127; IV, pp. 280 ff.; index, s.v. hiérarchies.

term "saint", a translation that opens the door to endless confusion and ambiguity, so much so that when the word is applied to God it is frequently translated as "protector". In fact, as is indicated by the Persian term *dūst* which is its translation in current usage, it always bears the sense of *Friend.* The idea originates in the verb form *tawallā*, which means "to take as a friend". Hence the definition given by Ḥaydar Āmulī: the *walī* is "he whose case God takes up in friendship".[12] A Koranic verse (7:196), for example, declares: "My Friend is God . . . He befriends the just." The idea of protection simply derives from this divine dilection.

The *walāyah*, as a spiritual qualification established by this act of predilection, is the equivalent of the term *maḥabbah*, meaning love or friendship. It is present in the *walī* under a double aspect. When the *walī* is regarded as the object of divine love (the *maḥbūb*, the beloved of God, he whom God has chosen to be his friend),[13] his *walāyah* is neither something he has acquired by himself, nor is it instigated by his own efforts. It is pre-eternal, being a gift of pure divine grace, in the sense that the first Imam—the Seal of the *Awliyā'*—was able to say: "I was already a *walī* (a beloved of God) when Adam was still between water and clay" (that is to say, did not yet exist). When the *walī* is regarded as the subject of love, as he who loves (the *muḥibb*, he who chooses God to be his friend),[14] he is obliged to "model the whole pattern of his behaviour (his ethos) on the divine pattern" (*al-takhalluq bi-akhlāq Allāh*). It is on this condition alone that he can be called a friend in the true sense. The *walāyah*, then, consists in the servant (*'abd*), the man, assuming the divine condition by ceasing to exist himself in order to arise again and exist in God; and he does this precisely "because God has chosen him to be his friend".[15] There is thus a distinct Johannine reminiscence in the spirituality of Islamic gnosis, which echoes

12 *N. al-N.*, § 606.

13 This is the state designated by the term *maḥbūbīyah*, an abstract noun formed from the word *maḥbūb*; it is the condition of the beloved, or *al-maqām al-maḥbūbī*, the *maḥbūbīyah* as a mystical station or dwelling (*maqām*).

14 This is designated by the term *muḥibbīyah*, an abstract noun formed from the word *muḥibb*: *al-maqām al-muḥibbī*, the condition of the lover as a mystical station or dwelling.

15 Hence the reply of the Imam Ja'far al-Ṣādiq to the impertinent man who wished to accuse him of pride: "Not at all! I am not proud, but since my own qualities have been obliterated by those of God, His greatness has banished mine and has taken its place." Cf. *Traités des compagnons-chevaliers* (*Rasā'il-e Javānmardān*). *Recueil de sept "Fotowwat-Nāmeh"*, published by Morteza Sarraf, with an analytical introduction by Henry Corbin, Bibliothèque Iranienne, vol. 20 (Tehran/Paris, 1973), p. 35.

the evangelist's verse: *jam non dicam vos servos sed amicos*. It is as though this reminiscence disclosed the secret tradition transmitted at the very origins of Islam by Khadījah, the Prophet's wife, and the monk Waraqah, her initiator.

It is by virtue of purely spiritual criteria which exceed the competence of men that the esoteric hierarchy is constituted within the entirety of these "Friends and Loved ones of God". At each period of the cycle of prophecy, the prophet, the *Nabī*, is at the summit of this hierarchy. He is the man who is "raised up (*mab'ūth*) by God for men in order to call them to God and deliver them from the darkness of ignorance". The prophetic mission takes two forms: there is the prophecy of instruction (*nubuwwat al-ta'rīf*), which consists in the initiation into the gnosis of the divine Essence, the divine Attributes and the divine Operations; and there is legislative prophecy (*nubuwwat al-tashrī'*) which, in addition to this, comprises the mission of reforming morals and of communicating a divine command. That is why we have, first the *Nabī* pure and simple (the equivalent, in the early periods of prophecy, of the *walī* of the Muhammadan period); then the *Nabī-mursal* (sent to a people, a town or a family); and above all, the *Nabī-rasūl*, the Envoy charged with the mission of revealing a new Law (*sharī'ah*).

For each *nabī*, the *walāyah* is the presupposition of his prophetic charisma, since without it there would be no grounds for seeing in him a manifestation of the Perfect Man. It is by virtue of this *walāyah* that his heir and successor, the Imam, may be regarded in his turn as a manifestation of the Perfect Man, and it is equally the intervention of the *walāyah* which marks the difference between the Shiite and the Sunnite conception of the Imam. The idea of the Imam (the "Guide" or hegoumenos) comprises *eo ipso* that of Caliph (*khalīfah*, a vicar, successor). This word may be understood to signify a succession from the Prophet in accordance with an order that is purely exoteric. In this case, the Caliph's mission is essentially the social and political one of a temporal leader, and it excludes any notion of the *walāyah*. This is the Sunnite conception. It is also possible, however, to understand the Caliph's function according to the sense in which it is said that Man, the *Anthropos*, is God's Caliph on Earth. Thus it was for the seven great legislative prophets, from Adam to Muhammad, and thus it was, too, for the Imams of each of the periods of the prophetic cycle. The caliphal function, being the result of the divine *walāyah*, is altogether independent of men's choice, and as such it invests the Imam with a sacral, metaphysical function, which is recapitulated in the idea of the "pole". Hence every Imam, like the Prophet whose successor he is, must be impeccable and immaculate (a notion that corresponds to the idea of the *anamartētos* in Judaeo-Christian prophetology). This is the Shiite conception.[16]

As we can see, this Shiite conception is not to be reduced to the idea of a fleshly descent or a political legitimacy. That is why it does not need any official acknowledgement on the part of men: the Imam is the Imam, even if confined to secrecy. If—like every previous prophet—the prophet of Islam (according to Twelver Shiism) had twelve Imams as successors, this is because together they form the eternal, metaphysical Muhammadan Essence (the *Ḥaqīqah muḥammadīyah*); the only meaning, function and basis of their earthly parentage, by fleshly descent, is the manifestation of their pleromatic and pre-eternal union. Consequently, it does not spring from the juridical or political contingencies of dynastic histories.

Just now we mentioned the term "pole" (*quṭb*). The notion is fundamental to the esoteric hierarchy, the keystone of the arch; and it dominates all attempts to establish correspondences. It is indeed possible to say, with Rūzbihān Baqlī of Shiraz, for example, that the *Awliyā'* are the eyes through which God looks at the world; and that consequently they are the mystical guarantors thanks to whom, unbeknown to men, our world can continue to be. The *pole* dominates their entire hierarchy; it is *par excellence* that on which the gaze of God rests in looking at the world, in every epoch; and therefore the pole, from which the whole esoteric hierarchy depends, is secretly but absolutely necessary in preserving the existence of the world. If it ceased for one instant to exist, our entire world would crumble. This is why it is homologous with the archangel Seraphiel who, in the archangelic tetrad which supports the cosmic Throne, possesses the function of maintaining *life* in general, the life of the cosmos. The *pole* has the task of maintaining life in the interior, spiritual sense, life in the true sense for man. This is the life which is henceforth invulnerable to the peril of the

16 This is why the Imamate is both a necessity and a divine grace, on the model of what is implied by the verse: "To Himself has your Lord prescribed Mercy" (6:54). Cf. *N. al-N.*, §§ 609–611. On the categories of the prophets, the concept of the Imam, and the relationship between prophecy and the Imam, cf. *En Islam iranien* . . . op. cit., IV, index, s.v.

second death, for it has passed the test of the mystical death, from which man arises capable now not of suffering his *exitus* but of living his death—that is, of passing through it as a living man. In short, "the *pole* is the cause of life—life in the true sense—for the men who people this world; it is the *place* where God looks for the vision that God has of the beings belonging to the visible and invisible worlds."

This polar function culminates in that of the major Pole, the major polar function (*quṭbīyah kubrā*) of the "pole of poles". This is the esoteric dimension of prophecy, and as such it can belong only to the Imam. Every Imam of each of the great prophets has had his turn at being the pole of poles. In the present, post-Muhammadan period, the qualification belongs to him who, as the esoteric dimension of the Seal of the prophets, is the Seal of all the Friends of God: the twelfth Imam, at present occulted, invisibly present to this world until the day of his advent. It is certainly on this point that the Shiite and Sufi conceptions of the esoteric hierarchy differ from each other, for the non-Shiite Sufis have separated the two notions, transferring to their idea of the pole the function originally reserved by Shiism to the Imam. Sunnite Sufism has thus managed somehow to found an Imamology without an Imam, something which would be akin to Christianity founding a Christology without Christ. As a result, there is a certain ambiguity at the summit of the esoteric hierarchy.

For example, Sufism refers to a personage below the major pole who is designated as *al-ghawth* (the help or aid), and we are told that he is the pole for so long as one looks to him for refuge and receives help from him. He is assisted by two Imams: one on his right whose gaze remains fixed on the *Malakūt* (the spiritual world), and the other on his left, whose gaze is fixed on the *Mulk* (the visible, phenomenal world), and who is called upon to succeed the *ghawth*. It is hard to see how these two Imams could belong to the prophetic pleroma of the Twelve. Moreover, one might well ask oneself what exactly is the relationship between the pole called *ghawth* and the major pole. Ḥaydar Āmulī hints at least at the answers to these questions. It is understood that supposing there has been a pole in correspondence with each of the seven great prophets, then the seventh pole is the "pole of poles", the most eminent and perfect of them all. At present he is the Muhammadan Seal of the Friends of God, the twelfth Imam, the Mahdī to come, announced by the Prophet when he said, "If there were only one day left to the world, God would prolong that day until the appearance of a man of my lineage, whose name will be my name and who will fill the earth with peace and justice, just as until then it had been filled with violence and tyranny." We are told that the nearer someone approaches to this pole of poles, the greater is his authority, and such is the case with regard to the pole called *ghawth* and its two Imams. It is as if Shiism were to integrate to its own esoteric hierarchy this triad composed of the *ghawth* (temporarily called pole) and its two Imams, subordinating it to him who, mysteriously and invisibly present, remains until the end of our cycle the "pole of poles", the twelfth Imam.[17]

The other members of the esoteric hierarchy may now be distinguished. There are the four *Awtād* (plural of *watad*), the four pillars or cosmic "tent-posts", who stand at the four cardinal points of the world and on whom rests God's gaze when he looks at the world. Their persons are the centre of a whole network of correspondences which "balance" the symbolism of the cosmic Temple and that of the Temple of the Ka'bah transfigured into a spiritual temple. These four *awtād* in fact correspond to the four archangels who support the cosmic Throne or Temple: Seraphiel, Michael, Gabriel and Azrael. In the same order, each of them corresponds to the heart of one of the four great prophets, Adam, Abraham, Jesus and Muhammad. Each represents one of the four corners (or pillars, *arkān*) of the Temple of the Ka'bah: the Syrian, the Occidental, the Yemenite and the Iraqi, in which the Black Stone is set.[18]

There are the seven *Abdāl*, literally the "substitutes", "those who permute". They are called this for several reasons: first because they are the "substitutes" of the *poles* of the seven climes; then because, withdrawn into their subtle bodies, they can abandon their physical bodies whenever they wish, without anyone noticing their absence or the fact that that physical body is merely a substitute for their real presence; or, again, because as one of them is recalled to the superior worlds, a member from the rank below takes his place, or is substituted for him.[19] All this hierarchy is thus penetrated by a continuous ascending movement.

17 Cf. *N. al-N.*, §§ 612, 626–627. On the "pole of poles", see *En Islam iranien . . .* op. cit., IV, book VII: 'Le XIIe Imâm et la chevalerie spirituelle'.

18 *N. al-N.*, §§ 612–618. Compare this with the structure of the correspondences between the corners of the earthly Temple of the Ka'bah and those of the Temples of the higher worlds; see below, the study 'The Configuration of the Temple of the Ka'bah as a secret of the spiritual life, according to the work of Qāḍī Sa'īd Qummī (1103/1691)', pp. 212 ff., 224 ff., 229 ff.

19 *N. al-N.*, §§ 612, 616–617.

There are also the forty *Nujabā'* or spiritual princes, and the three hundred *Nuqabā'* or spiritual leaders, whose name is the same as that designating the leaders of the twelve tribes of Israel. For the time being, I will leave the mysterious personages who are called the *Rukbān* or *Rukkāb*, the horsemen or knights of the Invisible (see below, section V).

As we must confine ourselves here to a brief exposition, without going into the details of the many variants, I will only call attention to the schema of the esoteric hierarchy established by a great Iranian Sufi Shiite of the thirteenth century, Sa'duddīn Hamūyah, as reported by Ḥaydar Āmulī. This hierarchy of *Awliyā'* or Friends of God comprises seven degrees: 1. The group of three hundred *Nuqabā'*, men of God who, like all the *Awliyā'*, remain *incognito* for the majority of men. 2. The group of forty *Nujabā'*. 3. The seven *Abdāl*. 4. A group with five members, of whom we are told simply that they assure the continuity of being. 5. The four *Awtād*. 6. The triad formed by the *ghawth* and its two auxiliary Imams. 7. The supreme pole or pole of poles. The total gives the figure of 360, which corresponds to the 360 degrees of the celestial Sphere.

This hierarchy of seven ranks is the support of multiple correspondences: 1. The supreme Pole, being the first theophanic manifestation (*maẓhar*), corresponds to the First Essence of the spiritual world which is the First Intelligence. 2. The triad of the *ghawth* and its two Imams corresponds to Nature, the *Materia Prima*, and the body; while its two Imams, considered separately, are set in correspondence with the Spirit and Soul of the world. 3. The correspondences of the four *Awtād* were noted above. 4. The group of five symbolize respectively those unities of the universe constituted by the *Jabarūt* (the world of the archangelic Intelligences); the *Malakūt* (the world of heavenly Souls); the *Mulk* (the world of phenomena); the *mundus imaginalis* (*'ālam al-mithāl*) or world of absolute Imagination (*'ālam al-khayāl al-muṭlaq*); and finally, the Perfect Man. 5. The seven *Abdāl* correspond to the seven stars and other heptads. 6. The forty *Nujabā'* correspond to the "forty dawns during which the clay of Adam was fermenting". 7. The 300 *Nuqabā'* correspond to the 300 remaining degrees of the Sphere, the 300 days of the year.[20]

But in fact Ḥaydar Āmulī, with Shiite inspiration, prefers to think that the entirety of these hierarchical degrees can be reduced to two groups:

20 Ibid., §§ 622–623, 628.

one of *seven*, which is the number of the great prophets, and one of *twelve*, the number of the twelve Imams, the *Awliyā' par excellence*, who, as all initiates (*khāṣṣah*) know, are the causes of the persistence and order of the spiritual world.[21] Moreover, this schematization facilitates an application of the science of the Balance that enables us to establish more rigorously a system of correspondences which are not simply metaphors. Indeed, just as the order and persistence of the exterior world or "exterior Heaven" are due to the *seven wandering stars*, or planets, and the *twelve* fortified castles (*burj* = πύργος, a high tower) or signs of the zodiac, so the persistence and order of the spiritual world or "interior Heaven" rest on the *seven* prophets and the *twelve* Friends of God *par excellence.* This rhythm of seven and twelve, heptad and dodecad, is expressive of a fundamental law of being, the very "balance" of being. Thus, as the planets have their "houses" in the twelve zodiacal constellations, each prophet had his twelve Imams, spiritual dwellings of the religion revealed by him.[22]

While he follows his master Ibn 'Arabī very closely, Ḥaydar Āmulī nevertheless tends to lay an emphasis of his own on the correspondences of these hierarchies. Both of them, however, agree in placing at the origin of the group of seven the "seven Angels ecstatic with love" (*al-Malā'ikah al-muhayyamah al-sab'ah*) whom God created in the eighth Heaven. These seven Angels are the theophanic forms of the seven divine Names, called the "seven Imams of the Names", of which the seven great prophets were also, in virtue of their high level of knowledge, the forms of manifestation (*maẓāhir*) in this world, just as the seven climes receive from the seven planets the influx and signatures that they communicate to their inhabitants. On the other hand, at the origin of the group of twelve are twelve Angels whom God created in the ninth Heaven, the unconstellated Sphere (the Heaven *Aṭlas*), and of whom the signs of the zodiac in the eighth Heaven or Heaven of the Fixed Stars constitute not the effigies, but the forms of manifestation, or dwellings. It is from these twelve Angels that the twelve Friends of God *par excellence*—that is to say, the group of twelve Imams—receive the higher knowledge which they transmit to men, in the same way that the twelve zodiacal signs communicate to the inhabitants of the different climes the influx and energy they receive from the twelve angelic entities of the ninth Heaven.[23]

21 Ibid., § 629.
22 Ibid., § 630.
23 Ibid., §§ 631, 637.

When the science of the Balance is applied to prophetology, it necessitates in this way the interiorization of angelology and astronomy. Yet the identical rhythm disclosed by these exalted sciences proceeds from the very mystery of the theophany, and this is the point emphasized by Ḥaydar Āmulī. In the case of the group of *Seven*, we have to take into account the following. To re-ascend to the mystery of the theophany is to re-ascend to the secret of the pluralization of the unique Essence into multiple forms of manifestation or multiple theophanies. The sacrosanct divine Essence—true Being in its true abscondence—has "infinite perfections of essence; by virtue of each perfection it has an Attribute or qualification; by virtue of each Attribute, it has a Name; by virtue of each Name it has an Operation (determined and determining); by virtue of each Operation, it assumes a particular theophanic form (*maẓhar*); by virtue of each theophanic form, it conceals a certain esoteric secret (*sirr*); by virtue of each esoteric secret there is a certain science which corresponds to it; by virtue of each science there is a certain wisdom (*ḥikmah*, theosophia) which corresponds to it; by virtue of each wisdom there is a certain statute (*ḥukm*) known to the divine Essence alone." This is why a Koranic verse declares, "He gives wisdom to whom he pleases. He who has been given wisdom has been given an immense good. But only those gifted with intelligence give thought to it" (2:269). Those "gifted with intelligence" are the *Nabīs*, the Imams, the whole assembly of the *Awliyā'*, the gnostics—in short, humanity's spiritual elite.[24]

The divine Names and Attributes form, therefore, a hierarchy which corresponds to the perfections of the divine Essence; and although they are infinite, their sources are determined. These consist of seven fundamental divine Attributes: Life (*ḥayāh*), Knowledge (*'ilm*), Power (*qudrah*), Will (*irādah*), Speech (*kalām*), Hearing (*sam'*), and Sight (*baṣar*). These Attributes postulate seven Names: the Living (*ḥayy*), the Knowing (*'ālim*), the Powerful (*qādir*), the Willing (*murīd*), the Speaking (*mutakallim*), the Hearing (*samī'*), the Seeing (*baṣīr*). These seven Names are what are called the "seven Imams of the divine Names",[25] and are so many major theophanic modes in the spiritual and exterior worlds. In fact, the list of these

24 Ibid., § 632.
25 Cf. *Kleinere Schriften des Ibn al-'Arabī* ed. H. S. Nyberg (Leiden, 1919), pp. 73 (the seven Imams of the Names), pp. 113–114 (the pole, the Imam), and pp. 30, 33–36, 48–49, 170 of the Arabic text.

seven Imams includes variants (see the table below). In the spiritual world, these epiphanic forms are the seven great prophets: Adam, Noah, Abraham, Moses, David, Jesus and Muhammad. In the exterior world, and corresponding to the "seven Angels ecstatic with love" of whom the seven prophets are the forms of manifestation, there are the seven planets: the Sun, Jupiter, Mars, Saturn, Venus, Mercury and the Moon. There are also the seven climes, corresponding to the order of the seven planets; the seven Earths and the people who inhabit them; the seven degrees of hell (see below, section IV); the seven days of the week, and various other heptads.

On the one hand, then, there are the seven great prophets, whose mission is to reveal a Book, and who correspond to the seven Imams among the divine Names: 1. Adam is the form of manifestation (*maẓhar*) of the divine Name "the Living".[26] 2. Noah is that of the divine Name "the Willing". 3. Abraham, that of the divine Name "the Powerful". 4. Moses, that of the divine Name "the Speaking". 5. David, that of the divine Name "the Hearing". 6. Jesus, that of the divine Name "the Seeing". 7. Muhammad, that of the divine Name "the Knowing". On the other hand, says Ḥaydar Āmulī, "if you have studied this deeply, you will have understood that each of the seven celestial Spheres is equally the form of manifestation of a divine Name", and that together they manifest seven divine Names which, with one exception—the Knowing—are different from the seven Imams named above. 1. The Heaven of Saturn is the form of manifestation of the Name "the Provident" (*razzāq*). 2. Jupiter's Heaven is that of the divine Name "the Knowing". 3. Mars' Heaven, that of the divine Name "the Triumphant" (*qahhār*). 4. The Sun's Heaven, that of the divine Name "the Light" (*Nūr*). 5. Venus' Heaven, that of the divine Name "the Configurator" (*muṣawwir*).[27] 6. The Heaven of Mercury (Hermes), that of the divine Name "the Shaper" (*bārī*). 7. The Moon's Heaven, that of the divine Name "the Creator" (*khāliq*).[28]

26 "Adam is the epiphanic form of the Name *the Living*, because he is the first individuality of the human species to be made manifest in visible existence; he lives by the Life of the Creator, and through him the whole world is alive, in accordance with the verse: 'I have breathed my Spirit into him' (15:29), and with the *ḥadīth* of the Prophet: 'God created Adam according to his image'" § 634.

27 Cf. the Koranic verse 59:24: "He is the Creator (*khāliq*), the Shaper (*bārī*), the Configurator (*muṣawwir*)".

28 *N. al-N.*, §§ 633–634. Elsewhere, Ḥaydar Āmulī indicates certain variants that he finds perfectly acceptable. For example: "Each of the prophets, *Awliyā'*, Imams, is

Following the order in which the author enumerates the correspondences, we can recapitulate them in the following table.

The 7 Heavens	7 Imams of the divine Names	The 7 prophets	7 Imams of the divine Names
Saturn	the Provident	Adam	the Living
Jupiter	the Knowing	Noah	the Willing
Mars	the Triumphant	Abraham	the Powerful
Sun	the Light	Moses	the Speaking
Venus	the Configurator	David	the Hearing
Mercury	the Shaper	Jesus	the Seeing
Moon	the Creator	Muhammad	the Knowing

It should be added that each of the seven climes is the form of manifestation of one of the seven planets, and that the temperament of that clime's inhabitants corresponds to the temperament of the planet. Each of the seven climes corresponds to one of the seven prophets, to one of the seven poles. Ḥaydar Āmulī is of the opinion that no one before him has established such a complete system of correspondences. However, one might remember that the Ismailis have excelled in this art. In associating prophetology and astronomy, our author's profound conception is that if the order and system of the universe are regulated by the course of the seven planets through their zodiacal houses, then the order and system of the spiritual world rest on the seven prophets, whose twelve Awliyā'—those called the Imams, poles, or heirs (*awṣiyā'*)—are the stages in the course of its religion. This profound unity is revealed and justified by the balance of

in actuality the form of manifestation of one of the divine Names, and to all intents and purposes he is the form of manifestation of the totality of Names, in accordance with the verse: He taught Adam the totality of the Names (2:31). In actuality Adam was the form of manifestation of the Name *the Knowing* (*'alīm*), and in potentiality he was the form of manifestation of all the Names. In actuality Noah was the form of manifestation of the Name *the Clement* (*ḥalīm*); Abraham was that of the Name *the Provident* (*razzāq*); David was that of the Name *the Strong* (*qawiyy*); Moses was that of the Name *the Manifested* (*ẓāhir*); Jesus was that of the Name *the Hidden* (*bāṭin*); Muhammad was that of the Name *the Wise* (*ḥakīm*)" § 745. Or again: "If you say that Adam is the form of manifestation of the Name *the Living* (*ḥayy*); Noah that of the Name *the Powerful* (*qādir*); Abraham that of the Name *the Hearing* (*samī'*); David that of the Name *the Seeing* (*baṣīr*); Moses that of the Name *the Speaking* (*mutakallim*); Jesus that of the Name *the Willing* (*murīd*); Muhammad that of the Name *the Knowing* (*'alīm*), this is perfectly acceptable" § 746.

the epiphanic forms: the seven Attributes correspond to the seven divine Names or Imams of the Names; to the seven Names correspond the seven planets, the seven prophets, the seven poles, and so on.[29]

In reality, the thought of Ḥaydar Āmulī is too close to that of Ibn 'Arabī for there to be any serious difference of opinion between them, on this point at any rate. Thus, having presented his own point of view with regard to the system of seven, Ḥaydar Āmulī limits himself to mentioning a schema proposed by Ibn 'Arabī and based on the seven *Abdāl*. These are the seven mysterious personages committed respectively to the safeguarding of the seven climes. They are assisted by the angelic being that rules over each of the seven Heavens, and they receive the influx of spiritual energy emanating respectively from each of the prophets who, according to the recital of the *Mi'rāj* (the Prophet's heavenly ascent during a night of ecstasy), dwell in each of these Heavens. Here, Abraham, Moses, Aaron, Idris (identified with Enoch and Hermes), Joseph, Jesus and Adam are named. In the heart of each of the seven *Abdāl*, each *day* and each *hour*, there occurs a theophany which is determined according to the patron saint of that hour and day, that is, according to the esoteric secrets concealed in the movements of the seven Heavens, and their assignment to their respective prophet.[30] This would seem to indicate something in the nature of an hourbook or an esoteric liturgical calendar.

This, broadly speaking, is what Ḥaydar Āmulī has to teach us about the Balance of the Seven. Where the Balance of the Twelve is concerned, he proceeds in the same way, starting with his own point of view, and continuing with an exposition of an extremely complex system of angelologic astronomy to be found in the writings of Ibn 'Arabī. He has already shown us how the Twelve originate in the twelve angels created primordially in the ninth Heaven or *aṭlas* Heaven.[31] These angels receive the spiritual influx from, and thus correspond to, both the twelve Friends of God who are the twelve Imams, and the twelve signs of the zodiac. This dodecad marks the equilibrium and equity which conform to a primordial divine ordinance: it is the very balance of being. One finds it again in the

29 Ibid., § 635.
30 Ibid., § 636.
31 The root *ṭls* connotes the idea of erasing (writing for example); the word *ṭils* signifies a page from which the writing has been erased; *aṭlas* means that which is totally bare, glabrous, like the ninth Sphere which is non-constellated.

number twelve of the leaders (*nuqabā'*) of the tribes of Israel,[32] in the twelve springs which gushed from the rock of Horeb when it was struck by Moses' rod. It is also the reason why each of the great legislative prophets was succeeded by twelve heirs (sing.*waṣī*) or Imams. Adam, Noah, Abraham, Moses, David, Jesus and Muhammad each had their twelve Imams —the list of them, already established by Mas'ūdī,[33] is well-known in Twelver Shiism. Unfortunately, even though the names of the twelve Imams of the Seal of the prophets are well-known, the names of the others have largely been disfigured by the copyists and can be recognized only with difficulty. Nonetheless, it is possible, Bible in hand, to identify some of them. And it is this which is disconcerting. For it is hard to believe that our Shiite gnostics could have invented this altogether; they must in this respect have been heirs to a Judaeo-Christian gnostic tradition, passed on by the Prophet himself, and which as yet we have been unable to trace.[34]

Thus, each of the seven legislative prophets had the duty of preparing and educating a spiritual heir (*waṣī*) or Imam, to whom he would confide the esoteric secrets of his prophecy, of the Book which had been revealed to him. In this way the heir would succeed him as a witness and a guarantor (*ḥujjah*) before his people, and his community would not dispose arbitrarily, at the whim of each man's caprice and fantasy, of the Book and its hermeneutic. (As a Shiite, Ḥaydar Āmulī holds that it was the rejection of the Imam by an entire section of the community which has unfortunately brought on the confusion and corruption reigning in Islam.) The twelve heirs (*Awṣiyā'*) or Imams (guides) of each prophet had thus to preserve his Word, his Logos, and to keep alive his *sharī'ah* for the entire cycle during which his *da'wah* (his call, *kerygma*) prevailed, until the coming of a new prophet or, in the case of the twelve heirs of the

32 Cf. the verses 5:12: "God received the promise of the children of Israel. We have raised up twelve leaders from among them"; and 7:160: "We divided them into twelve tribes." Cf. Nicolas Séd, *La Cosmologie Juive*. I. *La mystique cosmologique* (Sorbonne thesis 1970, typescript), pp. 374 ff., "Le symbolisme zodiacal des douze tribus".

33 In his *Kitāb Ithbāt al-waṣīyah* (Najaf, n.d.).

34 *N. al-N.*, §§ 638–645. Needless to say, this transmission of every prophet's heritage (*waṣīyah*) through the medium of twelve Imams must not be confused with the Prophet's ancestry back to Adam, and the transmission of the "Muhammadan Light" from prophet to prophet. The question of Judaeo-Christian antecedents has been reappraised in new terms in Jean-Claude Vadet's 'Les Ḥanīfs, "La plus grande Loi de Moïse", les Saintes Myriades et la naissance de l'exégèse islamique', in *Revue des Études juives* (April–December 1971), pp. 165–182.

Muhammadan period, until the final appearance of the twelfth of them. They are the guardians of the divine cause.[35] The Book is a silent Imam; the Imam is the Book speaking, because he proclaims its *ta'wīl*, its hermeneutic. The pleroma of the twelve Muhammadan Imams is the Seal of the *walāyah* of all the Imams who are the heirs of the previous prophets. And the Seal of the Muhammadan Imamate is the twelfth Imam, the Mahdī to come, announced by the Prophet himself.[36]

This use of the Balance of the Twelve is in fundamental correspondence with the concerns of a Twelver Shiite thinker. Ḥaydar Āmulī goes on to show us how it is used by Ibn 'Arabī, in the deployment of his angelologic astronomy. In the beginning the Most-High God established an archangelic heptad, known as that of the "Angels ecstatic with love", who are apparently identical to the Cherubim (*Karūbīyūn*). He appointed one of these Cherubim to be a chamberlain, and confided to him the whole science of his Creation. This Angel is the epiphany of this very science. One is inevitably reminded here of the "Cherub on the Throne" in Hebraic Gnosis, called also Metatron, Yahohel.[37] Here the Cherub, prince of the celestial Court, is designated, by a letter of the Arabic alphabet, as the Angel *Nūn*, in reference to the Koranic verse 68:1 which contains the adjuration: "By the *Nūn* and by the Pen, and by that which they write." In fact, appointed to this Angel, God has established beneath him another Angel, the Pen (*qalam*) or Scribe (*kātib*), who receives the epiphany of divine science through the mediation of the Angel *Nūn*. In its transmission from one Angel to the other, the divine science becomes more limited: it passes from a state of knowledge that is global and synthetic to an order of analytical understanding concerned with the details of beings. Whereas for the Angel *Nūn* the divine epiphany is brought about by the Name "the

35 The *ūlū'l-amr*, in preference to the banal translation "the holders of authority". *Amr ilāhī* here signifies the *res divina*, the divine object—the "cause", according to the etymology of the word.

36 *N. al-N.*, §§ 646–650. There are numerous *ḥadīth* in which the Prophet announces that twelve Imams will come after him, or that after Ḥusayn (the third Imam) there will be nine Imams, of whom the ninth will be the *Qā'im*, the Imam of the Resurrection. On the dodecad, or group of twelve, as a law of being, bringing into correspondence the structure of the Imamate and that of the Temple of the Ka'bah, cf. my study on Qāḍī Sa'īd Qummī, cited above (note 4).

37 Cf. Gershom Scholem, *Les Origines de la Kabbale*. trans. Jean Loewenson (Paris, 1966), index, s.v. Chérubin, Yahohel; see also *3 Enoch or the Hebrew Book of Enoch*, ed. and trans. Hugo Odeberg (Cambridge, 1928), pp. 82, 189 ff. of the Introduction, and pp. 172 ff. of the translation.

Knowing", in a unique and universal theophany, for the Angel who is the Pen or Scribe it is brought about by the divine Name "the Powerful", in a double theophany. In fact, as one descends in the hierarchy of the Intelligences, the number of theophanies is mutliplied, uniqueness being a sign of ontological superiority. The Angel who is the Pen or Scribe is appointed to compile and write the great Book of being. A sacrosanct Tablet (*Lawḥ*) has been prepared for him, on which he has to write all that will come to pass, up till the day of the Resurrection. Elsewhere, Ibn 'Arabī says that the sacrosanct Tablet bears the same relation to the Intelligence called the Scribe as Eve bore to Adam.[38] The number of the forms of knowledge and science that the Angel scribe is commanded to write correspond to the figure of the 360 degrees of the celestial Sphere multiplied by itself.[39]

Next, God has established twelve governors of his Creation, whom he impelled to descend from the supreme Sphere (the ninth Heaven), giving them as dwelling-places twelve fortified castles similar to the tall towers built onto the ramparts of a city. These castles are the twelve zodiacal constellations in the eighth Heaven. He removed all the veils between them and the "sacrosanct Tablet", so that they are able to see, written on the Tablet, their names and respective ranks; just as they are able to see, written in themselves, all the events to come until the day of the Resurrection.[40]

Below these twelve governors dwelling in the supreme Heaven are established twenty-eight chamberlains who are in their service. Their respective dwellings are the twenty-eight stations occupied successively by the Moon in the course of each lunar month. Their number corresponds to the number of letters in the Arabic alphabet, and it will of course recur later in the "balance of the twenty- eight".[41] The twelve chamberlains, in their turn, have established their delegates, who are seven *nuqabā'* (or spiritual leaders) in the seven Heavens (the moving Intelligences or Souls of the seven Heavens). These *nuqabā'*—a term we have already encountered in the nomenclature of the esoteric hierarchy—have the task of extracting and actualizing that which is potential in the twelve governors. Also in the service of the latter are those whom Ibn 'Arabī calls the

38 Cf. *Kleinere Schriften* . . . , op. cit., p. 49 (on the *Arwaḥ muhayyamah*, the Spirits ecstatic with love) and p. 55 of the Arabic text.
39 *N. al-N.*, §§ 651–652.
40 Ibid., § 653.
41 Ibid., § 654.

"guardians of the Temple" or "templars" (*sadanah*),[42] in addition to myriads of auxiliaries comprising twelve categories which correspond to the twelve governors. Their names appear in the Koran, and Ibn 'Arabī is thus in a position to systematize Koranic angelology for the first time. The names of the twelve categories of angelic beings are as follows. There are "those who repulse" (37:2); "those who recite" (37:3); "those who distribute" (51:4); "those who are sent" (77:1); "those who disperse" (77:3); "those who seize" (79:1); "those who extract gently" (79:2); "those who precede" (79:4); "those who swim" or "float" (79:3); "those who deliver the word" (77:5); "those who conduct the affairs of the universe" (79:5); "those who are ranged in order" (37:1).[43]

The idea is, then, that everything inscribed on the "sacrosanct Tablet" requires the intervention of these angelic hierarchies in order to pass into a state of actualization in this world. It is they who are responsible for the penetration into this world of the dispositions of the "decree" (*qaḍā'*) and the "destiny" (*qadar*) inscribed on the sacrosanct Tablet, but they have no power to allow the penetration of anything which is not written on this Tablet. All these hierarchies are subordinate to the twelve chamberlains, excepting, of course, the "Seven Spirits ecstatic with love", who are God's intimates. The majority of men sees only the dwellings of these intermediaries; but, says Ibn 'Arabī, it is given to the spiritual elite to see them in their dwellings, in the same way that most men see the heavenly bodies without seeing either the persons of the chamberlains or the *nuqabā'*.[44]

42 On this term *sadanah* (templars), cf. *Kleinere Schriften* . . . , op. cit., p. 74, and pp. 36–38 of the Arabic text.

43 *N. al-N.*, § 658. Nevertheless, Haydar Āmulī cuts short the quote from Ibn 'Arabī and does not go into detail in naming the twelve categories of Angels. This does not make it less important to know their names in order to understand diagram no. 8 (here, fig. 1). The quote is taken from Ibn 'Arabī's *Futūḥāt* I, p. 296. "There are those who, day and night, each morning and evening, rise up from God and from us to God, and speak only good about us. There are those who intercede for whoever is on Earth, and there are those who only intercede for believers, because they are filled with divine zeal (or divine jealousy), just as those who intercede for anyone on Earth are filled with mercy (. . .). There are those who are in charge of inspiration and who send knowledge into the heart (. . .). There are those who are in charge of the formation of that which God causes to happen in the womb; there are those who are in charge of breathing life into the Spirits; those whose function it is to cherish and provide . . . There is nothing in the world whose occurence God has not entrusted to the Angels' care." Ibn 'Arabī goes on to enumerate the twelve categories of angelic entities mentioned in our text, and which are also mentioned in *Kleinere Schriften* . . . , op. cit., pp. 76–78 of the Arabic text.

44 *N. al-N.*, §§ 657–665.

Ḥaydar Āmulī apologizes for having quoted Ibn 'Arabī at such length, but he had to do this in order to authenticate the manner in which he himself conceives of the place of the Twelve Imams of Shiism in terms of the "balance of the seven and the twelve". He is now in a position to construct a first diagram (fig. 1 = diagram no. 8; cf. below, the detailed description in the Appendix), in which he brings the spiritual world of the seven prophets and the twelve Imams into correspondence with the heptads and dodecads of the exterior world.

The following is a very brief description of this first diagram.[45] Beginning at the top and reading from right to left, we read in sequence, in the twelve small circles inscribed on the circumferent ring, the names of the twelve Signs of the Zodiac—the respective dwellings of the twelve Angel-governors—entered in the exterior hemicycle of each circle (the Ram, the Bull, the Twins, and so on). In the interior hemicycle of each little circle are the names of the twelve angelic categories in the service of the twelve Angel-governors who dwell in the twelve signs of the zodiac (those who repulse, those who recite, those who distribute, and so on). The twelve are arranged in groups of three. On the outer part of the ring, between each triad, is inscribed one triad from among the twelve months of the year. At the top on the right are Muḥarram, Safar, Rabī' I, etc. On the inside of the ring are four of the divine Names: the First, the Last, the Revealed, the Hidden. In the centre is a double circle also forming a ring, with seven small circles inside it. In the outer hemicycle of each small circle are the names of the seven planets. Beginning from the top, these are: the Sun, Jupiter, Venus, Mercury, the Moon, Mars, Saturn. In correspondence with these, with their names inscribed in the inner hemicycle, are the Intelligence, the Soul, Nature, the *Materia Prima*, the body, the Throne; the Firmament. At the centre is a little circle bearing the inscription: the manifested world (whose system of correspondences is represented by the diagram). To the side, in the corners of the figure, are four circles, each with a double inscription: 1. The Intelligence. Man. 2. The Soul. The Angel. 3. Nature. The Genie(*jinn*). 4. The body. The animal (the living creature).

Before proceeding to the next diagram, which shows the system of

45 This is described in more detail at the end of this essay, in the Appendix which accompanies the reproduction of the diagrams as they appear in the Arabic context of *N. al-N.* Note the absence in this first diagram of the "twenty-eight chamberlains".

correspondences in the spiritual world, we must follow the deliberations of Ḥaydar Āmulī.[46] Here the balance of the seven and the twelve will in some way establish the balance between the temporality of spiritual, esoteric time, and that of historical, exoteric time.

Like our authors Ḥaydar Āmulī and Ibn 'Arabī, we must bear in mind the idea which in Islamic theosophy corresponds to the idea of the pre-existence of the *Logos* in Christian theology. Here, this pre-existing Logos is called the *Ḥaqīqah muḥammadīyah*, the eternal Muhammadan Reality, Logos, Light and Holy Spirit of Muhammadan prophecy (in the Shiite perspective, it is composed of Fourteen Aeons of light: those of the prophet, of his daughter Fāṭimah, and of the Twelve Imams). This Muhammadan Spirit, designated as the *Spiritus Rector* (*al-Rūḥ al-mudabbir*), pre-exists in the world of Mystery (*'ālam al-ghayb*), the non-manifested spiritual world; and this was the Prophet's meaning when he said: "I was already a prophet when Adam was still between water and clay [did not yet exist]."

This idea imposes another: that of the *reversal* of time, which itself presupposes that the form of time is cyclical. A first cycle runs its course bearing the Name "the Hidden" (*al-Bāṭin*: the Hidden in relation to us), in the sense that the prophetic Muhammadan Reality or Essence is present in an occult, secret and esoteric way in the mission of all the prophets of the "religions of the Book" who preceded the manifestation of Muhammad. This can be seen as an exemplification of the motif of the *Verus Propheta* in Judaeo-Christian prophetology. In saying "I was already a *prophet* before Adam was created", not simply a "man" or a "being", the Prophet meant that he was already the holder of the prophetic charisma *before* all the prophets who were, respectively, so many "forms of manifestation or epiphany" (*maẓāhir*) within which the eternal Prophet, the *Verus Propheta*, was secretly *hidden*. This cycle is fulfilled with his corporeal manifestation in this world. There then comes about a reversal of time with the inauguration of a new cycle, that of the Name "the Manifested" (*al-Ẓāhir*: the Manifested in relation to us). If the Prophet himself has declared that "time has a cyclical form" (*istidārat al-zamān*), it is in order to denote that at the moment of his terrestrial epiphany, time returned to its original condition, as it was when God created it (this relates to the idea of the *thema mundi*). The metaphysical Muhammadan Essence was at the origin

46 Ibid., §§ 663–665.

of the mission of the prophets, and in its earthly epiphany it is the final Seal of both prophecy and the prophets. The point which is simultaneously the final point of the cycle of prophecy, where Muhammadan prophecy remains occulted, and the initial point of the cycle of its manifestation, marks a moment of privileged equilibrium between the Hidden and the Manifest.

This idea of a point which is at once both initial and final, and which as such involves the idea of a return to equilibrium by means of the movement of time conceived as cyclical—this idea orients the analysis towards a perspective within which, under the notion of time (*zamān*), is seen to lie that of the balance (*mīzān*). The analysis is facilitated by a process made possible by philosophical algebra, or the philosophical science of letters (*'ilm al-ḥurūf*)—a process equally familiar to the Jewish Cabbalists. In effect, there is scope for the consideration that the consonants forming the word ZaMāN (time) are exactly the same as those forming the word MīZāN (balance). Now, the value of a word does not alter when one inverts the order of the consonants of which it is composed. In this case, the equivalence thus found between the concept of *time* and that of *balance* is corroborated by many Koranic verses where allusion is made to the Balance and the eschatological significance of the Balance.[47] The conclusion is that the beginning and the end of time relate to the zodiacal sign of the Balance. "Every cycle of time ends in the Balance"; and it is from the Balance that the other Signs are manifested. The Balance is the sign of the harmony of things and of divine equity, the notions of equilibrium and

47 Ibid., § 665. Ibn 'Arabī, in the context quoted by Ḥaydar Āmulī, introduces the Koranic verses as follows: "The prophet has said: I and the final hour are like these two (fingers). And God himself has said: We will establish the *balances* in equilibrium on the day of the Resurrection (21:47). And we are told: Weigh justly, and do not falsify the *balance* (55:9). And again: He has raised the Heavens and established the *balance* (55:7). Thus, by means of the *balance*, God has revealed in each heaven the function of that heaven (41:12). And by means of the *balance* he has distributed proportionately over the earth the foods that the earth produces (41:10). And God Most High has set up a *balance* in the universe for each thing: a spiritual balance and a material balance. The balance never errs. In this way the *Balance* enters into speech and into all the arts whose object is perceived by the senses. In the same way, it enters into Ideas, for the primary origin of terrestrial bodies and celestial bodies, and of the Ideas which they support, is found in the law of the Balance. Similarly, the existence of time and of that which is above time proceeds from the *Mensura divina* (*al-wazn al-ilāhī*) to which the Name *the Wise* (*ḥakīm*) aspires, and which is made manifest by the equitable Judge. After the Balance Scorpio is manifested, together with the *res divina* which God has placed in it. Then come Sagittarius, Capricorn, and so on."

equity being two aspects of the Balance. It might seem that Ḥaydar Āmulī ought to have constructed his diagrams in terms of the primary role played by the Balance. If he has not done so, it is because in reality, in this context, the Balance is more than a zodiacal sign. It is that metaphysical principle of which we spoke at the start, and which as such organizes the totality of the diagram and establishes the system of correspondences.

We can, in fact, read the next diagram without difficulty (fig. 2 = diagram no. 9, cf. Appendix). In the preceding diagram, we had the names of the twelve Signs of the zodiac (the dwellings of the twelve Angel-governors in the ninth Heaven), and in the little circles inscribed on the circumferent ring these were coupled with the names of the twelve categories of angelic beings in their service. Here, corresponding to them, and distributed in four triads, are the names of the twelve Imams of the period of Adam (Seth, Abel, Cainan, etc.; the other names, apart from Idris and Enoch, have suffered such mutilation graphically that we will not go into them here; see Appendix). Corresponding to these twelve Adamic Imams are the twelve Muhammadan Imams, from 'Alī al-Murtaḍā, the first Imam, to the twelfth who is at present hidden: Muḥammad al-Mahdī. Also in the circumferent ring, grouped into four intercalary triads and inscribed both above and below the line, are the twelve Imams of the Mosaic period and those of the period of Jesus.

We pass now to the central circle. In the preceding diagram, the seven planets were brought into correspondence with the seven unities of the universe or the universe-principles: the Intelligence, the Soul, Nature, etc. Here, we find the seven great prophets sent to reveal a Book. Each of them is doubled by the mention of whoever was the "pole" (*quṭb*) of his period; the seventh pole is the "pole of poles", the twelfth Imam of the Muhammadan period. The arrangement is slightly different from that of the central circle in the previous diagram. The little circle in the middle of this central circle bears the name of the prophet Muhammad, and the six others are grouped all around. This is because—as announced by the small tangential circle above—we are dealing with the spiritual world (*'ālam ma'nawī*). The position of Muhammad is right at the centre of the prophets, because throughout the cycle dominated by the name "the Hidden", these prophets were his epiphanic forms (*maẓāhir*).

Thus this position is intended to suggest to us that in spiritual circles the centre has the virtue of being the circumference as well (this is a peculiarity affirmed in the *Theology* attributed to Aristotle, and one whose consequences our spiritual masters have explored to the full).[48] Like the seven planets of the astronomical Heaven, the seven prophets are in some sense the "motive forces" in the spiritual Heaven, by means of which the spiritual being (*rūḥānīyah*) of the *Verus Propheta* continues to grow until the moment of his plenary terrestrial manifestation in the person of Muhammad.[49] Nevertheless, the rhythm of the prophetic periods, and hence the limits which, by marking the beginning and the end of each, distinguish the one from the other, are conditioned by the twelve Imams who constitute the pleroma of each period of prophecy. Thus the same science of the Balance enables us to grasp the correspondences between the function of the *seven* and the *twelve* in the astronomical Heaven (fig. 1) and in the spiritual Heaven of prophecy (fig. 2).

We grasp *eo ipso* the consequences and potentialities that arise in this way from the conjunction of the concept of *time* and the idea of the *balance*. In effect, it is the idea of the balance which gives time its cyclical form. The balance returns to equilibrium at the end of the cycle, and this equilibrium is the return of time to the starting point which then becomes once more the starting point of a new cycle. We said at the outset that the science of the Balance is the very foundation of the correspondences between the worlds: without the idea of the *balance*, there can be no worlds in correspondence with each other. The correspondences established by our authors would be impossible if the only image they possessed was of time as rectilinear and unlimited, like that of present-day evolutionism. Thanks to the Balance, it is possible to set in correspondence the figures which are found in every cycle, for they are then seen to be homologous. Our current schema of history possibly permits certain analogies to be made, but these in fact remain metaphorical because they lack both what establishes and what permits the science of the Balance.

Moreover, it is not enough to substitute (as did Oswald Spengler) the schema of a cyclical conception of history for the perspective of a linear evolution—the schema of a continual genesis, regulated by a historical causality immanent in the uninterrupted succession of phenomena. For then the question arises: how is understanding (the act of understanding)

48 Cf. the last part of my article, 'Le Motif du voyage et du messager en gnose irano-islamique' (unpublished).
49 *N. al-N.*, § 666.

possible from one cycle to another, if each cycle is self-contained? The science of the Balance permits an understanding which effects the passage from one cycle to the next; and it does so by stabilizing the flux of History and by establishing, through the system of correspondences that it equilibrates, a level of transhistorical permanence between homologous *dramatis personae*. The science of the Balance spatializes the succession of time by substituting for the order of succession the order of simultaneity, the unity of the "cupolas" of which we spoke at the start.

It is this that makes the diagrams constructed by Ḥaydar Āmulī, as well as the correspondences inscribed on them in the form of homologous figures, perceptible to us on the level of the *imaginal*. Thus, too, is revealed the eschatological significance of the Balance. In effect, it returns time to its origin, to that origin, we were told, which it is itself. It brings about a *reversal* of time, and hence there is nothing that is "irreversible" (that word which has been so abused in our day!). The science of the Balance does not, to be sure, permit a philosophy of history, because a philosophy of history can be perfectly agnostic and its mode of perception may stem from brute realism. On the other hand, it permits a historiosophy which is *eo ipso* a gnosis, and whose mode of perception is essentially a *visionary* one. If our authors speak of the growth of the "spiritual being" of Muhammad, in other words, of the *Verus Propheta*, this growth is operative and perceptible not on the level of common historical reality, but on the level with reference to which early primitive Christologies spoke of *Christos Angelos*.

This, broadly speaking, is what is suggested by the balance of the *seven* and the *twelve*, applied to the manifested world and the spiritual world, to the astronomical Heaven and the interior Heaven. Together they total *nineteen*, and it is on this number that the two universes are constructed, as Ḥaydar Āmulī will now attempt to show by deploying the "balance of the nineteen".

III. The Balance of the Nineteen

The deployment of the "balance of the nineteen" comprises three stages, traversing the "three Books" of which we spoke in the opening section of this chapter. A. In the first of these stages, the science of the Balance brings the "Book of Horizons" into correspondence with the "Book of Souls". B. In the second stage, the science of the Balance clarifies the corresponding structure of the third Book, the revealed Book: the Koran. C. During the third stage, the science of the Balance brings the structure of the interior Paradise into correspondence with that of the interior Hell.

A. Like the "Book of the Koran" (*al-Kitāb al-Qur'ānī*), both the "Book of Horizons" (*Kitāb āfāqī*) and the "Book of Souls" (*Kitāb anfusī*, cf. Koran 41:53)—in Paracelsian terms the "interior Heaven" and the "exterior Heaven"—are each seen to possess a numerical structure based on the number nineteen. Thus the hermeneutic of all three Books will among other things be directed towards establishing their correspondences with regard to the three numbers involved in their respective structures.[50] True, these three Books were written by the Angel who is the Scribe, at the dictation of the Angel *Nūn*, the "Cherub on the Throne"; but it goes without saying that our author considers their structure to be based on the actual nature of the numbers, and for this reason he refers at some length to the arithmosophy of Pythagoras, as expounded in the celebrated Encyclopaedia of the "Brothers of the pure heart" (*Ikhwān al-Ṣafā'*).[51]

"Know," he writes, "that the wise Pythagoras was the first to discourse on the nature of number. He said beings come into existence in conformity with the nature of number. Consequently, he who understands the nature of number, its species and properties, is in a position to know the various genera and species of beings." Necessarily, things are *one* with respect to Matter (*hayūlī*) and multiple with respect to Form (*ṣūrah*). There must be dyads (matter and form, the subtle and the gross, the luminous and the dark, etc.); triads (surface, line and volume; past, future and present, etc.); tetrads (the four natures, the four Elements, the four *awtād* or pillars of the cosmic tent); there must be pentads, hexads, heptads, decads, etc. Unfortunately, the dualists were fascinated by the dyad; Christians by the triad; natural philosophers by the tetrad; and so on. Pythagoras and his followers, on the other hand, dispensed justice where justice was due. They saw very clearly that the One is the cause of number, and that all numbers, small or big, even or odd, are constituted by the One. The One gives its name to every number; number persists because the One persists; number grows and augments by the repetition of the One. It is because a

50 Ibid., §§ 669, 688, 736. Ḥaydar Āmulī is referring here (§ 669) to his *Ta'wīlāt*, for which he made nineteen diagrams. I believe him to mean his great spiritual commentary on the Koran (*al-Muḥīṭ al-a'ẓam*); cf. my introduction to *La Philosophie shī'ite . . .*, op. cit., pp. 46 ff.

51 Ibid., §§ 670–674.

dyad is a dyadic unity, for example, that it is different from a triadic unity, and so on.

We find here, therefore, a reaffirmation of the old saying, *Ens et Unum convertuntur*: the concept of being and the concept of One are reciprocal, for each being only comes into being because it is *one* being. This ontological unity is invariable and has no second; the formula which expresses it is 1×1. Consequently, it makes possible the series of arithmetical unities which are constituted into unities subsequent to the arithmetical unity of the number One—that is to say, $1 + n$.

Thus, explains our author, two is the number of the First Intelligence (as the second existence); three is the number of the universal Soul; four is the number of Nature; five, the number of the *Materia prima*; six, that of corporeal volume; seven, that of the Celestial Sphere; eight, that of the Elements; nine, that of the three natural kingdoms, that is to say, the mineral world (corresponding to the order of tens), the vegetable world (corresponding to the order of hundreds), and the animal world (corresponding to the order of thousands). We can now grasp the full significance of the statement that "every number contains in itself an esoteric secret which is not to be found in any other number." Now, the system of the world is ordered according to the number nineteen. When the theosopher ponders on the esoteric secret of the number nineteen, he discovers that if this number regulates the structure of the world, it is because the entire universe is in the image of God (*'alā ṣūrat al-Ḥaqq, secundum Formam Dei*). It is in the justification of this concept of the universe as *Imago Dei* that the secret of the number nineteen resides, as it is also in the same justification that there resides the secret of the law of correspondence between the three great Books written at the dictation of the "Cherub on the Throne", in other words, the Balance of a hermeneutic which is common to all three Books.

For our author, Ḥaydar Āmulī, it is evident that when the prophetic tradition states that "God created Adam in His image", one should understand Adam to mean the universe, the cosmos in its entirety, the *Makranthropos* (*al-Insān al-Kabīr, Homo Maximus*), that is counterbalanced by earthly Man as the microcosm. Since the cosmos itself is in the form of Man—of the *Anthropos*—and since Man is himself a universe, the *Imago Dei* must have reference to both: they are two homologous forms of the same theophany.

At this point, Ḥaydar Āmulī provides an excellent hermeneutic of the Koranic verse 41:53, where God declares: "We will show them our Signs on the horizons and within their souls, so that it will be clear to them that He is Being." It is a hermeneutic which, on the initiative of the verse, he puts forward in the first person.[52] "This verse," he says, "alludes to the two forms of the theophany (*ẓuhūr Allāh*). Its esoteric meaning is the following: *We will show them our Signs*, that is to say, our tokens and emblems which, in the world above and in the world below, together constitute the horizons, and which in the human world constitute the world of souls. *Until it is clear to them* that being in its entirety is composed of the epiphanic forms of my Essence, my Names and my Operations; and that in reality there can be nothing other than Myself, or, rather, that the *Other* does not possess being in reality, because the *Other* signifies, precisely, my own individualized and particularized theophanic forms, which subsist by virtue of my real, universal and absolute being, in the same way as what is limited subsists by virtue of the absolute, as the shadow subsists by virtue of the sun, and as the form of manifestation subsists by virtue of that which it manifests. For this reason I have said: *He is the First and the Last, the Manifested and the Hidden* (57:3). And I have said: *Whichever way you turn, there is the Face of God* (2:115). And I have also said: *All things are perishable except his Face . . . and it is to him that you return* (28:88). This is why the gnostics have said: Only God is able to be—God, his Names, Attributes and Operations." And here Ḥaydar Āmulī cites two well-known quatrains: "My Beloved has shown himself to me in every aspect / Thus I have contemplated him in every Idea and in every form / He said to me: Thus it is good. But when / Things are contemplated by me, it is you who are a copy of me." "Glory be to him who has manifested his humanity / Like a hidden secret of the brilliance of his resplendent divinity / And who has then appeared to us in the manifest state in his creation / In the form of someone who eats and drinks."[53]

52 Ibid., §§ 675–676.

53 L. Massignon attributes this quatrain to Ḥallāj, but neither Rūzbihān nor Ḥaydar Āmulī confirms this. It is not necessary to read a Christian meaning into the quatrain, although of course a Christian is at liberty to do so. It is even more permissible for a Shiite thinker to see in it an obvious allusion to the Imam, or else as envisioning the secret of divinity manifested in the beauty of ephemeral human beings (which is how Ḥaydar Āmulī understands it); for that is the secret of their "imperishable Face" (28:88), in virtue of which they are the epiphanic forms of divinity.

What is the reason for all this? Why this apparent digression? Ḥaydar Āmulī anticipates the reproach: the point of it all is that what is designated on the one hand as the universe, the cosmos, and on the other hand as Man, forms a Whole which is one and the same, constituted of all the theophanic forms. The supreme secret (*al-sirr al-a'ẓam*) is that the universe is "in the image of God" and that, for the gnostic, the Whole from one point of view is the divine Being, and from another point of view is the cosmic Adam or *Anthropos*, because the Whole reflects the Image of the hidden Treasure that created the world because it aspired to be known—to know itself in the mirror of creation. This is the secret of the first two Books, the "Book of Horizons" and the "Book of Souls".[54]

The science of the Balance can then effect a detailed proof of this. The exterior or manifested world obeys the rhythm of the number nineteen; it is in fact constituted by the Intelligence of the universe, the Soul of the universe, the 9 Celestial Spheres, the 4 Elements, the 3 natural kingdoms and, finally, Man. The total gives *19*. Or again, as we saw earlier, it is constituted by the 7 planets and the 12 signs of the Zodiac, which also total 19. This figure is also the number of man, of anthropology. Man is constituted by his personal intellect, his personal soul, ten faculties designated as the five external senses and the five internal senses, four souls—designated in Koranic terminology as "the soul which orders (evil)" (*al-nafs al-ammārah*), "the soul which censures" (*al-lawwāmah*, the conscience), "the inspired soul" (*al-mulhamah*), "the pacified soul" (*muṭma'annah*)—and lastly, three pneumas or spirits: vegetative (*rūḥ nabātīyah*), vital (*r. ḥayawānīyah*), and psychic (*r. nafsānīyah*). The total is nineteen. In the same way, the spiritual world is constituted by the seven great prophets and their twelve Imams, that is to say, . . . by the seven poles and the twelve *Awliyā'* or Friends of God. The total is again *19*.[55]

The correspondence between the world as *Homo maximus* and man as microcosm justifies the attribution to both of the *Imago Dei*, manifested respectively in their two theophanic forms. This correspondence is further expressed by the fact that the cosmos can be designated as God's major caliph, and man, the *Anthropos*, as the minor caliph. The inverse is equally true: man's caliphal function also embraces the universe, since the latter is manifested to and for man. It is this which effects the correspondence

54 Ibid., § 677.
55 Ibid., §§ 678, 684.

between the hermeneutic of the "Book of Horizons" and that of the "Book of Souls", to such a point that a cosmological verse like the Koranic verse 13:2, "God is He who has raised the Heavens without pillars that you can see", is equally applicable to the spiritual Heaven, the Heaven within. These invisible pillars are an allusion to the Perfect Man as the cosmic *Anthropos*, through whom the celestial Spheres subsist together with the Angels who are their moving Souls, like the visible pillars upholding a palace or a dome.

As for the invisible pillars which support the spiritual Heaven, they are to be understood as that which constitutes the Spirit, the Heart and the Soul of the world, that is to say, the metaphysical reality of that Perfect Man who is unknown to all save God, since "My friends are beneath my tabernacles (my cupolas, my domes). No-one knows them except myself." This *ḥadīth* again affirms itself here in order to remind us that the Perfect Man is exemplified at all the various levels of the esoteric hierarchy, which are these invisible pillars supporting the spiritual Heaven. We noted at the beginning of this study the terms by which they are designated. They are the prophets (*Nabī*), the Messengers (*nabī-mursal*), the Friends of God, the Imams, the poles, the caliphs, the pillars (*awtād*), the *abdāl*, and so on. But it is understood that the most eminent among them, those who determine the others, are the nineteen already mentioned—the seven prophets and the twelve Imams—who correspond to the nineteen of the external world, and on whom ultimately depends the movement of the periods which articulate a cycle; for this movement is the movement of the Balance brought back to the initial equilibrium.[56]

This, broadly speaking, is the "Balance of the nineteen" as a hermeneutic which brings into correspondence the two first Books: the "Book of Horizons" and the "Book of Souls". We must now apply it to the third Book, which is the revealed Book—the "Book of the Koran"; and we will see how the hermeneutic brings it into correspondence with the first two Books by means of the secret of the same number, *19*.

B. We can approach it initially by way of an analysis of the word with

56 Ibid., §§ 680, 683, 685. Cf. also the *ḥadīth* of the first Imam: "Know that the human Form is the greatest token (*ḥujjah*) of God before his creatures. It is the *Book* which he wrote with his hand. It is the *Temple* which he built with his Wisdom. It is the witness who bears witness for all the invisible, the evidence against all who deny. It is the *straight Road* that leads to all Good. And it is the road that lies between paradise and hell." § 682.

which Being expresses itself in the imperative mode. This is the KN (= *Esto!* not *fiat*) which, addressed to the thing already mysteriously present in its eternal virtuality, commands it *to be*. More precisely, the analysis involves the three consonants which make up the root of the verb KWN (to be): *kāf*, *wāw*, *nūn*.[57] When these three letters are multiplied by the three letters which compose, respectively, the name of each, the resulting figure is *9*. It is this number that regulates the structure of being with regard to both the esoteric and the exoteric, the visible world, or *Mulk*, and the world of the Soul, or *Malakūt*. Hence, on the one hand there are the nine celestial Spheres, and on the other the nine Angels who are the Souls which move them, giving a total of *18*. And this is what the theosophers mean when they speak of 18,000 worlds (a figure, moreover, as well-known in Ismaili gnosis as in the Jewish Cabbalah.)[58] Indeed, for Ḥaydar Āmulī the number *18* designates the "unities of the universe" or universe-principles, the order of thousands, symbolizing the multitude of parts which make up each one. When the Perfect Man is added to the number 18, the total figure of *19* is obtained.

We are led to the same conclusion when we analyse the *hexaemeron*, the six days of Creation, taking into account the Koranic verses: "One day for your Lord is like *one thousand* years in your reckoning" (22:47); and: "It is He who created the Heavens and the Earth and that which is between them, in six days" (25:60). The Heavens are the world of the *Jabarūt* (the world of the Intelligences and the divine Names). The Earth is the *Mulk*, the world of visible things. That which is between them is the *Malakūt* or world of Souls. The six days assigned to each of these three worlds gives a total of *18*. Since one day is equal to a thousand years, we arrive once again at the figure 18,000.[59] We shall see how in establishing certain correspondences, this figure possesses a decisive importance according to whether it

57 Ibid., §§ 686–687.

58 On the 18,000 worlds, see my book *L'Homme de lumière dans le soufisme iranien* (Paris, 1971), p. 162 [*The Man of Light in Iranian Sufism*, trans. Nancy Pearson, Boulder & London, Shambhala Publications, 1978, p. 109.] Cf. G. Scholem, *Les Origines de la Kabbale*, op. cit., pp. 476, 490; Nicolas Séd, *La Cosmologie juive*, op. cit., pp. 212 ff.

59 *N. al-N.*, §§ 702, 719–721. Ḥaydar Āmulī anticipates the possible objection: "Why not admit that the totality of the three worlds was created in six days, rather than that they were each created one by one in six days (whence 6 × 3 = 18)?" "I will reply: Because God Most High tells us in another place that such is the case; this he does in the following verse: Will you be unbelieving towards Him who created the Earth in two days? . . . and in four days he distributed proportionately over the Earth the foods which the Earth provides to those who require them (. . .) Next he

is thought to include Man, or whether, instead, Man is added to it so as to make a total of *19*. Here, Ḥaydar Āmulī observes that being (*kawn*), in relation to the nine levels deduced from it, is homologous to unity in relation to numbers (from one to ten, the progression starting again *ab initio* after ten), or to substance in relation to the nine accidents. Each time we have ten plus the nine levels, giving a total of *19*. Thus, we have the First Intelligence and the nine celestial Spheres, making up *10*, to which are added nine levels—the nine Intelligences which govern the Spheres—giving a total of *19*. Or again, we have the ten Intelligences, together with the nine celestial Souls that move the nine Spheres in an act of love towards the Intelligences from which they proceed; and here the total is again *19*.

Now it is on the basis of this same number—*19*—that, in correspondence with the "Book of Horizons" and the "Book of Souls", the "Book of the Koran" (*al-Kitāb al-Qur'ānī*) is constructed. It is true that the letters of its script number twenty-eight (the letters in the Arabic alphabet). Nevertheless, 14 of these (half of them, that is) belong to the world of the *Mulk*, the

disposed (Heaven) into seven heavens (in the space of) two days, and he revealed to each heaven its function . . .' (41:9–12). The questioner may now say triumphantly: "So God created Heaven and Earth in eight days (2 + 4+ 2), not in six!" But he has his answer ready: "Your conclusion is without value. The four days refer only to a complementary and supplementary creation, the creation of material substances. The separate spiritual substances transcend such measures." And this, for him, is the heart of the matter: where is the sense in taking these *days* to mean what the literalist commentators take them to mean, since "when" the Creation took place, neither day nor time existed? It is more to the point to understand the six days as six stages: mineral, vegetable, animal, man, genie, Angel; or, the *Jabarūt*, the *Malakūt*, the *Mulk*, the Living, the Genie, the Angel; or again: the Intelligence, the World-Soul, Nature, Matter, the Body, the Elements. The whole question, moreover, is dominated by the meaning of the word *day*. This can only mean the "divine day", which possesses two aspects: the days of lordship (*ayyām al-rubūbīyah*), and the days of divinity (*ayyām al-ulūhīyah*). Divinity is God's link with the man whose God He is in the spiritual order of things (*ma'nan*). Lordship is God's link with the man whose Lord (*rabb*) he is in the manifested (*ṣūratan*) order of things. That is why the gnostics say: lordship has a secret (*sirr*); if this secret were made manifest (and thus abolished), the relationship of lordship would be destroyed. Now the "day of lordship" is the day which, according to the verse 22:47, is equal to a thousand years in our reckoning, so each day of the hexaemeron can be reckoned as a millenium of lordship; while the "day of divinity" is equal to 50,000 years, which is the figure of a total cycle in Ismaili gnosis as well. This is attested by the verse: "The Angels and the Spirit ascend towards him in a day whose measure is 50,000 years" (70:4). §§ 722–725. These are brief observations on a theme which calls for the making of numerous comparisons. See *En Islam iranien* . . . , op. cit., IV, index, s.v. hexaéméron, jour.

visible world; these are the letters which possess diacritical marks. The remaining 14 belong to the world of the *Malakūt*; they are without diacritical marks and are the original letters. These are the letters which appear as mysterious sigils enclosed in a frame at the beginning of certain surahs of the Koran; sometimes they appear singly (monoliteral), and sometimes in groups of two (biliteral), three (triliteral), four (quadriliteral) or five (quintiliteral). There are thus five grades which, added to fourteen, give a system of 19 grades of letters.

Such is the system of letters in the Arabic script in which the Koran is written. But this is not all. Each surah is headed by a set phrase—the same phrase which is repeated by the believer before any undertaking: *Bism Allāh al-Raḥmān al-Raḥīm*: in the name of God the Compassionate, the All-merciful. This phrase is regarded as a recapitulation of the entire Koran. Now, in the Arabic script, it comprises *19* letters. Philosophical algebra sees in each of these letters the symbol of a stage in the descent of divine Mercy from one level of being to another. When added together, the seven and the twelve which we encountered in the preceding diagrams thus confirm the properties of their correspondences.

A rigorous transliteration of the nineteen letters of the Arabic script which constitute the *Basmallah* gives the following: BSM ALLH AL-RḤMN AL-RḤĪM.

The Prophet expressed himself in a striking manner on the virtues of this invocation: "He who desires immunity from the 19 henchmen of Hell needs to recite the *Basmallah*; for on the day of the Resurrection, God will make a paradise out of each of its constituent letters." Shortly, we will examine the practical implications of this statement. For this invocation does indeed recapitulate the entire Koran, and the first of its letters, *B* (the Arabic *bā'*) is itself the recapitulation of the *Basmallah*. Again, as the Prophet said: "God has made one hundred and four books descend from Heaven. The knowledge contained in one hundred of these books he stored in four of them: the Torah, the Psalms, the Gospel, and the Koran. The knowledge contained in the first three of these four books, he set down in the fourth, the Koran. He set down this knowledge in the *Mufaṣṣal* (the part from surah 49 to the end). This he set down in the *Fātiḥah* (the first, "opening" surah of the Koran). Lastly, he set this down in the *bā'* (B) of the *Basmallah*." Thus, the letter *bā'* recapitulates (totalizes) all that is in the Koran and in all the revealed celestial books. This is why it merits the observation made about it by the Prophet and the first Imam, and which is also attributed to several *mashāyikh*: "I see nothing without seeing the letter *bā'* written into it." And because all beings have been made manifest as from the letter *bā'*, the first Imam also said: "I call God to witness that, if I wished, I could produce a commentary on the letter *bā'* of the *Basmallah* equal to the load of seventy camels." Being is manifested by the letter *bā'*, and by the dot beneath the letter *bā'* the Creator is differentiated from the creaturely (the letter *bā'* on its own consists of a horizontal stroke with a dot underneath). To quote the first Imam once more: "I am the dot beneath the letter *bā'*."[60]

The letter *bā'* comes at the origin of being, and its esoteric secret makes it a symbol of the First Existence, designated as the First Intelligence, the Reality of Realities (*Ḥaqīqat al-Ḥaqā'iq*), the Supreme Spirit. Whereas the letter *alif* (which consists of a simple vertical stroke, with no ensuing ligature possible) symbolizes the unique divine Essence, alone and unseconded, the letter *bā'* symbolizes the primary Unity of all subsequent unities.[61] In the same way, each letter of the *Basmallah* gives its name to one of the existences of the higher and lower worlds. Ḥaydar Āmulī refers here to the long *khuṭbah* (homily) with which he opens his vast spiritual commentary on the Koran, a homily which is a typical example of "narrative theosophy". It begins as follows:[62]

"Glory be to him who has made the letter *alif*, alone, the origin of All and the symbol of the pure and absolute Essence; who has made the letter *bā'* the cipher of the First Determination, the First of all limited beings beneath absolute being, the first of its epiphanies; and who has made the other letters the symbols, respectively, of the other existences. He has written the entirety *qua* entirety on the pages of the invisible universes with the Pen of the primordial Will. He has given the name of *The Mother of the Book* (the archetype of archetypes) to the letters of the eternal

60 *N. al-N.*, §§ 689–690.

61 There is a serious problem implicit here. The first Intelligence is designated as the "Primary Existence", and as such is symbolized by the letter *bā'*. The pure divine Essence as the source of being, symbolized here by the letter *alif*, is thus beyond being, *hyperousion*. Elsewhere, as in the writings of Shaykh Aḥmad Aḥsā'ī for example, this state of things makes the letter *alif*, precisely, the symbol of the initial Determination, which is the Intelligence. Cf. *En Islam iranien . . .*, op. cit., IV, index, s.v. être, théologie apophatique.

62 The author refers here to his *Ta'wīlāt* (§ 690), and his *Ta'wīl* (§ 691); cf. above, note 50.

quiddities and individuations. He has composed its Verbs, perfect and imperfect, of the existence of beings. He has ordained the Signs of the universes of the Invisible and of the Visible in the Book of Horizons, to which refer the verses: By Mount Sinai! By a Book written on an unrolled parchment (52:1–3)."[63]

This Book is precisely the cosmic epic of Mercy propagating itself through all the stages of the revelation of being. The phenomenon of the world is thus a phenomenon of writing, a phenomenon of the Book. Hence the *ta'wīl* (the hermeneutics of symbols), when applied to this Book as the implementation of the Science of the Balance, is no other than the *ta'wīl* applied to the revealed Book; for the universe, unfolding to the rhythm of the *Basmallah*, is itself the book, the song or epic, of Mercy.

The following is a detailed presentation of the correspondences between the manifested world and the spiritual world, between the "Book of Horizons" and the "Book of Souls"—a presentation made possible by the letters of the *Basmallah*, which is itself the recapitulation, the quintessence, of the whole of the "Book of the Koran".[64]

a) With respect to the exterior manifested world, the schema of correspondences is as follows (see above for the 19 letters of the actual Arabic script for *Bism Allāh al-Raḥmān al-Raḥīm*).

1. B (the *bā'*) corresponds to the first Intelligence (the world of the *Jabarūt*);
2. S (the *sīn*) corresponds to the Soul of the universe (the world of the *Malakūt*);
3. M (the *mīm*) corresponds to the Throne (*'Arsh*): the ninth Sphere;
4. A (the *alif*) corresponds to the Firmament (*Kursī*): the eighth Sphere;
5. L (the first *lām*) corresponds to the seventh Sphere: the Heaven of Saturn;
6. L (the second *lām*) corresponds to the sixth Sphere: the Heaven of Jupiter;
7. H (the *hā'*) corresponds to the fifth Sphere: the Heaven of Mars;
8. A (the *alif*) corresponds to the fourth Sphere: the Heaven of the Sun;
9. L (the *lām*) corresponds to the third Sphere: the Heaven of Venus;

63 *N. al-N.*, §§ 692–694.
64 Ibid., §§ 696–697, 728–729.

10. R (the *rā'*) corresponds to the second Sphere: the Heaven of Mercury;
11. H (the *ḥā'*) corresponds to the first Sphere: the Heaven of the Moon;
12. M (the *mīm*) corresponds to the Sphere of Fire: the first Element;
13. N (the *nūn*) corresponds to the Sphere of Air: the second Element;
14. A (the *alif*) corresponds to the Sphere of Water: the third Element;
15. L (the *lām*) corresponds to the Earth: the fourth Element;
16. R (the *rā'*) corresponds to the animal: the first of the three natural kingdoms;
17. H (the *ḥā'*) corresponds to the vegetal: the second of the three natural kingdoms;
18. I (the *yā'*) corresponds to the mineral: the third of the three natural kingdoms;
19. M (the *mīm*) corresponds to Man, who recapitulates the Whole.

The author sets this forth in a diagram (fig. 3 = diagram no. 10, cf. Appendix). In the centre, a small circle bears the words: *al-'ālam al-ṣūrī* (the manifested world). On the circumferent ring, the nineteen "unities of the universe" which we have just enumerated are each symbolized by one of the 19 letters of the *Basmallah*, and balanced by the total of 19 made up of the 12 Signs of the Zodiac and the 7 Planets, which have already figured in the preceding diagram. However, through the inaccuracy or carelessness of the draughtsman, the celestial Spheres of the primary series are not exactly opposite the planets which correspond to them. There is a discrepancy weighing on the whole diagram (see Appendix), unless one is supposed to think of it as an adjustable figure (drawn on pieces of cardboard which revolve independently). But what counts first and last is, needless to say, the structure of the whole.

b) With regard to the spiritual world, each of the letters of the *Basmallah* is made to correspond respectively both with the *ḥaqīqah* (the spiritual or metaphysical reality), and with the form of manifestation of each of the 7 great prophets and each of the 12 Imams of the Muhammadan period,[65] who, together with the Prophet and his daughter Fāṭimah, make up the pleroma of the *Ḥaqīqah muḥammadīyah*. The schema of correspondences is as follows:

65 The *ḥaqīqah* or metaphysical reality of each Imam is specified by an adjective formed from his name (*murtaḍawīyah*, *ḥasanīyah*, *ḥasaynīyah*, *bāqirīyah*, *ja'farīyah* and so on), which can also serve as an abstract noun to designate his essence.

1. B (*bā'*) corresponds to the *ḥaqīqah* of Muhammad;
2. S (*sīn*) corresponds to the *ḥaqīqah* of Adam;
3. M (*mīm*) corresponds to the *ḥaqīqah* of Noah;
4. A (*alif*) corresponds to the *ḥaqīqah* of Abraham;
5. L (*lām*) corresponds to the *ḥaqīqah* of David;
6. L (*lām*) corresponds to the *ḥaqīqah* of Moses;
7. H (*hā'*) corresponds to the *ḥaqīqah* of Jesus;
8. A (*alif*) corresponds to the *ḥaqīqah* of the first Imam, 'Alī al-Murtaḍā;
9. L (*lām*) corresponds to the *ḥaqīqah* of the second Imam, Ḥasan ibn 'Alī;
10. R (*rā'*) corresponds to the *ḥaqīqah* of the third Imam, Ḥusayn ibn 'Alī;
11. H (*ḥā'*) corresponds to the *ḥaqīqah* of the fourth Imam, 'Alī al-Sajjād;
12. M (*mīm*) corresponds to the *ḥaqīqah* of the fifth Imam, Muḥammad al-Bāqir;
13. N (*nūn*) corresponds to the *ḥaqīqah* of the sixth Imam, Ja'far al-Ṣādiq;
14. A (*alif*) corresponds to the *ḥaqīqah* of the seventh Imam, Mūsā al-Kāẓim;
15. L (*lām*) corresponds to the *ḥaqīqah* of the eighth Imam, 'Alī al-Riḍā;
16. R (*rā'*) corresponds to the *ḥaqīqah* of the ninth Imam, Muḥammad al-Jawād;
17. H (*ḥā'*) corresponds to the *ḥaqīqah* of the tenth Imam, 'Alī al-Naqī;
18. I (*yā'*) corresponds to the *ḥaqīqah* of the eleventh Imam, Ḥasan al-'Askarī;
19. M (*mīm*) corresponds to the *ḥaqīqah* of the twelfth Imam, Muḥammad al-Mahdī.

This schema of correspondences is presented to the imaginative perception by another diagram (fig. 4 = diagram no. 11, see Appendix). The small circle in the centre signifies the spiritual world (*'ālam ma'nawī*). On the circumferent ring, in the outer segment of each epicycle, are the 7 great prophets and the 12 Imams of the Adamic period (Seth, Abel, Cainan and so on), each of whom is indicated by one of the 19 letters of the *Basmallah*. In the inner segment of the epicycles are the 7 poles of the great prophets and the 12 Imams of the Muhammadan period. (As in the preceding diagram, however, there is a certain discrepancy in the correspondences, although the structure as a whole remains unchanged; cf. Appendix).

These diagrams, then, disclose to our imaginative perception a vast system in which the correspondences are effected between the 19 degrees or levels of cosmology, and the 19 levels of prophetology and Imamology, each of which is indicated by one of the 19 letters of the *Basmallah*. In other words, we are shown the correspondences between the "exterior Heaven" and the "interior Heaven", between physical astronomy and spiritual astronomy, the "Book of Horizons" and the "Book of Souls". It is worth recalling at this point a statement by Paracelsus such as the following: "Should you wish to investigate the composition of man in its entirety, then you must realize that the bodies of the firmament are contained in the body of the microcosm. For the stars in the body of man, like the external stars, possess their properties, natures, courses and *situs*, and differ from them only in the substance of their form."[66] Similarly, the great mystical theosopher Simnānī spoke of the "prophets of your being".[67]

It is the nineteen letters of the *Basmallah* that enable Ḥaydar Āmulī to effect the correspondences between the Heavens of cosmology and the Heavens of prophetology, since they recapitulate both the manifested and the spiritual universes. If the *Basmallah* is here the Balance which verifies this correspondence, it is because the secret of the theophanies, the secret of the manifestations of the pure Essence (which, as we saw, is symbolized by the letter *alif*, there being no ensuing ligature possible), is ultimately identical with the secret of the manifestations, in the other letters, of this same *alif*. Ḥaydar Āmulī subjects this fundamental and original correspondence to an analysis of great subtlety, based on the Arabic spelling of the three words *bism*, *Allāh*, and *Raḥmān*, in which three *alifs* are in fact occulted or disguised.[68]

If we consider the Arabic spelling which is transliterated by BSM ALLH AL-RḤMN, we will realize that between the *B* and the *S* (the *bā'*

66 Cf. Paracelsus, *Paramirum* I, in *Sämmtliche Werke in zeitgemässer Kürzung* (!), ed. J. Strebel (St. Gallen, 1947), vol. V, p. 94. "He who has knowledge of the lower Sphere is called a philosopher, whereas he who has knowledge of the upper Sphere is called an astronomer. But they are both philosophers and astronomers, for they possess in common an art that is one and the same (. . .). Saturn is not only in Heaven but in the depths of the sea and in the deepest cavities of the Earth (. . .). He who has knowledge of Mars knows the property of fire, and *vice versa*. The philosopher apprehends in the one the essence of the other." Ibid., pp. 78–79.

67 On Simnānī, see *En Islam iranien* . . . , op. cit., III, pp. 275 ff., and IV, index, s.v. prophètes (les sept) de ton être.

68 *N. al-N.*, §§ 698–701, 730.

and the *sīn*) there should be an *alif* which current usage of Arabic spelling has abolished. Between the second *L* and the *H* (*lām* and *hā'*), there should be the *alif* of a *scriptio plena* (= *ā*), which is omitted in the spelling. Finally, between the *M* and the *N* (*mīm* and *nūn*) of the word RḤMN (*Rahmān*), strict orthography requires an *alif* which current spelling omits.

These three occulted *alifs* symbolize respectively the pure divine Essence, the divine Attributes, and the divine Operations. This same Essence is the cause of three levels: 1) the Unitude (*aḥadīyah*) of absolute, unseconded being; 2) the Unity (*wāḥidīyah*) which is the first in the series of unities and which marks the first limitation of being; this is the median level of the First Intelligence as the second hypostasis; 3) the limitation of the terminal being, which corresponds to the third hypostasis, the Soul, the level of the divine Operations designated as the level of the *rubūbīyah* or lordship. On this level is established the reciprocal relationship between the personal God or lord (*rabb*) and his vassal (*marbūb*), a relationship which renders them interdependent; it is the level of the "God created in the faiths".[69] How, then, in the three words *Bism*, *Allāh* and *Raḥmān*, is the letter *alif* able to "symbolize" with the theophanies?

It is in this way. Divine Being manifests itself in the multitude of its theophanies (*maẓāhir*). But this multiplicity is only such in virtue of the relationships and additions which are precisely what one eliminates when one affirms the esoteric or ontological *tawḥīd*, in other words when one affirms that divine Being alone *is*, in the true sense of the word. At the level of the theophanies, there is multiplicity and the *Other*, there is the relationship between the personal lord and his vassal—a relationship typified in the traditional words: "I was a hidden Treasure. I desired to be known, therefore I created Creation." At the same time, the essential, absolute occultation and secrecy of divine Being are affirmed in the verse: "God can dispense with [both] the universes" (29:6); and it is here that the symbolic pre-eminence of the letter *alif* becomes evident.

As we have already observed, the *alif* is formed by a simple vertical

69 On the designation of the first Intelligence—the second hypostasis—as the Merciful (*al-Raḥmān*), the metaphysical Anthropos, and of the Soul—the third hypostasis—as the All-Merciful (*al-Raḥīm*); and on the identification of *al-Raḥmān* with the Makranthropos (*al-Insān al-kabīr*), and of *al-Raḥīm* with the Mikranthropos (*al-Insān al-ṣaghīr*), cf. *La Philosophie Shī'ite*, op. cit., pp. 567–568. Moreover, the Imam is metaphysically identified with *al-Raḥmān*, *Homo maximus*, the "Light, father of Lights" (*al-Nūr abū'l-Anwār*); ibid., index, s.v. Imam.

stroke, of which one may regard the other Arabic letters as the horizontal elongation, incurvation, torsion, and so on. There is scope, consequently, for envisaging that the letter *alif* manifests itself in the other letters, and that this manifestation results in its determination by the form of each of the other letters. This implies the establishing of a relationship which, in its turn, entails both a multiplication and the fact that there are letters *other* than the letter *alif*. There is thus a perfect correspondence between the manifestation of divine Being in its theophanic forms and the manifestation of the letter *alif* in the diversified forms of the other letters. Consequently, every existing thing can be defined according to its correspondence with one of the letters: one may be designated by the *bā'*, another by the *jīm*, another by the *dāl*, and so on. The divine Essence (*dhāt ilāhīyah*, the divine Ipseity) is brought into relationship with each existing thing, and from this bringing into relationship arise the multiplication and the denomination of divine Being by the name of each existing thing (the name of the first Intelligence, the name of the Soul of the World, and so on). In the same way, a relationship is established between the letter *alif*, and each of the other letters, resulting in the multiplicity of the ABJAD (a, b, c, d), and in the denomination of the *alif* by the name of every letter (the *bā'*, the *jīm*, the *dāl* and so on are the names of the *alif*'s forms of manifestation).

Thus the manifestation of divine Being through the forms of the universe (*ṣuwar al-'ālam*) corresponds to the manifestation of the *alif* through the forms of the other letters. At the same time, here can be seen the ontological basis of the system of correspondences established in the last two diagrams (figs. 3 and 4) between the nineteen letters of the *Basmallah*, the nineteen levels of cosmology, and the nineteen levels of prophetology.

The three *alifs* occulted in the spelling of the three words *bism*, *Allāh* and *Raḥmān* can also be viewed as emblems of the three universes which are veiled within the *Basmallah*. These are the three "unities of the universe", the multiplicity of each of which is symbolized by the figure of one thousand. They are the mystical body of the *Basmallah*, in the same way that the angelic "holy myriads" are the mystical body of the Supreme *Nāmūs*, the "Law of fire" which was the first vision vouchsafed to the Prophet by the Angel—a vision that overwhelmed him and whose meaning was revealed to him by the monk Waraqah.[70] This "mystical body" of the

70 Cf. the article by J.-C. Vadet, op. cit.

Basmallah likewise leads us back to the nineteen worlds. In effect, the three "veiled universes" postulate the existence of three other worlds: the world of Knowledge (*'ālam al-'ilm*), the world of Will (*irādah*), and the world of Power (*qudrah*), each of which is ordained for another world that is its receptacle (*qawābil*): the Known (*ma'lūm*), the Willed (*murād*) and the Predetermined (*muqaddar*). The total number of worlds is 9. In virtue of the Balance which requires equilibrium between the hidden or esoteric (*bāṭin*) and the manifest or exoteric (*ẓāhir*), we should also take into account the three levels in the world of Intelligences (*Jabarūt*), the world of Souls (*Malakūt*), and the world of material bodies (*Mulk*). Here, once again, 9 + 9 = 18. When man's own universe is added, we have a total of *19*.[71]

In short, Ḥaydar Āmulī is of the opinion that the totality of worlds, from whatever angle and in whatever mode it is viewed, is 19, including Man. And he is fully aware of disclosing in this way the most extraordinary meanings (*ma'ānī*, ideas), "inspired by the Invisible, and for which there exists no precedent among the Ancients".[72] This is also the dominating sentiment in the third deployment of the "Balance of the nineteen", which equilibrates the levels of the interior paradise and the interior hell.

C. We have read, above, the advice of the Prophet: "He who desires immunity against the 19 henchmen of Hell needs to recite the *Basmallah.*" This is an allusion to the Koranic verse 74:30, which says that "above Gehenna stand nineteen [guards]." Ḥaydar Āmulī meditated at length on this verse, with regard to which two questions immediately arise: 1. What are these henchmen of Hell? 2. Why is their number limited to 19?

1. In order to reply to the first question, one must bear in mind the correspondence between the exterior Heaven and the interior Heaven, and hence between the exterior paradise and hell on the one hand, and the interior paradise and hell on the other; for it is in the inner meaning of paradise and hell as internal states of man that the answer will be found. It depends on man whether the Angels of his paradise are changed into the demons of his hell. All connection and attachment engender a perma-

71 *N. al-N.*, § 703. The Koranic verse 27:12, which commands Moses: "Put your hand inside your breast, and you will take it out all white without its being diseased; this will be one of the nine signs", is interpreted as referring to the nine exterior corporeal worlds, and the nine hidden spiritual worlds whereby Moses exercises his miracle-working powers over the former. § 704.

72 Ibid., § 705.

nent disposition or *habitus* (*malakah*, ἕξις) which "possesses" (*milk*) his interior being and becomes its "dominant".

Theology calls these *habitus* by the name of "Angels". But there are *habitus* which are excellent, valiant and beautiful, and it is these which are properly called "Angels"; and there are *habitus* that are vicious, craven and ugly. These go by the name of "henchmen" (*zabānīyah*) of hell, while the former are called by one of the names of Paradise—*Riḍvān* whose Angels they are. The correspondence between the two worlds is clear. The Angels signify the Powers (*al-quwā* or *al-quwwāt*, δυνάμεις) who are active both in the macrocosm and in the microcosm. As Ibn 'Arabī puts it, the Angels are the Powers of the *makranthrōpos*, of this "Great Man" (*insān kabīr*) who is the universe, just as in the microcosm, in the interior Heaven, the spiritual and psychic Powers are the Angels of man's existence; for within man the Powers of the cosmos are assembled and recapitulated in a condensed manner. It is with respect to these Powers that the *habitus*, the permanent dispositions of man, are ordered. The more a man is attached to this world, the more vicious and vile is his *ethos* or inner state. The less his attachment to this world, the more beautiful, strong and subtle his inner state. Why, then, is mention made of *19* connections and 19 *habitus*, based on the number of Angels who guard the threshold of paradise and the number of henchmen who are the guardians of hell?[73]

It is because the interior paradise and hell; precisely because of the correspondence between the exterior Heaven and the interior Heaven, are not extrinsic to this world. As the Prophet reminds us: "Paradise and hell are closer to each one of you than the clasp of his sandals." Inevitably, therefore, there is a correspondence between this paradise and this hell and the "nineteen" of the exterior Heaven, that is to say, the 12 signs of the zodiac and the 7 wandering stars. Our author stresses that this is clearly what astrology teaches when it relates man's attachments and his permanent dispositions to the signs of the zodiac. This is why, in one case as in the other, the whole complex forms a series of nineteen. The object of the mission of all the prophets, as of the contents of all the sacred Books revealed by Heaven, is the same: to induce man to free himself, to break all links with the nineteen. This was the meaning of the Prophet's utterance recommending the recitation of the *Basmallah* with its nineteen letters, so

73 Ibid., §§ 706–707.

that each of these letters might become a paradise for man on the day of his resurrection. Once he has broken his attachments, he escapes the nineteen henchmen who are hell and rejoins the nineteen Angels who are paradise.[74]

All worldly links must be severed in the name of an exclusive devotion to the service of the divine. Here indeed may be understood the traditional teaching of the mystics which originates in the utterance of the Prophet: "Die before you die." This mystical anticipation of death, this "death before death", is rooted in the idea that at the outset man's natural life is not, in this world, the life of his true nature. In order to live according to his true nature, he must undergo this voluntary mystical death, which is actually his second birth. Another utterance of the Prophet's states: "Human beings are asleep; it is when they die that they awaken." By means of this same utterance, Ibn 'Arabī (see below, section V) will finally offer us a dazzling insight into the meaning of the "science of correspondences". Here, sleep is ignorance and unawareness. Wakefulness is gnosis, the awareness of being awake;[75] it is to be an *Egregoros*.

A Koranic verse refers to this: "He who was dead and to whom we gave life, and whom we have set as a Light, so that he should walk with it among men—is this man like him who walks in darkness, and who will never emerge from it?" (6:123). Ḥaydar Āmulī comments on this: "He who has undergone the voluntary death of mystical initiation, whom we have made alive with the true life which is knowledge, gnosis, visionary power (*mushāhadah*), and whom we have set among men as someone who possesses knowledge, as a gnostic, as someone who sees (*mushāhid*)—is he like the man who is no more than a corpse amid the darkness of ignorance?" Life in the true and authentic sense is not life in the biological sense; it is Light, the Light which in the Koran always signifies knowledge, life, being.

Light is Being itself, and as such it is invulnerable to darkness and death. In order to liberate this Light and restore it to its invulnerability, it

74 Ibid., § 708.

75 *Yaqaẓah*. Cf. the name Ḥayy ibn Yaqẓān, which forms the title of one of Avicenna's mystical recitals, edited and translated in my *Avicenne et le récit visionnaire*, Paris, 1980, Berg International [*Avicenna and the Visionary Recital*, trans. Willard R. Trask, Spring Publications, Inc., 1980; University of Dallas, Texas. This translation has been made from the original 1954 French edition, not from the 1979 Berg International edition to which Corbin refers. The arrangement, however, of the text is the same in both cases.]

is necessary to pass through voluntary death, the mystical death. Our author understands the following Koranic verses (3:169–170) in their purely spiritual sense: "Do not think that those who have been killed on God's pathway are dead. No! they are living with their Lord; from him they receive their subsistence, and are filled with joy by the favour with which God overwhelms them." Thus, according to the *ta'wīl*, death is to be understood in a spiritual sense: one dies to the darkness and hence to death itself, in the natural sense, for this mystical death leads to a higher form of existence, to the immortal life which is maintained by the spiritual nourishment of knowledge, gnosis, inner revelation (*kashf*).[76] This is the significance that Ḥaydar Āmulī gives here to the "martyrs" fallen on the pathway of God; and in so doing he is perhaps close to the meaning ascribed to "martyrs" by a hermetic alchemist such as Zosimus, who was well aware that the birth and growth of the subtle body—of the body of resurrection within man—presupposes that the "martyr" passes through the dissolution represented by the stage of *nigredo*. This dissolution is here that of the many connections concealed in the nineteen.

Hence the conclusion: "He who in this world does not dissolve the ties resulting from his dependence on the twelve signs of the zodiac and the seven planets, remains, after his physical *exitus*, in the power of the *habitus* produced in him by those attachments which are designated as the nineteen henchmen of hell."[77]

2. Our first question has been answered by these considerations. It may appear that, because of the correspondence between macrocosm and microcosm, we have at the same time received the answer to our second question, as well: why is the number of these henchmen limited to 19? But in fact the question is one of far greater complexity, and there might even be something ridiculous in limiting these *habitus* to 19. In limiting the number of the *habitus* of man's inner being—that is to say, the Angels of his paradise or the henchmen of his hell—to 19, one is taking into account only global categories, the "unities of the universe" (as is the case when one speaks of the *Jabarūt* or the *Malakūt*); but when it comes to going into detail, and to visualizing particular things in all their singularity, only God knows their number and limits. As the Koranic verse 74:31 puts it: "No one knows the armies of your Lord save He alone." For this reason,

76 *N. al-N.*, §§ 709–711.
77 Ibid., § 713.

the multitude of these partial realities is not the object of our author's enquiry. The object of carrying out his enquiry into the number 19, encountered in the three great Books, is suggested to him by two references. One of these, in the Koran (69:32), alludes to a chain of 70 cubits; the other is contained in this utterance of the Prophet: "God has 70,000 Veils of light and darkness; if He were to raise them, the splendours of His Face would set alight any creature who met His gaze."[78] Are not this chain and these Veils related in some way to the 19, and especially to the 19 demons of hell, against whom one must guard by the recitation of the *Basmallah* and by substituting for them the 19 Angels of paradise?

Our author observes, firstly, that if the 19 letters of the *Basmallah* are, as the preceding diagrams have illustrated, an adequate cipher of the graduation of the system of the worlds—the manifest world and the spiritual world—a detailed realization of them is only achieved according to the system of the letters as a whole. He has already alluded to this when he recalled that of the 28 letters of the Arabic alphabet, the fourteen undotted letters relate to the *Malakūt* or spiritual world, while the other fourteen, which are furnished with diacritical marks, relate to the *Mulk* or manifest world. This is the system that we will be considering in conclusion, when we examine the "Balance of the twenty-eight". The theme of the 70,000 Veils of light and darkness has promoted a considerable body of literature among the mystical theosophers. What Ḥaydar Āmulī wishes to envisage here is the idea that both chain and veil denote all connection and attachment to this world, of which man must be free before his *exitus*. He considers that his great forbears, such as Ghazālī, Fakhruddīn Rāzī, Najmuddīn Kubrā, Najmuddīn Dāyah Rāzī, and Fakhruddīn 'Irāqī[79] were not able, in spite of their efforts, to explain the figure 70. By contrast, he says, "it happened that God opened the eye of our inner vision . . . so that we discovered and contemplated the state of things as it is in reality, and wrote a treatise in Arabic and a treatise in Persian on the subject, in which we explained it in various ways."[80]

78 Ibid., §§ 714–715.
79 On all these figures, see my *Histoire de la philosophie islamique*, part II: 'Depuis la mort d'Averroës jusqu'à nos jours'. (A shortened version of this can be found in *Encyclopédie de la Pléiade, Histoire de la philosophie*, III).
80 *N. al-N.*, § 716. This is most probably a reference to the treatise entitled *Risālat al-ḥujub wa- khulāṣat al-kutub* (Treatise on the veils and the quintessence of books). Cf. my introduction to *La Philosophie Shi'ite*, op. cit., pp. 40 ff., no. 15 of the bibliographical sketch.

His explanation as he presents it here is as follows. He recalls how one arrives at the total of 18 levels of cosmology (18 or 18,000 worlds), and how by adding the world of the Perfect Man one obtains the total of 19. Needless to say, as the science of the Balance demands, it must be understood that these 18 "unities of the universe" each comprises an exoteric and an esoteric dimension, that is to say, one aspect which pertains to the *Mulk*, the world manifest to the senses, and a counterpart which pertains to the spiritual world or *Malakūt*. When their double aspect is taken into account, the 18 "unities of the universe" give a total of 36. In accordance with the preceding method of calculation, these 36 "unities of the universe" are to be added to man's own universe, since this latter was added to the 18 levels of cosmology to give 18 + 1 = 19. Here, if we understand him correctly, Ḥaydar Āmulī proceeds by another course, inverse and complementary. The 18 universes are regarded as being the chains and the veils in relation to man, and it is with man that they become 19. Now, however, it is a question not of adding man to the sum of these universes, but of extracting him from it. To extract man from these universes so that he may constitute his own universe, free of chains and veils, amounts then, from the point of view here envisaged, to subtracting him from their totality. This gives 36 − 1 = 35.[81] These 35 are to be taken into account both in the "Book of Horizons" and the "Book of Souls", and this gives us the figure of 70—that is to say: 70 worlds, 70 veils, 70 chains, with respect to the global unities, but 70,000 Veils and 70,000 chains with respect to the detail symbolized, as before, by the order of thousands. *Quod erat demonstrandum*.[82]

This, broadly speaking, is how the "balance of the nineteen" is elaborated, verified as it is in the correspondence between the "Book of Horizons", the "Book of Souls" and the "Book of the Koran". Our author has indicated in passing how the 28 letters of the Arabic alphabet are linked to the 19 letters of the *Basmallah*, thus "ciphering" the genesis of the worlds. We will encounter this number 28 again in connection with the way in

81 If this were not so, it would be hard to see how, since man is not included in the 18 (he is added to make the 19th), the author could subtract him from the 36 (= 18 × 2) to get 35. If he is not there, how can he be subtracted? Ḥaydar Āmulī returns to the number 36 in connection with the "Balance of the 72" (that is to say, the 72 religious schools or groups before and since Islam), which for lack of space we cannot go into here. Cf. §§ 872 ff.

82 Ibid., § 717.

which, like Dante, Ibn 'Arabī apportions the 28 dwellings of Hell. But in Ḥaydar Āmulī, the "balance of the twenty-eight" fits into a vast whole which is one of the culminations of his prophetic historiosophy. Another culmination is the "balance of the seventy-two", which embraces the totality of the history of religion, both before and after Islam, in an inspired and grandiose perspective. Unfortunately, we have no room to describe it here.

IV. The Balance of the Twenty-Eight

The "balance of the twenty-eight" could be said in some sense to function at the heart of prophetology in general. It aims particularly at manifesting the pleroma constituted by the Muhammadan period of the prophetic cycle, and it does this by distinguishing the ideal topological correspondence between the levels that denote, respectively, the ancestors and the descendants of the Prophet of Islam. The undertaking is something quite different from that of a linear construction, vector of a philosophy of history that envisages either a necessary causality immanent in facts, or a purely contingent succession of these facts. In our case, "facts" are envisaged as ordered and dominated by a transcendental law, the superior law of a structure which determines things in the form of cycles (or "cupolas", as we said before). A homology exists between the respective stages of each cycle, and this makes it possible to bring the personages they locate into correspondence with each other. In conformity with a distinction which we have already established, the law itself, transcendental and transhistorical, is that of a historiosophy, not of a simple philosophy of history.

Prophetology in general acknowledges the existence of 124,000 prophets: not *Nabīs* who perforce have possessed the quality of Messengers, but *Nabīs* pure and simple. For each of these *Nabīs* there was a Friend of God (a *walī*) who was his spiritual heir (his *waṣī*). According to this order of things, there were 124,000 *Awliyā'* corresponding to the 124,000 *Nabīs*. But, as we already know, prophetology proper sees the seven great legislative prophets as occupying an incomparable rank. As we also know, each of them was succeeded by twelve Imams who were their spiritual heirs until the coming of a new prophet.[83] This applied also to the prophet of

83 Ibid., § 731.

Islam who, unlike previous prophets, was the *Seal* of prophecy and of prophetology, and whose twelfth Imam was and will be the "Seal of the *Awliyā'*" of his period. If this is the case, how is the Balance which equilibrates the ancestry and descendancy of the last of the legislative prophets to be established?

Our authors applied themselves to reconstructing the family tree of the prophet Muhammad back to Adam. Altogether it forms a chain of 51 links. Prominent positions are occupied by 'Abdul-Muṭṭalib, common ancestor of the Prophet and the first Imam; by al-Naḍr ibn Kinānah, from whom originated the tribe of the Qurayshites; and by Ishmael, son of Abraham, through whom we go back to Arphaxad, of the line of Shem. After this, it only remains to identify, beneath an orthography that is more or less accurate, the names which occur in the book of Genesis.[84] Ḥaydar Āmulī observes that of these 51 ancestors, 17 were prophets, 17 others were kings, and 17 more were *Awliyā'*[85]—a remark bearing witness to the perpetuation in Islamic gnosis of the arithmological virtues of the number *51*, considered as a multiple of 17 (17 × 3). The famous alchemist Jābir ibn Ḥayyān already regarded the corporeal world as "governed by the number 17, which is supposed to reproduce here below the image, admittedly distorted, of the celestial man".[86]

There are two further things to be noted. a) The ancestry of the prophet traced through the male line, from father to grandfather, is still an exoteric one; it leaves untouched the problem of his esoteric ancestry through the line of Khadījah, his wife, and of her cousin the Christian monk Waraqah,

84 Ibid., § 732. In fact, although 51 names are mentioned, Ḥaydar Āmulī lists only 46 of them. After the line of ascent from Ishmael to Arphaxad, the list accords with the Book of Genesis 11: 10–32.

85 Ibid., § 733.

86 Cf. Paul Kraus, *Jābir ibn Ḥayyān*, op. cit., II, pp. 216–217, 222–223, who has gathered together some suggestive comparisons. In the Nuṣayrī tradition, 51 (= 3 × 17) dignitaries stand at the gates of the town of Ḥarrān (the town of the Sabian hermetists, described in the manner of the heavenly Jerusalem) to receive the just who will inhabit Heaven (cf. the *Revelation of John*, 21:10 ff.). According to certain Jewish gnostics, there are 17 primordial Beings. According to the Shiite gnostic Mughīrah ibn Sa'īd (died 119/737), 17 is the number of people who will be resurrected at the appearance of the Mahdī, "and each of them will be given one of the letters of the alphabet composing the supreme Name of God". In the 153 fishes of the miraculous draught of fish (John 21:11), St. Augustine discerns a triangular number whose base is 17. The number 51 is the number of daily prayers said by the first Imam; it is also the number of treatises (17 of them on physics) in the Ismaili Encyclopaedia of the "Brothers of the pure heart" (*Ikhwān al-Ṣafā'*), and so on.

who initiated Muhammad into the meaning of his first vision. b) It is important to emphasize the position occupied by al-Naḍr, first ancestor of the Qurayshites; he is fourteenth in line, a position that will make it possible to establish, on the basis of the figure 28, the balance between the Prophet's exoteric ancestry and his esoteric descendancy in the person of the Imams.

Because the male ancestry described above is still exoteric, it does no more than retraverse the line of the Muhammadan Light (*Nūr muḥammadī*) which lies at the source of Muhammad's prophetic charisma. This pre-eternal, spiritual Light was transmitted from prophet to prophet, as a single Light unique to prophecy and to the Imamate ("I was, together with 'Alī, a single Light before God, before He created Creation"), until, from 'Abdul Muṭṭalib onwards, it splits into the two persons of the Prophet and the Imam. The purity of this Light excludes all tarnishing during the stages of its transmission, to such a degree that one must in passing exercise a certain precision with respect to the true identity of Abraham's father.[87]

The balance, then, of the Prophet's ancestry and descendancy is established on the basis of the figure 28. The importance for prophetology of the figure 28, already encountered in this context, is revealed at once. Indeed, the prophets mentioned in the Koran are 28 in number, and this number is *eo ipso* a distinguishing mark of the prophetology common to the "religions of the Book", to the Abrahamic "ecumenism" which covers the prophetic continuity from the Bible to the Koran. It is this continuity that permits the prophet of Islam to revive the scriptural antecedents of his own Revelation. The teachings to be inferred from the figure 28 are more easily foreseeable in that they have already been outlined. The number of prophets mentioned in the Koran conforms to the number that regulates

87 *N. al-N.*, §§ 733–734. The precision which our author brings to bear in passing is prompted by the Koranic verse 6:75, where it is said that Azar was the father of Abraham. Azar had been a worshipper of idols before being converted by Abraham, and it is absolutely out of the question that the Muhammadan Light, transmitted from prophet to prophet—which is, needless to say, a mystery deriving from subtle physiology—should reside in loins that are impure. In fact, Azar was Abraham's uncle, and the Koranic verse, says Ḥaydar Āmulī, merely confirms the Arabic usage of calling an uncle by the name of "father". Actually, Abraham was the son of Terah, and on this our author is in agreement with the Book of Genesis, 11:26. It is by virtue of the impeccability (cf. the concept of ἀνάμάρτητος in Judaeo-Christian prophetology) required of the prophets and the Imams that Ḥaydar Āmulī defends the memory of Abū Ṭālib also, who was both the father of the Imam 'Alī and the adoptive father of the Prophet.

the common structure of the three great books. The "Book of Horizons" comprises 14 levels: the 1st Intelligence, the 9 celestial Spheres, and the 4 Elements. Taking into consideration both the exoteric and the esoteric aspects, at the level of the *Mulk* and the *Malakūt* the total obtained is 28. The same is true of the "Book of Souls" and of the "Book of the Koran", which consists of the 28 letters. Equally, when one considers the 7 prophets in the "world of horizons" and in the "world of souls", taking into account both their metaphysical and their manifested aspects, the total obtained is again 28 (7 × 4).[88]

There is more than this. We have noted that the 19 henchmen of hell mentioned in the Koran had to be counterbalanced by the 19 Angels of paradise. In a similar manner, Ibn 'Arabī (whom Ḥaydar Āmulī quotes again at this point) saw a structure of hell counterbalanced by the structure of paradise organized in terms of the figure 28. The inhabitants of hell fall into four categories, for Iblīs-Satan's strategy is to assail men "from before and from behind, from their right and their left" (7:17).[89] Moreover, Gehenna is said (15:44) to have "seven gates", seven levels or circles, among which are distributed the four categories of "infernals". When this number (4) is multiplied by the number of circles (7), the result is *28*. Ibn 'Arabī's topography of Hell has been compared, by the great Arabist Asīn Palacios, to that described by Dante.[90]

These 28 infernal dwellings correspond to the 28 letters which make up the *kalimāt*, the words whereby unbelief and faith are manifested in this world; for God speaks and addresses each man through the faith or the lack of faith which is in that man, through his sincerity or mendacity; and evidence of God subsists in the world in the very words men utter, even if they utter them only to deny God. We have already seen how hundreds and thousands can serve to denote—symbolically, not statistically—the plurality concealed in each "unity of the universe". Here, each infernal dwelling is regarded as being made up of one hundred levels, which gives

88 Ibid., §§ 736–737.

89 Ibid., §§ 738–739. Cf. *Futūḥāt*, chap. 62: "Iblīs appears to the *mushrik* from in front; he appears to the atheist from behind; he appears to the proud man from his right; he appears to the hypocrite from his left, for that is his weakest side, and it is also the weakest of the four groups".

90. Cf. Miguel Asīn Palacios, *La Escatologīa musulmana en la Divina Comedia*, 2nd edition, (Madrid/Granada, 1943), pp. 144–148. The relationship of 4 × 7 is brought out in the diagrams on p. 147, showing the correspondence between the Islamic circles of hell and Dante's circles of hell.

a total of 2,800 dwellings. 28 hundred paradisiac dwellings correspond symmetrically to these 28 hundred infernal dwellings, for it is said: "Like a grain which produces seven ears, every ear bearing a hundred grains" (2:261), giving a total of 700. The blessed also fall into four categories: the prophet-legislators, the *Nabīs* pure and simple, the *Awliyā'*, and the ordinary believers. Once again, the number obtained is 2,800 (700 × 4). Thus, the scales which weigh Creation in the two worlds of paradise and hell are absolutely accurate. Consequently the figure of 28 prophets mentioned in the Koran conceals a profound wisdom, the same wisdom as that which has established between the two worlds correspondences of which we know practically nothing.[91]

There is, then, an essential connection between the science of the Balance as a science of correspondences, and the recognition of theophanies; for there is not a creature that is not the theophanic form (*maẓhar*) of one of the divine Names, and the science of correspondences consists in homologising the theophanies of a single divine Name at all levels of the universe as well as in each cycle of prophetic hierohistory. It is in this respect that the number 28 demonstrates its arithmosophical virtues, for, as well as denoting the number of the prophets mentioned in the Koran, it determines the structural homology between the two cycles formed by the ancestry and the descendants of the prophet of Islam. Ḥaydar Āmulī derives inspiration here from the subtle clues provided by a thirteenth-century author, Muḥammad ibn Ṭalḥa.[92]

While speaking above of the Prophet's 51 ancestors that go back to Adam, we mentioned the significance to be assigned to al-Naḍr ibn Kinānah as the founder of the tribe of the Qurayshites. This is because the Prophet declared that "the Imams who come after him shall be of the Quraysh". Thus, the Imamate of an Imam, even though he were an Arab, would be neither legal nor legitimate if he were a non-Qurayshite. Such a privilege doubtless bestows an incomparable dignity and nobility on the tribe of the Qurayshites, but it means *eo ipso* that in the Prophet's ancestry,

91 *N. al-N.*, §§ 740–741. On the number 28 as a perfect number in arithmology, see P. Kraus, op. cit., p. 199.

92 At that time, Muḥammad ibn Ṭalḥa (Kamāluddīn Abū Sālim) was one of the leaders of the Shāfi'ite school (he appears, in fact, to have been a crypto-Shiite, like so many others). He died at Aleppo in 652/1254–1255, at the age of 70. His main work, on the person of the Imams, *Maṭālib al-sūl fī manāqib Āl al-Rasūl*, was lithographed in Iran. He is also reported to have written a treatise on the supreme Name of God. Cf. *Rayḥānat al-adab*, III, p. 385, no. 96.

the line beginning with al-Naḍr, father of the Qurayshites, must be distinguished and set apart from the others.[93] Between the Prophet and al-Naḍr there are *12* links in the ancestral chain (to which links correspond the 12 Imams), from 'Abdullah, the Prophet's father, to Mālik, al-Naḍr's son. Thus, Mālik ibn al-Naḍr, at the summit of the ancestral line, corresponds symmetrically with the final point of the line of prophetic descendancy, which is marked by the twelfth Imam, Muḥammad al-Mahdī. If we now complete the twelve links of the ancestral chain with the two extremes of the Prophet and al-Naḍr, we obtain a total of 14 people.

This is clearly set out in the diagram provided by our author (fig. 5 = diagram no. 12; see Appendix). In the circumferent ring are the 51 names representing the line of ascent from Muhammad back to Adam; the names of these two last culminate at the highest point (for the end is a return to the beginning). In the central circle are inscribed the names of the 14 Qurayshites; in the small central circle is the name of the Prophet, linked by a written stroke to the name of his father. Round about, and reading from right to left, are the names of the 12 ancestors ending with Mālik al-Naḍr, whose name is joined by a written stroke to the small circle at the side which bears the name of al-Naḍr ibn Kinānah.[94]

In its turn, the diagram schematizing the Prophet's descendants corresponds strictly with the preceding diagram. Here we are once again reminded of the reason why the number of the Imams is limited to *twelve*. This necessary limitation possesses four aspects: a) It is symbolized in the 12 letters which make up respectively the double affirmation of the Islamic faith: the Affirmation of the Unique (LA ILH ILA ALLH = *Lā ilāha illā Allāh*), and the affirmation of the Prophet's mission (MHMD RSUL ALLH = *Muḥammad rasūl Allāh*). Now the Imamate derives from this dual

93 On al-Naḍr ibn Kinānah, ancestor of the Qurayshite tribe, see *Safīnat Biḥār al-anwār*, II, p. 424, s.v. *qrš*. He is not to be confused with al-Naḍr ibn al-Harth, *Safīnat*, II, p. 594, whose name is associated with a strange recurrence of Iranian fervour. He had gone to Persia, and announced to the Qurayshites on his return: Muhammad told you the story of 'Ād and Thamūd; I shall tell you the story of Rustam and Isfandyār. His audience found the story so beautiful that they ceased to listen to the Koran. It seems that he was a companion of Abū Jahl, and was killed by 'Alī after the battle of Badr, ibid., II, 210.

94 *N. al-N.*, §§ 747–751. The *situs* of the Prophet thus determines the equilibrium between his twelve Qurayshite ancestors and his twelve Imamic descendants. In connection with this, it will be observed that the first Melchizedek, who comes into *Enoch* II, is preceded by 12 priests (13 counting Nir, Noah's brother), and that the second Melchizedek, king of Salem, was the originator of a line of 12 priests. Cf. *Le Livre des secrets d'Hénoch*, ed. and trans. A. Vaillant (Paris, 1952), pp. 115–117.

principle, and those who assume it are *12* in number. b) The second aspect is the Prophet's choice of twelve men, and his announcement that twelve Imams would come after him.[95] c) The third aspect is represented by the prototype of the twelve leaders of the twelve tribes of Israel, of the twelve springs which gushed from the rock of Horeb, struck by Moses' rod. d) Finally, there is an aspect based on the equivalence, established earlier by the "science of letters" or philosophical algebra, between the words ZaMāN (time) and MīZāN (balance).

The progression of time marked by the revolution of the stars, especially by the revolution of the ninth Sphere, is necessary if the benefits which result from the stars' course are to propagate themselves in the terrestrial world. The course of the stars is regulated with reference to the computus of the twelve months and the twelve hours of the day and of the night. In the same way, by virtue of the perfect correspondence between the two worlds, the invisible action of the Imams on the spiritual world is regulated with reference to their number, which is *twelve*.[96] The time (*zamān*) of the Imamate is the balance (*mīzān*) which equilibrates the esoteric aspect of the Imamic lineage of the twelve Imams with the exoteric aspect of the lineage of the Prophet's twelve Qurayshite ancestors. When typified in the form of a cycle homologous to the preceding one, the time of the Imamate is to such a degree a "liturgical time" that each of the twelve hours of the day and of the night is under the protection of one of the Twelve. In contrast to chronological time, which flows in irreversible succession, liturgical time establishes that level of transhistorical permanence to which we referred earlier. It is perpetually there; it does not conceal a past which has passed away. Its very succession ensures not its flowing away, but its return. The present time of the Imamate is the mean-time of the hidden Imam, whose liturgical recurrences will continue until the "Day of the Resurrection".

In this way, the structure of the diagram showing the Imamic lineage, in correspondence with the line of Qurayshite ancestry, becomes immedi-

95 Ibid., §§ 753–754. "And that is why, on the night of the 'Aqabah (the summit of Minā where the Prophet was first acknowledged publicly), when the Messenger of God received the oath of his companions, he told them: Pick me out from amongst yourselves *twelve* leaders like the twelve leaders of the children of Israel. Which they did. So this became a custom to follow and a special number. Hence this saying of the Prophet's, expressed in different ways: the Imams after me will be twelve in number. The first of them will be 'Alī; the last will be the Mahdī."

96 Ibid., § 755.

ately recognizable (fig. 6 = diagram no. 13; see Appendix). In the circumferent ring are the 12 Imams starting with the twelfth, followed by those belonging to the line of the 51 who make up the lineage from Muhammad to Adam. The two names at the highest point—the point of origin and return—are here no longer those of Adam and the "Seal of the Prophets", but of Adam and the "Seal of the *Awliyā'* (*Khātim al-Awliyā'*), the twelfth Imam. In the preceding diagram, the central circle was inscribed with the names of the 14 Qurayshites—that is to say, of the twelve ancestors together with al-Naḍr, their origin, and the Prophet himself in the small circle in the middle. Here, in the small central circle, is the name of Fāṭimah, daughter of the Prophet and origin of the line of Imams. But because Fāṭimah is called the "mother of her father" (*Umm abīhā*), she is the origin both of the Prophet's ancestors and of his descendants. All around the little circle with her name are distributed circles containing the names of the twelve Imams; reading from left to right, these go from the 12th to the 1st Imam, who rejoins their source in the person of the Prophet. The Prophet's name occupies a small circle at the side, symmetrical to the one that in the preceding diagram contained the name of al-Naḍr ibn Kinānah, origin of the Qurayshite line.

On the one hand, then, there are the 12 Qurayshite ancestors, in addition to the initial figure of al-Naḍr and the final figure of the Prophet Muhammad. These give a total of *14*. On the other hand there are the 12 Imams, together with the Prophet and his daughter Fāṭimah, the Imams, origin who links their line with that of the Qurayshites. These, too, total *14* (the "Fourteen Immaculate Ones", the Fourteen Aeons of light of the *Ḥaqīqah muḥammadīyah*). The balance is exact: 14 + 14 = 28. The equilibrium of the balance is established on the basis of this number, which thus authenticates itself as the esoteric number of the Muhammadan period of the prophetic cycle, corresponding with the 28 letters, the 28 phases of the Moon, and so on.[97]

In conclusion, we will quote our author: "The light of the Imamate guides hearts and intelligences along the way of Truth (or the way of God, *ṭarīq al-Ḥaqq*), showing them clearly the goals on the road to salvation, just as the light of the Sun and the Moon guides the eyes of creatures along the ways of the visible world. It shows them clearly those ways which are well-

97 Ibid., § 758.

marked and easy, so that they can follow them, as well as those which are abrupt and perilous, so that they can avoid them. Both are guiding lights: one directs the eyes of the interior vision, and is the light of the Imamate; and the other guides the eyes of the exterior vision, and is the light of the Sun and the Moon. Each of these two lights possesses stations for its transference, its migration. The stations of the light which directs the eyes of exterior vision are the twelve Signs of the zodiac, of which the first is Aries and the last the sign of Pisces. This light is transferred from one to another of the twelve Signs, until it reaches the last Sign, the twelfth. Similarly, the stations of the light which directs the eyes of the interior vision, the light of the Imamate, are also limited to twelve, and are the twelve Imams: "*We offer these parables to men; only the Wise understand them*" (29:43).[98]

This Koranic verse, cited by our author in conclusion, confronts us with the ultimate question: what, basically, *is* this science of correspondences—correspondences which engender symbols and thus form the substance of the only true stories that are, perhaps, the parables? How is such a science of correspondences possible, and who therefore is capable of it? The answer, or at any rate an answer, to this question can be found in some extraordinary pages—yet are they not all extraordinary?—of the great work of Ibn 'Arabī.

V. The horsemen of the Invisible and the science of correspondences

At this point, let us take up some of the themes left to one side in the course of this study. We have been told that throughout their life in this world, men's mode of being is one of sleep. Could they, during this sleep, perceive the meaning and have an understanding of parables which, as the Koranic verse has just told us, are only understood by the Wise Ones? Who then are these Wise Ones? They are described to us by Ibn 'Arabī, in three marvellous chapters, as the "horsemen" or the "knights of the Invisible", and it is thanks to them that there can exist in this world a "science of correspondences".

In addition, when we made our brief survey of the esoteric hierarchy in Shiism and Sufism, we came across the categories of the *Awtād*, the *Abdāl*,

98 Ibid., § 757.

the *Nujabā'*, the *Nuqabā'* and so on (see above, section 2). There was one category that we deliberately omitted for the time being, since the appropriate moment to discuss it had to be deferred until now; and this, precisely, is the category designated by Ibn 'Arabī as the *Rukbān* or *Rukkāb*, the "horsemen".[99] Needless to say, it is a cavalry, or knighthood, whose function is strictly esoteric, a "cavalry of the invisible worlds" which is *incognito* to the eyes of men.

There are two categories of these horsemen. The first is made up of those who are mounted on great contemplations and sublime visions; the second is formed of those mounted on great actions, great enterprises. The two categories could be said to correspond on the one hand to a speculative, contemplative knighthood, and on the other to one devoted to practical activity. The first category, composed of contemplatives, is designated as that of the *Afrād*: the Peerless, the Incomparable, the Unique. On the level of man, they correspond to those Angels who were previously described to us as the "Angels ecstatic with love" for the divine beauty and glory (cf. *supra* the seven Cherubim who, in the Dionysian hierarchy, would more likely be the Seraphim; cf. also the *Seven* in the books of Enoch, the book of Tobias, the Apocalypse, the seven Source-Spirits in Jacob Boehme, and so on). These Angels are essentially dedicated to the celestial liturgy. The second category of knights, those devoted to practical activity, corresponds, on the level of man, to the Angels whose task it is to rule over a world and to govern the things of this world. As we shall see, it is thanks to them and to their equitation that something like a "science of correspondences" can exist.

We are told that to the knights of the first category God has entrusted a supernatural power,[100] and that this is why they conceal themselves beneath the veil of the pavilions of the Invisible (*surādiqāt al-ghayb*), or even beneath the veil of ways that are contrary to their state. In a sense

99 Cf. Ibn 'Arabī, *Kitāb al-Futūḥāt al-Makkīyah* (The Book of the spiritual Conquests of Mecca), I, pp. 199 ff., chapters 30–32. The vast critical edition of this, undertaken by Usman Yaḥyā, has not yet reached the passage in question. Ibn 'Arabī distinguishes between the *fursān*, the horsemen, and the *rukbān*, those who ride on camels or, to be exact, dromedaries (*hujun*), a sport at which the Arabs of Arabia are expert. Their group is associated with the taste for eloquence, for heroic poetry, for generosity—in short, for whatever is characteristic of the "chivalry of the desert". This is why Ibn 'Arabī chose the name of *rukbān*. In fact, throughout these pages as well as in the dictionaries we are concerned simply with "horsemen".

100 Ibid., p. 201.

they are "volunteers of disapprobation" (*malamātīyah*) should they judge it expedient in order to preserve their incognito; they are *Fityān* (plural form of *fatā*), a term whose appearance in this context is all the more distinctive in that it designates the members of the *futuwwah*—that is to say, of the Islamic equivalent of our Western phenomenon of chivalry and comradeship.[101] They are men who are absolutely free (*abriyā'*), free even of the authority of the Pole (*Quṭb*) that is the summit of the esoteric hierarchy: they are not at the Pole's disposal. On the contrary, they are themselves designated as *poles*, not because they are in charge of a group and rule over it as leaders—they are too highly placed for that—but because of their mystical status and their service to the divine. They exercise no command because they achieve full realization of their being in serving the divine. They are horsemen who move without movement, carried away by the sheer spontaneous impulse of their mounts. If they cover at great speed the distances which they are ordered to cover by divine command, the credit belongs to the steed which bears them, and on which they sit motionless in their contemplation. This is expressed by the Koranic verse 8:17: "When you shoot the arrow, it is not you, but God who shoots it." One cannot claim glory for something which is negative, and immobility is simply the negation of movement. They traverse spiritual distances, those perilous wildernesses, in their souls and by means of their souls, but they do not place their trust in their souls, for they are the Transported (*majdhūbūn*) by the divine attraction. Each night they undergo a spiritual ascension (*mi'rāj rūḥānī*). Like Abraham, their vision of the *Malakūt*[102] is direct, and it is to this that their immobility is due. They have no "bridge" to cross, for direct vision has no need of interpretations. We would say that they do not have to engage in "hermeneutical rides".

These "hermeneutical rides" devolve upon the horsemen in the second

101 Cf. *Traités des compagnons-chevaliers (Rasā'il-i Javānmardān). Recueil de sept "Futuwwat-Nāmah"*, published by Murtaza Sarraf, with an analytical introduction by Henry Corbin, Bibliothèque Iranienne, vol. 20 (Tehran/Paris, 1973).

102 Ibid., pp. 205–206. Cf. the Koranic verse 6:76: "This is how we caused Abraham to see the *malakūt* of Heaven and Earth". There exists a famous conversation on the subject of this verse between the fifth Imam, Muḥammad al-Bāqir, and his disciple Jābir ibn 'Abdullāh, who asked the Imam in what sense it should be understood that the *malakūt*—the supra-sensible world of Heaven and Earth—had been shown to Abraham. The Imam, by giving his disciple a brief visionary perception, *caused him to see* the Veils of light that are the respective spiritual universes of the twelve Imams. Cf. my *En Islam iranien . . .*, op. cit., IV. index, s.v. Jābir ibn 'Abdillāh, Voiles de lumière.

category. What exactly are they? Ibn 'Arabī puts us on the right track when he expresses his admiration for a Koranic verse that he continually re-reads and meditates upon. All the creatures in the universe are so many divine Signs, and "among these Signs", says the verse in question, "is your sleep during the night and during the day, and your expectation of the blessing of this sleep" (30:23). Why does Ibn 'Arabī consider this verse to refer *par excellence* to the second category of the "horsemen of the Invisible"? The reason is that in addition to speaking of sleep during the night, which is natural, it speaks of sleep during the day, excluding thereby all mention of a state of wakefulness. Herein lies the secret of that state of things described by the Prophet when he said, in a remark already quoted: "Human beings are plunged in sleep; it is when they die that they awaken". Contrary to profane opinion, death is not a falling asleep but an awakening. This can apply both to death in the mystical sense and to death in the physical sense of an *exitus*; and, as Ḥaydar Āmulī has explained, the purpose of the first death is that the second one should be a resurrection.

It is precisely this that is important for Ibn 'Arabī. Man's present condition in this world is such that the visions we see in sleep in the world of Night, and what we think of as our perceptions in the world of Day, are similar in that both visions and perceptions take place in a state of sleep, equally in the world of Night and in the world of Day. Thus both visions and perceptions, by the same token, require an interpretation, a hermeneutic; and it is for this reason that Ibn 'Arabī views this world as a *bridge*, as a stage to be traversed.

One Arabic root (*'br*) conceals in effect a valuable ambiguity. It means to cross, to traverse. In the second form (the causative, *'abbara*) it means to cross a bridge, to traverse a river, for example. In designating the act of crossing over from one side to another, the same verbal noun *ta'bīr* designates *eo ipso* the act of interpreting—the hermeneutic—because the *ta'bīr* or hermeneutic consists in making the crossing from the apparent to the hidden, from the exoteric (*ẓāhir*) to the esoteric (*bāṭin*). *Ta'bīr al-ru'yā*, the interpretation of visions and dreams, is one of the chief applications of the "science of the Balance". It is to make the crossing from the forms perceived in vision to the secret meaning of their appearance. The visions we see in sleep in the world of Night, as well as the perceptions we have in what we call the world of Day, require the same crossing to be made before we can perceive their secret meaning. The reason for this is that both are motivated by a secret purpose deriving from another world. This is why our present world—the world of Night and the world of Day—is a *bridge* which must be crossed. A bridge is a place of passage, not a stopping-place or a dwelling-place. One crosses over it, and it must be crossed if one is to understand the secret meaning, the invisible "correspondence" of what "takes place" on this side of it. This is the task assigned to the interpreters, the hermeneutists of the esoteric who are promoted to the rank of "horsemen of the Invisible".

Ibn 'Arabī goes on to recapitulate the situation which, in this world, keeps us in a state of slumber both at night and during the day. It may happen that someone sees visions in his sleep and dreams, still asleep, that he has woken up; and he dreams—thinking himself awake—that he is telling his dreams to someone who is also part of his dream. He goes on sleeping the same sleep, dreaming that he is interpreting what he has seen while asleep. Then he wakes up, and realizes that he has not ceased to be asleep, both while dreaming and while interpreting the visions of his dream.

The same thing is true in the case of the man the eyes of whose inner vision are opened while he is still in this world, before his *exitus*. From the moment of his great awakening, he realizes that he has always been dreaming, but he thanks God for granting him this sleep, as well as for the fact that he has lived in sleep both his visions and the interpretations of these visions. This is, perhaps, what we do when, like Ḥaydar Āmulī, we construct great diagrams of worlds and intermediary worlds; yet this, precisely, is the hidden meaning of the Koranic verse which speaks of "your expectation of the blessing of this sleep". To be forearmed against the decadence of dreams is to be capable of *crossing the bridge* with regard both to the dreams of Night and to those of the Day, since such is our condition in this world; and this crossing is effected by the "knighthood devoted to practical activity", a knighthood dedicated, as Ibn 'Arabī has told us, to great actions, great enterprises. Could there, indeed, be any undertaking greater than to dedicate oneself to the search for the correspondences between what we see in this world and the Invisible, the *ghayb*, the world of Mystery? For only this search can abolish the frontier which keeps our destiny captive.

Thus Ibn 'Arabī not only perceives that the Koranic verse (30:23), which speaks of the sleep of the night and the day, is a verse whose hidden purpose concerns above all the "horsemen of the Invisible"; he also perceives that the *time* of their undertaking is typified in the Koranic ṣurah which is entitled "Night of Destiny", for their undertaking is the realization of the hidden meaning of this Night. The "Night of Destiny" (liturgically speaking, one of the nights in the month of Ramaḍān) is the night on which the sacred Book, the Koran, descended into this world: the sacred Book whose homologies and correspondences with the "Book of Horizons" and the "Book of Souls" Ḥaydar Āmulī set out to discover.

The Koran says of this "Night of Destiny" that "it is worth more than a thousand months. On this Night, the Angels and the Spirit descend into this world together with all things. Peace accompanies this Night until the dawn" (97:1–5). Because the Night of Destiny is the descent of the Invisible into our world, it is during this Night, which continually recurs, that the "horsemen of the Invisible" ride; for it may be said that their ride is a *crossing of the bridge* to meet the Angels and the Spirit descending invisibly into this world. Of course, the bridge has always to be crossed again; but it is in this crossing that the "science of correspondences", as a hermeneutic of the Invisible, consists.

Paris, Saturday of Pentecost
June 9, 1973

Appendix

Explanation of the diagrams

The figures are numbered from 1 to 6. For each figure I have given the number of the corresponding diagram in my edition of *Naṣṣ al-Nuṣūṣ* (the Text of Texts) by Ḥaydar Āmulī (see above p. 58, note 8).

A. *Diagrams of the Seven and the Twelve*

Figure 1 = Diagram no. 8 (cf. p. 76).

I. *The Twelve*. 1. The circumference is made up of a double circle forming a ring. This ring contains twelve small circles or epicycles, each one cut in half by the inner circle of the ring. These epicycles are grouped in threes, each triad being separated by a space.

2. The outer section of each epicycle bears the name of one of the twelve Signs of the zodiac; the inner section bears the name of one of the twelve categories of Angel mentioned in the Koran and by Ibn 'Arabī.

The top group of three has: Aries (*Ḥamal*), Taurus (*Thawr*), Gemini (*Jawzā'*). Corresponding respectively to these are: those who repulse (*zājirāt*, 37:2), those who recite (*tāliyāt*, 37:3), those who distribute (*muqassimāt*, 51:4).

The left-hand group of three has: Cancer (*Saraṭān*), Leo (*Asad*), Virgo (*Sunbulah*). Corresponding respectively are: those who are sent (*mursalāt*, 77:1), those who disperse (*nāshirāt*, 77:3), those who seize (*nāzi'āt*, 79:1).

The bottom group of three has: Libra (*Mīzān*), Scorpio (*'Aqrab*), Sagittarius (*Qaws*). Corresponding respectively are: those who extract gently (*nāshitāt*, 79:2), those who precede (*sābiqāt*, 79:4), those who swim (*sābiḥāt*, 79:3).

The right-hand group of three has: Capricorn (*Jady*), Aquarius (*Dalw*), Pisces (*Ḥūt*). Corresponding respectively are: those who deliver (*mulqiyāt*, 77:5), those who conduct the affairs of the universe (*mudabbirāt*, 79:5), those who are ranged in order (*ṣāffāt*, 37:1).

In the section of the ring between the right-hand triad and the triad at the top are inscribed the names of the first three months of the year: *Muḥarram*, *Ṣafar*, *Rabīʿ I*. Below, within the circle, are the words: *Huwa al-awwal*, "He is the First".

In the section of the ring between the top triad and the left-hand triad are the names of the months: *Rabīʿ II*, *Jumādā I*, *Jumādā II*. Below, the words: *wa'l-Ākhir*, "and the Last".

In the section of the ring between the left-hand triad and the triad at the base are the names of the months: *Rajab*, *Shaʿbān*, *Ramaḍān*. Below, the words: *wa'l-Ẓāhir*, "He is the Manifested".

In the section of the ring between the triad at the base and the right-hand triad are the names of the months: *Shawwāl*, *Dhū'l-Qaʿdah*, *Dhū'l-Ḥijjah*. Below, the words: *wa'l-bāṭin*, "and the Hidden".

II. *The Seven*. In the centre of the diagram is a double circle forming a ring, with seven small circles or epicycles, each one divided into two by the inner circle of the ring. In the outer section of each epicycle (starting at the top and reading from right to left) are inscribed the names of the seven planets in succession; in the inner section of each are the names of the seven Principles.

The Sun (*Shams*): the Intelligence (*ʿAql*)
Jupiter (*Mushtarī*): the Soul (*Nafs*)
Venus (*Zuhrah*): Nature (*Ṭabīʿah*)
Mercury (*ʿUṭārid*): the *materia prima* (*Hayūlī*)
The Moon (*Qamar*): the body (*Jism*)
Mars (*Mirrīkh*): the Throne (*ʿArsh*)
Saturn (*Zuḥal*): the firmament (*Kursī*)

In the centre is a little circle bearing the definition of the diagram: "the manifested World" (*al-ʿālam al-ṣūrī*).

III. To the side, in the four corners of the ideal square in which the diagram is drawn, are four little circles, each with two inscriptions. Top right: the Intelligence (*ʿAql*); Man (*Insān*). Top left: The Soul (*Nafs*); The

Angel (*Malak*). Bottom left: Nature (*Ṭabī'ah*); The Genie (*jinn*). Bottom right: The Body (*jism*); The Animal (*ḥayawān*).

Figure 2 = Diagram no. 9 (cf. p. 79)

I. *The Twelve.* 1. As in the preceding diagram, the circumference is made up of a double circle forming a ring. This ring has twelve small circles or epicycles, each one cut in half by the inner circle of the ring. These epicycles are likewise grouped in threes, each triad separated by a space.

2. The outer section of each epicycle bears the name of one of the twelve Imams of the Adamic period. The inner section bears the name of one of the twelve Imams of the Muhammadan period.

The top triad has: Seth, Abel, Cainan. Corresponding respectively to these are: 'Alī al-Murtaḍā, Ḥasan al-Mujtabā, Ḥusayn *al-Shahīd*.

The left-hand triad has: Mīsham (*sic*), Shīsham (*sic*), Qādis (*sic*). Corresponding respectively are: 'Alī al-Sajjād, Muḥammad al-Bāqir, Ja'far al-Ṣādiq.

The triad at the base has: Qīdhūf (*sic*), Imalyakh (*sic*), Enoch. Corresponding respectively are: Mūsā al-Kāẓim, 'Alī al-Riḍā, Muḥ.-Taqī al-Jawād.

The right-hand triad has: Idrīs, Dīnūkh (*sic*), Nākhūr. Corresponding respectively are: 'Alī-Naqī al-Hādī, Ḥasan al-'Askarī, Muḥammad al-Mahdī.

In the space between each triad, inside the ring, are the names of three Imams from the Mosaic period (total: 12). Below these, inside the circle, are the names of three Imams from the period of Jesus (total: 12). Unfortunately, the names are mutilated and disfigured, and do not even tally with those given in the body of the text. What is essential to bear in mind is that the twelve Imams from each period of the prophetic cycle, from Adam to Muhammad, are brought into correspondence.

II. *The Seven.* In the centre of the diagram is a double circle forming a ring, with *six* epicycles, each cut in half by the ring's inner circle. In the outer section of each epicycle is inscribed the name of one of the *six* great legislative prophets who preceded Muhammad; in the inner section the "pole" (*Quṭb*) of each period is specified. The names, successively, are Adam, Noah, Abraham, David, Moses, Jesus. The name of the *seventh* legislative prophet, Muhammad as "Seal of the prophets", here occupies the small circle at the centre which, in the preceding diagram, was inscribed with the definition of the diagram. Here, the circle with the definition is transferred to above the circle of Adam, and is inscribed "the spiritual world" (*al-ʿālam al-maʿnawī*).

III. To the side, in the corners of the ideal square, are four small circles, also bearing two inscriptions. Top right: *al-Nabī* (the prophet); the Pole (*Quṭb*). Top left: *al-Rasūl* (He who is sent); *al-Ghawth*. Bottom left: *al-Walī* (the Friend, the Imam); *al-Fard* (the Solitary One, the Peerless One). Bottom right: *al-Khalīfah* (the Caliph); *al-Watad* (the Tent-Post).

B. *Diagrams of the Nineteen*

Figure 3 = Diagram no. 10 (cf. p. 92)

I. 1. As in the preceding diagrams (figs. 1 and 2), the circumference is made up of a double circle forming a ring. This ring has *nineteen* small circles or epicycles, tangential to each other, and each cut in half by the inner circle of the ring. The epicyle at the base, figuring the Heaven of the Moon, is isolated from the others, possibly because the draughtsman made an error in his calculations.

2. The outer section of each epicycle is inscribed with the name of one of the *nineteen* worlds. The inner section is inscribed with the name of one of the *seven* planets, and then with that of one of the *twelve* signs of the zodiac (total: 19).

3. Finally, forming a basis for the system of correspondences, above each epicycle and outside the circumference, is written one of the *nineteen* letters which make up the Arabic spelling of the *Basmallah*: BiSM ALLāH AL-RaḤMāN AL-RaḤĪM.

Above (p. 91 ff.) we reproduced the order of correspondence as set out by Ḥaydar Āmulī in his book (§ 696, pp. 312–313). This diagram, however, is irregular in one detail which we cannot explain: Saturn is relegated to the 19th position. The following is the order as it stands:

B: The world of the *Jabarūt*—The Sun
S: The world of the *Malakūt*—Jupiter
M: The Throne (*ʿArsh*)—Mars
A: The Firmament (*Kursī*)—Venus
L: Heaven of Saturn—Mercury

L: Heaven of Jupiter–The Moon
H: Heaven of Mars—Aries
A: Heaven of the Sun—Taurus
L: Heaven of Venus—Gemini
R: Heaven of Mercury—Cancer
H: Heaven of the Moon—Leo
M: Sphere of Fire—Virgo
N: Sphere of Air—Libra
A: Sphere of Water—Scorpio
L: Sphere of Earth—Sagittarius
R: The mineral kingdom—Capricorn
H: The vegetable kingdom—Aquarius
I: The animal kingdom—Pisces
M: The world of Man—Saturn

II. At the centre is a small circle explaining the meaning of the diagram: "The manifested World" (*al-'ālam al-ṣūrī*).

III. To the side, in the corners of the ideal square (as in the preceding diagrams) are four little circles, each with two inscriptions. Top right: the *Jabarūt*; the Intelligence (*'Aql*). Top left: the *Malakūt*; the Soul (*Nafs*). Bottom left: the *Mulk* (visible world); Nature (*Ṭabī'ah*). Bottom right: man; the Body (*jism*).

Figure 4 = Diagram no. 11 (cf. p. 93 ff.).

I. 1. As before, the circumference is made up of a double circle which forms a ring, and which has *nineteen* small circles or epicycles. These are tangential to each other, and each is cut through the middle by the inner circle of the ring. The bottom epicycle, however, as in the preceding diagram, is isolated from the others.

2. The outer section of each epicycle is inscribed with the name of one of the *seven* great prophets, and then with the name of one of the *twelve* Imams of the Adamic period, as these are spelt in the text and made unrecognizable, as we said, by a succession of copyists (cf. *Genesis* 5:1–32, the posterity of Adam: Seth, Enoch, Cainan, Mahalaleel, Jared, Enoch, Methuselah, Lamech, Noah). On the inner section, "the pole" (*quṭb*) is mentioned *seven* times, followed by the names of the twelve Muhammadan Imams.

3. Lastly, as in the preceding diagram, we have the key to the system of correspondences: above each epicycle and outside the circumference is written one of the *nineteen* letters which compose the Arabic spelling of the *Basmallah*, as above.

The diagram offers the following order, starting at the top and reading from right to left. Here again, there is a discrepancy between this order and that described above (p. 93 ff.), where we followed the order set out by Ḥaydar Āmulī in his text.

B: Adam—The pole
S: Noah—The pole
M: Abraham—The pole
A: David—The pole
L: Seth—the first Imam, 'Alī ibn Abī-Ṭālib
L: Abel—The second Imam, al-Ḥasan ibn 'Alī
H: Cainan (Qīnān)—The third Imam, al-Ḥusayn ibn 'Alī
A: Mīsham (*sic*)—The fourth Imam, 'Alī al-Sajjād
L: Shīsham (*sic*)—The fifth Imam, Muḥammad al-Bāqir
R: Qādis (*sic*)—The sixth Imam, Ja'far al-Ṣādiq
H: Qidhūf (*sic*)—The seventh Imam, Mūsā al-Kāẓim
M: Ilīmikh (*sic*)—The eighth Imam, 'Alī al-Riḍā
N: Inwkh (Enoch)—The ninth Imam, Muḥammad-Taqī
A: Idrīs (Enoch, Hermes)—The tenth Imam, 'Alī-Naqī
L: Dīnūk (*sic*)—The eleventh Imam, Ḥasan al-'Askarī
R: Nākhūr—The twelfth Imam, Muḥammad al-Mahdī
H: Jesus—The pole
I: Moses—The pole
M: Muhammad—The pole

II. At the centre is a small circle with the inscription: "The spiritual world" (*al-'ālam al-ma'nawī*).

III. To the side, in the four corners of an ideal square, are four small circles each with a double inscription. The names are the same as those in the corresponding cirlces in fig. 2.

c. Diagrams of the Twenty-Eight

Figure 5 = Diagram no. 12 (cf. p.. 108).

I. 1. Once again, the circumference is a double circle forming a ring. In a small circle at the top is written: "Cycle of the ancestors of the Prophet" (*dā'irat al-ansāb*).

2. Starting just to the left of this little circle, and reading from right to left, we find: first, the name of the Prophet (*Khātim al-anbiyā'*, the Seal of the prophets); next—continuing to read the names written in the ring—we go through the entire cycle which leads back finally to the name of Adam, written just to the right of the small circle at the top. Thus, the names of Muhammad and Adam open and close the cycle of ascent from ancestor to ancestor. Whichever direction is taken, the finishing-point of a cyclical vision of things leads back essentially to the starting-point. In this way, a fully-realized whole is achieved, a pleroma.

N.B. We read in Ḥaydar Āmulī's text (§ 733) that the total number of these ancestors is 51 (17 × 3). In fact, the text of § 732 gives only 46 names. In the rings of diagrams nos. 12 and 13, we find a further 2, 'Āmir and Ghābir, between the names of Sārūj (34th) and Arphaxad (35th); yet in spite of this, three more names are needed to bring the total up to 51.

II. The large central circle shows the Prophet's Qurayshite ancestry, which is contained within the Adamic descent shown in the circumferent ring, but it stops at the name of al-Naḍr ibn Kinānah, with whom the true genealogy of the Qurayshite tribe begins. Inside the large central circle are twelve small circles tangential to each other, together with a small circle in the middle which is linked by a written stroke to the one which is opposite and beneath it. A similar written stroke links the circle tangential to this last circle with another small circle on the outside, itself tangential to the large central circle.

This must be read as follows. We start with the small central circle inscribed with the name of Muhammad, and follow the written stroke downwards linking it with the circle inscribed with the name of 'Abdullah, father of the prophet Muhammad. From here we continue upwards from the base, going from right to left. Inscribed in succession in each small circle are the names 'Abdul-Muṭṭalib, son of Hāshim, son of 'Abd Manāf, and so on until we end up at the base once more, at the small tangential circle to the left of the circle of 'Abdul-Muṭṭalib, in which is written the name of Mālik. A written stroke links this with the small outside circle which is tangential to the large central circle, and which is inscribed with the name of al-Naḍr ibn Kinānah, founder of the Qurayshite line.

Thus the large central circle betokens the Prophet's *twelve* ancestors of Qurayshite lineage. When we add al-Naḍr and the Prophet himself to these, we obtain a total of *fourteen* figures; and this number forms the basis of the correspondence with the Prophet's descendancy (see following diagram).

III. To one side, in the corners of a perfect square, are four small circles, each with two inscriptions. Top right: Adam; al-Ṣādiq (Abū Bakr). Top left: Abraham: al-Fārūq ('Umar). Bottom left: Moses; Dhū'l-Nūrayn ('Uthman). Bottom right: Jesus; al-Murtaḍā ('Alī).

Figure 6 = Diagram no. 13 (cf. p. 110)

I. 1. The circumference is composed of a double circle forming a ring. As in the preceding diagram, we are told: "This is the cycle of ancestors" (*hadhihi dā'irat al-ansāb*). But the ancestry here is the Muhammadan Imamic lineage, "the Imams before they were Qurayshites".

2. Starting just to the right of the small circle at the top, and reading from right to left, we read first the name of the twelfth Imam (*Khātim al-Awliyā'*, the Seal of the Friends of God), Muḥammad al-Mahdī, then Ḥasan al-'Askarī, and so on until we come to the first Imam. 'Alī ibn Abī-Ṭālib, son of 'Abdul-Muṭṭalib, son of Hāshim, son of 'Abd Manāf, and so on. Here in succession are all the names which have already figured (fig. 5) in the Prophet's genealogy back to Adam, comprising in theory 51 names.

II. The large circle corresponds to that in the preceding diagram, where it showed the Prophet's Qurayshite ancestry. Here it shows his Imamic descent, the line of twelve Imams descended from Fāṭimah, the Prophet's daughter. Thus here, too, twelve small circles, tangential to each other, are inscribed in the large central circle. In the preceding diagram, these circles betokened the twelve ancestors intermediary between the Prophet and al-Naḍr ibn Kinānah; here they represent the twelve Imams of Muhammadan lineage. The small circle at the centre of the preceding diagram betokened the prophet Muhammad; here the same small circle is inscribed with the name of Fāṭimah his daughter. At the base of the preceding diagram was a small circle tangential to the large central one, with the name of al-Naḍr ibn Kinānah, founder of the Qurayshite line, and linked by a written stroke with the circle with the name of Mālik ibn al-Naḍr. The corresponding circle in this diagram is at the top, tangential to the large central circle, and inscribed with the name of the prophet Muhammad; it is linked, by a written stroke on the right, to the circle containing the name of the first Imam.

We read this as follows. Starting from the small circle at the top of the large central circle, and reading from right to left, we read in succession the names of Muhammad al-Mahdī (the twelfth Imam), son of Ḥasan al-'Askarī (the eleventh Imam), son of 'Alī al-Naqī (the tenth Imam), and so on, ending with al-Ḥusayn (the third Imam), brother of al-Ḥasan (the second Imam), both sons of 'Alī (the first Imam, whose circle is joined by a written stroke to the small outer circle containing the Prophet's name).

In this way, the equilibrium of the Balance is based on the number 28 (cf. the 28 letters of the Arabic alphabet, the 28 phases of the Moon, and so on):

The 12 Imams	the 12 Qurayshite ancestors	
Fāṭimah	al-Naḍr, father of the Qurayshites	
the Prophet	the Prophet	
Total: 14	Total: 14	14 + 14 = 28
(the "Fourteen Immaculate Ones")		

III. To one side, in the four corners of a perfect square, are four small circles, each with two inscriptions. Top right: al-Murtaḍā (the first Imam); the Pole (*Quṭb*). Top left: al-Ḥasan (second Imam); *al-Ghawth*. Bottom left: al-Ḥusayn (third Imam); *al-Fard* (the Solitary One, the Peerless One). Bottom right: al-Mahdī (twelfth Imam); *al-Watad* (one of the four pillars of the cosmic tent).

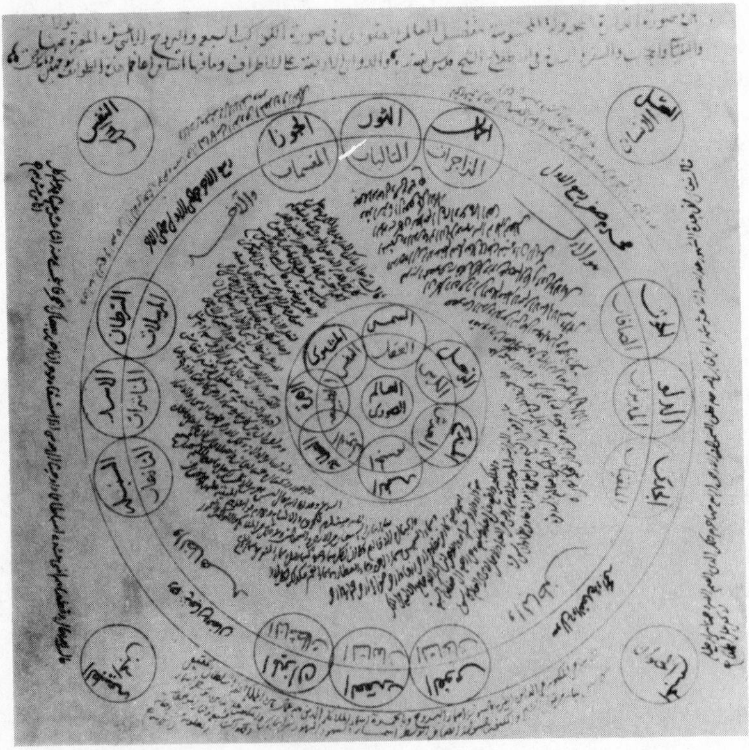

Figure 1 *Diagram No. 8*

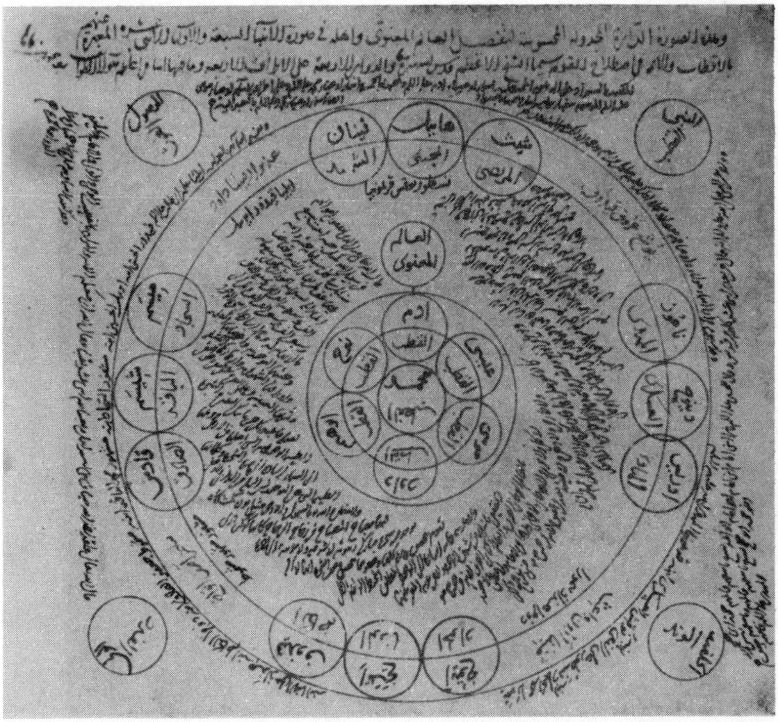

Figure 2 *Diagram No. 9*

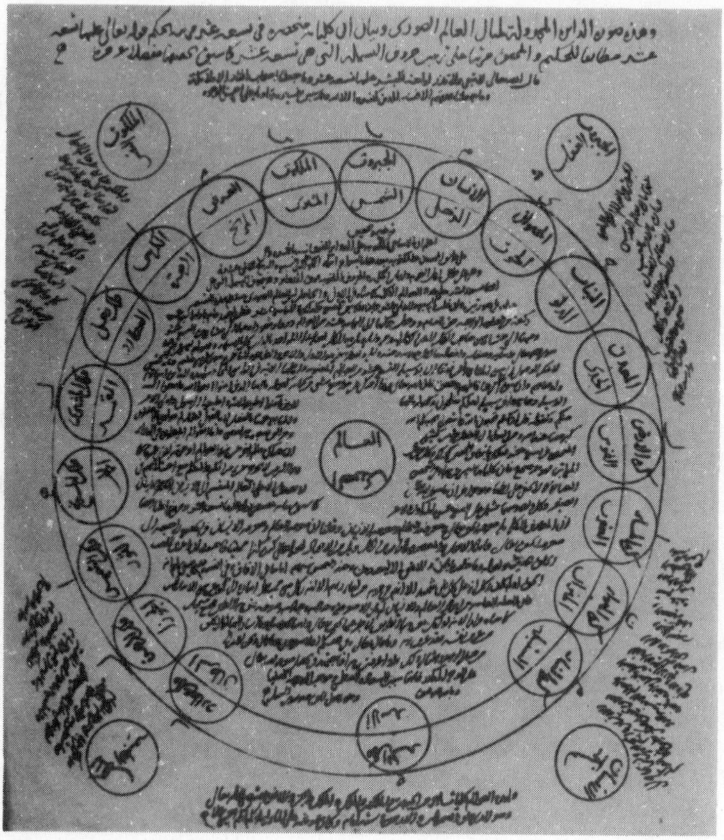

Figure 3 *Diagram No. 10*

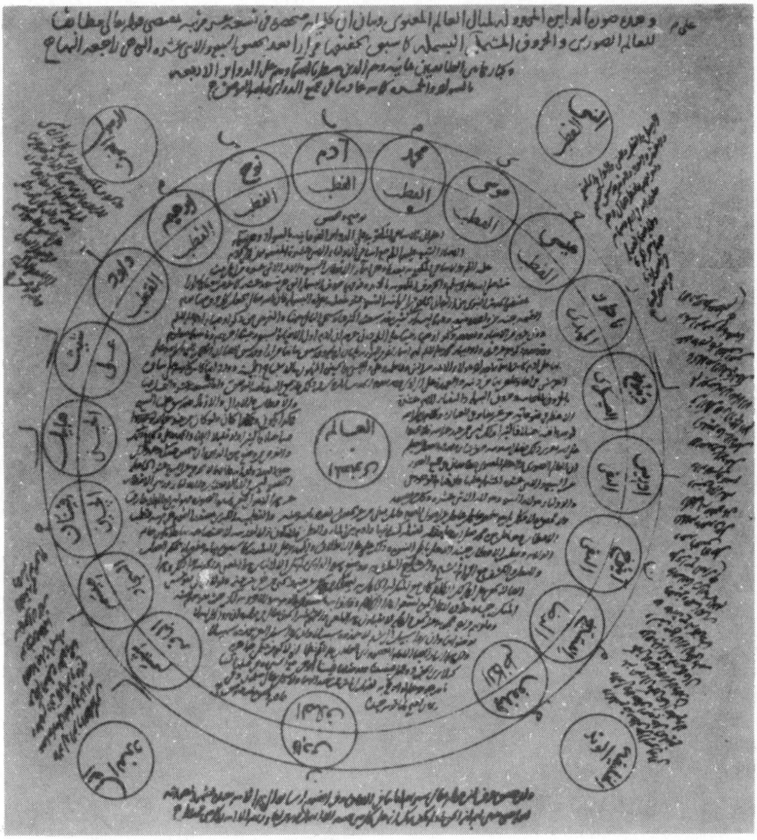

Figure 4 *Diagram No. 11*

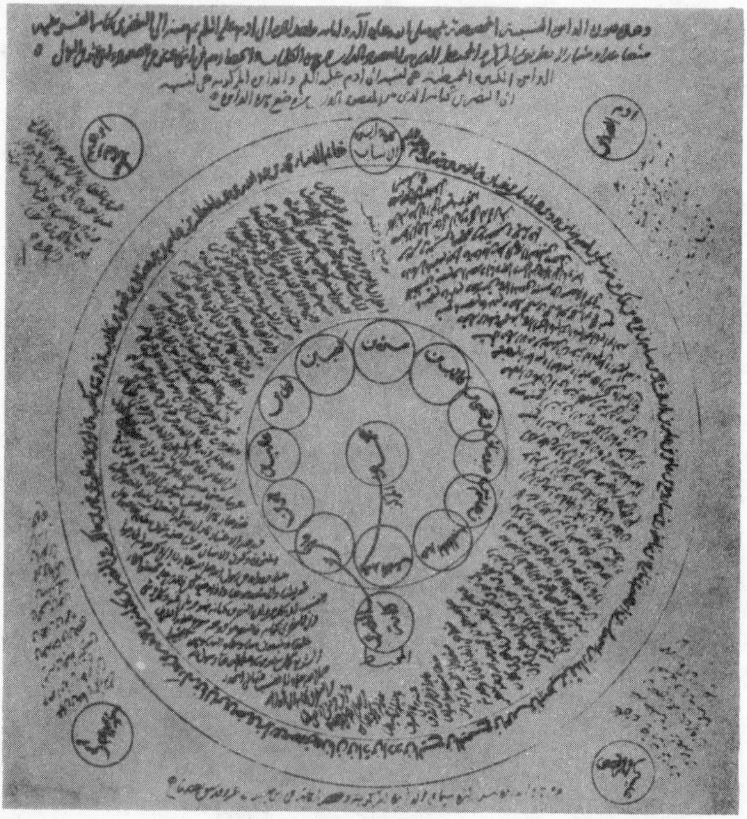

Figure 5 *Diagram No. 12*

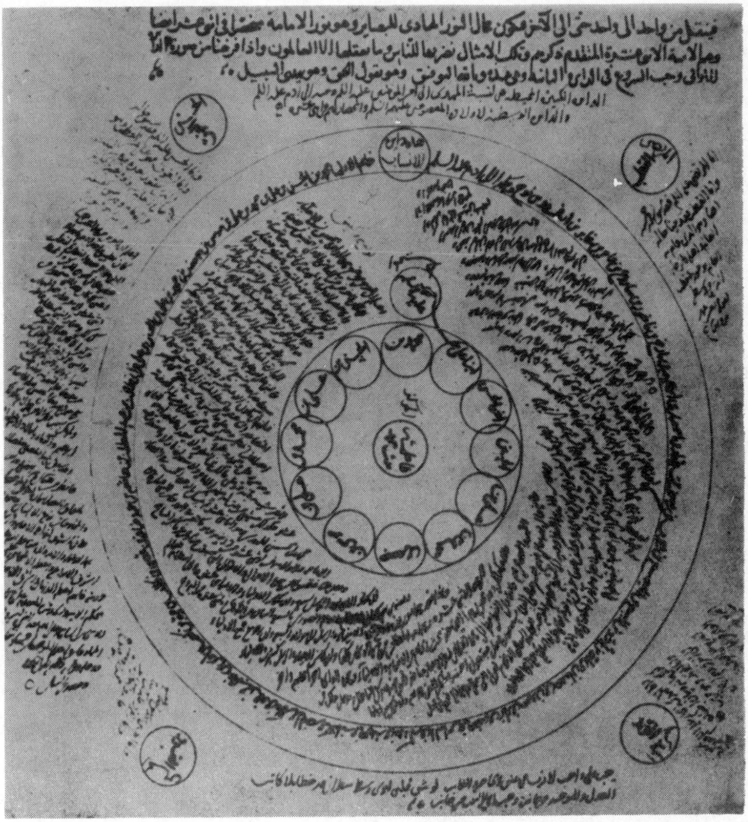

Figure 6 *Diagram No. 13*

3

Sabian Temple and Ismailism

1. Sabian Ritual and Spiritual Temple

1. *The Spiritual Temple.* The historian Mas'ūdī (tenth century A.D.), in a chapter of his book *The Plains of Gold* in which he describes the religious edifices of the Sabians,[1] reports that on the borders of China there is a Temple of immense height. The precinct wall of this Temple is pierced by seven gates, and it is capped with a seven-tiered dome. On the crown of this dome is set a kind of precious stone, vast in size and of a brilliance that illuminates everything within range. No one may come within ten cubits of it without falling dead; spears hurled towards the Temple turn back against the aggressor. Inside the Temple itself is a well with a heptagonal opening; anyone who leans over it is in danger of being overcome by a dizziness which drags him down into the abyss. Yet all around it runs an inscription proclaiming that the mouth of this well leads to the Treasury of books in which are preserved the sciences of Earth and Heaven, the chronology of times past and times future: "No one may enter here or draw on these treasures," it is said, "save he who is our equal in knowledge, power and wisdom." The Temple is built on a rock which rises out of the Earth like a high mountain. Anyone who beholds the Temple, the dome and the well is seized with a violent emotion in which impatience, sadness and an attraction that captivates the heart mingle with a fear lest something of this Temple may be destroyed or ruined.

Clearly, the identification of this Temple does not lie within the province of pure archaeology. In Arabic texts of mystical gnosis, the mention of China signifies the limit of the human world, of the world which man is

1 Cf. *Les Prairies d'or*, ed. and trans. by Barbier de Maynard, vol. IV (Paris, 1914), pp. 69 ff.

able to explore under the conditions of his ordinary awareness.[2] Mas'ūdī also describes another Temple, situated on the same borders:[3] a Temple divided into seven oratories and lit by seven large windows, before each of which stands an Image, or statue. These represent, respectively, the forms of five planets and of the two major luminaries, and each statue is made out of a substance and a colour (ruby, cornelian, emerald) that correspond to the action of the planet represented. All mystical and alchemical representations of the Sabian Temple preserve this architectural form.[4] It is in conformity with it that Suhravardī's *Recital of the Occidental Exile* intoduces us to the mystical pilgrim who is thrown into the depths of a dark well, a well dominated by a castle whose storeys rise one above the other into the heights of Heaven. In order to gain access to this castle, and to attain the "smaragdine vision" from the ramparts of the celestial City, the mystic must invert the norms of Day and Night. In other words, the dark depths of the well are no other than the Day of common awareness.[5]

The architectural form of this Temple with seven oratories and seven Images, into which one emerges out of a well of extraordinary depth, has, needless to say, been realized materially in one place or another. In any case, its laws are the same as those that govern the ideal architecture of Sabian Temples, each of which had to reproduce a celestial Temple and to guide the devout, through the contemplation of its form and by means of a

2 Cf. Commentary on the *Fuṣūṣ* of Ibn 'Arabī (560/1165/638/1240) by Kamaluddīn Kāshānī (died between 735/1334 and 751/1350–1351; Cairo edition, 1321 A.D.) p. 44, l. 16 ff.

3 Cf. *Prairies d'or*, op. cit., IV, 52.

4 For example, the *Book of the seven idols* attributed to Balīnās (Apollonius of Tyana), preserved for us by the alchemist Jaldakī. On this, see my report in *Annuaire* of the Section des Sciences religieuses de l'École pratique des Hautes-Études, 1973–1974, pp. 251–256; see also my article 'De l'alchimie comme art hiératique: Le Livre des sept statues d'Apollonios de Tyane, conservé en arabe par l'alchimiste Jaldakī' (*supra*, ch. II, n. 3). Cf. my earlier report on the 'Récit d'initiation et l'hermétisme en Iran', in *L'Homme et son Ange* (Paris, Fayard, 1984). See also in ibid. the famous Persian epic by Niẓāmī (535/1140–606/1209): *Haft Paykar* (*The Seven Beauties* or *The Seven Statues*), in the course of which King Bahrām Gōr successively visits, on each day of the week, a dome consecrated to the planet reigning over that day, wearing on each occasion a robe whose colour is that of the planet corresponding to it. Each dome, too, is of the colour determined by the star to which it is consecrated, and in each one there dwells one of the daughters of the kings of the seven climes, who bestows on Bahrām Gōr a recital of initiation.

5 Cf. Suhravardī's 'Récit de l'exil occidental', in my books *En Islam iranien: aspects spirituels et philosophiques*, vol. II (Paris, Gallimard, 1971–1972; 2nd edition 1978), p. 289, and *L'Archange empourpré: quinze traités et récits mystiques*, Documents Spirituels 14 (Paris, Fayard, 1976), VIII, p. 274.

particular ritual, to the person of the Angel reigning over the star. However, it does not greatly concern us whether or not archaeology is somewhere able to identify the remains of the Temple. What is important is the ideal configuration of these ritual monuments, into whose architectural form the soul projects her *imago mundi*, and thence proceeds to interiorize its every detail, assimilating it to her own substance through a meditation which thus enables her to construct her own microcosm.[6] In this sense the Sabian Temple is above all a Temple-archetype. Its ritual usage is best defined by an inscription, Platonic in tone, which in the year 332 A.H. Mas'ūdī was still able to read on the threshold of the great Temple of Ḥarrān: "He who knows himself is deified."[7]

This Temple-archetype is itself a threshold, *the* communicating Threshold between the celestial Temple and the Temple of the soul. Inasmuch as it is a material edifice, constructed in the image of the star or celestial Temple, it is the passage leading to the inner spiritual edifice. Because it *leads back to the source*, it is *par excellence* the figure and support of that mental activity designated in Arabic by the technical term *ta'wīl*, that is to say, an *exegesis* which at the same time constitutes an *exodus*, a going-out of the soul towards the Soul. In Islam, *ta'wīl*, the "exegetic leading back to the source", answers to that law of interiorization, that experiential actualization of symbolic correspondences, which, being an innate and fundamental impulse of the religious Psyche, leads the Spirituals of all communities to the same goal. In Islam, *ta'wīl* is put into operation by the *Bāṭinīs*, the esotericists or "interiorizers" of all persuasions; and as it is applied above all in alchemy, what it effects is the transmutation of external rites into the rites of the spiritual Temple.

From a dialogue introduced into his famous work by the historian of religions Shahrastānī (eleventh-twelfth centuries A.D.), it is evident that

6 Cf. Mircea Eliade, *Technique du Yoga* (Paris, 1949), pp 184–186.

7 *Man 'arafa nafsahu ta'allaha* (*Prairies d'or*, op. cit., vol. IV pp. 64–65). The technical Arabic term is the equivalent of the θέωσις of the Byzantine mystics. Nāṣir-i Khusraw gives the Persian literal equivalent "Khudā shudan" in *Kitāb-e Jāmi'al-Ḥikmatayn: le "Livre réunissant les deux sagesses" ou Harmonie de la philosophie grecque et de la théosophie ismaélienne*, text edited by H. Corbin and Moḥ. Mo'īn, Bibliothèque Iranienne, vol. 3 (Tehran/Paris, Adrien-Maisonneuve, 1953), § 94, p. 99 of the Persian text, l. 6. Cf. also the context of the citations in my edition of Suhravardī, *Oeuvres philosophiques et mystiques*, Bibliothèque Iranienne, vol. 2 (Tehran/Paris, Adrien-Maisonneuve, 1952; anastatic re-edition: Bibliothèque Iranienne, NS 2, 1977), *Ḥikmat al-Ishrāq*, § 117, p. 114, n. 4. It is hard to understand how Barbier de Maynard could have translated it as "he who knows God is in dread of him" (!).

the Sabian ideology of the Temple is an essential stage in this transmutation. It is the means whereby meditation can pass from the representation of the Temples or stars (*hayākil*) inscribed in the astronomical Heavens, and reproduced symbolically in the architecture of the earthly Temples, to the representation of a spiritual Temple, constituted by the coalescence of souls that take the place of the stars as receptacles and icons of the pure substances of the Light. The Sabians pictured the celestial Temples as governed by the Angels to whom their cult was addressed. In order for this transmutation to take place without degrading these beings of Light, but rather by raising the being of man to their level, the anthropomorphosis of the Temple is accompanied by a simultaneous angelomorphosis of man. In this sense, angelology represents a fundamental structure: it forms the ideal link permitting one to envisage the transition between Sabianism and Ismaili interiorism.

The term "Sabianism" is employed here deliberately without any of the precautions and reservations in which it is involved by historical criticism. Historically, we ought to distinguish carefully between the very different, not to say heterogeneous, phenomena which are grouped under this denomination. But if we were to conform to the science of history we should cease to be in accord with the phenomenology of Sabianism as it was considered, approved or condemned by those souls for whom it possessed a contemporary significance. Even though it means distinguishing between several sects, our Arabic or Persian authors use the term to denote both the religion of the "Sabians" of Ḥarrān (the ancient Carrhae in the north of Mesopotamia),[8] and the religion of those who are mentioned in the Koran and in whom it has been possible to recognize those more commonly known today as Mandeans. The term even incorporates a certain religion from Southern Arabia, practised by the Arabs from the country of Saba.

Nevertheless, although the discovery and consolidation of an ideal link between these religions were the task of meditation, a definite connexion was already present in the positive facts of history. The religion of the Sabians of Ḥarrān was an extension of ancient Syrian or Syro-Babylonian cults, reinterpreted in the light of elements borrowed from Neoplatonic philosophy;[9] and its great interest for the understanding of esoteric move-

8 Zarathustra (Zoroaster) and Buddha have both been represented as "Sabians".
9 Cf. in general D. Chwolsohn, *Die Ssabier und der Ssabismus* (St. Petersburg, 1856).

ments in Islam lies in the fact that it represents an intermediary between these ancient cults and the Nuṣayrīs. Before their conversion the Nuṣayrīs shared with the Ḥarrānians a great many religious forms, drawn from sources which were also those of ancient Gnosis.[10] At the same time, they present us with the unique example of a community won over to Islam not in its orthodox, official form, but directly in its esoteric and initiatory form, Ismailism, representative *par excellence* of Gnosis in Islam.

With regard to the Ismaili religion itself, whose articulation in the extreme form of Shiism can be traced back to the second/eighth century, we can now glimpse its supreme intellectual achievements through the publication of manuscripts which, for centuries, have been preserved over-jealously in private libraries.[11] What needs emphasizing here is, of course, its constitutive principle: spiritual exegesis. *Ta'wīl* postulates the principle of the Imam as guardian of its secret; his person is at the origin of the entire esoteric hierarchy which constitutes the "Ismaili Order",[12] each level of which corresponds to a rank in the celestial hierarchies. Lastly, the whole hiero-history developed by speculative Ismailism func-

---

More recently, see the paper by J. Pedersen, 'The Sabians' (in *A Volume of Oriental Studies presented to Edward G. Browne* . . . (Cambridge, 1922), pp. 383–391, which emphasizes the complexity of the sects (Mandeans, Mughtasilah, the Koran Sabians, Bardesanites, Manicheans, Elkesaites), which certain previous researches were too hastily inclined to identify. The term "Sabian" designates less a defined religion than a common name referring to several sects and signifying simply "gnostics". (Bīrūnī saw in it the synthesis of Judaism and the religion of the Mages.) On the other hand, L. Massignon ('Esquisse d'une bibliographie qarmate', in ibid., pp. 329–338) clearly perceived, in the "syncretistic story of the Sabians", the profound creative aspiration of the "myth which, in the East of the ninth century of our era, apparently played the same part in the diffusion of the Carmathian social conspiracy as Johann Valentin Andreae's (1616) myth of the *Rosicrucians* played in the West, during the seventeenth and eighteenth centuries, in the propagation of freemasonry" (p. 333; cf. L. Massignon, *Opera minora*, vol. I (Beirut, 1963), p. 632). [The two last-mentioned studies have been taken up again in *Opera minora*, vol. I, pp. 640–650 and 514–522.]

10 Cf. René Dussaud, *Histoire et religion des Noṣairīs* (Paris, 1900), p. 127. Cf. also L. Massignon, the article 'Nuṣayrīs' in *Encyclopédie de l'Islam*; 'Esquisse d'une bibliographie nuṣayrie' (in *Mélanges syriens* presented to M. R. Dussaud); 'Der gnostische Kult der Fāṭima im schiitischen Islam' (*Eranos-Jahrbuch* VI/1939).

11 Cf. my study, 'Le Livre du Glorieux de Jābir ibn Ḥayyān (*supra*, ch. II, n. 3), pp. 47 ff.

12 *Ahl-i tarattub*, the concept of an *Ordinatio*, hierarchy and ascent by levels, requiring the progressive typification of a celestial Order whose supreme level is represented by the *Ahl-i Waḥdah*, those who have reached the stage of unitude and whose actions typify the actions of the divinity itself. Cf. v.g. *Kalāmi Pīr, a treatise on Ismaili doctrine* . . . edited . . . and translated . . . by W. Ivanow, Islamic Research Association, no. 4 (Bombay, 1935), index s.v.

tions according to the Septenary, whose rhythm determines every phase of its cosmogony and eschatology.

When subject to a rigorous esotericism, a systematic and unlimited endeavour to achieve a state of interiorization connects with the idea of the alchemical Operation,[13] and results in the creation of a third world, or *mesocosm*, between the classic types of macrocosm and microcosm. This sacred cosmos is the place and instrument of the spiritual Ritual; its heavens are neither the heavens of astronomy, nor yet the inner heavens of pure subjectivity, but the esoteric heavens, rising in tiers to form the dome of the ideal Temple of the Imam, and revealing at every tier their angelic archetype. The unfolding of these heavens is thus both our starting point and the goal of our search. In the tenth century A.D., an intellectual society which called itself by the name of "Brothers of Purity and Lovers of Faith" left behind it a monument of Ismaili thought in the form of a vast encyclopaedia, consisting of 52 treatises.[14] Here, the invitation to enter into the new Temple is couched in terms which make explicit mention of ideal Sabianism, for there is a reference to Agathodaimon, whom the Sabians acknowledged as their prophet: "Will you not choose, oh my brother, to enter the Temple of Agathodaimon, in order to contemplate the heavens of which Plato spoke[15]—spiritual Heavens, not the visible heavens shown by the astronomers?"[16]

Thus, the themes to be meditated in order to effect such an entry are, essentially, the idea of the Temple, the idea of the Angel who governs it, and the *ta'wīl* or exegesis whereby one attains to the person of the Angel through the Temple. The transformation of the Ritual effected by *ta'wīl* culminates in an angelomorphic vision, a transfiguration of all figures, in

13 Cf. my 'Livre du Glorieux', (*supra*, ch. II, n. 3), pp. 59 ff.

14 Cf. Bernard Lewis, *The Origins of Ismailism* (Cambridge, 1940), pp. 17 ff. and index s.v.; W. Ivanow, *Ismaili Tradition concerning the Rise of the Fatimids*, Islamic Research Association Series, no. 10 (London, 1942), pp. 250–252. M. Adel Awa's interesting book, *L'Esprit critique des "Frères de la Pureté", encyclopédistes arabes du IVe/Xe siècle* (Beirut, 1948), came to my notice too late for me to make use of it here. The "Brothers" added to their encyclopaedia a secret Epistle or esoteric *synopsis* (*al-Risālah al-Jāmi'ah*); cf. W. Ivanow, *A guide to Ismaili Literature* (London, 1933), p. 31, nos. 14–15. Here I have used the manuscript in the possession of the Malek Library in Tehran, which was kindly put at my disposal. Unfortunately, I was not in time to use the first volume of the edition (Damascus, 1949) which we owe to M. Jamil Saliba.

15 This is a reference to the Plotinian ecstasy mentioned in the "Theology" attributed to Aristotle, to which all these mystical theosophers make favourable allusion.

16 Cf. *Rasā'il Ikhwān al-Ṣafā' wa-Khillān al-wafā'*, vol. IV (Cairo edition, 1928), p. 86.

the sense that once Interiority is achieved, it too is projected and objectivized in its turn in the world of celestial archetypes, a world which is both the substance of meditation and its fruit.

In this first section, we will attempt to discover how Ismaili angelology transfigures the Sabian idea of the Temple, how it explains the transcendent origin of the Ritual which must be led back to this same origin by *ta'wīl*. A first stage of this *ta'wīl* will be exhibited to us in the correspondence, established by the Brothers of Purity, between the religious ritual of Islam and an ideal philosophical ritual which could be that of Sabian theosophers.

2. *Sabian Ritual and angelology*. The ideal synthesis of Ismaili and Sabian thinking, as delineated by Shahrastānī, shows them to be both dominated by the same presupposition: the *Deus innominatus*—in Sabian terms the "Lord of Lords",[17] in Ismaili terms "He who cannot be reached by the boldness of thought",[18]—is of such transcendence that he can neither make himself known nor be known directly. The mediating beings who reveal Him are those essences of pure Light that philosophers call "Intelligences" (*'uqūl*), and that religious vocabulary designates as "Angels" (*malā'ikah*). The necessary plurality of the theophanies manifested through and in these celestial Figures does not alter the divine Unity in its essence. The Sabian representation is as follows. The mediators between the supreme Deity and human beings can only be spiritual in nature; they could not be men, not even Prophets, for a prophet is a being of flesh like all other men, and thus a creature composed of the Elements and of Darkness.[19] By contrast, Angels are Forms of pure and radiant Light,[20] whose nature is both passive and active, receptive and productive,[21] and whose state is one of total joy, beauty and beneficient goodness. Each of

17 Cf. Chwolsohn, op. cit., I, 717 ff., II, 420.

18 *Man lā tatajāsaru naḥwahu'l-khawāṭir* (der Unerkennbare); cf. R. Strothmann, *Gnosis-Texte der Ismailiten* (Gottingen, 1943), p. 55.

19 Cf. Chwolsohn, op. cit., II, 417, 420, 424.

20 Ibid., II, 424, 428.

21 This would lead us to conclude that the Sabians thought of the Angels as possessing a feminine nature; it also suggests that their cult might be linked to the ancient pre-Islamic Arabs, who believed that "the Angels are the daughters of God". Cf. ibid., II, 427, and Koran 16:57, 37:150, 43:19, 53:27. On the cosmogonic hierogamies described in speculative angelology (double aspect of the Angel *fā'il-munfa'il*), besides Suhravardī's *Hikmat al-Ishrāq* (see note 7), cf. H. S. Nyberg, *Kleinere Schriften des Ibn al-'Arabī* (Leiden, 1919), pp. 87, 130 ff., etc.

them observes and preserves in itself the divine Imperative that constitutes its being. The Sabians acknowledged, above all, the Seven Angels who rule over the Seven planets; each of them had his Temple (*haykal*), that is to say the form of the star, and each Temple has its Heaven or Sphere.[22] The relationship of the Angel with his Temple may be compared to that of the spirit with the body, with the difference that the Angel has total mastery over the Temple, and that this "body" is not his image, as the corporeal face is the image of a human being. (According to the Ismaili vision, the person of the Angel has the form of the glorified human body.)[23]

The Sabian conception of the Angel's absolute precedence, even over the rank and dignity of a prophet,[24] finds confirmation in the fact that the mediating universe of the Angel is both the place of origin of the souls in the terrestrial world, and the place of their second birth, the place whereto they "return". The world of the Angel and the terrestrial world confront each other like a person and his shadow,[25] to the extent that the truth of an earthly existence lies in its being the shadow of its Angel. Consequently, the chief concern of the soul is to achieve an intimate state of concordance with its Angel and to imitate it perfectly, so as to give free passage to the protection which the Angel can bestow upon it.[26] But the most direct way of existing "in the manner of the Angel" is to exist in the manner of the star which is the Angel's Temple—a type of devotion which is also to be found in the precept formulated by Agrippa of Nettesheim: *alicui stellae conformari*.[27] Generally speaking, this precept refers to the Platonic conception that souls are at first located in the stars, each of them in a different star which is its "partner" (σύννομον ἄστρον). It was this doctrine of a mysterious kinship between a particular human soul and a particular star that Aristotle sought to establish more firmly, by conceiving of their nature as a Fifth Nature, that of the Ether.[28] For its own part, Nuṣayrī

22 Chwolsohn, op. cit., II, 422.

23 Cf. Strothmann, *Texte* I, 1, pp. 6 and 7 of the Arabic text (cf. *infra* note 152).

24 As determined by the Angel's subtle and immaterial nature, which is precisely one of the violent reproaches levelled at the Ismailis and Carmathians by the orthodox. Cf. Dailamī, *Die Geheimlehre der Batiniten*, ed. R. Strothmann, Bibliotheca Islamica, 11 (Istanbul/Leipzig, 1939), pp. 73 ff.

25 Chwolsohn, op. cit., II, 427–428.

26 Ibid., II, 420.

27 Cited in C.-G. Jung, *Paracelsica* (Zürich, 1942), p. 165 n. 1.

28 Cf. R. P. Festugière, *La Révélation d'Hermès Trismégiste*, II: 'Le Dieu cosmique' (Paris, 1949), pp. 252–253, and p. 462, the translation of the passage from the pseudo-Aristotelian treatise on the World, 392 to l. 6 ff.

psychocosmology teaches that souls were originally stars and will once again become stars, or rather will return to being stars. This is expressed in a verse of their sacred book: "May God reunite us, us and you, in the Paradise among the stars of Heaven."[29]

The entire ritual, with its liturgical tones, burning of incense and perfume, and moral observances, is founded upon and directed towards this approach to the star. But these Temples in the sky are visible and invisible at different times. Thus the believer engaged in meditation must have before his eyes figures which correspond to them and which serve to support his devotion. Hence the necessity of building, here on earth, Temples whose correspondence in terms of structure, material composition and colour to the celestial Temple is guaranteed by astronomy and mineralogy. By means of this earthly Temple, meditation gains access to the celestial Temple, thence to the Angel who is its Lord, and thence to the Lord of Lords.[30]

Traces of these Temples built in the image of the stars have been preserved in the traditions of historians. The Sabians would have had circular Temples, dedicated to each of the five supreme Principles of their cosmology: Demiurge, World-Soul, eternal Matter, Space, and Time.[31] As for the temples of the planets, Saturn's was hexagonal in form; Jupiter's, triangular; Mars's, rectangular; the Sun's, a square; Venus', a triangle within a square; Mercury's, a triangle within a rectangle; and the Moon's, an octagon.[32] Each of these Temples was used, on the day specially consecrated to the star in question, for the performance of a liturgy involving garments whose colour corresponded to the planet, during which incense was burned in conformity with the importance which Sabians attached to the rite of perfumes. (During certain festivals, the rite consisted of sniffing roses.[33])

29 Cf. Dussaud, op. cit., p. 72 n. 1 (moreover, the stars were figured as bees, whence the title "Emir of the bees", that is to say, "Prince of the stars", in ibid., and 59 n. 3).

30 Chwolsohn, op. cit., II, 440.

31 There are variants in the numbering and designation of the Five Principles (Mas'ūdī, IV, 61, Shahrastānī [in Chwolsohn, op. cit., II, 446]) that it is impossible to analyse here. Cf. S. Pines, *Beiträge zur islamischen Atomenlehre* (Berlin, 1936), pp. 60–62 and 66–68, and Abi Bakr Mohammadi filii Zachariae Raghensis *Opera philosophica fragmentaque quae supersunt* collegit et edidit Paulus Kraus, Pars I (Cahirae, 1939), pp. 192 ff.

32 Chwolsohn, op. cit., II, 446 ff.; Mas'ūdī, IV, 62 ff.

33 Chwolsohn, op. cit., I, 195. The *ordo* and the liturgies had been dealt with in detail

We can find the details of this *Ordo* in the description of Sabian liturgies given by the author of the eighth century *Ghāyat al-Ḥakīm.*[34] They are described here not as collective celebrations which took place in the Temples, but as individual rituals, to be celebrated in an oratory which was private and appropriate to the star.[35] The intention was the same: to draw near to the star through a conformity of thought and gesture, thus making communion possible. The first injunction is as follows: "If you wish to converse in private with one of the Seven Stars, purify your heart of all corrupt beliefs and your vestments of all stain; render your soul limpid and clear."[36] Next, the ritual indicates the colour of the vestments to be worn, the kind of perfume to be burnt, the two invocations (some of great length) to be chanted, the second of which addresses the Angel of the star by name. The breath of an ardent devotion is often to be felt. In the liturgy of the Sun (*Shams*, feminine in Semitic languages) and its Angel, for example, the celebrant is directed to wear a robe of brocade, a diadem and a gold ring, since he must be dressed in royal finery in order to pray to her who is the Queen; and he addresses her in terms such as the following: "Hail to you, oh Sun, blessed Queen . . . resplendent, illuminating . . . you who concentrate in yourself all beauty, you who possess an authority over the six planets which makes them obey you as their guide and allows you to rule over them."[37]

---

in several works by the famous Sabian scholar Thābit ibn Qurrah (221/836–288/901); Barhebraeus had still been able to see some of those whose Syriac titles he mentions, v.g. in their Latin equivalent: Liber de lectionibus recitandis singulas septem planetas accommodatis; Liber de religione Sabiorum; Liber de distributione dierum hebdomadis secundum septem planetas; Liber de legibus Hermetis et de orationibus quibus utuntur Ethnici, etc. Cf. Chwolsohn, op. cit., II, 11 ff.

34 Pseudo-Mağrīṭī, *Das Ziel des Weisen*, 1. Arabischer Text ed. Hellmut Ritter, Studien der Bibliothek Warburg XII (Leipzig, 1933), pp. 195–228.

35 The word employed is *Munājāh* (ibid., p. 202 l. 8; it means telling a secret; an intimate conversation with the divinity, a confidential psalm). Cf. *En Islam iranien*, op. cit., vol. IV, general index s.v.

36 *Das Ziel des Weisen*, p. 195.

37 Ibid., pp. 216 ff. In order to differentiate between talismanic practice and philosophical Sabianism, it is vital to differentiate between the conjuration of the star and the invocation addressed by name to the Angel. For the liturgy of Saturn (Zuḥal), a black robe and mantle—the garments, it is said, of the Philosophers—must be worn, and an iron ring on the finger; the Angel invoked is Ishbāl (ibid., p. 203). For the liturgy of Jupiter (Mushtarī), a yellow and white robe must be worn, and a white mantle, and a ring of rock crystal; the Angel invoked is Rūfiyāel (in Persian, it is Ormazd who rules over this planet). Several liturgical formulas are suggested, one of which is very lengthy and very beautiful, and well illustrates the noble

In this way, Sabian devotion sets us in the presence of the Angels who govern the stars, or Temples of light, which are visible in the astronomical heavens. How, starting precisely from this point, can the transition be effected to the Angels who govern the spiritual Heavens of the esoteric Cosmos? The ideal place of this transition is the extraordinary dialogue instituted by Shahrastānī, to which we referred earlier. This dialogue is extraordinary because it is carried on not between one group which is ardently orthodox and another of "idolaters", but between two groups of speakers who possess far more an archetypal significance than a concrete historical existence, and who appear to have agreed secretly beforehand on the arguments they are about to exchange. These two groups are the *Ḥunafā'* and the Sabians. The *Ḥunafā'* (plural of *Ḥanīf*) are the representatives of religion in its most initial and pure state, the pure religion of Abraham who was neither Jew nor Christian but *ḥanīf muslim*: the religion created at the beginning of the world, before the Period of Adam even,[38] and which according to Ismaili eschatology will be restored by the Imam, lord of the Resurrection, when he closes the Cycle at the end of our own Period. There is also an ideal Sabianism, which Ismaili historiosophy conceives of as having been the first religion of "historical" humanity, and

---

fervour that this piety was able to inspire (ibid., pp. 204–211). For the liturgy of Mars (Mirrīkh), the garments must be red, a ring of copper must be worn, and the Angel invoked is Rūbīyāel (pp. 211 ff.). For the liturgy of Venus (Zuhrah), one wears a sumptuous white robe and a golden ring; the Angel invoked is Biṭāel (pp. 219 ff.). The liturgical colour of Mercury ('Uṭārid) is not indicated (in Niẓāmī's *Haft Paykar*, the king that day visits the blue dome, but blue and green are often confused in Persian); the Angel invoked is Ḥaraqiel (pp. 221 ff.). Lastly, for the liturgy of the Moon, the liturgical garment is white and must be reminiscent of the garment of a youth; the Angel invoked is Siliyāel (p. 224; the editor suggests that this is possibly a name formed from the Greek σελήνη, Seleniel?) I intend elsewhere to compare this planetary angelology with the corresponding Latin texts, e.g. with the *Steganographia* of Jean Trithème, abbot of the Benedictine monastery of Spanheim (1462–1516). Cf. Abel Lefranc, 'L'Origine d'Ariel', in *Cinquantenaire de l'École pratique des Hautes-Études* (Paris, 1921), pp. 347–356.

38 Cf. *Encyclopèdie de l'Islam* s.v. Ḥanīf. [Tr. from *Encyclopaedia of Islam*, 1st edn (4 vols. + supp., Leiden, Brill, 1913–38); 2nd edn as far as *lam* (4 vols. + fascs. + index, Leiden, Brill, 1960—present).] Cf. Pedersen, op. cit., pp. 390–391, the conclusions which show the synonymity of Ḥanīf and Sabian—the second term was substituted for the first, just as elsewhere the term "gnostics" replaced the designation "Ἕλληνες. Moreover, the dialogue introduced into Shahrastānī's work aims at a "recall to the source", and the perspective of *ta'wīl* dictates an order of things quite different from one in which questions of positive historical sequence need to be debated. (Of course, these *Ḥanīf* are not to be confused with the *ḥanīfite* rite deriving from Abū Ḥanīfah in orthodox Sunni Islam!)

which in our Cycle is the religion of the Adamic Period whose Imam was Seth.[39] This is why the Sabians themselves come to be designated as Ḥunafā'.[40] Thus there is no separation between the levels with which each speaker is respectively concerned; the point is the transition, or rather a "return to the source", which it is the task of *ta'wīl* to effect.[41]

This transition is effected by a series of arguments, built up broadly as follows. On the one hand, the Sabians affirm that the only mediators they acknowledge are the *Dii-Angeli*, or pure spiritual beings. Do they not, however, invoke the authority of Agathodaimon and Hermes (that is, we are told, of Seth and Idris or Enoch) as that of the Prophets who initiated them into their wisdom and their cult?[42] On the other hand, is not the cult rendered to the star, even if it be the Temple of the Angel and the method of access to him, a sin against pure spiritual Sabianism, since what it amounts to ultimately is the attributing of a mediating role to material Figurations, instead of reserving this role for pure spiritual beings? Constrained by these two objections, the Sabians find themselves being asked a crucial question: since they admit the assumption of Hermes,[43] who was

39 Cf. *Kalāmi Pīr*, p. 59 (p. 64 of the Persian text). Cf. also the period which corresponds to the "first day of the Creation" in the hexaemeron of the religious Cosmos, in Nāṣir-i Khusraw, *Jami' al-Ḥikmatayn*, op. cit., § 160.

40 For example, *Das Ziel des Weisen*, p. 204, l. 15: when praying to Rūfiyāel, the Angel of the planet Jupiter, one must hold in one's hand the "Book of the Ḥunafā'".

41 It has been suggested that Shahrastānī was perhaps himself Ismaili (cf. *Encyclopédie de l'Islam*, s.v.). However that may be, the end of the dialogue is, as regards this, very curious, and worthy of attention (*Kitāb al-milal*, lith. Tehran, 1288, pp 151–152). This is what the author says: "These exchanges between the two groups contain innumerable lessons. There yet remained in my thought corners which I would have liked to fill in, beneath my pen were secrets which I was on the point of revealing, but I abstained in order to speak of the sublime Hermes", or rather to call on the witness of Hermes, acknowledged by the Sabians to be their supreme authority, and to show that he was a pure *ḥanīf*, whose doctrine affirms that ontological perfection resides not in the stars but in the personal human Figures (*al-ashkhāṣ al-basharīyah*), which means passing from the "temple" of the star (*haykal*) to the human being as "temple". One should also note the close kinship between Shahrastānī's dialogue and a whole chapter (taṣawwur XXVII) of a book attributed to Naṣīruddīn Ṭūsī, cf. *The Rawḍatu't-Taslīm commonly called Taṣawwurāt* . . . Persian Text edited and translated into English by W. Ivanow, The Ismaili Text Society Series A, no. 4 (Leiden, 1950), pp. 175–187. Lastly, it is permissible to note that he who reported such a dialogue so "faithfully" was assuming a role analogous to that of Johann Valentin Andreae (cf. note 9).

42 Chwolsohn, op. cit., II, 433–434.

43 Cf. also the assumption of Hermes in Suhravardī's *Talwīḥāt*, § 83 of my edition (*Opera metaphysica et mystica*, I, Istanbul, 1945; anastatic re-edition in Bibliothèque Iranienne, NS 1, Tehran/Paris, Adrien-Maisonneuve, 1976), p. 108, and *En Islam iranien*, op. cit., vol. II, pp. 300 ff.

taken up into the angelic world, why do they deny the possibility of an Angel's descending from that world as a messenger of the Revelation, or even to put on a human body? But the central difficulty is clearly formulated: for the Sabians, perfection resided in stripping off humanity, whereas for the Ḥunafā', perfection was to be achieved by putting on the human form.[44]

Ta'wīl makes it possible to delineate a final solution to this problem. The Sabians already descend from the order of pure spiritual beings (*rūḥānīyūn*) to the material Temples (*hayākil*) which are their personal Figurations (*ashkhāṣ*); the Ḥunafā' acknowledge the Temples (*hayākil*) of divine beings (*rabbānīyūn*) in personal, human Forms (*ashkhāṣ*). This serves to initiate the whole *exegesis* leading from the Heaven of astral religion to the Heaven of the spiritual Earth, the Temple of the mediating Angel, and establishing the representation of the esoteric Heavens of the sacred Cosmos by the introduction of analogies which Shahrastānī's Ḥunafā' are quick to put into effect.[45] This signals the dissolution and disappearance of the anthropomorphism for which the Sabians were so ready to condemn the Ḥunafā': the anthropomorphosis of the Temple of the divinity is in reality made possible by an angelomorphosis of anthropology. It also puts an end to the scandal constituted, in the eyes of a Sabian, by the current Islamic affirmation that the prophet—in the final analysis, man—takes precedence over the Angel;[46] for it is now seen that the forms of the human condition are themselves but one of the stages in angelology. With great pertinence, the Sabians ask about the hierarchy (*marātib*) of intellects and souls; and the answer they are given refers to an adamology, a representation of Adam the true meaning of which will be unveiled to us in the Ismaili exegesis explaining the identity of the "Angels" that were commanded to prostrate themselves before Adam.[47]

44 *Libās*, an image essentially Ismaili; cf. for example *Kalāmi Pīr*, p. 65; Chwolsohn, op. cit., II, 436; lith. Tehran, p. 147.

45 Ibid., II, 342, and lith. p. 142. The spiritual (*rūḥānī*) element in the human person of the Messengers corresponds to the angelhood of the pure spiritual beings. Their individuality, their human "form", corresponds to the "temples" of the latter. The motion of these human star-temples symbolizes with the motion of the star-temples of Heaven: their institutions (*sharā'i'*) are the observance of the movements connected with the *ta'yīd ilāhī* (a characteristic expression in Ismaili vocabulary).

46 Cf. Wensinck, *The Muslim Creed*, pp. 200 ff.

47 Shahrastānī (lith. p. 142) mentions the distinction between the religion (*sunnah*) which issues directly from the creative Imperative (the world of *Amr*), i.e. the *fitrah* (cf. *Kalāmi Pīr*, index s.v., and *En Islam iranien*, op. cit., vol. IV, general index s.v.),

It is for this reason that, out of all the "Sabians", it is the Ḥarrānians who are held in particular favour, for they proclaim both the essential divine Unity and its pluralization in epiphanic Figures, visible in the stellar Temples of the mediating Angels as well as in the human Persons who typify them.[48] They also conceive of a cosmic alchemy that produces the Perfect Man as the epiphany of divinity—the same type of alchemy as that which produces the subtle humanity (*nāsūt*) of the Ismaili Imam; and so positive was this conception for them that the orthodox could hold them responsible, together with the Christians and the extremist Shiites (*Ghulāt*) for the idea of the Incarnation (*ḥulūl*).[49] The notion of the human

---

or Ḥanīfīyah religion mediated by the Prophets, and creatural religion (*khalqīyah*), which issues from the world of *Khalq*, mediated by the Angels. The response given to the Sabian question on the hierarchy of intellects postulates an onomaturgic Adam who might be comprehended within the context of the orthodox exegesis, were it not for the density of the allusion (p. 151) where the characteristic terms *Zuhūr* and *Kashf* (Unveiling, Manifestation) could refer to a concept to which the key is provided by Ismaili adamology. There is the universal Adam (*Adam al-Kullī*, Πανάνθρωπος, cf. Strothmann, *Texte*, p. 52 s.v.), and the partial Adam, or rather a plurality of partial Adams. The first Adam inaugurated the initial cosmic Cycle of Unveiling (*Ẓuhūr*, *Kashf*); each partial Adam, whose archetype he is, opens one of the "historical" cycles which succeeded each other. The universal Adam, or archetype, is himself an Intelligence or Angel of the primordial angelic world (*'ālam al-Ibdā'*); this Anthropos-Angelos (the archetype of the Imam-resurrector) is invested, by the tenth Archangel of the eternal Imamate, with the government of nature (cf. ibid., I, 4; II, 2, p. 20; XII, 37). We can note two consequences of this: 1) The name of Adam, as the archetype Adam, already refers to an angelic essence. 2) If, at the start of our Cycle, the "Angels" were ordered to prostrate themselves before Adam ("our" Adam, Biblical as well as Koranic), then the word "Angels" must have a different meaning from the one currently accepted (cf. *infra* note 67): a meaning which abolishes the opposition between prophetic and angelic mediation, as well as the question of precedence. Even if the Adam of our Cycle enjoys the precedence of an initiator, it is still the case that he had himself received the initiation of the Cycle of Unveiling which preceded the Cycle of Occultation that he inaugurated. His precedence over the "Angels" in his capacity as onomaturge thus calls for an exegesis other than the common Koranic one. These remarks on the subject are of course all too brief (cf. note 67).

48 Cf. Chwolsohn, op. cit., II, 442, and Shahrastānī, lith. Tehran, p. 157.

49 On the cosmic alchemy which produces the "subtle" humanity of the Imam, see Strothmann, *Texte* I, 2. Ma'ṣūm 'Alī Shāh, the author of a modern Iranian encyclopaedia of Sufism, saw in this an allusion to the doctrine of the Perfect Man (*Insān Kāmil*); cf. *Ṭarā'iq al-Ḥaqā'iq*, I, pp. 159–160. Here, in connection with the ideology of the Temple, is the violent reproach that Abū'l-Ma'ālī Muḥ. al-Ḥusayanī al-'Alawī directed at the Ḥarrānians, whom he speaks of as a sect of Mages, and whom he considers responsible, along with the Christians and the extremist Shiites, for the idea of an inhabitation or divine incarnation in a human "temple" (*ḥulūl*), a *unio mystica* (*ittiḥād*). The passage must belong to that section of the work (*Bayān al-Adyān*) which is missing in the only manuscript used for the editions (Persian chrestomathy by Schefer, and the 'Abbās Iqbāl edition, Tehran, 1312).

Temple exemplifies for them the structure of the astral world: "Just as the Seven (stellar) Temples are the Seven members of divinity, so our Seven human members are the Seven Temples of God: God speaks with our tongue, sees with our eyes, hears with our ears, grasps with our hands, comes and goes with our feet, acts through the intermediary of our arms and legs."[50]

Thus is made articulate the transition leading to the conception of spiritual Heavens which, although constituted according to the same model as the physical Heavens, are beyond the reach of sensible experience. Yet they are not on this account merely an allegory of subjectivity: they possess a reality of their own, of which the organ of apprehension *par excellence* is the metaphysical Imagination. The possibility of imagining them presupposes a modification in the structure of the angelology postulated initially by the Sabians. The celestial hierarchies are elevated by the introduction of a hierarchy of supreme Archangels, in relation to whom the Angels of the celestial Spheres are merely an intermediary hierarchy,[51] and who possessed a typification, which is no less perfect and legitimate, in the Angels of the esoteric Heavens that make up the sacred *mesocosm* of the Ismaili esoteric Church. The supreme archangelic universe is composed of Ten Archangels who emanate one from the other; of these, the Person of the First (*Sābiq*, the "Preceding One") is so totally the epiphany of the hidden divine Ipseity that all religious statements relating to God, to the Adored (*Al-Lāh*), are understood as referring to this Archangel.[52] Corresponding term for term with this hierarchy of Ten are, on the one hand, the hierarchy of the Angels who govern the heavens of our physical universe, and, on the other, the Ten levels or grades of the esoteric religious hierarchy, from the Annunciator (*Nāṭiq*) of each new religion, and the Imam, guardian of its esoteric meaning (*ta'wīl*), down to the *Mustajīb* or new initiate, whose rank corresponds in the physical cosmos with that of the active Intelligence which governs our Earth.[53] This

50 Chwolsohn, op. cit., II, 444; lith. Tehran, p. 158.

51 Cf. the triple hierarchy of the *Logoi* or Words (Major, Intermediate, and Minor) in Suhravardī's treatise, 'Bruissement des Ailes de Gabriel', in *L'Archange Empourpré* . . . op. cit., VII, pp. 234 ff.

52 Cf. Strothman, *Texte* III, 4–6, VII, 10, XII, 2, Ism 2 *in fine*, etc.

53 These correspondences receive detailed treatment from Ḥamīduddīn Kirmānī (died c. 408/1017, Iranian), in his *Rāḥat al-'Aql*, Ismaili Society, series C, no. 1 (1953), and from Idrīs 'Imāduddīn (died 872/1468, Yemenite), in his *Zahr al-Ma'ānī*, chaps. X and XIX. Cf. also Strothmann, *Texte* IX, 5, p. 82.

typification of the supreme celestial hierarchy in the esoteric hierarchy makes it possible to call the dignitaries of the latter (*ḥudūd*, lit. "limits"), from the greatest to the most humble, by the name of "Angels" (*ashkhāṣ rūḥānīyah, malā'ikah*).[54] All together, they form the Temple of Light of the Imamate, in a series of heavens which rise one above the other and which, from the "limited Heaven" (*maḥdūd*) to the "Heaven as limit" (*ḥadd*), are infolded with each other like those of the physical Cosmos.

In the physical Cosmos, each Heaven is set in motion by the aspiration of its Angel towards the Angel of the Heaven which constitutes its Heaven-limit; and this aspiration brings into being the Angel and soul of another heaven. In the same way, each hierarch, from the greatest to the least, brings into being the Angel of the esoteric Heaven or the grade that comes after him (his *Tālī*, follower).[55] Indeed, Ismaili authors[56] return tirelessly to this idea of the human condition as transitory and intermediate: the human being is nothing other than a potential angel *or* a potential demon. The ascension from one heaven to another of the sacred cosmos is each time a "resurrection" (*qiyāmah*); each time it constitutes a growth of the potential angel. Angelomorphosis is achieved from Temple to Temple, from Angel to Angel of those who rule the Heavens of the Temple of the Imamate. Hence the esoteric meaning of the famous formula (a variant of that which Mas'ūdī was able to read on the threshold of the great Temple of the Sabians): "He who knows himself (his "Anima" or *nafs*) known his Lord. To know oneself (one's *Anima*) is to know at every stage the Angel of the heaven which is the Heaven-limit of that stage, and which, by bringing

54 Cf. my 'Livre du Glorieux' . . . (*supra*, ch. II, n. 3), p. 58.

55 This is the esoteric meaning of the words of the Fatimid Imam al-Mu'izz: "A believer is not a true believer as long as he has not raised up (or 'resurrected') another believer like himself", Strothmann, *Texte* VI, 3 (p. 61 1.3–4), XII, 6 (p. 114 1.11).

56 For example, the Brothers of Purity, *Rasā'il* IV, 244: "Knowledge of the angelic operations is not possible for someone who belongs to the terrestrial world, unless he has first acquired knowledge of the essence of his own Anima (*jawhar nafsihi*). If he knows this, he can know all there is to know about Angels in the entire universe . . . By means of this knowledge, he is endued with the capacity to be moulded by the spiritual angelic Form, so that his actions may become the actions of the Angels." IV, 309: "When you exemplify, in the form of your being, the Testament which was left to you, the angelic Form will be perfected in you, and at the time of your Great Return (*ma'ād*) you will possess within you the ability to attain to this Form and dwell in it." IV, 165: The souls of gnostics "are Angels in potentiality; when they separate themselves from their bodies, they become Angels in actuality." This is the exact doctrine expounded by Nāṣir-i Khusraw in *Jāmi' al-Ḥikmatayn* (see note 7), chap. XI. Cf. also *Kalāmi Pīr* p. 92 of text l.8 (see note 17).

forth and drawing towards itself that which it limits, leads it into the presence of a new *Anima* and of a new Angel that is its Lord."[57]

Consequently, the Angel no longer has, as in the classic cosmology of Arabo-Persian Neoplatonism, a significance which is merely cosmological; it also possesses an anthropological significance. More precisely, the Angel is the term and the fulfilment of the Anthropos. Cosmology "re-emerges" in a universe of archetypes, where all is the transfigured human Figure. Angelology imparts to man the knowledge of his future condition; it reveals to him the secret of initiatory birth (*wilādah dīnīyah*), of his entry into the Temple of the Imamate. By the same token, it reveals and prescribes the Ritual of this Temple, which is also the Temple of Agathodaimon into which the Brothers of Purity invite one to enter. This Ritual will also arise from a "leading back to the source" of another ritual, from a *ta'wīl* similar to the *exegesis* which presides over the appearance of the physical Heavens and their Temples. The question then presents itself: whence comes the ritual which is to be transcended? In its reply to this question, angelology unveils to man his initial condition, that condition, precisely, which it invites him to regain by means of a *ta'wīl* which is a succession of resurrections. It is of these resurrections that the Ritual of the esoteric Temple is the ceremonial form.

3. *The transcendent origin of the Ritual.* Out of what past does the present human condition arise, for it to be linked with ritual observances which its "resurrections" must surpass by *leading them back* to their source, that is to say, to their *true meaning*? In their Encyclopaedia, the Brothers of Purity make solemn allusion to this past on a number of occasions, most notably when they set forth the secret of their association: "Know, oh my brother, that we are the society of the Brothers of Purity, beings who are pure, sincere and generous-hearted. We sleep in the *cave* of our father Adam[58]

57 Cf. the series of the Eight *Qiyāmāt* or Resurrections in *Zahr al-Ma'ānī* by Idrīs 'Imāduddīn, chap. XIX (cf. the citation in Ivanow's *Rise of the Fatimids*, p. 243, and Strothman, *Texte*, Idāh 11, pp. 153–154, and Ism 2–3 see note 99). On the work *Zahr al-Ma'ānī*, see my report 'L'Ismaélisme yéménite: l'oeuvre d'Idrīs 'Imaduddīn', in *Annuaire* de la Section des Sciences religieuses de l'École pratique des Hautes-Études, 1971–1972, pp. 257–260.

58 This is an allusion to the Seven Sleepers in the Koran, 18:18: "We turned them over sometimes to the right, sometimes to the left." The idea is of a *continuum*, a length of time proper to the mystical sleep, with the Events peculiar to it whose active Subject is God.

through the lapse of time during which temporal vicissitudes and the calamities of events turn us over, sometimes onto one side, sometimes onto another, until at last, after our dispersion through divers countries, there comes the moment of our meeting in the kingdom of the Master of the eternal Religion,[59] the moment in which we shall see our spiritual City rise into the air . . . the City out of which our father Adam, his wife and his posterity were forced to go."[60]

The cave of refuge and the spiritual City of Return confront each other. In the first of these, which is the first theme of Surah 18 of the Koran, it is easy to recognize the refuge where the Elect ("who are neither Muslims nor Jews nor Christians") sleep until the dawning of the Last Times.[61] In our text the "posterity of Adam", who took shelter in this cave, in no way denotes humanity in general, but only a specific fraction of humanity, whose composition is determined in the light of Ismaili sacred history. At the point of its fullest speculative development, this sacred history presents a schema made up of an innumerable succession of Cycles, in which Cycles of Unveiling (*dawr al-kashf*) alternate with Cycles of Occultation (*dawr al-satr*). The Cycle of Unveiling marks a state of beatitude and contemplative perfection; for the human beings living in such a Cycle, True Gnosis (*ḥaqīqah*) is proclaimed directly and openly, and the prescriptions of ritual are abolished. The soul has a direct and intuitive perception of pure spiritual Realities (*ḥaqā'iq*) through union with the light that flows over it from the First Archangel; the human body already enjoys certain glorious prerogatives pertaining to the "spiritual body".[62] The Cycle of Occultation is caused by the evil Desire of individual souls, who renounce their state of angelic individuality (*ashkhāṣ rūḥānīyah*) through an aberrant tendency which leads them to don the mask of material physical individuality

59 To compare this concept of *Nāmūs* in Ibn 'Arabī, see H. S. Nyberg, op. cit., p. 131 and pp. 102–103. Dailamī, op. cit., p. 73 l.5, saw in it nothing but a device dissimulating a state of topsy-turvydom, the overturning of the Koranic law.

60 *Rasā'il* IV, p. 85.

61 Cf. the most important study by L. Massignon, 'Les "Sept Dormants" apocalypse de l'Islam' (in *Opera minora*, vol. III (Beirut, 1963), pp. 104–118): an exemplary research into the "lines of spiritual force" underlying which is a topic of the imagination, and whose "knots" (the archetypes of C.-G. Jung) serve as "intersigns", enabling one to recognize and name the "consellations", as it were, in the multitude of events (cf. p. 115). With regard to the theme of the "person-archetypes" which we introduce here, cf. especially p. 109, where the Cave of the Seven Sleepers is identified with the Assembly of believers *personified* in Fāṭimah.

62 *Jāmi'ah* 25b, Strothmann, *Texte* I, 5, and X, 7; Idrīs 'Imāduddīn, *Zahr*, chap. XII.

(*ashkhāṣ ṭabī'īyah*). The Great Cycle (*al- kawr al-a'ẓam*), which includes the totality of the Cycles, and as to whose duration we are given the most dizzying figures,[63] began with a Cycle of Unveiling inaugurated by the Manifestation of the universal Adam, the πανάνθρωπος; each Cycle in turn is inaugurated by an incomplete Adam.[64]

Thus the "historical" Adam of our present Cycle, spoken of in the Bible and the Koran, is far from having been the first human being on earth. At the time of the grave symptoms which marked the end of the Cycle of Unveiling that preceded our Cycle—symptoms of the evil Desire of individual souls—the last Imam decided once more to impose the discipline of the Arcane, and to confer the Imamate on the young Adam whose father had himself died in the flower of his youth. Such is the extraordinary Ismaili exegesis (*ta'wīl*) of the Koranic verse 2:30, in which God addresses the Angels and says: "I wish to install a successor on the earth."[65] Yet just as—according to this exegesis—it is not the transcendent and unknowable God who speaks, but the *Imam*, so the Angels whom he addresses are not the spiritual Angels of the supreme celestial hierarchy, but the terrestrial Angels, human beings in the spiritual and glorious state of the Cycle of Unveiling; that is to say, they are the entirety of the *ḥudūd*, dignitaries or hierarchs, major or minor, of the Imam, who form his Temple or mystical body,[66] and whose descendants in the following Cycle will be no more than Angels, *or* demons, *in potentiality*. It is these privileged human beings, the terrestrial Angels, and they alone, who receive the command to prostrate themselves before Adam, their new Imam.[67]

Their vehement protests at the announcement of this investiture are undoubtedly motivated by the prospect of a state in which only symbolic Knowledge will be possible (for this is what it means "to be on Earth",

63 The Imam alludes to these in some passing remarks, certain of which estimate the Great Aion (al-Kawr al-a'ẓam) as made up of 400,000 Aions (*Kawr*) of 400,000 cycles (*dawr*) each! Cf. *Texte* I, 8 and II, 1.

64 Ibid., cf. index p. 52 s.v., and Idrīs, *Zahr*, chaps. XII and XIII.

65 Ibid., chap. XIII and *Texte*, Tuḥfah 2, p. 163.

66 *Jāmi'ah* 25b. Note the same word *majma'* in *Majma' al-Qā'im* (the Temple of the Imam, *Texte*, p. 21 l.4., or his Temple of Light, *Haykal Nūrānī*, ibid., pp. 6–7), and *Majma' al-Ṣābī'yīn*, the temple of the Sabians, in Mas'ūdī, *Prairies* IV, 64 (cf. note 141).

67 Cf. especially, again, *Texte* X, 23, pp. 100–101. *Eo ipso* the scandal is eliminated of man's taking precedence (in common anthropology) over the Angel. Just as the universal Adam is the initiator of the eternal Religion, so each partial Adam and each gnostic is a minor Angel, or an Angel in potentiality (cf. note 47).

esoterically speaking). But an even stronger motivation, surely, is the presentiment of the catastrophe which threatens the fragility of this form of Knowledge.[68] Here, we touch upon the mystery which the creative Imagination cannot fathom even were it to give shape to the most secret of psychic experiences. The attempt to attain knowledge beyond an eternal past, the memory of which has been wiped out by the vertigo of the abyss, traces a line of force which is pursued by the metaphysical Imagination of Baader, for example, in evoking the catastrophes which have left their traces in the universe and which we are unable, perhaps, even to picture to ourselves.[69]

The transition to the Cycle of Occultation, marked by the investiture of Adam and the restoring of the discipline of the Arcane, also ushers in the personage who is the personification, in this Cycle, of the eternal Antagonist, that Iblīs who before the beginning of Time caused the partial obfuscation of the Angel of Humanity, and who in the Period of Adam goes by the name of al-Ḥārith ibn Murrah.[70] In fact, he is one of the surviving dignitaries of the previous Cycle of Unveiling, one of the "Angels" of that period. As such, he knows that he himself is of an *essence of fire*. This means that he possesses a direct knowledge of the Truths of Gnosis. Adam, on the other hand, is made of *clay*, and this means that the knowledge assigned to him, the sole knowledge that he can and must transmit to those of the Cycle he inaugurates, is a hermeneutic of Symbols. Hence the refusal of al-Ḥārith to acknowledge Adam as the Imam (to "prostrate himself before him"), and his decision to provoke a catastrophe.

This malefic initiative possesses three aspects. It aims at provoking the young Imam Adam to transgress the limits of this Land of Paradise ("earthly Paradise"), where symbols burgeon and in which he is still allowed to dwell by the discipline of the Arcane. To this end, it incites him to aspire to the Knowledge reserved to the sublime Angels of the highest celestial hierarchies, that is to say, to the direct Knowledge of hidden Realities which constitutes in its own right the state of Resurrection (*'ilm al-Qiyāmah*).[71] It is precisely this Knowledge whose disclosure is reserved

68 "Will you place on the earth a being who will bring it into disorder and shed blood?" (2:30).

69 Cf. Eugène Susini, *La Philosophie de Franz von Baader*, II (Paris, 1942), p. 330.

70 Cf. Strothmann, *Texte* IV, 2 and X, 20, p. 101; Idrīs, *Zahr*, chap. XIII. On this partial darkening of the Angel, cf. also the symbolism of the "two wings" in my *Archange empourpré*, op. cit., VII, pp. 236 ff. (cf. note 101).

71 *Jāmi'ah* 20a.

for the Imam of the Resurrection (*Qā'im al-Qiyāmah*), who will come to conclude our Cycle and inaugurate a new Cycle of Unveiling. This Knowledge is the Gnosis that *is* Life, which is why it is represented in the Tree of immortality, whose fruit Adam is forbidden to taste—on pain of infringing the privilege of the Imam to come, and of inverting the cosmic order. Iblīs, however, can only arouse personal ambition in Adam indirectly, by appealing first of all to his generosity. Since the blessedness of the preceding Cycle was rooted in this disclosure of the Gnosis that constitutes the state of actualized Angels, this state must be restored, even if it means transgressing the sacrosanct Order of the necessary secret. So Adam "breaks the fast",[72] the vow of silence which is the ritual prescription *par excellence* of the esoteric Order.[73] "To break the fast" is to taste of the Tree of Knowledge that is the preserve of the actualized Angel. At the same time, it is to strip oneself of the protective veil of symbol; and this is how Adam appears before his own appalled dignitaries, in that state of terrifying nakedness which leaves him and his Temple of light defenceless in the face of the hate and vengeance of the Adversary. Thus all are forced to leave Paradise.

Having thus betrayed the secret of the Imam of the Resurrection to come, it is, conversely, by means of a pre-recognition of the Imam that Adam is enabled to hold a "secret conversation" with his Lord.[74] The anticipatory vision of the Epiphany to come thereby becomes the mediator for his nostalgia, for such a vision leads to the establishment of the "potential Paradise" (*jannah fi'l-quwwah*), the *da'wah* (literally "the Call") or Ismaili esoteric Church, into which those souls that are "angels in potentiality" must be received, and within which they can grow. These

72 Idrīs, chap. XIII; cf. also Massignon, op. cit., pp. 116–117: "To be nourished solely by the divine will is not only the vow of the *fast*, but also the complete guarding of the mouth, the vow of *silence*, which alone allows the heart, preserved from the world's tumult, to conceive the divine Word (like Mary's vow at the Temple, according to the Koran 19:27) . . . it is the Flight to the desert undertaken by the first Essenian and Egyptian hermits, the Solitude of God alone: *al-Ghurbah*" (cf. note. 92).

73 Cf. *Kalāmi Pīr*, p. 96 of the text. In the perspective of this exegesis, the fall of man and the fall of the Angels are not differentiated or opposed. But the fall of man is the fall of the human *Angel*, while the fall of the Angels is the fall of the angelic *man*. Anthropology can only be established, and is established, on the basis of angelology, which premisses both the preexistence and the supra-existence of the human person.

74 *Jāmi'ah* 20b.

souls constitute the "posterity of Adam"; they are the souls that together with Adam oppose the "posterity of Iblīs" and take refuge, like the Brothers of Purity, in the Cave—that is to say, in the Temple of the Imamate.[75] In this Temple, day after day, the esoteric Ritual must be performed; that is, the *exegesis* (*ta'wīl*) of the religious Ritual ascending, like a succession of resurrections, from one heaven to another in the mystical hierarchy. For Adam was initiated by the Angel sent to him into the arts and sciences with whose help he could cultivate an Earth on which symbols were able once more to blossom; and this blossoming has to spring from the hard soil of the letter and religious prescriptions of the Ritual: prayer at the five canonical hours, fasting, almsgiving, pilgrimage . . .

This is how it will be, say the Brothers in their secret Epistle, until the appearance of "the Child of Ishmael, that is to say, the Tree rooted in the earth and whose branches are lost in the heaven, the *lotus of the limit* (Koran 53:14) . . . until God brings to pass the Second Birth, and Creation returns to its source. Then the evil tree will perish . . . the Tree of direct Certitude will appear, around which the believers, the gnostics and the pure adorers of God will gather . . . when the Sun rises in its West, dazzling white after its eclipse. Then the Occident will become the Orient and the Orient will become the Occident . . . You will see the lights (of the beneficent stars) on the Earth of the Orient, while the Earth will be changed into a new Earth and the Heavens into new Heavens."[76] The "Sun rising in its West" designates *par excellence* the Imam of the Resurrection.[77] It is not impossible to see this as alluding to the imminence of contemporary events: the rising of the Fatimids on African soil. But there is a great deal more to it than that, for the text ends with these words: "when the Soul of the World manifests itself, and when the epiphany of individual souls outside their bodies of flesh is consummated." Thus what is in question is the manifestation of the Temples of Light at the time of

75 Cf. note 61, the assembly of believers personified in Fāṭimah.

76 *Jāmi'ah* 26a. Cf. Revelation 21:1; cf. also *Rasā'il* IV, p. 86: "May the Merciful One help you, and also the assembly of our brothers, to understand these indications and symbols; may he open your heart, expand your breast, purify your soul, illumine your intelligence, that you may contemplate, with the eyes of the inner vision, the True Realities (*ḥaqā'iq*) of these mysteries. So be no longer afraid of the death of the body when you separate yourself from it, for that itself is the life of the soul. For you are of the number of the Friends of God, of those who dare to desire death!" (and not of those who imagine themselves to do so—an allusion to Koran 62:6).

77 On the religious mystery concealed in the astronomical doctrine of the two opposing motions of the celestial spheres, see Paul Kraus, *Jābir ibn Ḥayyān* I, p. 1.

the Cycle of Unveiling which is to come, at the time of the final consummation of the Ritual by *ta'wīl*.

But it seems that, for the Brothers of Purity, this ultimate consummation of the Ritual entails a double phase of exegesis. They themselves describe to us the triple aspect of the *Ordo* of the divine service. There is the aspect which is prescribed by the religious law taken in its literal sense. There is the aspect which is practised by an ideal sect of philosophers who can be seen both as Sabians imbued with Neoplatonism and as pre-Ismaili theosophers. Finally, there is the Ritual as conceived and practised by the Brothers for themselves, which proclaims, in appropriate terms, the Ismaili exegesis of the Ritual. Both concept and practice are directed towards that metamorphosis of being which esoteric parlance designates as *qiyāmah*, resurrection, and whose mode of knowledge and awareness will reveal itself to us as a *mental vision of Person-archetypes*. We will thereby be enabled to envisage the nature of the spiritual experience into which angelology initiates, and which it both solicits and fulfils. An initial phase of this experience is revealed to us as an *exegesis* leading *from* the religious Ritual *to* the philosophical Ritual.

4. *Religious Ritual and philosophical Ritual.* The transition from one to the other of these is governed by the classic distinction, in Islamic theology, between *Islām* and *Īmān*.[78] The very word *Islām* connotes consecration and total submission to the divine will; it also involves strict observance of the religious rituals (the Five prayers, fasting, almsgiving and so on) which set the seal on the profession of the unitary faith (*tawḥīd*), and general conformity of one's life to the acts of the Prophet.[79] Īmān is conscious faith, the inner assent. If *Islām* and *Īmān* are the two faces of Religion, the Brothers of Purity are original in that they identify the degree of *Faith* with the "divine service of the Philosophers" (*al-'ibādah al-falsafīyah*), and thereby postulate positive religion—*Islām*—as a necessary prerequisite of the religious life: "Know, oh my brother, that as long as you remain imperfect in the cult of positive religion, it is in no way proper for you to take up the philosophical cult, for you could die by doing so." The believer (*mu'min*) is a true believer only if he has first been a *muslim*. When the time comes for the conjunction of the two cults, the initiate is given this solemn warning:

78 Cf. Wensinck, *The Muslim Creed*, pp. 23 ff., 94.
79 *Rasā'il* IV, pp. 301–302.

know that this is a work whose execution is extremely arduous, and which exposes the body to danger as well as demanding total renunciation of the soul. It involves renouncing all the facilities proffered by a world of familiar facts, in order to attain to the perception of the pure Essences, the True Realities (*ḥaqā'iq*).[80]

In fact, this conjunction is as yet no more than a preparation for the unfolding of the esoteric Ritual of the Brothers of Purity; it forms the first step of *ta'wīl*, the first stage of the *exegesis* which conducts thither. As such, it presupposes that the initiate has completely satisfied the prescriptions of the religious Ritual. Secondly, it introduces a liturgical calendar whose time is essentially measured according to the relative increase or decrease of Night and Day, while Night and Day themselves alternate with each other as symbols of esoteric and exoteric (*bāṭin* and *ẓāhir*), of the discipline of the arcane and revealed Gnosis.[81] There exists a correspondence between the divisions of the nychthemeron and those of the monthly and annual cycles: their liturgical recurrence obeys a ternary rhythm, followed each time by a period of withdrawal or silence. The correspondence also extends to the phases of a Period and of a Cycle of sacred history. This law of homology is essential to the understanding of the esoteric exegesis of the Ritual performed by the Brothers of Purity, for it establishes the cycle of sacred history as a cycle of cosmic liturgy.

The monthly ritual of the philosopher-Sages includes the celebration of three holy nights. The duration of each night extends from the hour which would correspond to our First Vespers until the hour of Second Vespers. These three nights are the first and middle nights of the month, together with one that falls between the twenty-fifth day of the month and the first day of the following month. They correspond to the phases of the moon; and indeed the cyclic correspondence between the time of the neomenias and that of the full moon appears in the Ismaili exegesis of these "liturgical Hours". Each night's ritual is split up into three nocturns. The first third of the night is taken up by a meditation in the personal oratory; this prolongs and confirms the official religious ritual, "so that there may be

80 Ibid., pp. 302 ff.

81 One must also take into account the ambivalence of each symbol. Esotericism may be the *night* of the mystery, but the reign of the letter may be the *night* of unawareness. The *day* may be the disclosure of the *mystery* in the sole Light of the Temple; it may also be the reign of *ready-made evidence*, of the clarity admitted and imposed by the common run of men.

purity upon purity and light upon light". The second third of the night is occupied by a meditation on the "cosmic text" under the starry sky, with the face turned to the Pole Star. The last third is devoted to the recital of a philosophical hymn (the "Prayer of Plato", the "Orison of Idrīs", that is, of Hermes, the "Secret Psalm of Aristotle"), whose texts we may one day be able to identify with the help of some manuscript. Finally, after the dawn prayer, the Sage invites his family and brothers to join him in celebrating agapae, and the day is passed in wise conversation.[82]

The choice of the Pole Star as *qiblah* points to the Sabianism of our Sages,[83] an impression confirmed by their annual calendar. The three periods, the three great liturgical solemnities, are astronomically determined by the sun's entry into the Sign of Aries, the Sign of Cancer and the Sign of Libra; that is to say, by the successive advent of spring, summer and autumn, which are followed by the silence and desolation of winter. In winter the Sages observe a strict "fast": it is the time during which the Elect slumber in the *Cave*. Here again the Sabian style of the ceremony is undeniable: at each festival the Sages gather in the Temple which is erected specifically for that festival, and whose architecture corresponds to the constellation reigning over that day; the colour and form of their garments conform to the same correspondence, and they eat only food that is equally appropriate to the day.[84]

What is revealed "ritually" to us here is the median and mediating position occupied by Sabian ideology; that is to say, the "Sabian Temple" is the ideal place where the official religious ritual is transmuted into the ritual of a cosmic liturgy, which itself serves as a prelude to the liturgy of the esoteric mesocosm of the Ismaili Order. On the one hand, the Brothers of Purity have no difficulty in showing the correspondence between the three great philosophical festivals and the religious solemnities: "If you meditate, oh my brother, upon the three days of the philosophic year . . . and carefully consider the festivals of the Islamic religion, you will find that they agree and correspond with each other." Corresponding to the festival of spring and renewal is the festival of *the breaking of the fast* (which concludes the month of Ramaḍān). To the summer festival corresponds

82 *Rasā'il* IV, pp. 303–304.

83 Cf. Chwolsohn, op. cit., II, 5, 59, 61, 222; also E. S. Drower, *The Mandaeans of Iraq and Iran* (Oxford, 1937), p. 18 n. 9.

84 *Rasā'il* IV, p. 305.

the festival of sacrifices (*'Īd al-Aḍḥā*), which falls on the tenth day of the month of pilgrimage (*Dhū'l-Ḥijjah*). The joy of this festival is quite different from that of the first festival, for it is mingled with hardship and fatique, sadness and lethargy; it is the noon hour, stifling and parched. To the autumn festival corresponds a festival not of orthodox Islam, but *the* festival *par excellence* of Shiite Islam: the solemn investiture of the Imam by the Prophet at Ghadīr Khumm, a testamentary act by which the Annunciator (*Nāṭiq*) of the religious Law entrusted its secret exegesis (*ta'wīl*) to his spiritual heir and to the Imams of his lineage. Corresponding to the time of sadness and of the Sages' retreat is the Departure of the Prophet to the other world, leaving his community to grief and mourning.[85]

On the other hand, one can readily perceive the hermeneutical advance towards the conception of Ismaili esotericism that is implicit in the calendar of the "festivals of the Philosophers". The festival of Spring, marking the point at which the equilibrium of Day and Night is broken in favour of Day, is celebrated by the Brothers in lyrical terms: springs gush, torrents once more fill their dry beds, sap rises to the topmost branches, the green fields are aflame with the brightness of flowers.[86] It is truly the time of a "resurrection" (*qiyāmah* in Ismaili terminology), that is to say the initial time of a Period in which a doctrine bursts forth, a Gnosis proclaimed by the angelic trumpets of the concert given, it is said, on this day of festival by the initiated Sages. The great festival of summer marks the start of Day's retreat before the encroaching Night; the joyous flowering of symbols begins to dry up on the Earth. The homily at the festival of autumn is short: "The measure of the Gnosis revealed is no more than is appropriate to such a Time." From now on, the Night of esotericism becomes the refuge of the Call (*da'wah*) to transcend the literalism of the Law and of all servitude to texts and men. This is the time of winter, which the theosopher-Sages pass in their *Cave*, observing the "strict fast" that once was broken, prematurely, by him whose posterity they are.

Thus, the "philosophical calendar" corresponds to the phases of *ta'wīl* or transcendent spiritual exegesis. The religious festivals *commemorate* an event. The speculative festivals *bring back* the Event, setting it *in the present.* The situation is actually experienced, determined by the star and the season, and projected into a Figure: the Temple, specially consecrated to

85 Ibid., p. 306.
86 Cf. ibid., p. 305.

each festival, in which the Sages assemble. *Īmān*, the inner faith in the sense intended by the Brothers of Purity, is a faith which transmutes; it does not commemorate, but effects and promotes the Event. This faith has the power to actualize Events because it transmutes them into symbols, preserving only their transcendence. It does not itself return *to the fact* or try to reduce it to its causes; it takes *the fact* along with it to *that which the fact indicates*.[87] Its exegesis of the calendar makes of the latter itself an exegesis, for the liturgical cycle actualizes, one by one, the calendar's permanent and original Figures. When *ta'wīl* raises itself onto an even higher level, the festivals will no longer be celebrated in the Temples of the Sabian theosophers. The Event will no longer be experienced merely as an event which survived or survives *after* people, but as *being* those very People. The Event, that is, is no longer simply *set in the present*: the soul itself becomes its *presence*. Thus, the lived situation will no longer be projected only into a Temple which serves as its Figure, but into the very reality of those Person-archetypes, the exegetes who *effect* the esoteric exegesis, and whose recurrence will be the actual cycle of the soul's calendar. By means of a conversion and an elevation which are characteristic of the mental vision, these Persons, as celestial archetypes, will be the Festivals themselves "in person", and they themselves will be the Time and the Temple of the festivals. This is the ultimate meaning of the ritual of the Brothers of Purity, as we shall see in the next section.

II. *The Ismaili Exegesis of the Ritual*

1. *The Festivals and Liturgies of the Brothers of Purity.* "Know, oh my brother, that we are the society of the Brothers of Purity, of all men the most fitted for the cult of religion . . . because it is we who have the most intimate knowledge of it . . . but we are also the most fitted for the philosophical cult, the most able to maintain it and to renew whatever may have degenerated in it."[88] The Ismaili exegesis aims at precisely this regeneration when it is applied, in its turn, to the cult of the Sages, whose ritual reflected an ideal Sabianism, and whose ceremonial and liturgical times

87 On this major aspect of psychic Energy which transmutes fact into symbol, cf. C.-G. Jung, *Über psychische Energetik und das Wesen der Träume*, 2nd ed. (Zürich, 1948), pp. 39–44; see also my 'Livre du Glorieux', op. cit., p. 84.

88 *Rasā'il* IV, p. 306.

make possible the transition from the Sabian ideology of the Temple constructed in the image of a star, to the Ismaili ideology of the human Temple as veil (*ḥijāb*) and sanctuary of a celestial Person of light (*haykal al-nūr*).[89]

"We have", it is said, "a third sort of year, the observance of which is peculiar to us. We too have three Days which we consider to be days of festival, and on which we instruct our brothers to gather together and celebrate. Know, oh my brother, that our festivals resemble, not literally but typologically (*bi'l-mathal*), the festivals of the Philosophers and religious festivals. This is because our festivals are of the nature of substances subsisting of themselves (*dhātīyah qā'imah bidhawātihā*); all actualization proceeds from, by and in them. They too are three in number: one comes at the beginning, one in the middle, and one at the end. There is a fourth, which is the most difficult to observe, the hardest to actualize."[90]

After mentioning the correspondences with the times of Islamic festivals and of the festivals of philosophical religion, as already described, the Brothers continue as follows: "Our festivals, oh my brother, are Persons who Announce (*ashkhāṣ nāṭiqah*), Souls in act and active, implementing, at the call of their Creator, the acts and practices revealed and inspired by Him. The first of our Days, and *the* festival *par excellence* of all our festivals, is the day of the appearance of the First *Qā'im* amongst us.[91] Corresponding to this day is the Sun's entry into the sign of Aries at the time of spring, of the blossoming and sweetness of life, when the heavenly Mercy of the Epiphany (*ẓuhūr*) descends to earth and dwells there, and when esoteric knowledge may be revealed. For us and for all our brothers it is a day of happiness. The second day is the Day of the resurrection (*qiyām*) of the Second *Qa'im*, the day when the Sun enters the sign of Cancer, the point at which days are at their longest and nights are shortest, for on this day the power of the oppressors has ceased and been consumed. It is a day of joy, happiness and good tidings. The third day is the Day of the resurrec-

89 On these *Hayākil al-Nūr*, see Ivanow, *Rise of the Fatimids*, p. 256 and p. 64 of the text of *Zahr* l. 9–10 (cf. notes 41, 44, 57, 66). The Prophets and Imams are the Temples of Light, and all the *ḥudūd* are oratories in this temple, limbs of this body, as the Seven stars were the limbs and the temples of the divinity which revealed itself in them.

90 *Rasā'il* IV, p. 307.

91 The word *Qā'im*, literally "he who stands up", *par excellence* denotes the Qā'im al-Qiyāmah, the Imam of the Resurrection; but each Imam, and even each member of the Order, is a Qā'im in potentiality. Cf. *Rise*, pp. 242–243 (54–55 of the Arabic text).

tion of the Third amongst us, and corresponds to the Sun's entry into the sign of Libra; once again the days and nights are of equal length. It is the advent of autumn, that is to say the resistance of error to truth, when the order of things begins to be inverted. Finally, there is a fourth day of sadness and desolation. On this day we return to our Cave, the cave of the discipline of the arcane (*taqīyah*) and of Occultation (*istitār*), to a state of things which accords with that described by him who instituted the Law, saying: *Islam began in exile and will be in exile again; happy are those who exile themselves.*"[92]

The appearance at this point of the famous *ḥadīth* immediately links the Brothers of Purity with all the ultra-Shiite ideology which developed around the figure of Salmān the Persian, or the Pure. Salmān typifies the case of the Stranger guided from distant lands by his own personal effort, and whose exile stamps him with the seal of a purely spiritual Islam, as opposed to all the legalistic pretensions and claims resting on a right of carnal descent. Jābir, the Ismaili alchemist, transposes these same attributes to the mystical figure of him whom he calls the *Glorious One*, who is allied to these "Strangers" whose spiritual condition in this world is none other than that of the Sethian Gnostics.[93] It is with reference to this condition of being strangers seeking refuge in the Cave from a world of ignorance and violence that the Brothers say: "This, precisely, is what we are subjected to in our time, until the hour comes of the Appearance, of free exit, of the Return after the Departure, just as the Sun, after the departure of winter, returns into the sign of Aries."[94]

The ritual that regulates the phases of the life of these Strangers offers scope for many forms of interpretation. One cannot entirely ignore the perspective it opens onto imminent contemporary events; but it would be a mistake to suppose that these events are able, by and as themselves, to exhaust the significance of what is involved here. In Ismaili historiosophy, no event is seen as affected by a contingency that lacks eternal significance. The drama is enacted on two levels, celestial and earthly, and this is the

92 *Rasā'il* IV, p. 308. On this ḥadīth of the Exile (*Ghurbah*, cf. note 72), see L. Massignon, 'Salmān Pāk et les prémices spirituelles de l'Islam iranien', in *Opera minora*, vol. I (Beirut, 1963), pp. 450–457, and *Biḥār al-Anwār*, vol. III (Tehran, 1306 A.H.), p. 292, l. 32 ff. (sentence attributed not to the Prophet but to the first Imam, and interpreted by the sixth Imam, Ja'far al-Ṣādiq).

93 Cf. my 'Livre du Glorieux', (*supra*, ch. II, n. 3), pp. 58 ff.

94 *Rasā'il* IV, p. 308.

very condition of the transformation of event into symbol. The contexts of the events exemplify on earth the drama of the eternal Archetypes, and it is only the latter that can explain the liturgical cycle of the Brothers' ritual.

For this reason, an interpretation which refers the phases of this ritual to a Cycle of Unveiling by no means excludes one that refers them to a Cycle of Occultation. This may be understood as follows. A Cycle of Unveiling follows on from the Great Resurrection (*Qiyāmat al-Qiyāmāt*), initiated by the seventh Imam of the seventh Period and bringing to an end a Cycle of Occultation such as ours.[95] This Cycle of Unveiling is followed, in its turn, by a Cycle of Occultation, of which ours is an example. According to this perspective, the third or autumn festival might well correspond to the crucial moment when Night prevails over Day, the moment when, at the decline of a Cycle of paradisal innocence, the evil forces of the Antagonist, the eternal Iblīs, begin to shake free and manifest themselves. It is, as we saw, the moment in which the dignitaries of the Order decide once more to impose the discipline of the arcane and the obligations of the Ritual—the moment in the Cycle immediately preceding ours, when the Adam of our Cycle was invested with the dignity and function of an Imam. The time which follows is not of course a day of festival, but a time of calamity and desolation, during which the Sages were obliged to take refuge in the "Cave". It is the time of the catastrophe which succeeded the day when Adam, the adolescent who in his folly broke the "fast", surrendered the secret and the vision of Paradise to the rage and mockery of Iblīs-Ahriman.

It must be admitted, nevertheless, that the conditions made possible by a Cycle of Unveiling—a mode of existence which is innocent, luminous and subtle—are totally beyond the reach, if not of our aspiration, at any rate of our actual psychical experience and, for the most part, of our boldest speculations and imaginings.[96] The texts at our disposal do not throw much light on the factors which determine the number of the three Persons who, in a Cycle of Unveiling, will succeed each other in the same

95 Needless to say, there were variations in the representations of sacred history (according to the periods of Ismailism: pre-Fatimid, Fatimid, Alamut and the Nizāri tradition, post-Fatimid Yemenite). We are not concerned here to study hitory stratigraphically, but to distinguish a schema which accords with the whole body of Ismaili speculative experience and with its resources.

96 Cf. note 62.

way as the three Festivals of the secret ritual of the Brothers of Purity.[97] But it is nonetheless true that the *law of homology*, already stated to be essential, is able here to lead us to a representation that gives coherence to the whole. The events of each Cycle, and of every period of each Cycle, are respectively homologous with each other. There exists a homology between the Great *Qiyāmah*, bringing to an end a Cycle of Occultation, and the lesser *Qiyāmah* which concludes each of the Seven Periods of that Cycle, when a religion which has exhausted its "appeal" in its previous form "revives" in the new religion proclaimed by a new Annunciator (*nāṭiq*).[98] Similarly, the name of *Qā'im*, resurrector, is reserved *par excellence* for "he who will rise up", the Lord of the Resurrection, at the close of the final Period of our Cycle. Yet each partial *Qā'im* at the end of each Period of the Septenary, as well as each Imam and each member of the Order, is also, potentially, Lord of the Resurrection, a limb of his mystical body, an oratory in his Temple of Light. Each Period of a Cycle is homologous to that Cycle; each *Qiyāmah* is in the image of the Great *Qiyāmah*. Moreover, each *Qiyāmah*, or resurrection, which is represented for each member of the Order by his elevation from one stage to another, is homologous with the Great Resurrection.[99] This is why the Brothers of Purity expressly emphasize the homology of their ritual with the phases of each human existence.[100] In the last analysis, all that matters is the loftiness of the horizon which the Event indicates, the Archetype which promotes the Event as such and which is exemplified in all the liturgical Cycles of events that are homologous with each other.

In this sense, and to this full extent, the three *Persons* mentioned by the Brothers as constitutive of their own *Festivals* are the homologues of the

97 This would give us a ternary rhythm, whereas the septenary is the rhythm of the schemas of periodization in Ismaili historiosophy (particularly for the Cycles of occultation). But in the perspective of precisely such a historiosophy, this is by no means a contradiction. We should call to mind Jābir's *Livre du Glorieux* (op. cit., §§ 2 and 3), where the rhythm is determined by the Triad 'Ayn-Mīm-Sīn, completed by the person of the Glorious One. Likewise, all is here regulated by the secret intention which places the Sabian theosophers in a mediating position between positive Islam and the Ismaili exegesis of the Brothers. Of all the festivals and commemorations of Islam, *three* have been retained, *plus* one day of mourning and expectation.

98 *Qiyāmah* or resurrection as the aim and end of religions (nihāyat-i adyān), cf. *Kalāmi Pīr*, p. 63 of the Persian text, l. 4 ff.

99 Cf. note 57.

100 *Rasā'il* IV, p. 307.

Three esoteric dignitaries who appear at the beginning of a Cycle of Occultation. These are, respectively: the Annunciator (*Nāṭiq*) of the new religion; his legatee, the depositary and foundation (*Waṣī*, *Asās*) of the pure spiritual meaning of his religion (the "festival" following which the Night of esotericism will get longer); and, finally, the first of the silent Imams (*ṣāmit*), the "festival" following which Night will preponderate over Day and the Order will have to seek the shelter of esotericism (the "Cave"). These silent Imams, from the first of the first heptad to the seventh of the seventh, are the keepers of the esoteric meaning whose communication to the souls called to their Order gradually matures, according to the degree to which they are able to assimilate this meaning, the fruit of the Resurrection.

One could go further and say that since each member of the Order, from the greatest to the least, merely exemplifies on earth a member of the celestial angelic hierarchy, these three superior dignitaries are the representatives on earth of the highest archangelic hypostases, to wit: the pair formed by the First and the Second Archangels—Intelligence and Soul of the World—from whom proceeds the third Archangel, the Angelos-Anthropos of Humanity. With him the cosmic catastrophe is precipitated, through his fatal tardiness in recognizing the divine Unitude (*tawḥīd*)—a tardiness which plunged him in darkness and which is symbolized in Suhravardī by the two wings of the Archangel Gabriel, one of light and the other of darkness.[101] This third Archangel fell to the rank of tenth in the supreme angelic hierarchy (which made him the *first* of our cosmos); and the entire history of our world represents the time spent in reconquering his original archangelic rank, aided by each of the "angels" who emanate from him. The last Imam (the *Qā'im*) of a Cycle is his surrogate: in his Temple of Light, all the souls of light, members of the Order who belonged to the Cycle, are *led back* by him to this Angel. The distance between the third *festival* or third dignitary alluded to by the Brothers, and the moment when they leave their cave (the *Occident* to which their souls have declined)—in other words, the moment of the appearance of the *Qā'im* (the Sun rising in the Occident)—is precisely the time during which the Redemption of the Angel is being accomplished through the maturing, in each soul, of an aptitude for the angelic state. One of its great phases

101 Cf. note 70.

(*Qiyāmāt*) is betokened by the Sun's re-entry into the sign of Aries. We are thus enabled to grasp the main features[102] of the cohesion between the ideology illustrated by the Ritual of the Brothers of Purity, and the entirety of Ismaili cosmology and sacred history.

For our purposes, we should concentrate on the succession of the personages in this sacred history, in so far as this succession constitutes the liturgical ceremonial of the ritual; for it is this which allows us to bring out the specifically Ismaili configuration of the "man and ritual" theme. If the same archetypes are exemplified in all the Cycles; if the Cycles and the events composing them are homologous with each other; and if these events *are* Persons, then all of these together must constitute and "temporalize" Time in such a way that it is by virtue of being the time of these Persons that it also becomes, properly speaking, liturgical Time as well. Simultaneity and coincidence exist between the recurrence of the festivals which constitute the Cycle of liturgical Time, and the recurrence of the individual Figures whose personal presence is projected onto the Cycle. The individual Figure is no longer confined to a moment in time, and does not fade into a vanishing past, for its own individual time is also a reversible time. In this cyclical presence is revealed simultaneously both the archetype of the individual and the individual as archetype; in other words, the individual case is an archetypal case every time.[103]

This recurrence of archetypal cases projects the hidden significance of the Cycles of sacred history onto a plane of *historical permanence*.[104] By means of it we can identify, in each generation, period and cycle, down to the completion of the Cycle of Cycles, the ἀποκατάστασις, the antagonists of the same drama: on the one hand the third Archangel in the primordial Universe ('ālam al-Ibdā'), the primordial Adam and all the incomplete Adams, and on the other hand Iblīs and all the Iblīs who came after him. And since this plane of historical permanence necessitates the recurrence of Persons who enact the *geste* of their archetype, it is this very recurrence which constitutes the ceremonial of the cosmic liturgical Cycle. The Persons are the festivals of this Cycle, and their recurrence is the recurrence itself of liturgical times. Because these festivals are the recurring

102 Notably in the *Zahr al-Ma'ānī* by Idrīs (ʿImāduddīn, chaps. IX–X, XX–XXI; cf. Strothmann, *Texte* IV, 2; Idāh I and index s.v. al-'Aql al-'Āshir (the tenth Intelligence).

103 Cf. my 'Livre du Glorieux', (*supra*, ch. II, n. 3), pp. 16–17.

104 A term used by L. Massignon in *Salmān Pāk*, op. cit., p. 467.

presence of the same archetype, they do not merely commemorate an Event which happened once for all in the past. The exemplifications of the archetype do not occur *in* time; they themselves determine their time "in the present" as gauge of their relationship with each other, as token of their specific individuality, an individuality irreducible to the abstract generality of a category.[105]

In the absence of this individuality, we would have only a banal system of rationalist propositions, propping up a philosophy of history. In complete contrast to this depersonalization, the ritual meaning of the *gesta mundi* performs, with respect to these *gesta*, a *ta'wīl* on each occasion; that is to say, it elevates the event to the level of symbol, and there discloses the *geste* of the archetype. That is why the festival in the liturgical calendar does not simply commemorate an event. It *is* that very event, and the Event *is* the Person who enacts the *geste* of the archetype. A striking illustration of this will be found below in the personalizing valorization of the Shiite Calendar. Another illustration is provided by the Mazdean calendar, where each day is called by the name of an Angel, inciting us to the discovery of what is meant by the "day of an Angel", that is, the day whose event *is* this very Angel. This meaning, in the case of the ritual as in that of the revealed text or of the cosmic text, very distinctly shows us how the spiritual *exegesis* or *ta'wīl* brings about the "return" *to* the archetype and *of* the archetype. By the same token, the ministry of this exegesis is understood as an angelic one, personified on earth, for example, in the person of Salmān the Persian, the Stranger whose role of companion-initiator to the Prophet[106] is repeated in each relationship of initiator to initiate, which, step by step, unites one by one the members of the Ismaili Order to each other. We have already mentioned, in fact, that the ritual of the sacred mesocosm is essentially a Cycle of resurrections, homologous with the Great *Qiyāmah*. The meaning that lies in conceiving a festival as a Person, the sense that each festival *is* a Person, is the promotion of that Person to a new 'resurrection', his elevation to a new heaven in the

105 Thus, something like a reversal of the notion of a time which imposes its measure: in this case, it is the soul that is the measure of *its* time. The same reversal is implied by a "chronology" which expresses the ideal interval between Zarathustra and Plato as being a period of 6,000 years. In the same way, the meaning of the Periods of Ismaili historiosophy cannot be reduced to the homogeneous time of the profane calendar.

106 Cf. my 'Livre du Glorieux', (*supra*, ch. II, n. 3), pp. 63 ff., and Massignon, *Salmān Pāk*, pp. 464 ff.

mesocosm—that is to say, his being born to an existence typified by the Angel who rules over that Heaven. This is the liturgical Cycle, celebrated in the spiritual Temple which is formed by the *da'wah*, the Ismaili esoteric Church.

What, one may ask, is the divine service *par excellence*, the liturgy which is celebrated by and for the "festivals" of this Cycle?

The Brothers of Purity do not fail to describe it, or rather to allude to it in veiled terms which we can, nevertheless, decipher by reference to other contexts. The sacrifice, they say, which they celebrate assembles and contains in itself all the virtues, both of the "religious" and of the "philosophical" sacrifice.[107] This is the sacrifice which was offered up by Abraham, "the ram that was obtained for him as ransom for his son and that had grazed for forty autumns[108] on the Earth of Paradise. If you are able to offer up in sacrifice a ram that has grazed on the Earth of Paradise an entire lifetime if necessary, then do so; do not relax, keep fighting for this, so that you may ultimately achieve your goal, may revive the exemplary cases and abide in the universe of God.'[109]

Thus the mental repetition of Abraham's sacrifice is presented as the act *par excellence* of an esoteric ritual of spiritual death and regeneration. But it is self-evident that the bent and the significance of this inner liturgy, which effects a transmutation of the soul, can be understood only within the context of the Ismaili exegesis. Who was the son that had to be sacrificed? What is the ram that was sacrificed in his place? Why had it grown up on the Earth of Paradise?

The Ismaili exegesis of Surah 37 refers, of course, to the order of the sacred mesocosm, established by Gnosis. The purpose of the usual Islamic

107 *Rasā'il* IV, p. 309.
108 The Brothers' text (309 l.11) has *kharūf* (forty sheep?). For this, read *kharīf* (autumn). Cf. Abū'l-Futūḥ Rāzī, *Tafsīr*, IV (Tehran edition, 1314 A.H.), p. 440 l. 28 ff. (*Chahal kharīf*). Forty autumns: that is, forty years. Cf. the passage where the Brothers represent the hierarchy of their Order as made up of four levels, each of which they address by a special vocative in the course of their treatises. The first corresponds to the age of fifteen ("Our merciful and candid Brothers"). The second corresponds to the age of thirty ("Our virtuous and excellent Brothers"). The third is reached after the age of forty ("Our eminent and noble Brothers"). The fourth level corresponds to the angelic faculty and is the result of an inner experience which can be attained only after the age of fifty. It is to the Brothers of this level that the Koranic verse is addressed: "Oh pacified soul, return to your Lord, pleasing and pleased", Koran 89:27–28 (IV, pp. 222–223).
109 Ibid., p. 309.

exegesis is to establish that the child to be sacrificed must be not Isaac but Ishmael. Yet according to the Ismaili perspective there is far more to it than this. Abraham had resolved to invest Isaac with his spiritual heritage, thereby keeping it from Ishmael, the child who by divine proclamation (37:101) had been characterized as the child of gentleness and patience. This is the meaning ascribed to verse 37:102: "My child, I dreamed that I was offering you up in sacrifice." But then a divine command alters this mistaken predisposition and orders Abraham to transfer his heritage to Ishmael: "And we ransomed him with a great victim" (37:107). Now this victim—traditionally this ram—is in fact no other than a metaphorical designation for Isaac himself.[110] What, then, is meant by the sacrifice of this Ram?

Here again the whole body of Ismaili Gnosis can be taken as a guide. By this Gnosis, Ishmael is regarded as the spiritual heir, the Imam who holds the secret of the Gnosis, while Isaac is a Veil: the veil or screen of the Letter which is placed before the Imam. The relationship between them corresponds to the fundamental distinction between the appointed and permanent Imam (*mustaqarr*, the *ordinarius*), and an Imam who is merely a depositary or curator (*mustawada'*), established as a kind of protection during periods of danger and apparently performing the functions of the true Imam, while the latter remains hidden.[111] Ishmael was the Upholder of the mystical meaning, of the esoteric science of *ta'wīl*, while Isaac was before him as a Veil, maintaining the science of *tanzīl*, of the revealed Letter and of positive religion. The same relationship is perpetuated in the course of their respective lineages,[112] and Ismaili historiosophy took upon itself the task of determining what the legitimate transmission was for each epoch. Whereas Moses established a new Law (*sharī'ah*), a new positive religion, the descendents of Ishmael continued and transmitted the esoteric message of Gnosis.[113]

Thus the spiritual ritual begins to assume a specific form. The ram which must be offered up in sacrifice is Isaac. This signifies the sacrifice of external evidence and literal faith (ẓāhir), of the prescriptions of legalistic religion, of material certainties, and of the justice of the Law. And whereas

110 Cf. Strothmann, *Texte* XII, 34, p. 128.
111 Cf. Bernard Lewis, *The Origins of Ismailism*, pp. 48 ff., and Strothmann, *Texte*, index s.v. *mustaqarr* and *mustawda'*.
112 Ibid., Tuḥfah, chap. III, pp. 164–167.
113 Ibid., p. 164.

tradition demands that the Ram must have grazed for forty autumns on the Earth of Paradise,[114] the Brothers go further and add: "an entire lifetime if necessary". We already know that by "Earth of Paradise" is signified the *da'wah*, the Ismaili Church as "potential Paradise". Here alone can the exoteric sense (*ẓāhir*) of religion grow and mature, for it is given substance by the inner and esoteric sense (*bāṭin*): it may grow for an entire human lifetime until it can be sacrificed at the moment when interiority is in full flower; for the mystery of the esoteric Church is accomplished in a cycle of Resurrections. Everywhere else in the official, external religious world, the letter can never be anything but the letter, the Law remains the Law. The ritual of the Ismaili Brothers of Purity thus culminates in an act of spiritual resurrection which liberates one from this Gehenna.

It may seem, perhaps, that the sacrifice of the Law's bondage is one which man would be only too happy to make. Yet it is represented by the Brothers as the culmination of an entire lifetime of effort. This is because, far from signifying an anarchic, negative freedom, obtained without anything being given in exchange, such a sacrifice can only be achieved at the end of a long period of inner asceticism. This is the meaning given to it by the great mystical poet 'Aṭṭār—who is suspected, moreover, of having possessed a knowledge of Ismailism—when he says: "If you profess the religion of Abraham (and if you are thus a pure Ḥanīf), the sacrifice of the son is a teaching which is addressed to you."[115] This teaching becomes imperiously evident from the moment it is viewed within the Ismaili perspective, in which Ishmael and his line represent the spiritual heritage, the perpetuation of the esoteric Imamate, while Isaac represents carnal descent and perpetuation of the Law. The religion of the Law, the social imperative, may prescribe the sacrifice of Ishmael—the sacrifice, that is, of the universe of the soul and its celestial mysteries. By contrast, to sacrifice the ram which is Isaac is to sacrifice carnal desire for earthly possession and descent, in exchange for the spiritual heritage. It is to renounce the child of flesh and blood in order to ransom the child of the Soul. It is to

114 On the age of forty, see note 108.

115 *Ilāhī-Nāme*, die Gespräche des Königs mit seinen sechs Söhnen . . . , ed. Helmut Ritter, Bibliotheca Islamica 12 (Istanbul, 1940), p. 59 v. 19. Cf. Fritz Meier, 'Der Geistmensch bei dem persischen Dichter 'Aṭṭār', Eranos-Jahrbuch XIII (1946), p. 295. Along with other Sufis, 'Aṭṭār was regarded by the Ismailis as a co-religionist; see Ivanow, *Guide*, no. CXXIV, pp. 104–105 and p. 118.

gather into oneself all the Soul's energies, to sacrifice the illusory terrestrial posterity which men naturally desire, in order to produce instead within oneself the child of the *Anima caelestis*, so that man himself becomes the Child of eternity, who can only be born and begin to exist within an esoteric kingdom (*bāṭin*) which is quite other than the exterior and visible universe.[116]

This engendering in the Soul of the *Puer aeternus* is the goal towards which the visions of mystics, from an 'Aṭṭār to Meister Eckhart and Angelus Silesius, are unanimously and strikingly drawn; and the Brothers of Purity, in accordance with their whole ethic, which could be termed *ad imitationem Angeli*,[117] refer to it at the conclusion of their Ritual: "Then the angelic Form (*al-ṣūrah al-malakīyah*) will be perfected for you, and on your Great Return (*ma'ād*) it will be ready for you to unite with it and dwell in it";[118] that is to say, so that you may then be in actuality the Angel whose birth in you only makes it potential here below. Thus, the *ta'wīl* of the ritual, like the operation of alchemy (which is an Ismaili application *par excellence* of the ritual), leads to the emergence of that Third World or mesocosm, born of a mediation which triumphs over contraries. All gnoses have aspired towards this world; it is proclaimed, for example, in an apocryphon of Clement of Alexandria, by Jesus, who replies to Salome's question as to when the reign of death will come to an end by saying "When masculine and feminine are one."[119]

If the "angelic Form" is the fruit of this sacred inner marriage of the masculine and feminine aspects of the Soul, the birth of that Form surely represents the passage, the *exodus*, leading from the Sabian ideology of the Temple to the Ismaili conception of the Temple of Light. It is no longer the luminescent forms of the stars shining in the night sky which are the temples of the hermeneutical Angels of the Divinity, but the Persons of the members of the Order, forming the Temple of Light of the Imamate. Through the angelomorphosis of man, the one divinity abides in man. The ritual celebrated by man in the Temple of his being is his own *metamorphosis*, the bringing to birth within himself of that Form of himself which conforms to the angelic archetype. Here, so to speak, lies the

116 Cf. Esther Harding, *Frauen-Mysterien einst und jetzt* (Zürich, 1949), the chapter on the sacrifice of the son, pp. 323 ff. and 373 ff.
117 Cf. the texts cited in note 56.
118 *Rasā'il* IV, p. 309.
119 Cited in E. Harding, op. cit., p. 376.

conclusion of the dialogue between Ḥanīf and Sabian, the New Testament of a spiritual Sabianism. It is of this that the Brothers of Purity are fully aware when, concluding the exposition of their own ritual, they call to witness "the fact that the ancient Sages used to build Temples on earth, typifying (*'alā mithāl*) the Temples which are built in Heaven."[120]

2. *The Esoteric Ritual and the Vision of the Person-archetypes.* The emergence of a new personal Form in man, "representing" or exemplifying an angelic archetype, is thus seen as the element which it is essential to understand, and which at the same time allows one to understand the ultimate significance of the esoteric Ritual—to understand, that is, the highest development of *ta'wīl*, the concrete transmutation effected by it. Unless we arbitrarily restrict the meaning of the word "mystical", it is difficult not to apply the quality of mysticism to this *exegesis* of the soul. But this mysticism differs profoundly from all mystical experiences of the annihilation of self in the divine absolute grasped directly and without mediation. In place of this abyss of negativity, it proffers a universe peopled with a multitude of celestial Persons, each of whom is a world.

It differs also, and equally, from what is frequently understood as esotericism, but which is basically nothing but a rationalist tendency to substitute an abstract meaning (idea, principle, law) for all personal figures or figurations (heroes, Angels, exemplary events). Such a substitution contributes to the dissolution of symbols, and consequently of the beings who symbolize, in order to promote impersonal generalities: once again, the celestial universe is unpeopled. In sharp contrast to this, Ismaili *ta'wīl* does not start with a symbolic personal figure and proceed to the enunciation of a general proposition. It starts with a factual reality given in physics, in history, in ritual or in religious prescription, in order to disclose the vision of the Person-archetype who confers stability and ontological validity on such data by elevating them to the level of symbols. Reciprocally, the mental vision of the Person-archetype presupposes the spiritual exegesis of the text, whether sacred or cosmic.[121]

Thus, all positive data are not done away with, but are transfigured in

120 *Rasā'il* IV, p. 309.

121 There is something similar in Swedenborg's *ta'wīl* of Scripture as the starting-point of his mental visions; cf. Ernst Benz, *Emanuel Swedenborg, Naturforscher und Seher* (Munich, 1948), pp. 326 ff.

and by the very figure that they represent. This being so, it is curious that the interiorizing Ismaili exegesis, into which the disciple was progressively initiated, has sometimes been thought to leave no more than a heaven peopled (!) with abstract symbols and phantoms without reality.[122] The opposite is the case: the Person-archetype is not the symbol, but that which is symbolized. It is the earthly, human person who, by gravitating towards his spiritual person (*shakhṣ rūḥānī*), his angel-hood (*firishtagī*), represents and typifies a hypostasis of the angelic world. He does not destroy this hypostasis by symbolizing with it; rather, he is called upon to answer for it on earth. Human gestures, human representations and imaginings, far from being abolished, are so many methods whereby man can be led to typify and exemplify in himself (*tamaththul*) a celestial existence. For example, if a celestial Person is represented by a particular gesture, or word, or phase of the ritual, then to observe these is already to exist in the manner of the transcendent Person. It is for this reason that the initiate must undertake to be faithful to these observances, at least in the Fatimid tradition of Ismailism.[123] In doing so, he is also affirming in his person the potential Paradise or Earth of Paradise, this Earth on which he is able to pasture the Ram that is offered up in sacrifice at the culminating point of a human life.

Consequently, what is perceived by mental vision on the horizon to which it reaches out are essentially personal Figures or else the relationships between them, relationships that communicate their archetypal value to the earthly relationships which are patterned on them. By way of example, let us consider the principle aspects of the Islamic Ritual. Mental vision perceives the Temple (*masjad*) as the figure of the Imam or of some superior dignity (*ḥujjah, dāʿī*).[124] The fifteen words of the Call to Prayer are "heard" as being, first, the Person of the Annunciator's spiritual heir (*waṣī, asās*), then the Persons of the six Imams of the first heptad (*mutimmah*), then the Persons of the seven Imams of the second heptad

122 P. Casanova, 'La Doctrine secrète des Fātimides d'Egypte', in *Bulletin de l'Institut français d'archéologie orientale*, vol. XVIII (Cairo, 1921), p. 148 n. 2.
123 Cf. the text of ibid., p. 152, and Strothmann, *Texte* Iḍāḥ 12.
124 Cf. Dailamī, op. cit., p. 43, who, in spite of his ardent hostility, works on sources at first hand and quotes from them frequently. He refers here (l.11) to the *Taʾwīl al-Sharīʿah* which he attributes to al-Muʿizz, the fourth Fatimid Imam (died 365/975); it has also been attributed to Abū Yaʿqūb al-Sijistānī (ibid., p. 118), and to Qāḍī Nuʿmān (Ivanow, *Guide*, no. 70).

(*khalīfah*[125]), and lastly the Person of the Imam of the Resurrection (*Qā'-im*). The four words of the *bismillah* are recited and understood as being the two supreme Archangels (*Sābiq* and *Tālī*) and the two dignitaries who typify them on earth (*Nāṭiq* and *Asās*). The seven letters of the same formula signify the six *Nāṭiq* of the six Periods of a Cycle, of which the *Qā'im* is the seventh. The *ablution* that precedes the Prayer is the return to Knowledge of the Imam; the water is the knowledge of Gnosis[126] which purifies one from all compromise with the literalists and the profane (*Ẓāhirī*). Each gesture of the ablution (touching the water to head, hands, nostrils and mouth) is a reference to one of the Persons in the esoteric hierarchy or else to his celestial Archetype. Similarly, each gesture, pronouncement and attitude of the ritual Prayer (*Ṣalāh*) refers to one of these Persons. The ritual Prayer, in particular, presented a rich hermeneutical potential.[127] Notably, the five "canonical Hours" represent the first two archangelic hypostases and the first three esoteric dignitaries of a Period (*Nāṭiq*, *Waṣī*, *Imām*). In the same way, in the Nuṣayrī ritual, recitation of the Names of the Five Persons of the Prayer (*ashkhāṣ al-Ṣalāh*[128]) is in itself a fulfilment of all the prescriptions, ablutions and recommendations attached to the celebration of the Prayer.

With regard to the ritual *fast*, we have already seen that it consists in observing the discipline of the arcane, "in keeping the secret of your Imam", in not surrendering anything imprudently to enemies and to the profane. *Almsgiving* (*zakāh*) is the communication of gnosis to him who is worthy of it, the initiatory relationship which is reproduced from the top to the bottom level of the mystical hierarchy[129] (the same ritual "alms-giving" is mentioned in the festivals of the Philosophers by the Brothers of Purity). The idea of almsgiving is linked with that of *pilgrimage* (*ḥajj*), because pilgrimage is the *exegesis* or *ta'wīl* par *excellence*, the *exodus* whereby the initiate gradually abandons the enslavement of primitive, literal beliefs, and progresses from the stage of *Mustajīb* to that of *Ḥujjah*.[130] Thus, there is a series of *Qiyāmāt* or resurrections, proceeding from a limited-Heaven

125 On this differentiation, see Ivanow, *Studies in Early Persian Ismailism*, The Ismaili Society Series A, no. 3 (Leiden, 1948), pp. 39–40.
126 Dailamī, op. cit., p. 44, "*al-'ilm al-ḥaqīqī*", cf. *Kalāmi Pīr*, p. 94 of the text, l. 17 ff.
127 Dailamī, op. cit., p. 45.
128 Cf. R. Dussaud, op. cit., pp. 68 ff. (ashkhāṣ al-Ṣalāt).
129 The theme of *Ta'wīl al-zakāt*, the work of the Yemeni Dā'i Ja'far b. Manṣūr al-Yaman (fourth/tenth century); cf. Ivanow, *Guide*, no. 40.
130 *Kalāmi Pīr*, p. 96 of the text.

(*maḥdūd*) to a Heaven-limit (*ḥadd*), which is "limited" in its turn by a new "limit" that must be crossed, in a perspective which extends beyond the very "limits" themselves of the terrestrial hierarchy. To enter the *da'wah* is equivalent to the pilgrim of Mecca entering the sacred and forbidden territory (*ḥaram*), which in this case is the Hallowed Place of Gnosis and Wisdom.[131] The *prayer for the dead* is the reviving, as though with the breath of Jesus, of a disciple whose spirit of truth (*rūḥ ḥaqīqah*) has been slain by a false doctrine.[132] The same goes for all the prescriptions of the Law: each one of them (marriage, divorce and so on) is "led back" by *ta'wīl* to the level of its true and superior significance.

It is on this superior level, also, that Ismaili ecumenism becomes intelligible. There could be no conflict between the celestial Archetypes, nor between the earthly symbols which represent them. That is why Abū Ya'qūb Sijistānī, for example,[133] is able to detect, in the symbol of the Cross, the "crossing" of the negative and positive phases of the Islamic Attestation of Faith (Non Deus nisi Deus). In the same symbol, too, the invisible celestial hierarchy and the terrestrial hierarchy "cross" in the persons of the two supreme Archangels (*Sābiq* and *Tālī*) and of their earthly typifications (*Nāṭiq* and *Aṣās*), who are represented respectively by the four branches of the Cross and also by the four words of the Attestation of the Unique. He is thus able to attribute an equal inner necessity to both symbols.

In this transcendent concordance—and the history of religions would have difficulty in finding an analogous attestation of it in the field of positive letters—is manifest the same sense of a *level of historical permanence* as that which is presupposed, as we saw, by the composition of a liturgical Cycle whose festivals are constituted by the actual recurrence of the celestial, spiritual Persons whom they typify. Likewise, the whole calendar is interpreted in this sense, and each of its moments is marked by the appearance of *its* Person. It is to be noted that it is a question not of the day or month being "consecrated to" a certain celestial patron, but strictly

131 Dailamī, op cit., pp. 46–47.
132 *Kalāmi Pīr*, p. 97 of the text.
133 *Kitāb al-Yanābī'* (The Book of Sources), Yanbū' 31 and 32, translated in my *Trilogie ismaélienne*, Bibliothèque Iranienne, vol. 9 (Tehran/Paris, Adrien-Maisonneuve, 1961), pp. 97–98 and 100–101. Cf. my article 'L'Ismaélisme et le symbole de la Croix' in *La Table Ronde*, no. 120 (Dec. 1957), pp. 122–134.

of exemplification. The Nuṣayrī Ritual[134] tells of the Prophet's rebuke to his companions who said Ramaḍān[135] was over: "Ramaḍān neither goes nor comes; it has no double (i.e. it is a unique archetype). To be sure, the *month* of Ramaḍān goes away and comes back (i.e. is the *repetition* of this Archetype), but Ramaḍān itself neither goes away nor comes back. Do not then say that Ramaḍān is over. In God's name! you do not know what Ramaḍān is. Say that the *month* of Ramaḍān is over."[136] In the case of what we called earlier the "day of the Angel", the *day* passes, but the Angel remains.

Who, then, is Ramaḍān? The same Nuṣayrī ritual tells us, in the course of the answers given to questions concerned with the *Persons* of the months and days and with their *Names*. Just as the first Person inaugurates the liturgical Cycle of the Brothers of Purity, Ramaḍān inaugurates the year in the person of ʻAbdallah ibn ʻAbd al-Muṭallib, father of the Prophet Muḥammad or prophet-Annunciator (*Nāṭiq*) of the sixth Period.[137] Since this is the "month" in which the revealed Book "descended" to earth, one can indeed see how its Person is the "father" of him who *annunciated* the new religion. Furthermore, each of the thirty days and each of the thirty nights of this month also have their person-archetype: thirty masculine personages for the days, and thirty feminine personages for the nights.[138] Likewise, every other month *is* a Person of sacred history. We thus perceive how excellent an exercise in speculative meditation it would be to effect the transposition, or *ta'wīl*, of each singular fact, in order to attain to the mental vision of the archetype.[139]

Of all the nights of Ramaḍān, there is one, called *Laylat al-Qadr*, the "Night of Destiny", which has a special dignity. During this night, the Koranic revelation is consummated, and for this very reason no one is

134 *Majmūʻ al-Aʻyād*, recently edited by R. Strothmann, *Festkalender der Nuṣairier* (Berlin, 1944–1948).
135 *Ramaḍān* in Arabic (with the emphatic ḍ). The Persian pronunciation is Ramazān.
136 Ibid., pp. 15–16.
137 Ibid., p. 12.
138 Ashkhāṣ ayyām (——layālī) Ramaḍān, ibid., pp. 13–14.
139 In the same way, meditation could attach itself to each of the divine Names in the person of their respective Angel, or to each letter of the Arabic alphabet as indicative of a cosmic force, visualized in the person of the Angel who is in charge of it (the names of the Angels are obtained by a combination of these letters furnished with the suffix *ʼīl* = *el*). This subject has inspired the composition of what one might call "breviaries of ecstasy" (e.g. the *Awrād ghawthīyah* by Shāh Muḥammad Ghawth, shaṭṭārī, Indian Sufism, sixteenth century).

rash enough to assign a place to it among all the nights in the month. By means of *ta'wīl*, this Night of Revelation becomes a Night of Transfiguration. It is said[140] that if you stay awake till dawn, you will have a vision of the Prophet and all his *ḥudūd* filling, in their rank of Glorified Ones, the Temple of the Resurrector,[141] and any wish you make within yourself at that moment is already granted. The asseveration is only apparently paradoxical; it concerns all those who are "actualized" in this Temple, and it signifies that after the Resurrection (*Qiyāmah*) which overthrows the tyranny of the Law (*Sharī'ah*), thought and imagination precede and *suscitate* the object that then becomes their symbol (because they already typify it within themselves), and do not merely track symbols down, as happens in the present human condition.

Even though one hesitates to assign a place to this night in the series of Nights in the month, because it surpasses them all by so much, the person-archetype of the night, who manifests this very transcendence, is clearly recognized. The Night of Destiny is the Prophet's daughter, mother of the holy Imams: "It is the typification of our suzeraine, Fāṭimah."[142] The Koranic text says: "The Night of Destiny is worth more than a thousand months. On this Night, the Angels and the Spirit come down to earth . . . Peace accompanies this Night until the dawn" (97:3–5). According to the Ismaili exegesis, each month is in fact a *ḥujjah*—that is, the dignitary who is the *Threshold* of Mercy and Knowledge, through whom one attains to the hidden essence and name of the Imam. Etymologically, he is "the Proof, the Sign", the Imam's visible double, who may receive in his name the oath of allegiance.[143] Fāṭimah was the *ḥujjah* of the Prophet's *Waṣī*, the foundation and principle of the Imamate. Therefore it is true that on this Night, in her person, the Angels and the Spirit—that is to say the entire line of Imams issuing from her and typifying on earth the angelic ministry —descend to earth. That is why it is true to say that "peace accompanies

140 Strothmann, *Texte* II, 3, pp. 20–21 of the text.

141 Cf. note 66.

142 Mathal 'alā mawlātinā Fāṭimah, *Texte* XII, 7, pp. 114–115.

143 This is one of the particulars whose great variations should be noted—variations extending from Fatimid Ismailism (in which *ḥujjah* was something like an actual dignitary, a specific office), to the reformed Nizārī Ismailism, which inclines to the religion of personal salvation. Cf. W. Ivanow, *Studies* (see note 125), pp. 40–44. The *ḥujjah* could even be a woman, a child, or even a book; cf. *Kalāmi Pīr*, p. XLV, and the concentrated, obscure little treatise *On the Recognition of the Imam* (Fāṣl dar Bayān-i Shanākht-i Imām), translated from the Persian by W. Ivanow, The Ismaili Society Series B, no. 4 (1947).

this Night until the dawn", meaning until the Manifestation of the *Qā'im*, the dawning of the new Cycle of Unveiling.

We now know, thanks to L. Massignon, a Nuṣayrī canticle (*qaṣīdah*) of extraordinary spirituality, in which Fāṭimah is glorified as being Initiation in person. Through her, the divine principle manifested in her father is manifested afresh in her sons. She unites feminine and masculine in herself: she is *al-Zahrā'* (She who dazzles with whiteness), and she is *Fāṭir* (in the masculine), Fāṭimah—Creator, or rather, she who "makes visible" the human form in which the divine is manifested through the Cycles.[144]

Because of the encounter to which the Ismaili exegesis of individual *eschatology* "leads back", this mental vision of Person-archetypes affects every existence in the profoundest depths of its being. In this sense, eschatology is no more than the goal, the culminating point of the exegesis of the Ritual. We can recall only one version here, a version which extends the visions of a Persian proto-Ismaili text (still in use today among the Ismailis of Pamir), and in which the soul is represented as respiralling through the levels of the cosmos to reach the level of Salmān and become the "Salmān of the microcosm".[145] As we have already seen, Salmān the Persian (*Salmān Farsī*), or Salmān the Pure (*Salmān Pāk*), is the Stranger, the Exile from afar, regarded by a long tradition as the Prophet's initiator-companion, who helped him become aware of the "exemplary cases of conscience" of previous prophets.[146] His person is the earthly typification both of the Angel Gabriel as the Angel of Revelation, and of the Angel or Spirit of exegesis. He is this Angel's earthly angel, performing, close to him whose companion he is, the angelic ministry of exegesis or *ta'wīl*. As the Prophet manifests the Law, *sharī'ah*, so he manifests the gnostic truth

144 Cf. L. Massignon, 'Der gnostische Kult der Fāṭima im schiitischen Islam', *Opera minora*, vol. I (Beirut, 1963), pp. 514–522. The name *Fāṭimah*, the numerical value of whose letters in the order of the *abjad* (290) is the same as that of the letters of the name Maryam, Jesus' mother, signals a recurrence which led L. Massignon (p. 521) to the problem of the reciprocal relations between the two figures. Another Night typifies Fāṭimah as the ḥujjah of the Imam: the first Night of the month of Rajab, which comes seventh in the order of the months (Strothmann, *Texte* II, p. 28). Similarly, the day and the night of the mid-sha'bān are respectively the exemplification of the Annunciator of the *Ẓāhir* (τα ἔξω, the Koran and the Law), and of the Waṣī, keeper of the ta'wīl (*bāṭin*, τα εἴσω, ibid., II, 8, p. 29).

145 A term employed in the Persian proto-Ismaili treatise *Umm al-Kitāb*; cf. my 'Livre du Glorieux', (*supra*, ch. II, n. 3) p. 71.

146 Massignon, *Salmān Pāk*, p. 31.

(*ḥaqīqah*) of the Imam; this is the meaning of the remark, attributed to the Imam: "Salmān proceeds from me, and I from Salmān."[147]

There are thus two aspects to Salmān the Pure: on the one hand he is seen as *ḥujjah* of the Imam in his eternal essence at the start of the Muhammadan Period, and on the other as signifying the status which the soul is invited to assume at the end of its "pilgrimage". In the merging of these two aspects, the intuition, like a flash of lightning, perceives who may be the person-archetype of the Soul that unfolds, and in which is unfolded, this new way of being and knowing that we have seen characterized as the disclosure of the angelic Form, whose peculiar function it is to typify in itself the celestial existences, and by this perfect symbolization to exist in a state in which its wishes are totally fulfilled.

The exemplary role played by Salmān with regard to the Prophet is repeated in the case of each initiate. It is actually said that "Salmān is one of the gates of Paradise". Indeed, "Salmān is the soul" (or the life, *jān*) of Paradise. And the scope of the mental vision is affirmed in the following remark: "If the soul of Paradise is a human being, then certainly the Person of Paradise (*shakhṣ-i Bihisht*) is by the same token a human being."[148] What, then, are this soul and this Person of Paradise?

Paradise as *Qiyāmah* (resurrection)—regarded either as being in the state of potentiality which is created here and now by the knowledge of gnosis (*ḥaqīqah*), or as being in its state of actuality beyond the limits of our world and our Cycle—is the mode of being which is spoken of in a Koranic verse: "The abode of the future world is the Living" (29:64). And the whole of this abode is the kingdom of the angelic substances (*rūḥānīyāt*), where, it is said, "the stones and the clods of earth will be granted the gift of speech". Now, as there is no being other than man that is gifted with the Annunciatory Word, this means that the future world possesses the human Form;[149] it means that at its every level the archetype of the Angelos-Anthropos is reproduced, and that all representations (minerals, plants, animals, landscapes) are spiritual forms projected by spiritual beings (*rūḥānīyāt*) and typifying, each in its own fashion, that same archetype in its various modes of being and knowing. The idea of typification

147 *Shanākht-i Imām* (see note 143), pp. 33, 42–44.

148 Ibid., p. 33, and *Haft-Bābi Bābā Sayyid-nā*, pp. 30–31, in *Two Early Ismaili Treatises*, Persian text . . . by W. Ivanow, Islamic Research Association, no. 2 (Bombay, 1933).

149 *Kalāmi Pīr*, p. 91 of the text, and *Haft-Bāb*, pp. 27–28.

(*tamaththul*) calls for an entire study to itself. For example,[150] it is said that for those who are admitted to this mode of vision, the *vestigium* of the divine Emanation is perceived in each atom of the terrestrial and celestial world (*mulk u malakūt*); and that when the direct perception (*mushāhadah*) of the Lights of the Essence of the Principle is typified or hypostasized (*mutamaththal*) in this way, it necessarily assumes "the most lovely of forms" (this, according to *ta'wīl*, is what is signified by the houris of Paradise). However, this also presupposes that the gnostic's entire person (*'ārif*) is typified according to this form in the mode of perfect union (*yakānagī*), since the contemplation of gnosis (*mushāhadah-'i dānish*) becomes, for the person contemplating, the Self of his own being (*'ayn dhāt-i ān shakhṣ*).

Thus, the mental vision of the Person-archetype accompanies and presupposes the typification of this Person in the person of the initiate. Hence we have a dialectic, each of whose stages elucidates the other, and whose few texts, scattered and obscure, present us with our problem and invite us to coordinate the elements of the vision which resolves it. The Lord, that is to say the eternal Imam in his essence, is epiphanized in the human Form.[151] All figures (Throne, *Kursī*, Tablet, Pen), as well as Paradise and Hell, are typified in human Persons; as we saw, the supreme Archangels also possess, in a pre-eminent sense, human Form,[152] and are exemplified on earth by the members of the esoteric community. To realize, in an ascending scale, these figures within oneself is to develop *angelhood*,[153] to attain to the level of the Angel (*martaba-yi firishtah*). In order to do this, one must see the Angel, that is to say, one must *see* his possible typification on earth. To follow him is to ascend the series of the eight *Qiyāmah* (the course of the Ritual). "If you wish to contemplate the Person of Paradise (*shakhṣ-i Bihisht*), you must contemplate the *person* who calls creatures to God and to divinity." This call, reproduced from Heaven to Heaven and from level to level of the mystic hierarchy, is what is meant by Salmān as "soul of Paradise" and "Person of Paradise".

We are indeed led even further and told that, so long as we do not thus grasp all reality in its personification and individuation, we cannot liberate

150 *Kalāmi Pīr*, p. 106 of the text.
151 *Haft-Bāb*, pp. 28–29.
152 Cf. note 23; *Kalāmi Pīr*, p. 92 of the text, l. 10 ff.; *Shanākht-i Imām*, p. 47 (where the use of the word *shakhṣ* is to be emphasized).
153 *Haft-Bāb*, p. 29, and *Kalāmi Pīr*, p. 92.

ourselves from vain representations. As this personification is accomplished by means of the growth of the spiritual or angelic person of the initiate, the latter can only see the Person of Paradise—and the Person of Paradise can only reveal himself as or in Person (that is, the initiate can only find Paradise in this Person)—if Paradise (Resurrection, Gnosis, Child of eternity) exists already in the initiate's own person. This leads to the extraordinary formula: "In order to punish the black stone, one will make a second black stone. In order to reward the white stone, one will make it into the person of Salmān, so that it may exist according to the model it has chosen for itself."[154] In other words, Salmān is the "Person of Paradise", and it is therefore up to the initiate to attain to the level of Salmān, and become the "Salmān of the microcosm".

Salmān's archetypal role is admirably illustrated in a conversation between the fifth Imam, Muḥammad al-Bāqir, and his confidant Jābir ibn Zayd al-Ju'fī,[155] from which we learn that Jābir can also become a Manifestation of Salmān, and thereby can also manifest, in his person, the Imam. Externally, Salmān resembles a closed door (*bāb*). His inner being (*bāṭin*) is the light of the Veil which is called "the Compassionate Merciful One". "When your mental vision is veiled to your inferior self, your spiritual person becomes visible in the brilliance of its Light". To model oneself on Salmān, support and vessel of this Light of the Imam, is to this extent to be his manifestation;[156] it is to attain to the person of Salmān. This latter, as "Person of Paradise", signifies the person of the Angel of which Naṣīruddīn Ṭūsī speaks elsewhere; and he becomes for all eternities the eternal Companion of the soul, when the soul, through its struggle to attain gnosis, "has revived its body"—that is, when it has united the corporeal with the spiritual, transmuting it by an influx of spirituality.[157]

There is thus something extraordinary about the remark that it is not Salmān who desires Paradise, but Paradise that desires the person of Salmān,[158] and that this happens at the Five liturgical hours of the Ritual.

154 *Haft-Bāb*, p. 31.
155 Not to be confused with Jābir ibn Ḥayyān; cf. the account of this conversation given in the *Zahr al-Ma'ānī* by Idrīs 'Imāduddīn, in W. Ivanow, *Rise of the Fatimids*, p. 254.
156 Cf. ibid., p. 63 of the Arabic text, l. 1 ff.
157 A major interest in this alchemy is elaborated in Rawḍatu't-Taslīm, taṣawwur XXI, p. 65. (See n. 41 *supra*).
158 *Kalāmi Pīr*, p. 107 of the text; cf. *Nafas al-Raḥmān*, a modern hagiography that we owe to Ḥusain ibn Muḥi Taqī Tabarsī Nūrī (lith. Tehran, 1285), chap. VIII.

The point is that in the absence of the archetypal person of Salmān there is no Paradise, because he is its Person and its Form. All the *Ḥudūd* of the potential Paradise are merely the shadows of the celestial *ḥudūd*. Through an Operation, identical to that of alchemy, which reveals the *bāṭin* (that which is hidden) of natural bodies, the *ta'wīl* of the Ritual aims at arousing (resuscitating) the inner, angelic, spiritual person, *hidden* behind the mask of the terrestrial personality, the Temple of Light hidden behind the Temple of the material body. This educative, "exegetic" role belongs to Salmān as Angel-hermeneut, the angel of the Exodus out of the earthly homeland of the letter. The potential Paradise in the heart of the "ḥadd" *desires*, with each time and gesture of the Ritual, the Person of the actual Paradise who is a new Salmān. To draw back the veil of the *terrestrial self* so that the Person, or primordial celestial individuality, may appear, is to typify (as in the conversation with the Imam al-Bāqir) the person of Salmān the archetype—just as the Glorious One, being likewise modelled on his Person, is the archetype for Jābir the alchemist,[159] and as each *Sābiq* in his turn is the archetype for his follower (*Tālī*), each "limit" (*ḥadd*) for that which it defines (*maḥdūd*) and attracts, and as in mysticism the Beloved is for the Lover. It is the person of the Angel who calls the soul to its Paradise by making it dwell in itself, and who accompanies it forever; for what *you see* is what your person manifests, or rather, what manifests itself *through* your person (according to al-Bāqir, the light of the Imam), not what your person might invent or create and which would thus be nothing but its illusion.

This angelomorphosis of vision and mode of being abolishes and by-passes the philosophical problem posed by viewing the angel of angelology as a "category", and by regarding its concretization as an illegitimate application of pure concept to experience, and hence as possessing only the appearance of reality. We are concerned here with more than a conceptual category or, rather, the concept already indicates a spiritual substance (*jawhar laṭīf, rūḥānī*), a person that it represents only momentarily (the same applies to the concepts of the times and gestures of the Ritual). Once its colourless generality is done away with, the concept allows the Person, of whom it was no more than a purely logical symbol, to come forth. This is not a mental operation whereby certain "universals"

159 Cf. my 'Livre du Glorieux de Jābir ibn Hayyān' (*supra*, ch. II, n. 3), § 6.

are hypostasized. On the contrary, a personal Individuality, anterior and transcendent, was momentarily hidden by this abstract universal appearance. The angelic form of knowledge leads to direct intuition of the singular and the personal, to the thought which envisions and to the vision which thinks individual archetypes. Just as humanity is only realized in persons (*mushakhkhaṣ*), and Divinity is only revealed in its archangelic and angelic hypostases, all reality is true (*ḥaqq al-ḥaqq*) only in so far as it expresses, heralds and reflects a hypostasis possessing the human Form; for it is by means of the mode of being and knowing of this Form that the Angel is made manifest; and it is through this same mode that it conducts this reality and this nature to its resurrection by reconstructing it in symbols.

These, broadly outlined, are the perspectives of *ta'wīl* which open onto the new dimension, one that transfigures the Ritual into an inner liturgy. This is trans-figuration in the literal sense of the word, for it aims at discovering the Figures of light who rule over times and gestures, just as the text of the Book, or the texts of Nature and of philosophical reason, lead to the same "trans-appearance". The vision of and nostalgia for this mesocosm, this universe peopled by an infinite multitude of angelic hypostases of light, was the support and nourishment of the Ismaili *da'wah*. To propose to the man called upon to join the esoteric community that his raison d'être was to typify on earth these existences of light was perhaps a wild dream, and a defiance of the laws of exoteric everyday life; only the inner man can bear witness to such a correspondence, visible only to those whose souls "trans-appear" to each other, but ridiculous in the eyes of the profane. It is the total transformation of existence into a liturgy. In the correspondence between the celestial hierarchies and all the hierarchs of the mystical Earth, from the greatest to the most humble, who fill the Temple of the Imamate, is to be found something of the sentiment of the Byzantine liturgy: ἡμεῖς τὰ Χερουβὶμ μυστικῶς εἰκνίζοντες.

Because, moreover, it was a question of the liturgical mystery of existence, the Ismaili Order could not break the discipline of the arcane during a Cycle of occultation. One does not expose the subtle, gentle light of the angelic world to the crude and glaring day of ready-made facts and social norms. It is not through addressing the multitude that one calls human beings to the "potential Paradise" of the esoteric community. Far from it: if the Call is thus betrayed in the false light of day, it provides men with the surest means whereby to aggravate their earthly Hell, for then the image of Paradise is bound to be a provocation, stimulating their fury of perversion and mockery. If, that is, they do not find it boring in the extreme, for this image is indeed the image of a *Paradise lost.* The history of Ismailism may be no more than one long paradox: it was harder for it to survive its triumphs than to recover from its setbacks. More than once, Ismaili writers have captured the image of their great and noble dream in striking terms. They were perfectly aware of its opposition to the law which is the curse of this world, the urge to dominate, the ambition and vanity of power which makes the soul the veritable habitation of Hell and which are truly the "punishment of the black stone by the black stone". The famous eleventh-century Iranian Ismaili, Nāṣir-i Khusraw, in his Persian translation of a Koranic verse (82:19) to which he gives an unexpected force, prefigures in this way the future Reign of the Spirit: "There will come a day when no soul will have command over any other soul, and on that day, yes, the Order will belong to God."[160]

Tehran, June 25, 1950

160 Cf. *Khwān al-Ikhwān* (The Table of the Brothers), ed. Yahyā al-Khashshāb (Cairo, 1940), p. 245; cf. also *Jāmi' al-Ḥikmatayn*, § 117 of my edition (note 7). Nāṣir-i Khusraw's entire book, entitled *Kitāb Wajh-i Dīn*, ed. Kaviānī (Berlin, 1925), is a long exercise in *ta'wīl*, leading from the external appearances to the true and secret face of the ritual prescriptions and religious traditions.

4

The Configuration of the Temple of the Ka'bah as The Secret of the Spiritual Life

according to the work of Qāḍī Sa'īd Qummī (1103/1691)

1. The Spiritual Forms

The themes that we ponder together in *Eranos* from year to year have the virtue of inducing in us, during the preceding months, a state of premeditation which is peculiarly favourable to lucid reaction. It was in this manner, and with regard to this year's theme, that I found myself reacting over the winter to two works on Balzac which had just come out. For, in their respective interpretations of the work of our great novelist, these two books form a contrast as striking as it is instructive for what we are about to discuss.

The first of these works is meant to be addressed to "people who are human enough not to limit their attention to literature alone"; yet it then presents us with a Balzac so dependent on nineteenth-century society that he occupies some quite minor position in it, like that of a clerk, and his society could very well have done without him. Because of his bias, the interpreter keeps us on the ground, or, more accurately, he refuses to rise, in dealing with Balzac's work, higher than the ground floor of the "Studies of Manners" where the archives are stored. There is no question of going up to the first floor, the floor of the "Philosophical Studies", "where one can discover a hidden order of things", let alone of going up to the second floor, that of the "Analytical Studies", where it is possible to "meditate on natural principles, and to see in what ways societies fall away from or approach the eternal laws of truth and goodness." It would be hard not to define this mutilating interpretation as counter-sense, because—to go no further—it contradicts Balzac's express statements.

By contrast, the second interpreter addresses himself to "people who are too human not to have been disheartened by the world", that is to say, by what is offered to them by sociology, demography and the economy; and if he leads us into the "Human comedy" as into a walled town, it is because "this walled town opens onto Heaven". It is this, and this alone, which is in accordance with Balzac's statements, when he foresaw that some people, faced with his painstaking collection and depiction of facts as facts, would imagine that he belonged to the school of the sensualists or the materialists. This is so far from being the case that he refutes such a school vigorously, adding: "I do not share the belief in the indefinite progress of societies. I believe in the progress of man over himself. Those who perceive in me an intention to consider man as a finite creature are therefore strangely deluded."

Here Balzac calls to witness his mystical masterpiece, *Seraphita*—"the actualization of the doctrine of the Christian Buddha", that is, of Swedenborg—as a sufficient response to all attempts to diminish the meaning of his work. In short, for the first interpreter Balzac is a prisoner of nineteenth-century society. He was created by it, and is therefore contingent and superfluous. For the second interpreter Balzac is the creator, he who "embraces within his work the society of the nineteenth century as well as that of other centuries. Society is his creation. It cannot do without him."[1]

If my reaction to this contrast has led me to stress it here, it is because it appears to me typical and exemplary, in the sense that it is characteristic of the situation we face when we try to understand what is implied by the ability to outline a spiritual world, to grasp, in a form and a figure, a world which is not within the scope of sensory perception. Indeed, for several generations Western man has exercised inexhaustible ingenuity in enclosing himself within his experience of this earthly world, carefully shutting off all exits through which he might leave it, even though it means lamenting his solitude and the absurdity of his condition. At the same time he persistently refuses to recognize that it is his own philosophies which have reduced him to this state. He means to stay on the ground floor, and systematically ignore the fact that there are, or might be, upper storeys.

Religious fact in itself postulates the existence of these upper storeys—

1 The first interpretation (the one which refuses to ascend any higher than the ground floor) is by André Wurmser, *La Comédie inhumaine*. The second is that of Maurice Bardèche, *Une lecture de Balzac*. For the terms in which the contrast is rendered, see Philippe Sénart's review of the two works in 'Combat' (Thursday, February 4, 1965), p. 9.

they are implicit in it. We are not less aware of the current peremptory assertion that the scientific study of religious fact cannot accept any appeal to a Revelation or any recourse to the intervention of a transcendent power. Obviously, it is impossible to discover in a fact something which one has started by denying it possesses. Considerable ingenuity has been employed in converting the *interpretation* of facts into established *fact*. For example, we have passed from evolution as an interpretation of a collection of facts to "the fact of evolution" (neglecting to note that the real *fact* was evolutionism). In turn, equal ingenuity has been employed in converting a *fact* into an *interpretation*, in order to reduce the original phenomenon (the *Urphänomen*) to certain elementary facts which are supposed to explain it. Religious fact, for example spiritual fact, is "explained" sociologically by the conditions of production and consumption, or psychologically by reference to the misfortunes of infancy and childhood, lived as a series of catastrophes. What is striking about our time is that so many people accept these explanations without noticing their ludicrous inadequacy as regards the object being explained. From the start, in effect, we are presented with unbalanced and atrociously mutilated forms, because our fundamentally agnostic science denies us recourse to a suprasensible dimension which alone makes it possible to perceive the integrality of a form. In the same way, the visible dimension of a being, its terrestrial biography, only ever reveals an infinitesimal part of its potentialities. We can speak of the configurative action of the Spirit, of form as a task to be accomplished by the Spirit (which is our theme in *Eranos*), with full meaning only if we are in possession of a space into which we can project the totality of this form. Such a space was known to the science of religions and to traditional theologies as the eschatological dimension, in which the spring of the arch is achieved—a spring which will never be ours so long as we remain on this side of our "scientific" proof.

In this connection, it is not mere chance that a text by Balzac should represent Swedenborg as the "Christian Buddha".[2] My essay on comparative spiritual hermeneutics brought out a remarkable convergence between Swedenborg's hermeneutics and the hermeneutics practised in Ismaili gnosis. This convergence occurred with regard to the necessity of there

2 Cf. my 'Herméneutique spirituelle comparée', in *Face de Dieu, face de l'homme* (Paris, Fayard, 1984): D. T. Suzuki's statement accords literally with Balzac's feeling about Swedenborg.

being an intermediary world between the sensible and intelligible worlds, a world I designate as the *mundus imaginalis*, the kingdom of subtle bodies, the "eighth clime", the limit "where spirit takes on body and where the body is spiritualized" (the kingdom of the *Geistleiblichkeit*).[3] In the absence of this world, the idea of subsistent spiritual Forms would be unthinkable. Yet prevailing opinion, philosophical or profane, maintains that what is spiritual does not possess form. Form is always that which confers a figure on matter, in the sense of "physical" matter.

In contrast to this, our first affirmation in connection with our present task must be the existence of spiritual Forms which subsist as such. This gives full weight to the thesis correctly propounded by a Swedenborgian thinker in the following terms:

"Here is the point in which philosophers and Christians have made the mistake, fatal not only to all *true* knowledge, but to *all* knowledge of spirit. It has generally been assumed that the only way to arrive at a true idea of spirit was to regard it as the opposite of matter in every respect. They reason in this way: Matter has form, therefore spirit has none. Matter has substance, therefore spirit has none. In this way they deny to spirit all possible modes of existence. The Christian stops here, and ends by simply affirming its existence, but denies that we can know anything more about it. But many push this destructive logic a step further, and deny the existence of spirit altogether. And this is the logical result, for denial can never end in anything but negation and nothing. This is inevitable; and the Christian escapes this conclusion only by stopping before he reaches it. We must admit that there is a spiritual substance, and that this substance has form, or we must deny the existence of spirit altogether. No other conclusion is possible."[4]

What emerges from the affirmation of such an unambiguous pneumatological thesis is the need for a space which, while remaining space, is not the space of the sensible universe—that is to say, of the universe identified by Cartesian dualists with spatial extension. Here we should bear in mind

3 On this theme, see my work *Corps spirituel et Terre céleste: de l'Iran mazdéen a l'Iran shī'ite*, 2nd edn (Paris, Buchet/Chastel, 1979); tr. N. Pearson, *Spiritual Body and Celestial Earth: from Mazdean Iran to Shi'ite Iran*, Bollingen Series XCI:2 (Princeton University Press, 1977). (*Translator's note*: this translation is not from the 2nd edition referred to by Corbin; however, this does not affect the work itself).

4 Chauncey Giles, *The Nature of Spirit and of Man as a Spiritual Being* (James Speirs, London, 1871), p. 6.

the thesis that Swedenborg reiterated so frequently in his vast work: in the spiritual world, as in the material world, there are spaces, even though nothing is evaluated there according to them. Everything is assessed according to states, "and as a result the spaces there cannot be measured as they are measured in the world; they are viewed in and according to the state of the interiors" (of the *internals*, rather).[5] In other words, spaces which are measured by inner states presuppose, essentially, a qualitative or discontinuous space of which each inner state is itself the measure, as opposed to a space which is quantitative, continuous, homogeneous, and measurable in constant measures. Such a space is an existential space, whose relationship to physico-mathematical space is analogous to the relationship of exitential time to the historical time of chronology.

Highly instructive, also, are the changes in the feeling for and expression of space in the figurative arts of Western man.[6] The problem was how to suggest the third dimension that is lacking in a plane surface. The solution involves recourse to a certain number of subterfuges which, as such, reveal the conscious or unconscious aspirations of those who employ them, and acquire thereby the value of "symbolic forms". These forms symbolize different things, the difference being perceived first of all in their arrangement according either to the laws of the *perspectiva naturalis*, codified by Euclid, or to those of the *perspectiva artificialis* of the Italian Renaissance. Euclidian optics, on the one hand, establishes a space which is discontinuous, in the sense that each region differs qualitatively from the other, deriving its position and qualification from the being which occupies it in its own right. An idea of this can be gleaned from the representtion of landscape in some great Roman fresco or Pompeiian decorative fragment, which gives us a sense of the great mural painting of Greece.[7] Each section of space has its own horizon, and the detail depicted there is *real*, as depicted, *for* that horizon. (In the physics corresponding to this, we have the concept of "natural place" as essential to all qualitative space, and which as such links up with the concept of "existential place". Let us recall the division of levels in the final scene of the second part of Faust: the "existential place" of *pater extaticus* and that of *pater profundus*; for it is a

5 Swedenborg, *De Caelo et ejus mirabilibus* . . . , art. 198.
6 See the study by Mme Liliane Brion-Guerry, 'L'Évolution générale de l'expression de l'espace dans la peinture occidental', in *Sciences de l'Art*, Annales de l'Institut d'esthétique et des sciences de l'art (Paris, 1964), pp. 47–71.
7 Ibid., mainly pp. 50 ff. and plate 1 (Pompeiian painting).

question of the place being *situated* by the inner state, the *internal*, the place where the being is "in its Truth", as it could not be *elsewhere*).

On the other hand, *perspectiva artificialis* presupposes a whole preliminary effort to unify space, culminating in a unified and homogeneous universe. The classical, central perspective is obtained at the price of this systematic optical unity. What is disturbing is that the way now lies open to all the illusions of the Baroque, to the science and ingenuity of *trompe l'oeil*. Disturbing, because if we set the forms of expression of space side by side with the secret sense of space corresponding to them, and expressible in pictorial form as well as in mental representation or visionary figuration, we have a comparison which begs a new question. Is not the position of the spiritual hermeneut, whose interpretation of Scriptural verses or of the signs and forms of the sensible universe goes deeper than the letter or the appearance, similar to that of the artist who is obliged to make a third dimension appear on a plane surface? The task of the spiritual hermeneut also involves a deepening of perspective: how, aided by the letter of the text or by sensible objects, is he to suggest their suprasensible—their "polar"—dimension, and thereby the integrality of their form? But then what space must he have available so that mental representation may escape the fate of *perspectiva artificialis*, and so that the "polar dimension" may not, in the final analysis, prove to be nothing but *trompe l'oeil*? For many of our contemporaries, given over defencelessly to their agnostic reflex, any evocation of a suprasensible world, of spiritual Forms which are more substantial than material ones, is indeed no more than *trompe l'oeil*.

Yet, if it *is* no more than that—no more than the illusion of a reality not worthy of attention—should not the cause or symptom of it be sought first of all in the fact that, with the exception of the school of Jacob Boehme and the Cambridge Platonists to whom Swedenborg so closely approximated, Western philosophy has lost sight of that intermediary world which, following the Persian Platonists, I designate as *mundus imaginalis* (*ʿālam al-mithāl*)?[8] For the space of this world is, precisely, the *qualitative*

8 On this theme, cf. my two works *Spiritual Body and Celestial Earth*, op. cit., and *En Islam iranien: aspects spirituels et philosophiques*, vol. IV (Paris, Gallimard, 1971–1972; re-edn 1978), general index s.v. mundus imaginalis. See also my '"Mundus imaginalis" ou l'imaginaire et l'imaginal', in *Face de dieu, face de l'homme* (*supra*, n. 2); tr. R. Horine, 'Mundus imaginalis, or the Imaginary and the Imaginal', in *Spring* (Zurich/New York, 1972), pp. 1–19; (reprinted by Golgonooza Press, Ipswich, 1975).

dimension of an inner state, and its substantial forms—Forms of light—do not constitute a *trompe l'oeil* beyond which abstraction is to be pushed even further, as though such a process must lead to a "liberating dematerialization" whose aim is to abolish forms and figures. One must indeed be deprived of this *mundus imaginalis* to believe that "dematerializing" forms amounts to abolishing them. On the contrary, the world of "subtle bodies" conceals the *true meaning* of immaterialization, and restores forms and figures to their archetypal purity. For what would a world without face or features—without, that is to say, a look—actually be? (One thinks of the Islamic precept: never strike at the face!)

In our day, there appears to be a tendency to think that by pushing abstraction *beyond* forms and figures, one is accomplishing something akin to the energy theories which, in physics, transform matter into energy. But in actual fact, Islamic theosophers have always been aware of the different states of matter, culminating in a "spiritual matter" to which they have given the name *Nafas al-Raḥmān* (the Breath of the Merciful One). They have spoken of the *mundus imaginalis*, of "subtle or *imaginal* corporeity" (*jismīyah mithālīyah*), of spiritual matter (*māddah rūḥānīyah*), terms which are the equivalent of the *spissitudo spiritualis* of the Cambridge Platonists, or of Oetinger's *Geistleiblichkeit*. For this reason, it was so much the less difficult for them to admit the existence of spiritual forms, and that these forms possess a face and a look. By contrast, the confusion occasioned by the absence of this subtle world engenders the need to free oneself from forms, the need for a liberation conceived as liberation with regard to the *object* on which classical perspective was based; for the object appears now as the stabilizing and *coercive* element of the space at whose centre it is. But why speak of "coercion"?

With the help of a Persian Platonist, the seventeenth-century Qāḍī Sa'īd Qummī,[9] an eminently representative Shiite philosopher, let us try

9 Qāḍī Sa'īd Qummī, almost completely unknown in the West until now, was one of the great Shiite philosophers and theosophers of Safavid Persia. He was born in the sacred village of Qumm, 140 kilometres south of Tehran, in 1049/1639. He spent most of his life there as a teacher, and died there in 1103/1691. His principal masters were Muḥsin Fayḍ (a pupil and son-in-law of the great philosopher Ṣadrā Shīrāzī) and Mullā Rajab 'Alī. His bibliography consists of about fifteen works, several of which are considerable in length. Only a few have been edited. He also had an excellent medical education. To distinguish him from his elder brother, also a philosopher, he is called in Persian by the alternative name of *Ḥakīm-i Kūchak*, meaning something like *Philosophus junior*. See *En Islam iranien*, op. cit., vol. IV, pp.

to grasp the idea of these spiritual circles, which differ from material circles in that their *centre* possesses the property of being simultaneously the *circumference*: for there is no doubt that in this lies the secret of spiritual forms and of the stability of their configuration. Swedenborg expressed it by saying that "each Angel carries its Heaven within itself", while our Shiite philosopher expresses it in the image of the "Throne stabilized upon the Water" and which stabilizes the Water the same time. In the world of spiritual forms there are as many of these *centres* embracing, or totalling, a universe, as there are spiritual individualities. The perspective here, properly speaking, is a *hermeneutical perspective*; in the Middle Ages, the science of perspective was considered fundamental for the same reason that here makes the science of perspective essentially a science of correspondences considered as a fundamental science, postulating a plurality of levels or stages of the universe which are homologous with each other.[10] This science of correspondences is equivalent to that elaborated in a treatise, entitled *De perspectiva*, in which the laws of optics are applied esoterically, that is to say, to suprasensible forms.[11] It enables us to witness the birth and amplification of forms and figures in correspondence with each other, recognizable even when they are transformed into each other, from level to level of the universe. To go "beyond" would be to pass into chaos and nothingness, to deny or violate the affirmation that all earthly things perish, whereas their Face of Light, or divine Face, lives forever (cf. Koran 28:88).

Iconographically, what is implied here is a *spatiality*, the sense and expression of which do not, it seems, figure in the evolution of the sense of space in the West. But I believe that I discovered recently, in a book by the Greek novelist Nikos Kazantzakis, evidence of such a figuration which is unexpected, appropriate and striking. The author tells how he once saw a Byzantine icon of St. George, in which "the fair-haired young hero, on his white horse and with his spear raised, hurled himself at the monster. All the bodies—St. George, the horse, the monster—were compact, muscular, crammed with intense matter. It was a real drama, a bloody

123–201, and Book III of my *La Philosophie iranienne islamique aux XVIIe et XVIIIe siècles* (Paris, Buchet/Chastel, 1980).

10 This science of correspondences, according to Swedenborg, derived from the immediate perception possessed by the men of the *Antiquissima Ecclesia*; cf. my *Herméneutique spirituelle comparée*, op. cit., I, §§ 2 and 3.

11 Cf. *En Islam iranien*, op. cit., vol. I, pp. 135 ff.

struggle. But in the air above this real St. George there was another St. George on the same white horse, with the same spear, against the same monster. Yet on this higher level of vision, everything was dematerialized, the bodies transparent, and through them you could see the flowering meadows and the pale blue mountains in the distance. It was a *more real* St. George than the real one, the astral body of the action, the pale and immaterial flower of matter."[12]

In this manner, the anonymous painter of the Byzantine icon spontaneously expressed his sense of a suprasensible space, dominating and enveloping our own; a level or horizon of the universe where forms are not abolished but transfigured, every mode of representation being true for the stage or the horizon at which it appears. We are talking, therefore, about a spiritual space, where forms subsist even more substantially, and more clearly figured, than in ours, since their pure "matter of light" exempts them from the caducity of our own unstable and corruptible matter. Once form is transmuted into symbol, its meaning becomes transparent, just as the bodies in the icon have become transparent to the flowers and mountains, as if signifying that from now on it is the form which contains its universe, being itself "a world in which our symbols are . . . taken literally".[13] What the painter of the St. George icon expresses here is the intimate sense that the figure, the object, far from being a "coercion", liberates him who contemplates it and meditates on it to a higher state of being, by opening up to him the new space which corresponds to such a state.

This sense of an object which, when contemplated on a higher plane, "a higher level of vision", liberates its own space and transfigures its own form, is to be found, I think, wherever in one way or another access has been left open to the *mundus imaginalis*. For example, the manner in which our Shiite philosopher, Qāḍī Sa'īd Qummī, exhorts us to meditate on the form of the Temple of the Ka'bah will prove a convincing illustration of this fact. First and foremost, however, it is important to bear in mind the premisses of this *figuration* of the Temple, a figuration which contains in itself the whole secret of the spiritual life, because it *figures* the stages of the mystical journey.

12 Nikos Kazantzakis, *Le Jardin des Rochers* (Paris, 1959); tr. R. Howard and K. Friar, *The Rock Garden* (Touchstone Bks, New York, 1969).
13 Cf. *Spiritual Body and Celestial Earth*, op. cit., p. XV.

Indeed, a meditation that transfigures its object from level to level of being is only possible if the schema of the world is one in which the universes rise in tiers of ever-increasing light and purity. This is exactly the cosmological configuration which is to be found in all Islamic theosophical tradition. In the work of the Shiite philosopher Qāḍī Sa'īd Qummī, who, as we shall see, applies this figuration to the esoteric meaning of the form of the Temple of the Ka'bah and the rites of pilgrimage, this is the traditional schema employed, but with a few original details. There are three categories of universe. First, there is the phenomenal world (*'ālam al-shahādah*), a realm where things are perceptible to the senses (*'ālam al-mulk*). Then there is the suprasensible world (*ghayb*), the world of the Soul or Angel-Souls, commonly designated *malakūt*: the "place" of the *mundus imaginalis*, whose organ of perception is cognitive imagination. And there is the intelligible world of the pure Intelligences or Angel-Intelligences, commonly designated *jabarūt*, whose organ of perception is the intuitive intellect.

Our philosopher relates these three categories of universe to three categories of space and three of time. There is the obscure, dense time (*zamān kathīf*) of the sensible world; the subtle time (*zamān laṭīf*) of the *imaginal* world of the *malakūt*; and the even more subtle time, the absolutely subtle time (*zamān alṭaf*) of the world of the Intelligence. The differentiation of these categories of space and time originates in as many specific differentiations of *motion*, from the motion of natural things in the process of becoming, to pure spiritual motion (*ḥarakah ma'nawīyah*). The differentiated spaces are themselves subsumed in the concept of an initial energy whose motion engenders the spatial form which is the origin of everything that assumes form in the world of being, whether spiritual or material. This energy is designated sometimes as *Nafas al-Raḥmān* (the Breath of the Merciful One), and sometimes as the primordial Cloud (*'amā'*).[14] Having established this initial schema, our philosopher is now

14 These themes are fully developed by Qāḍī Sa'īd Qummī in the monumental commentary he devoted to the *Kitāb al-Tawḥīd* by Ibn Bābūyah (died 381/992), one of the great classics of Shiite theology. I myself devoted a full year of courses to this commentary; cf. the report in *Annuaire* de l'École pratique des Hautes-Études (Sorbonne), Section des Sciences religieuses (1965–1966). The theme of time is elaborated in the commentary on the 2nd *ḥadīth* of chapter II of the book (*Sharḥ Kitāb al-Tawḥīd*, Persian ms. fol. 30 ff.; see *En Islam iranien*, op. cit., vol. I, pp. 179 ff.). The arguments are reminiscent of, while differing from, the categories of time in Proclus, from whom they passed to the Ismaili theosopher Nāṣir-i Khusraw,

in a position to conceive the reality of events and forms which, while not ceasing to be events and forms, possess a time and a space that are in no way those of the sensible world to which we are accustomed exclusively to relate our notions of event and form.

There exists between these three categories of universe a certain number of essential relationships, in that each higher universe is the cause of the one below it, and contains, in a manner more subtle and elevated, the totality of universes below it. Moreover, while thus containing and enveloping the totality of the universes below it, each higher universe is also the esoteric aspect (*bāṭin*) of this totality, its hidden, inner aspect or centre. Hence each being of the *mulk* has its own particular *malakūt* which governs and surrounds it, and which is at the same time within it (its "esoteric" aspect), just as each being of the *malakūt* has, in its turn, a *jabarūt* which dominates and surrounds it (envelops and contains it). In other words, each being has a *res divina* (*amr rabbānī*), a divine Word (*Kalimah ilāhīyah*) that is its own *malakūt*, its "esoteric aspect", the inner Man or secret archetypal reality, and that is simultaneously its Watchman or Guardian in that it is the cause which contains and encloses it.[15] As we will see shortly, this is the secret of the Pearl evoked by a Shiite *ḥadīth* which accords strikingly with the celebrated hymn in the *Acts of Thomas* (see below, III, 2).

One must be aware of all this in order to know a human being in his "integral" form (as opposed to that mutilated form of which I cited an example when speaking of Balzac at the beginning of this study). For these three worlds, or three categories of universe, are invested in the human being. Both the *jabarūt* and the *malakūt* are to be found in man; they constitute his essential, his real, his inner being, so that even when he withdraws from the phenomenal world which envelops him, he does not

and which have an exact correspondence in the cosmology of ancient Iran. Cf. my study 'Le Temps cyclique dans le Mazdéisme et dans l'Ismaélisme', in *Temps cyclique et gnose ismaélienne* (Paris, Berg International 1982); tr. R. Manheim, 'Cyclical Time in Mazdaism and Ismailism', in *Cyclical Time and Ismaili Gnosis* (London, Kegan Paul International and Islamic Publications Ltd., 1983).

15 *Sharḥ Kitāb al-Tawḥīd*, fol. 43 (the commentary on the 3rd *ḥadīth* of chapter II and on the 35th *ḥadīth* of chapter II). Qāḍī Sa'īd Qummī is insistent on this point: the *'ālam al-mithāl* is the world perceived by imaginative knowledge (*khayāl*) but it has nothing imaginary (*amr khayālī*) about it. It is perfectly existent (*mawjūd*), and has its own real joys and griefs. It is the *imaginal* world (*mithālī*). Our vocabulary must therefore be very precise, in order not to betray the intentions of our authors. See my article on the *Mundus imaginalis*, op. cit.

cease to subsist integrally as man. To comprehend the reality of the *malakūt* in man, its configurative or so to speak "ideoplastic" power, is to comprehend, in the light of Qāḍī Saʿīd Qummī's Shiite philosophy, that form is a work for which the Spirit is responsible. And in order to comprehend form in this way, we must envisage it in the dimension which, according to all our thinkers, situates man "in his Truth", his inalienable Truth or eschatological dimension.

Indeed, it is astonishing to note the way in which Qāḍī Saʿīd Qummī and his colleagues understand the "tomb", when Islamic eschatology speaks of it as spacious or narrow. We are not dealing here with the macabre: this "tomb" is not in a cemetery. It is what our philosophers conceive as the subtle body which is the *malakūt* within man, and with which man, after his *exitus* from the physical world, resurrects to this *malakūt*; for from this "tomb" he will resurrect yet again, at the time of the Great Resurrection, in order to rise to a higher level in the spiritual worlds. Such is the theosophical meaning, in Islamic eschatology, of the term *barzakh* (in-between, intermediary), as the state of the essential inner man who is separated from the elemental body that envelops him, and returns to his world, to which he is introduced in the state of his essential body (*jism ḥaqīqī*). The latter is designated as the essential body of light (*jism ḥaqīqī nūrī*) or *imaginal* body (*jism mithālī*)—although this, to be sure, is not in the least "imaginary".[16] The *imaginal* body of light is the *malakūt* of the physical body; and the totality of all the incorruptible and permanent corporeity of light (*jismīyah nūrīyah*) makes up the *malakūt* of the corruptible, material bodies of humanity.

The state of this subtle body of light depends on and results from the configurative or "ideoplastic" power of the soul. Its substance derives from all the soul's movements, that is to say from its habits and ways of being, its affections and behaviour, knowledge and wishes, aspirations, emotions, nostalgias and ardent desires. It is the body that the soul itself has formed and acquired for itself; it may be a body of dazzling light or of darkened light, a garden among the gardens of Paradise or a pit among the pits of Hell. This is what Islamic eschatology means in speaking of the width or the narrowness of a "tomb", and of "the interrogation in the tomb".[17] So far are we from macabre realism that our theosophers do not

16 *Sharḥ Kitāb al-Tawḥīd*, fol. 140b.
17 Ibid., fol. 139b–140, 140b–141b.

evade the question of what is meant by the current tradition according to which the bodies of the prophets and the Imams remain only "three days" in the tomb and are "taken up into Heaven". Does this mean that if one were to open the tombs of their sanctuaries one would find no remains? The idea would not even occur to him who has understood that it is not a question of such tombs or of such remains, but of the "body of light", and that the Heaven in question, as Qāḍī Sa'īd Qummī says, "is not the astronomical heaven over our heads".[18]

This *imaginal* body (*jism mithālī*), then, is as the soul has configured it. Throughout his earthly life, man is acting upon his own *malakūt*, and through this upon all the lower *malakūt*, that is to say upon the whole region of the spiritual world constituted by the fraction of humanity which, from century to century, is momentarily involved in the physical bodies of the phenomenal world. This, for our theosophers, is a conspicuous illustration of the concrete and formidable power of intervention which is described as the soul's configurative power—concrete and formidable because the eschatological dimension of the real man is dependent on it. We shall see how Qāḍī Sa'īd Qummī envisions the *malakūt* of the earthly Temple of the Ka'bah; and, since this *malakūt* is the configuration itself of the inner man, the esoteric meaning of the origins and of the rites of pilgrimage to this Temple must ultimately be sought in the direct configurative action exercised by man on his own *malakūt*. Because we moderns have lost the ability to imagine and envision, we must pay all the more attention to what is being said by the theosophers of Islam, to what is involved in the vision of the Temple that will be laid before us. We are confronted not merely with a conceptual representation, but with both a *vision* and a *configuration* of the *malakūt*, all the more "objectively real", it must be said, in that they are realized in the world of the Soul.

For example, we can speak with our theosophers of a "cycle of prophecy". This is a clear and rational concept, even though it envisages *sacred history*. But for them it is configurated and visualized in a real sense in the form of a Temple, homologous with the form of the earthly Temple, because this vision "takes place" in the *malakūt*, in the spiritual world of the Soul. Where a sociologist sees men in procession around a stone temple, our theosophers see Angels in procession from Heaven to Heaven around

18 Ibid., fol. 141b. Cf. also my *Spiritual Body and Celestial Earth*, op. cit.

archetypal, celestial Temples. Where we see a gathering of sages in meditation, the visionary perceives chariots and knights of fire—in short, everything that in the spiritual world is a representative correspondence. This, ultimately, is the whole difference between the phenomenology of the Spirit in Hegel and the visions in Swedenborg's *Diarium spirituale*. The visionary of the *malakūt* perceives the things of this world, but he perceives them as they are in the *malakūt*; he perceives them, that is to say, as men desire and configurate them in their secret reality, which is inaccessible to sensible perception but open to visionary perception. We should not be surprised, for example, by Swedenborg's concise description of a stroll through the streets of Stockholm as this town exists in the *mundus spirituum*, "in its Truth", which of necessity escapes sensible perception and rational understanding, for these are aware only of the hectic bustle of a city of this world. By contrast, its *real* state in the *spiritual* world inspires a dreary horror: most of the houses are shut up and silent, with lightless windows, because their owners are *spiritually* dead.

Such is the *real* state of things, which "trans-appears" on the "upper storey" of vision. Going back to the Byzantine icon of St. George described above, we recall that the reality of the young hero and his combat was shown to us on this upper storey of vision, as it "trans-appears" for the beings of light who people the *malakūt*. In short, if we are to achieve a phenomenology which is integrally true, we must see things and perceive each other as we would if we were "decorporized", at least momentarily, so that the appearance would actually be the *apparition* of what *is* in reality, with nothing external to misrepresent what is inward.[19] This is what our

19 One could go in depth into what there is in common between the *malakūt* and the first degree of the spiritual world in Swedenborg. In connection with the idea that a phenomenology of the spirit implies, in the end, an integral pneumatology, I quote some lines here from a book which is now extremely rare, by the Abbot Pierre Fournié, a disciple of Martinez de Pasqualis, published in 1801 in London (where he fled during the Revolution to continue his theosophical studies) with the title: *Ce que nous avons été, ce que nous sommes et ce que nous deviendrons* (cf. the treatise by Martinez on *Reintegration*): "Now, we should have the less difficulty in conceiving that Swedenborg was really among the good and evil spirits, and that he reported what he heard while conversing with them, in that we would be in exactly the same state if God were suddenly to disembody us altogether. That is to say that, being thus disembodied, we believe that since we are beings of eternal life, we could continue to see each other, and to speak of the divine and eternal realities as each of us sees, believes, lives and speaks of them in his present state." (Cf. *Arcana caelestia*, art. 1883). Quoted from M. Matter, *Saint-Martin le philosophe inconnu, sa vie et ses écrits, son maître Martinez et leurs groupes d'après des documents inédits*, 2nd edition (Paris, Didier et Cie, 1862), p. 53.

theosophers wished to signify and achieve by the *mundus imaginalis*, in that its corporeity of light is the *malakūt* within man. "To be in his Truth" for man depends on the configurative power that he derives from the *malakūt*, and which enables him to configure or disfigure it according to his modes of being, thinking and acting.

With a form of meditation which envisages the Temple of the Ka'bah as a sort of *mandala*, we are faced with a specific case. Meditation on the Temple will bring out structures that will prove to be homologous with other states of the Temple in higher universes. But to imagine, or render perceptible, these homologies, presupposes certain methods of figuration, inasmuch as these methods actually form the specific structures belonging to "an irreducible aspect of integral being"—an aspect called by the philosopher F. Gonseth *homo phaenomenologicus*. Meditation on the plan and the cubic form of the Ka'bah, as pursued by Qāḍī Sa'īd Qummī, presents us *par excellence* with a case where the structures in question, together with their homologies, "are realized through an elaboration which is geometric in character".[20]

With the help of our theosopher, we will try stage by stage to understand what is figured by the Temple of the Ka'bah when it is perceived by the organ of the active imagination: the reasons and meanings of its structure that interconnect the sensible and the suprasensible worlds, Nature and the *hierocosmos*. What, in consequence, is the esoteric significance of pilgrimage? What is accomplished, and to what does one give form "in the *malakūt*", the world of the Soul, when performing the rites of pilgrimage to the earthly Ka'bah? How is the secret of the Black Stone as a corner stone the secret of the *malakūt* within man? Lastly, we shall see how to enter the Temple is for the mystical pilgrim *eo ipso* to have "the power of the keys", the *potestas clavium* whereby spiritual man attains full self-realization. On the upper level of its icon, the Ka'bah rises as an invisible Temple of faith; it is the "place" of the spiritual exile (*ghārib*) who communicates from there with the higher worlds, and who is the man through whom God can still watch over this world—watch over it and care for it.[21]

20 Ferdinand Gonseth, 'La Morale peut-elle faire l'objet d'une recherche de caractère scientifique?' in *Revue universitaire de science morale*, 1965, no. 2, and 'Homo phaenomenologicus', in the review *Dialectica* 19 (Neuchâtel, 1965), pp. 40–69.

21 About twenty years ago, M. Fritz Meier made a full study in *Eranos* of the mystical aspects of the Ka'bah according to other authors; see 'Das Mysterium der Ka'ba,

II. *The Structure of the Temple of the Ka'bah*

1. *The Twelve Imams.* Very briefly, we must draw attention to the complexity which a study of this type of theme involves from the very beginning, since it has scarcely been explored before. Our goal could be defined as an application of the phenomenology of *form* (in the sense of the German *Gestalt*) to the traditional science of *correspondences* practised by all esotericists, from our Shiite theosophers, and their *ta'wīl*, to a Swedenborg.[22] The notion of a "field of perception" should be extended, and its objectivity established, so that it includes the notion of a "field of visionary perception". Imaginative perception could then be envisaged as laying hold of realities and events, both of this world and of higher worlds, in the forms which represent them in the intermediary world or *mundus imaginalis.* To start with, a number of premisses must be established. 1. First and foremost, the notion of form corresponds less to a given configuration which is the attribute of a thing, than to a functional definition of the *Gestalt* understood as a configurative ability or organizing principle, *vis configuratrix.* 2. It must be recognized that both notion and principle have their application well beyond the limits of sensory experience. 3. The "principle of transposition" must be acknowledged as fundamental, so that in passing from one level of the universe to another, the forms behave like a melody whose structure remains identical and recognizable when transposed into different keys.[23] 4. This is because the inner relationships of each whole, and the relationships between the wholes, are essentially functional relationships, so that geometrical relationships of the kind proposed by Qāḍī Sa'īd Qummī—for the engendering of the cubic form of the Ka'bah—are, essentially, functional relationships enabling us to move

Symbol und Wirklichkeit in der islamischen Mystik', *Eranos-Jahrbuch* XI (1944), pp. 187 ff. I myself have already had occasion to treat this theme at length in my book *L'Imagination créatrice dans le soufisme d'Ibn 'Arabī*, 2nd edn (Paris, Flammarion, 1977); tr. R. Manheim, *Creative Imagination in the Sufism of Ibn 'Arabī*, Bollingen Series XCI (Princeton University Press, 1969).* There are long and rewarding comparisons to be made, which we may not even attempt in this study. *(Translator's note: again, this translation is from the earlier (1958) edition of the work, but this does not substantially affect it).

22 Cf. my *Herméneutique spirituelle comparée*, op. cit.

23 Cf. *En Islam iranien*, op. cit., vol. I, pp. 143 ff., where I refer to the researches, unique of their kind, of my friend Victor Zuckerkandl, whose death is deeply to be regretted.

from one figure to another and from one level of universe to another.[24] The traditional science of correspondences links up with the phenomenology of forms to become a science of metamorphoses, within the limits of the three categories of universe mentioned above.

Especially typical is the way in which the Shiite theosopher Qāḍī Sa'īd Qummī, in the course of a monumental work which has hitherto remained in manuscript form, is led to envisage the causes and the engendering of the cubic form of the Ka'bah (the Arabic word *ka'b* denotes a cube). Our author is a Twelver Shiite, not an Ismaili Shiite. And among the traditional texts of Twelver Shiism that he commentates—among those of the *ḥadīth* that go back to the prophet of Islam—there are certain traditions which limit the number of Imams to *twelve* only. These Imams are the spiritual Guides who, coming after the Prophet, were to be the "Preservers" of the sacred Book and of the esoteric meaning of the Revelations. The limiting of their number to *twelve*, as we have observed elsewhere, *eo ipso* implies that the twelfth Imam, the Imam of the present time, is the "hidden Imam", the "awaited Imam". Our author undertakes to discover, in the structures themselves of the cosmos—that is to say, by a detailed implementation of the science of correspondences—the necessity for this specific number of *twelve* Imams. To his first attestation in this respect he gives the name "proof of the Throne" (*burhān 'arshī*). Later on, we will see that the figure of the Throne is equivalent to that of the Temple. Here we must note the following:[25]

The first being in the higher universe to emanate from the supreme Principle is a Light which contains all light (because all light is created from it). This Light of lights is described as the Throne (*'Arsh*), the Intelligence (*'Aql*, the *Nous*), Muhammadan Light (*Nūr muḥammadi*), be-

24 Cf. Wolfgang Köhler, *Psychologie de la forme*, Collection *Idées*, no. 60 (Paris, Gallimard, 1964); trans. S. Bricanier, from *Gestalt Psychology* (Bell & Sons Ltd., London 1930), especially pp. 177–180, 198, 207 ff. (although our own point of view in this context is not that of a psychologist).

25 For what follows, see Qāḍī Sa'īd Qummī, op. cit., fol. 136b–138b. The text forms part of the commentary on the 35th *ḥadīth* of chapter II of the book by Ibn Bābūyah (see above, note 14), which reappears as the 68th *ḥadīth* of another work by the same author, *Ṣifat al-shī'ah*, recently published in Tehran. This *ḥadīth* is essentially a conversation between the tenth Imam, 'Alī Naqī (died 254/868), and a disciple who went to find him at Samarra, in the camp where the Abbasid government was holding him prisoner. The disciple wishes to be certain that he has the Imam's approval for each of the articles of faith that he professes in his heart, with the result that the entire *ḥadīth* on its own forms a complete symbol of Shiite faith.

cause it is the Intelligence of the Fourteen Aeons of light that will be manifested to the terrestrial world in the form of the prophet Muḥammad, his daughter Fāṭimah, and the twelve Imams. The first being to emanate in the lower world is named the primordial Water, understood as ontologically prior to Water as one of the four Elements of our physical world. This primordial Water signifies the entirety of spiritual and material creatures, inasmuch as they are the contents of the intellection (*ma'lūmāt*) of the Intelligence. Further, by reason of the unity *sui generis* formed by the Intelligence and the object of its intellection, this Water is likewise known as the Throne. Now, if it is correct to picture the Intelligence as *surrounded* by its objects of intellection, with itself as their centre, it is no less true to say that it surrounds, contains and envelops them. Here the difference about which our author is so insistent, and which he ponders with the aid of the Theology attributed to Aristotle, makes its appearance: the difference between the material orbs whose centre is *surrounded* by their periphery, and the spiritual orbs whose centre, paradoxically, has the property of being "that which surrounds" (*muḥīṭ*).

The Intelligence is the Light, the Throne, the centre, knowledge as a unique, unquantifiable point, and at the same time it is also Water, the peripheral whole of all the objects of its intellection. The relationship of the Intelligence, as centre, with itself as the periphery surrounding and enveloping all the objects of its intellection, is expressed in the phrase "the Throne rests on the Water"; and this relationship is consolidated by *twelve* functional relationships which determine the cubic form which is both the *imaginal* form of the cosmic Temple and the sensible form of the earthly Temple of the Ka'bah. In other words: for the Throne, the Muhammadan Light, to be both the centre of the universe and the periphery containing it—in order, that is to say, for "the Throne to rest upon the Water" which it also stabilizes—these *twelve* functional relationships must exist; and their existence, as we will see, is assured by twelve human creatures of light (*bashar nūrī*), twelve sacrosanct persons of a superior humanity, namely the *twelve* Imams. Twelver Shiite Imamology is thus the *form* or *vis configuratrix* organizing the universe whose constitutive factors are represented by the two symbols of *Light* and *Water*.

We can now examine in detail the method whereby we proceed from the figuration of the orb of the Throne to the figuration of the *cube*. In considering the figure of a circle as it presents itself to our sensible perception, we see that several diversified aspects, or dimensions, appear as soon as we draw lines out from the centre to the periphery. Four of these aspects are essential, and result from the intersection of two lines that pass through the centre and are perpendicular to each other. They are essential because they divide the circle into four semi-diameters, and represent thereby the four metaphysical limits inherent in all creation, beginning with the Throne itself. The Throne is surrounded in this way by *four* limits that face each other, since it has a beginning (*awwal*) and an end (*ākhir*), an inner or esoteric aspect (*bāṭin*) and an external or exoteric aspect (*ẓāhir*). The first two limits are understood from the extension of its total time (the *Aion*, *dahr*, "time of times"), and the second two from the extension of its total space ("space of spaces"). Thus the original point of Knowledge, of the Throne, ends in four points which are designated as the *supports of the Throne* (cf. fig. 1).[26] It is commonly said that the supports or bearers of the Throne are *four* in number, and in certain Shiite traditions they are signified or represented as lights, the "four lights of the Throne", whose colours indicate that they are, respectively, the origin of each region of being which is symbolically linked to this colour: red light, green light,

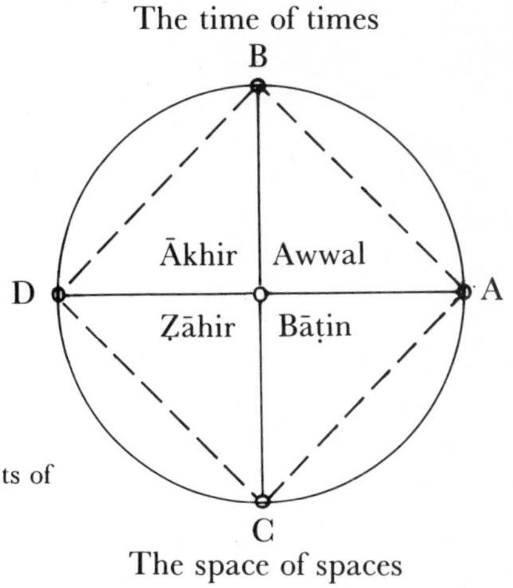

Fig. 1. The four limits of the creatural world

26 In all, Qāḍī Sa'īd Qummī's manuscript contains, in the way of figures, only the little plan of the Ka'bah reproduced here as fig. 5 (ms. fol. 178b). But it seemed to us that the understanding of his system of correspondences and homologies would be greatly assisted by a very few diagrams. We have therefore included some in strict accordance with the indications given—as strict, that is, as his frequent allusiveness permits.

yellow light, and white light. This is one of the great themes of Shiite theosophy.[27]

Let us join up these four points by the chords underlying the arcs of the respective circles, and follow the three phases of the mental operation whereby Qāḍī Sa'īd Qummī brings out the cubic form of the Throne or Temple. This operation is based on the principle that everything in the lower world is an image and a projection of something in the higher world, and that consequently the four limits are manifested in the suprasensible world before being manifested in the sensible world, in virtue of the correspondence establishing the "principle of transposition". Let us imagine that the square inscribed within the circle in fig. 1 (defined by the points ABCD), representing the suprasensible world (*ghayb*), accomplishes a "descent" (*tanazzul*) through a projection of itself onto the lower level which represents the world of sensible phenomena (*'ālam al-shahādah*), and which is defined by the points A′B′C′D′. Four straight lines (AA′, BB′, CC′, DD′) join up, respectively, the four angles of the higher level with the four angles of the lower (cf. fig. 2). At this point the supports of the Throne which is Knowledge are doubled from four to eight, as alluded to in the Koranic verse 69:17: "On that day, *eight* bear the Throne of your Lord."

Secondly, we must note the four straight lines (AB, BD, AC, CD) that interconnect the four limits of the suprasensible world and mark the unity and coherence of the spiritual world, thus permitting the coherent procession of the multiple of the lower world from the unity of the higher. Thirdly we must take into account the four straight lines on the lower level (A′B′, B′D′, A′C′, C′D′) which interconnect the four limits of the world below and mark thereby its organization and coherence.

This threefold operation gives us the *eight* angles that are the "supports of the Throne", plus *twelve* lines and *six* surfaces contained between each pair of lines. Qāḍī Sa'īd Qummī observes that the four points or metaphysical limits, the four lights, arising from the central point, must therefore be at the origin of the cubic form of the Throne or Temple (*uṣūl al-*

27 On these four lights or pillars of the Throne, see my work on Ibn 'Arabī, *Creative Imagination . . .*, op. cit., pp. 373–374. See also my edition of Mullā Ṣadrā Shīrāzī, *Le Livre des Pénétrations métaphysiques (Kitāb al-Mashā'ir)*, Bibliothèque Iranienne, vol. 10 (Paris, Adrien-Maisonneuve, 1964), pp. 166–167, 214 ff., 219 ff. of the French translation. Here again, a comparative analysis is needed. In connection with this, see *En Islam iranien*, op. cit., vol. I, book 1, chapter V.

muka''ab al-'arshī). These *twelve*, *six* and *eight* situate and stabilize this cubic form, thus bringing it about that "the Throne rests upon the Water".

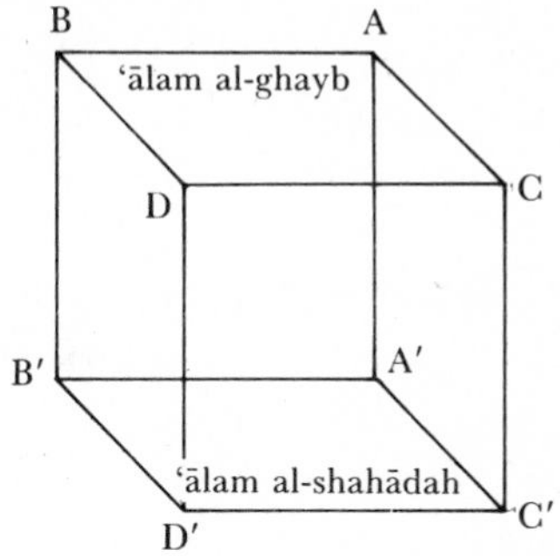

Fig. 2. The cube

Of what specific structures are we made conscious by this geometrical elaboration? Or, in Shiite terminology, what is here the consummation of the *ta'wīl*, of the symbolic hermeneutic? Our author suggests the answer straightaway when he invites us to consider the cubic form of the Temple, which totalizes and interconnects spiritual and material realities, as a unique Emanation proceeding from the supreme Principle; that is to say, as a human person, as the *Anthropos* who is God's vicar with regard to what he envelops and contains eminently within himself. In other words, the figuration of the Temple of the Ka'bah is likewise the figuration of Shiite prophetology and Imamology, because in both cases the same functional relationships are preserved.

We should thus bear two things clearly in mind. On the one hand, we have the question: in what way is the figuration of the Temple an imitation of the structure of the spiritual orbs, in which the centre is also that which surrounds? On the other hand, we should remember that Shiite prophetology reproduces, broadly speaking, the main features of the Judaeo-Christian prophetology expressed in the idea of the *Verus Propheta*, who hastens, from prophet to prophet, towards his resting-place, a resting-place identified with the Last Legislative Prophet and the final Seal of prophecy. However, the essential and irremissible characteristic of Shiite prophetology is that it bases the prophetic mission on the inner, esoteric meaning of the prophetic message. This is expressed in the idea of the *walāyah*, the "divine dilection" that renders sacred all the "Friends of God" and invests the Imams as ministers of the esoteric meaning of the prophetic missions. In the case of the *Nabīs* or prophets, the prophetic vocation (*nubuwwah*) is added to the *walāyah* from which it derives and which is superior to it because it is at the "centre" of each "Friend of God". This, broadly speaking, is the relationship between *nubuwwah* and *walāyah*.[28]

Hence, when Qāḍī Sa'īd Qummī invites us to reflect upon the general form of the Temple as the figuration of a human Person, the *Anthropos* or "Perfect Man", first divine Emanation and God's Vicar (*Khalīfat Allāh*) over all Creation, he specifies that by this we should understand him who was the final Seal of legislative prophecy (*Khātim al-nubuwwah*), and as such the plenary terrestrial manifestation (*maẓhar*) of the *Verus Propheta*—of, that is, the "Muhammadan Light" (*Nūr muḥammadī*), *Nous* or *Logos* of the primordial Pleroma. Shiite prophetology sees the "Seal of Prophecy" as recapitulating and totalizing the entire body of previous prophets and their prophetic missions, because he is the Seal of the *cycle* of prophecy (*dā'irat al-nubuwwah*). Hence the diagrams, as for example in Ḥaydar Āmulī, that arrange the series of prophets in the form of a circle. This, however, does no more as yet than give us the "peripheric" function of the primordial Muhammadan Light. It is the *walāyah* inherent in it which is both the *central* point and the *circumference* of the Temple of prophecy.

We must thus envisage the Muhammadan Light as essentially a bi-unity, typified in the two persons of the Prophet and the Imam. The Prophet expresses the aspect of this Light that is turned towards men (the prophetic mission *ad extra*), whereas the Imam expresses the aspect that is

28 On the relationship between *nubuwwah* and *walāyah*, and in general on the prophetology and Imamology here presupposed, see my *Histoire de la philosophie islamique*, vol. I, Collection *Idées*, no. 38 (Paris, Gallimard, 1964); see also *En Islam iranien*, op. cit., vol. I, book 1, chapter VI. On page 259 of this work, there is a diagram constituted by three concentric circles: the circle of the *walāyah* is in the centre, *surrounded* by the circles of the *nubuwwah* (prophetic vocation) and the *risālah* (prophetic mission). However, since all prophetic missions and vocations have their source in the *walāyah*, and there is no *nabī* who is not first a *walī* (one of the "Friends of God"), it is equally true to say that the *walāyah* surrounds the whole. The word *walāyah* has a Latin equivalent in the word *affinitas*. The link of *spiritual affinity* denoted by the *walāyah* corresponds in Shiism to the Christian notion of *communio sanctorum* (cf. below, IV).

turned towards God (that is to say, the return to the source by means of the inner esoteric sense of the Revelations). The Muhammadan Light as the centre of the circle of prophecy is the esoteric aspect of all the prophecies recapitulated in the final prophecy, that of the Seal of the prophets; and this esoteric aspect is typified in the Shiite conception by the person of the Imam. In fact, the mission of each prophet includes an esoteric aspect: each legislative prophet has been followed by *twelve* Imams. But the Imam, or esoteric aspect, was sent only secretly to earth with each previous prophet. It is only with the final Seal of prophecy that the Imamate is made publicly manifest in the person of the twelve Imams. And it is precisely in the person of the twelve Imams, as constituting the centre and esoteric aspect of the final prophecy, that the Muhammadan Light is both centre and circumference of the Temple of universal prophetic religion. The *twelve* Imams of the present *cycle* of the *walāyah*, which succeeds the previous *cycle* of prophecy,[29] are in effect the link between the prophetic religion of the cycle previous to the Seal of the prophets and that of the cycle of the *walāyah*. The Twelve Imams are the *vis configuratrix* that confers its form on the Temple of permanent prophetic religion, because their Imamate is the esoteric sense of all prophetic Revelations.

Thus, just as we were shown, a short while back, that the point of origin, in virtue of its creatural nature, was surrounded by four metaphysical limits which it engenders (fig. 1), so here the point of origin which is the Muhammadan Light spontaneously develops four limits (aspects or dimensions, *jihāt*), which circumscribe the previous cycle of prophecy and are typified in four of the great prophets: Noah, Abraham, Moses, and Jesus. In similar fashion, it develops four limits defining the cycle of the Imamate inaugurated by the closing of the cycle of prophecy with the Seal of the prophets. These four limits are here the Prophet himself (in his empirical person, *wujūd 'unṣurī*), together with the three first Imams: 'Alī ibn Abī Ṭālib, Ḥasan ibn 'Alī, and Ḥusayn ibn 'Alī (fig. 3). So, just as earlier we had the *eight* angles of the cubic form designated as the "supports" of the cosmic Throne or Temple, here we have the *eight* supports of the Throne of the Muhammadan Light, the permanent pro-

29 Cf. the preceding note. It is possible to perceive here the fundamental difference (in principle and consequences) between the Imamology of Twelver Shiism, limiting the number of Imams strictly to *twelve*, and Ismaili Imamology (which does not reocognize the force of the principle of the *ghaybah*). Cf. my *Trilogie ismaélienne*, Bibliothèque Iranienne, vol. 9 (Paris, Adrien-Maisonneuve, 1961), index s.v.

phetic religion of humanity. And as the inner cohesion of the higher level, then that of the lower level, and lastly the interconnection between them, were seen to be assured by the *twelve* straight lines and *six* surfaces that engender the cubic form, so here the *twelve* Imams homologically assume the same functional relationships for the cubic form of the Temple of prophecy. By means of the Imamate, which is the esoteric aspect of prophecy and its heart, the Throne or Muhammadan Light is "stabilized upon the Water". It is impossible to add or to take away anything from these *twelve*. Finally, just as the geometric figure of a cube comprises *six* surfaces, the names borne by the *twelve* Imams are *six* in number: three were called *Muḥammad*, four were called *ʿAlī* two were called *Ḥasan*, one *Ḥusayn*, one *Jaʿfar*, and one *Mūsā* (Moses).[30]

This, broadly speaking, is the geometric elaboration described by Qāḍī Saʿīd Qummī as "the proof of the Throne", a proof that brings to light a structure which shows why of necessity the Imamate should consist of not more than twelve Imams. From here our author proceeds to deal with two further points, points which have equally been pondered by all Shiite theosophy and which I can only mention in passing.

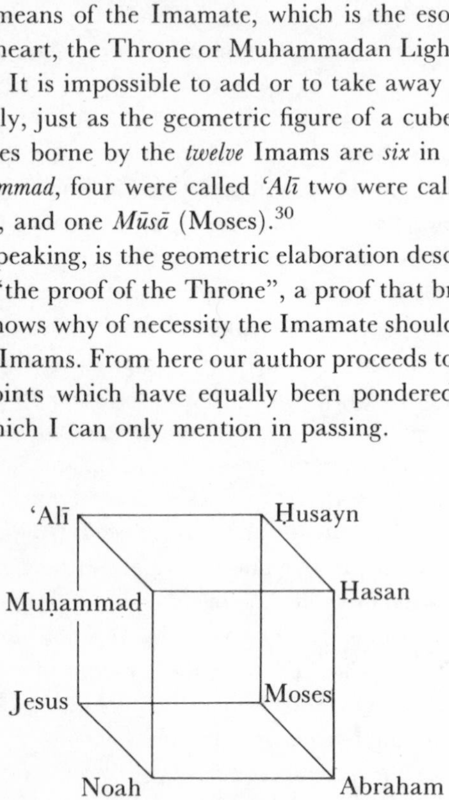

Fig. 3. The eight supports of the Throne

30 For the reader who is not necessarily familiar with these figures, the three Imams who have been named *Muḥammad* are the fifth Imam (Muḥ. al-Bāqir, died 115/733), the ninth Imam (Muḥ. al-Jawād, died 220/835), the twelfth Imam (Muḥ. al-Mahdī al-Qā'im, in "occultation" since 260/864). The four Imams who have been named *ʿAlī* are the first Imam (ʿAlī ibn Abī-Ṭālib, died 40/661), the fourth Imam (ʿAlī Zayn al-ʿAbidīn, died 92/711), the eighth Imam (ʿAlī Riḍā, died 203/818), and the tenth Imam (ʿAlī Naqī, died 254/868). The two Imams who have been called *Ḥasan*

From the first of these there results a homology of functional relationships between the supreme Heaven and the *twelve* strongholds or Signs of the zodiacal Heaven (the firmament) on the one hand, and between the supreme Heaven of prophecy and the pleroma of the *twelve* Imams on the other.[31] The principle is invariable: everything in the lower world is a projection and an image of something in the higher world; everything in the higher world is the Spirit (*rūḥ*) and the essence-archetype (*ḥaqīqah*) of something in the world below. From the supreme Heaven among the astronomical heavens, or ninth Sphere, emanate energies which are shared out between the twelve signs of the zodiacal Heaven that lie along the course of the Sun and Moon of the sensible world. In the same way, the universal Heaven of light of the higher world, which envelops the totality of intelligible and sensible Spheres and is the Throne of the essence-archetypes and of the divine Words (*Kalimāt ilāhīyah*), must necessarily create twelve strongholds of light, the dwelling-places or stopping-places of the Sun of the final prophetic mission and of the Moon of the esoteric aspect, or Imamate. These twelve Signs of light are the twelve Imams, in whom is ramified the existence of the Muhammadan epiphanic form (*taqāsīm wujūd al-mashhad al-muḥammadī*).

A second point emerges when we reflect on the position of the sun in the astronomical Heaven, which is the Throne in a form perceptible to the senses; when we reflect, that is to say, on the sun from the point of its rising at the time of the spring equinox to the point at which it terminates a twelve-month course—the Moon, on the other hand, completes its course in the space of one month. Similarly, the Sun of the final prophecy progresses and is made manifest by the twelve months which are the twelve Imams. Each Imam, therefore, corresponds to a lunar month, because the Imamate is the night of esotericism; and the Imam is a Moon in the heaven of the *walāyah*, that is, the nocturnal heaven which is the esoteric aspect of prophecy (*bāṭin al-nubuwwah*).

Thus, through the projection of a hermeneutical perspective—that is to say, of a disposition of correspondences, a field of vision arising no longer

are the second Imam (Ḥasan al-Mujtabā, died 49/669), and the eleventh Imam (Hasan al-'Askarī, died 260/874). The third Imam, *Ḥusayn* Sayyid al-Shuhadā' (martyred at Karbalā in 61/680), was the only one of his name, as were the sixth Imam, *Ja'far* al-Ṣādiq (died 148/765), and the seventh Imam, *Mūsā* al-Kāẓim (died 183/799).

31 For what follows, see Qāḍī Sa'īd Qummī, op. cit., fol. 138b–139.

from sensible experience but from imaginative spiritual perception—we are induced to meditate upon a series of impressive applications of the principle of "the transposition of forms". We are induced to meditate upon the manner in which the functional relationships are preserved when one moves from the geometrical structure of the cube to the relationship of prophecy with the Imamate, which together make up the Temple of prophetic religion; or when one moves from the relationship of prophecy with the Imamate to the relationship of the supreme Heaven with the signs of the zodiac, or else to the relationship of the year with its twelve months. These last confer on Shiite Imamology the traits of what the history of religions designates elsewhere as "theology of the *Aiōn*". The spirit of Shiite theosophy is characterized, one might say, by a remarkable configurative power. This power reveals figurations and correspondences which we merely mention here, since to do anything more we would have to study them in the light of a phenomenology of Form (*Gestalt*), and for this purpose we would have to renew the traditional science of correspondences.

We can now anticipate the esoteric significance of the pilgrimage to the Temple of the Ka'bah as the *centre* of the terrestrial world, *containing*, homologically, all of creation. The form of the Ka'bah is the very form of the cosmic Throne or Temple, as it is also the form of the Imamate or *malakūt* of this world, of its esoteric or suprasensible aspect. For the mystical pilgrim, the pilgrimage and the rites of pilgrimage performed at the Temple of the Ka'bah have a direct configurative action on the formation of his body of light, on his body's *malakūt*—that is to say, on the attainment of his total form, in the sense that his body of light becomes simultaneously centre and periphery of his essential, total being. We must, therefore, go on to consider the plan and the construction of the Ka'bah.

2. *The Plan of the Temple of the Ka'bah.* Qāḍī Sa'īd Qummī reflects on this plan in the course of some densely-packed pages of the same great work we referred to above, pages which follow those that we have already drawn from, and in which is revealed the totality of esoteric meanings of the pilgrimage to the Temple of the Ka'bah in Mecca.[32] In the preceding

32 We explained above (note 25) how the *ḥadīth* is introduced which is commentated here by Qāḍī Sa'īd Qummī. The profession of faith which the disciple makes known

figurations we moved from the cosmic Temple to the spiritual Temple of prophetic religion, whose edges and surfaces are the twelve Imams, and which is the *malakūt*, or supra-sensible aspect, of this world. In the same way, while retaining the same figurations and functional relationships, we now move from the structure constituted by the archetypal figures of cosmogony to the plan of the earthly Temple of the Ka'bah,[33] thus discovering why this Temple takes on a cubic form, as indicated by its Arabic name. It is always the same principle that is called into play: the forms of light (*ṣuwar nūrīyah*), the higher figures, are imprinted on the realities below, which mirror them. (We should note that, geometrically speaking, the considerations here adduced would remain valid even if the object of meditation was the form of a Greek temple.)

On the higher plane of Reality-archetypes, which together constitute Nature—not, as yet, the specific Nature of our terrestrial world, but Nature as the epiphanic form of the divine Will of manifestation—we encounter four limits that correspond to the four metaphysical limits referred to above (fig. 1). Here these limits are named respectively universal Intelligence, universal Soul, universal Nature, and universal Matter (Matter which is not as yet that of our physical world, but which embraces all the subtle and "spiritual" states of the *Materia prima*). "When," says our author, "these aspects or dimensions of the higher Lights are reflected

---

to the Imam, and the explanation given by the latter, naturally lead the conversation round to the five fundamental religious practices of Islam: Prayer, Almsgiving, Pilgrimage, Fasting, and the *Jihād* as spiritual combat. On each of these articles Qāḍī Sa'īd, in his role as commentator, has written a veritable treatise explaining the *asrār*, that is to say, the spiritual, inner and esoteric meaning. Together these five treatises form as it were a book which can be considered separately, and which has even been edited recently as such by M. Sayyid Muḥ. Bāqir Sabzavārī with the title *Asrār al-'ibādāt wa ḥaqīqat al-Ṣalāt* (Tehran, 1339 A.H.). We have given particular emphasis (see above, note 14) to the study of the third of these treatises, the *Kitāb asrār al-Ḥajj*, or "The Book of the esoteric meaning of Pilgrimage", which contains seven chapters. For the study of the first chapter which follows, cf. ms. fol. 177–179.

33 Let us call to mind the Koranic verses concerning the Ka'bah, which our author does not fail to mention at the beginning of his elucidation. "The first Temple to be founded for men is that which is Bakkah, the blessed Temple" (3:96) (Bakkah is another name for Mecca). "God has made the Ka'bah into the sacred House, to be a station for men" (5:100). "Pilgrimage is incumbent upon man as an obligation towards God" (3:97). "Perform the circumambulation around the antique Temple" (22:29). And a remark made by the Imam Riḍā: "The Temple was founded as the centre of the terrestrial world, beneath which the Earth is spread like a carpet. Every wind that blows in this world comes from the Syrian corner of the Temple. It is the first demarcated field to be established on Earth; because it is the *centre*, the obligation to be fulfilled is equal for Orientals and Occidentals."

on the Earth of receptiveness (*arḍ al-qābilīyah*) for the manifestation (*ẓuhūr*) of the divine Lights, then the four corners of the blessed Temple of the earthly Ka'bah take form."

Furthermore, two of these four divine reality-archetypes (*ḥaqā'iq muta'-aṣṣilah ilāhīyah*)—namely, the Intelligence of the universe and the Soul of the universe (fig. 4)—are on the *oriental* side of the ideal Reality (*mashriq al-ḥaqīqah*), "because they both belong to the horizon of the world of pure Lights, and are the Orient in which the Sun of the esoteric spiritual senses (*shams al-asrār*) arises". The two others—universal Nature and universal Matter—are on the *occidental* side. The Light rises with the first two—Intelligence and Soul—which are its Orient, the divine Day; and wanes, sets and is hidden in the last two quarters of the cycle—universal Nature and universal Matter—which are its Occident and correspond to the Night. The four limits together form the *nycthemeron* of cosmogony. Out of this night, from the occidental horizon, the Light will rise in a new dawn, when the "dense and obscure time" (*zamān kathīf*) of our world comes to an end.[34] When the Koranic verse 55:17 speaks of the "Lord of the two orients and the two occidents", it refers to these two oriental and two occidental horizons. Thus, the strict law of correspondences requires that, in the plan of the terrestrial Ka'bah, the corners should be arranged in accordance with the same order of relationships: two of them—namely the Iraqi corner, in which the Black Stone is embedded, and the Yemenite corner—are on the oriental side, and two of them—the Occidental corner and the Syrian corner—are on the occidental side (fig. 5).

We will now go through the same process as before (fig. 2), and be mental witnesses of the "descent" (*tanazzul*), or rather of the "projection", of the Reality-archetypes onto the earthly plan of the Ka'bath. Each corner of the higher plan enters into correspondence with a corner of the lower terrestrial plan by means of a straight line which represents one of the Elements. These straight lines (or pillars, *arkān*) themselves define the sides of an ideal Temple whose height, for the imaginative perception, enables Heaven and Earth to communicate with each other.

A. Let us picture the Temple of the Ka'bah as a person facing the pilgrim who approaches it from the north side (we have just been asked to think of the Temple as the theophanic person of the Seal of prophecy). It

34 On the symbol of the sun rising in the West, see Paul Kraus, *Jābir ibn Ḥayyān*, vol. I, in *Mémoires* de l'Institut d'Egypte, vv. 44–45 (Cairo, 1943), p. L.

is the revealed divine Face that "faces" the pilgrim, who thus fulfils the injunction: Meet my face (*istaqbil wajhī*). To the *right* of the Temple envisaged as a person facing the pilgrim (but to the latter's left), that is to say, on the *oriental* side and towards the north, is the *Iraqi corner* in which the Black Stone is set, a symbol, as we shall see, which contains the whole secret of the Temple and of man's spiritual life. With regard to its position in the Temple building, it is said that the Black Stone is "God's right hand". On this corner rests the dimension which establishes a correspondence between Nature, meaning here our earthly physical world, and the Intelligence of the universe (fig. 6). We have already seen that the primordial Water symbolizes the objects of intellection of the Intelligence, the lights of this Light. It follows therefore that among the four Elements of our physical world, the element of *Water* is born of the dimension which links Nature *imaginally* with the Intelligence; and the vertical line that represents it in the cubic form of the Temple typifies this functional relationship (the Arabic word *rukn*, pl. *arkān*, serves to designate the stone as well as the column, or pillar, and each of the four Elements). In addition, it is beneath this corner that the living water rises up out of the well called *zamzam*.[35]

B. Also to the right of the Temple, that is to say on the *oriental* side towards the south (the "back" of the Temple, envisaged as a person facing the pilgrim approaching it) is the *Yemenite* corner (or pillar) (fig. 6), corresponding to the dimension that links Nature with the Soul of the world or Spirit of the universe. It is situated at the end of the side contiguous with the corner of the Black Stone, which corresponds to the Intelligence, for it is through the "divine dimension" of the Intelligence that the Soul proceeds from it.[36] Thus the Yemenite corner (*rukn yamānī*) is

35 The designation of this corner as *Iraqi* should be understood in a very broad sense, as encompassing not only Arab Iraq and Persian Iraq (*'Irāq 'ajamī*), but extending the latter as far as the province of Fars (Persia). This is why our author quotes a *ḥadīth* here, which is the pride of Iranians: "Were knowledge (v.l. religion) as far away as the Pleiades, there would always be men from Fars who would reach it." This *ḥadīth* has a prominent position in the commentary on the prologue to Suhravardī's "Oriental theosophy" (*Kitāb Ḥikmat al-Ishrāq*).

36 In connection with this homologation, it is worth remembering the doctrine of the procession of the Intelligences in Avicenna. The first Intelligence (and after it each of the others) performs an act of triple contemplation. From the contemplation of its Principle there proceeds another Intelligence. From the contemplation of its own being as necessary through its Principle (what the author here calls its "divine dimension") proceeds a Soul which moves its Heaven. From the contemplation of

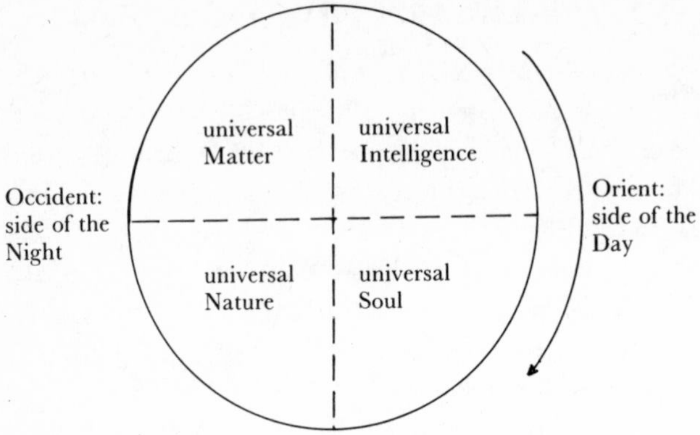

Fig. 4. The nycthemeron of cosmogony

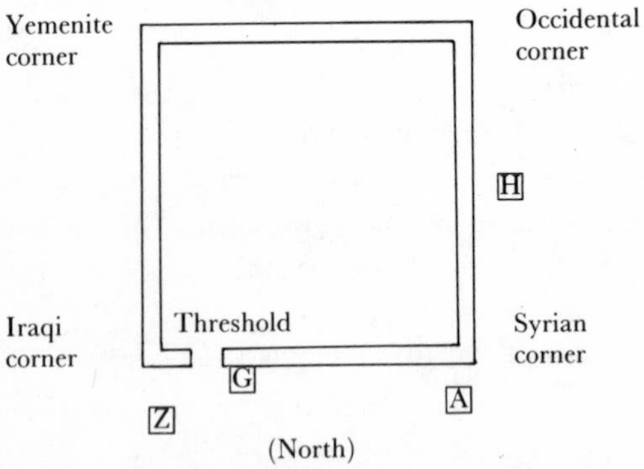

Fig. 5. The plan of the Temple of the Ka'bah according to Qāḍī Sa'īd Qummī. The Temple is envisaged as a person facing the person approaching it from the north side. The Orient is thus on the left-hand side of the diagram. H = the Ḥijr of Ishmael. G = the "station" of the angel Gabriel. A = the "station" of Abraham. Z = the well Zamzam (cf. below, §4)

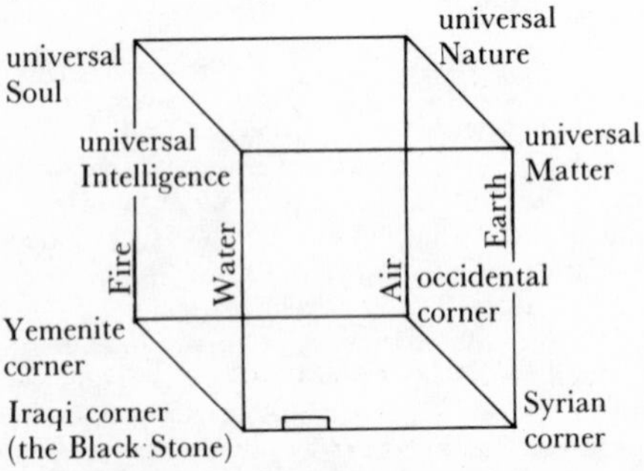

Fig. 6. Correspondence of the plan of the Ka'bah with the plan of the Reality-archetypes

also to the "right of the Throne" (*yamīn al-'Arsh*).[37] Moreover, the element of *Fire* is produced in our physical world from this dimension linking Nature with the Soul of the world or universal Spirit, a functional relationship typified by the Yemenite "pillar".

C. The *Syrian corner* on the *occidental* side, to the left of the Temple envisaged as a person facing the pilgrim, but to the latter's right when facing the Temple facade (fig. 6), corresponds to the dimension linking the Nature of our physical world to universal Matter; for this universal Matter, which embraces all creation both spiritual and material, proceeds from the Intelligence through its "creatural dimension" (in the way that the Soul proceeds from the Intelligence, as we saw, through the "divine dimension" of the latter). Now the principle of the Earth, the element Earth, is produced in our physical world by the relationship of Nature to universal Matter; indeed, this relationship engenders that which is most able, in our physical world, to manifest the Reality-archetypes with stability. It is typified by the Syrian pillar of the Temple.

D. There remains the *occidental corner* at the back and to the left of the Temple (still envisaged as a person facing the pilgrim). This corner corresponds to the dimension linking the Nature of our physical universe with itself as universal Nature, on the level of the Reality-archetypes. Its position in the *imaginal* functional space of the Temple is self-explanatory. It is situated between the Syrian corner, where the relationship between terrestrial Nature and universal Matter is established, and the Yemenite corner, where the relationship between terrestrial Nature and the Soul or Spirit of the universe is established. This is so because what we call Nature in our world results from the breathing into universal Matter of the Soul or Spirit of the world. Thus the element *Air* is born of the relationship of earthly Nature with itself as universal Nature; at the same time, given that the manifestation (the *vestigia*, *āthār*, active traces) of Nature is produced in Matter, the effect of this relationship is made manifest in the Syrian corner. As one tradition has it: "The wind blows from the Syrian corner, south wind and north wind, west wind and east

---

the possibility of its non-being, should it regard itself as fictitiously separated from its Principle (what the author here calls its "creatural dimension"), proceeds the subtle matter of its Heaven. Cf. my *Avicenne et le Récit visionnaire*, new edn (Paris, 1979); tr. W. R. Trask, Berg International, *Avicenna and the Visionary Recital*, (Texas, Spring Publications Inc., 1980).

37 Hence the qualification of wisdom as "Yemenite theosophy"; cf. below, note 54.

wind; that is why this corner (or "pillar") vibrates in winter as in summer, by night as well as by day; for the wind has its source in the Breath of the Merciful One (*Nafas al-Raḥmān*), and this Nature is the physical form of the manifestation of this Name (the Merciful One)."

In short, it is from these correspondences, when established and justified, that there emerges the image of a cosmic Temple, which itself is the form of manifestation of the "Sublime Throne" within the universal Nature of the "universal body" (*jism kullī*). These correspondences can be perceived with the help of a geometrical elaboration whose basis is the cubic form of the Temple of the Ka'bah, and which, according to Qāḍī Sa'īd Qummī, is *eo ipso* the explanation of this Temple.[38]

3. *The Celestial Archetype of the Temple.* In spite of all that we have already written, the mystical phenomenology of the form of the Temple is far from complete. We have been enabled to perceive the cubic form of the Temple of the Ka'bah, but a more difficult problem remains. This is the correspondence of the earthly Temple of the Ka'bah with its celestial archetype, the spiritual Temple in the spiritual universe. Qāḍī Sa'īd Qummī knows that here he must deploy the powers of a form of thought that is essentially intuitive.[39] The problem is this: although unquestionably there are spiritual forms more real and more substantial than the material forms perceptible to the senses, how are their structures to be homologized with each other, given the difference between them, of which, as we saw, our author is so aware? In effect, the characteristic of spiritual forms is that their centre is both that which *is surrounded* and that which *surrounds*, that which *is*

38 Continuing to apply the principle that everything in the sensible world is a *form* (*ṣūrah*) belonging to the higher universes, Qāḍī Sa'īd elucidates yet more traditional homologies. The Temple on earth corresponds to the Temple in the fourth Heaven (*al-Bayt al-ma'mūr*, Koran 52:4), and it is square in form (*murabba'*) because the words on which Islam is founded are *four* in number, the four *tasbīḥāt* or formulas of glorification (*tahlīl*, *takbīr*, *tasbīḥ*, *taḥmīd*). The three dimensions of the cube are likewise homologized with the three aspects of the *Tawḥīd*: the aspect of the Essence (*tawḥīd dhātī*), the aspect of the Attributes (*tawḥīd ṣifātī*), and the aspect of the Operations (*tawḥīd fi'lī*). Cf. op. cit., fol. 178b–179.

39 Here begins the second chapter of *Kitāb asrār al-Ḥajj*, whose position in Ibn Bābūyah's *Sharḥ Kitāb al-Tawḥīd*, fol. 179–181 of our ms., was specified in note 32 above. According to the long title he gives to the chapter, Qāḍī Sa'īd is well aware of his change of level. In all that follows, he will henceforth address himself to the intuition, through a method of exposition "foreign to rational understanding". The reflections which fill these chapters are "modest virgins, in no way suited to the vigorous maleness of men with rational knowledge".

contained and that which *contains*, whereas in the case of material forms, the centre is purely and simply that which *is surrounded*. The form of the earthly Temple must, therefore, conform finally to this ambiguity of the centre in the spiritual forms; for only then can the material form be elucidated in a spiritual form, and the earthly Temple of stone be transfigured into a spiritual Temple of faith.

Apart from other sources, the celestial archetype of the Temple of the Ka'bah is to be found in traditions that go back to the Shiite Imams. Two motifs represent it: the Tent descended from Heaven, and the white Cloud.

A tradition going back to the fifth Imam, Muḥammad al-Bāqir, recounts how when Adam fell from Paradise, he complained to God about the solitude and wildness of the places in which he found himself. God then caused a pavilion to descend, a single tent from among the tents of Paradise. The angel Gabriel set up this tent upon the site which was to be that of the Temple of the Ka'bah. The surface of the Tent exactly covered the area to be covered by the future Temple, and the corners of the Tent coincided with those of the Temple. The central pillar of this heavenly Tent was a rod of *red* hyacinth. The four tent-pegs were of pure gold, and were *yellow*. The ropes were woven of threads as silky as hair, and were *violet*. Here traditions vary. Sometimes it is the Angels who build the Temple of the Ka'bah in imitation of the celestial Tent. Sometimes it is God himself who builds it so that Adam, together with the seventy thousand Angels commanded by God to bear Adam company, might process around it. In any case, at the four corners of the earthly Temple were placed four foundation stones, originating respectively from Ṣafā, Mount Sinai, Salem or Kūfah, and Abū Qubays (the place where Adam halted on arriving in Arabia). We will shortly see how these four stones possess a decisive significance for the spiritual form of the Temple.

Another tradition, going back to the sixth Imam, Ja'far al-Ṣādiq, recounts how when Adam was "reconverted" to God, the angel Gabriel came to him and took him to the future site of the Temple. Here a white Cloud (*ghamāmah*) descended and overshadowed them. The angel ordered Adam to trace with his foot a groove outlining on the earth the exact area covered by the shadow of the white cloud. This was to be the perimeter of the Temple of the Ka'bah. We will encounter the context of this *ḥadīth* later on, in the elucidation of the esoteric meaning of the rites of pilgrimage.

As for the traditions which contain a reference to the secret of the Black Stone embedded in one corner of the Kaʿbah, these likewise assume significance in the context of the first pilgrimage undertaken by Adam in the company of the angel Gabriel.[40] "In all this," declares our author, "there are mystical secrets, access to which is denied to the best-trained intelligences, let alone to those minds which delight in placid torpor. As regards us," he adds, "we will show here, with divine help, a ray of that light, for the benefit of him who decides to attempt the ascent of this mountain and to reach its lofty summit."

It is from this summit that one may discern how it is possible to establish the correspondence, or homology, between the forms of spiritual things or beings and the forms of material things or beings. The starting-point, says Qāḍī Saʿīd Qummī, is the most perfect and stable form of all: the *sphere*. Let us at once observe with our author that in the present case we do not move from one category to another in moving from the spherical to the cubic form, because the latter simply locates certain functional relationships whose supports are inscribed within the sphere. In particular, in this respect, one must make no mistake when the spherical form is attributed to spiritual beings: what is being expressed in this manner is not a geometrical relationship as such, but a functional one. This is not to say that spiritual beings have the form of a ball with a certain diameter. It means that each Angel, or each human form of light, or the subtle *imaginal* body, is not "in Heaven" but carries its Heaven within itself, just as each demonic entity carries its Hell within itself.[41] Qāḍī Saʿīd Qummī is insistent upon this point: the spherical form, roundness, is not one which pre-exists and is imposed on spiritual beings. The spherical form which

40 We will find the context of this *ḥadīth* below, section III, § 3. The author cites here two other traditions in which the symbol of the red hyacinth is substituted for that of the white Pearl (he himself remarks on their identity of meaning). According to one tradition: "The Black Stone has two eyes, two ears, a mouth and a tongue (which is why the Black Stone is *witness* to the "judgement" of man). It happened that as Adam passed by it in Paradise, he struck it with his foot. When he was forced to descend, as it was of gleaming red hyacinth, he kissed it. This is why the pilgrims today kiss the Stone as they pass it." According to the other tradition: "When Adam had descended close to the mountain of Abū Qubays, he complained to God about the wildness of the places in which he found himself, and that he no longer understood what he used to understand in Paradise. Then God caused a red hyacinth to descend. He placed it on the site of the Temple, and Adam walked around it. Its radiance was such that signals (or emblems) were made in its form, and it became a sacred object." *Sharḥ*, 179b.

41 Cf. my *Herméneutique spirituelle comparée*, op. cit.

we perceive here below—the sphericity of the universe in its totality and of the heavens that compose it—is a form derived from spiritual beings, a form which is the manifestation in our own space of the intimate law of their being.

This being said, it may further be specified that if the most perfect and stable of forms is sphericity, this is because the relationship between spheres consists in the fact that they surround each other: the spheres of our universe (Heaven and Elements) are englobed by and encased in each other. Otherwise—if, for example, they were juxtaposed—there would either have to be another body between them or else a void, a hypothesis excluded by traditional physics. Furthermore, each of these spheres which are encased in each other possesses a superior degree of subtlety and light in relation to those below it and which it envelops; each sphere is duller and more opaque than the one within which it is encased. The truth of this law is made evident as one descends from the supreme Sphere, the manifested Throne of the Reality-archetypes—so pure that it is not even constellated—to the immense Heaven of the Fixed Stars (which contains, besides the mass of constellations, everything that we nowadays call the galactic universes), and then from planetary Heaven to Heaven until one reaches the elementary Spheres that surround the Earth.[42] In the spiritual world also there are ideal Spheres that surround each other, in the sense that the cause completely surrounds that of which it is the cause.[43] "Down below" likewise, what is inferior has a lesser light, and appears duller in relation to what is spiritually superior.

Here we are faced with the question whose terms we defined above: in what sense can one speak of a correspondence or homology between the centres of the spiritual Spheres and the centres of the material Spheres, when in the spiritual Spheres the centre is both *that which is surrounded* and

42 Qāḍī Saʿīd observes here that the Prophet never uses the word Heaven (*samā'*) to designate the Spheres (sing. *Kursī*, *'Arsh*), which are outside and above the planetary Spheres that form our solar system; *Sharḥ*, 179b.

43 All this accords perfectly with the *Theology* said to be by Aristotle and with Avicenna's commentaries. Cf. G. Vajda, 'Les Notes d'Avicenne sur la "Théologie d'Aristote"', in *Revue thomiste* II (1951); see also my *Avicenna and the Visionary Recital*, op. cit., p. 54. See also *En Islam iranien*, op. cit., vol. IV, general index s.v. Théologie dite d'Aristote. Qāḍī Sa'īd Qummī himself wrote a commentary on the famous *Theology*, which has hitherto escaped the attention of researchers. It should be edited, for it is a significant testimony to the Neo-Platonists of Safavid Persia. For more details, see my *La Philosophie iranienne*, op. cit.

that which surrounds (the Angel being the centre of the Heaven that he contains), while in the material Spheres the centre is by definition that which is surrounded? In our world, says Qāḍī Sa'īd Qummī, what is below (i.e. the Earth) is the centre in relation to what is above it and surrounds it. This is the reverse of what happens in the world with respect to which it is "down below"—that is to say, the reverse of what happens in the spiritual world; for there it is what is above that is the centre, but a centre which is no less capable of being that which surrounds; while what is below in the spiritual world, although in the position of being *that which surrounds*, is as such *that which is surrounded*. So how is one to establish a homology of forms?

The answer to this question depends on the application of the phenomenology of Form to the traditional science of correspondences and, together with this, the possibility for spiritual forms to reveal themselves as such, as of right and in the plenary reality as forms. In order for this to happen, a double correspondence must in principle be established.

A. A correspondence between the centre of the material form and that of the spiritual form inasmuch as this is a *surrounded* centre; and B. a correspondence between the centre of the material form and that of the spiritual form inasmuch as this is a centre that *surrounds*. In order to perceive intuitively that the Ka'bah, being the centre of the earthly world, is also that which surrounds it (the surrounded-surrounding, the enveloped-enveloping),[44] one must perceive "imaginally" that its structure is homologous with the structure of the Temples of the spiritual world, the Temples of light. This is what the motifs of the celestial Tent and the white Cloud are intended to suggest. Finally, there enters into this very structure an element represented by the four corner-stones, an element which "dematerializes" and transforms the Temple of stone into a spiritual Temple of faith. The inner, spiritual form—the form of light—as the centre assembles and totalizes the "data"; it is itself the "giver of the data", the external data surrounding the centre of the material form. It is

44 On these expressions, see my *Creative Imagination in the Sufism of Ibn 'Arabī*, op. cit., pp. 279 ff. Like Ḥaydar Āmulī, Qāḍī Sa'īd Qummī was steeped in the writings of Ibn 'Arabī, with whom the Shiite theosophers early discovered their affinity. Nevertheless, there was one point on which they were unable to compromise and over which they were forced to criticize him, namely the person of the "Seal" of the *walāyah*, (*khātim al-walāyah*) who can only be the Imam. Cf. my article 'Ḥaydar Āmulī, théologien shī'ite du soufisme', in *Mélanges Henri Massé* (University of Tehran, 1964), and *En Islam iranien*, op. cit., vol. III, Book 4, chapter I.

not *in* the light, but is the light, the act of light, and this is the centre which as such possesses the virtue of surrounding. (The passage from material form to spiritual form corresponds to a process of intussuception, as when a glove is turned inside out: the inside becomes the enveloping surface.)

A. On the one hand, then, the material centre—the site of the Temple of the Ka'bah as centre of the terrestrial world and of the geocentric universe of the Spheres—by virtue of its homology with the centre of the intelligible Spheres, has the privilege of manifesting the Temple (*Bayt Allāh*, the "House of God") in correspondence with the Throne of the sovereign Unity (*'arsh al-waḥdānīyah al-kubrā*). This latter is the pure intelligible Temple (*al-Bayt al-'aqlī*) around which the pure sacrosanct angelic Intelligences process (the *Angeli intellectuales*).

B. On the other hand, this terrestrial centre of the corporeal world corresponds to the Glorious Throne (*'Arsh majīd*) in the world of the Soul, that is to say, the supreme Sphere, which is the first to be affected by the action of the World-Soul. This supreme Sphere is the body which surrounds and envelops the universe (*jism muḥīṭ bi'l-kull*). The Glorious Throne itself corresponds to the Sublime Throne (*'Arsh a'ẓam*) or Intelligence of the universe, a correspondence based on the fact that, if the Intelligence is the centre of the intelligible Spheres, it simultaneously envelops, surrounds and contains those same Spheres whose centre it is.

The homologation of category A establishes a correspondence between the centre, and the centre as *surrounded* (*muḥāṭ*), between the earthly Temple of the Ka'bah, around which the pilgrims walk in procession, and the Temple of sovereign Unity, around which the Angels process. The homologation of category B establishes a correspondence between the centre, and the centre as *surrounding* (*muḥīṭ*): the Sublime Throne contains the intelligible Spheres, the Glorious Throne contains the astronomical Spheres, the Temple of the Ka'bah contains, homologically and within its "imaginal" structure, the totality. Thus, says Qāḍī Sa'īd Qummī, this double correspondence is reflected from above down to the earthly Temple; and he adds: "All this contains a mystery about which no one up till now has, to my knowledge, said more than I have just said" (and we admit to sharing this opinion, so abstruse is our author's text at this point).[45]

45 There are, besides, some variants between our ms. fol. 180 and the text edited by M. Sabzavārī, p. 177. It appears as though the editor incorporated into this text certain marginal notes present in the manuscript he was using. I cannot make a

Thus, no matter where the nature of the Throne or Temple (the notions overlap) is realized—whether in the spiritual or in the material world—it will always possess a comparable structure. The structure of the Tent which descended from Heaven, and which the angel Gabriel set up for Adam, is the structure of a spiritual form which contains its universe within itself. Our author undertakes a detailed examination of this. The *ḥadīth* of the fifth Imam specified that the central pillar of the Tent that came down from Heaven was made out of *red hyacinth.* In fact, it typified the Throne of the sovereign Unity, whose central pillar is the Supreme Divine Form revealed (*al-ulūhīyah al-kubrā*), which, in this context as in Ismaili theosophy, is the first Intelligence of the pleroma, the supreme *Nous.*[46] It is by virtue of this *Nous* that summits and abysses, Heavens and Earths, exist, as witnesses to this Unity. It is represented by the *red* hyacinth because it totalizes two aspects. It is *divine* because it is the initial theophany of the *Absconditum*, and this divine aspect is absolute light. But at the same time it is also *creatural*, and every creatural aspect is Darkness. It encompasses both the aspect of the worshipped and that of the worshipper, postulated by the very concept of divinity. According to the physics of our authors, the colour *red* derives from the mingling of *whiteness*, as an aspect or dimension of the Light, with *blackness*, as an aspect or dimension of Darkness. This is the motif which Suhravardī introduces so arrestingly at the beginning of the mystical recital he entitles *The Purple Archangel*—that is, having the purple colour of the morning or evening twilight, when day is mingled with night.[47]

This Tent is supported and stabilized by four tent-pegs (*awtād*)[48] typify-

detailed comparison here, so I limit myself to hoping for a forthcoming critical edition of Qāḍī Sa'īd Qummī's great work.

46 On the word *ulūhīyah* as a designation of the divinity manifest in the first Intelligence of the pleroma as a support for the name Allah (*Deus revelatus*), see my *Trilogie ismaélienne*, op. cit., pp. 160–161, and my book *Creative Imagination in the Sufism of Ibn 'Arabī*, op. cit., pp. 112 ff. and 293–294.

47 Cf. my translation of the 'Récit de l'archange empourpré', in *L'Archange empourpré: quinze traités et récits mystiques*, VI, Documents spirituels 14 (Paris, Fayard 1976), pp. 201–213. Compare, too, the symbolism of the two wings of the angel Gabriel, one of light and the other of darkness (ibid., VII, pp. 236 ff.). This should be related to the notion of the procession of the Intelligences; see above, note 36.

48 The *Awtād* also figure in the esoteric hierarchy, whose structure probably derives from the image of the celestial Temple. Cf. my *Trilogie ismaélienne*, op. cit., index s.v.; my book *Creative Imagination in the Sufism of Ibn 'Arabī*, op. cit., p. 45 note 15; my study on Rūzbihān Baqlī of Shīrāz in *En Islam iranien*, op. cit., vol. III, pp. 35 ff.; and my

ing universal Nature which, by means of its four aspects (cf. above figs. 1 and 4), maintains the order of the material universe. Their colour is the *yellow* of gold because universal Nature is both close to the intelligible Lights, and finds rest on the Earth of materiality (*arḍ al-hayūlānīyah*), where it consolidates itself and leaves traces which take on the "tincture" of the laws of physical reality.

The ropes of the celestial Tent, described as being woven of threads as fine as hair, are the irradiations of the Light of the Soul (*ashi''at Nūr al-Nafs*) as a hypostasis emanating from the Intelligence, and they originate in the "crenelles" (*sharafāt*) of the higher world. They are *violet* in colour because of their intermediate position between the world of being at the level of the pure Imperative—that is to say, the world of the cherubic Intelligences—and the world of Matter and Nature. Just as for our authors the colour red results from the mingling of light with darkness (white with black), the colour *violet* results from the mingling of the colours *yellow* and *red*.

In short, the structure of the celestial Temple described in the *ḥadīth* of the fifth Imam typifies the rank and position of the Supreme Intelligence or *Nous*, designated above as "Muhammadan Light", *Nūr muḥammadī*. It is the centre of the All, and as such it simultaneously surrounds and envelops the totality of the intelligible and material Spheres. As the central pillar of the Temple of sovereign Unity, it is the Sublime Throne which is God's Temple on the level of the intelligible world (*jabarūt*). It is the initial Temple, the Temple in its idea-archetype, founded for a seraphic humanity already in possession of the rank of Angel (*al-anās al-'aqliyūn*, which designates the persons of light in the pleroma of the Fourteen Most Pure Ones), as well as for the Angels of the superior hierarchies, whom traditional theosophy describes as the *muḥayyamūn*, those who are "made ecstatic by love".[49]

Because all the universes symbolize with each other, this same Temple exists in every universe in a form that corresponds to that universe. Below

---

L'Homme de lumière dans le soufisme iranien (Chambéry, Ed. Présence, 1971; distr. Libr. de Médicis, Paris); pp. 87–88; tr. N. Pearson, *The Man of Light in Iranian Sufism* (Boulder and London, Shambhala 1978), pp. 56–57.

49 This should be compared with the use of the same term in Ibn 'Arabī; cf. my *Creative Imagination* . . . , op. cit., pp. 311 ff. and 314. One could also refer to other contexts, for example to the celestial Temple described in the *Book of Enoch*, XIV, 10 ff., LXXI, 5 ff.

the world of the Intelligence, and on the level of the world of the Soul (*malakūt*), is the Glorious Throne (*'Arsh majīd*), the Temple of God around which the Proximate Angels (*muqarrabūn*) go in procession. Furthermore, the form of manifestation of this Glorious Throne, supreme Sphere or ninth Heaven, is the limit between the space in which we orientate ourselves in accordance with sensory data, and the *mundus imaginalis*. The world of the Soul is this *mundus imaginalis*, and it contains the Image-archetype of each thing and thence the Image-archetype of all the temples and sanctuaries where the name of God is celebrated. At the level of sidereal Nature, in the fourth Heaven (the heaven of the Sun and, in Jewish gnosis, of the archangel Michael[50]) is the Temple called *Bayt al-Ma'mūr* (the temple frequented by the Angels). Originally this was the Temple of the first earthly Ka'bah, but at the time of the Flood it was carried off by the Angels to the fourth Heaven and disappeared for good (like the Holy Grail) from the eyes of men;[51] it became the Temple around which process the Angels who are the motive Souls of the Spheres (the *Angeli caelestes*: here heliocentrism assumes a role in angelology).

Finally, at the level of the earthly world there is the Ka'bah. But, as we have just observed, the present Ka'bah built by Abraham is only the imitation (or "history", *ḥikāyah*) of the Ka'bah that was built in the time of Adam. It is the Temple of God in the world of sensible phenomena, on the material Earth, and it is homologous with the other Temples because it is the homologue on earth of the archetypal centre (*markaz aṣlī*). The Prophet records, in one of the recitals of his celestial assumption (*mi'rāj*): "It was as if I were then contemplating your own Temple here, for every archetype has its image". In the earthly Temple of the Ka'bah as the image of the archetypal Temple, explains Qāzī Sa'īd Qummī, the Black Stone corresponds to the pillar of red hyacinth (the mystical reason for this will shortly be seen, for the Black Stone is the secret of the Temple by virtue of being the secret of the spiritual life of man and of his pilgrimage). The Temple walls, and the veils with which they are covered at the time of the great pilgrimage, correspond to the violet tent-ropes, for in the macrocosm the "veils" signify the levels in the hierarchy of souls.

There remain the four mysterious corner-stones, whose provenance, as

50 Cf. W. Bousset, *Die Religion des Judentums im späthellenistischen Zeitalter*, 3rd edn (Tübingen, H. Gressman 1926), p. 327.
51 Cf. the *ḥadīth* cited in my *Herméneutique spirituelle comparée*, op. cit., note 149.

we saw, are four different mountains: Mount Ṣafā, Mount Sinai, Mount Salem, and Mount Abū Qubays. Their symbolic function is determinative: the transfiguration of the material Temple into a Temple of light, a spiritual Temple of faith. Qāḍī Sa'īd Qummī explains that these corner-stones correspond to the four tent-pegs of the archetypal Tent, of gold in both substance and colour. They typify four lights from among the lights of the *walāyah* (*anwār al-walāyah*). It is thanks to these lights that the universe of being (*'ālam al-wujūd*) subsists at all, for the *walāyah* is the "divine dilection" which sanctifies the "Friends of God", those through whom God still watches over and cares for this world. The four lights in question were those of Abraham, Moses, Jesus and Muhammad. In connection with this our author cites a tradition which makes its appearance fairly frequently in Shiite texts: "According to the Torah, the *Light* came (or as one variant has it: the Lord [*al-Rabb*] came) from Mount Sinai. This light arose over Sā'ir. It shone from the mountain of Fārān." It is of value to us to be able to identify in this tradition, where the proper names are simply Arabized, the exact translation of two Biblical verses (Deuteronomy 33:2–3).[52]

For our Shiite theosophers, this *light* is the light of the eternal prophetic Reality, of the *Verus Propheta* who found support from prophet to prophet, down to Muhammad who was the Seal of prophecy (see above, fig. 3). That it comes from Sinai is a reference to the mission of Moses. Its rising over the mountain of Seir (Sā'ir) is the symbol of the mission of Jesus; its splendour shining on the top of Mount Paran (Fārān) typifies the final prophetic mission of Muhammad. It is this light, also, which confers upon the four corner-stones the mystical significance that elevates the transparent spiritual Temple above the form of the earthly one.

A. The epiphany (*ẓuhūr*) of the Light of prophecy began with Adam and attained perfection in Abraham, through whom the religion of the pure believers (*millah ḥanīfīyah*) was made manifest. Abraham was neither Jew nor Christian; the religion of Abraham corresponds to the fundamental constitution of man as originally willed by his Creator (the *fiṭrah*). The stone in the *Syrian corner* comes from Safā because it was on Safā that Adam appeared to Eve (after their exile from Paradise), and because it was here too that Abraham halted at the end of the migration which he undertook

52 Cf. Deuteronomy 33:2/3 (Moses' great prophetic benediction): ". . . the Lord came from Sinai, and rose up from Seir unto them; he shined forth from mount Paran . . ."

in obedience to the divine summons for him to leave his country. This is indicated by the Koranic verse 14:37: "Oh our Lord, I have established a part of my posterity in a barren valley, close to your sacred Temple" (cf. fig. 7).

B. The stone from Sinai clearly alludes to the rank and mission of Moses with respect to proclaiming the pure prophetic religion and the institution of the divine Law (*sharī'ah*). It is in the *Occidental corner*, which is reserved for Moses as a result of a subtle exegesis of the Koranic verse 28:44, where Muhammad is told: "You were not on the *occidental* side (of Sinai) when We charged Moses with his mission."

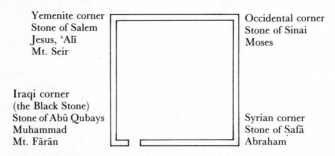

Fig. 7. The four corner-stones of the Temple of the Ka'bah, each one corresponding to a prophet

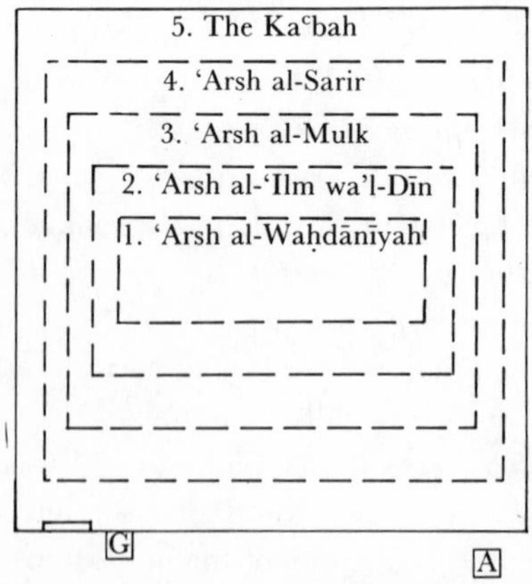

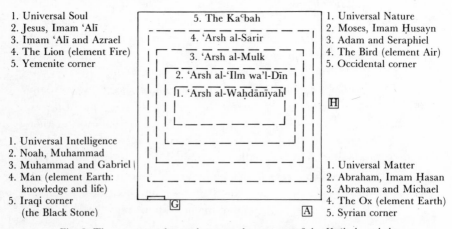

Fig. 8. The correspondences between the corners of the Ka'bah and the corners of the higher Thrones or Temples

C. The stone from Salem (Salām) symbolizes the rank and mission of Jesus. This is in the *Yemenite corner*, which is to the south and on the *oriental* side. A Koranic verse states: "Maryam retreated from her family towards a place situated in the *Orient*" (19:16), and we already know that in this retreat of Maryam's "towards the Orient", Ismaili gnosis sees one of the esoteric moments which are at the origin of Christ's mission.[53] The Yemenite corner also suggests the reason why the mystical qualifications of "Yemenite" and "Oriental" should be bestowed on one and the same theosophy.[54] Here, Twelver Shiite gnosis stresses another aspect: just as Jesus was the Seal of the *walāyah* (divine dilection and initiation) imparted to the prophets who succeeded each other after Adam, so the first Imam, ʿAlī ibn Ali-Ṭālib, was the Seal of the universal *walāyah* imparted to *all* the "Friends of God" (*Awliyā' Allāh*), prophets and non-prophets. Thus, he is a substitute for Jesus (*Qā'im maqām, locum tenens*), he who "answers for" him, just as the twelfth Imam, the Imam of the Resurrection, in his turn "answers for" the entire line of the prophets. In other words, the Imam ʿAlī is in the same relation to Jesus as the twelfth Imam is to all the Imams and prophets. (Hence the names of Salem and Kūfah associated in the attestation of the stone's origin.) Thus at the Yemenite corner of the Temple, on the oriental side, Shiite meditation brings about the unification of a prophetic Christianity with its own Imams, a unification also heralded in the fact that Christ's return must of necessity be preceded by the appearance of the twelfth Imam. Moreover, the plan of the heavenly Jerusalem with its *twelve* gates corresponds to that of the Temple with its *twelve* Imams.

D. Still on the oriental side, there remains the *Iraqi corner*, the corner in which the Black Stone is embedded, and whose "pillar" typifies the relation between all earthly things and the higher world of the Intelligence. Since Abū Qubays was the place where Adam halted, this provenance is doubtless a reminder that the secret of the Black Stone is linked to the drama itself of Adam (see below). But Qāḍī Saʿīd Qummī essentially

53 On Ismaili christology, see my *Herméneutique spirituelle comparée*, op. cit., 10.

54 In virtue of the tradition stating that "faith is from Yemen and wisdom (theosophy) is Yemenite (*al-īmān yamānī wa'l-ḥikmah yamānīyah*)". Hence, for example in Mīr Dāmād, the notion of "oriental theosophy" (*mashriqīyah* or *ishrāqīyah*) coincides with that of "Yemenite theosophy", meaning a theosophy which is inspired: a mental vision of the beings of light, not simply theoretical speculation. Like Maryam, the theosopher goes "towards the Orient", in the direction marked by the corner where the meeting takes place between Jesus and the first Imam. Cf. note 37 above.

considers that this corner marks the completion of the Temple (*tamām al-Bayt*), and that it typifies the perfection attained by the *res religiosa*. The function assumed by the Iraqi corner within the Temple as a whole corresponds in this way with that of the Seal of prophecy, with whom the mission of all the previous prophets is finally completed.

This is how the configuration of the Temple of the Ka'bah is shown to be homologous with that of the Temples of the spiritual universes. This Temple, the centre of the terrestrial world, is the centre *surrounded* by the procession of believers in this world; but at the same time it is the centre *which surrounds*, because it is the Temple of the eternal prophetic Religion. From being a material form situated at the centre of our world, the Temple becomes the spiritual form that surrounds and contains our world in its totality. Its corner-stones, the four great prophets, elevate it, as the immaterial Temple of faith, above its material configuration, so that it overhangs it (as in the Byzantine icon of St. George the immaterial body of the young hero contained the whole universe of his combat). The thought of Qāḍī Sa'īd Qummī shows a similar élan: as the material Ka'bah rests on its corner-stones, so the Throne or Temple of eternal Religion, the hierocosmos, subsists through its great prophets; and this is why the eighth Imam, 'Alī al-Riḍā, said: "The divine Religion will never perish so long as the Temple of the Ka'bah endures", the Temple, that is, of faith which is the religion of the prophets. The same statement is made in the Koranic verse 5:97: "God established the Ka'bah as the sacred Temple to be erected in perpetuity for human beings."

The Temple of the Ka'bah, explains our author, is so perfectly the spiritual Temple of faith that it could only disappear if the Imam ceased to exist—the "hidden Imam", that is, who is the mystical *pole* of the earthly world of men, without whose existence humanity would not even be able to keep itself in being; for the hidden Imam is the *pole* that invisibly gathers around himself those through whom God still "cares for" this world.[55] This precisely is the spiritual Temple which remains forever in this world, by virtue of the invisible presence of the hidden Imam. Here *par excellence* it is proper to speak of the "Cloud over the sanctuary"

55 Cf. *En Islam iranien*, op. cit., vol. IV, Book 7. The existence of the invisible Imam as the mystical *pole* of humanity is absolutely necessary if humanity is to continue to exist. This idea is affirmed over and over again in the *ḥadīth* (especially by Kulaynī) as in all the Shiite authors.

(Eckhartshausen). Finally, when we have understood the secret of the Black Stone, we will understand that the secret of the Temple is the secret of man, and that he who has grasped it has the keys of the Temple in his possession: on him has been bestowed the *potestas clavium*.

4. *The area surrounding the Temple: the "stations" of the angel Gabriel and of Abraham.* The little plan drawn by Qāḍī Sa'īd Qummī (see above, fig. 5) contains three hitherto unremarked attestations.[56] To the left of the Temple when facing it, and thus to the *right* of the Temple envisaged as a person facing the pilgrim—in the *oriental* part of it, therefore—just beside the threshold, is a site marked by the letter *G*. This is the place or "station" (*maqām*) of the angel Gabriel. In the *occidental* part of the Temple, to the left of the "person" of the Temple (but to the right of the person facing it), in front of the Syrian corner, is a site marked by the letter *A*. This is the place or "station" of Abraham. Finally, still in the occidental part, is a site marked by the letter *H*. This is the *ḥijr* of Ishmael, or the house of Ishmael (*Bayt Ismā'īl*), where he buried his mother Hagar and where he himself is buried.[57] These three sites possess an outstanding significance in connection with the structure and function of the Temple of the Ka'bah as a spiritual Temple, that is to say, as a Form whereby the mystic attains to the fullness of his being. Our author consequently sets about discovering the reason for their respective *situs*.

The place of the angel Gabriel is explained by the prominent part played by this Angel with respect to Adam, when, after his exile from Paradise, Adam discovered the secret of the Black Stone (cf. below, III, 2). The Stone is embedded exactly there, in the pillar establishing a communication between the earthly Temple and the world of the Intelligences (fig. 6) whose most eminent figure is the angel or archangel Gabriel. As the initiating angel of the prophets in general, and particularly of the Seal of the prophets to whom he transmits or dictates the text of the Holy Book, the angel Gabriel figures largely in the writings of Islamic theologians and philosophers. He is both the angel of Knowledge and of Revelation, Holy Spirit and active Intelligence.[58] It follows that his place

56 Here begins the third chapter of *Kitāb asrār al-Ḥajj*, op. cit., fol. 181–182.
57 Cf. *Safīnat Biḥār al-Anwār* I, p. 225.
58 One could write a sizeable monograph on the figure and role of the angel Gabriel in the theology, philosophy and theosophy of Islam, as well as in Islamic spiritual life

should be at the threshold of the Temple, on the *oriental* side, by the pillar of the Black Stone, because, explains Qāḍī Sa'īd Qummī, it is he who receives the mystical pilgrims on their arrival there. "He makes their perfect spirits mount up to the world of the beings of pure light, he brings them into the presence of the Master of the house." He it is who brings them "into the neighbourhood of the Temple of God which is in the world of the Intelligence (see above, II. 3) . . . Those who take refuge in the Temple enclosure the Angel leads into delicious shade (Koran 4:57), into a place of safety (44:51). On those that possess the aptitude for it he sheds knowledge which derives from the Principle who is the source of all Emanation (*al-Mabda' al-fayyāḍ*). He leads those who thirst after high spiritual knowledge (*ma'ārif ḥaqīqīyah*) to the wells of sweet clear Water, to the living waters of the *Kawthar* (108:1)".

Furthermore, on the *occidental* side of the Temple is the house of Ishmael. Our author sees this as a symbol of what is frequently expressed in Arabic by saying that the son is the secret (*sirr*, the esoteric meaning) of his father. This is how the person of Abraham is to be approached in order to understand his place and function on the occidental side of the Temple of the Ka'bah, in front of the Syrian corner or "pillar". It is here that the symbolic justification of this "station" of Abraham's leads our author into a full-scale recapitulation of the homologies whereby the visible and invisible universes symbolize with each other, in the course of which the supports or "bearers" of each of these "Thrones" are also homologized with each other. The nomenclature differs somewhat from the previous one (see above, II, 3), but the correspondence is easily established.

1. There is what Qāḍī Sa'īd Qummī here calls *'Arsh al-Sarīr*, and which is identifiable without difficulty as the eighth Heaven, the immense heaven of the Fixed Stars (the *Kursī* or *Firmamentum*). This is the "Throne in the firmament" where the constellations of the zodiac are distributed. Furthermore, and most remarkably, we see the reappearance here, in our Shiite theosophers, of explicit traces of Ezekiel's famous vision. Mullā Ṣadrā Shīrāzī, for his part, has preserved a tradition explaining the division of the signs of the zodiac by the four figures of Ezekiel's vision.[59] These four

in general. In the *Diarium spirituale* where Rūzbihān Baqlī described his visions, this figure often recurs, entrancing the visionary with the beauty of his features. Cf. *En Islam iranien*, op. cit., vol. III, pp. 47, 48, 50–52 and 63.

59 Cf. Ezekiel 1:10 and Revelation 4:7 (the vision of the four "living creatures", *ḥayyoth*).

figures—Man, Lion, Eagle, and Ox or Bull—are here the four supports of the Throne or Temple of the firmament (fig. 8).

2. There is the Throne or Temple of the visible cosmos (*ʿArsh al-Mulk*), the Throne in the Sphere of Spheres or supreme Sphere, which englobes the totality of the universes that are manifest to the senses. We may recall that this universe is defined by four limits (fig. 1, the limits which engender the cubic form). These four limits, which apply to all beings, are respectively designated here as the volume of a being (*jism*, or its configuration, *ṣūrah*); its spirit (*rūḥ*); its nourishment and growth; and its level of realization. These are the four corners of the Temple or Throne of the *Mulk*. Their homologues and also their supports are an archangelic tetrad and a tetrad of prophets (that is, in the *malakūt* and also in the hierocosmos): a. Adam and the archangel Seraphiel are the supports of the forms of beings at the moment when the spirit is breathed into them; b. Muhammad and Gabriel are the supports of the spirits and of their realization; c. Abraham and Michael ensure the subsistence of beings; d. the Imam ʿAlī and Azrael determine eschatologically their final level of realization.[60] There are *eight* supports, therefore, for the *ʿArsh al-Mulk* (fig. 8).

3. There is the Throne of Knowledge and Religion (*ʿArsh al-ʿIlm waʾl-Dīn*) which, as we already know, also possesses *eight* supports (see above, fig. 3). These are four great prophets from among the ancients—Noah,

Ṣadrā Shīrāzī develops this theme at length in his monumental commentary on Kulaynī's *Uṣūl minaʾl-Kāfī*, in connection with the verse of the Throne (*Āyat al-Kursī*) referred to in the *ḥadīth* of the Imams (cf. *Kāfī*, *K. al-Tawḥīd*, chapter XX, on the *ʿArsh* and the *Kursī*, and Ṣadrā Shīrāzī's commentary, lith. Tehran n.d., pp. 309 ff., 314 ff.). It is evident that Qāḍī Saʿīd Qummī, fol. 181b, was familiar with this commentary. A comparison should one day be made between all that has been written in Islamic theosophy about the "Throne" and the mystique of the "Throne" (the *Merkabah*) in Jewish gnosis. Cf. Gershom G. Scholem, *Les Grands Courants de la mystique juive* (Paris, 1950), pp. 53 ff; tr. *Major trends in Jewish mysticism* (New York, Schocken, 1976). See also *3 Enoch or the Hebrew Book of Enoch*, ed. and trans. H. Odeberg (Cambridge, 1928), index s.v. Ezekiel's vision and the vision of the Apocalypse are the source of the "tetramorph" in Western iconography; magnificent examples of it exist in Coptic and Carolingian art, signs of a Christendom in which the initiatic tradition was still alive.

60 In order to simplify the schema, Azrael is here allotted the function which our author doubles in the functions of Riḍwān and Mālik. The Imam's eschatological function should be returned to the body of Shiite doctrine; cf. for example Abūʾl Ḥasan Sharīf Isfahānī, *Tafsīr Mirʾāt al-Anwar* (Tehran, 1375 A.H.), p. 9 (on this work, see my report in *Annuaire* de l'Ecole pratique des Hautes-Études, cited in note 14 above). Shiism, as the religion of the *walāyah*, is the religion of love as regards the theophanic persons or forms (*maẓāhir*) who are the twelve Imams. The love or the hostility he bears them *makes* the paradise or the hell within man.

Abraham, Moses and Jesus—and on the other side the four Muhammadan figures: the prophet Muhammad and the first three Imams, 'Alī ibn Abi-Ṭālib, Ḥasan ibn 'Alī, and Ḥusayn ibn 'Alī.[61]

4. There is the Throne of Sovereign Unity (*'Arsh al-waḥdānīyah al-kubrā*), whose supports (see above, fig. 6) are four in number: Intelligence, Soul, Nature and Matter (the Intelligence or Sublime Throne is the central pillar of red hyacinth).

Thus, there is symmetry between *'Arsh al-waḥdānīyah* and *'Arsh al-Sarīr* (of Ezekiel's vision), in that they each have *four* supports, and there is symmetry between *'Arsh al-Mulk* and *'Arsh al-'Ilm wa'l-Dīn*, each of which possesses *eight* supports. This in no way compromises the correspondences of all the Thrones or Temples amongst themselves.

With this recapitulation completed, and Abraham's rank among the supports of the other Thrones or Temples specified, the meaning of his place in the area surrounding the earthly Temple of the Ka'bah should be quite clear.

This meaning is linked essentially to the function of the spiritual Temple. Abraham is there first of all because the prophets and the Imams are the "Face of God" (*Wajh Allāh*), and by orientating oneself towards them one turns towards God. But more precisely, Abraham's place is there on the left, on the *occidental* side of the Temple envisaged as a person *facing* the pilgrim, because this occidental *situs* conceals Abraham's exemplary mystical significance, whereby Abraham, builder of the Temple, makes the pilgrim fit to approach the Temple (*potestas clavium*) and to be introduced by the angel Gabriel into the spiritual world. His place is there in front of the Syrian corner, whose stone comes, as we saw, from Ṣafā, where Abraham dwelt in exile. He is associated "functionally" with the archangel Michael because, although the subsistence and growth of beings in general devolve mystically upon the archangel Michael, the subsistence and growth of believers and the children of believers devolve upon Abraham the prophet. Now, in the physiology of the human body, nutrition is a process pertaining to the "left (or occidental) side", because food travels, or "emigrates" (*ightirāb*), in the person whom it nourishes, by way of the left side—which is the side of the heart.

61 M. Sabzavārī, ed. cit., p. 184, note 1, refers, in connection with this theme, to texts by Kulaynī, Naṣīruddīn Ṭūsī and Ibn Abī Jumhūr Aḥsā'ī. Unfortunately, we cannot expand on this here.

Moreover, Abraham is called the intimate Friend of God (*Khalīl*) because the ground of his being is intimately involved with his love for God and the love of his God is intimately involved with his being,[62] in an intimacy comparable to that of food when it mixes with and is assimilated into the body of him whom it nourishes. Seen in this light, Abraham's position with regard to the mystical physiology of the Temple envisaged as a person is surely on the left side, the *occident* or *maghrib*. The *maghrib* is the place of *setting* and *exile*: thus, the double implication of the root of the Arabic word (*gh-r-b*: the setting star and the exile who emigrates) gives rise to the whole mystical meaning of the personage of Abraham. Abraham is he who goes into exile towards the "supreme horizon" (*al-ufq al-mubīn*, the horizon where the Angel appeared to the Prophet, Koran 81:23); he disappears from himself and is concealed from both universes. A *ḥadīth* of the sixth Imam declares "Islam began in exile and will once more be in exile as at the beginning. Happy are the exiles!" Abraham typifies the spiritual exile whose place is not in this world; and the spiritual exile, the stranger to this world, becomes the instrument through which God still watches over this world. As one tradition has it: "It is through the prophets that God watches over men", and according to an inspired (*qudsī*) *ḥadīth*, famous among the mystics of Islam, it is of this exile and stranger that God said: "I am the eye through which he sees, the hearing through which he hears, the hand with which he feels, the foot with which he walks. . ."

The mystic whom Abraham typifies by the involvement of his intimate being with divine love is the spiritual man whose person, in concealing itself from this world, simultaneously becomes the West or Occident of the divine Light (*maghrib Nūr Allāh*), that is to say, becomes the mystical place where this Light declines, exiles itself, and conceals itself in this world in order to dwell in this world. Thus the drama of Adam exiled *into* this world achieves its dénouement in Abraham exiling himself *from* this world; for it is in Abraham exiled *from* this world and a stranger to it that the divine light will itself be exiled *into* this world. If the divine Light did not thus exile itself into this world, concealed in those who exile themselves

62 On the reasons for associating the prophet Abraham with the archangel Michael—reasons which also make him worthy to be called an intimate friend (*Khalīl*), and thereby illuminating with the light of Islamic mysticism the "philoxenia" of Abraham in the famous icon by Andrei Rubliev—see my *Creative Imagination* . . . , op. cit., pp. 315–316.

from this world in order to be, without men's knowledge, the receptacles of this Light, God would cease to watch over this world, to "care for" it. It would be hard to find a more beautiful symbol than this placing of Abraham on the "occidental side" of the Temple to signify that man, in contemplating the form of the spiritual Temple of faith, configurates his own inner form of light, after the example of Abraham the exile building the Temple of Light. This is what we have called the *potestas clavium* bestowed on the believer. From this point onwards, the mystical meaning of the pilgrimage and the rites of pilgrimage present themselves in all clarity to the inner vision.

III. *The esoteric meaning of the pilgrimage to the Temple of the Ka'bah*

1. *The procession "in Heaven"*. A traditional teaching among the spiritual masters of Islam says that there are two sorts of pilgrimage: one is the pilgrimage of the community of the faithful (*'awāmm*), who travel in order to visit the Holy Places, and the other is the pilgrimage of the initiated mystics (*khawāṣṣ*), and is the desire for the Face of the divine Friend. Just as exoterically there is a Temple of the Ka'bah which orientates the gaze of created beings (a Ka'bah which is their *Qiblah*), so esoterically there is a Ka'bah which is the object of contemplation of the divine gaze, and this is the heart of man. The material Temple is the Ka'bah around which the pilgrims walk in procession; the Ka'bah of the heart is the place where the divine graces process. The first is the goal of pious travellers, and the second is the place where the pure Lights descend. The former is the house, the latter the Master of the house. For each of us there is a direction (*Qiblah*) towards which he orientates himself, and which is his personal Ka'bah. Whichever way he turns, he meets the face of the Friend, the Face, that is, with which the *Deus absconditus* is revealed to him and becomes for him the *Deus revelatus*. This Face, which mysteriously reveals the Ineffable in the lineaments of the Friend, is what is known in Shiism as the Imam, and could be said to be the secret at the heart of Shiite spirituality[63]—the secret that we will discover when the pilgrimage has been explained.

63 This is a faithful summary of a long Persian annotation by M. Sabzavārī, op. cit., p. 184, and it testifies to the spiritual sense of a present-day Iranian theologer. The Koranic verses with which it concludes are among the most popular in Shiite

THE CONFIGURATION OF THE TEMPLE OF THE KA'BAH

The earthly Temple of the Ka'bah, being a centre, is the place around which the ritual circumambulations are performed. The Temple possesses a celestial archetype, and the ritual too possesses one, since every centre is homologous with every other, and the circumambulation is associated with the actual idea of the centre. Qāḍī Sa'īd Qummī explains[64] how around the archetypal centre, the initial Temple in the intelligible world, goes the procession, made up—as we saw above (II, 3)—of a seraphic humanity of pure Light and of the Angels of the highest hierarchies who, through unassuaged nostalgia and an ecstasy of love, encircle in their flight the area surrounding the Sublimity. In the same way, the pilgrims walk in procession around the Temple on the Earth of absence and separation, in commemoration and as a reminder of the state of this superior seraphic humanity (the Fourteen Most Pure Ones). The initial divine Intention manifests itself from universe to universe by manifesting *eo ipso* the constant correspondence between the things above and the things below.

Nevertheless, between the supreme degree of the Temple in the world of the Intelligence and the plane of terrestrial Nature where the Temple of the Ka'bah rises, there are many intermediate stages, and it is here that the drama is played out, the symbolic story whose dénouement is the building of the earthly Ka'bah. There is a long traditional recital on this theme which goes back to the fifth Imam, Muḥammad al-Bāqir. The drama "in Heaven" begins at the moment when God announces to the Angels: "I will install a vicar on Earth" (2:30), thus announcing the appearance of Adam, of the earthly human Form, in the capacity of God's Caliph in the universe of Nature.

This episode "in Heaven", as meditated in Ismaili gnosis, is the key to sacred history; but for Ismaili as for Twelver Shiite gnosis, the Angels to whom God makes this announcement are not the Angels of the higher hierarchies.[65] For Qāḍī Sa'īd Qummī, the Angels in question are those of

---

spirituality: "Everyone has a part of heaven towards which he orientates himself" (2:148), and "Whichever way you turn, there is the Face of God" (2:115): the Face which is the Imam, he who *guides*, because in it is revealed the Friend. Herein is contained the sum of Shiite mysticism.

64 Here begins the fourth chapter of *Kitāb asrār al-Ḥajj*, op. cit., fol. 182 and 182b.

65 Cf. my *Hermèneutique spirituelle comparée*, op. cit., note 149, on the interpretation given by Ismaili gnosis, using the text of the *ḥadīth* of the Imam Ja'far, of the episode "in Heaven", where his father, the Imam Muḥ. al-Bāqir, beside the Ka'bah itself, teaches a mysterious stranger about the Temple's celestial origin.

the physical universe (*Malā'ikah ṭabī'īyah*), who are the *malakūt* of our visible world—the *malakūt*, as we said, "where our symbols are taken literally". These are the Angels who are seized with amazement and fear in the face of the divine announcement of the *khalīfah* entrusted to terrestrial Man. For it seemed to them that because of the purity of their nature there was nothing that could surpass it in nobility, and that this spiritual *khalīfah* should have come to them. "Will you," they ask, "establish on Earth a being who will create disorder and shed blood?". . . "I know," came the reply, "what you do not" (2:30). Then they understood the limit of their knowledge and the insufficiency of their power. The divine reply is seen by them as the effect of a divine displeasure, as though the divine Light were being veiled from them. That is why, explains the recital of the Imam, they sought refuge close to the Throne where seventy thousand Angels come each day; they went around it in procession for *seven* days or *seven* thousand years. This variant of days or years possesses little significance when it is a question of "subtle time" (*zamān laṭīf*); only the number *seven* is important, because it always symbolizes in this episode the interval of lost time to be made up, the "lost time of eternity" which is redeemed by the *seven* periods or "millenia" of the cycle of prophecy.[66] This, explains our author, is why *seven* ritual circumambulations are performed around the earthly Ka'bah, one for each *millenium*.

Since the Angels are those of the physical universe, the Throne around which they go during this episode is the Temple of the Soul of the universe; the Temple, that is, in the world of the *malakūt*, described in the form of its physical manifestation as the Glorious Throne (the ninth Sphere; see above, II, 3). Its symbolic description signals both its difference from and its similarity to the Temple or Throne of the Sovereign Unity, symbolized in the Tent descended from heaven. The Throne of the *malakūt* or Temple in the world of the Soul is made, explains the Imam's recital, of a marble of immaculate *whiteness*, exempt from all the impurities of physical material modalities (a Temple, therefore, made of the all-subtle matter of the *mundus imaginalis*). Its roof is of *red* hyacinth. We have already seen how the colour red derives from the mingling of Light with Darkness, and that it symbolizes the state of being in which the Divine, that is light, mingles with the creatural darkness. Furthermore, this roof is

66 On this point, cf. my *Trilogie ismaélienne*, op. cit., index s.v. sept.

the reality itself of the world of the *malakūt*, its "soul" (*al-nafs al-malakūtīyah*), because the soul is like a diadem placed on the body, like the flowerhead of a plant or the roof in relation to the Temple. The columns of the Temple are here made out of *green emerald*, because they are the traces emanating from the outpouring of the Soul of the universe over the universal body, and because the colour *green* is more or less the mean between *white* and *red* (as in the Temple of the Sovereign Unity the *violet* colour of the ropes was the mean between the *yellow* gold of the world of Intelligences and the *red* resulting from the mingling of the Divine with the Creatural).

Every detail, every colour, of the structure of the Temple is rich with a symbolism that should be explained with the help of many comparisons. We cannot do this here; we can only emphasize some suggestive points. God looked with love on the initiative taken by the Angels of the *malakūt*, and commanded them to "descend to Earth" in order to build a Temple there which would be the image (the imitation, *ḥikāyah*, the "history") of the Temple in the world of the Soul. This was the Temple around which Adam, and then his children, performed their perambulations in imitation of the Angels of the *malakūt*. Yet at the time of the Flood, the Angels carry off this Temple on earth and transfer it to the fourth Heaven.

The profound significance of the Flood, not as a geological event but as a spiritual cataclysm, is made apparent in this transference of the Temple. Brought to earth by the Angels, like the Holy Grail of our Western traditions, the Temple is swept away by the Angels from men's gaze when the latter have become incapable or unworthy of seeing it.[67] Abraham, the spiritual exile, will rebuild a Temple on earth on the foundations of the vanished Temple. This is how the Abrahamic pilgrim, in performing the external rituals, knows that his true pilgrimage is being accomplished around an invisible Temple within the space of the *malakūt*.

2. *The secret of the Black Stone and the motif of the Pearl.* From here we pass to the ultimate and decisive question: what is the function of the spiritual Temple with respect to the esoteric meaning of the rites of pilgrimage, when these are perceived as configurating the Temple's spiritual form? In

67 On the spiritual meaning of the *Flood* and the story of the removal of the Ka'bah to Heaven by the Angels, see note 65 above. See also §§ 6 and 9 of the same study (the theme of Noah and the Flood as it is treated by Swedenborg and in Ismaili gnosis).

the absence of this form the pilgrimage would not possess an esoteric meaning, for man configures both his own spiritual form through that of the Temple, and the Temple's spiritual form in accordance with his own inner form. This conformity or *symmorphosis* of the spiritual Temple with man, by virtue of which the invisible Temple is man's spiritual form, is the secret of the Black Stone. The Black Stone is the secret of the Temple and the secret of man, the esoteric aspect of both. The configuration of each of them, in the state of a spiritual form that is more truly subsistent than the material form which is temporarily visible, depends on a pilgrimage accomplished throughout an entire lifetime; for an entire lifetime is needed to "give form" to the spiritual Temple. The Black Stone is in some sense the key to the celestial Temple.

In the course of a conversation with one of his disciples,[68] the sixth Imam, Ja'far al-Ṣādiq, asks: "Do you know what the Stone (*al-ḥajar*) was?" No, the disciple does not know, and the Imam goes on to explain it to him in a symbolic recital which, for all its seeming simplicity, possesses a remarkable density of allusion. The undertaking or pact (*mīthāq*) mentioned in the recital is, in Shiite terms, the triple attestation of the Unique of Uniques, the exoteric mission of the prophets, and the esoteric mission of the Imams;[69] this is the totality expressed, as we saw, by the spiritual form of the Temple. Moreover, in order to understand the recital of the Imam Ja'far, we must perceive, like Qāḍī Sa'īd Qummī, the allusion it makes to three levels of universe to which this undertaking is proclaimed, because the reality of Man is manifested successively at each level of the descending hierarchy of the universes: in the world of the Intelligence, in the world of the Soul—the subtle corporeity of the *mundus imaginalis*—and in the physical terrestrial world. Shiite hermeneutics has reflected on this undertaking—the pact and its consequences—by joining together two Koranic verses: that in which God asks all humanity, which is mystically gathered together, "Am I not your Lord?" (7:172), and the verse containing the statement: "The trust that we offered to sky, earth and mountains, all have refused to shoulder, they trembled to receive it. Man has agreed to shoulder it: he is violent and ignorant" (33:72). If indeed, as Ḥaydar Āmulī explains, man had need of a sublime folly in order to accept the burden of such a trust, this sublime folly was to degenerate into a folly

68 Here begins the fifth chapter of *Kitāb asrār al-Ḥajj*, fol. 182b–184.
69 Cf. *En Islam iranien*, op. cit., vol. IV, general index s.v. mīthāq.

pure and simple which made him violate it. The secret of the trust confided to him is what all Shiite gnosis has attempted to express in its esoteric Imamology. I recall this very briefly here, because Adam's betrayal and the secret of the Black Stone are connected.

"The Stone," explains the Imam,[70] "was once an Angel among the princes of the Angels before God. When God received the Angels' undertaking, this Angel was the first to take his oath and agree to the pact. So God chose him to be the trustworthy follower to whom he could entrust all his creatures. He caused him to absorb, to "swallow", the pact and confided it to him in trust, and on men He laid the charge of renewing each year in front of this Angel their agreement to the pact and to the promise He had received from them. Thus God placed this Angel with Adam in Paradise, to make Adam mindful of his undertaking and so that he could renew his agreement every year before the Angel. When Adam had betrayed and had departed from Paradise, he forgot the promise and the undertaking that God had received from him . . . And when God had returned to Adam (Koran 2:37), he gave to this Angel the appearance of a *white pearl*, and he cast the pearl out of Paradise towards Adam, when Adam was still on the Earth of India." The tradition according to which the man Adam appeared in Ceylon is common in Shiism; in Ismaili gnosis it is applied to a primordial and universal Adam, *Pananthropos*, who is not yet the initial Adam of our present cycle.[71] The island of Ceylon signifies only an initial stage in the coming of physical terrestrial man.

The recital continues. Adam notices this *pearl*; he becomes familiar with it but does not recognize it, seeing it as nothing but a stone. But with divine permission, the *pearl* begins to speak: "Oh Adam! do you recognize me?"—"No."—"Surely Satan (*Shaytān*) has triumphed within you, since he makes you forget the memory of your Lord." At this moment the *pearl* assumes his original form, as the Angel who was Adam's companion in Paradise. "Oh Adam! where are your promise and your undertaking?" Adam starts; the memory of the divine pact returns to him, and he weeps. He kisses the white pearl—the Angel—and renews his agreement to the promise and the pact. Then God gives to the white pearl, pure and

70 The text of this *ḥadīth* is given in the great encyclopaedia of Majlisī, *Biḥār al-Anwār*, vol. VII (Tehran) p. 339, and *Safīnah* I, p. 225.

71 On the differentiation between the spiritual Adam (*Adam rūḥānī*), the universal Adam (*Pananthropos*), and the partial Adam who inaugurated our present cycle of occultation, see my *Trilogie ismaélienne*, op. cit., index s.v. Adam.

splendid, the appearance of the Stone (for such is the appearance it wears in a world given over to Darkness), and this is the Stone that Adam carries on his shoulder as far as Arabia. He makes this journey in the company of the angel Gabriel, a fact whose significance will shortly become apparent. When he is tired by the weight of the Stone, the angel Gabriel relieves him of it and takes his turn at carrying it—a magnificent symbol, seeming to say that only another Angel can momentarily relieve man of the burden of the Angel, that is to say of the pact that involves all his destiny with regard to the spiritual world. Each day and each night, Adam renews his mystical undertaking to this Stone that had been the testimony of his Paradise, and in whose company he advances until he arrives at the site of the Temple in Mecca. Here, as we know, in obedience to the divine command, the Angels of the *malakūt* of our world erected a Temple in the image of the Temple that had been their refuge "in Heaven", and the Black Stone is embedded in the corner of the Temple whose mystical correspondences have already been pointed out to us. On this spot, the recital continues, God received the undertaking of the sons of Adam, and we are present at the repetition—or the continuation—on earth of the drama that took place "in Heaven".

We are in agreement with Qāḍī Sa'īd Qummī that there is no doubt that the Imam's recital explains the secret of the white Pearl ("white" here meaning wholly pure and splendid) by the deployment of this secret in three settings: the world of the Intelligence, the world of the Soul, and our physical world. On each level, human beings exist in a form whose subtlety progressively decreases; on each of these levels, they utter the triple undertaking in a language that corresponds to their modality of being on that level. On the level of the world of pure angelic Intelligences, their utterance is in the language of these Intelligences. This is the first episode in our recital, where it is said that the Angel who was later to be concealed in the form of the Black Stone was the first of the Angels to reply. Next, we pass to the level on which corporeity comes into existence still in its wholly subtle form, the form of the body of light (*jismīyah nūrīyah*) of the *mundus imaginalis*. The "clay" out of which the human creature is made on this level is the subtle clay of the "Earth of light" (*ṭīnah arḍīyah nūrīyah*; cf. the *Terra lucida* in Manichaean gnosis). But because the corporeal form now exists, there is a *centre* which is distinguished from the surrounding periphery (cf. above, the difference between spiritual and material orbs). This plane of subtle corporeity is symbolized in the traditions by *red hyacinth* or *white pearl*, and it is one aspect of the celestial Throne or Temple (cf. above, II, 3 and III, 1, on the symbolism of *red hyacinth*).

At this level of manifestation of the human being, the *central* part of his clay of light is precisely the Angel whom God gave to Adam to be his companion and witness, who was charged with making him remember the divine pact, and before whom he had every year to renew it "in Paradise"; for this was the Angel whom God had caused to absorb or swallow the pact—the Angel, in other words, to whom He had confided the pact in trust. The jewel at the centre of man, says Qāḍī Sa'īd Qummī, is designated as the "Angel" (*malak*), because his rank or degree of being is the esoteric and the invisible, the *malakūt* of the world which is manifest to the senses. The jewel that utters and remembers the divine pact is the *malakūt* within man, both the corner-stone of the Temple (the Black Stone embedded in the Iraqi corner), and the Angel concealed within man's apparent material form (the *centre*, the *Earth of light*, the *Paradise* within man, or else that which holds the *keys* to it). According to Qāḍī Sa'īd Qummī, "To all that is inner and esoteric pertains authority over what is outer and exoteric, to educate and direct it (whence the question asked of Adam by the Angel: Has Satan, then, triumphed within you? . . .) And by the Angel we mean that which possesses this anteriority and authority, by virtue of the fact that he is the *centre* of the human being, before the other parts were constituted according to the norms proper to them." In Shiite terms, this centre is the Imamate within man. For this reason the jewel, as it is in itself, retains its purity, white pearl or red hyacinth, in its state as "body of light", unalloyed by any foreign admixture.

However, we read that after Adam left Paradise, the divine mercy cast this white pearl towards him. This means that this priceless pearl descends "from the hieratic world of the Throne and of the body of light" into the elemental physical world. Of necessity, therefore, it puts on the "robe", or appearances, of the dark world into which it is cast. The earth of India where it lands has a precise significance: among all the levels of the manifestation of being, it is the level which is the *occident* of spiritual entities (*maghrib al-arwāḥ*), the level where their nature of light is occulted. That is why Adam fails to recognize the pearl: on this level it is veiled, occulted, by the darkness of men's sins, by their obsessive pursuit of the pleasures of their ephemeral, physical existence. He recognizes it only when it assumes its original form; that is to say, when he has himself stripped it, divested it of its garment of darkness, in the same way as he strips the object perceived by the senses in order to attain to the vision of the intelligible. But he is capable of this stripping off only when the Stone has prompted his remembrance. His senses merely perceive the Black Stone; it is through his imaginative spiritual perception that he attains the vision of the Angel, of the white pearl, and remembers.

It would be impossible for us not to recall here a famous chapter of the Gnostic book of the *Acts of Thomas*, entitled *The Hymn of the Soul* or *The Song of the Pearl* (several episodes of which have their exact equivalent in Suhravardī's *Recital of the Occidental Exile*). The recital of the Imam Ja'far Ṣādiq is a striking example of the Pearl motif in Twelver Shiite gnosis. Without doubt this motif has characteristics peculiar to it, which a detailed comparison would reveal. The "pearl" in the *Acts of Thomas* can be seen as a symbol of the soul itself, and as a symbol of the gnosis[72] that the soul must attain and which is the soul's salvation. In our Shiite text, the "pearl" symbolizes man's spiritual *centre*, his Angel: that is, both what his remembrance must make him rediscover, and that which prompts the remembrance. The recovery of the "pearl" *is* this act of remembering. The object of the act is expressed in Shiite terms as the pact, the triple Attestation referred to earlier; but such an Attestation is the expression of a spiritual totality (see above, II, 1) which, figured in the form of the Temple, possesses as its corner-stone the Black Stone—the Stone, that is to say, in which man rediscovers the jewel or Angel concealed within himself. The homology or correspondence between the configuration of the Temple and the form of the spiritual life is therefore perfect.

The pilgrimage that leads Adam, in the company of the angel Gabriel, into Arabia and to Mecca, is the preparation for the third and final scene, in which the secret of the Black Stone is revealed on the level of our present earthly world. For an Islamic theosopher, the symbolic significance of this journey is immediately obvious, as a journey in the course of which spiritual entities finally decline in their occident. In this theosophy, the function of the angel Gabriel is a primordial one. He stands, as we know,

72 Cf. Reinhold Merkelbach, *Roman und Mysterium in der Antike* (München und Berlin, 1962), pp. 310 ff., 315 ff. See also my book *The Man of Light in Iranian Sufism*, op. cit., pp. 22 ff.

at the Temple threshold, close to the corner in which the Black Stone is embedded; he is the Holy Spirit and the Angel of humanity; human souls in this world emanate from his "wing of light";[73] and he is the angel of Knowledge, whose illumination projects the intelligible forms onto our intellects. It is thus altogether appropriate to typify, in the pilgrimage where Adam and the angel Gabriel are associated, the entire process of the descent of the white Pearl into this world, where it is metamorphosed into the appearance of the Black Stone—the form, that is, in which it appears to sensible perception and in which man must learn to recognize it, unless he is unfortunate enough to live his whole life through without doing so. The Black Stone, says the recital, was placed in the corner of the Ka'bah (where we located it in our previous figurations). And it was there that God received the undertaking of the sons of Adam, "to warn us," writes Qāḍī Sa'īd Qummī, "that all begins again from the beginning". The "drama in Heaven" in fact begins over again on earth with each man:[74] his divine pact, his departure from Paradise, his act of recollection, and his search for the lost Paradise. It is the Angel within him that makes the undertaking, the Angel whom God caused to "swallow" the pact in his celestial preexistence; and it is he, the external man, who betrays it. Each son of Adam must in his turn complete the pilgrimage, that is to say, he must rebuild the spiritual form of the Temple, in order to attain his own centre. He must rediscover the secret of the Black Stone which is also the secret of the Angel; for this Stone—which the pilgrims kiss in passing, as did Adam when he recognized it—fulfils the same function in the material Temple of the Ka'bah as does the Angel at the centre of man. The "functional relationship" is identical on both sides, and permits meditation to pass spontaneously from one to the other (cf. above, II, 1).

Then the Black Stone turns back into the white Pearl, the signature of Paradise, the Angel or Imamate within man. It depends on man whether

73 Cf. notes 47 and 58 above.

74 This is the sense in which the Imam Ja'far's *ḥadīth* should be understood, as Qāḍī Sa'īd has fully realized (fol. 183b). In the last part the "terms" are repeated, precisely because the same drama happens over again. The *ḥadīth* finishes with these words: "Because of his love for Muhammad and his people (the Imams), God chose this Angel from among all the Angels and caused him to swallow (*alqama-hu*) the pact (*mīthāq*). And this Angel will come on the day of the Resurrection; he will have a tongue which speaks, eyes which look; he will witness to those who come to him in that place and who have kept the pact." *Sharḥ*, fol. 183. Cf. the text cited above, note 40.

he recovers his centre, or whether he loses it and remains forever in a state of disequilibrium. The arrival at this centre is the esoteric meaning of the rites of pilgrimage. These are performed in the same way as the rites of an initiation mystery, at the end of which the mystic enters the Temple, because he has repossessed himself of the *potestas clavium* that offers him access to the lost spiritual world.

3. *The esoteric meaning of the visits to the Holy Places.* At the start of this recital of initiation, we are once again in the situation that arose previously (II, 3), in the recital of the white Cloud.[75] It is the whole of this recital, as reported in a tradition that also goes back to the Imam Ja'far, which now makes its appearance as a recital of initiation. The moment evoked here was (in the recital of the White Cloud) that in which the angel Gabriel had led Adam to the site of the Temple of the Ka'bah, and a white Cloud above them had cast its shadow on the ground. This Cloud was the image of the Glorious Temple "in Heaven", and the Angel had commanded Adam to trace with his foot a groove which outlined on the earth the exact area covered by the shadow; the future, earthly Ka'bah would coincide with its dimensions and would thus be the image of the celestial Temple. The intervention of the angel Gabriel at this point is particularly significant. For all our theosophers, the drama of Adam, his "descent" from Paradise, is the drama itself of Knowledge. As we recalled a moment ago, Gabriel is the angel of Knowledge. It is his illumination (*ishrāq*) which, when we perceive sensible objects, brings forth in the soul the intelligible form of these objects which is the form of knowledge: that which we know in reality, that which is grasped by our act of knowing. His initiatory role with regard to the Adam who has understood the secret of the Black Stone becomes immediately comprehensible. He initiates Adam into the esoteric meaning of the visit to the holy places which surround the site of the Temple. This visit then becomes the inner pilgrimage, the pilgrimage of

75 Here begins the seventh chapter of *Kitāb asrār al-Ḥajj*, fol. 186–187b. We have been unable to include in our text the contents of chapter 6, which nevertheless comprises several most interesting points. Noteworthy among these are the question of the meaning of pre-existence, and the question of the exclamation made by the pilgrims as they enter the sacred territory: *Labbayk! Labbayk!* (I am here! I am here! offering myself for Thee). Where, and in what world, does this cry resound? In the sensible atmosphere or in the pure spiritual air?

the heart just referred to: the pilgrimage of an entire lifetime, whose goal is the construction of the Temple's spiritual form.

Shiite theosophical traditions, both of Ismaili theosophy and of Twelver Shiism, are agreed that the drama of Adam is *the* drama of Knowledge.[76] Qāḍī Saʿīd Qummī gives us the broad outlines of this drama, and we know by what has already been said that it is continuously being performed (it attains its dénouement only at the end of the pilgrimage). The violence done by Adam to the trust reposed in him, which he wishes to lay hold of for himself; the betrayal of the undertaking which the Shiite terms relates to the triple Attestation: this constitutes the drama of Knowledge. For what Adam wished to lay hold of for himself was Knowledge that he, Adam, was not in a position to possess, because its object was as yet not manifest on the level on which it needed to be manifest in order for the knowledge of it to be actualized. For such knowledge to be actualized, its object would have had to be manifest on a level lower than that on which it was in fact manifest. For Ismaili gnosis, Adam's act of violence is a wish to attain to pure esotericism without the intermediary of symbolic figures. For Shiism in general, what was at issue was the knowledge reserved for the seraphic humanity of the Muhammadan Imams, the eschatological secrets that could be revealed only by the twelfth and last Imam. All other objects of knowledge, all the other trees in the Garden of Knowledge, were accessible and permitted to Adam, except for this one forbidden Tree.

When an object of knowledge is actualized for the knowing subject, it becomes a part of him, as food becomes part of the subject who feeds on it (as in the example of Abraham, whose intimate being is nourished by his divine love; see above, II, 4). By "eating" of the forbidden knowledge, Adam becomes in some sense heavy or pregnant with the subtle realities (*laṭāʾif*) of this knowledge; and these realities demand to be manifested by Adam, to be brought to light, as they are known by him. But this cannot happen on the level of Paradise (the *mundus imaginalis*), because on this

76 On the drama of Adam as the drama of Knowledge according to Ismaili gnosis, see my *Herméneutique spirituelle comparée*, op. cit., the whole of § 8. For Twelver Shiite gnosis, see *En Islam iranien*, op. cit., vol. IV, general index s.v. Adam—la faute d'Adam (sens ésotérique de la) selon le shīʿisme. A similar conception occurs in what amounts to an entire Western theosophical tradition (van Helmont, Swedenborg, and others). Cf. van Helmont's thesis of the *Intellectus adamicus* (that the drama of Adam, by forcing knowledge to "descend", shattered the integrity of the soul's organs which enabled it to perceive directly the spiritual and celestial equivalents of things).

level they *are* the forbidden Tree. It can only happen on the level of the world of sensible phenomena (*'ālam al-shahādah*). But this *eo ipso* presupposes the simultaneous descent of the knowing subject, so it is in fact inadequate to say that the descent from Paradise was Adam's punishment. One should say, rather, that by "eating" of the forbidden Tree, Adam *eo ipso* descended from Paradise, descended, that is, into the world of illusion and deceit (*dār al-ghurūr*).

In other words, we could say that for Adam, for man, to "eat" of the forbidden Tree is to perpetuate the violence that consists in *naturalizing* the things of the spirit. It is to wish to make the spiritual world knowable in the manner and on the level of natural things, to wish to possess it by force as material objects are possessed. But because the attempt is doomed to failure, man becomes in return a prey to his deep-seated agnosticism. His desire for conquest is turned against himself in the form of his doubt: does this spiritual world exist? It is thus assuredly *the* fundamental drama of Knowledge, its *permanent* drama, which can be confronted only by the *witness* of spiritual forms subsisting on the level and in the world proper to them. It is thus possible to see, with our authors, a profound meaning in the Imam's recital which, on the "morrow" of Adam's departure from Paradise, puts him into the safekeeping of Gabriel, the angel of Knowledge. It is also why the angel Gabriel is at the centre of so many recitals of personal spiritual initiation in Islam, for he is designated, by Qāḍī Sa'īd Qummī and his colleagues, as "the help of souls, their instructor, he who bears God's messages to their destination, the guide who leads back to Paradise".

The initiation is an initiation into the esoteric sense of pilgrimage and its rites: an initiation into the "first" pilgrimage completed by the "first" earthly human being. We have been made aware of the mystical significance of the journey from India to Arabia undertaken by Adam in the company of the Angel, up until the moment where they are both "in the shadow of the white Cloud". They will travel together to the holy places around Mecca visited today by pilgrims: from Mina to al-'Arafāt, from al-'Arafāt to al-Muzdalifah, from al-Muzdalifah to Mina, to return to the site where the Temple will henceforth stand. But through the initiation imparted by the Angel, each of these stages is transfigured and becomes a stage of the heart's pilgrimage towards the personal Ka'bah. They are thus the elements of what methods of meditation know as "composition of place".

We will follow the itinerary of the mystical pilgrimage from its beginning, as it is described in the *ḥadīth* of the Imam Ja'far. When the angel Gabriel was sent to Adam, who was in despair about his exile from the world of the realities of light, he led him towards the place where the Temple was to stand. Qāḍī Sa'īd Qummī explains: the world in which Adam now finds himself is constituted by the *traces* of the realities of light, the images of spiritual archetypes. But one can only arrive at the sources of the archetypes through their derivatives; to approach the "divine Face" is to walk round about the sanctuary, to seek refuge in its enclosure. As we know, sanctuaries of God exist in every universe, and in each case their constitution is homogeneous with the universe in question. In this way, each Temple is the image-imitation (the *ḥikāyah* or "history")[77] of the Temple that exists on the level of the universe superior to it: the exoteric (*ẓāhir*) is always as it were the frontispiece or title-page (*'unwān*) of the esoteric. In our world, constituted by the four Elements, the Temple of God that corresponds to earthly needs is the Ka'bah. To go there is the equivalent of what, on the level of pure knowledge, is described as the initial representation of a form (*taṣawwur*); for as long as a thing has not *taken form*, as long as one does not *represent* it to oneself, it is not possible to orientate oneself in its direction. Symmetrically, on the level of mystical vision (*shuhūd*) and spiritual realization (*taḥaqquq*), this corresponds to the entry upon the Way, the undertaking of the "journey leading from God to God" (*sulūk mina'llāh ilā'llāh*).[78] This is the moment, we may recall, in which there comes down over Adam and his angelic companion the mysterious white Cloud, defined by our author as "the Cloud of mercy, heavy with the beneficent rain which aids

77 On the implications of the Arabic word *ḥikāyah*, see the prologue to *Herméneutique spirituelle comparée*, op. cit.

78 The idea of this "journey" corresponds to a traditional schema. Mullā Ṣadrā Shīrāzī's great philosophical and theosophical encylopaedia is entitled "The high theosophy (or higher philosophy) concerning the *four* spiritual journeys". These are 1) The journey from the created world towards God. 2) The journey from God towards God through (or with) God. 3) The journey from God towards the created world through (or with) God. 4) The journey from the created world towards the created world, but through (or with) God. The mystical journey to which Qāḍī Sa'īd Qummī here refers (see also note 88 below) would correspond to the second journey in Ṣadrā Shīrāzī's terminology. Cf. my edition and translation of the *Livre des Pénétrations métaphysiques*, op. cit., p. 30 of the French text.

the growth of the new creation".[79] On the instructions of the Angel, Adam traces with his foot a mark in the earth which is the outline of the future Ka'bah, to the exact measurement of the shadow cast onto the ground by the Cloud "descended from the spiritual Heaven". In this way, the form or configuration of the Temple of God in the world of the Intelligence is imprinted onto the terrestrial world. Moreover, Adam's action in tracing the outline of the earthly Temple in the exact image of the celestial Cloud, signifies that the form of the earthly Temple must homologically enclose all that is enclosed by the celestial Temple. "Nothing in the world of light was left out, was not configured in the most beautiful of forms."[80] It is already being suggested here that the form of the Temple, as the homologue of the spiritual Forms, is a *centre* which, as such, simultaneously envelops and contains all things.

Following this, on the Angel's instructions Adam traces the limits of the sacred territory (*ḥaram*) surrounding the Temple as centre; that is to say, explains Qāḍī Sa'īd, the limits reached by the light of the red hyacinth whose colour has been explained as a conjunction of the divine with the creatural. In fact, it is through the intermediary of the knowledge within man that his universe receives its light. This knowledge is the Throne and the Light within him; and it is through man as the knowing subject that the universe is felt, imagined, and becomes intelligible. It is thus through man and for man that a sacred landscape is created, whose *imaginal* topography is marked by the hierophanic places. And as Adam's initial action in tracing the groove corresponds to the representational knowledge (*'ilm taṣawwurī*) through which a form comes into being, ever since then the pilgrims, on arriving at the Temple, walk around it once before visiting the places of devotion that surround it. These are the places to which the angel Gabriel takes Adam, in order to initiate him into the esoteric meaning of the rite he is made to perform.

1. The Angel first took Adam to *Mina* (a valley near Mecca), which is the chief place of devotion. Qāḍī Sa'īd Qummī attributes this priority to

79 The text continues: ". . . and aids the growth, out of the Earth of receptivity, of the plant which is man, as this Koranic verse has it: God has caused you to grow out of the Earth like a plant" (71:17). *Sharḥ*, fol. 186b.

80 It is in these very words (*fī aḥsan ṣūrah*) that the Prophet characterizes his personal theophanic vision. Cf. my book *Creative Imagination* . . . , op. cit., pp. 272 ff.

the actual name of the place, which he interprets as meaning *desire.*[81] All movement, whether spontaneous or voluntary, is preceded by the desire to attain to the object envisaged. To contemplate the traces of the divine response to Adam's tears—to contemplate, that is, on the terrestrial soil, the projection of the shadow cast by the white Cloud, and the course of the groove which defines the site of the Temple of the Ka'bah in its image, to ponder on the order of procession around it—all this is exceedingly apt to arouse the desire to advance and approach. Hence we learn, as a first eloquent testimonial, that what the angel Gabriel shows Adam in this place is the site of the mosque of Mina, because, explains our author, "in following the road that leads to God, the first thing to manifest itself in the *heart*—God's 'greatest Temple' (*Bayt Allāhi'l-akbar, Domus Dei Maxima*)—is ardent desire. After that come the methods of approach and their implementation". Here, then, is Adam, or more simply man, engaged, under the Angel's guidance, "in the heart's pilgrimage" towards the personal, spiritual Ka'bah. And the first stage, which determines the entire subsequent pilgrimage, is ardent desire.

2. From Mina, Adam and the Angel go to *al-'Arafāt*, a mountain about twelve miles from Mecca, as today's pilgrims continue to do. To go to al-'Arafāt, explains our author, is to have escaped from the place and level at which one was. It signifies entry upon the Way, completion of the first step in the process of uprooting oneself from the Earth of exile, in redeeming the distance implied by the transgression of the undertaking. The pilgrim arrives at al-'Arafāt at the *hour of sunset.* Adam stands at the head of the valley, while the Angel tells him: "Now that the sun is on the point of setting, acknowledge your fault." This means, explains Qāḍī Sa'īd Qummī: "Now that the Sun of truth (the spiritual Sun) is veiled from your eyes because of the betrayal you have perpetrated, your own hour is the hour of the evening twilight, for the darkness of your fault is around you and your sun is on the point of disappearing in the West. Acknowledge that you are estranged from your Friend only because you considered that you yourself were yourself (that you were sufficient to yourself in order to be yourself, *bi-ḥisābi-ka anna-ka anta*)." There is an arresting contrast here.

81 The root *mnā* has the meaning of to determine or to test. The fifth form, *tamannā*, means to wish or to desire. Obviously, one must place oneself within the perspective of Qāḍī Sa'īd's use of names.

Abraham, as we saw, was to be the occident of the divine Light; but this was so because the violence of his love had exiled him from himself. Because he was spiritually exiled *from* this world, the divine Light *exiled him to himself*: he was the mystical occident in which this Light was occulted and dwelt invisible. Abraham, or the mystic whom he typifies, carries this Light within him. Adam, on the other hand, was exiled *into* this world, because he had loved himself. Thus the Abrahamic symbol is inverted: it is no longer the divine Light which is exiled *into* him; it is he, Adam, man, who is exiled *from* this Light, and his "occidental exile" will last until the "dawn" (the hour of *Ishrāq*), at the end of the night of vigil which marks the next stage of the pilgrimage to al-Muzdalifah.

First the mystical pilgrim descends from al-'Arafāt; that is to say, he leaves behind him the viewpoint at which his own self was under the illusion that it was sufficient to itself in order to be itself. He passes by a group of *seven* mountains, typifying for him the *seven* or *seventy* thousand veils of light or spiritual stations that remain between man and his God after he has freed himself from the level of the carnal soul and nature. On each mountain, Adam, in obedience to the angel Gabriel's instructions, utters the *takbīr four* times (the formula, that is, of *Allāh akbar*: God is supremely great), in order to abolish the *four* limits that determine them,[82] and so that the "Face" of his Lord may reveal itself beyond the veils of his occultation.

3. The pilgrim then arrives at *al-Muzdalifah*. Geographically speaking, this is a hill situated between al-'Arafāt and Mecca, at about an equal distance from Mina and al-'Arafāt, where the pilgrims go on their return from al-'Arafāt to spend the night (from the 9th. to the 10th. of the month of pilgrimage or *Dhū'l-Ḥijjah*), setting out again next day at dawn for Mina. A Koranic verse (2:200) expressly prescribes that the pilgrims must here perform a rite of "recollection" of God (*dhikr*). This station of the pilgrimage has several names.[83] The actual root of the name al-Muzdalifah (*zlf*, *'zdlf*) means to advance or approach. If, therefore, it is also named *Jam'*, meaning "reunion", the mystic at once understands it as an allusion

82 Here one should call to mind the properties of the tetrad in the Pythagorean arithmetic known to our authors, which are such that the number four determines the structure of all forms of being: the four supports of the Throne, the four Elements, the four natural Qualities, the four ages of human life. Cf. M. Sabzavārī's note in op. cit., pp. 223–224.

83 Cf. my introduction to the *Livre des Pénétrations métaphysiques*, op. cit., pp. 43 ff.

signifying that this mystical station is the station of approach, coming after the station of separation that preceded it. Qāḍī Sa'īd also explains the name *Jam'* by the liturgical fact that the pilgrims here "reunite" two canonical Prayers, the Prayer of the sunset (*maghrib*) and the Prayer of the coming of night (*'ashā'*) (the hours corresponding to the hours of Vespers and Compline in the Christian liturgy). It is thus self-evident that the "approach" must take place at the station of "reunion". In his treatise "on the esoteric meanings of Prayer"[84] our author has already explained that these two Prayers are prayers of "vigil, in the period of waiting for the spiritual Sun to rise in the Orient of proximity and conjunction" (*mashriq al-qurb wa'l-wuṣlah*). Adam, and in his person the mystical pilgrim, spends the night of vigil at al-Muzdalifah in waiting for this dawn, the dawn of the "Morning of the Presence" (*ṣubḥ al-ḥuḍūr*), rising among the glories of the "Face" of the divine Reality (*subuḥat wajh al-ḥaqīqah*) over the Darkness of the world of Nature.

At the hour of the coming dawn, the Angel instructs Adam to make a sevenfold confession of his fault, in order that all trace of the Darkness that held him prisoner may disappear; and he instructs him to ask God, in a sevenfold adjuration, to "return to him". Each of these *seven* acts removes one of the *seven* veils between man and the divine Face; or it marks the symbolic completion, one by one, of each of the seven millenia or periods of the prophetic cycle, which are the measure of the "delay of eternity" signified by the descent from Paradise. With each of these seven acts Adam, the mystical pilgrim, ascends to a level of proximity, mounts towards the theophanic vision which blazes forth in the morning splendour of the dawn, in the spiritual "Orient" or *Ishrāq*, which has become, since Suhravardī's time, the name of mystical theosophy that deeply pervades, even today, the thought and spirituality of Islamic Persia.

The dénouement of the pilgrimage, as meditated by Qāḍī Sa'īd Qummī, concurs with the dénouement to which the meditation of Ibn 'Arabī bears equal testimony: the meeting with the divine *Alter Ego*,[85] the celestial pole in the absence of which the human *ego*, terrestrial pole of the bi-unity, would possess neither being nor truth. This is the very bi-polarity that

84 This is the *Risālah fī asrār al-Ṣalāt*, the first of five treatises which together make up the *Kitāb asrār al-'ibādāt*, op. cit. Avicenna and the great Shiite theologian Zaynuddīn 'Āmilī, *Shahīd-i thānī*, also wrote a treatise on this theme. We hope one day to make a comparative study of them.

85 See my *Creative Imagination* . . . , op. cit., pp. 383–385.

configures the Form in which the *Deus revelatus* is revealed to the heart of the mystic; for this Form must of necessity correspond to the norm of being of him to whom it is revealed. Without such a Form, there would never have been a theophanic vision for any prophet, not even for the Seal of the prophets.[86] Qāḍī Sa'īd here shows us Adam mounting through seven stages of ascent to the personal theophanic vision, to the moment, that is, in which the pilgrim *sees* that "he who is epiphanized, he to whom he is epiphanized, and the Form into which he is epiphanized (the theophanic Form) are one and the same reality (form a Unity)." This dénouement can also be expressed in the terms suggested by the story of the white *Pearl*. Because the Pearl is the Angel within man—the Angel whom God "caused to swallow" the personal undertaking towards Him, and who in each man is the guardian entrusted with the divine secret concerning that man—this "Angel" is also the *Form* necessarily assumed by God in revealing himself to man (which is why the Pearl is both gnosis *and* the Soul itself). This is the Form contemplated by the Shiite mystic as the *Imam*. Henceforth Adam is worthy to enter into the Temple (*istaḥaqqa dukhūl Bayt Allāh*) and to be perpetuated with the perpetuity of God (*al-baqā' bi-baqā'i'llāh*). The secret of the Black Stone, as we said earlier, is the key to the Temple.[87]

4. Next, the angel Gabriel, the angel of saving Knowledge or of gnosis, takes the road to Mecca again in the company of Adam. They pass by Mina once more, for Adam has now attained the goal of his *desire*. The rites performed there by Adam and by the pilgrims of today are of course rites in the spiritual sense. In the valley of Mina a peregrination is accomplished, in the course of which one makes a gesture of defiance at a figure representing Iblīs-Satan, at which one also throws stones (a ceremony known as the *jamrah*). Here it signifies that "the arrival at the sanctuary of the divine Sublimity" is the last moment in which Iblīs-Satan can try once again to triumph over the pilgrim, by making him stop at the awareness of being carried away, annihilated (*fanā'*) to himself and perpetuated with the divine perpetuity; for to contemplate oneself thus is still to contemplate one's self, while attributing to it the predicate of its divine

86 Cf. note 80 above. There are *ḥadīth* on this subject by the Imams, commentated by Ṣadrā Shīrāzī, which we propose to speak of elsewhere.

87 A comparison could be made here with the statements of 'Abdul-Karīm Jīlī and of Ibn 'Arabī, but this would occupy an entire book. See my *Creative Imagination . . .*, op. cit., pp. 386–387.

Alter Ego; so that instead of being *absolved* of its ego-ness, the self is exalted to the status of the *absolute*. The danger is an infinitely subtle one, and "the journey towards God *in the company of God*"[88] risks remaining unfinished. This is why the *sālik*, or mystical pilgrim, must annihilate even his annihilation, meaning that he must refuse so to consolidate himself in the awareness of a Unity that he no longer keeps *company* with his divine Companion in the mystery of their bi-unity. (If he did not annihilate his annihilation, the mystic would need only to consent to the exclamation of al-Hallāj: I am God!) Thus the angel Gabriel, "helper of souls", ordered Adam to stone Iblīs seven times, each time pronouncing a *takbīr* (whose esoteric meaning, as we saw earlier, has reference to the *seven* veils between man and God).

5. "Then Iblīs departed . . .", says the recital of the Imam Ja'far. "And the Angel took Adam to the Temple, where he ordered him to walk around it seven times." Our commentator explains: "This is the journey from God *in the company* of God towards created beings."[89] These final words convey to us the esoteric meaning of the pilgrimage. Let us observe, to start with, that the angel Gabriel and Adam had made a first visit to the future site of the Temple which, as another tradition informs us, was built on Earth by the Angels. Then Gabriel and Adam departed to visit the holy places, whose esoteric meaning, stage by stage, has just been imparted to us. Now, on their return, they come before a Temple, around which Adam is asked to walk seven times. This is the Temple whose future area Adam had defined by tracing with his foot a groove in the earth, which exactly outlined the shadow cast by the white Cloud. Everything happens, therefore, as though the time needed for the completion of the spiritual pilgrimage, the heart's pilgrimage towards the personal Ka'bah, was a measure of the time—the "subtle time"—during which the Angels erect the form of the Temple (see above, III, 1). The "form as a work of the spirit" is here the Ka'bah or Temple of the heart, invisibly built by the Angels.

88 Cf. note 78 above.

89 This mystical journey would correspond to the third journey in Ṣadrā Shīrāzī's terminology: see note 78 above. For the sake of brevity we have not mentioned the three days called *Ayām al-tashrīq* (fol. 187b and p. 229 of the printed edition). Since the word *tashrīq* means "to turn towards the Orient", Qāḍī Sa'īd's hermeneutic finds a straightforward application. During these nights, Adam conducts the darkness of *ego-ness* to its permanent place of *setting*, and the spiritual Sun (*shams al-ḥaqīqah*) *rises* over Adam's person.

This is the Temple that the pilgrim, Adam, circles seven times. These seven circumambulations can correspond to the seven organs or subtle centres of the inner man as the "greatest Temple of God", the inner man being clothed successively with the seven divine Attributes whose names are the "Imams of the Names".[90] Likewise, explains Qāḍī Sa'īd Qummī, to complete these seven circumambulations is successively to put on the "seven veils" which, as we were told earlier, mark the distance between God and created being. Several of the previous rituals were aimed at eliminating the veils interposed by Creation between the divine Face and created being. But now that the divine Face has appeared with the "Morning of the Presence", the pilgrim puts on these same veils. What does this mean? The reply to this question lies in calling the seven circumambulations "a journey from God, *in the company of* God, *towards created beings*". Everything happens, in fact, as though the arrival at the centre which is the Temple were the re-entry, or at any rate the potential re-entry, into Paradise, in such a way that creation is not simply returned to its origin, but everything begins again from the beginning. This *re-creation* is the "journey towards created beings",[91] but this time it is creation as it would have happened if Adam, man, instead of departing from Paradise, had remained from the beginning to make this journey "in the company of God". This is why the new creation necessarily escapes men's eyes in the visible world, for it is an event that takes place in the *malakūt*; it is the creation of spiritual forms which in essence are visible only to the eyes of the heart.

Thus the pilgrim, Adam, walking round the sacrosanct *pole* which is the Temple, embraces in his mystical procession the totality of intelligible and sensible circles. In so doing, explains Qāḍī Sa'īd Qummī, it is as though he had at his disposal the higher and lower universes. As our author has persistently reminded us all along, this is precisely the virtue of the centre in spiritual circles (the Throne stabilized upon the Water): in them the

90 Cf. my *Creative Imagination* . . . , op. cit., p. 387 note 20.

91 Cf. note 89 above. This new creation is symbolized in the fact that at the end of Adam's pilgrimage of initiation, "his wife was once more permitted to him. Then the nuptial unions were legitimate between the primordial Reality-archetypes, from the Principle of Principles to the horizon of the universe in the process of becoming, that from these unions might derive the derivations foreseen in the cosmic order", fol. 187b. These are the "five nuptial unions", the great cosmogonic acts; see my *Creative Imagination* . . . , op. cit., p. 362 note 20, and H. S. Nyberg, *Kleinere Schriften des Ibn al-'Arabī* (Leiden, 1919), p. 87.

centre as such is what envelops and englobes that which surrounds it. Herein lies the secret of the configuration of the Temple as a spiritual form, imitating and reproducing the "Sublime Temple" in the world of the Intelligence. No one enters the Temple save he who possesses the "power of the keys", and this "power of the keys" (*potestas clavium*) is none other than the "ardent desire" typified in the station at Mina, the station which marked the entry upon the Way. The Way is that which leads to the truth of the personal theophanic vision, in the form, that is, which corresponds to the level and to the norm of the being to whom it is revealed. This is the secret of the white *Pearl*, the heart and centre of the personal Ka'bah, restored to the radiance of its original form after having been the Black Stone embedded in the material Temple. This is why we said that the secret of the Black Stone is the secret of the Temple as the secret of man—the secret of the Temple which man builds in building his own invisible inner form, his "body of light" or, in the *malakūt*, his "Temple of light".

It would thus appear that, under the guidance of Qāḍī Sa'īd Qummī, we have extracted all the substance of the spiritual instruction contained in the *ḥadīth* of the Imam Ja'far, and have understood what is meant by pilgrimage as "the pilgrimage of the heart", whereby man attains within himself to the plenitude of his spiritual form.

IV. *Potestas clavium*

If we have understood it correctly, the symbolic recital of the Imam Ja'far should appear to us as something quite other than a curious or edifying document, and the work of Qāḍī Sa'īd Qummī as something quite other than an interpretation addressed exclusively to Iranian initiates of seventeenth-century Shiite theosophy. To sum up very briefly what is intimated, we may say that the transformation of the material Temple of the Ka'bah into a spiritual and personal Temple of the Faith; the virtue of a secret being made explicit from stage to stage and leading to the personal theophanic vision as the entry itself into the mystical Temple; the fact that this secret is also the secret of the "power of the keys", the keys of the personal, spiritual Temple—where the pilgrim penetrates only after a long Quest, which is the reconquest of his Paradise (and it is no mere chance that so many of the works by our authors have similar titles, beginning with a Persian book by Qāḍī Saʿīd Qummī entitled *Kalīd-i Bihisht*, the Key of Paradise): all this ultimately delineates a Way which, as we cannot but remark, converges with that which, in Western traditions centred on the Holy Grail, has been called the Way of "the secret Church", in the sense of the Church concealed in the "secret shrine" of the soul.[92] In the work of our Shiite theosopher we have likewise encountered the idea of the secret Temple, to which all mystical pilgrims make a pilgrimage—all who together form the *corpus mysticum* of the *walāyah* (Ismaili gnosis speaks of the "Temple of light" of the Imamate), that is to say, all the "Friends of God" (*Awliyā' Allāh*), all the prophets, all the Imams and all their "friends". The uninterrupted succession of this mystical Assembly is still described as *silsilat al-ʿirfān*, the "affiliation of gnosis".

To be sure, neither the "Secret Church" nor the *silsilat al-ʿirfān* denotes a constituted body or a form of social institution, with offices and archives, registers and degrees. In one of its aspects, the Shiite concept of the *walāyah* corresponds to the idea of the "communion of saints" in Christianity. Affiliation to this mystical body presupposes neither ritual nor initiation ceremony. It is in fact the "candidate" who commits himself, as people once committed themselves to the quest for the Grail, or the pilgrim Adam formulated and renewed his undertaking to the "Angel", the secret of the Black Stone that he carried with him. The reality of the heart's pilgrimage is realized invisibly, in the *malakūt*. Its effects are realized in the formation of the *jism mithālī* or *imaginal* body, and all these "bodies of light" together make up the invisible brotherhood. This brotherhood possesses a form, and even an organization and a structure, but all in the *malakūt*: the members of the esoteric hierarchy spoken of in Shiite theosophy are known to God alone. It has been said of this invisible Church, the *Ecclesia spiritualis*, that "the powers of Hell will not prevail against it", and Qāḍī Saʿīd Qummī, in a similar vein, reminds us of the words of the Imam al-Riḍā: "Divine Religion will not perish so long as the Temple of the Kaʿbah endures"—words referring to the immaterial Temple of faith, whose guarantor and guardian is the twelfth Imam, the *Hidden Imam*. Guardian of this Temple, he is concealed from the eyes of men, as is the Holy Grail since its disappearance in the spiritual city of "Sarras", on the border, that is, between the *malakūt* and our world. The reason given

92 I am thinking particularly of the work by A. E. Waite, *The Hidden Church of the Holy Graal* (London, 1909), pp. 639 ff.

in both cases for this occultation is the same: men were no longer able or worthy to see the Grail, as they had become unworthy and unable to *see* the Imam. In both cases, there is the same invitation to ponder on an occultation that bears upon the actual situation of our world.

In the present context, what is in question is a world in which the awareness it is possible to have of spiritual Forms subsisting in a spiritual universe, and preserved from the vicissitudes of our changing fashions, has been so ravaged, devastated, even annihilated, that there is scarcely any point even in wondering whether the Byzantine icon of St. George, mentioned at the beginning of this study, can still possess a meaning for it, or whether this meaning could be the *true* meaning. For it is possible currently to read certain phrases alluding to "the fires of the spirit which today illuminate only an empty Heaven", or referring to the Paradise whose meaning Qāḍī Sa'īd Qummī has just revealed to us as something "in which the Church no longer believes, and of which she no longer dares to speak". I quote from memory and without references, but only because these statements, gathered at random, also lacked them. And it is symptomatic of our world that statements such as these should merely register the facts accepted by the common consciousness. How can one propose, to a world which has lost all sense of the *malakūt* and for which the *mundus imaginalis* is no more than imaginary, that it should meditate on the configuration of the Temple under the guidance of Qāḍī Sa'īd Qummī, seeing that for such a world there is no longer even a Temple upon which to meditate? This is the reason why, also at the beginning of this study, I spoke of the mutilation inflicted by a recent interpretation on the work of Balzac, because it was peculiarly symptomatic of the ravages which have annihilated in our consciousness all traces of a spiritual universe.

For this reason, the theme of the "power of the keys"—the keys which would enable man to open up the way to himself once more—confronts us with ever-increasing urgency, as does the true meaning of what Qāḍī Sa'īd has shown to be the esoteric meaning of pilgrimage. This pilgrimage becomes identified with life itself once it is understood that the secret of the Temple and of the Temple's form is the secret of man: of the inner man, that is, or spiritual individuality, the goal of whose quest is the attainment of his Truth, of the theophany that corresponds with his being, when the dawn of the spiritual Sun rises over al-Muzdalifah. Only he who has understood this holds the keys of the Temple and may enter it; and "to enter" means to go towards God or towards created being "in the company of God". Thus, where sociology envisages and analyses only the collective rite of a social religion, drawing crowds of pilgrims to Mecca each year, the Shiite mystic perceives the invisible reality of an altogether different pilgrimage. This is the return of Adam to his Paradise, by means of which he restores to the *malakūt* all that he had forced to descend from it when he "ate" of the forbidden Tree, when, that is, he himself descended from the *malakūt*. What is implied here is both the re-establishment of knowledge of the spiritual world, and its re-establishment on the level proper to it. Yet instead of this, the "descent" is continually aggravated because all our science, all our system of knowledge, is directed towards the unlimited exploitation of the Nature that "descended" from Paradise with man, and such an exploitation is accompanied by a radically agnostic attitude with regard to all that is signified by the *malakūt*. The further man extends his dominion—the more his ambition seeks to deploy itself on the scale of what it terms *cosmos* and *cosmic*—the more man is condemned to introduce into his own life so-called scientific rigour, with the result that the forces of collectivization and socialization exert themselves unopposed, and the human being is given no initiative to enter upon the quest for his spiritual individuality, for *his* Temple. Indeed, the very idea of such a quest is done away with, and with it all idea of a *potestas clavium* which would enable individual man to find a way out of the circle to whose constraint that which used to be called the *soul* has now succumbed.

There has been no lack of warnings over the centuries; they form, indeed, a long Western tradition denouncing the dangers which threaten the spiritual individuality, a tradition represented by those who are known world-wide as the Spirituals of Protestantism. In the sixteenth century Maître Valentin Weigel wrote an entire treatise on the question of *potestas clavium*, centred on the hermeneutic of the evangelical verses (Matt. 16:18–19). Weigel, too, affirmed that the inner man, the new creature, is himself the Tabernacle or Temple, and that every believer, by virtue of the faith in his heart, possesses the *potestas clavium*. This is because the *key* of the kingdom is the Holy Spirit, which is granted to all believers, and the key is *eo ipso* given to all those who possess the faith typified by the Apostle Peter. Thus the words addressed to Peter are addressed in his person to all who have such a faith, since every believer, through his faith, *is* Peter.[93]

93 Cf. Valentin Weigel, *Von der Vergebung der Sünden oder vom Schüssel der Kirchen*, in

The same doctrine is affirmed with equal strength by him whom Kant himself, in his private correspondence at any rate, called "the divine Swedenborg". Swedenborg teaches that, for all those who live according to the inner meaning of the divine Word, there is no doubt that everything said concerning the *potestas clavium* applies to the power possessed by the faith that is in every believer. This is so because what the person of Peter represents and typifies is the faith that proceeds from love, as the Truth proceeds from the Good. This is the rock, the *petra* (let us recall the secret of the Stone according to the Imam). The "power of the keys" is the power of faith, because it is the faith proceeding from ardent desire that opens the kingdom. This faith is designated by the Latin word *fervor*, fervour. It does *not* mean that certain men have the power to admit other men "into Heaven" or to exclude them from it.[94]

Is humanity, then, condemned to fall unceasingly behind or below itself, too feeble to sustain the victories of fervour? Its *lack of desire* so effectively prevents it from choosing the way out which ardent desire for the kingdom (*malakūt*) could alone open for it, that what it increasingly manifests seems to be less the "nostalgia for Paradise" explored by Mircea Eliade, as a scornful aversion to the whole idea of it. This aversion is expressed, among other things, in the "agnostic reflex", so deeply rooted in Western man that it has overcome even present-day theologians, and has largely contaminated Oriental man. If Qāḍī Sa'īd Qummī and his Shiite colleagues saw the drama of Adam as *the* drama of Knowledge, is it not in fact the drama that is acted out when the only goal envisaged by knowledge is power, and when the so-called "human" sciences are envisaged as "techniques of man", regulating every detail of his life?

In our time the Grand Inquisitor has been secularized; he no longer speaks like a theologian, in the name of a transcendent God and of a magisterium whose power extends to the beyond. He speaks like a sociologist and a technocrat, in the name of collective norms, limiting all finality to this world. And by the same token, something has grown worse since the time of Weigel, of Swedenborg, of Dostoevsky even. For the "secret Church" of the soul, the *Ecclesia spiritualis*, could once fight against

Sämtliche Schriften, ed. W. E. Peuckert und W. Zeller, Part II (Stuttgart, F. Fromann, 1964), chap. VIII, pp. 30 and 33; chap. IX, pp. 35 and 38, and the final dialogue, pp. 88, 93, 95.

94 Cf. Swedenborg, *Arcana caelestia*. art. 9410 (Exodus 24:11) and *Apocalypsis explicata secundum sensum spiritualem*, art. 8.

the Grand Inquisitor with the superior weapon of high spiritual knowledge. It possessed the free power capable of configurating spiritual forms, and this was its own *potestas clavium*, its own guarantee of the objectivity and superiority of the invisible world it was configurating. But today it is this very knowledge that lies in ruins. Once, one fought against the Grand Inquisitor with the superior weapon of personal faith. How can the man disarmed by agnosticism fight against a Grand Inquisitor who is both secularized and a sociologist?

This is the tragedy of our times, and it makes what we read in the works of a Shiite theosopher such as Qāḍī Saʿīd Qummī eminently pertinent. It is a tragedy so fundamental that the opposing forces are symbolized quite spontaneously in the consciousness of the most clear-sighted among us. In conclusion, I will call on the witness of one of those exceptional books which have scarcely appeared before they are forgotten, and which must then be given into your hands by a friend. I allude to the book by Hans Schmid-Guisan, the French translation of which appeared shortly before the war with the title *Comme le jour et la nuit.*[95] It cannot be summarized here; the main theme only can be indicated. From beginning to end, this book is permeated by a spirit possessing a rare power to configurate symbols. In it, the opposing forces of which we are speaking are grouped and confront each other under their respective symbols: *Collectivopolis* and *Individua*.

There is an island, somewhere in an unnamed sea, divided into two halves by a mysterious high wall. On one side is *Collectivopolis*, whose strictly geometrical layout gives an impression of coldness and force. On the other side is *Individua*, looking not so much like a virgin forest as a huge abandoned park—something like a sacred wood. For a long time the island was governed by two kings, brothers who resembled each other so closely in physical appearance that their subjects believed they were serving under one and the same king. Then a terrible revolution made it manifestly impossible to maintain the *condominium*. Henceforth, one brother reigns over *Collectivopolis*, where the life of the individual has no other goal or *raison d'être* than to serve the good of the collectivity. The

95 This is a posthumous publication: Hans Schmid-Guisan, *Comme le jour et la nuit*, a translation of *Tag und Nacht*, with a foreword by C.-G. Jung (Paris, Denoel, n.d.). It is unfortunate that there should be neither the date of printing nor the date of the edition. The introductory note, signed M. Schmid-Guisan, is dated Basel, 1937.

other reigns over *Individua* where, by contrast, everything is directed towards fostering the growth of the individual. Henceforth, too, the great majority of the population leads a double life, divided between the two provinces of the island. At different points in the high wall are secret doors, heavily bolted, through which one passes from one province to the other: one finds them disguised behind a chapel altar, in a hospital room, even in the office of the sovereign of *Collectivopolis*. This is because there are very few people who can abstain from leading a double existence and can spend their life in one half of the island. But the most difficult thing to decide is the appropriate moment for passing from one half to the other. For he who lives as a free man in the town of *Collectivopolis* is a slave in *Individua*. Conversely, he who has gained his freedom in the country beyond the wall is reduced in *Collectivopolis* to a state of slavery.

These are the broad outlines of something that cannot be summarized, and they speak sufficiently for themselves. Their inner meaning is no less clearly signified by the symbolic forms which delineate the topography of each half of the island, as well as the beings who inhabit them or who pass secretly from one to the other: pass from the world of Day and the norms of consciousness to the world of Night, where these norms are abolished by the passionate pressure of the forebodings of the unconscious. For *twelve* days and *twelve* nights, the narrator takes us on a journey like that of Dante. We have not the time here to go with him on this twofold and fearful excursion, nor to explain the symbols inspired by his genius. I retain only the final scene, which is played out on the highest peak of *Individua*, whence one can survey all the symbolic landscapes at a glance.

We are on the edge of the crater of a still-active volcano, whose full extent we are prevented from taking in by the swirling smoke that rises from the furnace. And yet the road of *Individua* goes up to it, goes through it and beyond. On the approaches to the crater one comes across people lying here and there in exhaustion, people who had not the strength to stand *Collectivopolis*, but who for all that have not succeeded in gaining total freedom in *Individua*. Here is an apparently resolute man who has got as far as the crater. In spite of the solemn command whose echo resounds through the rocky hollow, he throws himself into the furnace and is swallowed up. Is this, then, to be the sole ending reserved for the supreme effort of those who have arrived at the highest peak of *Individua*? Not so; but he alone will cross the abyss whose firm resolution is not the illusion of despair. And this is the ultimate lesson that the book has to teach us. Once again a man is advancing towards the furnace. His moving dialogue with the voice of the Invisible enjoining him to stop is evidence of supreme renouncement and of a supreme act of love. While the narrator, seized with giddiness, turns away his eyes, his guide tells him: "Look!" And indeed, "the man is not swallowed up. His foot rests upon a miraculous bridge thrown over the furnace." Where is he going? The narrator may not follow him, for he is told: "It is forbidden to anyone who—like you, and like the gentle reader—has only followed this road as a disinterested observer, to go any further along it." If only his guide would at least explain to him where this bridge *leads*, but he is merely told: "To a place where there is no wall to divide our lives inexorably into two opposing halves . . . where harmony, triumphing over struggle and conflict, makes the heart blossom with pure joy; where at last, surmounting the darkest clouds, merciful to just and unjust alike, shines an unchanging sun."

The whole meaning of this poignant book appears to me to lie in this *bridge* which is finally thrown over the abyss; and it is not by chance that this bridge should awaken in our mind the image of the Chinvat Bridge, as it is configured in the eschatology of ancient Zoroastrian Persia.[96] For in the image of the bridge, which takes shape spontaneously in the consciousness of the author at the end of the vision of the twelfth night, I believe we can perceive the *present* meaning of all that we learned from the pilgrimage of our Shiite theosopher, up until the moment when the spiritual Sun dawned over al-Muzdalifah, and the pilgrim was worthy to approach the Temple.

At this point, before the bridge flung miraculously over the abyss, we must once more ask ourselves the question: will the inner man give way before he has attained his victory? Will he prefer instead the multiple disguises of the agnosticism which leaves him finally weaponless in the presence of the Grand Inquisitor sitting in *Collectivopolis*? The "country beyond the wall", *Individua*, with all its topographical details (shade and rivers, oratories and secret temples, valleys and high peaks, and so on) is one of the most perfect symbols of the unconscious to spring from the imaginative perception of a present-day author—a perception that itself enables him to discern the "bridge leading to the beyond". Why, then,

96 Cf. my *Spiritual Body and Celestial Earth*, op. cit., pp. 26 ff., 42 ff., etc.

should it be the case, acording to others, that the "modern" discovery of the unconscious (not in fact as "modern" as one would like to make out) should have closed a door forever, that it should exclude man permanently from the possibility of knowing "a reality spiritual in itself"? An agnostic statement as peremptory as this one does not simply appear out of proportion to the metaphysical methods at its disposal. It also carries an infinitely serious responsibility, for it can cause the so-called liberating discovery to collapse under its own triumph. If man owes his personal *potestas clavium* to this discovery of the unconscious, a *potestas clavium* powerful enough to configurate the bridge over the abyss, how, at the same time and in the name of this same discovery, can one try to deprive him of this power, having just given it back to him? This is the deprivation brought about by the agnosticism which dares not pronounce its name, when it says that the keys do not open any door, or that the door opens onto nothing, or that the bridge leads nowhere . . . Or, since the "modern" discovery disowns itself in this way, is it not likely that it reveals to man something for which he had already been long indebted to a different authority?

This other authority lies, perhaps, in all that we have learned to call the *malakūt* of this world, as a spiritual world at once invisible and concrete, both because it is peopled by substantial spiritual forms, and because it shows that the meaning of this life for man lies in being able to exercise a configurative action on his own *malakūt* or "body of light". Our Shiite theosophers, such as Qāḍī Sa'īd Qummī, see the supreme stage of personal initiation or trans-consciousness (*sirr*) as being the revelation that every theophanic form corresponds to the being of him to whom it is revealed; but they never confuse this correlation with a causality devolving solely upon him to whom the form is revealed, any more than Swedenborg's notion of correspondence abolishes the existence "in itself" of the higher level when symbolizing with the lower. The confusion would be as absurd as the confusion of supra-existence in the *malakūt* with a claim to attain immortality by preserving the status of the natural physical body (through a perfect equilibrium of secretion, elimination,, etc.). It would be to confuse a precarious perpetuity with what is called eternity.

It is in the *malakūt* that the essential work of man is accomplished, for the phenomenon of the world, as man reveals it to himself, depends above all and in the final analysis on the vision he has of his own *malakūt*. One can only act upon the external form assumed by the phenomenon of the world by acting upon the inner form or *malakūt*; and such action is only possible where there is an affinity of *ardent desire*. In the language of Qāḍī Sa'īd Qummī, we would say that in order to change something together, we must set out together on the pilgrimage to *Mina*. So I can conclude no better than with the words of the great Swabian mystic, Friedrich Oetinger, who belongs to the tradition of the other spiritual masters mentioned here. His words have all the virtue of a motto: "My God, grant me the boldness to change what it is in my power to change, and grant me the modesty to bear what it is not within my power to change."[97]

Paris, July 31, 1965.

97 I know these beautiful words of Oetinger's only from a citation in a note in the review *Offene Tore* (Zürich, Swedenborg-Verlag, 1965), part I, p. 13 (ed. note); a citation which is given, if not textually, at least in accordance with the sense.

5

The *Imago Templi* in Confrontation with Secular Norms

1. The Imago Templi *at "the meeting-place of the two seas"*

A great Jewish writer of our time, Elie Wiesel, has chosen as the epigraph to one of the most poignant of his books, *Le serment de Kolvillag*,[1] the following quotation from the Talmud: "If peoples and nations had known the evil they were inflicting on themselves by destroying the Temple of Jerusalem, they would have wept more than the children of Israel." I was still pondering the far-reaching implications of these lines when, in a recent work,[2] I came across another epigraph, taken this time from the historian Ignaz von Döllinger: "If I were asked to name the *dies nefastus* in the history of the world, the day that would come to my mind would be none other than October 13, 1307" (the day when Philip the Fair ordered the mass arrest of the French Templars). A few pages further on, the same work makes mention of "a legend whose setting is the amphitheatre of Gavarnie in the Pyrenees, where six knights of the Temple lie at rest in a chapel. Every year, on March 18—the birthday of the last Grand Master of the Order— a knight of the Temple is seen to appear, whose shroud is replaced by the famous white cloak with the four-triangled red cross. He is in battle apparel and holds his lance in rest. He walks slowly towards the centre of the chapel and utters a piercing call, which re-echoes around the amphitheatre of mountains: 'Who will defend the holy Temple? Who will deliver the tomb of Christ?' At his call, the six entombed Templars come alive and stand up, to answer three times: 'No one! No one! No one! The Temple is destroyed.'"[3]

The lamentations of the Talmudist sages and the doleful cry resounding

1 Élie Wiesel, *Le Serment de Kolvillag* (Paris, Ed. du Seuil, 1973), p. 6.
2 Pierre Mariel, *Guide . . . des Templiers* (Paris, Table Ronde, 1973), p. 7.
3 Ibid., pp. 131–132.

through a Pyrenean amphitheatre echo each other, in that each of them sets the same catastrophe at the centre of world history: the destruction of the Temple, of the same Temple. Nevertheless, over the centuries a triumphal Image occurs and recurs, opposing this despair with the tenacity of permanent defiance: the Image of the rebuilding of the Temple, the coming of the New Temple, which assumes the dimensions of a cosmic restoration. The two images, of the destruction and of the rebuilding of the Temple, are inseparable one from the other. They draw on the same source, and they configurate a vision of the world which in both its horizontal and vertical dimension is dominated by the Image of the Temple, *Imago Templi*, and which conjoins the destiny of the city-temple and the destiny of the community-temple in the body of the Knights Templar.

I use the term *Imago Templi* in order to typify and stabilize a specific intention in a Latin form *ne varietur*, thus avoiding the vicissitudes of translation. I should therefore explain how this *Imago Templi* has in the end come to impose itself on me as a student of Islamic gnosis, not by leading me away from this gnosis, but on the contrary by allowing me to penetrate to the heart of that for which I am seeking. In explaining this, I will also be delineating the successive stages of the present study.

Unlike modern philosophers of History, visionary theosophers always have someone—a personal messenger—who comes to give them instructions and to be their guide. Where does he come from? In the famous recital of Ḥayy ibn Yaqẓān, composed by Avicenna, the messenger—the Angel—on being asked by the visionary whence he comes, replies: "I come from the TEMPLE", or, to be precise, from *Bayt al-Maqdis*. This latter term, which is the literal Arabic equivalent of the Hebrew *Beth ha-miqdash*, means, to be sure, the "sacrosanct house"; but as we know, the symbol of the dwelling-place is commonly used to denote the temple.[4] The Arabic term designates Jerusalem; but the answer given to Avicenna refers not to the Jerusalem of this world, but to the celestial Temple of which the earthly Jerusalem is the image. We hear the same answer given in Suhravardī's visionary recitals.[5] Often, indeed, for the sake of precision,

4 Cf. H. Corbin, *Avicenna and the Visionary Recital*, trans. W. R. Trask (Texas, Spring Publications Inc, 1980), pp. 137 ff. See also copyright page of this translation: vol. II of Corbin's original 1954 edition is not included in it.

5 Cf. Suhravardī, 'Le Vade-mecum des fidèles d'amour', chap. V (the response of

we get the expression *Nā-Kujā-ābād*, the "country of non-where", or *Rūḥ-ābād*, the "country of the Spirit".[6] Thus the question arises: at what boundary or limit does the meeting take place between the visionary and the Angel "who comes from the Temple?" Hence, too, at what boundary or limit is this Image of the Temple disclosed to the visionary, so that he receives the revelation of the Angel who belongs to the Temple?

Our mystical theosophers have explained themselves with extreme clarity on this point, and in doing so show themselves to be in profound agreement with all visionaries of the "New Temple". What is in question is a world which conditions a fundamental spiritual experience, the secret of which initially escapes us Occidentals because for us this world has for some centuries been a lost continent. It is the world situated midway between the world of purely intelligible realities and the world of sense perception; the world that I have called the *imaginal* world (*'ālam al-mithāl, mundus imaginalis*) in order to avoid any confusion with what is commonly designated *imaginary*.[7]

Let us be quite clear about this. Our visionary theosophers—Suhravardī's *Ishrāqīyūn*—are no less aware than we are of the perils of the *imaginary*. I will recall briefly the metaphysics of the Imagination in, say, Suhravardī. The Imagination possesses a twofold aspect and fulfils a twofold function.[8] On the one hand there is the passive imagination, the imagination that "re-presents" or "re-produces" (*khayāl*). As such the imagination is, quite simply, the storehouse that garners all the images perceived by the *sensorium*, this latter being the mirror in which all the perceptions of the external senses converge. On the other hand there is the active Imagination (*mutakhayyilah*). This active Imagination is caught between two fires. It can submit docilely to the injunctions of the estimatory faculty (*wahmīyah*), in which case it is the *rational animal* that assesses things in a way related to that of animals. The rational animal can and in

---

Love to Zulaykhā), in my anthology of fifteen treatises by Suhravardī entitled *L'Archange empourpré*, Documents spirituels 14 (Paris, Fayard, 1976), IX, pp. 306–307.

6 Ibid., index. See also H. Corbin, *En Islam iranien: aspects spirituels et philosophiques* (Paris, Gallimard, 1971–1972, new edn 1978), vol. IV, general index s.v. Nā-Kojā-ābād, Rūḥābād.

7 Ibid., s.v. imaginal. See also H. Corbin, 'Science traditionnelle et renaissance spirituelle', in *Cahiers de l'Université Saint-Jean de Jérusalem*, I, 1975.

8 Cf. Suhravardī, 'Les Temples de la Lumière', 7th temple, the French translation in op. cit. (note 5), II, pp. 63–66.

fact does fall prey to all the deliriums and monstrous inventions of the imaginary, obstinately rejecting the judgement of the intellect. Yet the active Imagination can, on the contrary, put itself exclusively at the service of the intellect—of, that is to say, the *intellectus sanctus* as this functions in both philosophers and prophets. In such a case, Imagination is called cogitative or meditative (*mufakkira*; it should be noted that this is another name for the active Imagination, the *productive* Imagination).

The whole task consists in purifying and liberating one's inner being so that the intelligible realities perceived on the *imaginal* level may be reflected in the mirror of the *sensorium* and be translated into visionary perception. We have, I think, already gone a considerable distance beyond the limits imposed by psychology. That we do in fact go beyond these limits is all the more important for us because the vision of the Angel, and thence of the *Imago Templi*, does not emerge from the negativity of an *unconscious*, but descends from a level of a positively differentiated *supra-consciousness*. This order of imaginative perception is described by Ḥaydar Āmulī, the great Shiite interpreter of Ibn 'Arabī, as being that of "intellective Images", metaphysical Images (*amthilah 'aqlīyah*). It is the key which can open up to us the metaphysic of the *Imago Templi*.

Ibn 'Arabī greatly extended the metaphysic of the Imagination.[9] He agrees perfectly with Suhravardī in affirming the reality, plenary in its own right, of the intermediate world of the *barzakh*, the world in-between. His name for it is the Koranic "meeting-place of the two seas" (*majma' al-baḥrayn*).[10] He sees it as the place where the world of pure Ideas in their intelligible substantiality meets with the world of the objects of sense perception. It is the world where everything that appeared inanimate in the world of sense perception comes alive, the world to which Moses came before meeting his initiator (*Khez̤r, Khaḍir*). In short, it is at "the meeting-place of the two seas" that the *Imago Templi* reveals itself to the visionary.

9 Cf. H. Corbin, *Creative Imagination in the Sufism of Ibn Arabi*, trans. R. Manheim, Bollingen Series XCI (Princeton University Press, 1969).

10 Cf. Ḥaydar Āmulī, *Le Texte des Textes*, commentaire sur les *Fuṣūṣ al-ḥikam* d'Ibn 'Arabī, les Prolégomènes, Bibl. Iranienne, vol. 22 (Tehran/Paris, 1974), p. 24 of my French Introduction. The expression is from the Koran; cf. Koran 18:59 ff. Moses, in the company of his young servant, goes on a long journey in order to reach "the meeting-place of the two seas". When they reach it, the fish that they intend to eat escapes and "makes its way freely back to the sea". The boy thinks that it is the devil who made him forget the fish, whereas Moses says: "This is exactly what we were looking for." Immediately afterwards, Moses meets Khez̤r (Khaḍir), his initiator.

Having said this, we are better able to define our subject, to say what it is and what it is not. In speaking of the *Imago Templi*, I intend to remain at the level of a phenomenology, a "temenology" if I may risk the word (from the Greek *temenos*, a sacred precinct), which exists at the level of the imaginal world (*'ālam al-mithāl*), the world in-between (*barzakh*), at "the meeting-place of the two seas". I once had occasion, in relation to the Mazdean transfiguration of the Earth by the *imaginal* perception of the Light of Glory (the *Xvarnah*), to speak of an *Imago Terrae* as a mirror reflecting the *Imago Animae*.[11] Similarly, the case of the *Imago Templi* at "the meeting-place of the two seas" implies a situation which is above all *speculative*, in the etymological sense of the word: two mirrors (*specula*) facing each other and reflecting, one within the other, the Image that they hold. The Image does not derive from empirical sources. It precedes and dominates such sources, and is thus the criterion by which they are verified and their meaning is put to the test.

According to our philosophers' premisses of the metaphysics of the imaginal, the *Imago Templi* is the form assumed by a transcendent reality in order for this reality to be reflected in the soul at "the meeting-place of the two seas". Without such a form, this reality would be ungraspable. However, the *Imago Templi* is not allegorical but "tautegorical"; that is to say, it should not be understood as concealing the Other whose form it is. It is to be understood in its identity with that Other, and as being itself the thing which it expresses. It will thus be clear that we do not intend to take up the task of the psychologists, still less to subject the *Imago Templi* to the categories of positive historical criticism.

At "the meeting-place of the two seas", one is outside the process of becoming, outside historical causality and the norms of chronology, of filiations whose justification depends on archives and legal documents. This is because at "the meeting-place of the two seas" we are in the "eighth clime", a "clime" whose events and recitals take place in the *Malakūt*, the world of the soul and of visionary awareness. In the *Malakūt*, the only documents are the testimonials of the soul. Neither history in the normal sense of the word nor a philosophy of History is composed of the visions projected by the celestial world onto the mirror of the *sensorium*.

11 Cf. my *Spiritual Body and Celestial Earth: from Mazdean Iran to Shiite Iran*, trans. N. Pearson, Bollingen Series XCI:2 (Princeton University Press, 1969), index s.v. *Imago Animae*, *Imago Terrae*.

Equally, without the category of the *imaginal*, one is deprived of these visions and of their significant reality. The only history we are concerned with here—sacred history or hierohistory or hierology—does not come to pass in the continuous time of chronological causality which is the time of secular history. Each manifestation of the *Imago* constitutes a unity in itself, without requiring a "transfer of power". It is itself its own time. The successive times of these manifestations are, rather, part of the *tempus discretum* of angelology, a discontinuous time. For this reason the link to be discerned between them is amenable neither to historical criticism nor to historical causality. On each occasion, what occurs is a *re-assumption* by the soul, a decision, a *reconquest*. These unities of discontinuous time are the times of the *Imago Templi*: they irrupt into our own time and confer the dimension of eternity upon the scissions they produce. It is through this rupturing of time that the truth of all history can finally shine forth; for through it history is liberated and transmuted into parable.

The following tradition is the most striking of all. When the Temple of Solomon was set on fire by Nabuchodonosor (Nebuchadnezzar), the priests, holding the keys of the Temple in their hands, went up onto the roof of the sanctuary. From there they cried in the face of heaven: "Lord of the world, since from now on we can no longer perform our office in this Temple, take back the keys into your hand". And they threw the keys up into the sky. A hand appeared in the sky and took hold of the keys.[12] I think that a significant correspondence to this may be seen in our own Grail cycle. The epic concerned with the *geste* of Galahad ends with a mystical scene in the spiritual palace of Sarras: a hand appears in Heaven and takes hold of the Holy Grail, which from that time onwards is invisible to this world, in the time of this world.

Yet the *Imago Templi* survives. When man has fashioned his inner being in such a manner that the *Imago Templi* becomes manifest to him, he is *eo ipso* at "the meeting-place of the two seas"; it is here, and nowhere else, that the keys of the Temple can be restored to him in person.[13] It was in this way that they were restored to Suhravardī who, in Islamicized Iran, wished to recall from its exile the theosophy of Light professed by the

12 Friedrich Weinreb, *Die Rolle Esther* (Zurich, Origo-Verlag, 1968), p. 19.

13 Cf. my study 'The Configuration of the Temple of the Ka'bah as the Secret of the Spiritual Life according to the work of Qāḍī Sa'īd Qummī (1103/1691)', section IV: *Potestas clavium*, published above.

sages of ancient Persia. In the case of Davānī, one of his followers, visionary perception even makes Persia (*Fars*) a "kingdom of Solomon", and Persepolis a centre of spiritual illumination in the tradition of Solomon.[14] This is why the quest of the seeker into Irano-Islamic gnosis should itself guide him back to the primordial hierophany of the "Temple to come". This is the *Imago Templi* as it was manifested to the visionary perception of the prophet Ezekiel, and on which the community of Essenes at Qumran was to model its entire theology of the Temple and the new Temple.

Hence, although there are always vestiges of history hidden beneath the veil of what are called "legends", it is not by following these uncertain signs that we will rejoin the knights of the Temple referred to at the beginning of this study. But we will observe that the *Imago Templi*, forestalling all empirical perception, possesses in itself such power that it makes the fact, *a parte ante* and *a parte post*, of the filiation of the knighthood of the Temple quite inescapable. In both directions, the filiation is established through the conjunction of the initiatic idea with the idea of a spiritual knighthood. In both directions, this must be seen as the awakening of the *Imago Templi* to the awareness of itself, and then it will be understood how the links of ancestry and descent which are claimed to exist are not such as can be traced in archival documents. *A parte ante*, the *Imago Templi*, as it acquires an awareness of itself through the Templar knighthood, claims to descend from the primitive Judaeo-Christian community of Jerusalem, and through this from the community of the Essenes. *A parte post*, it determines the resurgence of the Templar idea in the eighteenth century, as in the great work of Willermoz, in the dramatic epic conceived by Zacharias Werner and, above all, in Swedenborg's revelation of the *Nova Hierosolyma*. These are all hierophanies of the *Imago Templi* which frustrate the explanations as well as the negations of positive historical criticism, because the *Imago* precedes and rules over all historical judgements. Thus historical criticism is in no position to explain this persistence of the *Imago Templi*. In order to do so, it would itself need to stand at "the meeting-place of the two seas", in the place where the night-sentries keep watch on the walls of the Temple, waiting for the withdrawal of night and

14 Cf. A. S. Melikian-Chirvani, 'Le Royaume de Salomon. Les Inscriptions persanes des sites achéménides', in *Le monde iranien et l'Islam*, vol. I (Genève/Paris, 1971), pp. 1–41.

the coming of dawn. Likewise, it is only by satisfying the requirements of a hermeneutic altogether different from historical criticism that we will be in a position to evaluate the hierophanies of the *Imago Templi* which form the tradition of the Temple.

In this way, too, we may perhaps perceive how the secret norm determining the recurrence and persistence of this *Imago* is precisely that which is capable of confronting the secular norms of our own times, because it is the Witness that challenges the desacralization of the world.

II. The Imago Templi *and the destruction of the Temple*

1. *The world as the crypt of the Temple.* We observed at the outset of this study how, in the visionary recitals of Avicenna and Suhravardī, the Angel encountered at "the meeting-place of the two seas" replies to the visionary's question "Where do you come from?" by saying, "I come from the Temple"—that is to say, from the heavenly Jerusalem. This reply sets the tone for the entire visionary composition, enabling us to perceive its difference with regard to an *Imago Templi* which is the *Imago* of the cosmic temple.

This latter is the Image of the world-temple well-known in the cosmic mysticism of pre-Christian antiquity. For example, Manilius (first century A.D.), in the prologue to his *Astronomica*,[15] prays in the temple of the world, "for the world too is a sanctuary, and Manilius is its priest". Likewise, at the time of Manilius, the image of the temple of the world was, not exactly a commonplace, but rather a ruling belief: the *Imago templi mundi*. For Dion Chrysostom, the wellsprings of belief in God lead back to the spectacle of the cosmos. For Plutarch, "the world is a most holy temple . . . Man enters into it on the day of his birth and contemplates in it . . . the sensible objects fashioned, says Plato, by the divine Intellect as copies of intelligible realities". Cleanthus compares "cosmic religion to an initiation. The star-gods are mystical figures with sacred names". The world is "a temple filled with a divine presence, a temple in which one must behave with the holy reverence of an initiate". But this motif, as A. J. Festugière observes, is already to be found in Aristotle, in a remark concerning the mysteries of

15 For the quotations gathered together here, we are indebted to A. J. Festugière's concentrated chapter 'Le monde, temple de Dieu', in his work *La Révélation d' Hermès Trismégiste*, vol. II (Paris, 1949), pp. 233–238.

Eleusis, where he says that "the first effect of initiation into the mystical temple of the world is not knowledge, but an *impression*, a sense of reverent awe and wonder at the sight of the divine spectacle presented by the visible world".[16]

Whatever there may be in common between this vision of the world-temple, assimilated to the Eleusinian temple of the mysteries, and the *Imago Templi* in Suhravardī, we are made aware of the profound difference between them by the reply of the Angel stating that "he comes from the Temple". This visible world is no longer itself the temple; it is the *crypt* of the Temple, or cosmic crypt. The initiation conferred by the Angel consists in showing the initiate how to leave this crypt[17] and reach the Temple to which the Angel belongs, and to which the initiate, by virtue of his origin, also belongs. Inside the crypt he is merely an exile. The meaning and function of the physical heavens of astronomy are to guide the initiate to the supra-sensible heavens of the spiritual world, to the heavens of the Temple (the *Malakūt* that was revealed to Abraham; Koran 6:75).

Suhravardī is emphatic on this point. There are several ways of regarding the heavens. One of these is common to men and beasts. Another is that of the men of science, the astronomers and astrologers, who see the heavens with the eyes of the heavens. Finally, there are those who see the heavens neither with their eyes of flesh nor with the eyes of the heavens, but with the eyes of inner vision.[18] In them the organ of the inner vision is an *Imago caeli* that does not originate in empirical perceptions, but that precedes and governs all such perceptions. It determines the whole way of viewing the heavens, of seeing them, in fact, as the *Imago Templi*, which is to see them at "the meeting-place of the two seas". This is why the *Imago Templi* is not subject to the vicissitudes of the history of positive astronomy: it is not a chapter in the history of science.

Like their world (*Jabarūt* and *Malakūt*), spiritual beings are always described as sacrosanct, as "hieratics" (*qudsī, quddūs, qiddīs*), because they form the Temple (*Bayt al-Maqdis*) in relation to this world which is itself

16 The following remark of Seneca's sums this up: "There are mysteries into which one cannot be initiated in a single day. Eleusis has secrets that are shown only to those who go back to it and see it for a second time. No more does Nature reveal all her mysteries at once." Quoted in ibid., p. 237.

17 Cf. my *Avicenna and the Visionary Recital*, op. cit., pp. 17–18 ff. Compare Suhravardī's 'Le Récit de l'Archange empourpré', the French translation in my anthology *L'Archange empourpré*, op. cit., VI, pp. 201–213.

18 See Suhravardī, 'Un jour, avec un groupe de soufis . . .', in ibid., XI, p. 374.

the crypt of the Temple. They constitute a double hierarchy, originating in the three acts of contemplation of the First and highest of the hierarchic Intelligences—the Intelligence that Suhravardī always calls by the name it has in Zoroastrian angelology, in which it is the First Archangel to proceed from Ormazd: Bahman (Avestan *Vohu-Manah*, Greek *Eunoia*) or Bahman-Light.[19] From the three acts of contemplation of the First Emanant or first Intelligence, there proceed a second Intelligence, a heaven, and the Soul that moves this heaven. This same ternary rhythm is repeated from Intelligence to Intelligence down to the Ninth, and from heaven to heaven, from the Sphere-Limit—the Sphere of Spheres—to the heaven of the Moon. When it reaches the Tenth, the process is as it were exhausted. The Tenth is what philosophers call the active Intelligence, whereas theologians and theosophers call it the Holy Spirit. Both are in agreement about this identification. This Intelligence-Holy Spirit is the archangel Gabriel of the Koran, the messenger of the inspired revelation of the prophets, who is also the Angel of the human race, the Angel from whom our souls emanate.

The hierarchical Intelligences are so many hypostases, and are named the Cherubim (the *Angeli intellectuales* of the Latin translations). The Souls that move each heaven are the *Animae* or *Angeli caelestes*.[20] An impulse of love prompts the *Animae caelestes* to resemble the Intelligences whence they proceed, and it is through this impulse that each of them implicates its heaven in its motion. For this reason, the relationship between the two hierarches is typified sometimes as the relationship between a love that dominates (*qahr*) and a love that obeys (*maḥabbah*; from this point of view Suhravardī calls the *Angeli caelestes* the "celestial faithful of love"), sometimes as the relationship of parent and child, and sometimes as that between teacher and pupil.

It is this relationship, too, which organizes the hierarchic Intelligences in, so to say, a symbolic manner so that they form an Order of the celestial Temple. It should be noted that Suhravardī typifies it as an Order of *futuwwah*, or Sufi Order. Each higher Intelligence is the master (*pīr*) that initiates the Intelligence that follows it: it instructs it like a teacher his

19 On the theory of the procession of the Intelligences, see my *Avicenna and the Visionary Recital*, op. cit., chap. II, 'Avicennism and Angelology'. See also *En Islam Iranien*, op. cit., index s.v. Bahman, Intelligences.

20 Cf. principally Suhravardī, 'Les Temples de la Lumière', and 'Livre d'heures', the French translation in *L'Archange empourpré*, op. cit.

pupil; it inscribes it in the register (*jarīdah*) of its pupils; it bestows on it the symbolic cloak (*khirqah*) of its investiture,[21] etc. The gradation here corresponds exactly to one found in an Ismaili text.[22] From level to level of the hierarchy, each God in turn has his God until we attain the "God of Gods", who is the "God of being in its totality", according to the terms that Suhravardī employs. This is why spiritual ascent to the God of Gods is not possible for man unless he first unites himself with the Angel from whom he emanates, his celestial parent and his guide. This is the meaning of all Suhravardī's romances of spiritual initiation. It is to go out of the Temple crypt in order to enter the Temple.

This brief survey enables us to perceive how the same *Imago Templi* governs the relationship of each Intelligence to its "Temple" (*maskin*, its dwelling-place) or heaven, including the relationship of Gabriel, as the Angel of humanity, to the "Temples of Light" which are human spiritual individualities. Each heaven or Temple of heaven is composed of three things: the cherubic Intelligence from which this heaven emanates, this heaven that is the scope of its nostalgia; the Soul that moves it with a view to assuaging this nostalgia; and, finally, the heaven itself, whose subtle matter is condensed into the star it bears. The astral liturgies composed by Suhravardī should be compared with the famous astral liturgies celebrated in the temples of the Sabians.[23] The liturgy specifies the Intelligence that is the sovereign of each heaven; it invokes its moving Soul and glorifies the beauty of the heaven in question.[24] But the hymn is not addressed to the "astral mass". The liturgy is consummated in the *Malakūt*; the star is a "person" only because it possesses a Soul, a Soul of which it is not the image, and which itself pertains to the *Malakūt*. Unlike human souls, this Soul does not possess sensible perception; but the *Anima caelestis* has over human souls the advantage of possessing the active Imagination

21 Suhravardī, 'Le Bruissement des Ailes de Gabriel', French translation in ibid. Compare this with the initiation ritual of the *futuwwah*. See *Traités des compagnons-chevaliers, recueil de sept "Futuwwat-Nāmeh*, Persian text published by M. Sarraf, with an analytical Introduction in French by H. Corbin, Bibl. Iranienne, vol. 20 (Tehran/ Paris, 1973).

22 This is the conversation between 'Amalāq the Greek and his master Kostā ben Lūqā; see *En Islam iranien*, op. cit., vol. II: 'Sohravardi et les Platoniciens de Perse', pp. 133 ff., 262, 284.

23 Cf. my study 'Sabian Temple and Ismailism', published above.

24 See *En Islam iranien*, op. cit., vol. II, pp. 126 ff., the psalm composed by Suhravardī in praise of the archangel Shahrīvar and the lord Hūrakhsh. See also the liturgies in 'Livre d'heures', in *L'Archange empourpré*, op. cit.

in its pure state, and consequently it never succumbs to the delirium of the estimatory faculty and of the senses, as do human souls. The image that it possesses of its heaven is an *Imago Templi* in all its purity.

2. *The destruction of the Temple crypt.* As for our souls, they emanate from the Angel of the human race whose theurgy they are, as each heaven is the theurgy of the Intelligence from which it emanates. They are "temples", called by Suhravardī "Temples of Light". The Angel who is both the Holy Spirit and the Angel of humanity bears the same relationship to these "Temples of Light" as does each Cherub to its soul and its heaven. The word *haykal* (temple) is often used to designate the external habitation, the material body of the building which contains the Light and whose destruction sets this Light free. In effect, it designates the human microcosm itself as a spiritual individuality, just as the Twelve Imams are called "temples of the *tawḥīd*"; that is to say, according to the esotericists, temples of theomonism.[24a] At the heart of each temple of Light conceived in this sense is a sanctuary that Suhravardī calls the *khāngāh*—a term again borrowed from Sufism and normally used to mean a lodge of Sufis.

In Suhravardī's visionary recitals, the spiritual man withdraws into the *khāngāh*: there, the meeting with the Angel takes place.[25] This amounts to saying that the *khāngāh*—the sanctuary of the temple which is the microcosm—is situated at "the meeting-place of the two seas". It is here that the visionary is visited by the flashes of light in which the experience of Suhravardī's "oriental theosophy" culminates. When the presence of these lights is prolonged—when they become permanently present—the state attained is designated by Suhravardī as *Sakīnah*. This word is precisely the Arabic equivalent of the Hebrew *Shekhinah*: the mysterious divine presence in the Holy of Holies in the Temple of Solomon.[26] Thus, the Arabic equivalent to the term *Shekhinah* is used by Suhravardī to signify this Presence in the Temple of Light, in the *khāngāh*, the sanctuary of the human microcosm.

24a We should note that the idea of the spiritual individuality of man as the temple was a theme already familiar to the Stoics and to Philo. Cf. R. J. McKelvey, *The New Temple* (Oxford, 1969), pp. 53 ff.

25 Cf. principally Suhravardī, 'Le Bruissement des Ailes de Gabriel' and 'Un jour, avec un groupe de soufis', in *L'Archange empourpré*, op. cit.

26 On the *Shekhinah*, see principally Gershom G. Scholem, *Les Origines de la Kabbale*, translated from the German by J. Loewenson (Paris, 1966), index s.v.

These human temples of Light are at present in exile, in the crypt of the celestial Temple. Herein lies the difference from the sense of the world experienced as a temple in the religion of pre-Christian antiquity. The sages of antiquity prayed in a temple that was intact; the prayer of Suhravardī's sage rises from the depths of the temple crypt, because he has been exiled from the Temple. We are situated between two catastrophes: one is the premise of salvation, the other is perhaps irremediable. The first is the descent into exile; this is something we will return to, because it determines the persistence of the *Imago Templi*. The second is in some sense the sending of the exile himself into exile: this occurs at the moment in which the world ceases to be experienced as the Temple crypt. This is not simply the destruction of the Temple, but the destruction of the Temple crypt: the crypt in which the exiles awaited their return to the Temple.

Some have spoken of an astronomical revolution, but the phrase does not exactly cover what is at issue here. The issue here is the cessation of a hierophany, the hierophany of the *Imago Templi*; a cessation that involves the ruin of the *Imago caeli*, which above all determined the superior mode of contemplating the heavens of which Suhravardī spoke to us a little while ago. The split between angelology and astronomy is not just an episode in the history of science; it signifies the destruction of the Temple from which the Angel-messenger declared that he came. It is true that this destruction is only effective for those who believed or believe themselves to be bringing it about, for in fact the perception of the supra-sensible celestial Temple, and the angelology governing this perception, do not depend on the history of astronomy. For, as I said above, the *Imago caeli* does not derive from empirical perceptions: it precedes and directs such perceptions. To destroy the *Imago caeli* is to change the very mode of perception and create thereby a hiatus, a breach which misleads the historian. The world has ceased to be the crypt of the Temple. The destruction of the Temple begins with the dispeopling of the crypt. Once the crypt has been dispeopled of the presences that inhabited it, the Temple itself is open to attack. But the final process must be traced back to its distant origins.

We were speaking earlier, with reference to the *Imago Templi*, of two mirrors which face each other and reflect within each other the same Image. It is one of these mirrors, the *Imago caeli*, that has been destroyed:

nothing less than this, certainly, but also nothing more. But this destruction of the *Imago caeli*—of the Temple crypt—was made possible only by the shattering of the symmetry exhibited, first, by the triadic structure of the celestial temples (Intelligence, Soul, and subtle body of the Sphere), and, second, by the triadic structure of gnostic anthropology: spirit, soul and body. This anthropological triad was gradually eclipsed in Western Christian thought. What remained was the dualism of soul and body, or of spirit and body, of thought and extension—a dualism for which Descartes could not then be held responsible. This anthropological destruction has a striking parallel in the destruction wrought in the sphere of celestial physics by Averroes in his desire to be a strict Aristotelian. The consequence of this was in effect the disappearance of the second angelic hierarchy, the hierarchy of the *Angeli caelestes* or *Animae caelestes* as affirmed by Avicenna and Suhravardī. Since the world of the *Animae caelestes* marked the threshold of the *Imaginal* world, the sovereignty of the active Imagination or *Imaginatio vera* was as a result entirely overthrown, and with it that whole world of the Soul, the world in-between, medial between the *Jabarūt* and the *Mulk*.

From that moment on, the way lay open to a vision of the world which, being no longer a vision governed by the *Imago Templi*, was to end by no longer perceiving in the *cosmos* anything apart from immanent and purely mechanical laws. Without the world of the Soul there is no *Imago*. Thus man had lost his own soul as the heavens had lost theirs: there was no longer an active Imagination to secrete and reflect in the *sensorium* the metaphysical Images of intelligible realities, revealed to it on its own level. What remains is an imagination whose products are now declared to be merely *imaginary*, the fantastic productions of the *phantasia* —in short, unreal. Never again will it raise man to "the meeting-place of the two seas". The ordeal of exile no longer exists; instead, there is a deliberate refusal to feel exiled, a rejection of the idea of the world as the crypt of the Temple—a rejection that heralds the devastation of the *Imago Templi*. Such a devastation is a *sine qua non* for the ascendancy of the norm that induces the desacralization of the world, its "disenchantment" in the etymological sense of the word. (*Die Entzauberung der Welt* was the title of a book which appeared between the two world wars.) What will be the future of this norm?

We can envisage a reply to this question only if, by means of the double negation of refusing the refusal which desacralizes the world, we return to the moment in which the *Imago Templi* affirms itself not as an image to be destroyed, but as the instrument of salvation enabling us to leave the crypt. We must rediscover the *meaning* of the crypt. When the *Imago Templi* is destroyed, one is no longer even aware of being in the depths of a crypt. The world is "disorientated": there is no longer an "Orient". One thinks one is out in the open, that there is neither an above nor a below. By contrast, for all our mystical theosophers the world has an "Orient" and is "orientated"; there is an above and a below, not necessarily in the sense of geometrical distance, but ineluctably in the sense of a metaphysical distance. This is so because entry into this world is perceived essentially as an entry into the world of exile, as a "descent" from the Orient of the Temple to the Occident of the world as the crypt of the Temple.[27] The *Imago Templi* is then there so that the visionary, withdrawing into his *khāngāh*—the sanctuary of his microcosm—may recollect his origin. Unlike the sage of antiquity, he experiences his entry into this world as a rupture. It is exile far from the Temple. The Angel's whole message is to remind him that an exile does not delay when his family calls him back, that he must return in haste. This is the whole theme of Suhravardī's recital of the "occidental exile", as well as of several other recitals.

3. *Entry into the world of exile.* There is fundamental agreement between Suhravardī's hermeneutic of exile and that emphasized by a contemporary Cabbalistic master, Friedrich Weinreb, in his many books. I do not say that this agreement is surprising—far from it: it is to be expected and is therefore all the more significant. Destruction of the Temple means entry into the world of exile. In short, both for the master of *Ishrāq* and for the Cabbalistic master, the destruction of the Temple is the actual occasion of our birth into this world which is the world of exile, but also the world through which we have to pass if we are to reach the new Temple. The

27 This is the whole theme of pre-existence that we find in Suhravardī. In his exoteric treatises, the skaykh al-Ishrāq adopts a position opposed to this idea. In all his esoteric treatises, on the other hand, which take the form of symbols and parables, the idea of pre-existence is implied. See for example 'L'Epître des hautes tours', where it is said towards the beginning that "return implies the anteriority of presence. We do not say to someone who has never been to Egypt: 'Return to Egypt'" (*L'Archange empourpré*, op. cit.). We believe that by distinguishing between the natures of the different treatises of Suhravardī, we resolve an ambiguity that was already troubling Mullā Ṣadrā Shīrāzī.

destruction of the Temple is the end of the "previous life" and of the "previous world".[28]

The history of humanity begins with the exile, which in its turn begins with the destruction of the Temple. There is a striking recital dealing with the descent of the *Neshāmah*[29] (man's celestial soul, one of the souls that dwells with God, the idea of which is extremely close to the Zoroastrian idea of the *Fravarti/Forūhar*). This soul is asked to animate a human being whose embryo is in the process of growing. The soul is aware of all it will have to give up in order to "descend" to earth, but only through its descent will the human being be marked with the divine seal and bear within him the *Imago Dei*. For this reason, the soul too traverses the same road as God until the return from exile. The *Shekhinah* in exile is "the totality of all the suffering of all time and of the suffering of all creatures in all the worlds". As long as Creation endures there will be exile, up till the time when the last *Neshāmah* has descended into this world. The Angel who accompanies the *Neshāmah* during its descent reveals to it that it will find him again at the end of its passing through the world of exile, that he will be there to take it back "home". He tells it that all it learned of the meaning of Creation in its existence "before this world" will be plunged into oblivion, like a temple destroyed. Its garment of light will become a garment conditioned by the form of time. Yet in its exile the *Neshāmah* will be in unison with the exile of the *Shekhinah*. Imitating the gesture of the priests on the roof of the Temple of Solomon when it was being devoured by flames, the Angel throws the keys of the Temple back into the heavens.

To know these things is *eo ipso* to avoid confusing the apparent history of humanity with the history conveyed to us in the divine Logos, the Word of the prophets; for the latter history is played out on another plane and cannot be measured with the yardstick of our world and our life. Our measures are valid only for the world of exile, because they are provided by the very form of the exile. By means of the Word—of the divine Logos—sacred history reaches down to us as "on a boat connecting the different worlds". In fact, this Word exists in different worlds, in the realities belonging to different levels. It also has the virtue of conferring another existence on each reality: "The Images produced by the Word (the Logos) dwelling in such and such a reality are the symbols and

28 Friedrich Weinreb, op. cit., p. 35.
29 Ibid. See the admirable pages 20–32 of this book.

parables of those Images which exist in another reality."[30] The same applies to the *Imago Templi*. To understand it, as we said at the beginning, is to reach "the meeting-place of the two seas".

Who will reach it? The reply to this question is given in an equally striking hermeneutic relating to the saving of Moses from the waters; for one of the symbolic properties of Water is to typify the sense of time and of engulfment in time. Pharoah's aim is to make all male children who sink into time succumb to the indifferent uniformity of all that is encased in time, and to prevent them from rising to the height of the worlds revealed by the divine Word. They are to drown in the waters of secular, one-dimensional history. The little "ark" in which, according to esoteric tradition, his "celestial parents" saved Moses, was in fact the divine Word, and Moses was preserved from the flux of historical time. What Pharoah wanted, on the other hand, was that only "normal man" should survive—the man who conforms absolutely to the norm of a world which, above all, does not wish to know that it *is* in exile.[31]

The analyses of the *sacred*, for which we are indebted to the sociological philosophies or philosophical sociologies from the nineteenth century to the present day, strike us as being in perfect conformity with the intentions and dispensation of Pharoah. Even when they agree in thinking and saying that "history is nothing other than the profanation of the sacred [and that] it is therefore the decadence and decomposition of a previously given reality",[32] it is no less the case that the content they attribute to the notion of the sacred is of an alarming poverty, because it is reduced to purely formal aspects. This is because these analyses have themselves taken on the form of the world of exile to such an extent that they can no longer even be aware or perceive that it is a world of exile. And yet the majority of our contemporaries live according to ideologies spawned by these analyses. At this point there is a preliminary question to be asked. If History is nothing other than the profanation of the sacred, in the sense that the profane, which used to be mute, has now itself *taken possession* of the Word, how is it possible to speak of the sacred using a Word which is itself desacralized, a Word which, in its very nature, profanes and is

30 Ibid., pp. 35–36.

31 Cf. Friedrich Weinreb, *Die jüdischen Wurzeln des Matthäus Evangelium* (Zürich, Origo-Verlag, 1972), pp. 40–41.

32 Cf. J.-F. Marquet, 'Sacré et profanation', in *Bulletin de la Société ligérienne de philosophie*', (1973), pp. 54 ff.

profane?[33] This profane and profaning Word is in fact incapable of expressing the sacred, and the norm of the sacred of which it professes to be the judge; for how can a consciousness which is entirely theoretical and ratiocinative, for which no hierophany possesses any reality, *really* perceive such a hierophany, for example that of the *Imago Templi*? In practice and in truth, only Moses can speak of the sacred—every Moses who is "saved from the waters of History".

Sociologists and philosophers of History, on the other hand, are the docile followers of Pharoah. They are men as Pharoah wishes them to be—they conform to his norm. They are unaware that their dialectic can relegate "the past to the past" only in the temporal world of the "waters of History". Whoever does not free himself from the norm which recognizes only the historical, which acknowledges as true only that which is in time and in the documents of History, will never understand, for example, that what sacred history (hierohistory) recounts in the Revelation on Mount Sinai is not an event which only took place in, let us say, the year 2449 after the Creation. The Revelation on Sinai dwells intemporally within man, within every Moses who has been saved from the waters. The foundation lives within us, it is that whereby we exist in truth and in reality. For this reason it is no less true to say that the Revelation on Sinai exists also before the beginning of the world.[34]

4 *The norm of those exiled from the Temple.* We have now been given the key to the recurrences of the *Imago Templi*. There is no need to evince these recurrences in terms of a material, historical filiation, or to explain them in terms of an external historical causlity. It must be repeated that the norm of these recurrences is not written down in legal documents; it is an inner norm, written in the hearts of those who are exiled from the Temple. Likewise, the goal towards which we are guided by Suhravardī's "Recital of the Occidental Exile" is a mystical and eternal Sinai, a Sinai which

33 Mircea Eliade, in *Fragments d'un journal* (Paris, 1973), p. 310, initiates an entire inquiry into the question raised here. We ourselves would express the contrast in the following terms. Profane history sees mankind as mankind has created itself; History is the creation that man regards as his own, and of which he is the result. Sacred history or hierohistory reascends to events that are prior to the world, prior to the destruction of the Temple, because it is by this Temple that I was created, and its *Imago* exists within me. This is the key to my hermeneutics, the sacred norm which determines the ascent from world to world.

34 F. Weinreb, *Die jüdischen Wurzeln*, op. cit., p. 42.

merges with the cosmic mountain of *Qāf*. At the end of his adventure, the exile rediscovers the Angel who, as we already know, is the Holy Spirit, the archangel Gabriel as the Angel of the human race. He is thus the "celestial parent" from whom the soul of the exile emanated. Above the Sinai of the Angel of humanity, other Sinais rise in tiers—temples of the hierarchical Intelligences that antecede him, up to the "God of Gods". At the summit of the first Sinai, the *Shaykh al-Ishrāq* situates the Great Rock which some Shiite traditions also describe as the "Green Emerald". This Rock is the oratory, the temple of humanity or the Tenth hierarchical Intelligence.[35]

This great "rock" is designated by the Arabic term *ṣakhrah*, and it is so essentially allied to the *Imago Templi* and to the tradition of the Temple that, as we shall see, it is at the origin of the denomination of the Knights of the Order of the Temple. It has given its name to the building constructed on the site of the Temple and which is still called, even today, *Qubbat al-Ṣakhrah*, the "Dome of the Rock". Thus the *Imago Templi*, in Suhravardi also, is rooted in the deepest traditions concerning the Temple. Very ancient Jewish traditions tell us that this holy rock was the initial point—the starting-point—of Creation, the original Centre around which the earth developed concentrically. Jacob rested his head on it while he slept and dreamed of the ladder linking Heaven and Earth, which the Angels ascended and descended (Gen. 28). It corresponds to the position of the Holy of Holies in the ancient Temple. This is why the place marked by the rock is seen as the entrance to the higher world or, rather, as already part of it. It is through the holy rock as the foundation stone that Heaven and Earth exist and communicate with each other. It was consequently already at Bethel before Jacob found it there.[36]

The idea of such a communication between Heaven and Earth thus determines the current notion according to which the earthly sanctuary is situated at the *nadir* of the celestial Temple, which is at the *zenith*. This notion is illustrated by Jacob's vision of the ladder, and is to be found in all the hierophanies of the Temple. Suhravardī's recital of the Occidental Exile ends at the great rock of the mystical Sinai, on the summit of the

35 Suhravardī, 'Récit de l'exil occidental'; see *En Islam iranien*, op. cit., vol. II, pp. 270–294, and *L'Archange empourpré*, op. cit., VIII, pp. 267–287.

36 Cf. R. J. McKelvey, op. cit., pp. 188–192. See also J. Massingberd Ford, 'A possible Liturgical Background to the Shepherd of Hermas', in *Revue de Qumran*, no. 24 (March 1969), pp. 540–541, note 34.

cosmic mountain of *Qāf*, on the threshold which opens onto all the worlds beyond—therefore at "the meeting-place of the two seas". It is thus the perfect exemplification of a traditional *Imago Templi.* Moreover, we also know that the rock on which Jacob rested his head was actually made up of *twelve* stones, and that God subsequently immersed this composite stone in the sea, so that it might be the centre of the Earth.[37] One cannot but recall here the meditation of a Shiite gnostic such as Qāḍī Sa'īd Qummī on the twelve edges of the cubic form of the temple of the Ka'bah, which are interpreted as typifying the pleroma of the Twelve Imams. The cubic temple of stone is then transfigured into a spiritual temple, the centre of the earthly world, the terrestrial homologue of all the temples of the celestial universes.[38]

We referred above to the concept of the "Temples of Light" in Suhravardī, which make the microcosm—man's spiritual individuality—a temple of Light. The concept expands to take in an entire community. A Koranic verse (7:159) says: "Among the people of Moses there is a community which is guided by the Truth and which thereby practises justice". By means of this personal *ta'wīl*, Suhravardī transposes the idea of this community of the elect to the ancient Persian people, the people of sages whose doctrines he revived in Islamic Iran, as he expressly puts it, without having had a predecessor in carrying out a project such as this.[39] The *Imago* of the spiritual Temple—of the community-temple—enables Suhravardī to link the *Khusruvānīyūn* of ancient Iran with his own disciples, the *Ishrāqīyūn*, in Islamic Iran. In Ismaili gnosis we also encounter the idea of the "Temple of Light" of the Imamate, constituted by all the forms of light present in the initiates, the high dome or "Sublime Temple of Light" being formed by the Imams themselves.[40] As the community-temple the spiritual Temple has its own architecture. We shall come across the equivalent in the *Imago Templi* of the Essene Community of Qumran.

In this way the *Imago Templi* of Islamic Iranian gnosis, with Suhravardī as its great mediator, leads us back to the primordial hierophany of the

37 Ibid.
38 See my article on the spiritual interpretation of the temple of the Ka'bah in Qāḍī Sa'īd Qummī, published above. We cannot go into the details of this interpretation here.
39 Suhravardī, 'Le Verbe du soufisme', chap. XXII, French translation in *L'Archange empourpré*, op. cit., p. 170.
40 Cf. H. Corbin, *Trilogie ismaélienne*, Bibl. Iranienne, vol. 9 (Tehran/Paris, 1961), index s.v. Temple de lumière de l'Imamat.

Temple: it allows us to perceive this hierophany through it. The *Sakīnah*—Arabic equivalent of the Hebrew *Shekhinah*, and signifying the steady illumination dwelling permanently in the "Temples of Light"—is identified by Suhravardī with the *Xvarnah*, the Light of Glory in Mazdean religion. This Light of Glory passes from the heroes of the heroic epic to the heroes of the mystical epic, to the community which, among the ancient Persians, was the homologue of the community of the elect among Moses' people. The great rock of the Temple of the Angel, to which the pilgrim of the "Occidental Exile" ascends, has the very name of the rock which was the foundation-stone of the Temple of Solomon. I remarked above how for one of Suhravardī's followers, the fifteenth-century Jalāl Davānī, Persepolis became one of the main spiritual centres of Iran, and Persia became a Solomonic kingdom.[41] At the same time, in the north-west, in Azerbaijan, the temple of Shīz, the great sanctuary of Fire where the sovereigns of Sassanid Persia were consecrated, became the Throne or Temple of Solomon (*Takht-i Sulaymān*). Even in the absence of written documents, the *Imago Templi* supplies us with persuasive testimonials about itself.

One essential factor stands out over and above everything else. We spoke earlier of the hermeneutic which adds depth to the notion that the destruction of the Temple is the occasion of our birth into this world of exile, since the exile follows on the destruction of the Temple. All the catastrophes, then—the destruction of the Temple of Solomon in 586 B.C., the destruction in 70 A.D. of the second Temple, which had been rebuilt by Zerubbabel, and the destruction of the Temple of Shīz—are only so many episodes in the history of the exile. To be sure, the norm of those who are in exile remains centred on the rebuilding of the Temple, because their norm is to fight against the desacralization of the world. But this rebuilding will be definitive and imperishable only if it is the building of the Temple to come, beyond the time of this world. The destruction of the Temple is the original catastrophe. Its rebuilding can only be a cosmic restoration.

This is the significance of the vision and theology of the Temple in the prophet Ezekiel—a vision that provided the archetype on which was modelled the ethos of the Qumran Community. Ezekiel's vision is the reply to the knights of the Temple, to their cry of despair in a lonely amphitheatre of the Pyrenees.

41 Cf. A. S. Melikian-Chirvani, art. cit., note 14.

III. Ezekiel and the New Temple as a cosmic restoration

The *Book of Ezekiel* appears indeed to be that which, more than any other, offers us the perfect *Imago Templi*. This is further confirmed by the fact that it was the book on which the Essene Community of Qumran modelled its own conception of the Temple, in relation to which its ethos was determined in the face of secular norms and of the catastrophe of a profaned Temple. Our first task must therefore be to compare the theology of the Temple in Ezekiel with that professed by the Essence of Qumran. In this we will be guided by the remarkable piece of research undertaken by a Japanese theologian, Shozo Fujita.[42] Although this work is unfortunately unedited, it is truly a model of Temple phenomenology.

For Ezekiel, as for the Community of Qumran, the vision of the Temple unfolds into a drama whose starting-point is the ruin of the Temple and the reasons for it, and whose culmination is a vision of the New Temple, the building of which is the prelude to the apotheosis of a cosmic restoration. Here is disclosed the perspective of an eschatology which is already realized in and through the celestial liturgy, a liturgy in which the members of the Qumran Community participate.

The theology of the Temple in Ezekiel comprises four major phases: 1. The ruin of the Temple deserted by the *Shekhinah* and by the Glory of Yahveh; 2. The spiritual Temple of the exile: God himself is now the Temple; 3. The return of the Glory and of the *Shekhinah*: the restoration of the Temple; 4. The vision of the New Temple on the high mountain as the visionary perception of a cosmic restoration.

1. *The ruin of the Temple deserted by the Shekhinah.* The sin of Israel, which led to the destruction of the Temple built of old by Solomon, was its apostasy to other gods. Thus it was essentially a sin against the Temple, and the Temple was the place of this apostasy: ". . . .and behold northward at the

42 Shozo Fujita, *The Temple Theology of the Qumran Sect and the Book of Ezekiel: their relationship to Jewish Literature of the last two centuries* B.C., *(Princeton University Dissertation, Ann Arbor, 1970, Xerox University Microfilms); henceforth abbrev. to Temple Theology.* As this thesis has unfortunately remained unpublished, we are glad of the present opportunity to make its content and its outstanding quality known.—Ezekiel, we may remember, was among the first group of exiles deported to Babylon. Thus, exile creates the background to his vision of the destruction and the final restoration of the Temple, a vision which confers a unique character on Ezekelian Temple theology.

gate of the altar this image of jealousy in the entry . . . Son of man, seest thou what they do? even the great abominations that the house of Israel committeth here, that I should go far off from my sanctuary?" (Ezek. 8:5–6). This is why the condemnation of Israel is symbolically described as the departure of the Glory of the Lord (*Kevodh Yahveh*) from the Temple,[43] and why Ezekiel has the vision of the Glory leaving Jerusalem. This Presence of Glory signified the personal presence of Yahveh, and that was why the Temple constituted an area which was completely consecrated, separated, closed in upon itself: nothing profane of any description was to be associated with it. This ideal *Imago Templi* is the basis of Ezekiel's theology of the Temple. Its profanation cannot but induce the divine Presence—the *Shekhinah*—to depart from it; and this desertion is the real catastrophe in the destruction of the Temple, because the *Shekhinah*, the mysterious divine Presence, is what makes the Temple the "representative" of the kingdom of God on earth. Its departure is thus what brings about the destruction of the Temple: "I no longer have a dwelling upon earth". This destruction implied, together with the exile of the *Shekhinah*, the suspension or cessation of the activity relating to the realization of the Kingdom (the cessation of the activity of the divine Right Hand),[44] for the Temple, as the ideal centre of the world, was the centre from which God ruled over the world, the centre of the cosmic theocracy.

Furthermore, just as the divine condemnation began with the Temple, so the work of divine restoration had to begin with the Temple. The vision of the New Temple fills the last chapters (40–48) of the *Book of Ezekiel*. "Thou son of man, shew the house to the house of Israel, that they may be ashamed of their iniquities: and let them measure the pattern" (Ezek. 43:10). In the course of these long visionary chapters Ezekiel's *Imago Templi* is defined: the image of a supernatural Temple beyond our time

43 For what follows, cf. ibid., pp. 19–26.

44 Cf. H. Odeberg, *3 Enoch or the Hebrew Book of Enoch* (Cambridge, 1928), chap. XLVIII, p. 154, note 1. The real catastrophe in the destruction of the Temple was the departure of the *Shekhinah* and its absentation from the earth, because its presence in the Temple had made it the "representation" of the kingdom of God on earth. God withdraws his *Shekhinah* from the Temple and this is why the Temple is destroyed. "God no longer possesses any dwelling-place on the earth". We spoke above of the comparison to be made in the work of Suhravardī between the Arabic *Sakīnah*, the Hebrew *Shekhinah*, the Persian *Khurrah* (Avestan *Xvarnah*, Light of Glory), and the Hebrew *kavodh*. This should form the subject of a phenomenological (we do not say historical) inquiry.

and our space. It is not to be confused, therefore, with the second Temple, built by Zerubbabel in 515 B.C.

2. *God himself as the Temple.* The promise of the new Temple arises out of the very abyss of its destruction; for, if that destruction were definitive, it would no longer give rise to anything but what goes today by the name of "the theology of the death of God". The theology of the Temple can never accept such a death. The promise of the New Temple comes not from a theology of the death of God, but from a theology of exile; and this inspires a motif in Ezekiel which anticipates the most elevated intuitions of spirituality. In this theology of exile it is God himself who becomes the temple of his faithful; for there were some who sighed and groaned because of the profanation of the Temple (Ezek. 9:8). These are "the remnant of Israel", the last righteous men. The Angel-scribe was ordered to "set a mark upon [their] foreheads" (Ezek. 9:4), as a guarantee of immunity and protection. To all the others the Eternal can say, "I will profane my sanctuary, the excellency of your strength, the desire of your eyes" (Ezek. 24:21), for the love of such as these for their temple is no more than superstition. But the divine Presence which has deserted the Temple will remain in the country of exile among the exiles. "Again the word of the Lord came unto me, saying, Son of man, thy brethren, even thy brethren, the men of thy kindred, and all the house of Israel wholly, are they . . . Although I have cast them far off among the heaven, and although I have scattered them among the countries, *yet will I be to them as a little sanctuary* in the countries where they shall come" (Ezek. 11:14–16).

So there is a promise of a divine Presence in the countries of exile.[45] Those who are exiled, who have received the mark of the Angel on their foreheads, are the true heirs of Israel. God is identified with the Temple. The Temple on the earth of exile is only temporary. God is not, of course, identified with the physical building; rather, it is the idea of the spiritual Temple which is heralded by the prophet Ezekiel and which will be realized in the Community of Qumran. The spiritual Temple is the establishment of a spiritual and personal bond between Yahveh and his people: "And they shall be my people, and I will be their God" (Ezek. 11:20). This spiritual proximity is in no way hindered by spatial distance

45 For what follows, see Shozo Fujita, op. cit., pp. 34–43.

or by dispersion into the countries of exile, for it signifies the habitation of the Torah in the heart through the heart's renewal: ". . . make you a new heart and a new spirit: for why will ye die, O house of Israel? For I have no pleasure in the death of him that dieth, saith the Lord God: wherefore turn yourselves, and live ye" (Ezek. 18:31–32).

Even more than the Torah, it is God himself who dwells in the heart: ". . . yet will I be to them as a little sanctuary". God himself is the spiritual Temple that dwells with the exiles.[46] There is a conjunction between the renewal of the human heart and the establishment of the new Temple that, as a spiritual Temple, presages and heralds the spiritual worship that a spiritual Israel will offer up to God "upon a very high mountain" (Ezek. 40:2). This is the perfect *Imago Templi*: the spiritual Temple as the place where spiritual worship is celebrated.

The Glory of Yahveh has departed from Jerusalem and dwells among the exiles, in Babylon or other places. Yahveh has become the spiritualized Temple, but he has nonetheless promised that when he returns to the new Temple where he will dwell forever, he will restore the Glory to it. This is a new phase in the templar theology of Ezekiel.

3. *The return of the Shekhinah.* As we have already observed, the destruction began with the Temple and with the departure from it of the *Shekhinah* or Glory. Similarly, the restoration begins with the Temple and is the return of the Glory of the Lord to the new Temple.[47] "And the glory of the Lord came into the house by the way of the gate whose prospect is towards the east" (Ezek. 43:4). As the Glory, carried by the Cherubim, had withdrawn by the Temple's eastern gate (Ezek. 10:18–19; 11–23), so on its return it enters the Temple by way of the eastern gate. Now ". . . behold, waters issued out from under the threshold of the house eastward: for the forefront of the house stood toward the east, and the waters came down from under from

46 This verse from Ezekiel (11:16) allows us to be specific about what we should understand by "spiritualization" of the Temple. We will return to this later (see below, note 121). Here, Shozo Fujita (p. 41, note 1) tells us: "An object can be said to be *spiritualized* when it is interpreted in accordance with some predominant theological or religious concept. The adjective *spiritual* describes a state or an action which is attributed to the Spirit of God or to the human spirit as opposed to the flesh. It is also used as a synonym for the word *spiritualized*. In this dissertation, the word *spiritual* has been used in the first sense, but it is used here in the second sense."

47 Shozo Fujita, op. cit., pp. 44–69.

the right side of the house, at the south side of the altar" (Ezek. 47:1). This water and this East are essential components of the *Imago Templi Novi*, for it is the water that fertilizes the wilderness and enables the fishes to live. We also encounter the fountain of the Water of Life at the foot of the mystical Sinai, the temple of the Angel of humanity in Suhravardī's "Recital of the Occidental Exile".[48] The restoration of the world, and the return from the state of ruin to the state of Paradise, depend on this living Water. It should be noted that this power of regeneration and transformation has its source at the threshold of the new Temple, and that this threshold faces the East.[49] As Shozo Fujita observes, this is not a geographical location but a theological image, which forms the typological counterpart to the "wilderness of the land of Egypt" (Ezek. 20:36): "And, behold, the glory of the God of Israel came from the way of the east: and his voice was like a noise of many waters: and the earth shined with his glory" (Ezek. 43:2).

Here, too, the tone of the setting is the same as that of the *Ishrāq*, of the morning splendour of Suhravardī's "Oriental theosophy". The visionary Ezekiel experiences the rays of the rising sun as a vehicle bearing the Glory of Yahveh,[50] and it is with the rays of the rising sun that Yahveh enters his Temple through the eastern gate (Ezek. 43:4): "So the spirit took me up, and brought me into the inner court; and, behold, the glory of the Lord filled the house" (Ezek. 43:5). The eastern gate was opened only

48 Shozo Fujita, ibid. p. 49, reminds us that the description of the Temple in the 'Letter of Aristeas' (see below, section IV, B, 2) mentions a natural spring welling copiously out of the Temple precinct. Tacitus (*History* 5:15) speaks of the Temple's *fons perennis aquae*. The same image of a stream of water coming out of the Temple of Jerusalem occurs in some pre-exilic psalms, e.g. Pss. 46, 65 (Fujita, p. 50). The rivers mentioned in Rev. 22:1 and I Enoch 26:2–3 derive from Ezek. 47 (ibid., p. 51). We are reminded here of Suhravardī's 'Récit de l'exil occidental': the Spring of the Water of Life at the foot of the mystical Sinai, which is the temple of the Angel-Holy Spirit.

49 Even though there is evidence that at a given moment a solar cult, severely condemned by the prophet Ezekiel, was celebrated in the Temple of Jerusalem, this did not necessarily lead Ezekiel totally to reject the association of the sun's glory with the presence of Yahveh. See Shozo Fujita, ibid., p. 24, note 1, and p. 52.

50 Ibid., p. 53, note 1. Shozo Fujita here refers to the studies of J. Morgenstern, suggesting that a golden image of Yahveh stood in front of the Holy of Holies in the Temple until it was removed at the time of Asa's reform in 889 B.C. The reflection of the sun on this image during the spring and autumn equinoxes was "the glory of the Lord". But later on the same scholar admits that there was only an empty throne in the Temple *devīr* . . . We may recall the association in Suhravardī between the concepts of *khurrah* (Light of Glory) and *Ishrāq* (Light of dawn).

on the Sabbath and during the new Moon (Ezek. 46:1); for the rest of the week it was kept shut: "This gate shall be shut, it shall not be opened, and no man shall enter in by it; because the Lord, the God of Israel, hath entered in by it" (Ezek. 44:2). The closed door is henceforth a symbol to us of the fact that God will never again desert his Temple.[51] Because there will be no more idolatry, the eternal divine Presence—the eternal *Shekhinah*—will reign supreme, and by the same token the *Imago Templi* is the *Imago Paradisi*.[52] Thus, in the pages of the *Book of Ezekiel*, we rediscover the motif of the destruction of the Temple signifying the fall from Paradise.[53]

The restoration of the Temple brings us to the ideal of the city-temple to come: "I . . . will set my sanctuary in the midst of them for evermore. My tabernacle also shall be with them: yea, I will be their God, and they shall be my people" (Ezek. 37:26–27). Here the Temple is truly the place of the ever-continuing Presence (*mishkan*):[54] "I was a sanctuary for them" in the time of exile; "My dwelling is now with them forever". Let us observe that it is not on account of Israel, but on account of his own sacrosanct Name that God will restore the Temple: "And the heathen shall know that I the Lord do sanctify Israel, when my sanctuary shall be in the midst of them for evermore" (Ezek. 37:28).

On whom, then, will fall the privilege of being the priests of this Temple? The full sacerdotal ideal of the prophet-priest Ezekiel manifests itself at this point. His prayer will be fulfilled by the "sons of Light", the knight-priests of the Community of Qumran, and by all their emulators, those whose entire inheritance consists in God alone. The last chapters (40–48) of the *Book of Ezekiel* clearly demonstrate the ideal of the city-temple, anticipating the heavenly Jerusalem of the Johannine Apocalypse. The city-temple assumes the dimension of a cosmic restoration.

51 Ibid., p. 55.

52 Shozo Fujita, ibid., p. 59, reminds us of the main texts in which the image of Paradise serves to describe the blessings of the divine Presence (*Shekhinah*): the oracle of Balaam (Num. 24:3–9), the prophetic message in Isa. 11, Ezek. 47:6–12, Joel 3:18.

53 Cf. above, section III, 2.

54 Shozo Fujita, in ibid., p. 63, stresses the concept of the Temple (*miqdash*) as the divine dwelling-place (*mishkan*). A comparative research should be undertaken into the use in similar texts of the words *bēth* and *hēkhāl* in Hebrew, *bayt* and *haykal* in Arabic (*bayt al-maqdis, bayt al-muqaddas, bayt al-maʿmūr; hayākil al-nūr, hayākil al-tawḥīd*). Cf. in Qāḍī Saʿīd Qummī the designations of the Temple in accordance with the forms that exemplify it in each universe. Cf. my study 'The Configuration of the Temple of the Kaʿbah', op. cit., section II, 3: *The celestial archetype of the Temple.*

4. *The New Temple.* Let us repeat that the delineation of the Temple found in Ezekiel furnishes us with the image not of a historical Temple, but of the Temple as it will be at the time of the final restoration, envisaged as a cosmic restoration.[55] The vision which inaugurates the book situates us on the level of visionary perception: ". . . as I was among the captives by the river of Chebar . . . the heavens were opened, and I saw visions of God" (Ezek. 1:1). The opening of the heavens is what we encountered previously, expressed in the phrase "the opening of the *Malakūt*", and it can only occur at "the meeting-place of the two seas" (cf. above, sections I and II). Similarly, chapters 40–48, which describe the vision of the new Temple "in the land of Israel . . . upon a very high mountain" (Ezek. 40:1) make no mention of Zion or of any tradition of Zion, nor do they refer to the ancient Temple or the ancient city: the perspective is an entirely new one. The stream of water which, as we saw, flows from beneath the threshold of the Temple, on the Eastern side, brings about the cosmic restoration, the return to Paradise. Paradise is thus connected with the high mountain, which is henceforth situated in the Garden of Eden.[56] This vision locating the final Temple on the high mountain of Paradise is peculiar to Ezekiel, for the *Book of Genesis* (2–3) contains no reference to a mountain in the Garden of Eden.

Upon this high mountain will be planted the "tender branch" that typifies the messianic prince and, with him, the future messianic nation, which will grow to the height of a noble cedar (Ezek. 17:22–23): "And the desolate land shall be tilled, whereas it lay desolate in the sight of all that passed by. And they shall say, This land that was desolate is become like the garden of Eden" (Ezek. 36:34–35). Here, then, the *Imago Templi*

55 Cf. Th. A. Busink, *Der Tempel von Jerusalem, von Salomon bis Herodes* . . . , vol. 1, *Der Tempel Salomos* (Leiden, Brill, 1970), p. 42, note 156. Here the author, after referring to the treatise *Middoth* (On the measurements of the Temple), which belongs to the second-century *Mishnah*, suggests that the delineation of the Temple in Ezekiel should be interpreted in the same sense. This sense should also be given to the description of the measurements of the new Temple in the Qumran texts. It was necessary to provide for the replacement of the old Temple because of its defilements, but this replacement is merely temporary, provisional upon the restoration of the new Temple. Cf. below, note 122. In his great work, Th. A. Busink provides diagrams reconstructing the first and second Temples, as well as a sketch of Ezekiel's ideal eschatological Temple.

56 Shozo Fujita, *Temple Theology*, pp. 70–71. Cf Ezek. 28:13/14: "Thou hast been in Eden the garden of God . . . Thou art the anointed cherub that covereth; and I have set thee so: thou wast upon the holy mountain of God".

proclaims the new Temple as the basis and the starting-point of the transfiguration of the land, because the temple is here, as in Babylonian religion, the "navel of the world". As the centre of the universe, too, it is situated "on a high mountain" because it is the link between Heaven, Earth and the sub-terrestrial world (the living Water welling up from below the threshold). This is an essential function, one which can also be interpreted in the sense we assigned above (in section II) to the destruction and restoration of the Temple. Already the cosmic symbolism can be detected equally in the form of the altar described by Ezekiel.[57]

In short, Ezekiel's vision of the new Temple sets before us the Temple's celestial archetype, or, in other words, the celestial Temple as the archetype—a concept which reappears frequently in later apocalyptic literature. In its nature the new Temple—the city-temple—is supra-terrestrial, and it is envisioned "as the frame of a city" (Ezek. 40:2). The mode of visionary perception of the new Temple corresponds to the mode of the initial vision (that of the divine chariot or *Merkabah*): "And above . . . was the likeness of a throne, as the appearance of a sapphire stone: and upon the likeness of the throne was the likeness as the appearance of a man above upon it" (Ezek. 1:26). This vision is one which *par excellence* pertains to the mediatory *imaginal*: it is a vision not of a terrestrial Temple, nor of an earthly Jerusalem, but of a city-temple whose origin is celestial: "The new Temple is described as pre-existing in the supra-terrestrial world."[58]

The city-temple—Paradise regained, the link between heaven, earth and the sub-terrestrial world—is characterized exclusively by the sovereignty of Yahveh, for it is through love of his Name that Yahveh restores the Temple. Ezekiel's message of the new Temple concerns Yahveh's continuing Presence in the midst of his people. He is the centre, and this is expressed symbolically by the central position of the final Temple in the universe. Ezekiel's concern is not to glorify the brilliance of its external appearance, but to herald the establishment of divine sovereignty in the universe, at its ultimate zenith. The temple is eschatological, essentially

57 Ibid., pp. 76 ff. Shozo Fujita suggests a comparison between this and the description of the Temple on the scroll of Gudea, even though the text of this scroll was composed long before Ezekiel. The temple is in honour of the god Ningirsu. In a dream Gudea receives the plan of the temple inscribed on a "tablet of lapis lazuli". The comparison of these details with those of Ezekiel's vision is extremely interesting in relation to the ideology of the Temple.

58 Ibid., p. 79.

theological in nature, the focus of Yahveh's creative activity. We would prefer to say that this creative activity takes place in hierohistory ("subtle" history or "hierology") rather than in History, for the secular eyes of History are incapable of perceiving this hierohistory, and secular historians either are unaware of it or else deny it. They can perceive it only as a mythological representation, and therefore as unreal.

The *Imago Templi* as the centre of divine action in hierohistory is the characteristic of Ezekiel's theology of the Temple, or templar theology, and as such it can be the object only of "inner" or esoteric perception. There are two great phases in this theology of the Temple. The first is when God himself becomes the Temple in the land of exile: a unique declaration which, as we saw, initiates a new relationship between God and the true believer of Israel, represented by the faithful posterity of Zadok. The second is when, on the summit of the lofty mountain, the final Temple appears as a supra-terrestrial Image,[59] divine in origin—the unprofanable dwelling of the Sacred. The eastern gate is shut. The last verse of the last chapter of the book ends with the name of the holy City. The new city-temple is named "the Lord is there" (Ezek. 48:35). The Vulgate translates it as *Dominus ibidem.*

IV. The Imago Templi *from Ezekiel to Philo; Meister Eckhart, Robert Fludd*

Our survey of the hierophanies of the *Imago Templi* now encounters a literature whose scope may well dismay the inquirer. I refer to the Jewish literature of the two centuries preceding the Christian era. Nevertheless, our brief inquiry must make and co-ordinate some soundings at least. Here again, Shozo Fujita's valuable thesis has prepared the way for us, and we shall continue to be guided by it, concentrating first on the Palestinian Jewish sources and then on those of the Hellenistic Judaism of the Diaspora. Let us bear in mind, once more, that our survey is that not of a historian but of a phenomenologist in search of evidence.

A. *The theology of the Temple in Palestinian Judaism.* The evidence gathered from Palestinian Jewish sources is disposed around certain great themes

59 Ibid., pp. 81–82.

which link up with those of Ezekiel, thus contributing to the construction of a theology of the Temple to which only a comprehensive conspectus could do justice.

1. *The exaltation of the Temple.* A whole group of books illustrates the motif which one may style "the exaltation of the Temple". As portrayed in the *Book of Ecclesiasticus* (the Wisdom of Jesus the Son of Sirach), the *Imago Templi* is associated particularly with the representation of Wisdom, *Sophia* as a hypostasis, common in wisdom literature (cf. Proverbs 8–9). In a splendid poem, Wisdom herself states that she proceeds from the mouth of God and that God appointed her to dwell in the holy Tabernacle, that is to say in the Temple. Moreover, as Sophia is also identified with the Torah, the fact that Sophia dwells in the Temple *eo ipso* signifies that the Torah dwells there as well (cf. Deuteronomy 10:5; "I . . . put the tables in the ark which I had made"). And the Son of Sirach utters an ardent prayer: "Have compassion upon the city of thy sanctuary, Jerusalem, the place of thy rest" (Ecclus. 36:15).[60]

The *Book of Daniel* contains an announcement of the restoration of the Temple, whose message is explained by the angel Gabriel to Daniel "presenting [his] supplication before the Lord [his] God for the holy mountain of [his] God" (Dan. 9:20): ". . . for thou art greatly beloved: therefore understand the matter, and consider the vision. Seventy weeks are determined upon thy people and upon thy holy city . . . to anoint the most Holy" (Dan. 9:23–24). Nevertheless, attention is focused on the earthly Jerusalem, and nowhere is the Temple interpreted symbolically.[61]

Because of disillusion with the second Temple, built by Zerubbabel in 515 B.C., the *Book of Tobit* exhibits as it were a nostalgia for the perfect *Imago Templi.* This second Temple, too, is no more than temporary, and

60 Shozo Fujita, in ibid., pp. 89–90, follows the version and the numbering of the Septuagint. The Vulgate version is as follows: "Ego [Sapientia] ex ore Altissimi prodivi, primogenita ante omnem creaturam . . . Ego in altissimis habitavi, et thronus meus in columna nubis . . . Tunc praecepit et dixit mihi Creator omnium, et qui creavit me requievit in tabernaculo meo . . . Ab initio et ante saecula creata sum et usque ad futurum saeculum non desinam et in habitatione sancta coram ipso ministravi. Et sic in Sion firmata sum et in civitate sanctificata similiter requievi, et in Jerusalem potestas mea" (*Liber Ecclesiastici* 24: 5, 7, 12, 14–15). "Et in omni sapientia dispositio legis" (19:18). "Miserere civitati sanctificationis tuae, Jerusalem, civitati requiei tuae" (36:15).

61 Shozo Fujita, op. cit., p. 95.

awaits the day when the final Temple will be built in all its ideal magnificence, radiant with the brilliance of sapphires and emeralds. Here again, what is envisaged, even in this idealized form, is the earthly temple, which will "physically" incorporate the divine Glory:[62] the city-temple that will receive all the peoples who have renounced their idols.

Rabbinical literature likewise presents an Image of the glorified Temple. Targumical texts (Jonathan, Onkelos) tend towards an idealization of the Temple (largely because they exemplify the hermeneutic known in Islamic gnosis as *ta'wīl*). The Temple of Jerusalem is the only Temple in which the divine *Shekhinah* dwells forever, and as such it is the source of all divine benediction. *Midrash* and *Talmud* envisage the Temple as a symbol of the glory of Israel and anticipate its restoration. We thus observe, with Shozo Fujita, that all these writings, apart from *Ecclesiasticus*, expect the magnificence of the ideal Temple to be the final restoration of the first Temple, the Temple of Solomon. They accord with Ezekiel where the sense of expectation is concerned. But they differ from Ezekiel in the sense that for him the first Temple had been utterly profaned, and thus the new Temple is not envisaged as being purely and simply the restoration of the first. This fundamental conception confers on the Temple a significance which is highly symbolical and theological, whereas in all the other writings the restored Temple at Jerusalem is idealized to such an extent that its theological significance, and hence the significance of the divine judgement pronounced on the first Temple, are eclipsed. By the same token, the *Imago Templi* is overlaid with lavish descriptions of the details of its external appearance, while the vision of Ezekiel did not dwell on this external appearance at all.[63]

2. *Hope in the future Temple.* This theme provokes a question which, depending on the answer given, will lead to two different conceptions of the

62 Ibid., pp. 96–97, according to the Septuagint version. The Vulgate gives the following, in the canticle of Tobit the elder after the disappearance of the archangel Raphael: "Beatus ero si fuerint reliquiae seminis mei ad videndam claritatem Jerusalem . . . Portae Jerusalem ex sapphiro et smaragdo aedificabuntur, et ex lapide pretioso omnis circuitis murorum ejus. Ex lapide candido et mundo omnes plateae ejus sternentur, et per vicos ejus alleluia cantabitur" (Tobit 13:20–22). "Omnis autem deserta terra ejus replebitur, et domus Dei, quae in ea incensa est, iterum reaedificabitur, ibique revertentur omnes timentes Deum, et relinquent gentes idola sua et venient in Jerusalem et inhabitabunt in ea" (14:7–8).

63 Shozo Fujita, op. cit., pp. 105 ff.

significance of the restoration of the Temple. The question is: who will be the builder of the new Temple?[64] According to some, he will be a Messiah of David's line, an idea going back to the *Book of Zechariah* (6:12). According to others, he will be God himself, an idea going back to the *Book of Ezekiel* (40–48). In the first of these cases, the *Imago Templi* represents a temple which will be essentially the restored Temple of Solomon; this is the image gleaned from the *Book of Tobit* (see above) and also from the *Psalms of Solomon*. In the second case, the future Temple will not be simply a restoration of the first. In virtue of its transcendent nature, it will be infinitely more glorious. The image of this Temple, whose origin is ultimately the vision of Ezekiel, is attested in *I Enoch*, in the *Testament of Benjamin* (*The Testaments of the Twelve Patriarchs*), and finally, and most importantly, in the writings of the Community of Qumran.

We must therefore note the similarities between Ezekiel and *I Enoch*. In both there is the idea that the new Jerusalem will have nothing in common with the old, but will descend or be brought down from Heaven.[65] In both there is the idea that since God himself is the builder, the new Temple will be infinitely superior to the first Temple, the Temple of Solomon. The origin of the final city-temple is celestial and transcendent.

3. *The young branch planted on the mountain.* Here the *Imago Templi*, inasmuch as it is an image of the eschatological Temple, is enriched by a motif which was to supply the Community of Qumran with one of the most significant themes in its theology of the Temple. We have already noted, in the *Book of Ezekiel* (17:22–24), the image of the "young branch" planted on the mountain of the Temple—a branch which is the principle of the growth and flowering of the new Israel. Originating in this image is the theme of the righteous men who together constitute, symbolically, the "planting of justice", and are offshoots of the "plant of eternal justice". In the *Psalms of Solomon*, in *I Enoch*, in the *Book of Jubilees*, in the *Testaments of the Twelve Patriarchs*, the righteous are symbolized as "plants of justice". Hence arises

64 Ibid., pp. 130 ff.

65 Ibid., p. 134, where the author refers to the Judaeo-Christian apocalypses: the *Revelation of John*, 21:10; *IV Esdras* 7:26, 13:36; *II Baruch* 32:2. Cf. *Le Livre d'Hénoch*, trans. F. Martin (Paris, 1906), pp. 233–236. Shozo Fujita, moreover, stresses the fact that in *I Enoch* the idea of the final Temple of Jerusalem is linked to the idea of God as the "good shepherd": it is his task to build the eschatological Jerusalem and to gather together all the children of Israel. The appearance of the final Messiah heralds the restoration of the *Imago Paradisi*.

the idea that the eschatological Israel will be "like God". In a Qumran document which has already been the subject of lengthy research, Melchizedek, a priestly, messianic and eschatological figure, is designated as one of the *Elohim*.[66] His precursor Abraham was the first "righteous plant". All the righteous planted after him by God, from age to age, are chosen from among the rest of the Jews and Gentiles, with the result that the theme of the plant of justice is indissolubly linked to the idea of divine election. By the same token, it appears to be inseparable from the idea of a *gnosis* and of the divine plan in hierohistory.

The plant of justice receives nourishment, in fact, from the Water that is knowledge, and this knowledge is the gnosis that unveils the secret of the divine mystery to the righteous who are called upon to inaugurate the new era. Thus the rise of these "plants of justice" is, if not the most important event, certainly one of the most important in the divine plan of hierohistory, whose secret meaning is registered on the "celestial tablets" so frequently mentioned (*I Enoch*, *The Book of Jubilees*, *Testaments of the Twelve Patriarchs*),[67] and which the Angels reveal only gradually to certain privileged men. We may say that these "Tablets" are the "code of theocracy in History",[68] but only if we specify that, as the setting of theocratic activity, History means something other than what is understood by the word as it is currently employed. This is why we said earlier that we would rather use the term hierohistory, in order to avoid all ambiguity. For the same reason, it is not enough to say that History has two dimensions—one vertical and one horizontal—in the sense that it must be interpreted not merely in terms of a "final end" (*eschaton*) but also in terms of an "up above". Precisely here one must specify that a vision of History which acknowledges that the events that constitute it possess a celestial archetype, confers on this History a *parabolic* dimension, a dimension which elevates all events to the level of parables. Eschatology cannot simply be an event which one fine day puts an end to the rectilinear perspective of secular history. Equally,

66 The eschatological Israel that is "like God" involves the theme of *imitatio Dei*; cf. ibid., p. 141 note 1. Here we may remember the sentence which recurs frequently in the Islamic mystics: *takhallaqū bi-akhlāq Allāh*, "model your ways on the divine ways". The Qumran fragment about Melchizedek (p. 140 note 3) has already been the subject of a considerable literature. We will return to it elsewhere in connection with its implications for Ismaili Imamology.

67 Cf. Hans Bietenhard, *Die himmlische Welt im Urchristentum und Spätjudentum* (Tübingen, 1951), pp. 231–254: 'Die himmlischen Bücher und Tafeln'.

68 Shozo Fujita, *Temple Theology*, pp. 142 ff.

the latter is incapable of grasping the eschatological dimension. What it offers is a caricature: a social messianism or popularized eschatology. We will have occasion to recall, when speaking of Qumran, the connection between realized eschatology and the *mysterium liturgicum*, between the existential meaning of eschatology and liturgical time.

Only when there is such a connection does the *Imago* of the final Temple acquire its authentic and existential significance, as the eternal theocratic kingdom. The final Temple, built in the middle of "the eternal planting of justice", will be the centre of the new world, where only the unique divine sovereignty will be recognized. The synthesis of the theme of the "planting of justice" and that of the restoration of the Temple—that is to say, the new Temple as God's planting, in which the "plant of justice" flowers eternally—establishes an *Imago* of the new world centred on the Temple, an *Imago Templi* which is faithful to the vision of Ezekiel. By means of this symbolism, the pact or alliance between God and men takes the form of the Temple—a form which we, for our part, will certainly not define as empirical, since it is a form which is *par excellence* the Temple's *imaginal form*, and is therefore experienced on the *imaginal level*, at "the meeting-place of the two seas". Thus, the Image of the future Temple (*I Enoch* and the *Book of Jubilees*) is inseparable from the restoration of the primordial Paradise. This fact is the root of all that is said below concerning the symbolism of the Temple theology at Qumran.[69]

4. *The celestial Temple and the cosmic restoration.* In this way we re-encounter the theme which marks the climax of Ezekiel's templar theology, the theme in which "the cosmic restoration and the Temple" are associated. The start of our inquiry here is a Jewish tradition according to which the Temple is destined to be "in Heaven" until the end of days.[70] What is this celestial Temple? The reply to this question embraces three phases: a. the celestial liturgy; b. the celestial *Imago Templi*; c. the link between the celestial Temple and the eschatological Temple.

a. The *Testament of Levi* (3:4) contains an account of the vision that he

69 Ibid., pp. 148, 150–151.

70 Other traditions situate the celestial temple "between heaven and earth"; ibid., p. 152, note 1. (Cf. what is signified here by "the meeting-place of the two seas"). On the celestial temple, cf. *I Enoch* 61:12.

had of the Temple of God in the highest heaven.[71] In the highest Heaven dwells the great Glory (ἡ μεγάλη Δόξα), far above all holiness, in the Holy of Holies of the celestial Temple. In the sixth Heaven are the "Angels of the Presence", who are its liturgies and who intercede for men. The idea of liturgy evokes the ritual observed by the priests in the Tabernacle and the Temple, but the angelic liturgy is purely spiritual and does not include any blood sacrifice. It may be objected that this is merely a spiritualized description of the earthly Temple, projected into Heaven. We believe this to be too facile a way by far of surrendering and conforming to the explanations of modern psychology. In total contrast to this type of explanation, it may be said that *to see* what our visionaries see is to see that the earthly Temple is never more than a projection on earth of the celestial Temple. This archetypal relationship will prove crucial for the theology of Qumran, inspiring the texts of its dazzling celestial liturgy. Philo also testifies to the idea of spiritual worship among the Essenes. It is perfectly correct to speak of the pre-Christian origins of spiritual worship.[72]

The "Angel of the Presence" plays a most important part in intertestamentary literature. He is the intercessor, the minister of the spiritual liturgy (*Testament of Levi* 3:5–6), God's Scribe, whose task in the celestial Temple is to write down the decrees which determine the destiny of the hierohistory of the world (*Jubilees* 1:27)[73]—this hierohistory which, through its hidden decrees, defies the secular norms of exoteric History.

b. Thus the celestial *Imago Templi* arises, in a form which accords with the scope of the angelic liturgy and with the hidden reality of a hierohistory that resuscitates from the fallen Temple the figure of the ideal Temple reserved for God, the Angels and the righteous.[74] Sacred cosmology, or hierocosmology, presents us with the vision of the ascent of this Temple into the heights—the vision of its vertical cosmic dimension. The Holy of Holies is in the seventh heaven. The sanctuary where the Angels of the highest rank celebrate their liturgy is in the sixth heaven. The vestibule of the Temple corresponds to the fourth and fifth heavens, where the lower-

71 According to one manuscript, the "seventh heaven"; ibid., p. 152, note 2. The numbering and function of the Heavens are different in the cosmological mysticism of Avicenna and Suhravardī.

72 Ibid., pp. 156–157. On the same concept of the celestial temple-archetype in Shiite gnosis, see my study 'The Configuration of the Temple of the Ka'bah', op. cit., notes 13 and 14.

73 We may also think of Metatron, of the "Cherub on the Throne", and so on.

74 Cf. H. Bietenhard, op. cit., pp. 130 ff., and index s.v.

ranking Angels assist the higher Angels in celebrating the eternal liturgy.[75] Here again, we will not say that the celestial Temple is an idealized projection of the earthly Temple; as the visionary knows, it is the celestial Temple which is the original, of which the earthly Temple is merely a copy. The archetypal relationship—whose importance for the Qumran Community we noted above—goes back ultimately to the vision of the new Temple in Ezekiel, to the idea of the celestial archetype of the Tabernacle as it impressed itself on the priest-theologian.

c. With regard to the significance of the celestial Temple as the eschatological Temple, the lived experience of this must be sought in the *mysterium liturgicum*. In *I Enoch* (chaps. 24–25), there is a description of a visionary journey towards the north-west, in the course of which Enoch sees seven magnificent mountains. The central mountain surpasses all the others: ". . . resembling the seat of a throne: and fragrant trees encircled the throne" (24:3); ". . . it reached to heaven like the throne of God, of alabaster, and the summit of the throne was of sapphire" (18:8). The Angel-guide, who is here the archangel Michael, explains to the visionary: ". . . it is His throne . . . when He shall come down to visit the earth with goodness" (25:3). Four things are to be noted here: the mountain is a link whereby communication is established between Heaven and Earth; it is the throne on which God is seated when He descends; it is, consequently, the mountain-temple; and from this mountain, divine grace is poured out over men. There is an analogous vision in Ezekiel (40:2).[76]

Among the fragrant trees one is without peer. The archangel Michael explains (24:4) that no mortal may touch its fruit until the day of judgement, when it will be transplanted close to the temple of the Lord (25:4–5) and its fruits will nourish the Elect. This tree is the *tree of Life*,[77] and we are

75 In the fifth heaven are "the Angels who bear the replies to the Angels of the Lord's presence". This is most likely a category of Angels who are inferior in rank to the latter, to whom it is their function to bear the prayers of men. The Angels of the Presence offer these prayers to God, then bear his replies back to the lower-ranking Angels, who in turn communicate them to men. In the Greek *Apocalypse of Baruch*, 11–12, the archangel Michael is represented as receiving the prayers of men which are brought to him from earth by the Angels. Elsewhere he is identified as being himself the "Angel of the Presence"; Shozo Fujita, op. cit., pp. 156–157. The essence of the angelic hierarchy can thus be expressed sometimes in liturgical terms and sometimes philosophically. We may also recall the superimposed Sinais of which the celestial Temple is constituted in Suhravardī's 'Recital of the Occidental Exile'.

76 Shozo Fujita, *Temple Theology*, p. 161.

77 R. H. Charles (ed.), *The Apocrypha and Pseudepigrapha of the Old Testament* (Oxford,

in the Garden of Eden. The exaltation of the mountain-temple assumes an eschatological significance: the vision anticipates not an empirical temple with a sacrificial ritual, but a celestial temple which communicates the heavenly benediction to the earthly temple, expressed symbolically by the transplanting of the tree of Life close to the temple of the Lord. This is why entry into the new Temple is an act both eschatological and liturgical.[78] The liturgical act consists in obtaining, in integrating to oneself the fragrance of the tree of Life, the source of long life, joy and sanctification. As the Garden of Eden was the centre of the world, so the new Temple—the restored Garden of Eden—will be the centre of the restored world. All is ready for the vision of the *Nova Hierosolyma* descending to earth at "the meeting-place of the two seas", *in mundo imaginali.*[79] To this vision of a spiritual Temple, perfectly concrete, but concrete in a spiritual state, we are summoned by the *Imago Templi* of the documents of the Hellenistic Judaism of the Diaspora.

B. *The theology of the Temple in Hellenistic Judaism.* These documents, which belong to the two centuries preceding the Christian era, testify to an unreserved exaltation of the Temple of Jerusalem, whose *Imago* nourished the nostalgia of the faithful scattered in the countries of exile. Moreover, the influence of Hellenistic thought, which saw ultimate value and ultimate truth in the invisible and the immaterial, made itself felt in a notable tendency to idealize the Temple. Other characteristics are the absence of the apocalyptic expectation of a future temple, and the lack—except in the case of the high priest Onias and of Philo—of a critical attitude towards the Temple of Jerusalem. While such an attitude was by way of compensation to be responsible for the formation of the Community at Qumran, in Onias and Philo the motives for it are different. Onias was unlawfully banned from the Temple; Philo concentrates essentially on the grandiose vision of the immaterial Temple.

1913), vol. II, pp. 200–204. Cf. Gen. 2:9, 3:22; Rev. 22:2, 14, 19; Ezek. 47:12; IV Esd. 8:52; Test. of Levi 18.

78 Shozo Fujita, op. cit., p. 162, note 2, recalls the entry of the Glory of the Lord (Ezek. 43:1–5) and the entry of the Messianic prince into the new Temple (Ezek. 46:2). Cf. the processional hymn of the first Temple found in Ps. 24:7, 9: "Lift up your heads, O ye gates; and be ye lift up, ye everlasting doors".

79 Ibid., p. 164. We find the same parallel between the garden of Eden and the new Jerusalem in the *Testament of Daniel* 5:12. In the apocalyptic description there is thus interpenetration and convergence between the earthly and heavenly Jerusalems.

All we can do here is to give a very brief summary of the documents analysed in detail by Shozo Fujita.

1. *The Septuagint.* The Septuagint version of the Bible demands a comparative study which is practically inexhaustible and also extraordinarily interesting, since any translation inevitably involves, to a certain extent, a hermeneutic.[80] While it emphasizes the exaltation of the Temple of Jerusalem, the Septuagint seems anxious to avoid any association of God with an earthly site or building. Where the last verse of the *Book of Ezekiel* concludes: ". . . and the name of the city from that day shall be, the Lord is there" (Ezek. 48:35; cf. above), the Septuagint prefers: ". . . and the name of the city, from the day that it shall be finished, shall be the name thereof" (τὸ ὄνομα αὐτῆς, the name of this city).

2. *The Letter of Aristeas*, which in fact recounts the "legend" of the *seventy-two* translators of the Bible into Greek, is a text in which Judaism "is expressed through the mouth of a pagan who is a devotee of Jewish worship and law". We are indebted to him for an ideal *Imago Templi*, an Image of "the Temple as biblical tradition, especially the priestly tradition, had impressed it upon the imagination and the veneration of pious Jews",[81] and which is in correspondence with the eschatological image: "And it shall come to pass in the last days, that the mountain of the Lord's house shall be established in the top of the mountains" (Isa. 2:2). With its sense of the universal vocation of the Jewish religion, which finds support in a symbolic hermeneutic, this text can be seen as a precursor to Philo. It is possible, and even probable, that the description of the Temple, of the solemnity of the ritual and the splendour of the liturgies, was influenced by the accounts of pious pilgrims. But it seems, also, that the apocalyptic image of the final Temple in Ezekiel has contributed here to the idealization, although this does not culminate in a theology of the Temple which can be compared to Ezekiel's.[82]

80 Shozo Fujita, op. cit., pp. 174 ff., gives some striking examples. Cf. Ps. 48:9, where God is said to be "in the midst of [his] temple" instead of "in the midst of his people".

81 Cf. Annie Jaubert, *La Notion d'Alliance dans le judaïsme aux abords de l'ère chrétienne* (Paris, 1963), pp. 322–329.

82 Shozo Fujita, op. cit., pp. 190 ff.

3. *II Maccabees* was originally a five-volume work written by a certain Jason of Cyrenia, of which we only possess a shortened version in one volume (second century B.C.). Its theme has been defined as the glorification of the Temple, which in this dramatic history functions as the central pivot of the action. It has also been said that it is a history in which the archetype of the event assumes more importance than the factual reality of the event itself.[83] In connection with this, we should bear in mind the observations made above about the necessity for a concept of hierohistory as parabolic (parahistoric) in contrast to profane, exoteric and literalist history. Here the drama of hierohistory consists of two acts, symmetrical in structure.[84] In Act I, the Temple is threatened by Heliodorus (3:9–39), desecrated by Antiochus (5:11–20), and finally reconquered and purified by Judas Maccabeus (10:1–8). In Act II, the Temple is threatened by Lysias (11:1–21), and Nicanor (14:31–15:27), and finally rescued by God (15:28–35). The two acts culminate in the establishment of a new solemn festival (10:5–8).

The two cycles of the drama are thus concerned with the threats against the Temple and its preservation by God himself. One can, it is true, distinguish certain features to be found also in Ezekiel's prophetic image of the mountain of the Temple, but the difference here is that the author is thinking essentially of the exaltation of the existing Temple (the second Temple, that of Zerubbabel). Moreover, there is as it were an adherence to Jeremiah's warning against all magical belief in the Temple: "Trust ye not in lying words, saying, The temple of the Lord, The temple of the Lord, The temple of the Lord [is here] . . ." (Jer. 7:4). Here, the Temple is not the end in itself, but merely the sign of the Presence of God among his people.[85] In accordance with the line of thought which is that of Philo and

83 Ibid., p. 193. D. Arenhoevel (quoted in ibid., note 4) speaks of a "geschichtslose Geschichtschreibung", a non-historical historiography. We thus appear to come back, in one way or another, to the concept of "subtle history", which we have emphasized here.

84 Following the analysis provided in ibid, pp. 193 ff. In relation to section VI below, we should point out the existence in the Scottish rite of a grade of "Knight of the East", which tradition traces back to the Maccabean period. At the time of initiation, the candidate is seeking for the sacred Treasure, after the profanation of Antiochus Epiphanes. Cf. A. E. Waite, *Emblematic Freemasonry* (London, 1925), p. 106.

85 Cf. these lines by F. M. Abel, quoted by Shozo Fujita: "The Temple is not an end in itself, but merely a means whereby to attain a higher end. But the fate of the people was conditioned by its behaviour with regard to God, and the fate of the Temple was conditioned by the fate of the people". For his part, D. Arenhoevel remarks,

is common to the literature of the Diaspora, we find here in the *Imago Templi* that the form of the spiritual presence takes precedence over all physical and local limitations. This line of thought goes back, to be sure, to Ezekiel (11:16): in the time of exile, God himself is the Temple (cf. above). In any case, we for our part believe that the opposition between the vision of the material Temple "localized" on earth, and the vision of the ideal spiritual Temple, is somewhat artificial, since in fact the *Imago Templi* as such is always perceived on the level of the in-between, of the *imaginal*—the level which we have already designated as that of "the meeting-place of the two seas".

4. *The temple of Leontopolis.* This would also appear to be the way in which the high priest Onias IV perceived the temple that he built at Leontopolis in Egypt,[86] during the exile imposed upon him by the advent of the Hasmonean dynasty. There is no doubt that he intended, as far as was possible, to make the temple he was building into an *image* of the Temple at Jerusalem. To the extent to which an eschatological meaning is assigned to the verses from Isaiah (19:18–19) in the letter that Onias addressed to Ptolemy Philometer and Cleopatra, quoted by the historian Josephus, the *Imago Templi* would have been an eschatological *Imago* for the community grouped around him. To this extent his perception of the Temple is in line with that of Ezekiel and of Qumran, with the difference that Qumran did not build a physical temple at all, but remained in expectation of the final Temple, to be built by God himself.[87]

5. *The Sibylline Oracles.*[88] Book III refers to Cyrus and then to Joshua ben Jehozadak, the high priest of the community which had returned from

with reference to *2 Macc.* 5:19–20: "Die eigentliche Geschichte des Buches ist die des Volkes; der Tempel ist wesentlich Symbol; in seinem Zustande offenbart sich der Zustand des Volkes"; quoted in ibid., p. 200 note 2. [The book's real story is that of the people; the Temple is essentially a symbol; in its situation, the situation of the people is made manifest.]

86 Ibid., p. 205. Whether the temple was built by the high-priest Onias IV, or previously by his father Onias III, has no bearing on the question. Cf. also S. H. Steckoll, 'The Qumran Sect in relation to the Temple of Leontopolis', in *Revue de Qumran*, no. 21 (Feb. 1967), pp. 55–70.

87 Shozo Fujita, op. cit., p. 211.

88 Ibid., pp. 211 ff. "The Sibylline Oracles are a collection of Jewish and Christian oracles of which twelve books have survived, namely, books I–VIII and XI–XIV." Cf. Annie Jaubert, op. cit., pp. 329 ff. See also Edgar Hennecke, *Neutestamentliche Apokryphen*, vol. II (Tübingen, 1964), pp. 500 ff.

exile.[89] At that time the Temple will be rebuilt as it was. The author uses hyperbole: not only Cyrus, but all the kings of Persia will lavish gifts upon it and embellish it with gold and precious metals. In the "Sibylline Oracles", the *Imago Templi* is seen as the symbol of the return to the Golden Age.[90] We must note, however, that in the "Oracles" it is the second Temple, Zerubabbel's Temple, which is exalted, whereas in Psalm 132:7–17, for example, it is the future temple, which will be built by the Davidic Messiah. The difference is resolved on the level of the *Imago Templi*: if the author visualizes the post-exilic community as the final messianic establishment, the implication is that he perceives the Temple of Jerusalem, of which he is a contemporary, as the restoration of the first Temple, the Temple of Solomon, in all its magnificence. The exaltation of the Temple thus links up with the exaltation in the *Book of Tobit* (14:5),[91] which we discussed above.

6. *Philo*, in his monumental work, has provided us with one of the greatest conspectuses of symbolic hermeneutics to appear among the "religions of the Book". To discover the *Imago Templi* in this work amounts to inquiring whether and how this Image is present in it on the *imaginal* level. The fact that Philo uses the terms *allegory* and *symbol* interchangeably tends to complicate the inquiry, insofar as we try nowadays to distinguish precisely between them.[92] But whether allegorical or symbolical, Philo's hermeneutic is aimed essentially at revealing the hidden meaning (the *baṭin* of Islamic gnosis). And since the hidden meaning is nothing other than the letter raised or transmuted into symbol, and perceived henceforth on the level of the *imaginal* world, the symbol itself is no longer something behind which hides the thing symbolized. It is, quite simply, the form assumed on this level by the transcendent reality, and this form *is* this reality. Thus,

89 Zech. 6:11–14. On this passage from the *Book of Zechariah*, see below, note 158.

90 "Der Tempel hat in den jüdischen Sibyllinen sozusagen symbolhaften Charakter. Er ist die Verkörperung des goldenen Zeitalters, das längst vergangen ist, aber wieder mit Herrlichkeit für die Einen und Schrecken für die Anderen kommen wird." [In the Jewish sibyllines the Temple has a kind of symbolic character. It is the personification of the Golden Age now long gone, but which will come again—in majesty for some and terror for others.] P. Dalbert, *Die Theologie der Hellenistisch-Jüdischen Missionsliteratur* (Hamburg-Volkdorf, 1954), quoted in Shozo Fujita, op. cit., p. 213.

91 Ibid., p. 214.

92 Cf. *En Islam iranien*, op. cit., vol. IV, index s.v. allégorie, symbole.

instead of allegory, one could perhaps speak of *tautegory*. Far from being exhausted, these problems may not even have been properly formulated yet. The hermeneutics of Philo will have to be compared with those of Qumran, a comparison from which the Ismaili hermeneutic in Islamic gnosis must not be excluded.

Needless to say, for Philo the Temple of Jerusalem is the only authentic Temple on earth: one God, one Temple on earth. He also gives us a celebrated description of it. But the work of his true genius is other than this. Dominating his thought is the idea that notwithstanding the uniqueness on earth of the Temple of Jerusalem, on a higher level of vision there are *two temples*, the cosmic temple and the temple of the soul. We had occasion above (section II) to refer to the cosmic mysticism of pre-Christian antiquity, to the *Imago Templi mundi*. This theme is one which Philo accepts as self-evident,[93] even though he is specific about his own personal idea of the cosmic temple, which he sees as a philosopher.

One could in fact say that there is a double cosmic temple, because the cosmos includes both the sensible cosmos "which is the temple of the natures perceived by the senses", and an intelligible cosmos "which is the consecrated temple of invisible natures". One could also say that there is a unique temple constituted by a unique cosmos, "whose sanctuary is the most holy part of the essence of beings, that is to say Heaven" with all the intelligible natures that it comprises. On the other hand, the cosmic significance of the Temple of Jerusalem and of the parts which compose it is attested in Philo by reference to *Exodus* 25:40, where Moses is ordered: "And look that thou makest them [the tabernacle and all it contains] after their pattern, which was shewed thee in the mount". The tabernacle on earth (the Temple) is the image of the tabernacle in Heaven, the archetypal model which was revealed to Moses.[94] This motif also has roots in wisdom literature: the *Book of Wisdom* likewise saw in the Temple of Solomon "the image of the sacred tent".[95] The phenomenology of the *Imago Templi* is

93 Shozo Fujita, op. cit., p. 222. For what follows, see Annie Jaubert, op. cit., pp. 483–484. The quotes from Philo here are taken from this latter work.

94 Annie Jaubert, op. cit., p. 483, and the references given on p. 484, note 3. We have already alluded to the motif of the Temple-archetype in Shiite gnosis; cf. my 'Configuration of the Temple of the Ka'bah', op. cit.

95 "Et dixisti me aedificare templum in monte sancto tuo, et in civitate habitationis tuae altare, similitudinem tabernaculi sancti tui, quod praeparasti ab initio" (*Liber Sapientiae* 9:8).

completed by the motif of the Temple of Wisdom, the Temple that Sophia has built for herself (see above, section IV, A, 1, and below).[96]

The motif of the temple of the soul, or soul-temple, derives from the analogy that exists between the soul and the cosmos.[97] In his treatise on the *Cherubim*, Philo develops a detailed comparison between the human soul and the palace of a king:[98] "There is only one dwelling that is worthy (of God), and that is the soul prepared (to receive him). To speak in all justice, the dwelling of the invisible God is the invisible soul"; "The soul of the Wise Man activated by grace is a veritable altar . . . The sacred light burns on it always, unceasingly tended. For the light of the spirit is wisdom"; "God delights in altars without fire, on which the virtues dance in unison." "Ultimately," writes A. Jaubert, "the entire soul is the seat of a spiritual worship far preferable to the worship of temples. It offers up a true liturgy to its creator."

This liturgy is to be considered in relation to the double Temple: since there is a cosmic temple and a temple of the soul—a cosmos-temple and a soul-temple—there is also cosmic worship and worship of the soul, a worship that takes place in the macrocosm and a worship that takes place in the microcosm. In both cases, the temple is a spiritual one. In the books of wisdom (see above, note 96, *Proverbs* 9:1–2), hypostasized Wisdom, Sophia, was already building her temple and celebrating her liturgy in it. In *Ecclesiasticus*, Sophia, "come forth from the mouth of the Most High" and therefore identical with his Word, his Logos, "is described as a high priest officiating in the Temple of Jerusalem . . . She fulfils her liturgical function in the presence of the Lord (24:1–12) . . . She officiates mysteriously before the face of God like an Angel of the Presence, and her liturgical function is intimately associated with that of the priests of the Temple. We are close to a conception of the Logos-priest intimately related to the Temple liturgy."[99]

The high priest of the cosmic temple is the First-born, the divine Logos (θεῖος Λόγος). The high priest of the temple of the spiritual soul (λογική ψυχή) is man himself, man in the true sense (ἀληθινός ἄνθρωπος, *Homo*

96 "Sapientia aedificavit sibi domum, excidit columnas septem, immolavit victimas suas, miscuit vinum et proposuit mensam suam" (*Liber Proverbiorum* 9:1–2).

97 Cf. A.-J. Festugière, op. cit., vol. IV, pp. 213–216.

98 A. Jaubert, op. cit., pp. 488–489, summarizes and quotes the most salient parts of this treatise by Philo.

99 Ibid., p. 484.

verus).[100] "To the archangel and most ancient Logos, the Father gave the privilege of being intermediate between the creature and the Creator and separating the one from the other . . . And he rejoiced in this privilege, and exalted it, saying: I stood between the Lord and you (Deut. 5:5). In truth, being neither uncreated like God, nor created like you, but intermediary between these two extremes, I am a hostage for both . . ."[101] Because the Temple of Jerusalem is in the image of the celestial temple, there is of necessity a parallelism between the functions of Aaron and the functions of the Logos: "Like the Logos, Aaron is intermediary between God and man . . ." As the typification of the high priest, Aaron "officiated in the Temple of Jerusalem, the replica of the celestial sanctuary in which the Logos fulfilled its liturgical function. One sole and unique liturgy was unfolded through the mediation of the Logos and of Aaron in the sanctuary of heaven and the sanctuary of earth".[102]

It is true that Philo does not describe the angelic liturgy as it is described in the *Testament of Levi* (see above, section IV, A, 4); he does not make us participate in something of this nature. Nevertheless, the correspondence between the cosmic temple and the temple of the soul—between the cosmic worship and the worship of the soul—leads him to the notion of the "Aaron of the soul".[103] There is thus a triple Logos-priest. There is the First-born Logos, the priest of the cosmic temple; there is Aaron, typifying the high priest of the Temple of Jerusalem, who is both "the Logos of Moses and the Logos of God"; and there is Aaron, the Logos who is "Aaron of the soul". This illustrates the thesis first introduced above: "There are two temples of God. One is the cosmos, in which the high priest is God's first-born, the divine Logos. The other is the spiritual soul, whose priest is the true man; his sensible image is he who offers up the prayers and the sacrifices of the Fathers, who is clothed in the vestment whereon is reproduced the whole of Heaven, so that the cosmos may co-celebrate with man and man with the universe".[104] Just as the soul is the

100 Shozo Fujita, op. cit., p. 222. There exists in Arabic an exact equivalent to the term *Homo verus*: *al-Insān al-ḥaqīqī* (the "spiritual Adam" found in Ismaili gnosis or in Ḥaydar Āmulī, who follows Ibn 'Arabī).

101 A. Jaubert, op. cit., p. 485.

102 Ibid., p. 486.

103 "The Aaron of the soul": the expression is reminiscent of those found in the work of the great mystic Simnānī: the "seven prophets of your being", the "Jesus of your being", the "Muhammad of your being", etc. Cf. *En Islam iranien*, op. cit., vol. IV, index s.v. prophètes.

104 A. Jaubert, op. cit., p. 487, where the references to Philo are given.

inner holy City, the inner Jerusalem, so the worship of the soul is an inner worship, of which the sensible worship, celebrated in the material temple, is merely the *image*. We spoke above of the dignity of the soul-temple, integrally the seat of this spiritual worship. God delights not in the hecatombs offered up to him, but in the feelings of those who love him. The soul's liturgy is that in which the soul itself is offered up, and this is the only liturgy necessary. It consists, for the soul, in "engendering Abel", who belongs to God as to the First Cause, and in "rejecting Cain, the spirit of possessiveness that attributes everything to itself. The soul offers God its faith as a splendid gift, in festivals which are not those of mortal beings".[105]

Is it then correct to say that in the philosophy of the Temple in Philo, the *Imago Templi* is "dematerialized"?[106] It is to be feared that this mode of expressing oneself leaves out of account everything which is specific in the correspondence between the *corporeal* and the *incorporeal*. In point of fact, this correspondence overcomes all opposition between the corporeal and the incorporeal, for it enables one to grasp both of them simultaneously on the level which we have already designated as "the meeting-place of the two seas", the appointed place for hierophanies. In order for the material Temple and the immaterial Temple to *symbolize with* each other, both of them need to be lifted out of the isolation of a world without correspondence, and to be perceived on the level "where bodies are spiritualized and where spirits take on body" (Muḥsin Fayḍ): the level, that is, of the *spiritual body*. This in itself is the definition of the *imaginal* world, the world where, for Philo as well, the *Imago Templi* is made manifest.

In this world the *allos* (the other) of *allegory* is surpassed, because the *Imago* is the form in which both the *one* and the *other* integrally manifest themselves. This privileged imaginal form can also be called *tautegorical*. This, it seems to us, is the way in which one should read all of Philo, *living* the vast system of correspondences that he established: a synergy which is a syn-hierurgy (συνιερούργειν, the "concelebration" mentioned above), a union typified, as we saw, by the high priest's vestment. The system of correspondences in Philo, as in Swedenborg, is unending: the rites, the liturgical vestments and their colours, the altar with the incense, the seven-branched candlestick, the sanctuary, the ark, the priest's long violet

105 Ibid., p. 489.
106 This is Shozo Fujita's conclusion in op. cit., pp. 220 ff.

robes, the *ephod*, and so on. Philo searches for the hidden spiritual meaning —the esoteric meaning—of *all* corporeal objects (temple, vestments), of all liturgical gestures, in an attempt to discover a *universal* meaning in the Jewish temple and its worship.[107] To be sure, the *Imago Templi* that emerges is different from the visionary *Imago* of Ezekiel or of Qumran, but it leads in its own right to an authentic *interiority*: the Logos as high priest in the spiritual macrocosm corresponds to the true Man who is reborn in the spiritual soul. The two kingdoms—the two Temples—are one.

7. *Meister Eckhart*. It is only possible here to make a few brief observations. The search for the *Imago Templi* should be pursued throughout the Jewish esoteric tradition, for only then could a theosophy of the Temple be built up which would enable us to understand how and why the symbolism of the Temple overflows into Christian mysticism, how and why nostalgia for it remains the lasting source of Christian esotericism. The following are two examples of this.

Gershom Scholem, in an admirable book, has indicated one of those convergences that throw light upon the course of this inquiry. Recapitulating the process whereby the cosmological symbol of the Temple of the heavenly Jerusalem has become a mystical symbol for the author of the book *Bahir*, he writes: "Infinite divine Thought, that precedes and embraces all things, is the mystical 'temple' in which all spiritual beings have their place." This is the mystical place to which the prophet Habakkuk comes in the "delights" or "ecstasies" of his prayer: "Oh God! I have heard thy speech, and was afraid" (Hab. 3:2). *To hear* in Hebrew also means spiritual understanding. The supreme sphere of hearing is what one hears God say. The thought from which "ear and eye draw" is named "the king of whom all creation has need", the king who is withdrawn, miraculous, hidden in his temple, "and who has commanded that no one should ask for him".[108]

G. Scholem goes on to make the following comparison: "This symbolism, in which the Temple is the most profound divine thought, can be

107 Ibid., p. 224, note 2: "Philo said that sacrifices at the Temple were not just on behalf of the Jews, but 'for all mankind'" (*Spec.* I, 168, 190). "The Jewish nation is to the whole inhabited world what the priest is to the state" (*Spec.* II, 163), for it "has received the gift of prophecy and priesthood on herself of all mankind" (*Abr.* 98).

108 Gershom G. Scholem, op. cit., pp. 141–142. The author recalls that the prophet Habakkuk was regarded as the prototype of the mysticism of the *Merkabah* (the divine chariot of *Ezekiel* I). Cf. also ibid., p. 72.

understood all the better with the assistance of a very similar symbolism. This is the symbolism of the 'temple' by which, as by so many other metaphors, Meister Eckhart, some hundred and fifty years later, was to define the highest sphere of the soul, its 'knowledge by way of the Intellect'. The soul's noetic faculty (*Vernunftlichkeit*),[109] as Eckhart calls the highest aspect of the intellect, is its pure thought, in which it is in contact with the *intelligere* of God—in which it is the very Intellect of God. 'Where is God, if not in his temple where he reveals himself in his holiness? The temple of God is the Intellect. Nowhere does God dwell more patently than in his temple, the Intellect, as that other master [Aristotle] has said: God is an Intellect that lives in the knowledge of itself . . . for only there is it at rest (*Stille*)'."[110] As Scholem observes, the starting-point of the *Bahir* is different from that of Meister Eckhart, who proceeds from the concept of God in Aristotle, but the symbolism is the same.

The transition from the temple of God to the temple of the soul signifies the coming into contact of divine thought and human thought, since the *intelligere* of the soul in this temple is in contact with the *intelligere* of God. This contact is the source itself of all *speculative* theology, in the etymological sense of the word *speculum*: a catoptric mysticism. Meister Eckhart returns to the theme of the temple in a sermon on *Matthew* 21:12. The nobility of the human soul lies in the fact that it carries the *Imago Dei* within it (cf. Eckhart's idea of the "noble man"), and as such it is the Temple, from which all merchants and traders must be driven away. For ". . . God wants to have this temple empty, so that He alone may dwell in it. Hence this temple pleases Him so much, because it is so like Him, and He is so pleased to be in the temple if He alone dwells in it".[111]

109 It should be noted that in translating the German *Vernunft* from Meister Eckhart's text we use, not the term "reason", but the terms "intelligence, intellect". *Nous* is more than reason, and it is doubtless one of the misfortunes of philosophy, whether we are concerned with Meister Eckhart or with Hegel, that it has become customary to translate *Vernunft* as "reason". *Vernunftlichkeit* is the intellectivity of the *intelligere*. The speculative theologians of the Hegelian line used to call on *Vernunft* in order to vilify rationalism. Should this not warn us against equating *Vernunft* with reason? The "temple of God" is not the temple of the "goddess Reason".

110 G. Scholem, op. cit., p. 142, note 128, refers to Meister Eckhart, *Die deutschen Werke*, vol. I (1957), pp. 150 and 464.

111 The sermon 'Intravit Jesus in templum et cœpit eicere vendentes et ementes', in *Meister Eckhart: an introduction to the study of his works with an anthology of his sermons*, ed. J. M. Clark (Thomas Nelson & Sons, 1957), p. 127.

8. *Robert Fludd.* The second example is taken not from Christian mysticism properly speaking, but from the tradition of Christian esotericism. It testifies to the hierophanic presence of the *Imago Templi*, nostalgia for which, as we shall see, found expression in the various preoccupations of the "templar knighthood" (see below, section VI).

The famous theosopher and English Rosicrucian Robert Fludd (1574–1637) affirms the idea of the triple Temple. There is the Temple of Solomon; the Temple of the Holy Spirit, or soul; and the celestial Temple that is the spiritual palace, situated, like the temple in Ezekiel's final vision, "on the high mountain", which in this case is "the high mountain of initiation".[112]

V. The spiritual Temple and the Community of Qumran

Any attempt to construct or reconstruct a theosophy of the Temple, to explain the recurring hierophanies of the *Imago Templi*, will have from now on to dwell at considerable length on the Essene Community of Qumran, whose supreme legacy before its disappearance was the transmission, expanded into a vast literature, of the message of the prophet Ezekiel. It is barely thirty years since the first discoveries were made of the "scrolls" hidden in the caves of the Judaean desert, and already the research into them has reached such proportions that it is difficult for the inquirer to master the bibliography.[113] Here we are concerned with four points: 1. The Qumran critique of the existing Temple of Jerusalem; 2. The symbolism of the new Temple as a spiritual Temple; 3. The symbolism of the planting, the water, and the high mountain; 4. The motif of the celestial

112 Cf. Robert Fludd, *Summum Bonum*, p. 41, apropos of II. Sam. 7:6 ff. "Per quae verba intelligebat (rex David) templum materiale: nam testatur sacer textus quod David habuerit Templi materialis descriptionem spiritualiter a Digito Dei sibi descriptam: unde etiam arguere videtur se vidisse et artificum fuisse in domus super montem rationabilem fundatae structura: ut pote ad cujus exemplar non modo formatum erat tabernaculum fœderis et templum Salomonis, sed etiam ipse homo, qui dicitur templum Spiritus Sancti. Concludimus denique, quod unica domus istius constructio veri fratris adjumento sit occulti manifestatio, hoc est nupis Spiritualis, seu Sapientiae mysticae a lapide Patriarchae (quem vocat Domum Dei) revelatio, hoc est Domus seu Palatii Spiritualis super Montem Rationalem constructio, atque hunc lapidem Castellum mysticum Bethlehem vocamus, de quo sic loquitur Evangelista: Christus erat de Castello Bethlehem . . ."

113 At present, this bibliography comprises almost five thousand titles.

liturgy which, as "eschatology in action", dominates the whole of Qumran's spirituality, as well as all the spirituality that it inspired or will inspire.

1. *The critique of the Temple of Jerusalem.* As we know, the position adopted by the Community of Qumran stems from their severe critique of the Temple then in existence in Jerusalem, that is to say, the second Temple, built by Zerubbabel in 515 B.C. To the judgement which condemns this Temple and its priest irremissibly is opposed the vision of the celestial Temple, of which the Community is structurally the symbol and the anticipation. The theological ideas, images and expressions found in the Book of Ezekiel are used by the Essenes of Qumran in formulating and presenting their theology of the Temple. As we know from the document which goes by the name of the "Damascus Document",[114] it is because of the treason of those who have abandoned Him that God has turned away His face from Israel and from His Temple, and has delivered them to the enemy. Ezekiel said: ". . . because they trespassed against me, therefore hid I my face from them" (Ezek. 39:23).

This reactuation of Ezekiel's theology of the Temple is itself a remarkable instance of the spiritual hermeneutics practised at Qumran.[115] The events of the past are reclaimed from this past, not through an allegory which passes them over, but through a transference which makes them the archetype of ever-recurring events in which prophetic truth is accomplished. The abominations preceding the catastrophe and the destruction of the Temple of Solomon (586 B.C.) recur with the presence of the accursed priest, with the last priest-kings of the Hasmonean dynasty[116] and the profanation of the sacerdotal office of the Temple. But in Ezekiel, there is also "the remnant of the faithful", those who bear on their foreheads the mark imprinted by the Angel. It is they who, in their turn, form the Community of Qumran. Remarkably, we find the same diptych in an eighteenth century epic concerning templar knighthood: a drama in which the catastrophe is ratified by a condemnatory judgement counterbalanced by an apotheosis (see below, section VIII). Does not the *Imago Templi* become, in each of its recurrences, the drama of man succumbing to the

114 Cf. Shozo Fujita, op. cit., pp. 235 ff.

115 The *pesher*, which in many ways resembles the *ta'wīl* practised in Shiism and Ismailism.

116 This dynasty starts with Judas Maccabaeus (165–161) and ends, after several tragic reigns, with Mattathias Antigonus (40–37), tenth in the dynasty.

norms of the secular world before triumphing over them with the help of this same *Imago*?

The divine judgement condemning the Temple is one of the most important motifs in Ezekiel's Temple theology, and is a motif also found in the "Damascus Document". This correspondence illustrates the way in which the Community had an understanding "in the present" of the divine judgement executed in previous times by the Babylonians: a correspondence between the last days of the Hebraic monarchy in the sixth century before our era, and the abominations which put an end to the Hasmonean dynasty. Just as the Angel once received the order: ". . . set a mark upon the foreheads of the men that sigh and that cry for all the abominations that be done in the midst [of Jerusalem]" (Ezek. 9:4), God has now raised up for such men the "Teacher (or the Master) of Righteousness". Thus, the Community was able to trace its origins back to the period of the exile. The modern historian may be lost here; but for whoever perceives the hidden reality of hierohistory or "subtle history" as it was perceived by the Community of Qumran, this origin is true in a literal sense. The judgement that was brought of old against the first Temple corresponds to the judgement of the "end of days", that is to say, it corresponds to the time of the Community of Qumran, the time of "realized eschatology" (see below, § 4).

We will do no more than mention the motives which had prompted the secession of the Community. There was the evil spell hanging over the Temple through the presence of the wicked priest, who had ignobly and unlawfully usurped the priesthood, and who enriched himself through plundering.[117] There was the basic disagreement about the calendar which, while it may appear secondary to us, nevertheless possessed a fundamental importance for the Community, since on it depended the synchronism between the celestial and the terrestrial liturgy, and thence

117 We referred above (note 86) to the exile of the high priest Onias IV, who built the temple of Leontopolis in Egypt. This temple may perhaps have been built by his own father, the high priest Onias III, if it is admitted that he was not assassinated but exiled himself to Egypt. If this is the case, then Onias III was removed from his priestly office one year after the accession of Antiochus Epiphanes IV (175–164) because he was opposed to the latter's policy of radical hellenization. The result was the combining of the royal and high-priestly offices in the person of Simon Maccabaeus (142–135; cf. I Macc. 14:27–47). The Hasmonean dynasty thus became a dynasty of priest-kings "until a prophet to come would manifest the divine will" with regard to this situation. The situation was satisfactory with Simon Maccabaeus, but ceased to be so with his late successors.

between the celestial Temple and the earthly Temple. Both in doctrine and in practice, this synchronism was essential and fundamental. There were "Halachic" disagreements. Finally, there was the question of the authenticity of the sacerdotal lineage, the lineage of the faithful Sons of Zadok, who had been dispossessed by the Hasmonean usurpers. Confronting these negatives was the *Imago novi Templi*, contemplated by Ezekiel in his visionary ecstasy, and of which the Qumran Community felt itself to be the realization. True, this new Temple's defining characteristic, then as now, was that it was not yet realized—not in a "physical" sense, for in any case its reality is perceived on the imaginal level of vision, but rather in the plastic sense of its architectural detail. This was because the Community of Qumran felt that it was itself the new Temple, in so far as this was a spiritual Temple whose institution inaugurated the new era. And this profound assurance was rooted in the spiritual hermeneutic as it was lived at Qumran: a hermeneutic which simultaneously unveiled and realized the truth of the prophecies, for the Community was itself their culmination. Ezekiel's prophecy of the new Temple was being fulfilled in the Community of Qumran.[118]

2. *The symbolism of the new Temple*. The Qumran Community, having to confront the henceforth tarnished and desecrated second Temple from which it had cut itself off, was aware that it constituted, symbolically, the new Temple as a spiritual Temple.[119] *Miqdash adam*: the translation "human temple" is already eloquent. The translation suggested by B. Gärtner is more accurate: a "temple of men", that is to say, a temple "consisting of men". The Community, as the "house of God", bears the seal of eternity: the eternal Temple is henceforth in the process of realization within the Community. The sacrifices offered up in this "temple" which is constituted by the members of the Community are purely spiritual in nature, consisting in the strict observance of, and deepening penetration into, the hidden meaning of the Torah.[120] It is, indeed, a symbolic Temple, by contrast with the "material temple" which the high priest Onias IV attempted to

118 Cf. Shozo Fujita, op. cit., p. 259, note 1: the comparative plan of the structure of the new Temple as it is described in Ezekiel, and as it is actualized at Qumran in the feeling of the Messianic Community.

119 Ibid., pp. 263 ff., the lengthy analysis of the document *4 Q Florilegium*.

120 Cf. Bertil Gärtner, *The Temple and the Community in Qumran and the New Testament* (Cambridge, 1965), pp. 34–35 (abbrev. *The Temple*).

build at Leontopolis. At Qumran, it is the spiritual Community itself which sees itself as the "place" or ideal of the Temple. The *Imago Templi* is being actively realized; the Community, therefore, as a spiritual or theological temple, *is* the "new Temple".

Nevertheless, the idea of the "spiritualization of the Temple" must be given a precise meaning. The Community has no intention of breaking with the idea of the Temple and the worship celebrated in it. The "spiritualization,, consists in transferring the concrete entity—the Temple building—to a spiritual kingdom—the Community-temple—and in replacing the sacrificial rituals by a form of worship that consists of a life spent in observance of the Torah and of a liturgy of hymns and psalms celebrated in conjunction with the celestial liturgy. Needless to say, the term "spiritualization" in no way implies the idea of a lesser degree of reality, of a temple less "realistic" than the Temple of Jerusalem.[121] The opposite is true: the "spiritual" represents a degree of reality that is preeminent. Thus the idea of the Temple was never abandoned. On the contrary, it was reinforced by the idea of the regeneration of the Temple at the end of time. Like the primitive Judaeo-Christian community, Qumran retained both the idea of the Temple and the longing for it.[122]

The question now arises: how did the Community intend to realize, in its actual structure, its theological ideal of the "new Temple"? The two most important areas within the material Temple were the Holy of Holies and the sanctuary. Within the new Temple, these are represented respectively by the "sacerdotal circle" and by the circle formed by the rest of the Community; and these two circles are typified by Aaron and Israel. The firm and sure foundation of the "Temple constituted by men" is the truth—that is to say, the understanding in depth of the Torah and of the Revelation to which the Community owes its existence. From this under-

121 Ibid., pp. 18–19.

122 Cf. Ibid., pp. 26 ff., 44, 99 ff., and notes 46 and 55 above. Cf. also Shozo Fujita, op. cit., p. 42 note 15, pp. 267 ff. Th. A. Busink, op. cit., p. 42, note 156, makes timely reference to an article by Valentin Nikiprowetzky in *Revue des Études juives* 126 (1967), p. 25, which denies that the Qumran texts can lead to the idea that the Temple was to be abandoned definitively. "On the contrary, these texts would appear obviously to favour the opposite idea, the idea, that is, of a regeneration of the Temple at the end of time. This concept . . . alone keeps Qumran within Judaism." Similarly, the first Christians did not reject the Temple of Jerusalem; see H. Nibley, 'Christian Envy of the Temple', in *The Jewish Quarterly Review*, 1959, pp. 97–123. See also Georg Klinzing, *Die Umdeutung des Kultus in der Qumrangemeinde und im Neuen Testament* (Göttingen, 1971), pp. 92, 150 ff., 221–224.

standing proceed justice and judgement, since it is within this sanctuary that the "eternal laws" are preserved. The worship there celebrated consists not of holocausts but of a hymnology which is participation in the angelic liturgy.

For the Community, as we saw, hermeneutic penetration into the Torah consisted in experiencing itself as the realization of the *Imago Templi* proclaimed by the prophets. A verse in Isaiah, for example, says: "Behold, I lay in Zion for a foundation a stone, a tried stone, a precious corner stone, a sure foundation: he that believeth shall not make haste" (Isa. 28:16). This is the "rock of the Temple", the stone on which the Ark of the covenant rested in the Holy of Holies (reference has already been made to the "Dome of the Rock"; see above, section II. See also section VI below, in connection with the Knights Templar). The Qumran hermeneutic uses the plural: "tried stones". The "foundation" laid by God—the rock—are the "truths" made known to the Community by the hermeneutic of the Torah. The "tried stones" on which the New Covenant is based are the members of the Community;[123] for in purifying the members of the Community, the Holy Spirit confers on them an inner vision which penetrates into the mysteries of God.

Again, in Ezekiel, regenerate Israel will sacrifice to God "in mine holy mountain, in the mountain of the height of Israel" (Ezek. 20:40, 40:2). Here the Community, in relation to the mountain-temple, is spoken of as a temple containing two areas, the Holy of Holies and the sanctuary, corresponding to the priests and the people, Aaron and Israel. Ezekiel's prophetic conception is actualized in the new Temple as an eschatological Community, the symbolic new Temple. In this way, the image of the true Israel rises to confront the official Israel.[124] We will have occasion later to see how the persistence of this same *Imago Templi* is the source of the entire "templar" tradition at the heart of a Christianity which had ceased to be an eschatological community. In both instances, the norm of the Temple confronts the norms of a profaned and desacralized world.

Most striking of all, perhaps, is the bond thus established between spiritual hermeneutics and spiritual worship. The former, as a new Revelation, puts the Community in a position in which it experiences itself as

123 Cf. B. Gärtner, *The Temple*, op. cit., pp. 27, 77.
124 Ibid., p. 29.

the "place" where the prophecies are fulfilled.[125] The spiritual form of worship is the response to the mystery which is thus revealed. To study the Torah is to prepare the way of God.[126] This way can be understood in three senses: as the exodus from Jerusalem towards the desert of Judah (the place-names here acquire, typologically speaking, a permanent significance); perfect observance of the Torah; and preparation for the age to come. In effect, the Torah had been the supreme revelation of the divine mystery delivered through Moses. In their turn, the Hebrew prophets received revelations from the Holy Spirit, clarifying what had been revealed through Moses. In his own turn, the "Teacher of Righteousness" was the unique master who instructed the members of the Qumran Community in the divine truth. He was the "final prophet",[127] possessing a knowledge and a hermeneutic of the Revelation which were entirely new. Like Ezekiel, he combined three offices in his person: he was a priest of the line of Zadok, an inspired prophet, and a visionary of divine things. As such, the "Teacher of Righteousness" was truly a "new Ezekiel" and, to the extent to which these three functions were also ascribed symbolically to the members of the Community, it can fairly be considered an "Ezekelian community".[128]

Like Shozo Fujita, we believe that the answer to the question raised above is to be found here. What makes the Community into the "new Temple" is the new revelation that it received from God—the revelation not of a new Book, but of the true hermeneutic of the Book.[129] In the old temple of Jerusalem there was neither new inspiration nor personal dedication, but a false hermeneutics and a false practice of the Law. The symbolic Temple or Community-temple, on the other hand, was a new

125 We have spoken of this elsewhere as "prophetic religion" (*ḥikmah nabawīyah*); cf. *En islam iranien*, op. cit., vol. IV, index s.v., and note 115 above.

126 Shozo Fujita, op. cit., pp. 272 ff. See Otto Betz, *Offenbarung und Schriftforschung in der Qumransekte* (Tübingen, 1960), pp. 155 ff.

127 This concept should be compared with the concept in Shiite prophetology of the "Seal of prophecy". But insofar as he is charged with the mission of unveiling the hidden meaning of the Revelations, the "Teacher of Righteousness" combines in some way the function of a prophet with that of the Imam. Cf. *En Islam iranien*, op, cit., vol. IV, index s.v. Sceau.

128 Cf. Shozo Fujita, op. cit., p. 273.

129 Similarly, in Shiite prophetology the function of the Imam to come, the twelfth Imam, will not be to reveal a new Book, but to reveal the esoteric meaning (*bāṭin*) of all the divine Revelations. In the context of the theology of the "True Prophet", common to both Judaeo-Christianity and Shiite prophetology, the function of the "Teacher of Righteousness" could perhaps be compared to that of the Imam.

temple because it owed its birth to a new prophetic inspiration, a new revelation of the divine mystery.[130] This Revelation enabled the Community to think of itself as a sanctuary, as the Community-temple, for it felt itself to be the active realization of all the prophecies concerning the temple of Jerusalem. "To live within the Community would mean that the laity always behaved as though they were in the Temple, and that the priests always thought of themselves as being in the Holy of Holies".[131]

3. *The symbolism of the planting, the water, and the high mountain.* This constellation of symbols is what really determines the "Ezekelian" character of the Community. By means of a tropological hermeneutic, the images of Ezekiel's vision actually become the *active images* in terms of which the Qumran Community represents itself to itself. We have already alluded to the vision in Ezekiel (17:22–24) of the prince of the future city-temple as a "young branch" planted on the mountain of the Temple where the new Israel will flourish (cf. above, sections III and IV, A, 3). Hence the idea of the "planting of righteousness" or "eternal planting". The Community of Qumran, as the symbolic Temple, feels itself to be this planting.[132] The symbolism of the planting spontaneously evokes the symbolism of the water that nourishes the trees of life—that is, the Teacher of Righteousness and his disciples—and this Water issues from the "fountain of Mystery". The notion of mystery encompasses all the things that man is unable to see unless God himself reveals them to him. "There is a cosmic mystery of God (*Razi-el*),[133] a vast and profound secret that only the Teacher of Righteousness and his followers can at least recognize; and this knowledge or *gnosis* enables them to be the authentic lineal heirs of the "planting of righteousness". Their growth and prosperity are assured forever and without limit by the "living Water", that is to say, by the mystery.

We have already observed in Ezekiel (47:1–12) the visionary image of the Water welling up from beneath the Temple threshold on the eastern side, swelling into a powerful torrent which flows through the desert to the sea. By this torrent the parched earth is made fertile; a dead sea is

130 Cf. Shozo Fujita, op. cit., pp. 275–278.
131 A. Jaubert, op. cit., p. 159.
132 Cf. Shozo Fujita, op. cit., p. 279, with reference to 1 QS, 8:5.
133 Ibid., p. 282. Raziel is the name of the Angel who was Adam's initiator. Cf. Moïse Schwab, *Vocabulaire de l'angélologie* (Paris, 1897), p. 246. On *water* as a symbol of knowledge, see *En Islam iranien*, op. cit., vol. IV, index s.v.

transformed into a living sea. As the Angel, the visionary guide, measures it, it becomes too deep to be crossed. Similarly, a Qumran text says: "And they [the springs] shall become an unleashed torrent over all the banks, and shall go down to the fathomless seas".[134] The parallel is obvious. It indicates that the source of the torrent which fertilizes the parched earth is ultimately to be sought in the Temple. The Water that wells up from below the Temple threshold symbolizes the special revelation imparted to the "Teacher of Righteousness", and by means of this Water his Community thrives like the "Tree of Life".

It is from the symbolism of this Water, too, that the Community derives its sense of participation in God's "eschatological programme". This participation consists in the profound study and strict observance of the Torah, since this was "to prepare the way of God" (see above, the three meanings of such preparation), the Torah being precisely that which was symbolized by the Water—this Water that "issues from beneath the threshold of the house", that causes justice to flourish and transforms the land.[135] We agree with Shozo Fujita in thinking that when the Community refers to the "scroll hidden beneath the threshold" and to "the water that nourishes the plants in the dry land", it associates both these concepts with the prophetic image of Ezekiel contemplating the Water whose source is in the Temple. They knew that they were those in whom this prophetic vision found its fulfilment, and that, as the symbolic temple, their Community was the source in which God's "eschatological programme" was initiated.[136] But as we shall see later, the living within oneself of such a fulfilment of the prophecies is what was known as "realized eschatology".

Finally, the symbolism of the high mountain, too, both proceeds from and nourishes the experiential sense of "realized eschatology". The image of the new Temple on a high mountain—"on the high mountain of

134 Shozo Fujita, op. cit., p. 284, quoting 1 QH, 8:17.

135 Cf. *Zechariah* 14:8: "And it shall be in that day, that living waters shall go out from Jerusalem; half of them toward the former [i.e. Dead] sea, and half of them toward the hinder [i.e. Mediterranean] sea: in summer and in winter shall it be." Cf. *Joel* 3:18, *I Enoch* 28:9 (all these references to the river are based on the image of the current of water flowing out of the Temple in Ezekiel's vision). Cf. also Rev. 22:1–2: ". . . a pure river of water of life, clear as crystal, proceeding out of the throne of God and of the Lamb", flowing down the middle of the street in the new Jerusalem.

136 Shozo Fujita, op. cit., p. 287.

Israel"—is peculiar to Ezekiel.[137] The image of the high mountain-temple would thus seem to derive, at Qumran, from the Ezekelian *Imago Templi*. The mountain-temple is the symbolic temple constituted by the Community itself. The dominant note here is entirely spiritual. Qumran will not become a high mountain some day in the future: it is already a high mountain in the spiritual sense, a mountain as high as heaven. When a text says: "Thou [the Community] shalt be as an Angel of the Face for the glory of Elohim of hosts . . .", this corresponds strictly with the description of the celestial Temple and of the office of the Angels of the Presence in the *Testament of Levi* 3:4–6 (see above).[138] The *Imago Templi* is no longer a symbol referring to something beyond itself; it is realized in actuality, becomes the event itself (becomes, as we said above, not allegorical but tautegorical). As regards the synchronization of its divine service with the angelic liturgy, the Community is the place where eschatology is already and actively realized.

4. *The celestial liturgy and realized eschatology*. The connection indicated by this sub-title best illustrates the fundamental orientation of the members of the Qumran Community. If their entire life is dominated by the Word of God, it is because they are truly "existential interpreters of the Holy Scriptures".[139] The features which characterize the life of the Community derive from its eschatological hermeneutic of the whole of the Old Testament, and it is this lived hermeneutic which confers on the eschatological Community a permanent sacred status, an irreducible *life-style*. The Community of Qumran lived the eschatological salvation as something already accomplished "in the present". The Johannine community, as we will see later, did much the same. This mode of being, it has been said, implies the fulfilment of "five eschatological acts": resurrection, new creation, communion with the Angels, final deliverance from the power of death, and anticipatory ("proleptic") transference to the holy City.[140] This escha-

137 Ibid., pp. 228, 290. Even though it was to Ezekiel that the Qumran Sect owed the image of the new Temple on a high mountain, this image could equally have been inspired by other passages in the Old Testament: Isa. 2:2–4, Mic. 4:1–2.

138 Cf. also *I Enoch* 24:25, the high mountain as an apocalyptic image. Cf. Shozo Fujita, op. cit., pp. 290–291, the translation and analysis of 1 QSb, 4:25–26.

139 Cf. Otto Betz, 'The Eschatological Interpretation of the Sinai-Tradition in Qumran and in the New Testament', in *Revue de Qumran*, no. 21 (Feb. 1967), pp. 89, 94, 96.

140 Heinz-Wolfgang Kuhn, *Enderwartung und gegenwärtiges Heil: Untersuchungen zu den Gemeindeliedern von Qumran* (Göttingen, 1966), quoted with comments by David

tological anticipation was essentially *mysterium liturgicum*: the hymnology of Qumran, the experience of being transferred to the heavenly kingdoms and of singing hymns in the company of the Angels, constituted essentially a liturgical realization of the Community's eschatological status. The "five acts" mentioned above were performed "in the present" in the liturgical congregation. Communion and liturgical companionship with the invisible Angels are an essential aspect of "realized eschatology": they testify to the fact that the restoration of Adam as a glorious celestial being among the other celestial beings is already accomplished.[141]

The Qumran Community is not a multitudinary Church; it is "*the* Temple", not the chosen people in the ethnic sense of the word, but the coming together and union of chosen individuals. Like Israel on Mount Sinai, the members of the Community live in a *camp* which is Qumran (cf. Exod. 19:2, 16–17), awaiting the manifestation of God's Glory. Because the Community is the living sanctuary, and thus the "centre of the earth", it marks the boundary between the sacred and the profane. It is the fortress which the sons of Light must defend through incessant combat against the attacks of the sons of Darkness.[142] This combat is an eschatological one, and is carried on side by side with the angelic powers, since all beings of Light are partners in the same struggle. Thus, angelology governs the life of Qumran: the Angels are present at the council, at the liturgy, and in the combat. This communion and companionship with the Angels characterize the Qumran Community-temple and its spirituality. The highest expression of this spirituality is to be found in an "angelic liturgy", of which the text, to the great dismay of researchers, has so far at least come down to us only in a fragmentary and mutilated form.

Nevertheless, a fragment suffices to show how this ceremonial liturgy re-enacts each time the great moments of Ezekiel's vision of the divine Chariot (the *Merkabah*; Ezek., chapters 1–10). Even though the word *Merkabah* does not appear in these chapters of Ezekiel, they have furnished the Jewish mystical tradition with its central image of the Throne which is like a chariot. And G. Scholem has no doubts about the Essene origin of

---

Edward Aune, *The Cultic Setting of Realized Eschatology in Early Christianity* (Leiden, Brill, 1972), pp. 31 ff (abbrev. *Cultic Setting*).

141 Cf. ibid., pp. 41–42.

142 Cf. Otto Betz, art. cit., pp. 96, 98, 103.

the mystical current of the *Merkabah*, whose source lies in the first century before our era.[143]

"...The Ministers of the glorious Face in the Abode of the God of Knowledge fall down before the Cherubim and utter blessings while the sound of the divine wind rises . . . and there is a tumult of shouting while their wings cause the sound of the divine wind to rise. The Cherubim above the heavens bless the likeness of the Throne of the Chariot . . . And when the wheels turn, angels of holiness come and go between His glorious wheels like visions of fire. Spirits of supreme holiness surround them, visions of streams of fire similar to scarlet (*hashmal*); and shining creatures clothed in glorious brocades, many-coloured marvellous garments more brilliant than pure salt, spirits of the living God, unceasingly accompany the glory of the marvellous chariot".[144]

Just as the sons of Light fight side by side with the angelic powers, so they are included in the celestial armies in order to acclaim the divine Chariot-throne. It is thus possible to say that the theophanic vision described by Ezekiel (1–10) was lived actively, liturgically, by the Community of Qumran, and that in this sense the worship it celebrated was truly a celestial liturgy. It is true that in Ezekiel the vision of the divine Chariot is not a prophecy. But the Qumran hermeneutic, by virtue of being an existential tropology, was able to confer a prophetic significance on the Ezekelian vision of the Chariot.[145] The resurrection, as "realized eschatology", is not a fact which happens *in* history; it is *the* "liturgical mystery". The distinction between eschatology with respect to time and

143 Shozo Fujita, op. cit., p. 297. Cf. Gershom G. Scholem, *Jewish Gnosticism, Merkabah Mysticism, and Talmudic Tradition* (New York, 1960), pp. 1–30. "A new evaluation of the inner development of Judaism and its relation to the Gnostic movement should replace the rash and uninformed judgments that have hitherto prevented proper insight into Merkabah mysticism and Jewish gnosticism" (ibid., p. 83).

144 A. Dupont-Sommer, trans. G. Vermès, *The Essene Writings from Qumran* (Oxford, 1961), pp. 333–334. Shozo Fujita, op. cit., pp. 296–304, gives the translation and the comparison line by line with the text of Ezekiel. The state of the manuscript makes it difficult to read. Another translation would be: "The ministers of the Presence of Glory in the tabernacle of the *Elohim* of knowledge. The cherubim fall down before Him, and give thanks to Him, while the sweet voices of the *Elohim* rise into the heights . . ." The text testifies to a very complex angelology: Cherubim, Angels of the Face, Angels of holiness, Spirits of supreme holiness. For the image of the chariot, cf. I Chr. 28:18; for the rivers of fire, cf. Dan. 7:10. Cf. Dupont-Sommer, op. cit., p. 333, note 4, and p. 334, notes 1–5. See also the copiously annotated translation in J. Carmignac, E. Cothenet and Ḥ. Lignée, *Les Textes de Qumrān traduits et annotés*, vol. II (Paris, 1963), pp. 316 ff.

145 Shozo Fujita, op. cit., p. 305. Cf. above, note 115.

eschatology with respect to space is an artificial one. "Liturgical time", continuously recurrent and reversible—the time of the "angelic presence" —is both the rupture or "end" of linear chronological time, and the assumption of space.

J. Strugnell, to whom we are indebted for the *princeps* edition of the Qumran "angelic liturgy", was already aware of what we are attempting to explain here.[146] He made it perfectly clear that what is at issue is not an angelic liturgy at which a visionary happens to be present, but an earthly liturgy to which the Angels are summoned and at which they are present —a liturgy in which the celestial Temple is contemplated as the archetype of the earthly Temple. There is synchronicity—interpenetration—between the liturgy celebrated in the celestial Temple and that celebrated in the earthly Temple.[147]

Another aspect of the "angelic liturgy" of Qumran is brought out by the importance of the seven archangelic Princes of the divine heptad.[148] "The fourth among the Chief Princes shall bless in the name of the King's majesty all that walk in uprightness with seven words of majesty, and he shall bless the foundations of majesty with seven marvellous words . . . The fifth of the Chief Princes shall bless in the name of all His wonders all who know the Mysteries of the perfectly pure beings with seven words of His sublime truth . . ." This recurrence of the number seven in the angelic liturgy cannot but bring to mind the heptadic structure of the Revelation of St. John, and it thereby suggests that the function of the hymns in St. John's Revelation, its liturgical realization of the kingdom of God and of the last judgement, may be linked with the same liturgical phenomenon in the worship of the Essene Community at Qumran. The same experience of a realized eschatology is found in the liturgy both of Qumran and of the

146 J. Strugnell, 'The Angelic Liturgy at Qumran', in *Supplements to Vetus Testamentum*, vol. VII (Leiden, 1960). (The theme of the angelic liturgy should be the subject of an extensive comparative study. Cf. the nocturnal vision of the Emperor Henry II (973–1024) in the cave-temple of the archangel Michael: A. von Keyserlingk, *Vergessene Kulturen in Monte Gargano* (Stuttgart, 1970), pp. 112–113, and 185 note 88).

147 Cf. D. E. Aune, *Cultic Setting*, op. cit., p. 32 note 1. Hence, as we have already observed, the importance of the question of the liturgical calendar, on which Qumran and the Temple of Jerusalem were divided.

148 A. Dupont-Sommer, op. cit., pp. 330–331. Unfortunately, although the text of the hymnology from the fourth to the seventh celestial Prince is complete, that of the hymnology of the first three Princes is missing.

primitive Johannine community (see below, section VI).[149] What distinguishes the texts of the Qumran Community from all other apocalyptic literature (e.g. *Daniel* 12, *I Enoch*, *Testaments of the Twelve Patriarchs*) is that in place of the expectation of the resurrection of the dead there is the lived sense of a victory already achieved "in the present" over the kingdom of death. In this sense it is true to say that whoever lives in the Community of the sons of Light is already living in the last times. The eschatological experience of communion and companionship with the Angels is accompanied by a secret paradisal joy.[150]

It goes without saying that the Community of Qumran was thus fully aware of the presence of God's Spirit within itself. Some have wondered whether one could go so far as to say that this possession of the Spirit was itself also experienced as an eschatological gift, and this is a theme of controversy among Qumran scholars.[151] It seems to us, however, that in contrasting the Christian community, with its certitude of the *fait accompli*, with the Community of Qumran looking ahead to an advent of the Spirit that will bestow a more integral form on the visitations of Yahveh, we fail to consider what is implied by the simultaneity of the *jam* (already) and the *nondum* (not yet). Is Pentecost—the outpouring of the Spirit—a *fact* accomplished once and for all, or is it a *fact* which is still to come? The certainty that it is both *past* and *to come* is what has inspired all *paracletic* movements which could not accommodate themselves to the official Church, bogged down in History.[152] Such a certainty is also a nostalgia, and these two together have prompted the recurrence and the persistence of the *Imago Templi* in the face of the institutions and dogmas of the official Church (see below, section VI).

We would make a similar comment with respect to the question whether, when the Community asserts that it possesses an esoteric divine knowledge

149 D. E. Aune, op. cit., loc. cit. This is also the theme of Aune's admirable theological study: the realization "in the present" of eschatological salvation in the Qumran Community, in the 4th Gospel, in the Epistles of Ignatius, in the Odes of Solomon, in Marcion.

150 Ibid., p. 33, notes 1 and 2. We may recall here that Ismailism conceives of the entry into the Ismaili *da'wah* as entry into the "potential Paradise". Cf. my *Trilogie ismaélienne*, op. cit., p. 124.

151 Cf. D. E. Aune, op. cit., p. 34, where he discusses the work by H.-W. Kuhn, op. cit.

152 Cf. H. Corbin, 'L'Initiation ismaélienne ou l'ésotérisme et le Verbe', in *L'Homme et son Ange* (Paris, Fayard, 1984). See also my study 'L'Idée du Paraclet en philosophie iranienne', in *Face de Dieu, Face de l'Homme* (Paris, Flammarion, 1983).

(and the secrets of its angelology or of its fight against the sons of Darkness support such an assertiòn), this is not another aspect of its experience of the reality of eschatological salvation "in the present", in contrast to Jewish apocalyptic literature, which locates the acquisition of soteriological wisdom "in the future".[153]

Even when it is recognized that the "gift of gnosis" was seen as an "eschatological gift", there is still the need for a concept of *time* which validates the simultaneity of the *jam* and the *nondum*. We are familiar with the attempt made by present-day "dialectic theology" to "detemporalize" primitive Christian eschatology, but this is not what we are concerned with here. On the other hand, to affirm that the Qumran Community is the only one in which future eschatological salvation penetrates the present age, and then to go on to assert that the juxtaposition of future and present must itself be considered as determined and conditioned "temporally and historically",[154] is simply to relapse into historicism. It is to lose sight of all that is unique in the "liturgical mystery" lived as an eschatological experience; to lose sight of what is peculiar to the category of "liturgical time" in relation to chronological time, for which the simultaneity of *jam* and *nondum* is as unintelligible as the reversability of time. We believe that here it would be fruitful to introduce an analysis of the temporality of time, such as we have elsewhere elicited from Shiite gnosis.[155] It is as though our theological discussions in the West always stay on the level of "dense and opaque time" (*zamān kathīf*), when we ought to be bringing into play, above all in this case, ideas cognate with subtle time (*zamān laṭīf*) and hyper-subtle time (*zamān alṭaf*). This is the time of events on the level of the imaginal, the level of the "meeting-place of the two seas" where we initially situated the hierophanies of the *Imago Templi*.

Only if this *Imago Templi* is grasped on the level of the *imaginal* and in the time proper to it, is it true and justifiable to say that it is the hermeneutic of the Temple—the symbolism of the Temple—which enables the Qumran

153 Cf. D. E. Aune, op. cit., p. 35, in support of H.-W. Kuhn, op. cit.

154 Ibid., p. 36.

155 From the work in particular of Qāḍī Sa'īd Qummī, the outstanding Iranian Shiite thinker and spiritual master of the seventeenth century. Cf. *En Islam iranien*, op. cit., vol. IV, index s.v. *zamān*. We are indebted to Qāḍī Sa'īd for a remarkable analysis of temporality, which he schematizes in the three modes mentioned above (opaque and dense, subtle, and hyper-subtle).

Community to experience the *jam* and the *nondum* with the difference between them abolished and the abyss between them filled in. This is so because the Community experiences itself as the intermediary place uniting God's celestial habitation with his earthly habitation: the Temple of the kingdom, "the unique sanctuary where, in an intimately synchronized liturgy, the worship of men and the worship of Angels conjoin".[156] Needless to say, the symbolism of the Temple is not the *cause* which enables the Community to believe in the present realization of eschatological salvation. It is one of the modes—and an exalted mode at that—of envisaging the presence of the final salvation.[157]

Once this realized eschatology is seen as essentially linked to the motif of Paradise and of the restoration of Adam, the *Anthropos*, to the state of Paradise, it has to be safeguarded by a conception of a time which is other than the time of History; for otherwise the motif in question will be relegated to the *imaginary*, and will not be stabilized on the level of the *mundus imaginalis* as a reality *sui generis* in its own right: the reality in which the events of hierohistory or "subtle" history take place. For all visionary events take place and have their place in the subtle time of this subtle history, whenever the invisible world, disclosing itself to the seer, sets him in the company of the Angels.

This is what happens in the great visionary scene that takes up the whole of chapter III of the *Book of Zechariah*. The high priest Joshua is defended from Satan by the Angel of Yahveh himself. The Angels remove his soiled clothes and clothe him in festal garments (3:4). And the Angel of Yahveh utters the solemn promise in the name of the Lord of hosts: the Temple of Jerusalem, rebuilt and purified, will once more be filled with the divine Presence. It will once more be the place filled with the company of Angels, because there is no gap, no hiatus between the celestial and the earthly Temples. "Ecce enim adduco servum meum *Orientem*" (3:8). "Ecce vir, *Oriens* nomen ejus et subter eum *orietur* et

156 A. Jaubert, op. cit., p. 191.

157 D. E. Aune, op. cit., p. 37. But if one can say that what differentiates the concept of the *eschaton* as a *restitutio principii*, as professed at Qumran and in Jewish apocalyptic literature in general, in relation to other religions, is the conception of the theophanic nature of history, it is still necessary to specify that this is not History in the ordinary, current sense of the word, but a hierohistory; and the time of this hierohistory, in which the events proper to it take place, is no longer the time of profane history. The hierohistoric recital is by its essence a "hierology". Cf. below, note 170.

aedificabit templum Domino" (6:12).[158] This promise is addressed by the Angel to "Joshua the high priest, thou, and thy fellows that sit before thee" (3:8), who are described as "men who serve as signs or portents" (*viri portendentes*). This very same expression is used to describe the companions of the psalmist of Qumran.[159] There is a knowledge which man, through his communion with the Angels, is called upon to share. The Angels are the "knowers" *par excellence*. "You have charged man with an eternal destiny in the company of the Spirits of knowledge . . ." It is this that, a few lines above, made us keep the Latin of the Vulgate: *Ecce vir, Oriens nomen ejus*. The Angel's knowledge is knowledge of the *Orient* "in the Orient" of things, knowledge which is "oriental" in the metaphysical sense of the word: the *cognitio matutina*, a term whose exact equivalent is the *'ilm ishrāqī* found in Suhravardī, who resurrected the ancient Persian theosophy of Light in Islamicized Iran. *Oriens* is the type of man realized by all the sons of Light.

Naturally, the esoteric character of this knowledge or *gnosis* need not surprise us. It has long been known from the historian Josephus that the Essenes pledged themselves "not to reveal the names of the Angels", for this is one of the mysteries about which the initiate does not speak lightly in front of anyone. But this does not mean that, on the level of Qumran angelology, it is not fitting to note, as Annie Jaubert does so well, the expansive breath of cosmic communion which inspires the piety of the faithful. The word *ecclesia* is taken here, of course, in its etymological sense, connoting the idea of a liturgical assembly. It would therefore be simpler to say just "the Temple", since the union of the celestial and the terrestrial communities is, indeed, *the Temple*. Bearing this in mind, we can subscribe to the following lines: "On entering into the covenant of the Community, which was by definition the Covenant of God, the new member was involved in an immense *ecclesia*, both of Angels and of men, of which it could perhaps be said without paradox that it was more celestial than earthly. It was the communion of the sons of Light, of the sons of truth, of the "Saints", whether of heaven or of earth. Beyond was the world of darkness, where Belial and his troop of evil spirits exercised their perverse

158 What the Vulgate translates as *Oriens* is often translated as "branch". We prefer the former, with its distant echoes of the concept of the *Ishrāq* and the *Ishrāqīyūn* (the "Orientals") in Suhravardī (*'ilm ishrāqī*, "oriental" knowledge, *cognitio matutina*). Cf. above, note 89.

159 Cf. A. Jaubert, op. cit., p. 190.

rule. It is evident that whoever refused to enter the earthly assembly was thereby excluding himself from the celestial assembly."[160]

VI. The Imago Templi *and Templar Knighthood*

1. *Questions raised by the "jam et nondum"*. We have just emphasized that "eschatology realized in the present is experienced spiritually as a *fact*, as the simultaneity of the *jam* and the *nondum*. This simultaneity is constituted by and lived in the *mysterium liturgicum*, and postulates a liturgical time *sui generis* which is not the time of History. Liturgical time wrests eschatology away from the idea itself of historic-chronological time, of which eschatology, according to current opinion, is simply the final end, to be expected in an unforeseeable future. Recent researches have demonstrated what there is in common as regards this experience between the Essene Community of Qumran and the primitive Johannine community, that which produced the Johannine *corpus* (see below, § 4). We must limit ourselves here to this latter theme. The questions raised would assume their full amplitude if we could refer in detail to the theology of the primitive Judaeo-Christian community of Jerusalem, the Church of James, of which the Ebionite community is the extension. We shall be able to allude to it only in passing; but the inquiry must in any case confront themes of formidable complexity, and it is most important to specify the terms in which these themes are being formulated: historical or phenomenological. We must confine ourselves here to the perspective within which we can hope to understand the recurrence of the hierophanies of the *Imago Templi*.

The phenomenological relationships and affinities discernible, with regard to Temple symbolism, between the Qumran Community and the Johannine community, raise questions such as the following:

1. What is essentially common to the idea of the new Temple at Qumran and the same idea in the Johannine community, and what is the essential difference between them? What essentially creates this difference?

2. What does this difference tell us about the experience of time and history? Has hierohistory been brought to a close? In what way does the transition from eschatological Christianity to the Christianity of History influence the recurrence or the cessation of the hierophanies of the *Imago*

160 Ibid., p. 198.

Templi? If resurrection and eschatology are conceived and lived as located in the *mysterium liturgicum*, is it not clear that current conceptions of eschatology are inadequate?

3. On the other hand, is it not by grasping the common element in the eschatological experience of the Qumran and Johannine communities that the purposes and aims of all the *paracletic* movements which have arisen in the course of the history of Christianity can be explained? And cannot the birth of the concept of the *Ecclesia Johannis* as the third reign and Church of the Spirit be explained in the same way? Is there not an essential connection between a mystery of Pentecost both already come to pass and not yet come to pass, *jam* and *nondum*?

4. Is it not with reference to the purpose common to the paracletic idea and to the recurrences of the *Imago Templi* that a response will be given to the twofold lament heard in the beginning, the lament sounded in the Talmud and the lament which, echoing in a solitary Pyrenean amphitheatre, links the fate of the Temple with the fate of the Templar knighthood? Here, in particular, the inquiry becomes the concern of phenomenology.

2. *The theology of the Temple and the theology of the Church.* The primitive Christian community considered itself as the inheritor of the divine promises, as the ideal Israel confronting the Israel of history. The discovery of the literature of Qumran has had the result—still unforeseeable thirty years ago—of setting us in the presence of the lofty spirituality of a Jewish community which had a great deal in common with the *milieu* from which the primitive Christian community emerged. Each has its founder (for Qumran this was the "Teacher of Righteousness"), whose interpretation of the Scriptures is decisive for his community. Both communities have the same sense of eschatology. Both claim to be the true Israel. An important function is fulfilled in the thought of both communities by the same theme, that of the symbolism developed around the Temple. At Qumran and in the New Testament, this Temple symbolism involves three factors: a critique of the Temple of Jerusalem and of its sacrifices; the belief that the last days have begun; and the conviction of both communities that God dwells within it as he once dwelt within the Temple. Both have the sense of being the community-temple.[161]

161 B. Gärtner, *The Temple*, op. cit., pp. IX–X, 100.

Having said this, we must note that, notwithstanding that they share the symbolism of the Temple, there is an essential difference between the two communities, namely, the fact of faith in Jesus as the Messiah and the Son of God. The feature which distinguishes the symbolism of the Temple in the New Testament is that it is entirely dependent on faith in Jesus.[162] The texts of Qumran represent the Community as being itself the new Temple. The canonical Gospels stress the replacing of the Temple by a person—by Jesus as the Messiah. St. Paul and the authors of the other Epistles do, it is true, return to the idea of the community, and represent the Church as the new Temple; but the idea of this community owes its existence to the person of Jesus and is based on him.[163]

The innovation and difficulty arise precisely at the point at which there is a question of establishing the link between the pre-existing *Christos* and the person of the historical Jesus. On the one hand, Israel is God's first-born. There is the figure of the angel Metatron, of the "Cherub on the Throne", of the Son of Man, revealed and shown to Enoch as Enoch himself. But this revelation is effectuated through a celestial assumption, not through an earthly incarnation. On the other hand, there is the coming of the Messiah in the historic person of Jesus. Several centuries had to pass before Christian thought could stabilize its Christology. Here we will simply say that between the two extremes—the Community-temple of Qumran and the historical Christology of the Great Church—primitive Judaeo-Christian Christology represents something like a middle way: the Christology of *Christos Angelos* and of the *Verus Propheta*.[164] The fact that this was not the way followed by official Christology is doubtless the inner and decisive tragedy of Christianity, and is of great significance for our present inquiry.

In effect the connection, established and lived, between the new Temple and the messianic conception is replaced by the connection between the new Temple and the Christology of the New Testament. The community-temple is transformed into a *corpus mysticum*, the idea of the mystical body of Christ, of which Christians are the members. The two representations

162 Ibid., p. 101.
163 Ibid., p. 122.
164 Here, one should take into account all the conclusions to be derived from the researches of Martin Werner, *Die Entstehung des christlichen Dogmas*, 2nd edn. (Bern/Tübingen, 1953). We will return to this elsewhere.

appear to be separated by a very brief interval; but the interval suffices to contain the hidden reasons for a persistence and recurrence of the *Imago Templi* which make a conscious appeal to its Solomonic origins. It suffices to differentiate what one might call the spirit of the Temple from the spirit of the official Church, and to explain, in spite of the *hiatus* of its external history, the persistence over the centuries of a tradition of the Temple which has been sometimes latent and sometimes explicit. The norm of the Temple continues to inspire a theology of the Temple which sees itself as the esoteric aspect of the theology of the Church. This is what religious phenomenology may thematize as Christian esotericism and Templar tradition. These observations contain some elements of the reply to the first question raised above.

3. *Is all finished?* Is it in fact enough simply to speak of two ecclesiologies, as though the Qumran image of the Community-temple, the place of the divine Presence, were the equivalent of the *magisterium* of the Church with its assertion of canonical possession of the *potestas clavium*? The answer can, it seems, be reached by considering how the experience of *time* is lived differently on both sides. For the Qumran Community, as we saw, resurrection and eschatology are lived not as events occurring *in* History that has happened, but as a *mysterium liturgicum*, a celestial assumption. Liturgical time is reversible, and the events occurring in it do not belong to the historical time of irreversible chronology. They occur at "the meeting-place of the two seas", where the celestial Temple and the earthly Temple conjoin. They belong to hierohistory, to "subtle history". One cannot make History out of the events of "subtle history".[165] These events are both already over and still to come, and their end is always expected: lived eschatology consists in being "always in readiness". This essential expectation excludes the possibility of time being finished, as it is finished according to the meaning assigned to Christ's death and resurrection by a Christianity that, no longer eschatological, has lapsed into History. In this case, the events are past: "All is finished".

By the same token, the time of the Church, inaugurated after everything was accomplished, is the time of History, of irreversible history. In this

165 Most theologians and critics omit to question the concept of "history" and accept it as a *fait accompli*. There is thus no way out of the impasse. Cf. above, note 157, as well as the whole of this present study.

time of the Church, writes Annie Jaubert, "a consummation is exploited which has already been totally realized. There is no higher teaching to be expected, no other liberator. The world of consummation has been opened up by Christ's resurrection and one must incorporate oneself into it. We believe that this, ultimately, is the essential difference not just between Qumran and Christianity, but between all Jewish theology of the Covenant and Christian theology".[166] If the writer of these lines is right, the situation is serious, for it amounts to saying that the Jewish theology of the Covenant remains open to the future, while Christian theology is closed upon the past. These lines enable us, in fact, to grasp the moment when Christianity, having been essentially eschatological as the *mysterium liturgicum*, succumbed to the perils of History. If there is nothing left to expect, it means that hierohistory is over and done with. let us observe in passing that the denial of this ending to prophetic history or hierohistory is, likewise, all that differentiates Shiite Islam from Sunni Islam. Islamic prophetology inherited something from the Judaeo-Christian theology of the *Verus Propheta*, but extends the manifestations of the latter up till Muhammad, who then becomes the "Seal of prophecy". For Shiite gnosis, however, the closing of the cycle of prophecy marks the inauguration of the cycle of spiritual initiation. Something is left to expect, which is the appearance of the twelfth Imam. Ismaili gnosis, moreover, goes as far as to challenge the closing of the cycle of the manifestations of the *Verus Propheta*.[167] It is most important to note the analogy of the positions adopted here. There are those for whom the past is over. There are those for whom the past is still to come.

For if there is no higher teaching to be expected, this means that the New Testament has no literal sense beyond which one can go; that it is complete, an accomplished and acquired revelation, which one has only to put to use. This would seem to exclude the idea itself of Christian esotericism. But, if this is the case, statements such as the following are incomprehensible: "Therefore speak I to them in parables" (Matt. 13:13).

166 A. Jaubert, op. cit., p. 468. These lines provide a clear description of the situation as envisaged from the point of view of official Christology—Christology as it has prevailed "in history". But such a closure is exactly what our authors urge us to oppose and overcome.

167 Cf. *En Islam iranien*, op. cit., vol. IV, index s.v. prophète, prophétologie, *Verus Propheta*. See also H. Corbin, 'Un roman initiatique ismaélien du Xe siècle', in *Cahiers de civilisation médiévale* (January–March and April–June 1972), especially pp. 134 ff.

"Unto you it is given to know the mysteries of the kingdom of God: but to others in parables; that seeing they might not see, and hearing they might not understand" (Luke 8:10).[168] Where there is a parable, there is a meaning which is hidden, inner, "esoteric". There is, then, something to come: the events that will verify the prophetic *meaning* of these parables. We have already seen how all events, when they are elevated to "the meeting-place of the two seas", become parables. This was the line taken by the hermeneutics of the Joachimites, the followers of Joachim of Fiore.[169] This elevation, however, is not possible without the inspiration of the Spirit-Paraclete. Must we then say that the mystery of Pentecost is definitively accomplished, or that it is both *jam* and *nondum*? Such a simultaneity is verifiable only in a time which is other than the time of the history of accomplished facts : the "subtle time" of the *mysterium liturgicum*.[170] The paracletic idea is quintessentially Johannine; and without it, there is no reason for the recurrences of the *Imago Templi*. These recurrences are connected, in one way or another, with the idea of the "Church of John" as the reign of the Spirit-Paraclete, the final reign which is already being lived "in the present". These are all elements of the reply to the second and third questions raised above, which will be completed in what follows.

4. *Liturgical theophanies and christophanies*. Herein lies the extreme importance of the researches demonstrating what there is in common between the lived eschatology of Qumran, on the one hand, and of the primitive Christian community—or, more precisely, of the "Johannine community"—on the other. The element common to both these communities is the eschatological sense of the liturgical mystery. By the term "Johannine community" is meant what several theologians have designated as the "School of St. John",[171] the milieu in which the theology and eschatology of the "Gospel

168 Compare Isa. 6:9–10 (following the vision of the seraphim).

169 P. de Lubac, *Exégèse médiévale*, III, 459, sadly reproaches them for this hermeneutic, which he regards as their fundamental error. The opposition could not be more clearly marked.

170 Cf. above, note 157. On the equivocal, rather than analogical, use of the terms *time* and *history*, see my study 'L'Initiation ismaélienne ou l'ésoterisme et le Verbe', in *L'Homme et son Ange*, op. cit.

171 Cf. D. E. Aune, op. cit., p. 63, note 3 (note: we always use the term "Johannine" for everything deriving from the teaching that originated in the apostle John, and the term "Johannite" for everything deriving from the Order of Saint John of Jerusalem).

according to St. John" were developed in a context of worship, preaching and instruction. Such an eschatology is not a "datum" fitting into a system, but a vital affair of faith and relgious experience, whose outward expression is moulded by the modalities of piety and worship. This theological expression of it derives from the piety and spirituality of the Johannine community, from its thought and its religious experience; and at the centre of the religious life is the worship, the liturgy.[172]

The different modes in which eschatological salvation was conceptualized as a phenomenon realized "in the present", in the experience both of the individual and of the community, were determined by the current forms of Christian piety and worship.[173] As at Qumran, piety and worship in this case are those of an eschatological community. The experience of eschatological salvation "in the present" is a phenomenon which by its essence cannot be understood apart from the liturgical worship, and it is the latter which defines the community. Thus, eschatology and worship are *ab initio* inextricably intertwined. The celebration of the Last Supper, which was the central act of the liturgical community, was seen not only as the affirmation of events that had already occurred, but as the present anticipation of the eschatological consummation of the history of salvation.[174] This anticipation, then, was essentially a liturgical mystery, accomplished in a hierophanic time. Herein is revealed the phenomenological relationship between the writings of Qumran and Johannine literature.

We saw above (section V, 4) that this remarkable form of eschatology, "presently realized" in liturgical worship, implied, if not the presence of a gnostic component, at any rate a marked affinity with Jewish gnosis. This in itself implies that a Jewish gnosis existed before Christian gnosticism developed. For certain theologians, so-called "heterodox" Judaism is the background against which one can achieve a better understanding of the Gospel of John; a whole section, at any rate, of the Johannine community came from this background.[175] Some theologians, referring to the vision of Isaiah (Isa. 6:1 ff.), go so far as to view Johannine mysticism as an offshoot of the mysticism of the *Merkabah*.[176] The vision anticipated by the book of

172 Ibid., pp. 9, 64.
173 Ibid., p. 8.
174 Ibid., pp. 13, 16, 17.
175 Ibid., pp. 65–66.
176 Peder Borgen, *Bread from Heaven: An exegetical Study of the Concept of Manna in the Gospel of John and the Writings of Philo* (Leiden, 1965), pp. 3, 147, quoted in ibid., p. 91.

the *Ascension of Isaiah* presupposes a visionary ascension into heaven.[177] Likewise, the aim of the Gospel of John is not to preserve a historical memory of the earthly Jesus,[178] but to impart another "history" whose place and seat is the spiritual knowledge of the Johannine community. This "history" possesses a plenary reality in its own right, a reality which is certainly different from the outward history of events, but is no less real—is, rather, "even more real" than this outward history. The characteristics of the Johannine Jesus derive existentially from the activities—pneumatic, charismatic, prophetic—of the Johannine community. As a result, Christology determines eschatology, and eschatology becomes an aspect of Christology.[179] Johannine "history" is not divided into a series of periods and epochs, among which the period of the Church is qualitatively distinguished by the fact that it has been inaugurated by Jesus' earthly ministry. Jesus' true, eternal mission was not interrupted by his passion, death, resurrection and ascension; rather, these events together serve to broaden his ministry, to render it more effective, through the bestowal on the community of the gift of the Spirit-Paraclete, Jesus' *Alter Ego*. The limitations and particulars which characterize his historic mission are laid aside.[180]

These characteristics enable us to understand each event as originating in the *mysterium liturgicum* and lived "in the present" of liturgical time. Hence the phenomenological affinities between the "liturgical visions" of the Jewish prophets and the visions of the primitive Christian prophets,[181] which are so many eschatological transpositions in the celestial kingdom. In Israelite worship, the *theophany*, the "liturgical advent" of Yahveh, was the central event in the divine office. In the divine office of the Johannine

177 D. E. Aune, op. cit., p. 91: *John* 8:56 assumes a similar visionary experience on the part of Abraham.

178 Ibid., p. 67.

179 Ibid., pp. 84, 88.

180 Ibid., pp. 104–105.

181 The vision of the *sessio* (of the Son of man) *ad dexterum Dei* can be understood with reference to two perspectives. Either the prophet and the liturgical community see themselves as transported to the celestial kingdom (Hymns of Qumran, Apocalypse of Paul, Odes of Solomon), or the prophet and the liturgical community see the object of their vision as coming to them (vision of Stephen, initial vision of the Apocalypse, the Johannine community at the time of the farewell speech). "Regardless of precisely how the future is thought to be actualized in the present, the cult is the primary setting for that actualization. With this background, we may proceed to the interpretation of the *crux interpretum* for our hypothesis of the *visio Christi* as central point of the Johannine cultus, John 1:51."

community, the central moment was the *visio Christi*. In John 1:51, for example,[182] which is an independent fragment concluding the conversation with Nathaniel and alluding to the coming and going of the Angels between heaven and earth, the evangelist is not anticipating an event which is going to happen one distant day in the development of evangelical history. He is speaking of "the sort of event that the Johannine community experienced spiritually (pneumatically) in the context of the worshipping community." In the context of the charismatic liturgy, the temporal boundaries between present and future are abolished, and the glories of the future eschatological state, conceived as a restoration of the primitive paradisal condition, "are experienced as a reality in the present".[183] In the same way that the Jewish mystics wished to experience a *visio Dei* by way of anticipation,[184] the Johannine community experienced a *visio Christi* in its celebration of the liturgical mystery. Here, *theopany could only be Christophany.*

Thus the real question, as D. E. Aune, for example, posits it, cannot be one simply of acknowledging or of trying to reconcile or maintain a tension between the present and future elements; neither can it be one of superficial attempts to explain things by the supposed "transformation" of futurist eschatology into realized eschatology. Far from it: "the solution to the problem (of Johannine eschatology) consists in determining the function of this eschatology in the Johannine liturgical community, in determining the significance assumed by it for this community in relation to its

182 "Verily, verily, I say unto you, Hereafter ye shall see heaven open, and the angels of God ascending and descending upon the Son of man" (John 1:51). D. E. Aune, op. cit., pp. 96–97, recalls the exegeses of this which have been given. G. Quispel (quoted in ibid., p. 97, note 4) interprets this vision in terms of a background of esoteric Judaism—of, that is to say, *Merkabah* mysticism.

183 Needless to say, all theophanic visions and visionary experiences presuppose the "subtle body" of mystical anthropology as the organ whereby they are mediated. Cf. Odeberg, *The Fourth Gospel*, cited in ibid., p. 101: "In order to enter the highest heaven, the Celestial Realm, the ascending human being must change into fire, taking on a body of light, or, as it is also expressed, put on garments of light . . . There is also in mystic notions from different times and places of origin a common idea of an inner, spiritual body, sometimes viewed as merely latent in earthly men . . . sometimes as the conscious possession even during earthly life of the twice-born, who as a consequence are able to perceive and act both in the earthly world and the spiritual world."

184 Ibid., p. 99, note 1. Cf. b. Haggigah 14b: "The teacher of R. Jose the Priest says he saw them seated on Mt. Sinai; heard heavenly voices saying: Ascend hither, you and your disciples are destined to be in the third set (of angels) singing continually before the Shekinah."

religious values and hopes and with regard to the precise mode of conceptualization with which the community represented to itself this eschatology as already realized."[185]

This function and significance can be grasped with the aid of the analysis that we have summarized here, and they enable us to understand the connection between what is implied by Johannine eschatology "in the present" and the persistent recurrences of the *Imago Templi*. In the case both of the Community-temple of Qumran and of the Johannine community, the certainty of the presence of the Spirit makes possible the experience of realized eschatology. Given the precedence of the *mysterium liturgicum* over all other considerations and interpretations,[186] the "comings" and "returns" of Jesus would appear to refer in the first place to the liturgical "coming" that recurs in the form of a *visio Christi* during the celebration of the liturgy "in the Spirit", as the Johannine community celebrated it.[187]

The comings anticipated in liturgically realized echatology were not, of course, mistaken for the final act, the Parousia or "Second Coming", which is the end of eschatology itself, of the eschatology that has already begun. But it seems to us that without this actualization in the present, the Parousia would never occur at all. The Johannine scheme of things remains open: all is not finished. "He that believeth on me, the works that I do shall he do also; and greater works than these shall he do" (John 14:12). Such a man will have traversed the initiatic way of the second birth (John 3, the conversation with Nicodemus).

The promise of the coming of the Paraclete was not fulfilled in the past alone. The outpouring of the Paraclete, the mystery of Pentecost, is simultaneously *jam et nondum* in "subtle time". This is why it is renewed

185 Ibid., p. 102.

186 Ibid., p. 127. Cf. John 14:3, 18, 28. D. E. Aune, ibid., pp. 128 ff., recapitulates under six headings the interpretations that have been given of these verses.

187 Ibid., p. 129: "In our opinion, the 'coming' of Jesus in the relevant passages under discussion from John 14 refers primarily to the recurring cultic 'coming' of Jesus in the form of a pneumatic or prophetic *visio Christi* within the setting of worship 'in the Spirit' as celebrated by the Johannine community. The eucharist undoubtedly forms the central moment of this setting within the cult worship of the community in which the exalted Jesus, now present in Parousia splendor, pronounces both blessing and woe, salvation and judgment through prophetic cult personnel." Ibid., note 1: the *cheroubikon* hymn of the liturgy of St. John Chrysostom as a survival of realized eschatology.

each year for the knights of the Grail.[188] The entire Johannine *corpus*, both Gospel and Revelation (to say nothing of the *Acts of John*), forms the framework of the *Ecclesia Johannis* or Church of the Parclete: the vision of the celestial Temple, the *Nova Hierosolyma*, the Temple "of many mansions", as it continued to be envisioned by a Christianity whose nature was templar and knightly—in other words, esoteric and Johannine. In the perspective of the *Paraclete*, the three Abrahamic faiths can come together in the same city-temple. We have attempted to explain this elsewhere,[189] and it is indicated by the persistence of the hierophanies of the *Imago Templi*. This brings us to the reply to the fourth question raised above.

5. *Christian esotericism and the Templar tradition.* At this stage of our enquiry we are faced with a decision regarding the process whereby eschatological Christianity became Christianity *within* History. Was it because of the delay of the Parousia, that is to say, because the awaited Parousia did not take place, that people ceased to expect it and began to make history, to be *in* History? Or was it because it ceased to be awaited that the Parousia was delayed indefinitely and in the end has not taken place at all?

Here the phenomenologist effects a "Copernican" reversal of the question that confronts historians with regard to the transition from eschatological Christianity to historical Christianity—a transition that decided the fate of official Christianity for two millenia. For to go from "subtle time" to "opaque time" was to succumb to the temptation of History. The time of prophets and of prophetic visions was not *within* the time of History. The Copernican reversal of the question is made necessary by the existential phenomenology of the *Imago Templi* that we are attempting to elucidate. Faced with a Church which had become a historical power and a society in the time of this world, the longing for the Temple is a longing for the "place" where, during the liturgical mystery and at "the meeting-place of the two seas", eschatology was realized in the present—a present which is not the limit of past and future in historical time, but the *nunc* of an eternal Presence. This "realized eschatology" was the restoration of Paradise, the restoration of the human condition to its celestial status. The longing

188 *The Quest of the Holy Grail*, ed. Béguin & Bonnefoy, trans. P. M. Matarasso (Penguin Books, 1971), pp. 43 ff.

189 Cf. my study 'L'Idée du Paraclet en philosophie iranienne', op. cit., and *En Islam iranien*, op. cit., vol. IV, pp. 393 ff, 410–430.

found and finds a response in "Christian esotericism", because this esotericism is unable to conform to the norms of official ecclesiology, to accept that "all is finished", and hence cannot accept the norms of sociological religion. And it is in its broadest sense—that is to say, as implying some link or other with the recurrence of the *Imago Templi*—that one must grasp the recurrences of the word "templars".[190]

The Community of Qumran felt itself to be the new Temple, felt itself to be involved, alongside the angelic powers that were invisibly present in its midst, in the fight of the sons of Light against the sons of Darkness. This aspect of the Community makes it a perfect example of "Templar knighthood". A previous example had been furnished by the companions of Zerubbabel when building the second Temple: they also confronted the demonic counter-powers. An affinity has rightly been shown to exist between the ethic of Qumran and that of Zoroastrian knighthood. Ormazd could not defend the ramparts of the city of Light without the help of the Fravartis. The ethic of battle is the same in both cases: it does not consist in waiting for an eschatological event that will take place later, on some distant day. The battle fought by the beings of Light is eschatology itself in the process of being accomplished. This is the connection between eschatology "in the present" and the ethic of knighthood, and hence the connection between eschatology "in the present", in the process of being accomplished, and the Ezekelian vision of the celestial Temple: the defenders of the holy City are defending an *Imago Templi* that embraces both the celestial and the earthly Temples, and connects heaven with earth. In this way, we do not deviate from our initial hermeneutic (see above, section II), according to which the destruction of the Temple signified our entry into this world, and its rebuilding signified our departure from exile, our return to the original world whence we came.

Thus, an indissoluble connection is established between the *Imago Templi* and a Templar knighthood in its multiple forms. The *Imago Templi* polarized the Western esoteric tradition, and this is also why the image of the Temple knighthood—of the Order of the Temple—remains indissolubly linked to the concept of initiatic knighthood.

The "history" of it must therefore be the antidote to—the antithesis or

190 As serving to designate, in a broad sense, all those whom the tradition of the *Imago Templi* sees as the predecessors or the successors of the knights of the Temple—all those, that is to say, who in some sense are bound to the service of the Temple.

counter-history of—that History which, as we saw at the beginning, has been described as nothing less than the profanation of the sacred. To conceive of the sacred, of the divine, as constituting the immediate, the natural, the given, from which man will break free by becoming historical man—that is to say, by the *geste* of a History whose hero is man himself—is nothing other, perhaps, than to consent to the satanic inversion of the primordial order of things. Going back to the symbol we used earlier (see above, section II), it is to conform to the norms that Pharoah wishes to impose on men. If History-profanation is no more than the decadence and corruption of what was given to us originally, then we could say that in our day the disease has attained planetary dimensions. We could also say that, if this is the case, the idea of salvation is essentially and assuredly our deliverance from the perils of History. Reference was made earlier to the symbol of Moses saved from the waters of History. To save in a similar way is the function of the *Imago Templi*. Given that this is so, the transition, since the time of the Montanist crisis, from eschatological Christianity—the Christology of *Christos Angelos*—to a Christianity and a Christology *within* History, must surely strike us as fateful, a sign of the process of corruption. Does not this sign coincide with the refusal of gnosis? And is it not then the case that the secret of Israel, the secret of the "new Temple", communicated impartially to all nations, is a sign that the difference between the "Temple" and the profane has been abolished?

Unfortunately, all too frequently one hears people say that the Christian Revelation has no secret about it, nothing esoteric that needs interpretation. "All is finished", as we were reminded earlier. In accordance with this attitude these same people oppose the Christian revelation to gnosis and to the hermeneutic that accompanies gnosis. In compensation, we are told that the Christian mystery is unprofanable, because it requires one to be present at this mystery through the sacramental communion of faith. Any gnostic would see this contrast both as fragile and as painfully artificial, for it starts out by forgetting that in this same sense gnosis itself is also and *par excellence* unprofanable. It is not enough to hear the esoteric meaning uttered; it is necessary to be present at it through a new birth. Gnosis and palingenesis are inseparable, and this is also the sacramental sense of communion through gnosis. On the other hand, to separate the Christian Revelation from gnosis is precisely what lays the former open to profanation. The overwhelming desacralization that is occurring in our time gives us ample food for thought. A hostile attitude towards gnosis has led to forgetfulness or ignorance of the original relationship between the primitive Christian community at Jerusalem and Jewish gnosis. The same hostile attitude has inspired the statement that all Christian esotericism is doomed to defeat. Unfortunately, what we are witnessing today is the defeat to which we are condemned by the absence or the refusal of gnosis.

Protesting and testifying against this absence, on the other hand, is the persistence of the *Imago Templi* and its connection with the notion of an initiatic knighthood that is perpetuated from century to century, unknown to the majority of men. Exactly the same theme occurs in Islamic gnosis, both Shiite and Ismaili.[191]

We must emphasize once again that our inquiry here is not of the sort that a historian would conduct. The transmissions effectuated by the Temple traditions are not supported by legal acts, registered documents, and so on. Here above all it is necessary to proceed phenomenologically, allowing the traditions to tell us what they will, without losing sight of two things: 1) These traditions can tell us, better than any archival document, what goes on at "the meeting-place of the two seas", at the place, that is, where all spiritual transmissions—which are not, of course, simply transmissions of certificates or archives—*really* take place. 2) The moment the decision to filiate himself to a tradition becomes effective for a man of spiritual aspiration, the "historic" link between him and his predecessors is forged. He is their lawful heir and successor, whatever the chronological hiatus between them (we have frequently cited the case in point of Suhravardī, reviving the theosophical tradition of the sages of ancient Persia in Islamicized Iran).[192] This existential link is not "historical" in the current exoteric sense of the word, for it cannot leave any trace in any archive; but nonetheless it is formed once and forever in the time of "subtle history"—which could also be termed "parahistory", since it bears the same relationship to profane history as does the parable to all one-dimensional utterances. If the phenomenologist has some difficulty in making himself understood on this point by the historians, that is no reason for him to give up or to be discouraged!

The "templar" tradition—that is to say, the "subtle history" or "hier-

191 See *En Islam iranien*, op. cit., vol. IV, index s.v. *silsilat al-'irfān*.

192 Cf. my article 'Science traditionelle et Renaissance spirituelle', in *Cahiers de l'Université Saint-Jean de Jérusalem*, I (1975).

ology" of the Temple and of the recurrences of the *Imago Templi*—when confronted with the perils of History and with Pharoah's norms, reveals itself in the following terms. The aspirations of Christian esotericism were polarized in the historical Order of the Knights of the Temple, conceived as having been the seat of this esotericism. It goes without saying that the ancestry of this Order was the subject of inquiry, and in this inquiry the significant aspiration is revealed. For this ancestry was always traced back to the Temple of Solomon through the Essene community and other related communities. This is why we had to start by noting the "purposes" (in the phenomenological sense of the word) of the *Imago Templi* from the representation of this *Imago* in Ezekiel's theology of the Temple down to its representation in the theology of the new Temple among the Essenes of Qumran. So much for the ancestry of the *Imago Templi* in the Templar tradition, considered *a parte ante*.

At the same time, Christian esotericism could not consent to the destruction of the Temple, and neither could it agree that Philip the Fair had succeeded in bringing his evil act to a successful conclusion. Its only possible response was a challenge, echoing the desperate cry of the Templar knights that we heard at the beginning, resounding through the solitary amphitheatre of Gavarnie. *A parte post*, the succession of the Temple, down to the resurgence of initiatic knighthood in the eighteenth century, was assured by a series of links, the very choice of which increases our knowledge of the meaning and the "purposes" of the *Imago Templi*. This meaning and these purposes can still be perceived in the Temple of the Grail built by Titurel at Montsalvat, in Zacharias Werner's great dramatic poem, and in Swedenborg's *Nova Hierosolyma*.

We Occidentals have been over-forgetful, perhaps, of both the meaning and the tradition. But it has seemed to me important to bear them in mind, because I have heard it said too often that we in the West were destined to obey the norms of materialism and mechanization.

6. *Templar filiation "a parte ante"*. Let us situate the sparse historical data of which we can be certain—those that establish us *ab origine symboli*, at the birthplace of the symbol—at the centre from which the traditions *a parte ante* and *a parte post* radiate outwards. To begin with, there is the epistle addressed by St. Bernard to the first knights who formed the "Militia Crucifera Evangelica". Here the Temple of Solomon as the Temple of

Wisdom is already seen as the outward symbol of the inner temple, to whose building their Order was thus pledged from the start. The Temple must first be built in the heart. This link, emphasizing the vocation of the knights as builders, at the same time validates the relationship of modern templarism to the original Templar knighthood. This validation stems essentially and above all from the fact that both exemplify the same archetype, and that the "modern Templars" are no less the spiritual sons of St. Bernard than the Templars to whom he spoke of the Holy City and of the promise made at Zion. There are differences, of course, between the original Templars and, for example, the Templars of the Holy Grail (see below, section VII), but both share in the same heritage, constituted in the "treasures of Heaven".[193]

Secondly, there is the monument erected in the ancient and sacred precinct of the Temple—the monument known as the "Dome of the Rock" (*Qubbat al-ṣakhrah* in Arabic), though often and wrongly as the "Mosque of 'Umar". This monument owes its name to the fact that it is situated exactly on the rock which, according to tradition and to the opinion of a good many scholars, used to be in the Holy of Holies of the old Temple. By an act of donation on the part of the king of Jerusalem, Baudoin II, the building became *Templum Domini*, the church of the knights *Templar*, who were henceforth associated indissolubly with the Temple through their name. The building forms a regular octagon surmounted by a dome, and was the prototype of the Templar churches built in Europe. The dome itself was the symbol of the Order and figured on the seal of the Grand Master.[194]

From that time on this symbol was to be *par excellence* the *Imago Templi*, dominating the horizon of "templarism". The word "templarism" will be used here to denote the whole concourse of the hierophanies of the *Imago Templi* in Western consciousness—a concourse that phenomenology should analyse and contemplate while acknowledging at last the importance of this *spiritual fact*. It would be important to analyse what is expressed by the

193 Arthur Edward Waite, *A New Encyclopaedia of Freemasonry* (*Ars magna Latomorum*) (London, 1921), vol. II, p. 239 (abbrev. *Encyclopaedia*).

194 Cf. the article 'Kobbat al-Ṣakhra', in *Encyclopédie de l'Islam*. See also Th. Busink, op. cit., p. 12 and note 43. It is worth recalling some of the hierological traditions: Jeremy taking the stone with him to Ireland; King Edward III transferring it to Westminster Abbey, where, ever since, the kings and queens of England have been crowned upon this stone.

details and variants of the different versions of what seems to be, basically, one and the same tradition. What this tradition tells us is that the builder-knights are engaged in the same task as the builders of the first and second Temples. It testifies to the continuity of the endeavours that converge in the vision of the final Temple, the supra-natural Temple "on the high mountain" of Ezekiel's vision. It is for this reason that the building and rebuilding of the Temple postulate a continuing series of builders, who succeed each other not by means of archival transmission but through their common will. It is by virtue of this common will that they are the spontaneous heirs of each other and share the same secrets. This corresponds exactly to the idea of the continuing line of gnosis (*silsilat al-'irfān*) in the esotericism of Shiism, Ismailism, the *Ishrāq*, and Sufism, as well as to the idea which is the very secret of prophetology.[195] The continuity is determined by heavenly inspiration, which brings together what is constantly being dispersed by the vicissitudes of this world.

When these versions of the same tradition were put into written form—a tradition which is neither "history" nor "myth" nor "romance", in the sense assumed by these words in the dilemma by which historicism is imprisoned—nothing was yet known about the Essene Community of Qumran, although the Essenes themselves were known. What Templar tradition claims is precisely the heritage of the Essenes and, through them, of the Judaeo-Christian gnosis of the Church of James. This claim thereby implies that something is yet to come, that "all is not finished". We referred earlier to the Messianic perspective that dominates both the primitive Judaeo-Christian community and the entire body of Jewish gnosis. The messengers of this future possess differing qualifications, sometimes as hermits, sometimes as knights (as hermits and knights play the key roles in our own Grail cycle).

In this way, the *Traditio Templi* in itself presupposes a tradition of *Templar* chivalry, of a spiritual and initiatic knighthood. Because the continuity of this tradition does not arise from an immanent historical causality, it can be expressed only in symbols. Those who transmit it are raised to the rank of symbolical personages, and the events whose protagonists they are assume the status of parables. There is an episode which would seem to situate us *ab origine symboli*, reported by the fifth-century

195 Cf. *En Islam iranien*, op. cit., vol. IV, index s.v. Komayl ibn Ziyād (ses entretiens avec le Ier Imam), hiérarchie, Sohravardi.

Philostorgius, who was both a historian and an ardent defender of the Arian theological tradition.[196] The episode lies within the context of the abortive attempts to rebuild materially the Temple of Jerusalem. Some workmen descend, by means of a long rope, to the bottom of a well. They discover that rising out of the water is a column, and that on the column is placed a book wrapped in a linen cloth. The workmen take the book up, and on examination it turns out to be a copy of the Gospel of John.[197] It would be impossible to find a more concise and arresting symbol to express the link that connects the Temple of Solomon to Johannism in general, down to the Johannine temple of the *Nova Hierosolyma*. The expression of this continuity was the task of the transmitters, those known now as the Knights of the Morning and of Palestine, now as the Brothers of the Thebaid, now as the Sons of the Valley, and so on. Their intervention is sometimes direct and sometimes through intermediaries, because their true dwelling-place, like that of the esoteric hierarchies in Shiism and Sufism, is not a country that we can locate on our maps.

Very briefly, we will outline the versions of this Templar tradition *a parte ante*, previous, that is to say, to the Order of the knights of the Temple. According to this tradition, the latter are not the founders but the preservers, during an auspicious period (in the twelfth and thirteenth centuries), of an uninterrupted Templarism.

A. One version[198] introduces the "canons of the Holy Sepulchre", established in Jerusalem after the conquest of the Holy Land by the Crusaders. These canons were the depositaries of the secret knowledge of

196 Philostorgius (died after 425 A.D.) had composed a work on ecclesiastical history in ten books, seen from the Arian point of view. Unfortunately, only fragments of it survive. His Arianism brought him into close relationship with Judaeo-Christian theology. Cf. E. Preuschen, 'Philostorgius', in *Realencyklopädie für prot. Theologie und Kirche*, vol. 15, pp. 365 ff.

197 Cf. Arthur Edward Waite, *Emblematic Freemasonry and the Evolution of its Deeper Issues* (London, 1925), p. 107 (abbrev. *Emblematic*).

198 This version occurs in a manuscript discovered at Strasbourg in the last century and dating from 1760. Cf. René le Forestier, *La Franc-maçonnerie templière et occultiste aux XVIIIe–XIXe siècles*, published by Antoine Faivre with addenda and index (Paris, 1970), p. 68. This manuscript is valuable for the immense amount of material that it brings into play. Unfortunately, as the spirit of the author is firmly closed to any phenomenology of the events of the imaginal world, the implementation is faulty. His mocking and self-important tone makes painful reading of this work, which should be re-written. A. Faivre in his preface has rightly emphasized what needs emphasizing with regard to the events that took place "in illo tempore" (Mircea Eliade). Unfortunately, there are people who will always be incapable of understanding.

the Essenes "from whom they were directly descended". It was their brotherhood which had restored the primitive Order after the destruction of the second Temple by Titus in 70 A.D. When Hugh de Payens and his eight comrades-at-arms were established on the site which had been that of the Temple, the canons, realizing that they had the same end in view, joined with them and initiated them into the esoteric sciences. In this way the primitive Order was restored under the name of the Order of *Templars*. When Jerusalem was reconquered by the "Saracens", the headquarters were transferred to Cyprus. The historic Templar Order here resembles an episode in secular Templarism; but this major episode connects the Jewish and the Christian periods of the *Traditio Templi*,[199] of the hiero-history of the Temple from the time of Solomon.

B. Another version, which was current mainly in what went by the name of the "chapter of Clermont" in eighteenth-century France, is more specifically linked to alchemical symbolism and royal Art. After the Babylonian captivity, Esdras "was responsible for embedding a quadrangular stone in the foundations of the second Temple, a stone in which three hollows had been made. Each hollow contained a dish, and these three dishes (salt, sulphur, mercury) were the key to the great work".[200] What then occurs constitutes one of the motifs that are at the source of the modern resurgence of the Templar tradition known as the "Scottish rite". In effect, between the twelfth and the thirteenth centuries, four Brothers who were originally from Scotland came to Jerusalem, succeeded in prising out the quadrangular stone, and took it back to Scotland.[201] In recognition of this service, the King of Scotland, David II, appointed them to be "Knights of St. Andrew". The heirs of the four Scottish masters were the Templars, three of whom, after the suppression of their Order (see below, § 7), confided their secret to the "Knights of God and his Temple".[202] The *Historia Ordinis* here postulates a periodicity of history, analogous to the periodicity found in the Judaeo-Christian community and in Ismailism,

199 This schema corresponds to the "Discours" of the knight André Michel de Ramsay, the friend of Fénelon.

200 Le Forestier, op. cit., p. 86.

201 The rock on which the dome is built thus becomes the symbol *par excellence* of the alchemical work. It is worth considering here the relationship of the Black Stone with the Ka'bah, and the role it plays in alchemical symbolism. Cf. my study 'The Configuration of the Temple of the Ka'bah', published above, ch. IV, *Potestas Clavium*.

202 Le Forestier, op. cit., p. 87.

which regulates the successive manifestations of the *Verus Propheta*. The starting-point—Adam—and the septenary rhythm are the same in both cases, but the name and content of the seven periods are different. They are as follows: 1. The period of Adam. 2. The period of Noah (the Order of Noachians). 3. The period of Nimrod. 4. The period encompassing the first and second Temples. 5. The period of the Templars, put in possession of the esoteric science by the teaching of the four Scottish masters. 6. The period of persecutions and of the destruction of the Order. 7. The period of the resurgence of the Order of the Temple in the eighteenth century.[203] Here again, we observe that the Templars had been formed as such because they had been entrusted with an exalted transcendental science, transmitted from sage to sage since the earliest times.

C. The theme of a secret and superior authority, hidden behind the Order which is manifested in history, leads on to the idea of the knight-priests. This idea dominates the tradition of the *Clerici Templi*, systematically expounded in the eighteenth century by the Lutheran pastor Johann August Starck, who had worked on a massive collection of documents. Here we re-encounter the equivalent of the canons of the Holy Sepulchre (version A), but this time they are called the "canons of the Temple of the Lord" (*Canonici Templi Domini*). They served in the church that was built on the ruins of the Temple of Solomon, and it was their prior, Amaldus, who had received the knights in the quarter conceded to them by the King of Jerusalem. The link between the knights of the Temple and the canons of the Temple was effective from then on. The latter had inherited the esoteric sciences of the Essenes through the intermediary of seven hermits, descendants, across the vicissitudes of successive transmissions, of the primitive Essene community.[204] These hermits were the first people met by Hugh de Payens and his comrades. They preserved the tradition of a prophecy announcing that eternal Wisdom, *Sophia aeterna*, would manifest herself once more "in the ancient sanctuary of Jerusalem, when the

203 Ibid., pp. 88–90.

204 The role played by the seven hermits is reminiscent of the role of the seven *abdāl* in Islamic esotericism. These hierological data which emerge from "subtle history" refer us, such as they are, to the problem of the survival of the primitive Judaeo-Christian community of Jerusalem, the Church of James. What we now know, thanks to the Essene Community of Qumran, has given us a better *understanding* of what lay behind the claims to such a lineage. We would do well to ponder in this sense on the great work by Hans Joachim Schoeps, *Theologie und Geschichte des Judenchristentums* (Tübingen, 1949).

knights clothed in white come from beyond the seas to defend the holy City". Thus the new hierophany of the *Imago Templi* was proclaimed: the light of the *Shekhinah*—of the divine Presence—would once more dwell in the Temple. All, hermits and knights, had found refuge in Jerusalem with the canons of the Temple.

D. A fourth version takes the form of an epic of mystical knighthood, the "Knights of the Morning and of Palestine". The name itself is strikingly reminiscent of what is implied by the term *Ishrāq*, the keystone of the doctrine expounded by Suhravardī, the twelfth-century "resurrector of the theosophy of Light professed by the sages of ancient Persia". The *Ishrāq* is the dawning, the orient of the light, and hence the "oriental" light. The *Ishrāqīyūn*, Suhravardī's followers in Iran, are the "orientals" who stand at the "orient" of the Light.[205] Here, the Knights of the Morning and of Palestine are the most ancient knighthood in the world. They were scattered after the destruction of the second Temple, but they preserve their traditions, laws and liturgies in expectation of the event that will enable them to rebuild the Temple for the third time. The event seemed imminent during the time of the Crusades. The Knights of Palestine came out of their citadel, emerged from their retreat in the deserts of the Thebaid, and joined those of their brethren who had remained at Jerusalem in a state of vigilance. Their relations with these latter seem analogous to those which we shall find existing between the "Sons of the Valley" and the knights of the Temple (see below, section VIII), in which an invisible authority acts *incognito* through the intermediary of *dramatis personae* who are the visible manifestation of its existence (an idea, as we saw, which closely resembles that of the esoteric hierarchy in Islamic gnosis).

The Knights of the Morning were Essenes, healers, sons of the prophets and of Melchizedek, king of a supernatural Salem. Their brothers in Jerusalem were apparently a kind of *Militia hermetica*, who dedicated part of their quest to the realm of Nature.[206] Their connection with the Templars stems from the fact that they shared the same vision of the *Imago*

205 Cf. *En Islam iranien*, op. cit., vol. IV, index s.v. Ishrāq, Ishrāqīyūn. On the "Knights of the Morning and of Palestine", see A. E. Waite, *Encyclopaedia*, I, pp. 317–319. The epic of these "knights of the Morning" is the theme of the well-known work by Baron Tschoudy, *L'Étoile flamboyante*; cf. ibid.

206 This brings to mind, inevitably, the *Ikhwān al-Safā'* (the "Brothers of the Pure Heart") and their encyclopaedia, whose connections with Ismailism are now known.

Templi. We have said that beneath the solemn appearance of defending the Holy Sepulchre, the knights Templar pursued a secret objective, which was none other than the rebuilding of the Temple of Jerusalem. This was also the purpose of the "Thebaid Solitaries", who were in possession of the mystical measurements of the first Temple. Thus they were all "knights of the Temple", whose secret purpose was to have been achieved amidst the architectural splendour of a restored Jerusalem and of a sanctuary renewed under the aegis of a gnostic Christianity[207] (see below, section VII, the temple of the Grail). This version of the tradition also expresses therefore the sense of a *theosophia perennis*; those who testify to it have in common the idea of the restoration of the Temple, and regard themselves as the spiritual descendents of the Essene community.

E. A fifth version expresses the same idea. This is the version of the "Twelve Chosen Masters":[208] twelve Masters who, after the completion of the first Temple, formed a separate fraternity, governed by one of themselves, and were chosen in person to be the Temple guard.[209] Their Order managed to hold out until about the year 70 A.D., after which it lapses into obscurity. Some of them had embraced Christianity,[210] and it was their descendents who, in the twelfth century, joined with the knights of the Temple and with the knights of the sovereign Order of St. John of Jerusalem in pursuit of the same objective, which was to establish a Christian Temple modelled on the Temple of Solomon. This is the essential thing to bear in mind in our phenomenology of the *Imago Templi*: the intention to rebuild the Temple of Jerusalem was common both to the knights Templar and to the mystical brotherhoods, variously designated as the Brothers of the Thebaid desert, the Knights of the Morning and of Palestine, and so on.

To both of them is ascribed the secret intention of establishing, with the new Temple, a gnostic Church of the Elect, a universal metropolis corre-

207 A. E. Waite, *Encyclopaedia*, II, pp. 221–222.
208 A. E. Waite, *Emblematic*, pp. 144–146.
209 Cf. my study 'Science traditionnelle et Renaissance spirituelle', op. cit.
210 This is certainly an intimation of the relationships existing between the Jewish community and the primitive Judaeo-Christian community, the Church of James. We must emphasize yet again that these hierological traditions are of interest not because they provide material for a historical critique, but because they disclose the *sense* of a continuous manifestation of the awareness of the *Imago Templi*: of how this awareness finds itself again *ab origine*. To introduce psychiatry here is completely beside the point.

sponding, perhaps, to "the secret dream of the oriental patriarchs". This is doubtless the clue to what is meant by the longing for the Temple in the face of the tragedy of historical Christianity. To grasp the full significance of the claim to Essene descent, one must recognize behind it the presentiment of a Christianity that vanished too soon from external history, a presentiment that cannot capitulate before the violence of such history. After the death in 62 or 66 A.D. of James, first bishop of Jerusalem and the first "bishop of bishops", the Judaeo-Christian community, warned by an Angel, emigrated to Pella on the other bank of the Jordan. It thus escaped the torments of the siege that ended in the destruction of the Temple in 70 A.D., and it survived as the community of "Ebionites" until the fourth century. Meanwhile, however, a new Christianity began to gain ground, a Christianity so "different" that the doctrine and gnosis professed by the first apostolic community of Jerusalem, founded by the very people who had been Christ's companions, were described and reputed by the "fathers of the Church" to be an abominable "heresy".[211] It is one of those mortal paradoxes which receive too little attention.

For this reason, the longing for the Temple which is expressed in the *traditio Templi* and arrogates a line of descent for the Templar knighthood that goes back through the Essenes to the primitive Judaeo-Christian community, configurates a history that is "more true" than the official history of external facts. It is so much "truer" that it leads to the affirmation of an *Ecclesia Johannis* in opposition to the *Ecclesia Petri*, when this Church of Peter quite simply did not exist in the time of the Church of James.

The phenomenologist's task is now to discover a *counter-history* "more true than history in the evidence *a parte post* of the Templar tradition—evidence that confirms the secret survival of the Order of the Temple until its resurgence.

7. *Templar filiation "a parte post"*. As in the preceding case, we will note some historical traces of this secret survival after the official destruction of the Order of the Temple (the Grand Master Jacques de Molay died on March 18, 1314). We know that the Order of the Temple survived in Portugal as the Order of Christ. Traces of its survival are also found in Germany, mediated by the knights of St. Mary of Jerusalem, otherwise

211 On this paradox, cf. Hans Joachim Schoeps, op. cit., p. 342.

known as the Teutonic knights; this would explain the rapid success of the "Strict Templar Observance" in the eighteenth century.[212] And there are the even more specific traces to be found in Britain.[213] But our phenomenology of the *Imago Templi* aims essentially at authenticating different evidence, on the level proper to it. The role assigned to the four Scottish masters, mentioned above (version B), already indicates the importance of the "Scottish rite" in perpetuating the Templar tradition. It would be difficult to grasp its importance *a parte post* without bearing in mind its significance *a parte ante*, because the primitive Scottish rite paved the way for the role of the Scottish knighthood in the survival of the Temple. Its survival, assured by this knighthood, made possible the resurgence of the spiritual initiatic chivalry, the "Scottish rite", in the eighteenth century.

The primitive Celtic Church, prior to Romanization, is represented by groups of monks known as Culdees (cf. the German *Kuldeertum*).[214] The origin of this name is the Irish *céile dé*, of which the Latin equivalent was *Coli Dei*, *Deicolae*, that is to say, men of God: *viri Dei*, *amici Dei*.[215] The groups of companions called by this name seem, moreover, to have played a much larger role in Scotland than in Ireland. We gather from the documents that these companions combine the features both of secular clerks and of hermits or anchorites, finally appearing as Canons Regular (similar to the *Canonici Ordinis Templarii* of version C above). Assuredly, these autonomous groups of hermit brothers correspond to what we know of the original structure of the Celtic Church—a structure, unfortunately, which did not place it in a powerful enough position to resist the Romanization of the twelfth century. What is important here for our phenomenology of the *Imago Templi* is that these *Coli Dei* had a role to play on the Celtic side analogous to the role attributed on the eastern side, as we saw above, to the canons of the Holy Sepulchre, the spiritual descendents of the

212 Cf. J. Tourniac, *Principes et problèmes spirituels du Rite écossais rectifié et de sa chevalerie templière* (Paris, 1969).

213 The person of John Claverhouse, Viscount Dundee (whose brother gave the famous Benedictine Dom Calmet the great cross of the Order) would seem to be evidence that an Order of the Temple existed in Scotland down to 1689; cf. Waite, *Encyclopaedia*, II, p. 223.

214 Cf. 'Keltische Kirche' in *Realencyclopädie für prot. Theologie und Kirche*, vol. 10, pp. 234 ff.

215 On this denomination of "Friends of God" found in Islamic gnosis (*Awliyā' Allāh*) and in Rhenish mysticism (*Gottesfreunde*), cf. *En Islam iranien*, op. cit., vol. IV, index s.v.

Essenes. The appeal to a distant Celto-Scottish filiation parallels the appeal made to affiliation with the builders of the Temple of Solomon and the community of Jerusalem. It is as if the double line of descent, Hierosolymitan and Scottish, linked, *ab origine symboli*, the Church of James and the Celtic Church in the trials and misfortunes from which the Temple knighthood had to rescue them.

The *Coli Dei* are also included in the spiritual line of descent from the builders of the Temple of Solomon, the line of the Essenes, the gnostics, even the Manichaeans and the Ismailis.[216] They were established at York in England, at Iona in Scotland, in Wales, and in Ireland; their favourite symbol was the dove, the feminine symbol of the Holy Spirit. In this context, it is not surprising to find Druidism intermingled with their tradition and the poems of Taliesin integrated to their *corpus*.[217] The epic of the Round Table and the Quest of the Holy Grail have likewise been interpreted as referring to the rites of the *Coli Dei*. It was, moreover, to the time of the *Coli Dei* that is assigned the formation of the Scottish knighthood whose seat is typified by the mysterious sanctuary of Kilwinning, under the shadow of Mount Heredom in the extreme north of Scotland.[218]

In order to understand the significance of this, we must call to mind the three mystical mountains: Mount Moriah, Mount Sinai and this Mount *Heredom*. We will not find Heredom on our maps, just as Corbenik must be sought elsewhere than on the rugged slopes of Wales. The word Heredom has been explained by reading it as *Hierodom*, a transcription of ἱερός δόμος, the Holy House—an allusion to the Temple of Jerusalem or to the Order of the Temple. But it is equally possible to see it as a deformation of the Hebrew word *Harodim* that designates the officers, the foremen of works in the building of the Temple.[219] The Order of the Temple was first introduced into Scotland by King David I in the middle of the twelfth century.[220] The royal Order of Heredom of Kilwinning, or "Royal Order of Scotland", was revived in 1314 by King Robert I, the Bruce, and this

216 Waite, *Encyclopaedia*, I, pp. 161–165; *Emblematic*, p. 66.
217 Waite, *Encyclopaedia*, I, pp. 198–201.
218 Ibid., I, pp. 347–348.
219 Ibid., I, pp. 344–345. Cf. I Kgs. 5:15–16; II Chr. 8:10. It has also been suggested that the word *Heredom* consists of a suffix, "dom" (= hood, ship) appended to the word "Here" (or "Her"), derived from the Latin *herus* (master, chief, guide). If this were so, "Heredom of Kilwinning" would mean "knighthood of Kilwinning". Cf. R. S. Lindsay, *The Royal Order of Scotland* (Edinburgh, 1972), p. 10.
220 Waite, *Encyclopaedia*, II, p. 230.

revival, as we shall see, is closely linked to the survival of the Order of the Temple.[221]

Bearing these facts in mind, we will proceed to outline, very briefly, the schema of the tradition concerning the perpetuation of the Order of the Temple *a parte post*, remembering only that if, in the nature of things, counter-history is not history in the ordinary sense of the word, it is not therefore "myth". As was the case with the filiation *a parte ante*, there are several versions of the Templar filiation *a parte post*.[222]

A. The provincial Grand Master of Auvergne, Pierre d'Aumont, succeeded in taking refuge in Scotland with a few of his knights. They helped King Robert the Bruce win the victory of Bannockburn in 1314, which made Scotland independent of England. In gratitude, the King restored the Royal Order of Scotland and affiliated the Templars to it. The Order continues to exist today.

B. After putting up a valiant defence in some castles of the Order, Pierre d'Aumont had to flee his Province in the company of two commanders and seven knights, ten people in all. In order to escape recognition, they disguised themselves as masons. They finally found refuge in the island of Mull to the north of Scotland, where they met George Harris, grand commander of Hampton Court. Aumont was elected Grand Master in 1312 by the brothers who had taken refuge on the island.[223]

C. The version of filiation through the count of Beaujeu, nephew of Jacques de Molay, differs from the preceding versions, maintained in the eighteenth century by the "Strict Templar Observance". It forms the Swedish version of the Templar filiation, substituting Sweden for Scotland as the place where the secrets of the Temple were guarded. However, a variant of it exists which is interesting in that it links the names of Beaujeu and Aumont. On the instructions of his uncle, Jacques de Molay, Beaujeu—together with nine knights (making ten people in all, as above)—managed to save the secrets of the Order: the annals and secret papers, the crown of the kings of Jerusalem, the seven-branched gold candlestick, the exalted knowledge. These treasures were deposited in Cyprus, in the care of the canons of the Holy Sepulchre (see above, § 6, version A), who were still living there in the greatest secrecy. The knights

221 Le Forestier, op. cit., p. 781.
222 Waite, *Encyclopaedia*, II, pp. 219–220; *Emblematic*, pp. 173–179.
223 Le Forestier, op. cit., pp. 115, 160–163.

vowed to keep the Order alive secretly, as long as there existed "nine perfect Architects". On the death of Beaujeu, Aumont was elected Grand Master as in version B, and the Templar tradition was continued through Scotland.[224]

D. There is the version known as that of Eliphas Levi: before his death, Jacques de Molay organized and established an esoteric structure. He erected four metropolitan lodges: Naples for the east, Edinburgh for the west, Stockholm for the north, and Paris for the south.

E. There is a version which is quite unrelated to the preceding versions and unassociated with the Scottish tradition, according to which the successor named by Jacques de Molay was Johannes Marcus Larmenius of Jerusalem, who in turn was succeeded by his son, Franciscus Thomas Theobaldus Alexandrinus, and then by a whole series of Grand Masters.[225]

F. There is the whole Jacobite affair: the figure of the pretender Charles Edward Stuart and the Templar penetration of Ireland in the wake of the Scottish Jacobites.[226]

G. Independent mention must be made of the Order which still exists in England, and which goes by the name of "Military and Religious Order of the Temple and Holy Sepulchre".[227] As in the case of the Royal Order of Scotland, this is no honorary title, but denotes a spiritual and initiatic knighthood.

We can do no more than recall here the action of Jean-Baptiste Willermoz, in Lyons during the eighteenth century, whose objective was to establish an "inner Order", separate from the "Strict Templar Observance" in Germany. Willermoz' intuition was profound, and is in accordance with what is presupposed by the filiation of the Order of the Temple *a parte ante*. As we observed, this filiation, while constituting the strength of the Order of the Temple, establishes this Order as a single phase in a permanent Templar tradition. This was also to be the theme of Zacharias Werner's great dramatic poem (see below, section VIII). There was thus no need to restore in a material sense the historic Order of the Temple, as many wished to do. What was needed was to affirm one's spiritual descent by taking one's place in the tradition that the Order had made its own in

224 Ibid., p. 69.
225 Ibid., p. 944. Waite, *Emblematic*, p. 179.
226 Waite, *Encyclopaedia*, II, p. 225. Le Forestier, op. cit., index s.v.
227 Waite, *Encyclopaedia*, II, p. 225; *Emblematic*, p. 175.

the course of two centuries. This conviction resulted in the formation of the spiritual Templar knighthood, the "knights of the Holy City", the "Rite écossais rectifié".[228] J.-B. Willermoz professed a profound spirituality which was centred on the *Imago Templi.* In this sense his "instructions" are worthy of long study, as a textbook of Temple spirituality.[229] They lead to an interiorization that could profitably be compared to Philo's and to that of some of the masters mentioned above.

The ideal of the spiritual Templar chivalry had already been admirably formulated by the Chapter of Clermont: "Eques et frater hierosolymitanus scientiis divinis elatis maximam operam dare debet, ut in dies magis magisque luce mirifica et illuminationum divinarum scintillis incendatur et inflammetur." This is how it would be "until the day when the Order of the Temple retook possession of Jerusalem, thus making possible the rediscovery, in one of the caves of the Holy Mountain, of the store of integral esoteric knowledge".[230]

We should at this point consider the *Imago Templi* in Goethe—both in the unfinished poem entitled *Die Geheimnisse* (the Mysteries), which is about twelve Rosicrucian knights, and in the "Tale of the Green Serpent". The first we have written about elsewhere. In referring later on to Montserrat, Goethe himself pointed out the way which leads to Montsalvat and to the Temple of the Grail.[231]

Proceeding along this way, we come to the meeting-point of Celtism and Templarism, of Celtic tradition or hierology and Hierosolymite tradition or hierology (see above), within the perspective of the "Third Temple". The motif of the three temples dominates Templarism from the Ezekelian theology of the Temple onwards (see above, section III). The first two Temples, that of Solomon and that of Zerubbabel, were still built

228 On the assemblies of Lyons and of Wilhelmsbad, see Le Forestier, op. cit., pp. 476 ff., 610 ff.

229 The complete text of them has been published by A. Faivre as an appendix to his edition of the work by Le Forestier, op. cit., pp. 1021–1049.

230 Quoted by Le Forestier, ibid., p. 94, who remains completely oblivious both to the beauty and to the implication of these texts, whatever the place and time of their origin. In them the motif of the mystical Mountain reappears, as in Ezekiel's vision of the final Temple. We are not concerned here with historical or material verification, but with signs and inter-signs, as it were. One cannot but remember that it was precisely in the grottos and caves of the desert of Judaea that the "scrolls" of the Qumran Community were found, without which our phenomenology of the *Imago Templi* would not attain the *meaning* to which it aspires.

231 Cf. *En Islam iranien*, op. cit., vol. IV, pp. 405 ff.

by the hands of men, and needed masons and builders. The third Temple "on the high mountain", at "the meeting-place of the two seas", the city-temple of the *Nova Hierosolyma* (see below, section IX), is built by divine hands. What it requires is a knighthood dedicated to its service. Celtism and Templarism come together: in Wolfram's "Titurel", the Temple is conceived and the building of it is directed by Merlin, the Celtic prophet, who was initiated by Joseph of Aramithea into the mystical measurements of the temple-archetype, the Temple of Solomon. In the "New Titurel" by Albrecht von Scharfenberg, the architectural splendour of the Temple of the Holy Grail on the summit of Montsalvat bestows on us a fleeting vision of the Temple in Heaven.

VII. The Temple and the Templars of the Grail

For several generations, treasures of philological erudition have been expended in "explaining" the different aspects of the cycle of the Holy Grail. Unfortunately, no more than the indecent virtuosity of psychoanalysis is the method of literary historicism equal to the task that confronts us here. One would wish that, like the Bible, the entire cycle of the Grail poems could be read by "believers" not as a *corpus* but as the "Bible of the Holy Grail"—read as the Bible was read by such as Philo, Origen or Swedenborg. There are many people who have not seen, or do not wish to see, that the Bible has any esoteric meaning at all. Nevertheless, over the centuries this esoteric meaning, in all its aspects, has impressed itself on the reading of those who have known how to read. We will not take up the argument here, particularly since the argument between "those who see" and "those who do not see" cannot be resolved. A hermeneutic of the Grail which would coordinate and systematize the data of the *corpus* from beginning to end is a task which has yet to be undertaken. Here our only concern is with the *Imago Templi*. With what features is the Temple of the Grail presented to us?

For the sake of simplicity, let us say that the clearest description of the Temple, as the Castle of the Grail or *Gralsburg*, is given in the Germanic *corpus* of the "Grail Bible". In this *corpus*, the founder of the dynasty of the guardians of the Grail is King Titurel. The Temple is to be his creation. We referred above to the "Titurel" by Wolfram von Eschenbach; in his

"Parzifal", express mention is made of the Temple of the Grail[232] on the occasion of the baptism of Feirefis, the pagan half-brother of Parsifal.[233] Up to this point (Book V for example), it is merely a question of the dwelling-place or house of the Grail, the castle-temple as it were. And it is only in Albrecht von Scharfenberg's "New Titurel" (*Der Junge Titurel*), between 1260 and 1270, that the *Imago Templi* rises in all its architectural magnificence. (This great epic consists of 6,000 stanzas of 7 verses each, or 42,000 verses. No translation of it has yet been made, even into modern German.)[234] In it, the cycle of the Grail is developed into an epic of the Temple, whose climax is attained between the Temple of Solomon on Mount Moriah and the heavenly Jerusalem. The entire theology and spirituality of the Temple also attain one of their crowning-points on the heights of Montsalvat, the support of a hierophany which is the Temple of the Grail. Indeed, the teachings of Titurel amount to an entire theology of the Temple, as complete as the theology of Qumran and other elected places. This theology culminates in an eschatology that finally confers its full meaning on the knighthood of the Templars of the Grail in relation to the knighthood of the historical Templars. There is the description of the Temple; there are its correspondences; and lastly there is the theology of the Temple of the Grail.

1. *The description of the Temple of the Holy Grail.* The description is re-

232 In the final book, Book XVI: "They (Parsifal and Amfortas) prayed the king of Zazamanc . . . to enter into the temple where the Grail was kept." Wolfram von Eschenbach, *Parzifal*, trans. S. Tonnelat (Paris, 1934), vol. II, p. 332; English tr. H. Mustard, C. Passage, *Parzival* (New York, Vintage Bks., 1961).

233 Let us say once and for all that we are keeping to this form of the name, which has become classic since the time of Richard Wagner.

234 Albrecht von Scharfenberg, *Jüngerer Titurel*, Werner Wolf, in Deutsche Texte des Mittelalters, ed. Deutschen Akademie der Wissenschaften zu Berlin, vols. 45, 55. 61 (Berlin, 1955–1964); parts tr. A. U. Pope, 'Persia and the Grail', *The Literary Review*, 1957, pp. 57–71. Of especial interest is the excellent thesis by Gudula Trendelenburg, *Studien zum Gralraum im "Jüngeren Titurel"* (Göppingen, A. Kümmerle, 1972; abbrev. *Studien*). Lars-Ivar Ringbom in his great work, *Graltempel und Paradies: Beziehungen zwischen Iran und Europa im Mittelalter* (Stockholm, 1951; abbr. *Graltempel*), had already made full use of Albrecht's epic. His researches embrace all the prototypes, imitations and parallels of the Temple, from West to East, and he lays particular emphasis on the affinity between the "Burg" of the Persian Sassanids and the Gralsburg. The material employed is considerable. Nevertheless, with regard to the significance of possible conclusions, the boundary should be more clearly drawn between what is historical research properly speaking, and what is comparative phenomenology as such.

nowned.[235] In the country of Sauveterre (*Salva Terra*) rises a high mountain named Montsalvat.[236] King Titurel has surrounded this mountain with a high wall, and on its summit he has built a splendid castle, the *Gralsburg*. Here he decides to found a temple for the Grail.[237] Up to this moment, in fact, the Temple has not yet been established at any definite place, but floats between heaven and earth, held up invisibly by the Angels. The building incorporates all kinds of precious stones. Gold predominates, and the furniture is of aloe wood. The stones are chosen according to the standards of Pythagorean art and the science of Heraclius.[238] The rock of the mountain is onyx. When all the grass and earth are removed, the onyx surface shines as brilliantly as the Moon. One morning, there appears on this surface the complete plan of the Temple, projected from heaven. The plateau itself forms a base two toises thick.[239] Between the edge of the plateau and the Temple wall, there is a space five toises wide all around. Vertically, the building forms a high dome, supported by columns of bronze. It is completely covered with gold and precious stones, whose inner significance will be discussed later on. The windows are surrounded by beryl and luminous crystals. The panes are coloured or encrusted with precious stones, and dim the brilliance of the light. The roof is also of gold, encrusted with precious stones so that its glare should not blind the eye. The Temple of the Grail was built with the help of Heaven, like the Temple of Solomon, *Templum Throni Dei*, in Jerusalem, the stones for which were brought to the site already cut, so that no displeasing sound of hammer or chisel should be heard during the building of the Temple. The same goes for the builders of the Temple of Titurel: everything was sent to them by the Grail.

The high central dome is covered with sapphire, representing the celestial dome in all its azure brilliance. It is studded with carbuncles which sparkle in the darkness of the night like stars. It contains an image of the

235 L.-I. Ringbom, op. cit., pp. 21 ff., has a lengthy summary of it.

236 Here again, the form we are adopting once and for all is Montsalvat.

237 We cannot here recall the details of the hierology of the Grail: its descent from Heaven in the care of the Angels, the Templars who guard it, etc. Cf. the translation of *Parzifal* by S. Tonnelat, op. cit., book IX, vol. II, pp. 36 ff.

238 Rather than "Hercules", whose position in all this would be somewhat puzzling, whereas the name of the emperor Heraclius is familiar to all the alchemical tradition. He already appears in the Hermetic version of "Salaman and Absal"; cf. *Avicenna and the Visionary Recital*, op. cit., p. 210 note 10.

239 A toise was equal to about two metres.

Sun in gold and an image of the Moon in silver, both of which, set in motion by an ingenious and secret clock, perpetually progress through a marvellous zodiac. Golden cymbals herald the succession of the days.

The entire Temple forms a vast, high rotunda, divided into a number of chancels, each of which projects towards the outside. Some manuscripts give the number of chancels as seventy-two; others give it as twenty-two. We must again remember that both figures have their arithmosophical significance and can in no way be opposed to each other. To object to the gigantic proportions of the building with seventy-two chancels would be to forget that the Temple of the Grail is located at "the meeting-place of the two seas", on the "Earth of Light", and not in the world where the laws of physics prevail. In each chancel, the altar is *orientated*, that is to say, turned towards the East. The main chancel is also turned towards the East, and is double the measurement of the others (in the version of the twenty-two chancels, we thus have a total of $22 + 2$, or $12 \times 2 = 24$); it surpasses the others in sumptuousness, and is consecrated to the Holy Spirit. The one immediately beside it is dedicated to the Virgin Mary, that is to say to eternal *Sophia*. The third chancel is consecrated to St. John. The chancels that follow are dedicated to each of the other eleven apostles. The four evangelists are represented by four statues of Angels, whose high, widespread wings direct attention to the celestial Throne. Three portals give access to the Temple, one to the west, one to the south, and one to the north. Above the western portal is an organ of extraordinary construction and power.

Finally, at the centre of the rotunda is the Holy of Holies, a small building which, like a microcosm, reproduces the entire structure of the great Temple, except that instead of several chancels, it has a single altar. The towers flanking the great Temple on the outside are here replaced by ciboria holding images of the saints. In this Holy of Holies the Grail is kept, floating in suspension, so that the space below forms a large *sacrarium*. The architectural relationship between the great Temple and this microcosm is the perfect figure of the relationship between the outer and inner Temples in man as a microcosm. A meditation which interiorizes the vision of the Temple built by Titurel bestows on it its perfect mystical significance, and another relationship, which reduplicates this Temple, corresponds to it. The appearance of the whole Temple in fact corresponds to the appearance that a Gothic semi-rotunda would assume if it were made to form a perfect circle. As we will suggest below, there may be a profound esoteric meaning in the disappearance of the Templar churches, built in the form of a rotunda, and in the ascendancy of the semi-rotunda of a chancel opening onto the rectangle of a basilica.[240]

2. *The correspondences.* As conceived by Titurel, the Temple of the Grail is the image of the cosmic Temple.[241] There are three zones: intermediary, lower and upper. a) The intermediary zone is formed by the twenty-two (+ 2 = 24) and the seventy-two chancels. There are artificial trees filled with Angels and birds; the ground is covered with a forest of flowers, lilies and roses; the walls sparkle with the green of emeralds. The whole rotunda has the appearance of an enchanted garden, a transfigured Earth, an earthly Paradise. b) The lower zone is beneath the tiles which are crystal-plated, transparent as water. In this crystal sea, fishes and other creatures are made to move by an ingenious mechanism. c) The upper zone corresponds to the dome covered in sapphire, which represents the dome of heaven and its constellations. The Temple is thus the living representation of the cosmos: sky, earth and water. As in the preceding cases (see above, section III ff.), the Temple can be seen here as the link between the celestial, the terrestrial and the sub-terrestrial. As such, the Temple of the Grail is a sanctuary situated at the centre of the world, and Montsalvat is the mountain at the centre of the world.[242]

As we saw, Albrecht von Scharfenberg does not fail to refer to the Temple of Solomon. This he does not because there is an architectural correspondence between the two Temples—the Temple of Solomon was not the architectural archetype of the Temple of the Grail—but because he saw that the two Temples are the equivalents of each other.[243] The Temple of Solomon had been built as a dwelling-place for the *Shekhinah*, for the divine Presence. The Temple of Titurel was built as the dwelling-

240 Cf. Ringbom, op. cit., pp. 50 ff.
241 Ibid., p. 58.
242 Ibid., p. 247. In developing this motif, Ringbom undertakes to demonstrate the correspondences between the *Gralsburg* and the architecture of the castle-temple of Khosrow at Shīz in north-western Iran; cf. ibid., pp. 75 ff. Shīz (where the German archaeological mission has made some very important excavations during the last few years) is now called *Takht-i Sulaymān* (throne or temple of Solomon). We have already referred to the meaning of Persia (*Fars*, in the south-west of Iran) as the "Solomonic kingdom". Cf. above, section I note 14, and section III *in fine*.
243 Ringbom, op. cit., p. 57.

place of the Holy Grail. This may point to an aspect of the nature of the Grail which is worth reflecting on. The Temple of the Grail is not a building of ecclesiastical inspiration or finality. It is not a church among the other churches of Christianity. Likewise, the Grail cycle, whether its origin lies in the person of Titurel or in that of Joseph of Aramithea—the first Christian bishop—appears to know nothing of the Roman hierarchy. The Grail Temple is the realization, in the New Testament cycle, of the Temple corresponding to the building constructed by Solomon in the Old Testament cycle. This is why both Temples were built with the same direct divine assistance.

This being the case, it is here appropriate to reflect on the functional convergences between the rotunda of the Grail Temple and the building already mentioned (see above, section VI, 6), known as the "Dome of the Rock" (*Qubbat al-ṣakhrah*). This latter is supposed to be built on the site of the Holy of Holies in the Temple of Solomon, and it figures on the ancient seals of the Knights Templar. Its plan (the rotunda surrounded by an octagon) is the prototype of certain Templar churches, and the figure of the ideal sanctuary in the kingdom of a Christian Solomon. Yet, because of its origin, the building also appears as the sanctuary in the kingdom of an Islamic Solomon. The sacred rock has a function here which is homologous to that of the Black Stone in the Temple of the *Ka'bah*. The building is as it were a temple-reliquary, and the relic it preserves is this rock itself as *umbilicus Terrae*, the starting-point of all Creation and the site of the Holy of Holies.[244] The *Imago Templi* can be seen as the meeting-place of the great families of the Abrahamic tradition, of all the "communities of the Book" (*Ahl al-Kitāb*).

This convergence should be studied with the guidance of the vision of another temple, with reference to which the last chapter of the "New Titurel" says that it can be compared only with the Temple of the Grail. This miracle of architecture is the Palatine chapel in the land of the mysterious Prester John, an "Orient" that we would seek in vain to find on our maps, as literalist researchers have always been tempted to do. To this "Orient", mystical land of Prester John, Titurel and Parsifal were ultimately to transfer the Holy Grail, hidden from that time on from mortal eyes, like the Temple itself which heralded the heavenly Jerusalem.

244 Ibid., pp. 203–206. See also my study on 'The Configuration of the Temple of the Ka'bah', published above, pp. 235 ff.

Let us ascertain, at least, the direction in which the Quest of the Grail is to be pursued, and hence the meaning of the vocation of Titurel, builder of the Temple. It is through him that the transition from the Temple of Solomon to the heavenly Jerusalem of John's vision is consummated. The *geste* of Titurel is inseparable from the *geste* of the builders of the first and second Temples, Hiram and Zerubbabel, just as the three hierophanies of the *Imago Templi* are inseparable one from the other: the Temple of Solomon, the Temple of the Grail, and the Johannine Temple which is the heavenly Jerusalem. They are inseparable because each of them has reference ultimately to the spiritual temple, the "inner Church", the *Ecclesia Johannis*. Such also is the entire theology of the Temple of the Grail.

3. *The theology of the Temple of the Grail.* The interpretation of the Grail Temple is provided by Titurel himself in his great "speech from the Throne",[245] where he reveals his doctrine of the Temple. The speech is addressed to the young, so that they may put themselves at the service of the Spirit with the virtue demanded by the Grail. True, the interpretation that the poet, Albrecht von Scharfenberg, gives through the mouth of Titurel is not exhaustive; it is essentially concerned with the theological aspect, but it leaves the way open for subsequent interpretations.[246]

What strikes one initially is the age of Titurel. The poet gives it as four hundred years, yet he radiates the beauty, vigour and youth of a man of thirty. The secret of this youthfulness is Titurel's identification with his Temple: every man is always as old as his temple. The start of the construction of the Temple signalled a second birth for Titurel, a *dies natalis* on a higher level of being. The thirty years it took to build the Temple will be his age forever, the perpetual flowering of his youth. This is the norm of the Temple (cf. the lines by Vladimir Maximov which serve as the epigraph to this book).

The second thing that strikes us, coming before the great explanation of the Temple, is the importance assigned to the role of the archangel Michael. On the one hand, there is the evocation of the angelic cohorts

245 Stanzas 510–586. Gudula Trendelenburg, op. cit., pp. 73 ff., provides an analysis of these—an analysis the implications of which should be expanded into an entire book.

246 Ibid., p. 80.

fighting under the leadership of the archangel Michael, an evocation which forms the prelude to the hierohistory of the Temple: there is his descent onto the high mountain of Sauveterre and the migration to the same mountain of the Grail knighthood. On the other hand, there is presented, as an afterword so to speak, the image of the archangel Michael as he whose function is the "weighing of souls".[247] Just as the Qumran Community sensed in its midst the invisible presence of angelic powers, at whose side it waged war against the sons of Darkness, so the Templars of the Grail partner the celestial militia. In the thirtieth year of its construction, the *Imago Templi* leads the entry into battle. The weighing-up of what has been gained in the course of battle leads from meditation on the Temple that is being built to meditation on departure from this world. Hence the emphasis placed on the archangel Michael's double role.

An interiorizing meditation discerns a virtue in every stone of the Temple. It is this which, after the evocation of the Temple of Solomon described above, enables the poet, in his "speech from the Throne", to show the heavenly Jerusalem appearing through the Temple of the Grail. At the same time, the connection between the Grail and the vocation of those who guard it is confirmed. At each moment they offer to the Grail a pure heart. The Grail knighthood makes them into men whose soul has the virtue of a "diamond" (*adamas*). The word is not chosen at random: there is an esoteric connection between what one might call "sacred mineralogy" and mystical anthropology, the conception of man intrinsic in the theology of the Grail Temple.

Because it is made up of all the precious stones that exist, the Temple becomes the parable or the likeness of Man. The meaning of Titurel's Temple lies in promoting the formation in man of the Temple, in investing him with the *Imago Templi*. As the Temple is constructed of the most noble materials, so should man be, since God desires to dwell in the human soul. In the first place the parable concerns individual man. But it also becomes the parable of the human community when, through the invisible action of its knights, the Spirit makes the boundaries of the community of the Grail coincide with the totality of the human community. An essential part is played in the inner transformation of man by a meditation which interior-

247 This is a classic theme in the iconography of the archangel Michael, and represents him holding the Balance in his hand (for example on the portal of the Sainte Chapelle in Paris).

izes the virtue of each stone, deepening its symbolism.[248] The diamond has already been named; after it the twelve precious stones that Aaron wore when he entered the Temple are also specified. The invocation of the number twelve leads to the mention of the twelve apostles to whom Christianity owes its diffusion. (We could also think of the twelve precious stones at the foundations of the wall of the heavenly Jerusalem; *Revelation* 21: 19–20.)

There follows a reference to the effects of each precious stone both on the inner man and on his body. This sacred mineralogy signifies that when the secret of the Grail Temple is transposed to individual man, it becomes the secret of the purification and ennoblement of his whole person. Thus, to know what the precious stones "have to say" becomes the pre-requisite for participation in the nourishment provided by the Grail. It is true that the process is a circular one: man must acquire virtues in order to prepare a dwelling within himself for the Holy Grail, but these virtues themselves can come only from the Grail. Nevertheless, in revealing the relationship between the precious stones and man's essential being, the circuit reveals the relationship of man to the Grail. Until the Temple was built, the Grail could be touched only by the Angels. After it is built, it tolerates the contact of men, but only of those who have acquired the virtue of a *diamond*. These are the men who constitute the knighthood of the Grail.[249]

Such being the nature of the Temple, we are able to understand its rituals and liturgies. It is significant that, of the three great Christian feasts of Christmas, Easter and Pentecost, greater importance is assigned to Pentecost than to the other two (one line for the first two, but an entire stanza for the third). This is because Pentecost is the main feast of the Grail Temple. The principle chancel of the Temple is consecrated to the Holy Spirit (see above, § 1), and the spirituality of the Grail knights is dominated by the mystery of Pentecost. In "The Quest of the Holy Grail", it is on the eve of Pentecost, after the arrival of Galahad, that the Holy Grail manifests itself among the knights around King Arthur: ". . . there came a clap of thunder . . . Suddenly the hall was lit by a sunbeam which shed a radiance through the palace seven times brighter than had been

248 Cf. ibid., pp. 76–77, for some of the correspondences signified by the constituent parts of the Temple.
249 Ibid., pp. 78–79, 83.

before. In this moment they were all illumined as it might be by the grace of the Holy Ghost . . ." For a long time they were silent, then "the Holy Grail appeared, covered with a cloth of white samite; and yet no mortal hand was seen to bear it."[250] The next day, the Quest for the Holy Grail began.

The feast of Pentecost in the Temple of the Grail is not just a commemoration of the outpouring of the Spirit. We have already seen (see above, section V, 4) how in the Community-temple of Qumran the celestial liturgy was itself realized eschatology. Here, the liturgy of the Grail is Pentecost realized; it is the event "in the present". This is so because the outpouring of the Paraclete did not happen once for all in the past, but is still to come, and the community is still in expectation of it. Once again, the norm of the Temple here is the *jam* and *nondum*, already and not yet (see above, section VI, 1). Hence the necessity of the persistence of Christian esotericism (see above, section VI, 5), of which the Grail cycle is a monument. The *Imago Templi* of Titurel dominates every Paracletic perspective, including that of the *Ecclesia Johannis* of the Joachimites (see above, section VI, 2–3).[251] As we observed above, the Grail *before* the "time of Titurel" remained on high, carried invisibly in the hands of the Angels. The "time of Titurel" is the "time of the Temple", the recurrence "in the present" of the mystical liturgy. The Grail may now be touched by the hands of its knights, and can reproduce itself indefinitely in the future within each soul that has attained the required purity.

Attention was also drawn earlier (see above, section IV, 7) to the affinity that may be seen to exist between the *Imago Templi* of the heavenly Jerusalem in Jewish esotericism, and the idea of the mystical Temple in Meister Eckhart. Here once again, the similarity is obvious. "We may wonder whether Meister Eckhart the mystic, born in a epoch when the romance (the New Titurel) was written (between 1260 and 1270), was not himself touched by the light of the Grail and the Grail Temple, when he defines the uncreated part of the soul not only as a *scintilla* (spark) but as a castle (*castellum*), a small fortress (*Bürglein*)".[252] We may also recall the

250 *The Quest of the Holy Grail*, op. cit., pp. 43 ff.
251 Cf. the two studies cited above, note 152.
252 Cf. Helen Adolf, *Visio Pacis: Holy City and Grail. An Attempt of an inner History of the Grail Legend* (Pennsylvania State, 1960), p. 139, cited in Gudula Trendelenburg, op. cit., p. 85. Cf. above, section IV, B, 7, and notes 110 and 111. We may recall the concept of *Shahrestān-i Jān* (the castle of the Soul) in Suhravardī, the metaphys-

theme of the "noble man" in Meister Eckhart, of the chivalric ideal that informed an entire aspect of Rhenish mysticism in the fourteenth century.

The two numbers twenty-two (+ 2 = 24) and seventy-two, given as being the number of chancels in the Temple of the Grail, each possess, as we said, an arithmosophical meaning. It is not surprising that the space inside Titurel's Temple is of a size that makes it the measure, eschatologically speaking, of the entire human community. The number twenty-four is double the number of the signs of the zodiac, and suggests the correspondences between the Temple of the Grail and the cosmic Temple. But the number seventy-two corresponds to the number of peoples and of human tongues (seventy or seventy-two), as the Ancients traditionally represented them. The figure seventy-two is certainly contained, potentially, in the number twelve (12 × 6 = 72). In favouring it, preeminence is given not so much to its relationship with the cosmic dome as to the relationship of the Temple with the human race.[253] In Wolfram, the chivalric ideal already brought the knights of East and West together in the same knighthood. Eschatologically, the service of the Grail should bring together the whole of humanity in the Temple of Titurel. The Pentecostal mystery is "eschatology realized" in the Temple of the Grail (see above, section V, 4).

We also said above that, on the one hand, the secret of the Grail Temple was the Holy of Holies which exemplifies the relationship of the Temple with the Temple within man as a microcosm, and that, on the other hand, this secret lay in the form of the great Temple, which is a perfect round. This form has fascinated researchers. The Finnish scholar L.-J. Ringbom has traced its models, imitations, parallels and variations from Persia to the far West. According to him, the form of the temple in the round is essentially and *par excellence* the form of the sacred royal building. The concept of the priest-kingship, of the integral king as a priest-king—as in

ician *par excellence* of Light (*Shaykh al-Ishrāq*). The mystical meaning of Albrecht's epic should be gone into more deeply, and Gudula Trendelenburg's brief note on the metaphysics of Light and Gothic style needs developing, ibid., p. 112.

253 Cf. ibid., pp. 90–91, 193 ff., where numerous examples of the archetypical usage of the numbers 70 and 72 are quoted. It is worth noting that the diagrams in which the Iranian Shiite philosopher Ḥaydar Āmulī represents the 72 sects, schools and religions into which the human race is divided before and after Islam, correspond perfectly to the ideal plan of the Temple of Montsalvat with its 72 chancels. On the diagrams of Ḥaydar Āmulī, see my study on 'The Science of the Balance and the Correspondences Between Worlds in Islamic Gnosis', published above.

the case of the Grail king—provides him with the key which opens all the traditional sanctuaries whose form is related to that of the Grail Temple.[254] We observed that the shape of the entire Temple corresponds to that which would be assumed by a Gothic semi-rotunda if it were completed to make a perfect circle. Yet the chancel of the Gothic church—for example, Saint-Martin de Tours, or Saint-Rémi de Reims—consists of no more than a semi-rotunda opening onto the rectangle of the old basilica, so that the plan of the whole building is cruciform. The breaking, or rather the cutting-off, of the rotunda signifies the breaking of the whole formed by the sacerdotal kingship of the Grail or, in other words, the breaking of the unity formed by exoteric and esoteric, which are henceforth separated and dispersed. The whole drama and meaning of the Temple *ab origine* lies in the capitulation of the esoteric before the official norm and power of the exoteric Church.

The historian of traditional architectural forms can thus follow the progress of the *Imago Templi* from the Orient to its entry into the West, where the hearts of men are so hardened that it cannot survive. The Templar rotundas are destroyed. With a few exceptions, all that remain are the semi-rotundas, traces of a mutilated unity.[255] The exoteric is triumphant, and the idea of the royal Temple returns to the country whence it came, to the mystical "Orient" where it is received by him who is the guardian of the priestly kingship, the mysterious Prester John, who is not a ruler of this world. This is the last episode in the "New Titurel". Yet it must never be forgotten that the Temple of the Grail was only ever manifest at "the meeting-place of the two seas", in the Land of Light or *Terra Lucida*, the "eighth clime" which the *Ishrāqīyūn* call the "intermediary Orient". It was not and could not be "incarnated" in this world, in the sense that this word is misused today. In a single night, the Temple was transferred from this "intermediary Orient" to the "Orient" of the metaphysical world, to which Titurel and Parsifal transferred the Holy Grail.

If this "return to the Orient" possesses a symbolic virtue for the history of traditional architectural forms, it possesses it no less with respect to the temple within man—or, better, to the temple that is man. We come back

254 Gudula Trendelenburg, op. cit., pp. 98–99. See also Ringbom, op. cit., especially chap. X, pp. 140–178, 197–198.

255 Consider, on the other hand, the rotunda of Neuvy Saint-Sépulcre (Indre), the Round Church at Cambridge, etc.

in this way to the drama of the destruction of the Temple which, following a Cabbalistic master of our own time (see above, section II), we were made to envisage at the beginning of this inquiry, as the drama of our entry into this world. The rebuilding of the Temple is the work of a human lifetime; or, more precisely, one can only leave the world of exile by undergoing a second birth, signified by the rebuilding of the Temple. The transference of the Temple to India is the return of the soul to its country of origin.

Finally, this "return to the Orient" gives us the clue to the secret of the Grail knighthood. The "India" to which the knights withdraw in the wake of Titurel and Parsifal is not one which we can hope to find on the map. Traditionally, the word designates a distant Orient where the realm of the invisible Paradise begins. It would be futile and absurd to identify the Prester John of the Grail cycle with a ruler of this world, with, for example, a Mongolian or Ethiopian ruler, as happened in previous centuries. At the end of Wolfram's epic, Prester John is Parsifal's nephew; at the end of Albrecht's epic, the name and the honour are conferred on Parsifal himself.[256] Prester John is the ideal priest-king of the Johannine kingdom. The return of the Templars of the Grail to his kingdom is their return to invisibility, to a strict *incognito*.

One cannot therefore speak of the Temple of the Grail without opening one's inner vision and hearing to the musical dramas of Richard Wagner. Indeed, in the "recital of the Grail", Lohengrin voices the norm of strict esotericism to which every knight of the Grail is subject: "And its power is sacred as long as it remains unknown to all." The final scene of their "return to the Orient" suggests to us how best to envisage the relationship between the Templars of the Grail—in "Parsifal" and the "New Titurel" —and the knights of the historic Order of the Temple. The historic Order was the visible manifestation of a still more exalted knighthood that was unknown to men, the temporary trustee of a mission which, from century to century, these superior and unknown knights assign to those who are worthy. This is how J.-B. Willermoz, in the eighteenth century, himself understood the significance of the historic Order of the Temple in relation to a permanent Templarism that was superior to it—a relationship through which alone the historic Order could claim descent from the Order of

256 Cf. *En Islam iranien*, op. cit., vol. IV, index s.v. Prêtre-Jean.

Essenes. There is a striking correspondence between what is implied by this vision of things, and the occultation of the Grail knighthood.

The triumph of the *Imago Templi* lies in its thus emerging safe and sound from all failings, all betrayals, all enslavement to the norms of this world. Counter-history is ultimately more true than history. Once in occultation, the Templars of the Grail can assume other names. One such name is the "Sons of the Valley" in the great dramatic poem by Zacharias Werner.

VIII. The Imago Templi *and the "Sons of the Valley"*

1. *The critique of the Temple.* In Zacharias Werner's great drama, the *Imago Templi* is linked to the theme of the Temple's perpetuation, but it differs in two essential respects from the Templar tradition that we have already discussed (see above, section VI). 1. The tragedy of the historic Order of the Temple gives place not to a glorification pure and simple of the *Imago Templi*, historically represented by the Order, but to a critique of, and lamentation over, the descendence into which the Temple has fallen, and which motivates and governs the expectation of the new Temple. 2. As a result, Templar filiation is not seen as following directly on the historic Order of the Temple, as if it were simply a question of reviving this Order. Templar filiation is conceived as being the work of a higher Order, which is concealed behind the historic Order of the Temple, as well as behind all the known manifestations of Templarism. This hidden community is called by the author the "Sons of the Valley". The Templar heritage is ensured by their decisions; it is not engendered historically by the events of profane history. The new Temple is not the fruit of historical evolution.

As regards the first point, we are confronted with a critique of the Temple at a moment parallel to that found in Ezekiel and in the Community of Qumran. The historic Order of the Temple is guilty of betraying the orders of the "Valley", a betrayal which is like a repetition of the sin of Israel that violated and desecrated the Temple. Thus the tragedy corresponds to the first part of the *Book of Ezekiel* (see above, section III), which speaks of the judgement of God on the Temple and the resulting exile of the *Shekhinah*. But the destruction of the desecrated Temple is a necessary prelude to the coming of the new Temple, which assumes the dimensions of a cosmic restoration. The vision of the return from exile and the rebuilding of the Temple correspond in Zacharias Werner to the alchemical transfiguration of the martyr Jacques de Molay as prelude to the coming of the new Temple, which will be the work of the "Sons of the Valley". In both cases, the *Imago Templi* is manifested in two phases: the tragedy of its destruction, and the triumph of its restoration (see below, *Nova Hierosolyma*). The whole drama of humanity is contained within the drama of this *Imago Templi*, whose norm opposes the violations and profanations of History with the inviolability and sacredness of the Temple "on the high mountain".

As regards the second point, because the historic Templars were no more than temporary trustees of the secrets of the Temple, Zacharias Werner is led to adopt an attitude different from that which tends to exculpate the unfortunate Templars on the charges brought against them in the course of an unjust trial. The expectation of the new Temple presupposes a critique of the old one. It is not that the author goes over to the side of their sinister enemies, King Philip the Fair of France and Pope Clement V; but he attempts to explain their fate in terms of a superior logic, one which enables him already to proclaim the dawning of a new day. In effect, the tragedy of the historic Order of the Temple is raised to the rank of parable. In saying that this tragedy typifies all the drama of mankind, we are once again thinking of the essential meaning assigned from the start (see above, section II) to the destruction and the restoration of the Temple: entry into the world of exile, and departure from it. In Zacharias Werner's dramatic poem, the Templars of the fourteenth century are in fact no more than surrogates for the Templar masonry of the eighteenth century because, according to the author's vision, both of them were unfaithful to the mission with which they had been entrusted by the "Sons of the Valley".

In what did this betrayal consist? All the reproaches and criticisms levelled by Zacharias Werner at the historical Order of the Temple are in fact directed at his own eighteenth-century contemporaries, who are easily recognizable. The Knights Templar are said to have misused a secret knowledge that had been entrusted to them, and to have been about to reveal it at an untimely moment to the profane world. It was on account of this that the "Sons of the Valley" withdrew their protection from them, and they were abandoned to their destiny of destruction. They were not, however, utterly abandoned: a small remnant was preserved with a view to the future palingenesis.[257] In this, Zacharias Werner is simply following

257 A. E. Waite, *Emblematic*, p. 184.

Templar history according to the Scottish tradition (see above, section VI, 7). In fact, as we have just said, it is eighteenth-century Templarism which is at issue, because it is accused of having allowed itself to be corrupted by the radical application of the principles of the *Aufklärung*, the "age of Enlightenment". In the first place, he is thinking of the disquieting *Illuminati* of Weisshaupt in Bavaria, who had already provoked a violent reaction on the part of the "Strict Templar Observance", and whose political aspirations did indeed bring discredit on Templarism in general.[258] Secondly and more generally, the author has in mind the whole spirit of the Enlightenment in his critique of a degenerate Templarism: the reduction of religion to morality in the name of a rationalism and a criticism that so mutilate the high ideal of the Temple that it is no longer recognizable; a deism that opens the way to atheism pure and simple and unleashes the passions of egoism and personal ambition—in short, everything that the spiritual knighthood was charged and pledged to oppose.[259]

Obviously, it would be easy to speak of anachronism with respect to the role assigned to the fourteenth-century Templars as mouthpieces for the Enlightenment. But here the intentions of the playwright are not those of a historian. What he wishes to do is to synchronize the decadence of the *Imago Templi* with the ways in which it may be restored.[260] That is already clear from a very brief analysis of his great dramatic poem. This esoteric play—it deserves to be staged, although I do not know whether it ever has been—comprises two parts.

A. *The Templars in Cyprus*. The scene of action is Limassol (Limasso), the stronghold of the Order in the south of the island. In several scenes we are presented with the life of the Order and its ritual ceremonies, in a way which is intended to show us the deep-seated reasons for the Order's decadence. Its Grand Master, the virtuous Jacques de Molay, is unable to remedy the situation. Under a false pretext, Philip the Fair persuades the knights to come to France. The fateful decision is taken during a solemn

258 Cf. Louis Guinet, *Zacharias Werner et l'ésoterisme maçonnique* (Paris/The Hague, Mouton, 1962).

259 Ibid., pp. 321–324.

260 Friedrich Ludwig Zacharias Werner, *Die Söhne des Thal's, ein dramatisches Gedicht*. 1. Teil: 'Die Templer auf Cypern'; 2. Teil: 'Die Kreuzesbrüder'; Theater von F. L. Z. Werner (2 vols., repr. of orig. ed., Vienna, J. V. Wallishauser, 1813; the first edition is dated Berlin, 1803). The photocopy of the work came too late into my possession for me to be able to provide an analysis of it here, as I would have wished. I will return to it elsewhere.

chapter. All the necessary dispositions are made concerning the treasures, the ritual objects and the secret works. In the background we perceive the action of the unknown Superiors, the "Sons of the Valley", whose mysterious messengers Eudo and Astralis have the task of preparing Jacques de Molay for his fate, and the young knight Robert of Heredom for his mission. This is the young man who has been chosen to carry through the palingenesis of the Order, or rather its continuation after its destruction on the visible stage of History.

B. *The brothers of the Cross (Kreuzesbrüder)*.[261] This time the action is set in Paris on March 17–18, 1314. The theme is the trial of the Templars, their condemnation, and their appeal. But it is important to observe that Philip the Fair is merely the agent, accursed no doubt, but nevertheless the mere executive agent of decisions which are taken by an authority higher than his, the authority of the "Sons of the Valley". If the Order must disappear it is because it has overstepped the limits of its power. After an imprisonment lasting eight years, Jacques de Molay "understands the meaning of his tribulations and his death. He is received as a member of the Valley in the cave of Carmel, after which he undergoes martyrdom in a sort of apotheosis and mystical ecstasy". Robert of Heredom, after having been initiated as well, flees to Scotland with a few knights. In accordance with the Templar tradition, the *Imago Templi* once again makes the royal Scotland of Robert the Bruce into the sanctuary where the Temple is perpetuated.

2. *The "Sons of the Valley"*. What exactly does this name represent? It represents an exalted company of initiate Brothers, who constitute *ab origine* the secret Church of Christ—not unreminiscent of Eckhartshausen's "Inner Church".[262] For Zacharias Werner, it represents a brotherhood of "unknown Superiors", which was at work behind the Templar knighthood of the fourteenth century and is still behind the Templar knighthood of the eighteenth century. In fact, both of these knighthoods represent simply a temporary form of manifestation which is determined by the brotherhood of the Valley. When the Valley, because of a transgression, withdraws its protection from these forms, they are left defenceless before

261 L. Guinet, op. cit., p. 38, translates this as "Frères-Croix" (Cross-Brothers).
262 Waite, *Emblematic*, p. 184. Antoine Faivre, *Eckhartshausen et la théosophie chrétienne* (Paris, Klincksieck, 1969), especially pp. 374–386.

the attacks of the powers of this world. The Valley, which is a purely spiritual and secret power, has no part in the tide of becoming, and participates in human events only in a mediate sense, through the communities emanating from it and whose destiny it controls.

Thus, the historic Order of the Temple had been organized by the Valley into three hierarchical levels: a. the knights, men of action who were not even aware of the Valley's existence; b. the initiated brothers, who received esoteric instruction; c. the masters, who were in direct but secret communication with the "Sons of the Valley". The latter thus correspond, in a certain sense, to the knights of the Grail after their occultation in the kingdom of Prester John (see above, section VII, 3). More precisely, they correspond to those mysterious figures of Templar tradition, through whom this tradition traces the ancestry of the historical Order back to distant Essene origins. They are variously called the "Knights of the Morning and of Palestine", the "Thebaid Solitaries", the "canons of the Holy Sepulchre", the *Canonici Templi Domini*, and so on. They have all been mentioned before (see above, section VI, 6). Nevertheless, it is important to qualify the relationship: the "Sons of the Valley" did not simply have to ally themselves with the Knights Templar. The "Sons of the Valley" assign to these knights the mission which links them to the distant Essenes, to the original Judaeo-Christian community. When they withdraw their mission from the knights of the Temple in the fourteenth century, they themselves continue to exist as before, immutable in their Valley, the guardians of the *Imago Templi* in its ideal purity, ready to ensure its future palingeneses.

This "Valley"—"the peaceful, silent homeland of a community of Sages whose task was to sanctify and divinize the world"—is the valley of Jehoshaphat in the Holy Land, according to a Hermetic tradition, and its name appears in the Bible in the Book of the prophet Joel.[263] The word of three syllables that in Zacharias Werner's drama the Temple initiates whisper into each other's ears is obviously the word Jehoshaphat. How-

263 L. Guinet, op. cit., p. 102. Cf. Joel 3:2, 12 and 14. Cf. Jacob Boehme, *De Tribus Principiis*, chap. XIII, 11: "Der Engel des grossen Raths kommt in Josaphats Thal mit einer güldenen Bulla, die verkauft er um Oele ohne Geld; wer da kommt, den trifts." [The Angel from the Great Council comes to the valley of Jehoshaphat with a Golden Bull, which he sells for oil, not money; whoever comes will obtain it.] (Sämtliche Werke, Faksimile-Neudruck der Ausgabe von 1730, Stuttgart, 1960, 2ter Bd., p. 150.

ever, a significant fact emerges during the course of the extraordinary seance held, on the eve of the fatal departure for France, by the seven knights entrusted with the fate of the secret archives and sacred objects of the Order. At the moment of repeating the password, the youngest member of the Temple, young Gottlieb, as though discovering by inspiration the profound truth that the others have forgotten, utters these words: "Ich—in mir—wir sind—das Sein" (I—within me—we are—Being).[264]

The valley of Jehoshaphat is likewise located, not on our maps, but at "the meeting-place of the two seas" (see above, section II). Its very name confers on it an eschatological dimension, since it appears to the prophet Joel as the place of the Last Judgement.[265] The eschatological dimension is that of the *Imago Templi*, whose virtue is such as to make it the supreme and effective recourse of all innocent men condemned unjustly. It is the *Appellatio ad vallem Josaphat*.[266] We are reminded here of the last words of Jacques de Molay, summoning Pope Clement V and King Philip the Fair to appear before the judgement seat of God (both of them, as we know, died that same year).

Because it is situated at "the meeting-place of the two seas", in the place which *par excellence* is *median* and *intermediary*, the valley of Jehoshaphat also typifies the mode of knowledge that Zacharias Werner opposes to the rationalism which is destructive of the indissoluble unity of Creator and Creation, and to the deistic conception of God as separated from his creation and indifferent to it: a *Deus otiosus*. The starting-point must be the original intuition. In creating man, God entrusted him with the task of "completing the temple", this implying for man the obligation of becoming himself the Temple of God.[267] Instead, through his egoism, man builds a dwelling for himself, shattering in this way the unity of Creation. The centre of Creation no longer coincides with the centre of the divinity, for man henceforth locates this centre within himself. This dislocation is the consequence of pride, which manifests itself in the form of knowledge

264 L. Guinet, op. cit., pp. 106–107. Gottlieb's reply: "Gottlieb kann's nicht anders" (Gottlieb cannot do otherwise) echoes the very words of Luther before the Diet of Worms.

265 "I will also gather all nations, and will bring them down into the valley of Jehoshaphat", Joel 3:2. "Thither cause thy mighty ones to come down, O Lord. Let the heathen be wakened, and come up to the valley of Jehoshaphat", Joel 3:11–12. "Multitudes, multitudes in the valley of judgement", Joel 3:14.

266 L. Guinet, op. cit., p. 102, note 8.

267 Ibid., pp. 208 ff.

described by our author in his gnostic hermeneutic of the Tree of knowledge of good and evil. This is the form of knowledge which he is actually condemning in his own contemporaries when he attacks the Templars of the fourteenth century for accepting it. It is a form of knowledge that is discursive, analytical, falsely objective; that isolates and parcels out into autonomous components something which constitutes an essential unity. Moreover, it is a form of knowledge that wrongly arrogates to itself the privilege of being the only valid mode of knowing.

On the other hand (and here we perceive the profound influence on our author of the great theologian Schleiermacher), there is a mode of knowledge which is intuitive, divinatory, combining the action of imagination and feeling, and which as such is the mode, essentially, of religious knowledge.[268] This rediscovery of the *noetic* value and of the *mediating* function of the Image and the Imagination is of major importance, for Zacharias Werner thereby validates at once imaginative knowledge and the existence of that *mundus imaginalis* (*'ālam al-mithāl*) which fulfils a function (between the *Jabarūt* and the *Mulk*) so essential for the theosophers of Islam. Only a metaphysics of the *imaginal* can attain to "the meeting-place of the two seas", to the "valley of Jehoshaphat", as Suhravardī so admirably demonstrated (see above, section II). This mediating function of the active Imagination is essential for spiritual alchemy—that is to say, for the effectiveness of the alchemical operation viewed as a transmutation of the inner man. Moreover, it is this exalted science of alchemy that Zacharias Werner sees as the secret of the "Valley", the secret which transformed the martyrdom of Jacques de Molay into an ecstatic apotheosis.

The Order had but a single aim: the regeneration, the new birth, brought about by the re-establishment of the identity between macrocosm and microcosm. The all-powerfulness of the active Imagination (quite different, as Paracelsus says, from the "fantasy") puts into operation an alchemy which comprises simultaneously a conception of the world, an

268 Ibid., pp. 210, 292. For Zacharias Werner, faith as it is generally conceived in the Christian churches has a rational component that is too opposed to his idea of religion; its character is too dogmatic, too historical for him. Today we would add: too sociological. I quote, from memory, a recent invitation "to celebrate (the Eucharist) less and to share more (socially)". Well and good; but the second undertaking requires neither religious faith nor a Church, and it is hard to see how it could revive them.

ethic and an eschatology. And this is so whether it is a case of practical alchemy or speculative alchemy: the notion of *mediating* and *mediation* is the very foundation of the *Ars magna*. The philosopher's stone is to be found only through the *coincidentia oppositorum*, and this *coincidentia* can occur only through a mediatory term and on a mediating level (the level, as the Islamic theosophers say, "where bodies are spiritualized and where spirits take on body"). Mercury both engenders and resorbs contraries, and it is also one of the names for the Stone of the Sages. This stone has the power to destroy gross matter and to convert the body of man into a subtle body of a luminous essence, like the bodies of the Righteous in Paradise, or the body of the androgynous Adam before his Fall. The active Imagination is the organ of meditation that assimilates the *Opus alchemicum*, by which base metal is refined. In virtue of this assimilation, the Imagination is the mediator which brings about the refinement of whoever "spiritualizes himself until he reaches the final stage of mystical union".[269] Such is the secret of the *apotheosis* of Jacques de Molay and of the *Imago novi Templi*.

3. *Towards the new Temple.* In speaking of the Grand Master Jacques de Molay, Robert of Heredom called him "that great, poor, misunderstood heart". Despite his modesty and renunciation, which led him to submit to the fateful decision, taken by the Chapter, to return to France—a return whose consequences he foresaw—Jacques de Molay had to undergo the moral and physical sufferings of an unjust trial, as well as endure the distress of eight years in prison, in order to attain supreme purification.[270]

The interiorizing of the alchemical work leads, certainly, to a superior form of gnosis, to a knowledge of the unitive way. What characterizes this knowledge, however, is that it is not merely theoretical: it is the actual experience of the unitive way and of the mystical union. The three stages of the alchemical operation, whose secret is also the secret of the "Valley", have their spiritual correspondences: *nigredo*, the dark night of the soul; *albedo*, illumination, the birth of the *filius philosophorum*; and *rubedo*, the red of divine love, the hierogamy of the soul with her God. Jacques de Molay traversed and experienced these three stages of the mystical way. The final term of the Great Work is represented by Zacharias Werner as the

269 Ibid., p. 142.
270 At the Château of Chinon today, one can still make a pilgrimage to the Tour du Coudray where the Knights Templar were imprisoned.

Grand Master of the Templars being received into the bosom of the Valley. The transmutation of his inner being is complete; here below, he knows ecstasy, the union with God which is the prelude to the definitive union, consummated by death as a martyr. His transmutation is simultaneously the transmutation of the entire Templar Order. His death is redemptory, the philosopher's stone which transforms the base lead of the old Temple into the gold of the new.[271]

While Jacques de Molay embraces death in ecstasy, Robert of Heredom throws himself into the world of action which leads to the coming of the new Temple. In an extraordinary scene, the initiator, Adam de Valincourt, instructs him in the significance of earthly death. Defunct bodies liberate the "seeds of resurrection". When living beings disappear, they leave behind them a subtle body (Paracelsus' *corpus spirituale*, the *jism mithālī* or *imaginal* body of the Islamic theosophers). When the rose is subjected to the action of fire, burned to ashes and then diluted after fermentation, a bluish colour appears, followed by the astral form of the rose. This experiment is the same as that conducted by the great Christian Cabbalist F. C. Oetinger, using a sprig of balm—an experiment he found so overwhelming that he returns to it over and over again. "May the son of the Valley be annihilated—And may there spring from the worm-eaten Temple —A tree of life flowering in the eternal sacred wood of the Lamb."[272] Towards the end of the poem, Robert of Heredom is thus initiated by the Sons of the Valley and created Grand Master of the new Temple, which will be born again from the ashes of the old. He is the guardian of the secret *Palladium* until the time when men are sufficiently mature to acknowledge him, and worthy enough to receive the Light which the Valley revealed to Jacques de Molay on the eve of his martyrdom.[273]

Robert's name in chivalry refers us to the mystical mountain of Heredom in the north of Scotland, of which mention has already been made (see above, section VI, 7). The entire Scottish tradition is thus evoked, the part played by Scotland in the renaissance of the Order of the Temple after its destruction. The person of the young knight likewise comes to be integrated to the *geste* of the knights who, in the company of Pierre d'Aumont, were accorded in Scotland the protection of King Robert the Bruce and,

271 L. Guinet, op. cit., pp. 154–155.
272 Translation by L. Guinet, ibid., p. 156.
273 Cf. Waite, *Emblematic*, p. 184, note 2.

according to the tradition, continued the Temple there. After the sacrifice of Jacques de Molay, Robert of Heredom receives, from the hands of one of the Sons of the Valley, the coffer containing both the authentic doctrine and the bell of the primitive Church, which he will transmit to future generations. Six more knights who have become "Brothers of the Cross" are attached to him by the Valley, and the little company of seven men "ride out at daybreak, the symbol of rebirth, youth and strength", towards the castle of Heredom in Scotland.[274]

Then there rises up on the horizon an *Imago Templi* which resembles both the Temple of Titurel and the Church of the third reign, the *Ecclesia Johannis* of the Holy Spirit proclaimed by the Joachimites. All thought of politics is laid aside; nothing counts but man's spiritual powers and divine providence. The Temple which is at present still invisible will become the Temple of the whole human race: "And the globe became an immense church—On the evergreen grass of the tombs . . .—And from above the flaming winds this chorus resounded—And earth and water gave back a sonorous echo—And all beings thundered:—Life will overcome dreadful death." The symbol of the Cross fades before the ancient flaming Star, symbol of the Church of the Holy Spirit and of the Eternal Gospel: "Then to the sound of bells—To the accents of the choirs—The new sign—Will fade before the ancient emblem."[275]

It is astonishing that such a drama should never have tempted a musician.

IX. The Nova Hierosolyma. *Swedenborg*

1. *The celestial Temple and the new Jerusalem.* Zacharias Werner's great Templar epic ends with a triumphant celestial liturgy which assumes the dimensions of a cosmic liturgy. In the Revelation of John, the vision of the *Nova Hierosolyma* likewise sets us in the presence of a cosmic liturgy, a celestial liturgy in which we relive the mystery of an eschatology that is already visionally accomplished, as in the liturgies of the Community of Qumran (see above, section V, 4). In Swedenborg, the new Jerusalem as the *Imago Templi* heralds the coming of the *Nova Ecclesia.*

In the celestial Temple, John witnesses a magnificent liturgy which

274 Cf. L. Guinet, op. cit., p. 101.
275 Ibid., pp. 175–176. Cf. pp. 360–365.

unfolds in seven great scenes.[276] Recent research has shown that the dominant image in these grand liturgical scenes is without doubt the great Jewish feast of the Tabernacles.[277] Be that as it may, the heavenly Jerusalem is peopled by priest-kings. Ideally speaking, the Israelites are a people of priests (Exod. 19:6). In the vision of John, all the Elect are also a people of priest-kings (Rev. 20:6 and 22:5). The believer's status is simultaneously royal and sacerdotal[278] (like that of the knight-priests at Montsalvat). As was the case with the Community of Qumran, there is here an indissoluble union between the celestial and earthly liturgies: the believer in heaven and the believer on earth are united in the same liturgical act. The connection between "events in Heaven" and those which "take place" on earth is dramatically illustrated in the effects that the celestial liturgy can have on those who are on earth: "And the Angel took the censer, and filled it with the fire of the altar, and cast it into the earth: and there were voices, and thunderings, and lightnings, and an earthquake" (Rev. 8:5).

The Image of the celestial Temple and that of the new Jerusalem are indissolubly united in the Johannine vision. "Him that overcometh will I make a pillar in the temple of my God, and he shall go no more out: and I will write upon him the name of my God, and the name of the city of my God, which is new Jerusalem, which cometh down out of heaven from my God: and I will write upon him my new name" (Rev. 3:12). The new Jerusalem is none other than the new Temple of God. John thus reinterprets all the traditional expectation of Israel: "And I saw a new heaven and a new earth: for the first heaven and the first earth were passed away" (Rev. 21:1). This is truly a new creation; and the city-temple that comes down from heaven (21:2) is part of this new creation, and descends from newly-created skies. We can see from this that it is a question not simply of the rejuvenation and transformation of the old, but of the breaking-through of something that is outside and beyond history. Is this conception radically different from that of the *Rabbis* for whom the city was the celestial city-archetype?[279] We think not, because the descent of the city-archetype in any case marks a break or discontinuity in the course of things. It is hierohistory or "subtle history" breaking through and dissolving the norms

276 Cf. R. J. McKelvey, *The New Temple, the Church in the New Testament* (Oxford, 1969). The seven great scenes in question are *Revelation* 4:2–11; 5:8–14; 7:9–17; 11:15–19; 14:1–5; 15:2–4; 19:1–8.

277 Ibid., pp. 162–163.

278 Ibid., pp. 165 ff.

279 Ibid., p. 170.

of secular history. This hierohistory is also, by its essence, a radical innovation, a new creation, hitherto unseen. The true relationship is expressed, moreover, in a remarkable symbol.

2. *From the Temple of Ezekiel to the Johannine city-temple.* The symbol in question is a magnificent window in Chartres cathedral, which shows the apostle John perched on the shoulders of the prophet Ezekiel.[280] This symbol by itself makes the relationship between the vision and theology of the Temple in Ezekiel (see above, section III, 4) and the Johannine vision of the *Nova Hierosolyma* quite clear: fundamentally they are in agreement, but in the second new heights are reached. To reach these heights, however, it is necessary to be carried by Ezekiel himself higher than his own vision. "And he [one of the seven Angels] carried me away in the spirit to a great and high mountain, and shewed me that great city, the holy Jerusalem, descending out of heaven from God" (Rev. 21:10). Ezekiel, too, relates how "In the visions of God brought he me into the land of Israel, and set me upon a very high mountain, by which was as the frame of a city on the south" (Ezek. 40:2). The temple contemplated by the visionary Ezekiel is already a city-temple just as the city contemplated by John is a city-temple. Here, our inquiry should complete the parallel previously established (see above, sections III and V) between the Ezekelian theology of the Temple and that of the Community of Qumran, by establishing another parallel between the Qumran vision of the *Nova Hierosolyma* and the Johannine vision.[281] For the present we must confine ourselves to pointing out what there is in common between the Ezekelian and Johannine visions of the new Temple.

Common to the Temple in both visions is the geometrical layout, whose symbolism is such as to characterize an *Imago Templi* common to the esotericism of the entire Abrahamic tradition. In Ezekiel's city-temple, whose name is "the Lord is there", the four sides of the perfect square each have three gates (north, south, east and west): twelve gates in all, the

280 There is a beautiful reproduction of this in Paul Popesco's book, *La Cathédrale de Chartres*, Chefs-d'oeuvre du Vitrail européen (Paris, Bibliothèque des Arts, 1970), fig. 40, window 95 (south), and p. 140: "The evangelist appears like 'a dwarf on the shoulders of a giant', meaning that the evangelists are lesser then the prophets, but see further because they are more highly-placed."

281 Cf. Shozo Fujita, *Temple Theology*, pp. 306–316, the final chapter entitled 'The book of Ezekiel and the fragments of "New Jerusalem"'.

name of each corresponding respectively to the name of one of the twelve tribes of Israel (Ezek. 48:30–35). In the Revelation of John (21:12), the city-temple, the new Jerusalem descending from heaven, "had twelve gates, and at the gates twelve angels, and names written thereon, which are the names of the twelve tribes of the children of Israel". There are three gates in each of the four sides of the square. Furthermore, the city wall had twelve foundations, and on them were the twelve names of the twelve apostles (Rev. 21:13–14).

Another parallel completes this one. Twelver Shiite prophetology always establishes a correspondence between the number of twelve Imams, and the twelve heads of the twelve tribes of Israel, the twelve springs that gushed from the rock struck by the staff of Moses. And Shiite gnosis, most notably in the work of Qāḍī Sa'īd Qummī, meditates in this sense on the cubic form of the Temple of the Ka'bah, which corresponds to the form of the city-temple in Ezekiel and John. In the twelve edges of the cube, Shiite gnosis perceives the symbol of the twelve Imams, who are the spiritual temple because they are *par excellence* the ministers of the esoteric aspect of the prophetic revelation. The very structure of the Temple thus betokens the structure of the pleroma of the eternal prophetic Reality, and the Temple of the Ka'bah is transfigured into a spiritual Temple.[282] In this way there emerges an *Imago Templi* that is common to all three branches of the Abrahamic tradition. Through the mediation of their esotericists, they are finally reunited in the mystical Jerusalem, in the same spiritual city.

Next, there is the Johannine statement: "And I saw no temple therein [in the city]" (Rev. 21:22); for the Temple is the Lord God himself and his Christ. Jewish eschatology itself, it is true, makes the new Jerusalem into the symbol of the unity not just of Israel, but of humanity, and John relates his vision to this great hope by making the city-temple the centre of the world. But is not a future Jerusalem without a temple something unthinkable, unacceptable for the Jewish sense of piety?[283] In reply, Ezekiel himself and, closer to our time, Swedenborg, prepare the way for

282 Cf. my study on 'The Configuration of the Temple of the Ka'bah', published above. See also my 'Science traditionnelle et Renaissance spirituelle', op. cit. (*in fine*, on the meaning of the coat of arms chosen for the Université Saint-Jean de Jérusalem).

283 "Das zukünftige Jerusalem ohne Tempel, ein für die alte Synagoge unvollziehbarer Gedanke", Strack und Billerbeck, III, 852, cited in R. J. McKelvey, op. cit., p. 175 note 2.

the hermeneutic. Does not God say, in the Book of Ezekiel (11:16): "... yet will I be to them as a little sanctuary"? (see above, section III, 2). There are thus two essential aspects to be taken into account.[284]

a. It would indeed be disconcerting if the new Jerusalem had no temple. What John means is that the temple of the new Jerusalem is God himself and his Christ (Rev. 21:22), and the intimacy proclaimed in Ezekiel between God and man is experienced on an even higher level. The veils or barriers between God and men disappear in the new Jerusalem. "And they shall see his face" (Rev. 22:4).

b. Another aspect, leading back to the first, is that the new Jerusalem is itself the Temple: it is all Temple, the city-temple. Not only is God a temple for the believers, as in Ezekiel; the believers are also a temple for God (cf. the Community-temple of Qumran; above, section V, 2. See also Rev. 3:12: the believers become pillars in the Temple and bear the name of the new Jerusalem). The city-temple is in the form of a cube (as is also the Ka'bah; see above), like the Holy of Holies in the Temple of Solomon (I Kgs. 6:20). The new Jerusalem and the Temple are one and the same thing. Better still, the new Jerusalem is itself the new Heaven and the new Earth. Let us note, too, that when John speaks of God as the temple of the believer, and of the believer as the temple of God, he does not signify the same thing as when one speaks of the Church as the Temple of God. He is not describing the Temple alone, but the Holy of Holies, the most sacred part of the Temple. Thereby the necessity for Christian esotericism is also established (see above, section VI, 1–5).

Consequently, the Johannine *Imago Templi* is the symbol of the ultimate and final communion between God and his people, the fulfilment of the Ezekelian promise: "They will be his people and God himself shall dwell amongst them". The divine Presence—"the dwelling of God amongst them"—which believers are privileged to experience on earth, will not be taken away from them when they die. In the world to come they will still have that privilege. This is what it means to become "a pillar in the temple of my God" (Rev. 3:12), and to enjoy the immediate vision of the divine (Rev. 21:22, 22:4). There alone will the mystical epic of all Templar chivalry be consummated, for it is not in this world that man's goal and destiny are to be sought.

284 For what follows, see McKelvey's apposite observations in ibid., pp. 175–177, 187.

3. *The "Nova Ecclesia" in Swedenborg.* The entire spiritual *oeuvre* of the great eighteenth-century visionary theosopher Swedenborg is dominated by the idea of the *Nova Hierosolyma*, signifying the *Nova Ecclesia* whose annunciator and prophet it was Swedenborg's mission to be. His hermeneutic of chapter XXI of the Revelation is in some sense the recapitulation of his entire doctrine. "The whole of this chapter," he writes, "treats of the Lord's Advent, and of the new church to be established by him. It is this new church which is meant by Jerusalem . . ."[285] We should therefore study the whole doctrine of the new Jerusalem; but we will confine ourselves here to the commentary on the chapter in question, which has the virtue of reminding us of the laws of *imaginal* visionary perception (angelic hierognosis in Swedenborg). The hermeneutic of the *Imago Templi* illustrates how esoteric and exoteric, by virtue of these very laws, are inseparable.[286]

The heavenly Jerusalem is perceived first of all by the visionary of the Apocalypse as the holy city; immediately afterwards, he contemplates it as a young betrothed maiden. In the doctrine of Swedenborg the two images, superimposed one upon the other, are symbolic visions, an exemplary case of correspondence. The very idea of such a correspondence presupposes the ontological reality of what we, in common with our Islamic theosophers, have called the *mundus imaginalis* and, consequently, the necessary perception of things at "the meeting-place of the two seas". Symbolically or "representationally", the new Jerusalem is perceived as a city; in its spiritual reality it is perceived as a betrothed maiden. This, observes Swedenborg, is exactly what happens for the Angels when they see, read or hear in the Word something to do with a city. In the thought of the lower-ranking Angels, it is still perceived as a city. In the thought of the Angels of a higher order, it is perceived as the *Nova Ecclesia* with respect to the doctrine. But by virtue of the law of correspondences, which ensures the plenary reality *sui generis* of the visionary Images that immediately translate the inner state of those who perceive them, the holy city is perceived in the thought of the still higher-ranking Angels as a most beautiful maiden, clothed in garments that correspond to the attributes of

285 Emanuel Swedenborg, *The Apocalypse Revealed* (London, The Swedenborg Society (Inc.), 1878), vol. II, art. 880, pp. 705–706.

286 On Swedenborg's hermeneutics and the meaning of the *Antiquissima*, *Antiqua* and *Nova Ecclesia*, cf. H. Corbin, 'Herméneutique spirituelle comparée: I. Swedenborg. II. Gnose ismaélienne', in *Face de Dieu, face de l'Homme* (Paris, Flammarion, 1983).

the *Nova Ecclesia.* "Thus," declares Swedenborg, "has it also been permitted me to see the church.[287]

The events and content of the Johannine vision are likewise interpreted by Swedenborg according to the same hermeneutic, in which symbols are elucidated in relation to the inner states that determine the hierarchy of those who perceive them. John was "carried . . . away in the spirit to a great and high mountain" (Rev. 21:10). This signifies that John was carried off into the third Heaven, and that there the *Nova Ecclesia*, with respect to its doctrine, was made manifest to the eyes of his visionary perception, first as the image of a city and then as the image of a betrothed maiden. If "to be carried away to a high mountain" means to be carried off to the third Heaven, this is because it happens "in the spirit" and he who is "in the spirit" as regards thought and vision is in the third Heaven. The Angels of the third Heaven dwell on the mountains, those of the second Heaven on the hills, and those of the first Heaven in the valleys between the hills and mountains. The elevation to the third Heaven happens in an instant. It corresponds to a change of thought, that is to say of the visionary's total inner being.[288]

The new Jerusalem descends from Heaven "having the glory of God: and her light was like unto a stone most precious, even like a jasper stone, clear as crystal" (Rev. 21:11). What this means is that in the *Nova Ecclesia*, which is the *Nova Hierosolyma*, the letter of the Word had become translucent, so that its spiritual meaning was immediately apparent to the sight. For those who have entered into the spiritual intelligence of the Word, its spiritual meaning is made luminous in the light of their Heaven, a light which proceeds from the Lord as from the sun. For such beings, the same applies to the spiritual meaning concealed within each detail of the Word. We should follow Swedenborg's hermeneutic in detail with regard to all of the verses describing the New Jerusalem.[289]

287 Swedenborg, op. cit., art. 881, p. 708.

288 Ibid., art. 896, pp. 716–717. Swedenborg does not omit to compare the description of the city with those given in *Ezekiel* 40:2 ff. and *Zechariah* 2:2.

289 Ibid., art. 897, pp. 717–718. Swedenborg is here referring expressly to his work *Doctrina Novae Hierosolymae de Scriptura Sacra*; cf. *A Bibliography of the Works of Emanuel Swedenborg* (London, 1906), nos. 1790–1855. It seems necessary here to quote at least one other page of Swedenborg's where he comments on this Johannine vision of the heavenly Jerusalem. The quotation is taken from his fundamental work, *Heaven and its Wonders, and Hell: from things Heard and Seen*, London, J. M. Dent & Co., 1909 (*De Caelo et ejus mirabilibus, et de Inferno, ex auditis et visis*, Londini, 1758). The quotation illustrates perfectly Swedenborg's doctrine of the conjunction of

Let us merely observe, however, that his spiritual hermeneutic enables him to overcome the seeming paradox of a holy city in which the visionary sees no temple (Rev. 21:22). We must not think, he says, that in the *Nova Ecclesia*, the New Jerusalem, there will be no temple. No; what is meant is that in the New Jerusalem there will be nothing external (exoteric) whose inward (esoteric) meaning will be veiled. The reason is that although the word "temple" does indeed designate the *Nova Ecclesia* as the place of the celestial liturgy, in its highest sense it designates the Lord himself in the human manifestation of his divinity. Then "the Lord God is himself the Temple",[290] as we also read in Ezekiel (see above, section III, 2).

The fact that in this world there is a screen which separates inner and outer, esoteric and exoteric, is what creates the necessity for a Christian esotericism. The understanding that this duality is abolished by the *Nova Hierosolyma* is the essential perception that links Swedenborg to all the spiritual masters for whom the norm of the spiritual Temple signifies the coming of the Paraclete. Their agreement on this point unites the Joachimites of the eternal Gospel, the Jewish Cabbalists, and the Twelver Shiite theosophers who identify the coming of the twelfth Imam with the coming of the Paraclete. This is why we said above that the mystical Jerusalem is the spiritual Temple common to the three branches of the Abrahamic

---

Heaven with man through the Word: a conjunction of the spiritual meaning with the material meaning, of the exoteric with the esoteric. "Anyone who reads these words understands them merely according to the sense of the letter, according to which the visible heaven and earth are to perish, a new heaven is to exist, and the holy city Jerusalem with all its dimensions as here described is to descend upon a new earth. But the angels present with man understand these things quite differently, for they understand spiritually what man understands naturally. By the new heaven and new earth they understand a new Church. By the city Jerusalem coming down from God out of heaven, they understand its heavenly doctrine revealed by the Lord." Swedenborg goes on to give the spiritual meaning of all the details in the description of the New Jerusalem in the Apocalypse, and sums up as follows: "The natural ideas of man pass into spiritual ideas with angels, without their knowing anything of the sense of the letter of the Word . . . And yet the thoughts of angels unite with the thoughts of man, because they correspond to one another. They unite almost like the words of a speaker and the understanding of them by the hearer . . . Therefore, when angels think spiritually and man thinks naturally, they are conjoined almost like soul and body; the internal sense of the Word is also its soul, and the sense of the letter its body. Such is the Word throughout; hence it is evident, that it is the means of conjoining heaven with man; and that the sense of the letter serves as a basis and foundation." Op. cit., art. 307, pp. 143–144.

290 Swedenborg, *The Apocalypse Revealed*, op. cit., pp. 734–735.

tradition. The Temple as a "place of vision" is the ultimate intuition to which we are guided, through all its recurrences, by the *Imago Templi*.

TEMPLE AND CONTEMPLATION

There is no place here for anything resembling a conclusion, let alone an epilogue. The Temple is not yet completed. I would prefer to use the word "dénouement", but I would accompany it with this question. When what is at issue are the norms that reign in our world, in the present state of our civilization, might not the *Imago Templi* appear to us as "resolving", or *absolving* (in the sense that it sets us in the presence of an *absolutum*, an *absolute* because it *absolves* from the limits which block our world off from the horizon of the spiritual worlds) the horizon of the world beyond?

It is significant that the Latin word *templum* originally meant a vast space, open on all sides, from which one could survey the whole surrounding landscape as far as the horizon. This is what it means to *contemplate*: to "set one's sights on" Heaven from the *temple* that defines the field of vision. By the same token, the idea of contemplation introduces the idea of *consecration*. The term was actually used above all to designate the field of Heaven, the expanse of the open Heaven where the flight of birds could be observed and interpreted. Perhaps the idea of the cosmic Temple, which we have come across several times in the course of our inquiry, should be viewed in this light. Thus sacralized, the word *templum* finally came to mean the sanctuary, the sacred building known as a *temple*, the place of a divine Presence and of the contemplation of this Presence. Thus, the Latin *templum* became the appropriate word with which to translate the Hebrew and Arabic expressions that we met with at the start (*Bēth ha-miqdash*, *Bayt al-Maqdis*; see above, section I), which connote the idea of a divine dwelling-place; whereas, through its distant etymology, the word itself connotes the idea of a place of vision. The *temple* is the place, the organ, of vision.

Our inquiry, which embraced the theology of the Temple both in Ezekiel and in the Essene Community of Qumran, has presented us with this thesis: God himself is the temple of believers—and, reciprocally, believers are themselves the temple of God. This is the whole motif of the man-temple, the community-temple. To be the man-*temple* (one should say *templatio*, *templificatio hominis*) is to be oneself a space of *contemplation*, and thence a *consecrated* space. It is here, in the man-temple, that the *Imago Templi* manifests itself, because in the man-temple the *Imago Templi* is the mirror reflecting the *Imago Animae*, and because in this sense contemplator, contemplation and temple are one. There is thus an indissoluble link between Israel and the idea of the Temple, not only because Templar hierologies lay claim to a descent that goes back ultimately to the first Temple of Solomon, but also with regard to the essence of that which makes the temple.

When I say that we owe the Temple to the people-temple, I am thinking particularly of the late Hebrew etymology that was given to the name of Israel, in perfect accordance with the thought of Philo. Moreover, this etymology accords perfectly with that of the word *templum*, for the meaning it assigns to the name Israel is man-temple: "He who sees God". The word thus designates "the race of seers", and "Israel thus became, by definition, a people of *contemplatives* dedicated to the vision of divine things". As Philo explains, "The eye of the soul, which is the most transparent, pure and piercing of all, which alone is permitted to see God, bears the name of Israel." Through this philosophical transposition, the concept of Israel is expanded to mean a spiritual and mystical Israel, representing both the assembly of holy, "seeing" souls, and the individual soul, the soul's intellective part, the νοῦς or διάνοια, the thought of the sage "who sees God and loves him". Vision surpasses sound: the ears become eyes. Philo explains further: at the time of the theophany of Sinai, it was said that "all the people saw the sound" and did not understand it, "for if the voice of human beings is received by the hearing, the voice of God is received by the sight, like a light."[291] We could say the same of active *contemplation*. When man is thus, man is truly the Temple.

And it is when man is thus that we can speak of the dénouement, that is, of the resolving, absolving function of the *Imago Templi*. This is not, of course, a resolution that can be produced with a great flourish of dialectic. As we envisaged at the start of this inquiry (see above, section II), the destruction of the Temple now appears as the destruction of the man-temple, and thence as the desacralization of man and of his world. We grasp the full extent of the tragedy when we recall that, in the course of this inquiry, we have been told over and over again that the Temple was

291 Annie Jaubert, op. cit., pp. 411–412.

the place through which Heaven and earth were in communication, the intermediary *locus* "at the meeting-place of the two seas", linking Heaven with the earth. The destruction of the Temple is destruction of the field of vision: contemplation collapses for lack of space, for lack of a horizon beyond this world. Heaven and earth have ceased to comunicate: there is no longer either temple or contemplation.

From then on the knot of agnosticism tightens around the consciousness, shutting it off from itself. This is the reign of the "normal" man, of the man, that is, who conforms to the norm of Pharoah (see above, section II). The world of such a man is a world that "God no longer looks upon", that is no longer his concern. An eminent Iranian shaykh, from whom I have learned much,[292] went so far as to say to me, some time before he died, when we were speaking about the confident pessimism of Shiite traditions: "Never forget! The day will come when one will no longer be able even to utter the name of God in this world." For many of our contemporaries, that day is already here. The Temple is destroyed. There is no longer any link between Heaven and earth.

The norm of our world can assume all manner of names: sociology, dialectical or non-dialectical materialism, positivism, historicism, psychoanalysis, and so on. There is nothing, not even parapsychology, that does not oppose a savage refusal to any so-called "spiritualist" consequence that one might be tempted to deduce from one's observations and discoveries. The knot which paralyses our awareness is well-tied. The difficulty is that most men live outside themselves, even though they may never have gone outside themselves, for the good reason that they have never been inside themselves. Of course, there is no lack of therapies to make them go inside themselves; but if these are successful, it is often even more difficult to make them come out of themselves. Deprivation in the external world is followed by sterile stagnation, endlessly hammering out the contours of a false subjectivity. I would say that the virtue of the *Imago Templi* lies in making us be *within ourselves outside ourselves*. For we must not confuse introspection, introversion, with contemplation: there is no *contemplation* without the Temple. The virtue of the *Imago Templi* lies in delivering the man-temple both from the dangers of an invasive sociology, and from the dangers of a subjectivity which is its own thrall. It unties the

292 I refer to Sarkār Aghā (Shaykh Abū'l Qāsim Ibrāhīmī, who died in 1969). On him and his work, see *En Islam iranien*, op. cit., vol. IV, pp. 248–255.

knot because it re-establishes communication between Heaven and earth, opening up for all men the spaces beyond.

The norm of the Temple may doubtless appear fragile or absurd in a world like ours, and the state of the "guardians of the Temple", of the contemplatives "at the meeting-place of the two seas", may seem infinitely precarious. Nevertheless, the norm that they follow itself bears witness to another world, as for the Essene Community of Qumran it bore witness to the fact that the celestial cohorts were fighting by the side of their earthly partners. What will the future of this norm be? The answer, it seems to me, comes at the end of Albrecht von Scharfenberg's great epic, "The New Titurel" (see above, section VII). Here, there is an episode which has all the impact of a parable of the *Imago Templi.* When Titurel and Parsifal take the Holy Grail back to the East, they pass through a certain city. Parsifal leaves the inhabitants of this city with an *image* of the castle-temple of the Grail at Montsalvat. And with the aid of this single image, the inhabitants set about building their own Temple of the Grail.

This *Image* is also what remains to us. No more; but no less. No less, because it provides the answer to our question: what will happen in the future to the norm of the Temple? And it answers this question because this Image is imperishable, to the extent that we see it rise triumphant in the "waste land", from an earth that is spiritually more devastated than the domain of the Grail ever was before the coming of Parsifal. I call to witness the extraordinary vision of the castle-temple at Montsalvat which comes in one of the most moving pages written by Alexander Solzhenitsyn. Here the *Imago Templi*, rising like a challenge to dominate the norms of a hostile landscape, can be contemplated in all its purity. The vision takes the form of a study made by a painter who is trying to set down the moment when Parsifal "contemplates" the castle-temple of the Holy Grail for the first time.

"In shape the picture was twice as high as it was long. It showed a wedge-shaped ravine dividing two mountain crags. Above them both to right and left, could just be seen the outermost trees of a forest—a dense, primeval forest. Some creeping ferns, some ugly, menacing prehensile thickets clung to the very edge, and even to the overhanging face of the rock. Above and to the left a pale grey horse was coming out of the forest, ridden by a man in helmet and cape. Unafraid of the abyss the horse had raised its foreleg, before taking the final step, prepared at its rider's command to gather itself and jump over—a leap that was well within its power. But the rider was not looking at the chasm that faced the horse. Dazed, wondering, he was looking into the middle distance, where the upper reaches of the sky were suffused with an orange-gold radiance which might have been from the sun or from something else even more brilliant hidden from view by a castle. Its walls and turrets growing out of the ledges of the mountainside, visible also from below through the gap between the crags, between the ferns and trees, rising to a needle-point at the top of the picture—indistinct in outline, as though woven from gently shimmering clouds, yet still vaguely discernible in all the details of its unearthly perfection, enveloped in a shining and lilac-coloured aureole—stood the castle of the Holy Grail."[293]

This visionary page written by Solzhenitsyn is evidence that the *Imago Templi*, the image of the castle-temple left to mankind by Parsifal, will never be lost. It is in some sense the response to the *geste* of Parsifal, and both together are the response to the desperate cry of the Templar knights that we heard echoing at the start in an amphitheatre in the High Pyrenees. Together they reply: No! the Temple is not destroyed forever. This was known to Suhravardī also, with whom we began this discussion and with whom it is right that we should end it. Suhravardī composed an entire "Book of hours" in honour of the "guardians of the Temple", who are unknown to the majority of men. They guard a secret Temple, and those who find their way to it can join in the invocation which returns, like a refrain, in one of the most beautiful psalms composed by Suhravardī: "O God of every God! Make the litany of the Light arise. Make the people of Light triumphant. Guide the Light towards the Light. Amen."[294]

Paris, Thursday July 25, 1974

293 Alexander Solzhenitsyn, *The First Circle*, trans. Michael Guybon (Collins & Harvill Press, London, 1968), p. 259.
294 Cf. Suhravardī's 'Livre d'heures', of which extracts are translated in my anthology entitled *L'Archange Empourpré*, op. cit.

Index

A

INDEX

C

D

E

F

G

H

hermeneutic(s), 15, 25, 28–31, 37–40, 53, 55–6, 72, 114–15, 172, 185, 188 190, 203, 207, 236, 251n., 270, 277, 279, 283, 294, 301, 304–5, 316–18, 320, 322, 339–40, 382; gnostic, 375; "hermeneutical rides", 113; of Koran, 37–40; of symbols, 151; of "three books", 81–96
Hermes, 69, 143, 156
Hermeticism, 1, 100, 373
hexad, 82
hexaemeron, 87
hierarchy, angelic, 57; celestial, 146–7, 150; of divine names, 68–71; esoteric, mystical, 57, 59, 66, 74, 86, 111, 136, 146–7, 153, 178, 254, 348; of Intelligences, 74, 144
hierocosmos, 226, 298
hierohistory, subtle/sacred/symbolic history, counter-history, para-history, 59, 107, 136, 155, 164, 174, 195, 233, 268, 278–80, 292, 296, 298, 302, 313, 326, 328, 332, 341, 369, 379–80; angelic hierognosis, 383; Celtic, 355; Ismaili, 149, 165n., 174
hierophany, 19, 269–70, 275, 280–81, 292, 308, 325; of *Imago Templi*, 270, 275, 280, 311, 325, 328, 338, 343, 348
ḥikāyah, both "history" and "imitation", 15, 28–9, 32, 222, 235, 245
ḥikmah, *see* wisdom
Ḥiram, 362
historicism, 325, 344, 356, 388
Historiosophy, 81, 103; Ismaili, 142, 160, 164–5
history, 80, 142, 267–8, 278–80, 292, 296, 298, 302, 322, 324, 326, 331, 338–41, 379–80; of astronomy, 271, 275; evangelical, 336; philosophers of, 264, 280; of religions, 103, 173; of science, 271, 275; time of, 326
"holy myriads", 96
Holy of Holies, 318, 359, 366, 382
Holy Sepulchre, 349; Canons of, 351–3
homology, 59, 155, 162, 240
Horeb, rock of, 72, 109
hours, liturgical, 172, 179
Hugh de Payens, 347–8
Ḥujjah (Witness, guarantor), 72
Human Comedy, The, 184; *see also* Balzac
humanity, subtle (*nāsūt*), 145, 149
Hūrakhsh, 273n.
Hūrqalyā, 31
Ḥusayn ibn ᶜAlī, 3rd Shiite Imam, 10, 45–7, 73n., 93, 119, 122, 125, 205–6, 230; as pillar of red light, 43; *see also* Karbalā
Ḥusaynī al-ᶜAlawī, 145n.
hyacinth, red, 41, 44, 230, 234, 239, 246
hymn, 156, 315
hymnology, 156, 316, 321

I

Iblīs, 106, 151–3, 156, 161, 164, 250–1; posterity of, 153, 164
Ibn ᶜArabī, 21, 23, 33, 58, 60, 67, 71, 73–8, 98–9, 103, 106, 111–12, 114–15, 218n., 249, 266
Ibn Bābūyah, 192n., 199n.
Ibn al-Fāriḍ, 54
icon, 135; Byzantine, 190–1, 196, 226
ᶜĪd al-Aḍḥā (feast of sacrifices), 157
ideas, pure, 266
ideologies, so-called modern, 56
idolatry, 289
Idrīs, 71, 79, 119, 143; "Orison of", 156
Idrīs ᶜImāduddīn, Yemeni philosopher, 146n., 164n.
Illuminati of Weisshaupt, 371
image, 134, 275–6, 278–9, 308; archetype, 222; intellective (*amthilah ᶜaqlīyah*), 266, 276; of Hidden Treasure, 85; of time, 59; visionary, 383
imaginal, 265, 268, 276, 291, 297, 303–4, 314, 325; corporeity, 189, 194; form, 200, 297; metaphysics of, 265
imaginary, 265, 276, 326

J

K

L

M

N

O

P

Pen (*qalam*) (*cont.*):
sacrosanct, 30, 39, 73–4, 90; *see also* Intelligence, First
Pentecost, 324, 329, 337, 364, 366
perception: sensible, 241, 266, 273; visionary, 81, 269, 284, 384
period (in Ismaili sense), 142–3, 157, 162, 172
Persepolis, 269, 283
Persia, *see* Iran
person(s): archetypes, 154, 158, 165, 169–71, 175; celestial, 169–71, 273; celestial, of light (*haykal al-nūr*), 159–61; five, of prayer, 172; human, 145, 180, 203; of Paradise, 179; spiritual, 173–4; theophanic, 210
perspectiva artificialis/naturalis, 187
Peter (apostle), 256; Church of, *see* Church
phantasia, 276
Pharoah, 47, 279, 340, 342, 388
phenomenon: of being, 11; of world, 261–2, *see also* world
phenomenologist, 392
phenomenology, 1, 135, 196–7, 208, 214, 267, 329, 343; of colours, 7–8, 15, 24, 33–4; and Copernican reversal, 338; of *Imago Templi*, 305–6, 355n.; religious, 331; of Temple, 284
Philip the Fair, 263, 342, 370–1, 374
Philo of Alexandria, 274n., 292, 298, 300, 302–9, 355, 387
philosophy: natural, 82; prophetic, 53
philosophy of history, 56, 81, 103, 165, 267
Philostorgius, 345
physics: celestial, 276; traditional, 217
physiology: mystical, of Temple, 231; subtle, 105n.
pilgrim, mystical, 133, 211–13, 219, 246, 248–50, 252
pilgrimage, 172–3, 177, 192, 195, 197, 208, 216, 232, 235, 240–53, 260; esoteric meaning of, 255; of heart, 253
pillars, invisible (of spiritual Heaven), 86
pīr (master), 272
Pisces (sign of zodiac), 111, 118, 121
place: natural and existential, 187; holy places, 227, 232, 242–4
Plains of Gold, The: *see* Mas[c]ūdī
planets, 67, 69, 76, 92, 100, 133, 139, 141
planting (symbol), 318–19
Plato, 137, 165n., 270; "Prayer of Plato", 156
Platonic, 134, 139; Platonism, 4
Platonists: Cambridge, 188; Persian, 188–9
pleroma, 381; Muhammadan, 103, 123; primordial, 204; of each period of prophecy, 80; of twelve Imams, 73, 282
Plutarch, 270
pneuma, the three, 85
pole (*quṭb*), 64–5, 86, 113, 120, 122; sacrosanct, 252; seven, 70–1, 93; of poles, 79
Pole Star, 156
positivism, 388
potestas clavium, 197, 227, 230, 232, 242, 253–62, 331
Power (*qudrah*): divine attribute, 68; world of, 97
Powerful (the), divine name, 68
Powers, *al-quwwāt* = *dynameis*, 98
Prayer, ritual, 172
Predetermined (the), divine name, 97
Presence, divine, 286, 326, 382; "morning of P.", 252, *see also* *Shekhinah/Sakīnah*
Prester John, 368
principle: of Principles, 252n., supreme, 140, 199, 203; of transposition, 198, 202, 208
Proclus, 7
Programme, eschatological, of God, 319
Prometheus, myth of, 50
prophecy: cycle of, 176–7, 234; esoteric dimension of, 64; legislative, 62; Muhammadan, 77, 105, 110
prophet(s), 53–4, 62, 64–8, 72, 86, 91–2, 107, 121, 226, 250, 254, 272,

Q

R

S

T

U

V

vegetable (world, kingdom), 55, 92, 121
veils: human Temple as, 159; 70,000, of light, 101–2, 113n., 248; veiling God, 74, 252
Venus, 69–70, 76, 91, 118, 120, 140
Verbs, 91
Vernunft, 310; *Vernunftlichkeit*, 310
Verus Propheta, 77, 80–1, 203–4, 223, 330, 332, 347; Judaeo–Christian theology of, 332
Virgo (sign of zodiac), 117, 121
vis configuratrix, 200, 205
vision, inner, 32, 101, 111, 114–15; Johannine, 380; liturgical, 335; of *malakūt*, 195–7; mystical (*shuhūd*), 245; of Person-archetypes, 154, 158, 174, 178–81; prophetic, 319; smaragdine, 133; theophanic, 250, 253, 336n.; *visio Christi*, 336–7; *visio Dei*, 336, 382
vision of Isaiah, 334
visionary: awareness, 267; perception, 81; visionaries, 265
Vohu-Manah: *see* Bahman
Vulgate, 292, 293n., 327

W

Wagner, Richard, 357n., 368
wahmīyah, (estimatory faculty), 265
Waite, A. E., 254n., 302n., 343, 345n.
walāyah (*dustī*), 41–3, 61–2, 204–5, 207, 223, 225, 254; seal of, 225; *see also* Imam
walī (pl. *awliyā'*), 60–2, 66–8, 70, 85, 103–4, 107, 110, 120, 205, 225, 254, 351; *see also* Friends of God, Imam
Waraqah (monk, initiator of Khadījah), 62, 96, 104
waṣī, pl. *awṣiyā*, heir, 163, 172, 175, 176n.
Watchman, 193
Water, 16–18, 24, 31, 41, 92, 121, 190, 200, 211, 291, 318–19; of Life, 288; of history, 279–80; primordial, 200, 211
way, from God to God, 245, 247, 253
Weigel, V. 256–7
Weinreb, Friedrich, 268n., 277–9, 280n.
Wensinck, 144n., 154n.
Werner, Zacharias, 269, 342, 354, 369–78
"White Cloud", Recital of, 215, 218, 247–8, 251
Wiesel, Elie, 263
wilādah dīnīyah, initiatory birth, 148
Will (*irādah*), divine creative (*mashī'ah*), 39; divine attribute, 68; of divine manifestation, 209; primordial, 90; world of, 97
Willed, *murād*, 97
Willermoz, J. B., 28, 269, 354–5, 368
wisdom: *ḥikmah*, 68, 173; soteriological, 325
Wisdom, Book of, 305
Word, 72, 177, 384; divine, 257, 279; see also *Kalām*, Verbs; as *Logos*, 72, 193, 306; of prophets, 278
world: corporeal, 104; of day, 259; of illusion, 244; opaque (*kathīf*), 6; of night, 259; of phenomena, 192, 222, 244; phenomenon of, 91, 262; of realities of light, 245; sensible, 32, 68–9, 192, 197, 238–9, 252; spiritual, 67–8, 77, 79–80, 85, 93, 101, 109, 120, 122, 195, 197, 218, 244–5; suprasensible, 32, 192, 197
Wurmser, A. 184n.

X

Xenakis, 50

Y

Yahohel, cherub: *see* Angel (Metatron)
Yahveh, 284–8, 291–2, 324, 335
Yaḥya, Osman, 58n., 112n.
young branch, 295–7

Z